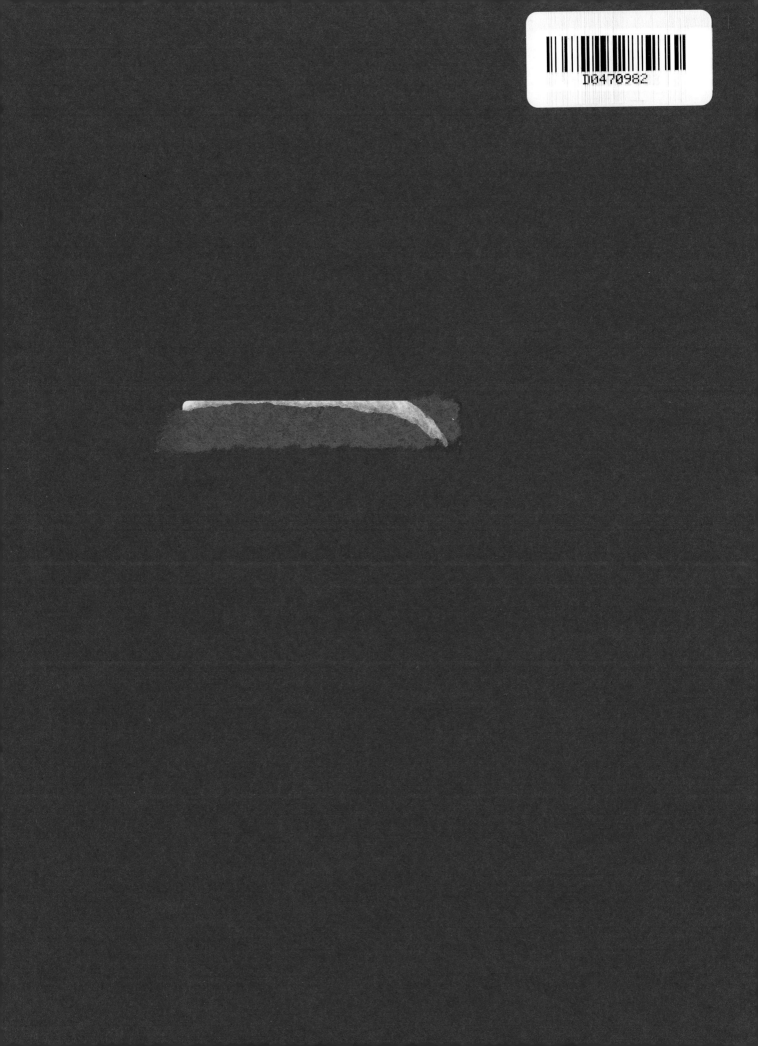

An American Anthropologist in Melanesia

VOLUME I: FIELD DIARIES

An American Anthropologist
in Melanesia

||||||||||||||||||||||||||||||||||||||||||||||||||||||||||||||||||||||||||||||||||||

A. B. Lewis
and the
Joseph N. Field South Pacific Expedition
1909–1913

||||||||||||||||||||||||||||||||||||||||||||||||||||||||||||||||||||||||||||||||||||

Edited and Annotated by
Robert L. Welsch

University of Hawai'i Press
HONOLULU

Library of Congress Cataloging-in-Publication Data
An American anthropologist in Melanesia : A. B. Lewis and the Joseph N.
Field South Pacific expedition, 1909–1913 / edited and annotated by
Robert L. Welsch.
    p.   cm.
    Includes bibliographical references and index.
    Contents: v. 1. Field diaries — v. 2. Appendixes.
    ISBN 0–8248–1644–7 (alk. paper)
    1. Ethnology—Melanesia.   2. Lewis, A. B. (Albert Buell), 1867–
—Diaries.   3. Material culture—Melanesia.   4. Melanesia—Social
life and customs.   I. Welsch, Robert L.   II. Lewis, A. B. (Albert
Buell), 1867–   .
GN668.A44   1998
306'.0995—DC21   97–39219
                                  CIP

Published with the support of the
Maurice J. Sullivan & Family Fund
in the University of Hawai'i Foundation

Designed and typeset by Northeastern Graphic Services, Inc.

FRONTISPIECE: Launching canoe in which A. B. Lewis traveled
from Bukaua to Lokanu and back, at Wusumu [Busama].
The canoe is from Bukaua, A-32032 (339).

To the memory of Albert Buell Lewis,

    whose earlier work made this book possible,

and

For Sarah, whose constant love

    and encouragement made this work a reality

Contents

||||||||||||||||||||||||||||||||||||||||||||||||||||||||||||||||||||||||||||||||||||

Volume I: Field Diaries

||||||||||||||||||||||||||||||||||||||||||||||||||||||||||||||||||||||||||||||||||||

Preface

||||||||||||||||||||||||||||||||||||||||||||||||||||||||||||||||||||||||||||||||||||||||||||||||||||||||||

This work was conceived in 1987. John Terrell, curator of Oceanic archaeology and ethnology at Field Museum of Natural History—and at the time chair of the Department of Anthropology—invited me to have a look at the A. B. Lewis Collection to see if this large collection of Melanesian material culture could be drawn upon to motivate new anthropological field research in New Guinea. Terrell wanted to demonstrate in some concrete and empirical way that the ethnological collections Field Museum had cared for and housed for most of a century still had relevance for anthropology and for important anthropological questions. He suggested that I have a look at Lewis' field notes, his photographs, and the thousands of objects he had collected during his expedition to Melanesia to see if any of these materials might be interesting avenues to pursue. I knew Lewis' name from his collection and some of his publications; even the lab in which I had previously cataloged collections at Field Museum was prominently named the A. B. Lewis Oceanic Laboratory. But like most anthropologists, I knew virtually nothing about Lewis when I began poring over his field diaries and his many other field notebooks stored in acid-free boxes in the departmental archives.

It was immediately clear from these expedition diaries that Lewis had collected much richer field data than I had assumed from his 1921 exhibit cases, which were not deinstalled until 1989 and which I had seen periodically since I was an undergraduate. As I perused these barely legible diaries, his "dusty" old collection in its long-outdated exhibit cases was transformed: it became a complex historical document, complete with photographs and many of the very objects his diaries described. What's more, as I consulted maps, gazetteers, and other reference works, it was clear that Lewis had not only assembled an enormous collection, but had encountered—as a trained anthropologist—a slice of Melanesian history that no other American anthropologist had experienced. As my research on Lewis and his collection progressed, it was clear that the Joseph N. Field South Pacific Expedition, occurring as it did immediately before Bronislaw Malinowski set off for Papua, happened at a critical moment in the history of anthropology. Thus, it seemed that through Lewis' expedition diaries—which had been neglected for so many decades—we could gain new insights about the ethnology of Melanesia, about the history of the Southwest Pacific, and about the development of anthropology and anthropological research methods.

And so, the present work was initially conceived. The idea for it remained inchoate for the next two or three years because the collection did suggest a very different kind of traditional society in Melanesia than I had expected. Instead of the multitude of hostile, isolated communities constantly at war with one another as most anthropologists had depicted the small-scale societies of New Guinea, Lewis described numerous small communities that had regular and frequent interaction with one another for trade in economically and socially important objects.

His research on the North Coast of New Guinea was especially intriguing because he had documented the exchange of so many different kinds of things and had purchased examples of most of the items that were routinely "traded."

Since 1987, John Terrell and I have developed an ongoing research program—the A. B. Lewis Project—that combined analysis of collections at Field Museum with new fieldwork in New Guinea. Our museum-based research was supported by the National Science Foundation (BNS-881-9618), Northwestern University, Field Museum of Natural History, the Thomas J. Dee Fund at Field Museum, The School of the Art Institute, Walgreen Corporation, and private donors. Terrell and I conducted our first joint expedition to Aitape during the 1990 Walgreens Expedition to the West Sepik, which served as a reconnaissance survey and demonstrated that there was still a great deal to be learned through fieldwork in this region about what Lewis had called trade.

In 1993–1994 I spent nearly a year in the field on the collaborative A. B. Lewis Project Expedition, which was supported by the National Science Foundation (DBS-9120301), the National Endowment for the Humanities (RO-22203-91), Field Museum, and the Papua New Guinea National Museum and Art Gallery. Joining me in the field for about five months each were John Terrell and Wilfred Price Oltomo, senior technical officer at the National Museum and Art Gallery. We were joined for a shorter period by Michael Reupana and Alois Kuaso, students at the University of Papua New Guinea.

During this phase of the research, I was able to document continuity with what Lewis had observed about relationships along this coast. In 1909, for example, Lewis saw Tumleo and Ali Islanders giving earthenware pots, shell rings, and smoked fish to their partners in mainland villages; the islanders received sago and other garden produce from their mainland friends. In 1993 I accompanied Ali Islanders on visits to their friends in mainland villages; during these visits they brought earthenware pots and smoked fish. On some occasions, I even helped the Ali people bring back the sago, betel nut, and garden products that their mainland friends had given them. Despite considerable change in the political, economic, and social context of life on this coast since 1909, people were still actively participating in the kinds of intergroup transactions Lewis had reported during his research. To find out how these relations worked and why they were still alive in 1993–1994, I conducted 130 interviews with older residents of eighty villages about their "friends and family networks" along the coast. I also brought hundreds of photographs of objects in the Lewis Collection back to the villages where he had bought them to see if I could upgrade his documentation. In many instances, villagers today could add to what Lewis recorded about the collection and about Lewis' field photographs. To update Field Museum's holdings from this region, Wilfred Oltomo helped me assemble a new collection of about two thousand items, which were divided up between the National Museum and Field Museum.

While I was conducting interviews along the coast, Terrell was conducting a survey of archaeological sites in the same region, aimed at elucidating the extent to which the networks we were observing (and which Lewis had observed early in the century) could be linked to evidence of transactions in the prehistoric record. We found evidence of some kinds of economic (and friendship?) networks in the form of 1,472 obsidian flakes (1.517 kg) that had originated in quarries in New Britain and the Admiralty Islands some 500 to 900 kilometers to the east. In addition, some of the 10,644 potsherds—including at least one Lapita sherd—as well as some of the 75 chert flakes, 23 pieces of worked shell, and 10 stone or shell adzes or axes also suggest that such materials too were being exchanged or traded in prehistoric times. This preliminary survey of prehistoric sites has motivated further archaeological research around Aitape planned for 1996 and supported by the National Science Foundation. We now call this set of collaborative research projects the Field Museum's New Guinea Research Program, in which the A. B. Lewis Project, the archaeological project, and a planned biological project are components.

Although these museum-based and field research projects were not directly aimed at producing this two-volume work, they have enhanced my understanding of the Lewis Collection and Lewis' field notes considerably. Since the A. B. Lewis Project has relied so heavily on an appreciation of Lewis' collection together with its supporting documentation and photographs, work with the collection, work with the diaries and other field notes, and new fieldwork made up three mutually supportive and inherently related facets of the same research effort. Without the opportunity of retracing some of Lewis' footsteps along the Aitape coast, I could not have appreciated the subtleties of some of his comments, much less his general perspective. For these and other reasons I owe a great debt of gratitude to all of those institutions, organizations, agencies, and individuals who facilitated our work in the A. B. Lewis Laboratory and on two expeditions to New Guinea.

More directly related to the present work was a catalog grant awarded by the National Endowment for the Arts in 1990 that was intended to facilitate making and printing up the many photographs needed for this volume. Field Museum was forced to decline this award because of the so-called obscenity clause. Nevertheless, Willard L. Boyd and Jonathan Haas, the museum's president and vice-president for research and collections, respectively found funds to assist this effort despite the loss of grant support. I deeply appreciate the confidence that both Field Museum and the endowment had in this work. Without such support this volume would be visually much less rich, not to mention less informative.

During these years since 1987, the concept for the present work grew and developed in many different ways. In the early years, I tossed out—to a patient and encouraging John Terrell—one vague and incompletely formed idea after another about what these diaries and the collection they helped document might mean. At times, it seemed that I could not grasp the significance of Lewis' (often) cryptic comments because I knew too little about the political and economic histories of the colonies he visited. At other times, I sensed that the people he casually mentioned in his text—most of whom were unknown to me—were critical in understanding what Lewis was experiencing and what conclusions he was drawing from these experiences. And, early on, it often happened that I had little or no sense of what kind of collection Lewis was trying to assemble and what his underlying purpose might be. Thus, I began research along a number of avenues that would help me contextualize and understand more of what these diaries and objects had to tell. These various lines of research proved to be far more convoluted and challenging than I had imagined in 1987. And these inquiries took me to many individuals and institutions both inside and outside Field Museum.

I want to acknowledge the assistance of the following individuals for their help with different aspects of this project:

Janet Miller and Janice Klein, at different periods registrar and departmental archivist, made available to me diaries, field notes, correspondence, and departmental records relevant to Lewis and the J. N. Field Expedition. Mary Ann Johnston, museum archivist, helped me comb many accession files, director's files, correspondence files, and other boxes in the archives to find material for this work.

Field Museum volunteers have been of tremendous help over these years, and their consistent efforts too often go unacknowledged. Dee Aiani, John Cox, Ann Gerber, Jeanne Martineau, Sam Mayo, and Irmgard Nirschl-Rauch put in many long hours on the Lewis Project as Field Museum volunteers; they have helped in numerous ways to pull together, identify, and retrieve objects, photographs, and references that I needed over the years. Josephine Faulk helped with proofreading and correcting my original draft of the diaries and assisted with efforts to match up Lewis' collections with different parts of his diary. Peter Buol assisted with translations from the German, particularly the "Notice" reproduced in Book 1. Ralph Cowan helped me understand tabletop photographic work and took one of the photographs reproduced here. John "Jack" MacDonald has assisted in so many ways with the text, mock-ups, and photos for so many years that it is impossible to thank him adequately. Finally, to James Coplan, who was my first volunteer on the Lewis Project and my most loyal supporter in the early years, I owe a great debt of gratitude for his efforts, which were provided as more than just time and talent.

Two undergraduate interns from Northwestern University—Anne Charbonneau and Larry Saviers—assisted in the project in various ways; Anne was largely responsible for identifying and pulling together the many obscure sources about missionaries in the New Hebrides. Three interns from The School of the Art Institute of Chicago—Deborah Beckles, Abigail Mack, and Caroline Price—assisted early on with photographs and analysis of certain parts of the collection. Rebecca Kammerer from St. Augustana College assisted by pulling together some sources about Germans Lewis met in Eitape. Howard Eisenberg from the University of Wisconsin at Madison and Trudy Barry of Northeastern Illinois University helped with analysis of parts of the collection.

As graduate students in the Department of Anthropology at Northwestern University and as A. B. Lewis Fellows working on the project in 1989 and 1990, Leslie Ashbaugh, Barbara Hsiao, and John Nadolski have each assisted with many different aspects of this work.

The Department of Photography at Field Museum deserves special credit for the enormous task of setting up, photographing, and printing the new images required for this volume as well as for helping me inventory all of the Lewis expedition photos and printing up those needed here. Photoarchivist Nina Cummings has been a tremendous help throughout the research and was fundamental in explaining how these images have been cataloged, stored, copied, and reproduced over the years; in addition she graciously provided spare prints of Lewis images when she came across them and has been supportive of the research since 1987. Ron Testa, former museum photographer, was also helpful early on in identifying images and in inventorying this collection of photographs. His successor, John Weinstein, has also supported this project, despite the considerable time it has required of his staff. Weinstein photographed about a third of the object photos reproduced here. James Balodimas photographed the majority of the images of objects in the Lewis Collection and printed up most of the photos reproduced here. Diane Alexander White also printed a considerable number of photos for this project and has from time to time offered other advice about tabletop work and how best to reproduce Lewis' images. I am greatly indebted to all of these talented individuals who have performed yeoman's service in making this work a visually informative and interesting one.

Margaret Baker and David Willard of the Department of Zoology assisted in tracking down and identifying for me a number of zoological specimens that Lewis had collected in Melanesia.

Mavis Blacker, James Foerster, William G. Grewe-Mullins, Christine Gross, Sheryl Heidenreich, Lanet Jarret, Catherine Sease—all members of the Department of Anthropology—assisted the research in various ways. Peter Lowther and James W. Koeppl of the Computing Department, and Dorothea Vicari in the Development Office also assisted with different aspects of the project.

I was fortunate to be able to talk with Rupert Wenzel, zoology curator, and the late anthropology curator, Donald Collier, both of whom as students had known A. B. Lewis at Field Museum in the 1930s. Their recollections, observations, and insights were especially helpful in understanding the course of Lewis' career.

Lewis' cousins—Dorothy Lowrie of Lake Geneva, Wisconsin; Dr. James Anderson of Monroe, Ohio; Martha Benham of Clifton, Ohio; and Margie Mesloh of Tulsa, Oklahoma—

offered many details of the family's oral traditions as well as a tour of Clifton's historical sites. During a visit I made to Clifton, they let me stay in the Benham home, the house where Lewis' mother had grown up. The family also gave me access to a rich correspondence with Lewis' late cousin Merle Rife, whose recollections and interest in family history filled in several key gaps. The family has been supportive, encouraging, and enthusiastic about my research on A. B. Lewis and his expedition from the beginning, and I am grateful for their encouragement and interest.

In particular, I want to thank Lucille T. Morris, recorder in the Registrar's Office at the College of Wooster, for details about Lewis in their files. Also, thanks to Maxine Sullivan, registrar of the University of Chicago, for assistance in deciphering some of the details about his coursework at her institution. Bill Fisher of the Geographic Society of Chicago kindly helped me hunt through the society's scrapbooks, memorabilia, and minute books for details about Lewis' membership and involvement with his organization.

The Field Museum Library was the most important starting point for my background research on Melanesia, the individuals Lewis met during his expedition, and the history of the discipline. Michele Calhoun was especially helpful in tracking down obscure sources and references as well as in understanding my needs early on, sometimes before I myself recognized them. Janeen Devine was especially diligent in tracking down obscure sources through inter-library loan. Other members of the library staff, but especially W. Peyton Fawcett, Kenneth Grabowski, Michael Trombley, and Benjamin Williams, have assisted in finding citations, references, and sometimes dusty volumes tucked away in forgotten corners of the library. To all of these individuals my thanks for helping when it counted.

Besides the Field Museum Library, the University Library at Northwestern University and the United Library of Seabury-Western and Garrett-Evangelical Theological Seminaries in Evanston, Illinois, the Regenstein Library at the University of Chicago, and the Center for Research Libraries in Chicago have proved the most valuable and constant source for needed references.

In addition to these most important library resources, I have consulted works in many other libraries around the world including the following:

Baker Library, Dartmouth College, Hanover, New Hampshire; Burke Library of the Union Theological Seminary, New York; Catholic Theological Union Library, Chicago; Chicago Heights Public Library, Chicago Heights, Illinois; Chicago Historical Society Library; Chicago Public Library; Clifton Historical Society, Clifton, Ohio; Evanston Public Library, Evanston, Illinois; Library of Congress, Washington, D.C.; Library of the Society for the Divine Word, Techny, Illinois; Loyola University of Chicago Library; Michigan State University Library, Lansing; National Anthropology Archives, at the U.S. National Museum of Natural History, Washington, D.C.; National Archives Regional Branch, Chicago; National Archives, Washington, D.C.; National Library of Papua New Guinea; The New Guinea Collection, in the Michael Somare Library, University of Papua New Guinea; New York Public Library; Newberry Library, Chicago; Papua New Guinea National Archives; The Robert Goldwater Library, The Metropolitan Museum of Art, New York; University of Hawai'i Library, Honolulu; University of Kansas Library, Lawrence; and University of Michigan Graduate Library, Ann Arbor.

The following organizations and museums kindly made available archival materials that have facilitated my research for this work:

Archives of the Franciscan Mission, Aitape, West Sepik Province, Papua New Guinea; Department of Africa, the Americas, and Oceania, The Metropolitan Museum of Art, New York; Department of Anthropology, American Museum of Natural History, New York; Department of Anthropology, Australian Museum, Sydney; Department of Anthropology, Bishop Museum, Honolulu; Department of Anthropology, U.S. National Museum of Natural History, The Smithsonian Institution, Washington; The Fairbanks Museum, St. Johnsbury, Vermont; The Hood Museum of Art, Dartmouth College, Hanover, New Hampshire; The National Museum and Art Gallery, Port Moresby, Papua New Guinea; Peabody-Essex Museum, Salem, Massachusetts; The University Museum, University of Pennsylvania, Philadelphia.

I am especially grateful to the following reference librarians at Baker Library and Special Collections, Dartmouth College, for help in checking references when the manuscript came back from the copyeditor: Ridie W. Ghezzi, Robert Jaccaud, William McEwen, Lois Krieger, and Cynthia Pawlek. Not only did they help me confirm obscure citations when I was far away from my original reseach notes, but many of them had helped with references needed to complete the penultimate draft of the manuscript. Jennifer Nelson at the Storage Library at Dartmouth also helped me find sources in both 1991 and 1995. Special thanks to my colleague Gregory Finnegan, formerly reference librarian at Baker Library, but now on the staff of Tozzer Library, for his help with sources in 1994.

My special thanks to the people of Melanesia, whose parents and grandparents assisted A. B. Lewis in his work. Thanks also to the people of Papua New Guinea and Indonesia, especially those living on the north coast of the island of New Guinea, who have assisted my colleagues and me in the field. In particular, I want to thank Adolf Woichom of Ali Island and his family, who welcomed us into their home and looked after us in 1993–1994. They accepted, with considerable patience, the challenges of having a team of foreign researchers live with them for a year on Ali; they hold a very special place in our hearts. We also appreciate the logistical support and friendship of those in the provincial government of Sandaun Province and the missionaries and staff of the Diocese of Aitape, especially Father Timothy Elliot and Bishop Brian Barnes, whose hospitality we enjoyed on many occasions.

Many colleagues have offered suggestions, assisted with specific questions, or made comments on various parts of the manuscript: David Akin, Kathleen Barlow, Christine Behrmann, Lissant Bolton, Bennett Bronson, Donald Collier, Barbara Conklin, Susan Crawford, Ross Day, Valerie Free, Kellen Haak, Thomas Harding, Jackie Lewis Harris, Debbie Haynes, Mary Taylor Huber, Terence Hays, Adria Katz, Adrienne Kaeppler, Phillip Lewis, David Lipset, Nancy Lutkehaus, Tamara Northern, Margaret Rodman, Paul Roscoe, Roger Rose, Abe Rosman, Paula Rubel, Michael French Smith, James Specht, Pamela Stewart, Gabriele Stürzenhofecker, Robin Torrence, James W. VanStone, James B. Watson, Virginia-Lee Webb, Maria Wronska-Friend, and three anonymous readers of the manuscript. Special mention is due John Terrell, who, in addition to getting me started in this project and collaborating with me in the museum and in the field, has frequently offered advice and constructive criticism throughout the writing and rewriting of this manuscript.

I am especially grateful for the help and encouragement provided by my editor at the University of Hawai'i Press, Pamela Kelley, who has worked with me to shape this complex and cumbersome manuscript into a cohesive and logical whole. Joanne Sandstrom copyedited the manuscript, removing unwanted repetition, eliminating many inconsistencies, and greatly improving the flow of my text. Cheri Dunn and Keith Leber, managing editors, helped the manuscript through an intricate production process with good humor and aplomb. I also wish to thank Director William Hamilton for supporting this project as well as for arranging funding for production. And I want to acknowledge the enthusiastic encouragement of Colins Kawai, marketing director, and his wonderful sales and marketing staff. In these beleagured times for academia and the arts, to have the full support of such a talented and erudite university press has been a boon; to work with such a pleasant group of people has been a joy.

Finally, I want to thank Field Museum for permission to publish Lewis' diary, correspondence, and photographs together with related correspondence and other archival material.

Thanks also to the library of the American Philosophical Society for permission to publish two of Lewis' letters, the originals of which are in the Professional Papers of Franz Boas. I also want to express my gratitude and thanks to the anonymous donor whose financial support has helped facilitate publication of photographs in this volume.

Special thanks are due to the Claire Garber Goodman Fund for the Anthropological Study of Human Culture, administered by the Department of Anthropology at Dartmouth College, for helping with funds for indexing. Thanks also to Debbie Hodges, who compiled the index and helped me catch some of the many typos and inconsistent spellings that inevitably creep into a work of this size.

I appreciate the encouragement and moral support I have received throughout the writing of this manuscript from my parents Russell L. and Carmen Castillo Welsch and from Mr. and Mrs. J. William Stack. To Eleanor D. MacCracken, who shares with me a special interest in the Pacific Islands and its peoples, my thanks for her warm and enthusiastic support over the years since I began research for this work. And last but by no means least, I want to acknowledge the constant support of my wife Sarah Leslie Welsch, who has been with me through every phase of this long and complex work.

In a project that has involved the assistance of so many individuals over such an extended period, I have undoubtedly neglected to mention some individuals by name. I apologize for any oversight, which was surely inadvertent.

To all of the individuals and institutions who have offered assistance, my heartfelt thanks. Their contributions and assistance have clearly enhanced the final product; any shortcomings are, of course, my own.

Textual Note

||||||||||||||||||||||||||||||||||||||||||||||||||||||||||||||||||||||||||||||||||||||||||||

When A. B. Lewis wrote these diaries, he never intended them for publication, nor would he ever have imagined that his raw, unanalyzed, and sometimes contradictory comments would be read by others outside the laboratories and workrooms of Field Museum. The diaries were intended as documentation, not as introspective reflections about how Lewis experienced the diverse peoples of Melanesia. For the most part, his notes were intended only as aides-mémoire to help him jog his memory or as a record of the information he would need when preparing exhibits from his collection. He clearly used these notes during installation of his large exhibition, which opened in 1921. Later, he also used them when writing his monograph, *The Ethnology of Melanesia*.

Lewis' diaries were written every day or two, whenever he found time to sit down and dash off a few observations about where he had been, what he had done, whom he seen or talked with, what he had collected, and what he had observed about the people, their culture, and their way of life. They were composed when he was tired from a long day's work in a difficult environment. He was often fatigued from travel by foot, by canoe, by cutter, or by small steamer. He was periodically sick with fever and malaria. As his collections grew, he was frequently tired from cataloging, moving, shifting, and packing his specimens. And throughout almost four years in the field, Lewis was nearly always exhausted from the research itself; each day was mentally challenging and taxing as he interacted with villagers who knew little of white-skinned people. Buying specimens and getting documentation from people who had no idea what anthropology was or why outsiders might be interested in local customs, local names for things, or their commonplace, handmade objects were exhausting and personally taxing chores.

Because his notes were almost always written when he was tired, they take the form of sparse, abbreviated comments about his observations. Throughout the diaries, Lewis employed a variety of abbreviations and shorthand comments. He inadvertently misspelled proper names and ordinary words. And although he employed a more or less systematic orthography for rendering native words and names, he records these names differently in different places as he heard them pronounced differently or heard them more clearly.

Lewis' expedition diaries are contained in seven small notebooks, written in pencil—often faint—in a scrawled hand. The diary text in each of these notebooks is reproduced here in its entirety, each as a separate "Book." None of the diary text has been deleted, abridged, or abbreviated. The inside covers of several of these diary notebooks contain a few—mostly disorganized—notes: names, word lists, bibliographic references, addresses, and the like nearly always without a specific context. A few of these notes from the covers have been added to the text as footnotes, although most have not been reproduced here.

xvii

Lewis organized his diary notes chronologically as daily entries, each headed with the day of the week and date. I have regularized these daily headings to make reading easier. On three or four occasions, Lewis inscribed the wrong date or day of the week. Such mistakes have been corrected; a footnote is included if such correction might be relevant to the order of events or Lewis' interactions with others. The diaries from the first year or so of the expedition (especially in books two and three) are more detailed and include word lists and the like. (In the last years of the expedition, Lewis wrote most of his extended entries and lists in separate notebooks, reserving his diaries largely for an account of where he went, who he saw, and what he collected.) These detailed entries and lists are usually set off in the diary by topic headings, which have been reproduced here. Several of these headings appear in the margin at the top of the notebook page and were intended to help Lewis find these sections in his notes later. In such cases, these topic headings have been inserted within the diary text where they belong. In editing this material, I have added a few topic headings [within square brackets] to assist the reader when Lewis' own headings by themselves would be misleading.

Following standard Department of Anthropology procedures, a departmental secretary at Field Museum typed a transcript of Lewis' diaries on his return from Melanesia, just as she typed up the notebooks containing his lists of specimens and photo captions. These typescripts had been used as the principal reference for the Joseph N. Field South Pacific Expedition for more than half a century, although all three types of transcripts contain numerous errors, particularly in the rendering of place names, names of individuals, and local words. Throughout, I have used the original expedition notebooks for transcribing, proofreading, and editing these diaries because the early typescript contains far too many errors, misunderstandings of Lewis' original intent, and the like to be useful by itself.

Lewis' spelling conventions have been preserved throughout the diaries, (e.g.) "cocoanut," "fibre," and "Pigeon English." My own introductory texts, however, conform to modern usage and thus use the more familiar spellings, "coconut," "fiber," and "Pidgin English" or simply "Pidgin." In about two dozen instances, Lewis misspelled very common, ordinary words, apparently when he was exhausted and writing hastily. Such trivial misspellings, which take the form of transposed letters or substitution of one consonant for another, have been corrected without comment, unless there seemed to be some possible question about Lewis' actual intent. Where Lewis omitted a word or two, particularly such words as [of the], [and], and the like, the text has been augmented in square brackets. In such cases nothing has been deleted. My intention was not to alter Lewis' text, but to make it clearer.

Lewis misspelled a number of the nearly three hundred personal names mentioned in the diary text. Where possible, these have been corrected in the text with a footnote to indicate Lewis' original spelling. This convention was adopted out of respect for the individuals mentioned, but Lewis' actual rendering is given to allow future scholars the opportunity of checking my identifications of these individuals. As an example, the editor of Malinowski's diary misinterpreted at least one of the expatriates mentioned by Malinowski (Ryan was the hotelier and publican, Tom Ryan, not assistant resident magistrate Henry Ryan; 1967, 9), and such mistakes are possible here as well.

One of Lewis' most frequent abbreviations is the ampersand. Because the abbreviation disrupts the flow of the text for many readers, I have replaced it, writing out "and" nearly everywhere (exceptions being in the proper names of firms, with Mr. & Mrs., and when the text is intended as an abbreviated note about the contents of his shipments). The ampersand has been retained in names of firms where it was standard usage at the time.

Lewis frequently used numerals in sentences rather than spelling out numbers. Numerals have been retained except in a few instances where spelling out numbers makes for greater clarity and readability. Such a use of numerals retains the feel of the original without affecting the meaning or clarity of the text.

Punctuation was more problematic. Lewis used many commas in his diaries, far more than is customary in modern, carefully crafted writing. His commas have been retained, except in a handful of cases, mostly instances in which Lewis seems to have revised his intended thought or sentence while writing. His commas, cumbersome as they may seem today, do set off phrases, clauses, and other meaningful units in his sentences, which tend to be longer and wordier than would have been the case if he had carefully edited and rewritten his text.

Another convention that Lewis frequently used has not been retained. This is the use of a comma, followed by a dash and a space, where a comma or an em dash would be more customary today. This complex punctuation has been simplified as either a comma or an em dash. These changes make the text more readable for modern readers without significantly affecting the feel of the original text.

Throughout the diaries Lewis frequently left blank spaces in the text, which he (presumably) intended to fill in later, after he had learned someone's name or a local word. In some cases, Lewis actually did fill in these blank spaces, but many—probably most—were left unresolved. Such lacunae illustrate how many new experiences and observations Lewis had as he moved constantly from place to place. In addition, these lacunae illustrate how hard it was to get information about a place after he had left. Where the original names or words are uncertain, I have inserted a line _____ instead of a blank space in the text as in the original. Throughout the edited text, anything in square brackets [thus] is my addition or my explanatory text, while any text in parentheses is by Lewis. Lewis' occasional use of square brackets—usually inside parentheses—is rendered here {thus}.

Only rarely did Lewis underline the names of ships or the titles of books or journals in his handwritten text. Here, for the convenience of the reader, both have been italicized. Occasionally, Lewis underlined vernacular terms or set them off in quotation marks in his text; these too I have set in italics. Pidgin, Malay, German, French, and Dutch terms, but not titles or proper names, are similarly italicized. Standardization of these usages generally follows Lewis' practice in work published during his lifetime; rigid adherence to the original in such matters would offer no particular insight into his growing understanding of Melanesia during the expedition.

In contrast to these conventions, I have retained Lewis' spellings of all vernacular words, including those in Pidgin and Malay, even when Lewis' rendering is incorrect for its time or when modern usage follows a different orthographic convention. When Lewis renders the Pidgin term for a kind of government-appointed headman *(tultul)* as *tulil,* it indicates how new he was both to Pidgin and to the German colonial system within which such headmen operated. When Lewis systematically spells the Pidgin term for anything associated with the secret men's cult as *tamburan,* which contrasts with the modern usage of *tambaran,* we catch a glimpse of how much Pidgin has changed and become systematized since the first decade of this century, when it had no fixed orthography.

Similarly, I have retained Lewis' spelling for all local place names, even when his spelling varies, typically settling in on a preferred spelling after a few days of hearing and writing down the name. Many village names did not have a standard spelling in 1909, and even when they did Lewis was recording the names phonetically as he heard them; his spelling thus offers some insights about how village people pronounced place names at the time and also about Lewis' growing familiarity with these village communities. Because the villages Lewis visited are generally not the places anthropologists have tended to study since the Second World War, many place names will be unfamiliar to a good many readers. Some names will be unfamiliar to most readers because they refer to places now called by different names or with different pronunciations. But whether names are familiar or not, retention of Lewis' original rendering offers a consistent point of reference against which his observations are made.

Diacritics have proved to be the most difficult domain in which to maintain loyalty to Lewis' text, textual consistency, and clarity for readers. Lewis seems to use a more or less systematic orthography, though an idiosyncratic one. He uses the macron (¯) for long vowels and the breve (˘) for short vowels, as well as an accent (´) for syllabic stress. For words with two or more syllables, Lewis was rarely consistent in his use of these three diacritics, typically introducing all of the length and stress marks in the first instance and gradually dropping all the diacritics as he repeatedly wrote down the word in his daily notes. But he is just as likely to reintroduce one or another diacritic, or even all of them, in later occurrences of the same word. In most cases such variation has little to do with his changing perception of how the name or word was pronounced; the diacritics took extra effort, and he largely dropped them after the pronunciation had been established.

Here the following convention is followed. Vowel length, if indicated in the original, is marked in the first occurrence of a vernacular term or local name. Stress, if indicated, is introduced (instead of vowel length) on the next occurrence of the word—or on the first occurrence if no vowel length is indicated. Subsequent usages are reproduced without diacritics, unless Lewis has introduced a new rendering of the word. This convention allows the edited text to adhere to Lewis' rendering of obscure vernacular words within the publisher's technical constraints, without excessively burdening the reader with a plethora of cumbersome diacritics. Lewis indicated a few diacritics on consonants, but these are unusual and pose fewer difficulties either for the publisher or for the reader.

All correspondence included in this volume is reproduced following the same guidelines as described above. In a few instances, the letters have been abridged and a paragraph or section has been deleted because it deals with unrelated topics. Such abridgments, however, occur only among the early correspondence 1906–1907 in Appendix 2 (Volume II); all expedition correspondence is reproduced in its entirety.

Abbreviations and Short Titles

American Anthropologist	*American Anthropologist.* 1898+. Washington: American Anthropological Association.
Amtsblatt	*Amtsblatt für das Schutzgebiet Deutsch-Neuguinea.* 1909–1914 (fortnightly). Simpsonhafen (later Rabaul): Kaiserliches Gouvernement.
ANU	Australian National University, Department of Anthropology and Sociology. 1968. *An ethnographic bibliography of New Guinea.* 3 vols. Canberra: Australian National University Press.
DKB	*Deutsches Kolonialblatt: Amtsblatt für das Schutzgebiete in Afrika und der Südsee.* 1890+ (fortnightly). Berlin: Reichskolonialamt (Kolonialabteilung des Auswärtigen Amtes).
Encyc. Ned-Indië	Encyclopaedisch Bureau. 1917+. *Encyclopaedie van Nederlandsch-Indië.* Ed. S. de Graaff and D. G. Stibbe. 5 vols. plus supplements. Batavia: Encyclopaedisch Bureau van Nederlandsch-Indië.
FBPP	Microfilm collection of the professional papers of Franz Boas. Originals at the American Philosophical Society, Philadelphia, Pa. Indexed in the two-volume *Guide to the microfilm collection of the professional papers of Franz Boas.* Wilmington: Scholarly Rescources Inc. in cooperation with the American Philosophical Society, 1972.
FMNH Annual Report	*Field Museum of Natural History Report Series.* 1894+ (annual report of the director; title varies). Chicago: Field Museum of Natural History.
NKWL	*Nachrichten über Kaiser Wilhelms-Land und den Bismarck-Archipel.* 1885–1898. Berlin: Neuguinea Kompagnie (by Asher & Co.)

PART
ONE

Introduction

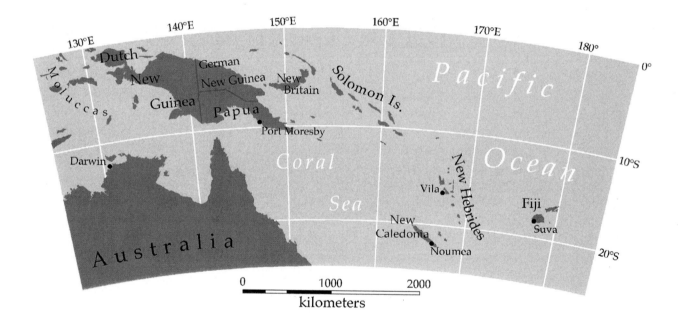

0		1000		2000	

kilometers

The Joseph N. Field South Pacific Expedition of 1909–1913

In the spring of 1909, Albert Buell Lewis (1867–1940) set off from Chicago on an expedition to the South Sea islands. The Joseph N. Field South Pacific Expedition, as it was later called in honor of its patron and financial backer, was an anthropological expedition formally sponsored by Field Museum of Natural History. At the time, Field Museum was a young but up-and-coming museum that had pretensions of competing with older, more established natural history museums on the East Coast, particularly the Smithsonian Institution in Washington and the American Museum in New York. By sending A. B. Lewis to Melanesia for a few years, Field Museum administrators hoped to acquire hundreds of rare and valuable ethnological specimens, which were becoming increasingly expensive and difficult to obtain on the international curio market.

A year earlier, in 1908, Anthropology Curator George A. Dorsey had made a whirlwind around-the-world tour, during which he visited the remote colony of German New Guinea for two months. On his return, Dorsey told Field Museum administrators and trustees about the kinds of magnificent and rare specimens that were still available for a modest cost in New Guinea and the other Melanesian islands. Museum director Frederick J. V. Skiff liked what he heard; so did the board of trustees. And so, at Dorsey's suggestion A. B. Lewis—the Department of Anthropology's newest assistant curator and one of Franz Boas' students—was sent off to Melanesia and the wilds of New Guinea to document what he could of native life through collections, through photographs, and through field notes.

Four years later, Lewis returned to Chicago from his first (and only) period of anthropological fieldwork. He had assembled the largest single collection of Melanesian material culture ever made in the field. Containing more than fourteen thousand objects and nearly two thousand photographs, his collection is still the premier American collection from Melanesia. It remains one of the most important research and reference collections of Melanesian material culture in the world. This book is the story of Lewis' remarkable collection.

From the beginning, Field Museum administrators viewed this South Seas expedition primarily as a cheap way of adding to their collections objects whose value was certain to rise in coming years. The expedition was also part of George Dorsey's grand plan to build up his department's collections. By 1909 Dorsey had headed the Department of Anthropology for a decade, during which time he had already nearly doubled Field Museum's ethnology collections

3

by mounting expeditions and through purchases from curio dealers. In proposing a South Seas expedition to Director Skiff and the trustees, Dorsey stressed its urgency, noting the growing international competition among museums in Europe and Australia to obtain material culture from New Guinea and the Melanesian islands. And now, on Dorsey's recommendation the museum sent Lewis off on what would become one of the museum's most extraordinary and successful ethnological expeditions.

But while Albert Lewis was extremely successful as a collector during these four years in Melanesia, both he and Dorsey had always viewed the South Seas expedition as principally a scientific effort. For both of these anthropologists, acquiring and documenting specimens for the museum's collections were basic and integral parts of field research. Like most American anthropologists of their day, Dorsey and Lewis had been trained in zoology and human biology before pursuing careers in anthropology. Field Museum's holdings of material culture from around the world were thus seen as essential data for subsequent study and analysis, in the same way that the museum's zoology and botany collections were. In these years before the Great War—as the First World War was generally known until the 1940s—anthropologists routinely went on research expeditions, and most collected material culture for museums during these expeditions. Of course, anthropologists also collected a variety of other kinds of cultural, linguistic, and biological data; but during the decade or two before the Great War, collections of material culture were an integral part, if not always the most important result, of anthropological fieldwork.

Here as we follow Lewis on his travels during four long years in the field, we are able to glimpse an important part of the history of American anthropology as it was emerging. He was the first American anthropologist to conduct systematic research in the region, and he was exploring and investigating problems that were shaping the discipline in both the United States and Europe. We have a rare opportunity here to observe how an early student of Franz Boas dealt with logistical, practical, and theoretical problems in the field.

This was an important time for the discipline of anthropology, as new field methods were being established and field researchers were developing more systematic ways of collecting anthropological data. It was also an age of self-conscious "science" in anthropology. Most anthropologists came into anthropology with training in some other scientific field, and most were attempting to make anthropology as rigorous and "scientific" as these other sciences with careful recording of data, improved notations and definitions, accurate measurements, plotting of distributions, and through systematic collections.

In the end, intensive ethnographic research would position itself as the most systematic and "scientific" field method for anthropology. But the pattern of research set by Bronislaw Malinowski during the Great War—the so-called ethnographic method—would dominate the discipline only by marginalizing other methods and field strategies as "speculative history," that is, as studies not based on careful, systematic, and rigorous observations.

Such claims by functionalists, especially Radcliffe-Brown (1958), were largely self-serving attacks on the style of analysis used by the British historical school, particularly Rivers (1914), Perry (1923), and G. Elliot Smith (1928). Radcliffe-Brown attacked the admittedly fanciful conclusions of these three diffusionists, not only casting doubt on the unproved assumptions that guided their analyses but also impugning their data as unscientific. Both Radcliffe-Brown and Malinowski were thus able to dismiss historical and regional problems for which it was claimed there were only "a few, a very few" facts (see Lowie 1937, 223).[1]

Radcliffe-Brown and Malinowski portrayed "historical ethnology" as having no rigorous facts or observations, distinguishing it from their own "social anthropology," in which one observes customs and practices directly and therefore can explain them by showing their relationship to other observed customs, practices, and institutions. Ironically, while the ethnographic method certainly did involve actual observations, ethnographic monographs written in the "ethnographic present" were also speculative reconstructions of "traditional" societies, described largely as ethnographers imagined communities might have been before becoming involved in the broader colonial society and global economy.

But when A. B. Lewis set off for Melanesia, functionalist studies were still many years in the future. Many anthropologists were working in Melanesia in the period immediately before the Great War, and each was building on common field methods by developing various kinds of systematic and structured research protocols. In these diaries we see how A. B. Lewis was elaborating on and improving the standard methods of what I will refer to as the "expedition period" in anthropological research, a period that extended from the 1890s until shortly after the end of the Great War.

By the label "expedition period" I mean to suggest a period in the history of anthropology characterized by a particular field strategy, the anthropological or ethnological expedition.[2] As a field method, expeditions emphasized extensive (rather than intensive) field research. This is not to say that anthropologists were uninterested in local field data, but merely that the problems most field anthropologists tackled in the field were regional ones, often aimed at documenting the regional distribution of particular cultural traits. To document such distributions required fieldwork very different from the kinds of village-based research most American, British, Australian, European, and Canadian anthropologists have routinely conducted in Melanesia since the Second World War.

To fully appreciate and understand the pioneering research of early anthropologists like Lewis before the First World War, we must recognize that their research questions and field objectives were very different from those of most anthropologists working half a century or more later. None of the now classic functionalist ethnographies would appear in print until 1922, and the intellectual challenges for these early anthropologists were quite different from those goals many of us have come to assume as the natural object of anthropology.

During the expedition period, anthropological research was oriented toward understanding and explaining observed cultural distributions, and there was a constant quest for defining and describing the world's culture areas as one way of coming to terms with cultural variation. There was little concern with functional explanations to account for the presence of a particular trait or feature in terms of its function or how it might operate within a certain social setting. If functionalist explanations were invoked, they were invoked as an explanation for a broad class of phenomena, such as magic, religion, the levirate, or the couvade. Instead, anthropologists tended to seek evolutionary, diffusionist, or other historical explanations for the distribution of traits they observed during their fieldwork.

Even in the early years of the expedition period, anthropologists were willing to consider a variety of causes for the presence or absence of particular cultural features, including biological explanations. This willingness is obvious from the results of the Cambridge Expedition to Torres Straits (Haddon 1901–1935), which show that anthropologists were ready to consider genetic, linguistic, and even environmental factors. By and large, however, evolutionary or culture-history models dominated the discipline, which found itself increasingly faced with growing mountains of survey data to sift through and analyze.[3]

As the expedition period wore on, anthropologists attempted to develop a variety of new field strategies and methods. Perhaps the best known of these was W. H. R. Rivers' (1910) "genealogical method," which he initially intended as a simple and reliable survey technique that could produce comparable field data from many places during his extensive travels in the Solomon Islands. Rivers (1914) used the rich kinship data from his Melanesian survey in his magnum opus, *The History of Melanesian Society*. But even though Rivers' analysis in this work was later vigorously criticized as speculative history, largely based on supposition and conjecture, his genealogical method became the standard method for collecting kinship data throughout the rest of the century.[4]

In other quarters methodological advances were being made with other kinds of field data. S. H. Ray (1892, 1893, 1895, 1896, 1907) and Georg Friederici (1912, 1913) were exploring various comparative methods that used linguistic data from Melanesia. Haddon attempted to develop a strategy he called "anthropogeography" (Haddon 1900a, 1906; see also Seligman and Strong 1906), though he is probably best known for his comparative studies of art and material culture (e.g., 1894, 1900b, 1920, 1923), which were essentially culture historical in tone. And Seligman (1910) produced a series of short comparative ethnographies of various Melanesian-speaking peoples in southeast Papua in an effort to document the cultural variation of a group of peoples he assumed were closely related.

Neuhauss (1911a) made photos of hundreds of villagers (front and profile shots) intended for anthropometric study. Similarly, both Lewis and Dorsey collected hundreds of skulls for essentially the same purpose (Hambly 1940a, 1946). Speiser (1923, 1991) attempted to understand the culture history of the New Hebrides using stylistic and material culture data, while his cousin Fritz Sarasin (1916–1922, 1917; Sarasin and Roux 1929) used an approach rooted in natural history methods combining comparative studies of material culture with anthropometry to study the culture history of New Caledonia.

Lewis was also concerned with documenting cultural variation in Melanesia. His fieldwork largely focused on variation in material culture: styles, designs, materials, uses, manufacturing processes, and so forth. His diaries often note what kinds of objects he saw in particular villages in addition to those he actually purchased for his collection. At times he seems almost obsessed with documenting such variations in material culture, an interest that is far removed from the work of most ethnographers today. Such a preoccupation was an effort to be rigorous; he was building a "systematic museum collection," filling in some of its inevitable lacunae with observational data about the items, styles, and designs he saw. He clearly saw his fieldwork as primarily aimed at building not just a museum collection but a research collection that he and others could study and analyze for many years to come.

In part, Lewis' interest in material culture emerged because he was a museum curator responsible for assembling a collection for Field Museum. But he also believed that material culture offered a good data set for studying cultural variation and culture history. Material culture was not the only possible data set Lewis might have studied, but for him it was as worthy and as accessible as most other possible data sets. Indeed, his concern with documenting local variation in material culture from village to village suggests that he felt that objects provided a particularly appropriate arena in which to study the processes of diffusion and interaction among communities with different cultures.

Similar research concerns had been the focus of his doctoral dissertation about Native Americans on the coasts of Washington and Oregon (Lewis 1906b). And Lewis' New Guinea research seems partly to have emerged from the same questions and problems that had motivated Boas and his colleagues during the Jesup North Pacific Expedition on the American northwest coast and the coasts of northeast Asia. These research questions concerned the culture history of broad regions or areas. And like many of the early Boasians, Lewis attempted during his fieldwork to identify culture areas or clusters of peoples that shared cultural features either because they shared a common past or because they had experienced cultural contact or diffusion.

Everywhere he went in Melanesia Lewis saw how rapidly indigenous ways of life were changing. In all of Melanesia, only in one village on the remote upper Sepik (or Kaiserin

Augusta) River were villagers unfamiliar with steel tools; everywhere else steel had already replaced stone tools. Thus, there was considerable urgency in building as complete a collection as possible to document traditional material culture, which was rapidly being replaced, supplemented, or modified with imported European goods.

Lewis believed that when objects were part of a systematic collection, they offered valuable clues about the diverse local and external factors that had shaped the communities from which the objects were collected. In this respect, his work drew upon many of the same assumptions that still inform archaeological research. For the modern period, beads, cloth, and steel, which he increasingly saw in Melanesian villages as part of their contemporary material culture, were prima facie evidence of the particular kinds of colonial situations in which these communities now lived. By the same token, Lewis assumed that objects unadulterated with beads, cloth, or paper would embody evidence of cultural influences that had spread across the countryside and from island to island before the arrival of Europeans.

This unmistakable aspect of ongoing change had an important effect on Lewis' fieldwork and the collection he was assembling. He had not come to study acculturation; for that he could have stayed home and visited Indian reservations like so many of his American colleagues. Here he wanted to make a systematic collection that would shed light on traditional cultures that were still thriving, even though they were experiencing rapid change as a result of European contact.

Concerned with documenting a traditional way of life, Lewis was thus concerned with building a collection that self-consciously depicted what I will call the "ethnographic past." He eschewed objects that illustrated the acculturative process in favor of "traditional" things, which included both old pieces and those recently made with traditional materials.

Decades later Malinowski and his students would write monographs in the "ethnographic present," extrapolating from what they saw to describe a traditional society they had never seen, usually one that had never actually existed. Here, for somewhat different reasons, Lewis self-consciously collected objects that had in fact been made and used by Melanesians as evidence of an "ethnographic past" he knew no longer existed, but whose objects were still present. He was, in fact, trying to find an authentic past by extrapolating from what he could see was changing.[5]

Lewis seems to have had a much more profound awareness of the importance of intervillage trade in shaping patterns of cultural similarity and difference than many of his anthropological colleagues. He recognized that different communities spoke different languages, had different specialized products, and exhibited differences in their local cultures; yet in spite of, or perhaps because of, such differences, communities often interacted to trade various kinds of objects, foodstuffs, and raw materials. Unlike many other museum-based anthropologists of the day, Lewis was keenly aware that the particular style, artistic motifs, or materials of a particular object were not necessarily a direct reflection of some local cultural expression; similarities could as easily be the direct result of trade, the borrowing of a style from another area, or shared traditions. These possibilities were repeatedly demonstrated to him throughout his four years in the field.

The distribution of peoples, cultures, and languages in New Guinea and the Melanesian islands proved far more complex than Lewis (and other anthropologists) may have anticipated. Ultimately, if Lewis was unsuccessful in accounting for Melanesia's diversity, the lack of success perhaps has less to do with his own failings than with the sheer complexity of the problem at hand. Melanesian diversity is certainly more complicated than the pattern of cultural variation Boas and his colleagues had studied during the Jesup Expedition. Even today no other scholar has as yet succeeded in accounting for Melanesia's remarkable cultural, linguistic, and biological diversity (see, e.g., Terrell 1986).

Although most anthropologists continued to collect objects from their study communities until the 1940s and even into the 1950s, museum collections became less and less central to the discipline after the Great War.[6] The shift to functionalism nearly brought an end to museum-based anthropology because most museum collections were assembled as data for comparative, regional studies and thus had little to say about local, functionalist questions.

The four years A. B. Lewis spent in Melanesia were critical ones for the discipline. During this period anthropologists were just beginning to shape anthropological research into the form we know today. Every anthropologist or ethnologist in the field—Lewis among them—was actively exploring new field methods, developing new research strategies, and addressing new anthropological problems. Most researchers conducted ethnological surveys of one kind or another, but there was no single set of anthropological problems to study, nor was there a single fieldwork method. Thus, while some anthropologists were experimenting with increasingly localized field studies, others—including Lewis—were conducting a variety of even more extensive studies in the field.

As the discipline was struggling to find a common research agenda, individual researchers were busy collecting data that would fill in the vast blank spaces on the ethnological map. In 1909, much of the globe was—anthropologically speaking—virtually unknown; practically nothing was known about the vast majority of Melanesia's communities. Thus, almost any kind of survey added important new data about almost any part of the region.

For A. B. Lewis, "Melanesia" comprised all the islands from New Guinea to Fiji. This region included the colonial territories of Dutch New Guinea (now Irian Jaya, a province of Indonesia), German New Guinea and Papua (now the independent state of Papua New Guinea), the Solomon Islands, the New Hebrides (now Vanuatu), New Caledonia, and Fiji. Although this was primarily a geographic definition of the region, it reflected a general awareness that the inhabitants of all of these island groups shared certain superficial physical features: dark skin and curly or kinky hair, features they did not appear to share with neighboring peoples in the Pacific, Australia, or Southeast Asia. At the turn of the century, it was generally assumed that the peoples of this vast region would share many cultural, linguistic, and biological characteristics.

As it happens, many cultural commonalities extend across many, though not all, of the region's peoples. But linguistically the region exhibits no homogeneity whatsoever: its six million people speak over a thousand mutually unintelligible indigenous languages. It is estimated that more than one-quarter of the world's languages are spoken in Melanesia. This is an extraordinary number of different languages, a fact that never failed to perplex early researchers. Today, anthropologists working in the region generally accept Melanesia's linguistic and cultural diversity as a given; but when Lewis set off for the Southwest Pacific, no one had any idea that Melanesia's communities spoke so many different languages or exhibited so much cultural variation.

In 1909 anthropologists had much to learn about the peoples of Melanesia, and most researchers were actively collecting field data that would allow them to identify the most important regional characteristics. It is certainly the case that early in the century a number of scholars overinterpreted their data, but the transition from regional surveys to village-based ethnography following the war led scholars largely to abandon their previous interest in regional, comparative, and processual problems. Now, half a century after the ethnographic method became the dominant field method and the ethnographic monograph became the standard anthropological field report, we know a great deal about many particular societies, communities, and ethnic groups. But we know little more than did Lewis and his contemporaries about the historical, developmental, and interactive processes that have continued to influence these communities.

Anthropology's infatuation with the (now discredited) "ethnographic present" and the society (ethnic group or ethno-linguistic group) as the fundamental unit of analysis led most researchers to minimize the importance of both the historical and the regional context within which their study communities were situated. More important still, this preoccupation with local ethnographic problems has led many of us to dismiss the problems that the discipline was actively trying to solve in the years before the Great War.

For example, although we know a great deal about many individual languages spoken in Melanesia, we are hardly any closer to explaining why one-fourth of the world's languages are spoken by 0.1 percent of the world's people. Similarly, we know only a little more now about how isolated from or how connected to their neighbors Melanesian communities were. Nor, despite shelves of ethnographies, do we yet have any detailed understanding of just which cultural characteristics vary and in what ways these characteristics vary throughout Melanesia. How is it possible that cultural and linguistic diversity have persisted in spite of intermarriage, trade, and other kinds of interaction between communities with different languages or different cultures? We can ask this question about both the precontact Melanesian world and the postcolonial world of the late twentieth century.

A. B. Lewis assembled an enormous collection of Melanesian material culture. He viewed these objects as research data that (he hoped) would help him answer some of these research questions. Throughout his four years in Melanesia, Lewis tried to obtain what he called "a connected view" of the communities he visited. He never collected data for a detailed ethnography but instead assembled data in the form of thousands of ethnographic specimens with reliably documented provenience. Shortsightedly, when the discipline abandoned "speculative history" for ethnography, it simultaneously abandoned ethnographic museum collections, not to mention the actual (nonspeculative) historical context of the colonial period that has continued to shape these same communities. As some of my own work with the Lewis collection shows, these objects offer direct, tangible evidence about Melanesian societies; they are a valuable data set that continues to offer insights about many of the regional and historical problems that originally interested A. B. Lewis and his contemporaries (see, e.g., Welsch 1995, 1996; Welsch and Terrell 1991, 1994, 1996; Welsch, Terrell, and Nadolski 1992; see also Terrell and Welsch 1990a, 1990b).

When Lewis returned to Chicago in the spring of 1913, more than three hundred crates and boxes of his specimens were waiting for him; others were still on their way. The mass of material he had assembled was so great that the Department of Anthropology had been forced to close one of its public galleries just to store the growing mountain of packing crates. For Director Skiff and his board of trustees, this mass of crates represented a welcome, not to mention valuable, addition to Field Museum's collections. For Dorsey these objects became the largest Pacific collection in the United States and enhanced his department's professional reputation. They justified his confidence in Lewis and demonstrated the value of Dorsey's own long-term program to build up his department's collections by sending his curatorial staff off on expeditions.

For Lewis, these crates represented years of hard work assembling a systematic data set. They had been long, arduous, and physically taxing years. He had spent four years on the move, visiting hundreds of villages, eating whatever mix of tinned goods and local vegetables was available, sleeping on his bedroll wherever he was given space. With difficulty he had surmounted bureaucratic obstruction and social ostracism. He had endured numerous bouts of malaria and diarrhea. At one point he had even been confined to bed for six weeks while recovering from an attack of (usually fatal) blackwater fever that had nearly killed him. And throughout these years he had faced continual problems over transportation both for himself and for his collection, often finding himself stranded while waiting for a ship, a cutter, or an outrigger canoe that could take him to his next destination.

While in the field Lewis had often planned how he might use his specimens in a new, exciting, and innovative exhibition that would illustrate a traditional Melanesian way of life that he knew was rapidly changing and in some places disappearing. He appreciated the artistry in his collection, but for him these pieces were not merely beautiful examples of Melanesian art or simply a rich and varied body of material suitable for exhibition. These specimens were a scientific resource, a body of data he thought would continue to offer insights about Melanesia's extraordinary diversity for years to come. They were scientifically valuable because when taken together they constituted a collection rich in types, in varieties, and in numbers of objects, all of which he had systematically assembled to document as many different parts of Melanesia as possible.

For Lewis, documenting the lives and material culture of Melanesian peoples required information about the objects he was collecting. He kept a daily journal or expedition diary that outlined his activities and what he observed in the villages. In this field diary Lewis kept notes about how different objects were made or used, jotted down other information about material culture, and entered remarks and observations that provoked his interest. As he moved about the region he kept a systematic log of his collection, a list of numbered specimens with notes about each piece (usually indicating where a piece was collected and made), local names, and other notes as appropriate. These specimen lists, together with his field diary and other notes, provided information about specific pieces and were the notes he used to catalog the collection on his return. By today's standards the documentation of his collection is limited to be sure, but his documentation is generally much better than that of other researchers and collectors of his day.

Lewis also took along a camera and tripod. Throughout the expedition he photographed ordinary village life. Some of these photos depicted the people's daily dress, their ornaments, and occasionally their physical type. Others illustrated local architecture, house styles, and the

A. B. Lewis' field notes: Archival box of notes in folders; seven diary notebooks (one open) with a glass plate negative and some negative envelopes, at left; twenty small notebooks containing specimen lists, photo captions, word lists, and miscellaneous notes (one specimen list open), at right. A-112401.

A page from one of A. B. Lewis' notebooks with designs on paddles collected at Cape Merkus, New Britain. GN-86760.

arrangement of houses in the villages. Still others showed villagers making things, building houses, or engaging in daily subsistence activities. Some were merely candid shots of life in the villages.

These expedition photographs offer unique views of Melanesians as they were before the First World War. Unlike the posed images made a decade later by the Australian photographer Frank Hurley (Specht and Fields 1984), Lewis' photos show conditions exactly as he found them, illustrating varying degrees of European influence on native life. He made no effort to reconstruct the past or to portray a more traditional way of life.[7] He was not taking professional photographs but making images that he could later use to study and analyze with his specimens to understand the material culture of the diverse peoples of Melanesia. It seems unlikely that when taking these pictures Lewis expected many of them to be good enough for publication; they were primarily intended as a study collection. For this reason he urged Charles Carpenter, the museum photographer, not to destroy any of his negatives because "many poor ones show things of importance," including some with very badly cracked emulsion.

Altogether Lewis took just over 1,900 photographs, of which some 1,561 images have survived. Toward the end of the expedition Lewis began to experiment with nitrate films, which

A. B. Lewis at Friedrich Wilhelmshafen
(now Madang), German New Guinea,
1910. A-33645.

could be exposed more easily than the cumbersome 4-by-5-inch glass-plate negatives he used for almost 90 percent of his photographs. Lewis had to process all of these negatives himself in the villages, a laborious and difficult task that caused him considerable consternation throughout the expedition. These images comprise the largest single collection of photographs of Melanesian life made before the First World War.[8] This feat is all the more remarkable because Lewis had had little photographic experience before he left Chicago in 1909.

Lewis viewed his photographs, his field diary, and his specimen lists as essential and integral parts of his collection. Individually, each part of the collection—the specimens, the photos, and his field diaries together with his other notes—provides important data about the Melanesian communities he visited, but when taken together, the whole is considerably greater than the sum of its individual parts.

This work tells the story of the Lewis Collection by combining all its integral parts. The centerpiece is Lewis' expedition diary, a journal outlining his daily activities during fieldwork. The original diaries consist of seven small, pocket-sized notebooks, each of which covers a different period in his travels and a different part of Melanesia. Lewis wrote this daily log in pencil, often barely legible, and intended it only for his personal use as a straightforward record of his work in the field. He did not write this text expecting it ever to be published, a fact that explains its abbreviated character and its intensely matter-of-fact style.

It is not a soul-searching analysis of Lewis' struggles in the field; in fact, it would appear that Lewis specifically excluded most personal details from his diary, probably because he expected his field diary to remain at the museum with his collection as part of its permanent documentation. As such, he would undoubtedly have felt it appropriate to excise personal reflection, complaints about either Dorsey or the museum's administration, and similar concerns from the expedition's formal record. Unlike Malinowski's diary (1967), which records the ethnographer's intensely personal and psychological experience of fieldwork, Lewis' diary is almost completely committed to day-to-day discussions of his work. Here Lewis offers no insights whatsoever into his inner state, nothing about the psychological aspects of fieldwork, and very little about the personal trials and challenges that confronted him.

Of somewhat more interest for the personal side of his experience in the field are his letters in the expedition's correspondence file (most of them to Dorsey and other colleagues at Field Museum). About twenty-five of these letters have survived. They refer to the same period as his seven diary notebooks but offer a more personal account of what Lewis experienced. These letters do not offer many more insights into Lewis' inner state than the diaries, but they give more expression to what he was feeling as well as more details about the frustrations of fieldwork and the countless other difficulties that he experienced during this epic journey.

Organization of This Work

This work comprises two volumes. Volume I consists of seven major sections or "Books," each representing one of Lewis' original diary notebooks. Except for the shortest (Book 1), each book is further divided into two or three parts. Each part deals with a special geographic area, a specific theme, or a particular issue. Initially, the reader may feel that this partition of Lewis' diaries disrupts the natural flow of his text. But because of the abbreviated and highly contextualized character of his diary entries, the reader who hopes to understand the context of Lewis' work, what he was doing, and whom and what he was seeing needs to have more background.

Each section of the diary opens with an explanatory introduction that sets the stage for Lewis' text. These comments provide some historical background about the different Melanesian colonies Lewis visited, notes about influential people he met, and an explanation of the circumstances and conditions he encountered in different places. Some consideration has also been given to the many other scholars and researchers he saw during the expedition because of the important role such encounters may have had on the history of the discipline.

Throughout, special attention has been given to how Lewis developed as a field researcher during the expedition. Although he had been a graduate student of Franz Boas, when he left Chicago in 1909 Lewis had never conducted his own field research. He had undoubtedly heard Boas describe the trials, tribulations, and successes of fieldwork, but Lewis himself had had no firsthand experience of ethnological, ethnographic, or anthropological field research. Naturally, it took Lewis some months to develop his own research style, establish his own field methods, and figure out ways of dealing with the discomforts of life on expedition. Understanding how Lewis grew and developed as a field researcher is particularly important for evaluating the enduring significance of his collection. But the story of how Lewis matured as a fieldworker is neither a unique nor an isolated event. At the time most anthropologists were similarly developing their own field methods and were maturing as researchers as well; Lewis' story is a particular example of what was happening throughout anthropology as the discipline was evolving.

One striking fact that emerges from Lewis' diaries is that although anthropologists often worked independently before the Great War, they seem to have encountered one another frequently. Anthropologists were not as isolated from other scholars in the field as we (in the late twentieth century) may assume they were. This fact has important implications both for the apparent independence of reported observations made by different anthropologists and for the growth and development of anthropology, as researchers may well have influenced one another during a time when new methods and novel ideas were actively being shaped in the field.

Selections from Lewis' "letters from the field" follow these introductory notes. Each letter deals more or less directly with the events covered in the diary and shows a more human side of both Lewis and his work. These letters from the field also tell a quite different story about the actual events and difficulties he encountered. It is only in his correspondence—usually following some provocation or frustration—that we get a glimpse of what Lewis was hoping to accomplish scientifically and the broader goals he had for later analysis of the collection.

This volume is illustrated throughout with two kinds of photographs: those that Lewis took in the villages are interspersed with recent photos of objects in the collection made for this volume by the museum's Department of Photography. Although his diary text offers a kind of running caption and discussion about these images, the images are essential for understanding what Lewis was observing and what he was doing in the field. Lewis made many simple pencil sketches and maps in his diary and other notebooks, and a selection of these sketches is also included among the figures that illustrate the text.

Lewis' expedition photographs offer unique views of village life in many of the places he visited. The selection of objects in the Lewis Collection provides an illustrative sample of the kinds of material he collected and examples of the documentation he provided. In most cases, the photo captions are drawn from his original field notes.

Book 7, the last of Lewis' diaries, concludes with a short section titled "The Long Road Home: From Batavia to Chicago." This section contains two letters Lewis wrote Dorsey during his journey home, describing his travel plans and his continued enthusiasm for his research and for the collection he had assembled. Both letters are filled with logistical details about shipping and about smaller collections he had purchased to fill in gaps in his own collection, but they also reflect the excitement of a seasoned field anthropologist returning home from a successful period of fieldwork. Each is followed by Dorsey's cordial reply, which describes the reaction to Lewis' expedition back at the museum.

The first section following the diaries ("Return from the Field") explains the Gargantuan task of unpacking, numbering, cataloging, labeling, and finally exhibiting the collection that confronted Lewis when he returned to Chicago. There is every reason to believe that on his return to the museum his initial enthusiasm was quickly dampened as he contemplated the enormous amount of work awaiting him. Not only did he face the prospect of working up his own collection of well over 14,000 pieces, but he was responsible for cataloging several other substantial collections that Dorsey had arranged just before Lewis left in 1909 or in his absence. These collections included a collection from Richard Parkinson, the German ethnologist residing in German New Guinea; two collections from Captain Voogdt of the New Guinea Compagnie; a collection Dorsey had purchased in 1912 from Umlauff, a curio dealer in Hamburg; and Dorsey's own German New Guinea collection, obtained in 1908 but as yet uncataloged. Together these additional collections numbered more than 10,000 items, yielding a total of some 25,000 objects that awaited Lewis' attention.

The monumental effort of processing his collection consumed virtually all of Lewis' time at the museum for five years and then some. During the period from 1913 to 1919, he cataloged 25,000 objects, installed 50 exhibit cases, and wrote more than 3,000 exhibit labels. He gave a few public lectures illustrated with lantern slides made from his negatives, but throughout this period of more than six years he published nothing about his field research. His responsibilities at the museum almost certainly account for his not being a more prolific and better-known anthropological author.

The main text of this volume concludes with an examination of Lewis' place in the discipline of anthropology. This Conclusion situates the Joseph N. Field South Pacific Expedition into the context of a discipline that was already changing before the Great War and that would be completely transformed in the first decade or two after the war. Lewis' work has been largely ignored by anthropologists for many decades, in part because he wrote little and as a museum curator had no students to appreciate and to carry forward his seminal work. But his work has also been ignored and often dismissed because—after his return from Melanesia—the discipline abandoned expeditions, surveys, and comparative or historical studies in favor of intensive, local ethnography.

The concluding chapter therefore attempts to explain why the work of A. B. Lewis and his contemporaries and expeditions like the J. N. Field Expedition of 1909–1913 seem remote from modern research and recent research problems. I think the comprehensiveness of this shift from extensive to intensive and from broad, regional studies to narrow, village-based projects was short-sighted. By abandoning historical and regional research we have simultaneously abandoned entire families of research questions that are still both relevant and unanswered.

Volume II contains several appendixes. The first contains a brief biographical sketch of A. B. Lewis, together with a complete list of his known publications and his posthumous publications and editions, along with a list of reviews and commentaries on his work.

Appendix 2 ("The Early Correspondence of A. B. Lewis, 1906–1907") contains twelve letters to, from, and about Lewis written in 1906 and 1907. During these sixteen months, Lewis was finishing his dissertation at Columbia University and looking for employment at Field Museum. These letters demonstrate the early origins of Lewis' reticent and at times self-deprecating style. They also illustrate how different the discipline of anthropology was in 1906, when employment as an anthropologist was difficult to find, when fieldwork was almost totally dependent on the direct financial support of wealthy patrons, and when virtually the whole world was available for research by an enterprising anthropologist.

Appendix 3 ("Who Was Who in Melanesia, 1909–1913") provides a series of biographical sketches of about 280 individuals named in the text of Lewis' diary, field notes, and photo captions. To appreciate many of the abbreviated references to most of these named expatriates requires considerable background information about many individuals whose lives and significance to the history of Melanesia are obscure to most anthropologists and art historians, and probably to many Pacific historians as well. These biographical entries are provided to help readers interested in these diaries as a historical resource, because Lewis—who knew full well whom he was writing about—rarely explains who the people he met in Melanesia were. The field diaries are a unique historical document about Melanesia before the First World War, but most readers will find them more interesting and easier to follow and understand if they know who the people were that Lewis encountered during his travels. While reading the diaries, readers may want to refer repeatedly to these biographical sketches.

Appendix 4 provides a summary (in table form) of all the cataloged items in the Lewis Collection, numbering some 14,385 objects in 12,041 catalog numbers. This list is provided as a shorthand guide to the collection and its documentation. It offers a breakdown of the collection according to object type and the locality where each was collected, allowing interested researchers to determine quickly whether the collection contains material of particular types or from particular areas. This list demonstrates the character of the Lewis Collection as an attempt at a systematic research collection. Excluded from this listing are some four hundred pieces that were exchanged with the Australian Museum in Sydney for Aboriginal material. About two hundred other items were apparently brought back to Chicago but were discarded and never cataloged because they had been destroyed in shipping or were thoroughly eaten by insects; these items are also excluded from this table. All cataloged material, including some items that have been subsequently exchanged or deaccessioned, is reflected in the table.

Appendix 5 contains a comprehensive list of the more than nineteen hundred photographs Lewis took during the expedition. For each image this list provides the negative number, locality, and caption and notes whether the image has survived.

Together, these materials are an invitation to scholars and the indigenous peoples of Melanesia to make use of this impressive collection for better understanding Melanesian life, culture, history, and especially Melanesian art and material culture.

Albert Buell Lewis: The Early Years

A. B. Lewis (hereafter ABL) was born 21 June 1867 in Clifton, Ohio, a village of three hundred people in central Ohio, not far from Springfield.[9] ABL was the only child of Charles Boughton Lewis and his wife, Anna E. McKeehan, who were married in 1864.[10] The families of both his parents were solid, well-to-do, Presbyterian citizens of this rural farming community.[11] ABL's grandfather, Bennett Lewis, had been one of Clifton's original proprietors and for many years was the village's largest landowner.[12] Tragedy struck the family when ABL's mother died on his second birthday.[13]

ABL's father remarried about 1872. The following year, Charles and his new wife, Susan M. Waddle, began their own family when Harry, the first of ABL's six half-siblings, was born. ABL maintained a warm relationship with his two brothers and four sisters and corresponded with them during his travels in Melanesia.

Beginning his education at Clifton Union School, ABL attended classes in this four-room schoolhouse from first grade until he completed high school.[14] He was an exceptionally bright student and is said to have been the only pupil at the school ever to have received marks of 100 in all his subjects. He graduated in 1887 in a class of three students.

After the death of family patriarch Bennett Lewis in 1876, the family's ties to Clifton began to wane. Uncle Ezra, who had been a clerk in his father's dry-goods store, set off in the 1870s to find his fortune in California; he eventually settled at San Jose and became a merchant. In 1883 Aunt Harriet set off for Canton, China, as a missionary with the Presbyterian Board of Missions; in 1918, although in her eighties, she was still in the Chinese mission field. About 1884 ABL's father moved his family to Santa Ana, in Orange County, California.[15]

Of the Lewis family, only Uncle Storrs was left in Clifton by 1885. ABL stayed on in Clifton to finish high school, living for two years with Uncle Storrs and his family, then joining his father in Southern California after graduation. In 1890 ABL returned to Ohio to begin his college studies at the University of Wooster, a well-respected Presbyterian liberal arts college.

ABL's quiet temperament and self-effacing reserve were probably shaped in part by the several disruptions in his early life—the death of his mother, his father's remarriage, and his family's move to Southern California—and in part by his own superior academic abilities and interests.

Undoubtedly, Wooster was an attractive college because of its strong Presbyterian associations, but ABL was probably drawn to Wooster for other reasons as well. Ohio had an especially large number of liberal arts colleges, several of which were near Clifton and thus well known to ABL and his family. At the time, California had few colleges and universities, and none would have been as well known or would have seemed to offer as good an education as those back home.[16]

ABL's class at Wooster was small, although with forty-two students in his class (thirty-four men and eight women) it was substantially larger than his high school. Here he pursued the classical program, completing his studies in 1893. At Wooster he established an interest in biology, a subject in which he excelled. During his senior year he was appointed assistant in biology, a position whose duties probably involved setting up and straightening up the biology lab.[17]

In 1893 ABL continued his studies in biology, enrolling for the autumn term at the University of Chicago. Although the University of Chicago had only recently opened (in 1892), it already offered the possibility of more advanced training in the sciences than did Wooster. During the academic year ABL largely took courses in the sciences, especially chemistry, geology, and zoology. In June 1894 he completed his bachelor's degree (A.B.) in biology and was among the first graduates of the college.

Following graduation, he continued his science curriculum from 1894 to 1897 with assistantships at the university in biology (1894), in histology (1895), and in bacteriology (1896). During these three years he took courses often associated with medical training in anatomy, physiology, morphology, osteology, and embryology, as well as courses in paleontology, botany, zoology, geology, chemistry, and geography. ABL was clearly headed for a career in biology or medicine during these extremely rigorous years at Chicago. It is unclear what interest ABL had in anthropology during these years. But even if he had wanted to study anthropology, at that time there were no anthropology programs in the Midwest, and it would be another thirty years before the University of Chicago would have an anthropology department or a proper anthropology curriculum.

In 1897 ABL followed his career trajectory in the biological sciences by accepting a teaching position at the University of Nebraska in Lincoln. Here he taught zoology for five years, first as a fellow (1897–1899) and later as an instructor (1899–1902). But as a bright, thirty-something academic, ABL seems to have wanted more from life than being a lowly paid instructor who could afford no better than to be a lodger in someone else's house in Lincoln, Nebraska. At the time, the University of Nebraska would have seemed to him a remote and unimportant university, far from his home in Ohio and even farther from his family in California. In describing this phase of his life, ABL later wrote of teaching zoology in Nebraska that "I accidentally got started in that line, and had to stay by it till I got enough money ahead to make the break." In all likelihood he had become interested in anthropology and had begun to consider a career in that discipline before arriving in Lincoln, or perhaps soon afterward.

While the shift from zoology to anthropology may now seem like an abrupt change in discipline, it is unlikely to have seemed such a major shift at the time. Anthropology training in the United States was essentially limited to Harvard and Columbia. In both programs anthropology students received considerable training in somatology, human anatomy, and physical anthropology, courses ABL had already completed at Chicago. It was probably these studies that had drawn ABL's attention to anthropology in the first place (Hambly 1941), even though in graduate school he soon became caught up in what we now call cultural anthropology. His interest in cultural anthropology may also have been enhanced by his Aunt Harriet's letters from China and through contacts with Native American groups in Southern California during the summers.

In the end, ABL applied and was admitted to graduate school at Columbia University to study anthropology. There he began his first formal studies in the field and there he became a student of Franz Boas, the father of American cultural anthropology.

From Columbia University to Field Museum

When ABL arrived at Columbia in 1902 for the fall term, Franz Boas was the university's leading (and practically the only) anthropologist. Boas had taught anthropology at the university since 1896 and had been appointed professor of anthropology in 1899. When Boas arrived at Columbia he had arranged a simultaneous curatorial appointment for himself at the American Museum of Natural History. This arrangement insured close ties between the two anthropology departments, a relationship that persisted even when Boas' own interest in the museum began to wane.

Previously (1888–1892), Boas had been at Clark University, where he taught Alexander F. Chamberlain, his first graduate student to receive the Ph.D. From 1892 to 1894 Boas was in Chicago, working under Frederic W. Putnam on anthropology exhibits for the World's Columbian Exposition. When Field Columbian Museum was founded in 1893, acquiring a large part of the collections Putnam had assembled for the fair, Boas stayed on and supervised new installations of the material in one of the old exposition buildings. But he left Chicago in 1894 following an acrimonious dispute with Field Museum director Skiff.[18] In 1895 Boas obtained an appointment in New York at the American Museum of Natural History. The following year he started at Columbia, beginning a long-term relationship with the university that would last until his death in 1942 and have a profound impact on the young discipline of anthropology.

Although the anthropology department was still very small when ABL began his studies at Columbia, the first decade of the new century would see many changes in the department. It brought many bright, young members of the faculty together with a group of promising graduate students and in effect established the new discipline of anthropology as part of the modern American university. Most of these key developments occurred during ABL's four years of study at Columbia.

In one of his early letters (reproduced in appendix 2), ABL mentions five men with whom he had worked or studied at Columbia besides Boas: Professors Livingstone Farrand, Clark Wissler, Adolph Bandelier, Marshall H. Saville, and Berthold Laufer. All of them came to the department after ABL had begun his studies with Boas. Farrand had long been at Columbia in the psychology department when he was appointed professor of anthropology in 1903. Wissler, Saville, and Bandelier also joined the department in 1903, and Laufer arrived two years later.

It was a very young faculty. Only Bandelier—whose appointment was actually at the American Museum rather than at the university—was a mature scholar; he was sixty-three years

18

old in 1903 when he returned from a decade of research in Peru. Of the others, Farrand and Saville were the oldest. But they were only thirty-six when they joined the faculty. As it happens both were born the same month and year as ABL—June 1867; Farrand was a week older and Saville three days younger than ABL. Of the others, ABL was three years older than Wissler and seven years Laufer's senior. For ABL it was a young faculty indeed.

But despite their relative youth, it was a distinguished group that Boas had recruited. Aside from Farrand, they were all, like Boas, deeply involved in museum-based research. Yet, also like Boas, all of them conducted a considerable amount of field research.[19]

The year before ABL arrived, the department had awarded its first Ph.D. to A. L. Kroeber, who immediately left to take up a position in Berkeley's newly established anthropology department. Thus, while ABL missed having Kroeber as a fellow student, he sat in seminars and classes with an impressive group of other students, including among them William Jones, F. G. Speck, Robert Lowie, Alexander Goldenweiser, Edward Sapir, and Fay-Cooper Cole.[20] It is notable that of these early students of anthropology, only Goldenweiser subsequently had no important ties to a museum.[21]

Anthropology at Columbia involved studies that often considered material culture as appropriate data for analysis. Material culture was routinely used as an important marker of previous cultural connections, a topic of interest to the early Boasians. There were close relations between the university and the American Museum of Natural History. Faculty members at Columbia often had appointments at the museum, and the museum's curatorial staff often taught at the university. These ties clearly shaped the directions and kinds of research Boas' early students conducted after leaving Columbia.

In June 1905 Boas wrote ABL asking him to present a preliminary account of the ethnology of the Columbia River tribes in relation to their neighbors during their autumn seminar (FBPP, FB to ABL, 18 June 1905). Boas must have discussed the subject with ABL earlier in the spring. This research may have originally been ABL's proposed thesis topic. Quite possibly, Boas had suggested the topic to him because the subject fit so nicely with Boas' own work on the Jesup North Pacific Expedition. In any event, by the summer of 1905, ABL had already begun research on what would become his dissertation.

This thesis, "Tribes of the Columbia Valley and the Coast of Washington and Oregon," was a library study whose object was to "bring together the more important facts known regarding the natives of this area, group them according to culture areas, and see if they throw any light on possible movements of peoples and cultures." ABL would have liked to have conducted his own original fieldwork, but the cost put such a field trip well out of his reach. As it was, he had been forced to supplement his small savings by working. Wissler, for example, had used him as a research assistant at the American Museum, and Farrand had hired him to do some of the research and writing of various encyclopedia and dictionary entries.

Like most scholars and students who worked with Boas in this period, ABL began by defining the region's culture areas. But from the outset he faced a perplexing intellectual challenge. His research dealt with a diverse collection of peoples that had previously been discussed as a mix of Northern California and Northwest Pacific slope cultures. Rather than write of these communities exclusively in terms of what they had borrowed from their northern and southern neighbors, ABL approached their culture as an example of local development.

ABL did not deny borrowings from neighboring groups but turned the problem on its head and saw neighboring cultures and communities as part of the environment within which the Columbia River tribes had developed. Clearly, the importance of the Chinook at the mouth of the Columbia, who were renowned traders and middlemen within the region, encouraged him to conceptualize the area as one with its own internal dynamic rather than as a set of peoples whose culture was entirely derived from more important neighbors. For its time, this was a sophisticated analysis of a perplexing problem and one that would likely have been missed had his work come from field research. As we shall see, this study was an important testing ground for understanding complex cultural relationships in a context where much obvious trade and other kinds of interaction occur.

Before ABL had completed his dissertation, he met George Dorsey, curator and head of the Department of Anthropology at Field Museum of Natural History, which had only recently changed its name from Field Columbian Museum. Dorsey had been at the museum for a decade and was actively trying to develop his department by building up its collections and developing its staff. He often tried to achieve both ends at once, building his department by hiring assistants, researchers, or assistant curators who could be sent off to get more collections.

Early in 1906, when Dorsey went to New York to visit the American Museum, he met ABL, who was soon to become the fourth Boas student to complete a doctorate. In 1905 Dorsey had hired William Jones, Boas' third Ph.D. student; Columbia was a natural place to scout new talent for his department's growing staff.

Over the next months there followed an exchange of letters between Dorsey and ABL in which they discussed the possibilities of employment at Field Museum. Dorsey kept ABL dangling for many months but finally hired him a year later, in March 1907. During this time Dorsey tried unsuccessfully to find one or another wealthy Chicago patron to provide funds for ABL to go off on an expedition. In 1904 Dorsey had successfully found such money for Fay-Cooper Cole, who had not even begun graduate school. Dorsey, who moved comfortably in Chicago's highest social circles, felt confident he could do the same for ABL.

But Dorsey had more trouble finding funding than he had expected. After completing his dissertation, ABL was forced to find something productive to occupy his time. Preferring to wait for a position at Field Museum, ABL declined an offer to be as an assistant editor at the *New International Encyclopedia,* only to be forced to throw in his lot for the summer with an archaeological project in southern Ohio. Thus, he joined William C. Mills, who was excavating Seip mound that season. ABL found the excavation hard physical work with little intellectual stimulation. Nevertheless, he was employed for the summer and was able to spend some time with his Uncle Storrs Lewis before returning for the fall to New York, where Boas seems to have found him some additional research work that allowed him to pay his rent.

What is most important in this correspondence (reproduced in appendix 2) is that Dorsey consistently envisioned that ABL would come to Field Museum planning to go off on an expedition. Dorsey seems to have had many possible ideas about where he might send ABL, but no firm decision was made. In these letters, including one soon after ABL had joined the museum's staff, Polynesia, Melanesia, South America, Africa, the Pacific Northwest, and the Malay region are variously mooted as possible destinations. The diversity of this set of fieldwork destinations illustrates how open the discipline was at the time. Vast regions were—anthropologically speaking—virtually unknown, and choice of field site depended more on being able to interest a wealthy patron in a specific region than on developing a particular research problem.

In the end, it was more difficult to attract a patron than Dorsey had expected. To snatch ABL up before he was hired by some other institution, Dorsey hired him as an "assistant" to replace one of the department's preparators who had recently died. This was not Dorsey's original intention, but when the museum administration offered him no funds for another assistant curator and no patrons seemed forthcoming, this was the best Dorsey could do.

And so in the winter of 1907, ABL returned to the Windy City to catalog collections for fifty dollars a month. For some months he worked primarily with African material collected by

C. E. Akeley in British East Africa and some German collectors in Togo and the Cameroons. It looked as if ABL too was headed for Africa. But even on this point Dorsey was vague, and as always, Dorsey continued to keep his cards close to his chest.[22]

Mounting the Expedition

George Dorsey liked traveling and did a lot of it. He routinely made trips to the East Coast or out to visit Native American communities in the Western states. He also made frequent trips to Europe. On many of these trips he purchased collections or attended conferences or conducted his own collections-based research at other museums.

In the spring of 1908 he set off on a round-the-world trip that kept him away from the museum for nearly eight months (Dorsey 1909a). During these travels he visited Europe, Egypt (where he accessioned ancient mummies, a tomb, and other antiquities), India and the Dutch East Indies (where he obtained collections of textiles), Australia (where he arranged for an exchange of specimens), German New Guinea, the Philippines, and finally Guam, on his return to Chicago.

He had planned to stay a month in German New Guinea, but when offered the opportunity of joining Governor Hahl's patrol across Bougainville (Dorsey 1909b; *American Anthropologist* 1908 (10), 504), which would be the first crossing of that island by a European, Dorsey extended his stay for a second month. These arrangements allowed him ample time to visit the north coast of the New Guinea mainland (Kaiser Wilhelmsland) with Capt. H. Voogdt of the New Guinea Compagnie, including an ascent of the Sepik River. He also had a chance to meet Richard Parkinson, whose now classic book, *Dreissig Jahre in der Südsee,* had been published the previous year (1907). (Dorsey later arranged to purchase important collections for the department from both Parkinson and Voogdt.)

During these travels, Dorsey purchased more than two thousand specimens; he later bragged about how his "loot" had filled the tiny steamer *Siar* to overflowing. Throughout his stay in German New Guinea, the colonial government and the New Guinea Compagnie were more than accommodating. Other members of the expatriate population also extended him a warm, inviting hand. When he left the German South Seas colony, he decided that Melanesia seemed to be one of the most promising field areas for one of his assistant curators. This, finally, was an expedition for A. B. Lewis.

Meanwhile, back in Chicago ABL continued to catalog African material and comb publishers' book lists for suitable volumes to add to the departmental library. When Dorsey returned, however, things began to change. Dorsey informed ABL of his intentions and instructed him to start boning up on the South Seas material in the library. Then Dorsey turned to Director Skiff and his wealthy Chicago friends.

Just before Christmas 1908, Dorsey wrote to Skiff outlining his plan for a South Seas expedition, nominating ABL to head the expedition. Skiff agreed, provided that Dorsey could raise the funds, so Dorsey went around Chicago's high society in search of a patron. He found his patron in Joseph N. Field, the older brother of the museum's founder, Marshall Field of department store fame.

Joseph Field's son, Stanley Field, was president of the museum's board of trustees. And it was probably through Stanley Field that Dorsey was able to interest the elder Field in his department's growing South Seas collections. Dorsey expected funds of $5,000.00 per year for three years; on this basis, Skiff and the board agreed that Dr. Lewis should make himself ready for this long expedition.

And so in March and April 1909, ABL purchased a camera and other things to outfit himself for an extended stay in the tropics. Days before ABL's departure, Dorsey wrote ABL formal instructions outlining what was expected of the expedition (reproduced below). Dorsey recommended that ABL divide his time, spending a year in German New Guinea, a year in Papua and the Melanesian islands, and a year in Dutch New Guinea. So at the age of forty one, untried and untested in the rigors of fieldwork, ABL readied himself for what would be one of the longest anthropological expeditions ever mounted. Still single, ABL had no wife or children to keep him from an extended period of fieldwork. He seems to have been dating at least one Chicago woman before he left, but this incipient relationship did not survive his four years in Melanesia. Two years after his return from the field, ABL married Gertrude Clayton of Chicago, but he had no family commitments before setting off on the expedition.[23]

ABL left Chicago on 8 May 1909 bound for Fiji via the West Coast and Hawaii. The Chicago newspapers announced his departure on their front pages, but this exciting Field Museum story about a new scientific expedition was overshadowed by tragic news that had been received the previous day: William Jones, the museum's assistant curator and ABL's fellow student at Columbia, had been murdered by natives during fieldwork in the Philippines.

When Dorsey interested Joseph Field in the South Seas he also encouraged him to allocate part of these funds toward the purchase of collections from Parkinson and Voogdt. When ABL left Chicago, the Field family had not yet given the money that would fund the expedition, though it was expected in the near future. Within two months Mr. Field had offered his donation to "defray the expenses of the South Sea Islands Expedition." This was how great museums were able to mount such expensive expeditions before the Great War.

FIELD MUSEUM OF NATURAL HISTORY
CHICAGO

December 22, 1908

Mr. F. J. V. Skiff
Director, Field Museum of Natural History

Dear Sir:

Of all the countries recently visited by me New Guinea impressed me as most deserving immediate attention. I believe that nowhere else in the world is ethnological investigation so imperatively demanded, and that nowhere else can so great and valuable a mass of museum material be secured at such a reasonable expenditure of money. With the material which I secured in German New Guinea and with that which I hope we may acquire from Captain Voogdt our collection from that region already ranks among the greatest in the world. But even in German New Guinea are great stretches of territory entirely unexplored. From English New Guinea we have important collections, but they are representative of only one or two localities. From Dutch New Guinea we have next to nothing.

New Guinea, as a whole, is in the peculiar position of a country freshly opened, but where it is possible to travel with safety and with a fair amount of comfort, and where the natives are willing to part with the objects of their material in exchange for the cheap knives, hatchets, axes, adzes, beads, looking glasses, etc., of German manufacture. In other words, the conditions there are absolutely ideal for museum collecting. One or two institutions are already aware of this fact and Berlin and Hamburg, especially, are taking advantage of it, but so far they have practically confined their attention to German New Guinea.

New Guinea is the largest island in the world; it is densely inhabited; it contains, probably, sixty distinct centers of culture; its material culture is amazingly rich, especially in material of high museum value. We have it easily within our power to make from New Guinea the greatest and most valuable collection ever to be made. But conditions are rapidly changing, and the old carved ghost houses, masks, countless ceremonial paraphernalia, the stone, bone and shell tools, native costumes, great carved ceremonial drums, carved shields, the wonderful headdresses of birds of paradise, etc., all of these will rapidly disappear. We are in a position to do in New Guinea to-day what might have been done, for example, among our western Indians sixty years ago. I strongly favor taking immediate advantage of this almost unique opportunity.

In Dr. Lewis we have a man eminently fitted to undertake this work. He knows, as few, if any, men know, the literature of this vast territory.[24] Better than this he has spent months in overhauling, examining, classifying, and cataloguing all our material from that region. He will at once catalogue and arrange the material which I collected along the middle New Guinea coast and on the Kaiserin Augusta River.

I recommend that $15,000.00 be appropriated for the purpose of collecting and investigating the cultures of New Guinea; the sum to be expended during three years, and that of this sum $5,000.00 be made available for Dr. Lewis on March 1st, and $5,000.00 on each of the two succeeding years. Should you approve of this recommendation, I would propose that Dr. Lewis leave Chicago on April 1st, or shortly thereafter, and proceed directly to English New Guinea, spending from six to ten months in an ethnological survey of the entire coast; that he then proceed to German New Guinea, penetrate the interior, especially on the Ramu and Kaiserin Augusta Rivers, spending in German New Guinea approximately six months; and that the remainder of the three years, about twenty months, be spent in Dutch New Guinea. I am confident in the belief that, as a result of such an expedition, our Institution would secure material for publication and for exhibition purposes of enormous value and extent. I make this recommendation now in order that Dr. Lewis may have ample time in which to make preparation for a long absence.

> Yours respectfully,
> Geo. A. Dorsey
> Curator of Anthropology

FIELD MUSEUM OF NATURAL HISTORY
CHICAGO

May 5, 1909

Dr. A. B. Lewis
Assistant Curator
Department of Anthropology
Field Museum of Natural History

My dear Dr. Lewis:

Some time ago, as you are aware, I recommended to the Director that the sum of $5,000.00 be appropriated to defray your expenses and work of collecting for an ethnological investigation in Melanesia. At that time I suggested that this work be continued for two additional years. The Director has approved of my recommendation, and the sum of $5,000.00 less $600.00 which will be used for the purchase of some specimens from New Guinea, is now at your disposal. You will consider then that the sum of $4,400.00 is an appropriation with which you are to carry on work until a year from May 7, the supposed date of your departure from Chicago.

While I fully hope and expect that the two additional sums of $5,000.00 each will be appropriated to carry on the work for the first, second and third years, yet it will be well for you to bear in mind that we are certain only of this first appropriation.

You will proceed to Melanesia by route which we have agreed upon, and at once begin your work. I realize the impossibility of directing from this point the exact plan or even scope of your investigations. All the details of this must be arranged on the spot by you. As you are to proceed via Fiji you will ascertain on arrival there if you think it advisable to stop off for one month in order to have a look at the Fijians and possibly supplement our collection. I am inclined to doubt the advisability of this, but will leave the matter to your judgment. From Fiji, I assume that you will go to Sydney, and thence to Herbertshöhe, the capital of German New Guinea, where you will report to Governor Hahl, and take his advice in general as to the safety of regions under his jurisdiction, and discuss your plans with him freely, for I am of the opinion that he is greatly desirous of aiding our work, and from his knowledge of conditions can be of great service to you. How rapidly you move about through the German possessions will depend upon circumstances and on your judgment on the spot. I am inclined to think that our collections from the coast region are sufficiently complete, except two or three areas, about which we have already talked, and in these areas you will only do such work as seems necessary to make our collections adequate. I think it highly desirable that you should, on the coast of German New Guinea, secure as many of the large carvings from the ceremonial houses as possible. I should also be very glad, if the opportunity presents itself, for you to ascend the Kaiserin Augusta River. Should you desire to settle down in any one spot in German New Guinea for any long stay of several months, you will be the best judge. I should say, in general, that you might devote one year to the German possessions, making, if possible, a trip to Gardner Island for New Ireland carvings, and one or two trips into the interior of New Britain and a trip to the Admiralty Islands; that the second year might be spent in British New Guinea and in the Melanesian Islands on the east, such as New Hebrides, New Caledonia, British Solomons, etc.; that the third year be expended in Dutch New Guinea and the adjacent islands to the west.

I should be glad if at the end of every six months you will forward to the Director a brief report of your movements, together with an itemized account of expenditures to date, sending in at the same time such vouchers as you have. You have already received from the office instructions as to the shipping of your collections. These will be held unopened here until your arrival, unless you should direct either Mr. Simms or Mr. Owen to have them unpacked and placed in storage.

Should you at any time feel that a continued stay in the tropics is impairing your health, you are at liberty to take the steamer and go to Brisbane or Sydney to recuperate.

Please bear in mind that during the next three years I shall probably be absent from the Museum and that you will address your reports that you may make from time to time, together with the account of your monies, to the Director's office, to which should also be sent all invoices and bills of lading.

You are not expected, out of your funds, to prepay freight on any of your collections.

With all your collections of specimens you will, of course, gather such data as will be needful for the proper labeling thereof. In connection with your collections, you will, of course, conduct ethnological investigations, which will have to deal with the general culture of Melanesia or such phases or special sides of its culture as you deem worthy of investigation.

You will at all times zealously regard your health and safety by every possible safeguard, wherever necessary employing native constabulary, etc.

Wishing you a most pleasant and profitable journey and expressing the hope that you will maintain perfect health and find your work agreeable and interesting, I am

Very truly yours,
Geo. A. Dorsey
Curator of Anthropology

{From the Field Museum Minute Books}

2 July 1909. The following communication was read:

Mr. F. J. V. Skiff, Director
Field Museum of Natural History, Chicago

My dear Mr. Skiff:

I take pleasure in enclosing a check for $10,000.00 which is a donation of Mr. Joseph N. Field to defray the expenses of the South Sea Islands Expedition.

This money can be used to pay for the Parkinson material received from Capt. Voogdt and for the appropriation made at the first of the year to defray the expenses of Dr. Lewis' Expedition.

Yours very truly,
Stanley Field

The secretary was instructed to notify Mr. Joseph N. Field that his contribution was received by the trustees with much gratification and to express to him their full appreciation of his well directed generosity.

In view of the contribution made by Mr. Jos. N. Field and the funds placed at the disposal of the Museum for the purpose stated, the Director was instructed to purchase the Bismarck Arch. ethnological material from R. Parkinson, which on account of lack of funds it was ordered at the meeting held May 10, 1909, not to purchase.

Further, to arrange to purchase a certain collection of New Guinea ethnological material from Capt. H. Voogdt for the sum of $2,400, less $52.78 advanced freight. (This payment, however, is not to be made until Jan. 1910). All of this material is already in the possession of the Museum.

Further, to return to the General Fund the sum of $4,400 appropriated for the expedition of Dr. Lewis to the South Sea Islands on January 18, 1909, on which expedition Dr. Lewis has already embarked.

PART
TWO

The Field Diaries of
A. B. Lewis

Fiji

VANUA LEVU

Bua

Taveuni

VITI LEVU

Ba

Ra

Nandi

Rewa River

Viria

Bau

Nadroga

Suva

Nausori

Cuvu

Navua

Rewa

Sigatoka

Lau Group

Lakeba

Kadavu

Kabara

Matuku

Book 1

Fiji

||||||||||||||||||||||||||||||||||||||||||||||||||||||||||||||||||||||||||||||||||||||||||||||||||||||||||||||||||||||||||||||

9 June 1909–8 July 1909

On 8 May 1909, ABL left Chicago by train for California. After a day or two in San Francisco he embarked on a steamer for Hawaii, spending a week in Honolulu. Finally he set off for the South Pacific, heading initially for Fiji. His first port of call was Suva, capital and largest city of the British Crown Colony.

Like the *Odyssey* or the *Aeneid,* ABL's diary begins in medias res. The first book opens in Suva on 9 June, a month after his departure from Chicago. Although it is not clear exactly when he arrived in Fiji, it was probably about 1 June. He may have spent a few nights in one of the Suva hotels, but within the first week or so he sought out more economical lodgings, an arrangement suitable for a month's stay. And so ABL seems to have settled in at Mrs. Johnston's boarding house on one of Suva's side streets. This he could use as his home base for the several excursions he was planning into the surrounding countryside. He began assembling what he could of field gear and getting a feel for Suva. During these first weeks, ABL seems to have met quite a number of people in town, all of whom seemed more than happy to be of assistance. These included planters, government officials, photographers, and curio dealers, many of whom were old Fiji hands and members of the recently formed Fijian Society, a group that met periodically in Suva to discuss aspects of Fijian culture and history. Finally, on 9 June 1909 he began his field diary.

In many respects ABL's experiences in Fiji bear little resemblance to his experiences elsewhere in Melanesia. Fiji was, of course, ABL's first real fieldwork experience, and such differences are partly a consequence of his relative inexperience and naivete in the field. But the differences between ABL's fieldwork in Fiji and in the other Melanesian colonies also reflect the fact that of all the Melanesian territories, only Fiji had already become a mature and established colony.

Fiji was the oldest and most developed colony in Melanesia.[1] Europeans had been settling there for nearly a century. By 1874, when King Cakobau and twelve other chiefs signed the deed of cession transferring the sovereignty of Fiji to Great Britain, Europeans had already been deeply involved in Fijian political and economic affairs for a quarter-century.[2] Of all the places ABL visited in Melanesia, only New Caledonia had the sort of European development and settlement he found in Fiji, and as a consequence his experiences in these two colonies are more similar to one another than to his work elsewhere. But the contrast between Fiji and other parts of Melanesia may appear even sharper because, while elsewhere ABL was drawn to remote and undeveloped areas, in Fiji his activities centered on the most developed parts of the main island, Viti Levu: Suva, Sigatoka, Rewa, Nasori, and Bau.

Before he arrived in the colony, ABL already knew about Fiji's violent past. In Suva, old settlers would have repeatedly told him about the brutal wars of the nineteenth century that brought the rise of Cakobau, a minor chief from the small kingdom of Bau who became paramount chief or *tui viti* over virtually all of Fiji. Bau was a tiny island off the southeast coast of Viti Levu, "scarcely a mile in length, and with the exception of the summit, which serves as the deposit of all the dirt and refuse, is covered with houses disposed in irregular streets, reminding one, in a degree, of the poorer parts of some of our West India towns" (Erskine 1853, 185). But by 1850, after waging a series of bloody wars with the other six Fijian kingdoms or *vanua* and assisted by guns and a few European beachcombers, Cakobau achieved control over nearly the entire archipelago.

Cakobau's wars with Rewa and Verata on the Viti Levu mainland were among the most brutal.[3] After one battle in 1839 the victorious warriors from Bau brought 260 of their dead enemies back to Bau for a great celebration and cannibal feast.

> Many women and children were taken alive to be kept for slaves. About 30 living children were hoisted up to the mast head as flags of triumph. The motions of the canoes when sailing soon killed the helpless creatures, and silenced their piercing cries. Other children were taken alive to Bau that the boys might learn the art of Fijian warfare by firing arrows at them and beating them with clubs. [David Cargill, from Schütz (1977, 159)]

But soon after Cakobau's rise to power, he faced growing opposition from both British and American trading interests, leading to a blockade of Bau by British warships in the early 1850s. In 1854, largely as a way of gaining both European and Tongan allies, Cakobau converted to Christianity. In becoming a Wesleyan, he made Christianity the new religion of Bau and ordered the destruction of heathen temples. He prohibited many traditional rituals and practices, simultaneously encouraging his people to attend services at the mission, which gained an important base on Bau itself.

ABL's reasons for remaining in the developed parts of southeastern Viti Levu probably had to do with two issues. The first concerned his instructions from the museum; the second had to do with the historical importance of Bau, Rewa, and Sigatoka in Fijian history. Given his instructions and his interest in the important chiefly kingdoms of Fiji, the decision to visit areas near Suva was a reasonable one, even if this strategy now tends to make his activities in Fiji seem anything but a systematic attempt to document traditional Melanesian culture.

Dorsey's instructions regarding Fiji had been explicit. He doubted whether a stopover in the colony would be productive (meaning that traditional specimens would be hard to obtain and most would be expensive), but he gave ABL the option of a month's stay in Fiji should the latter find anything of consequence there. ABL undoubtedly would have liked to have accompanied John Waters on a trip into the mountains, but such a trip would have taken more time than ABL could spare; furthermore (according to Waters), there was little to be collected there. Thus, ABL confined his activities to areas he could reach fairly easily from Suva, and these areas just happened to be the traditional kingdoms of most consequence.

As ABL met various old Fiji hands and read a few early accounts of the islands, it would have become clear that Bau and Rewa were the two most important kingdoms on Viti. To these could be added their sometimes allied, sometimes vassal states at Nasori and Sigatoka, providing a list of the major areas involved in the brutal wars of the mid-nineteenth century, renowned for their cannibal victory feasts. And, of course, old settlers like David Wilkinson, Simeon Lazarus, A. H. Ogilvie, and Humphrey Berkeley almost certainly steered him toward these historically important areas.[4] It was probably only on arriving in these now developed communities that ABL realized his work on Fiji would not be what he had hoped for, as everything he saw was strongly influenced by the Methodist mission, sugar and banana production, and other European enterprises.

In 1909 Fiji's population was about 135,000, of which about 90,000 were Fijians, roughly 35,000 Indians, and some 5,000 or 6,000 of European or part-European descent (Coulter 1967, 35ff.). The plains and deltas of southeastern Viti Levu, which attracted ABL's attention, were organized economically around sugar production and a few other plantation crops, for which Indian laborers had been imported beginning in the late nineteenth century. Native Fijians were engaged in many kinds of agriculture, including banana production, subsistence gardening, and small-scale truck gardening. Fijian commoners seem to have been less involved in producing sugar than were Indian laborers, European planters, or Fijian chiefs. ABL's excursion to Sigatoka was set against a background of boatloads of bananas being readied for export to New Zealand, while his sojourn at Rewa and Bau was set amid the vibrant sugar industry with vast fields of cane, sugar mills, and various kinds of secondary development, such as Brandyork's store and the industrial high school.

ABL came to Fiji to study traditional Fijian material culture. He did not intend to study its export economy, the lifestyles of Europeans, or the cultural and economic changes that were sweeping through native Fijian communities. Thus, it is ironic that these latter issues dominate the first pages of his diary. In Fiji he moved at first in a world centered on Europeans. His diaries record anecdotes about his comings and goings and offer some feel for the intensity of at least two domains dominated by Europeans: the relatively fast paced commerce of Viti Levu and the activities of the Methodist mission. In both domains Fijians played either minor or subservient roles.

In the latter part of the first notebook, the focus of his diary shifts to village life. ABL increasingly offers observations on mundane matters of material culture. Occasionally he comments about status relations within Fijian society, influenced as it was by the formal governmental structures and appointed headmen (the *buli*s) and nobles with quasi-hereditary titles (the *ratu*s) or positions on government councils (the *roko tui*s).

Historians are likely to be disappointed by ABL's comments about colonial Fiji. He offers little analysis of relations between Europeans and Fijians and only the slimmest of anecdotes about the relations between Fijian nobles and commoners. I doubt that ABL had more than a vague sense of how Fijian society was organized, either in traditional terms—a topic that clearly interested him—or in the modern colonial context of 1909—a topic that may have been useful for him, but that would have held little interest for his research. Even ABL's thoughts about agriculture, exports, and commerce are more anecdotal and abbreviated than they would have been had these topics genuinely interested him.

Perhaps most striking about ABL's records of his first days in Fiji is what is absent from his account. Throughout his month in Fiji, ABL never mentions the presence of Indians in Viti Levu, although he must surely have seen hundreds of Indians laboring in the sugar fields and in the mills.

This lacuna also reflects ABL's initial concept of fieldwork. He was charged with the task of making a large museum collection that would illustrate the culture and achievements of Melanesians. ABL took seriously his responsibility for assembling a world-class collection, much as other Field Museum curators were doing in other parts of the world; but this meant that neither the Indian laborers nor the structure of the modern Fijian economy held much interest for him. As a result he wrote very little about such topics in his field diary.

Such omissions and truncated accounts of what ABL must have seen and heard reflect where ABL placed his research priorities: he had come to the South Seas to study traditional Melanesian culture, especially material culture, art, and technology, not to study colonialism or Fijian culture change. His field diary clearly shows us these biases. His decision to concentrate on the old kingdoms of southeast Viti Levu had thus been the wrong one, as these communities emphasized the latter set of issues rather than the former. And these concerns are probably what led ABL to his unusual manner of acquiring (and documenting) specimens from Fiji.

Building a Collection: Lessons Learned in Fiji

During his month in Fiji, ABL had his first opportunity to acquire ethnological objects for Field Museum. Compared with his collections from the other Melanesian colonies, his Fiji material is mediocre at best. He collected very little of it himself. Large parts of it, in fact, were purchased from a few curio dealers in Suva, especially from the well-known and respected photographer John W. Waters.

ABL's Fiji collection, which numbered only 257 objects, was by no means the only part of the Lewis Collection purchased from local European residents. In nearly every colony ABL visited he bought similar small collections from colonial residents, usually to represent communities or specimen types he could not obtain himself. Typically such purchases represented villages or districts he could not visit on his own for lack of time or adequate transport, or they contained material that was now scarce or no longer made, such as stone clubs. Before the Great War it was customary for museums to acquire collections of material culture from curio dealers, and Dorsey regularly purchased material for the museum from dealers and long-time residents all over the world. In Fiji, then, ABL was clearly following a pattern he had often observed in Chicago.

After making some purchases from Waters' stock in Suva, ABL asked him to collect additional material on his next collecting trip. But ABL also asked Waters to collect examples of baskets, earthenware, raw materials, and a variety of utilitarian objects that Waters rarely collected on his own because there was no market in Europe for such common and mundane items. In addition ABL asked Waters to record the Fijian names for objects sent on to Field Museum and to identify the materials used in each piece. ABL even asked Waters to make notes on use and function. (It is a tribute to Waters that he not only made an effort to provide such documentation, but he offered notes on the distribution of object types in Fiji. Waters was the only one of ABL's delegated field collectors to provide "museum-standard" documentation.)

Although ABL did himself obtain a few specimens in villages around Sigatoka, Rewa, and Bau, he turned all of these objects over to Waters for shipping, with the understanding that Waters would send along descriptive notes about the entire collection, whether purchased from Waters or not. The only extant specimen list for ABL's Fiji collection is one written by Waters in a small notebook. This list is probably more complete in its descriptions of materials, uses, and indigenous names than it would have been had ABL written the list himself. But unfortunately, Waters' list comingles objects that ABL bought in the villages with those purchased from Waters or Lazarus, another dealer in Suva. As a result, information about provenience is less precise for the pieces Waters did not collect than if ABL had provided a separate specimen list.

Throughout his expedition ABL was forced to turn over his specimens to someone else for packing and shipping, especially as his collections got larger and more cumbersome. But leaving the documentation to someone else was uncharacteristic behavior for the man who would assemble the largest single field collection from Melanesia. Later when ABL left money with traders or missionaries to make small collections for him, he was often forced to rely on (typically limited) documentation and notes made by these collectors, particularly when specimens were sent directly to Chicago. But he never again entrusted the documentation of his own collections to anyone else. After leaving Fiji, he assumed responsibility for documenting his collection, which would become one of the best-documented prewar collections from Melanesia. Indeed, ABL's documentation is what sets the Lewis Collection apart from most other collections from the period.

While in Fiji, ABL seems to have reflected a great deal on how he was going to build a systematic collection. During this month, as he tried his hand at buying objects in the villages and selected material from dealers in town, he considered various collecting strategies. By the time he left Fiji he had formalized what became his philosophy of collecting in the field, and he wrote about this subject to Dorsey a few days before his departure for Sydney. In this letter (reproduced below) we find ABL's only explicit statement of how he understood different kinds of collections. He explains his sense of what makes a strong, systematic ethnological collection, primarily by illustrating why his Fiji collection was not a systematic collection, but merely a "type collection." (One senses in this discussion of collections the wise but subtle guidance of John Waters mixed with ABL's own museum experience and training. In this sense, Fiji was very much a training ground for him.)

Faced with limited funds and a scarcity of fine old specimens, ABL was forced to decide what kind of collection he could afford to buy to represent Fiji. In his letter to Dorsey, he tried to explain why his collection was somewhat limited in the number of large carved pieces. In the process he outlined his understanding of what made an ethnological collection systematic.

For ABL, systematic collections should be as complete as possible in types, varieties, and specimens. A systematic ethnological collection should thus include examples of every major object type, including rare and unusual types as well as inexpensive, commonplace items—such as baskets, mats, and pots—which were of little interest to most curio dealers and collectors in 1909. The best systematic collections should display the range of variation in designs, styles, materials, motifs, and the like for each type of object, illustrating with many examples the variety within each type. By containing many examples of different types and differing varieties within each type, a systematic collection documents both the range of variation and the typical or modal variety of different kinds of objects.

ABL had sufficient funds for a modest "type collection," but his collection contained few examples of unusual object types. Had he been able to afford more, he would have increased the number of varieties of different types of carvings, such as clubs, headrests, and wooden bowls. But he would have preferred to obtain a more systematic collection, such as the one Waters showed him. This collection contained many seeming duplicates of types and richly illustrated the range of variation in kinds of objects and in the designs within each type to be found in Fijian material culture. For ABL this became a goal for his collections from other parts of Melanesia, where funds and time were not so much an issue.

Anthropologists and the Position of Fiji among Pacific Cultures

Fijians have always presented a classificatory conundrum for anthropologists keen to sort the world's peoples into neat racial, ethnic, or culture-area groupings. On the one hand, Fijians have rather dark skin, frizzy hair, and a history of fierce warfare and cannibalism, all characteristics that have been commonly associated with Melanesia. On the other hand, the Fijian language is closely related to Polynesian languages like Tongan and Samoan; additionally, Fijians had unmistakable chiefs and social hierarchies, and they were traditionally preoccupied with special tabus for their hereditary nobility, characteristics that many still associate with Polynesia rather than Melanesia. None of these so-called Polynesian features are absent from Melanesia, however.[5] Hereditary chiefs, social hierarchies, and status-based tabus are even found in some communities in Melanesia that speak Non-Austronesian languages, thus making the classification of Melanesia and Polynesia even more complex (see Terrell 1986).

Largely on linguistic grounds many anthropologists now classify Fijians as Polynesian, although it is still not obvious that language should take precedence over all other human characteristics. But in 1909 the matter was much less clear, and ABL consistently saw Fiji as the easternmost outpost of Melanesia. Even as late as 1932, when ABL published his monograph, *The Ethnology of Melanesia,* he treated Fijians as Melanesians in his discussion. ABL clearly defined Melanesia in cultural rather than linguistic terms, and he was among the first to consider the range of variation in social and material forms found in all parts of the southwest Pacific from Dutch New Guinea to Fiji. He saw Fijians as falling comfortably within the range of cultural variation that became for him the hallmark of Melanesian cultures.

For the anthropologists of 1909, language was not the definitive marker of broad ethnic associations that it has become since the Second World War. At best, language was but one cultural characteristic to consider when sorting out the world's peoples into culture areas, tribes, or other cultural groupings. The presence of particular cultural traits—often items of material culture such as the bow, betel nut, or kava—were routinely seen as markers of broad culture areas that linked communities speaking different languages. For many researchers such markers were as important as physical characteristics in defining culture areas; and racial types and cultural traits were seen as more important in defining culture areas and ethnic groupings than was language. But perhaps most important, such cultural classifications had a purpose: associations among culture traits were expected to elucidate the origins and culture histories of diverse communities, to provide order in a confusing mélange of cultural variation by exposing its history.

In this respect modern classifications of Pacific peoples into societies, cultures, ethnic groups, and ethno-linguistic units have different objectives from those schemes developed before the Great War. Modern classifications are aimed at description rather than explanation. By defining the inhabitants of a set of communities as the "X people," whether X is understood as a society, a culture, an ethnic group, or an ethno-linguistic group, anthropologists today are attempting to distinguish the X from neighboring communities, many of whom may be generally similar. The goal is to describe the set of communities for whom cultural generalizations can be expected to hold (Watson 1967), that is, to identify those communities who share certain essential traits. Rarely do these modern classifications overtly define units larger than a single ethnic group. The diverse classifications of the early twentieth century, in contrast, were aimed at illuminating the (pre)historic trajectories and migrations of peoples on the basis of one or more significant traits thought to be survivals from an earlier era.

Today, classifications of societies and cultures are typically based on similarities in language.[6] For our generation, language is the *only* cultural survival widely accepted as having any utility for tracing culture history—an assumption with which ABL would have strongly disagreed. And for anthropologists of the late twentieth century, language has been accepted (often implicitly) as *the* principal marker of cultural similarity. Associations marked by similarities of language are implicitly (and usually uncritically) assumed to tell us about a great deal more than language history: they are assumed, often in naive ways, to document racial and cultural history (see, e.g., Kirch and Green 1987; Moore and Romney 1994; but cf. Welsch, Terrell, and Nadolski 1992; Welsch and Terrell 1994; Welsch 1995, 1996).

As ABL's teacher Franz Boas (e.g., 1940) long ago taught us, the characteristics of race, language, and culture are independent of one another. Such characteristics may be associated, but it is naive to assume that linguistic associations are inevitably good indicators of either cultural or racial characteristics (Welsch, Terrell, and Nadolski 1992). Clearly ABL did not assume that any single trait or dimension defined either essential Melanesian characteristics or Melanesian culture history. Those who would define Melanesia in terms of a single dimension, such as language, or according to a dichotomy between ascribed and achieved leadership (e.g., Sahlins 1963), would do well to consider the broad range of variation that ABL observed in the field. In both his diaries and his monograph it is clear that he saw no strict dichotomy between big men and chiefs, since he saw hereditary leaders in many of the communities he visited in New Caledonia, the New Hebrides, the Solomon Islands, the Bismarck Archipelago, and in various parts of New Guinea.

Colleagues in the Field

During his month in Fiji ABL met the first two of many anthropologists he would encounter during the J. N. Field Expedition: the young British anthropologist A. M. Hocart and the American cultural anthropologist Roland Dixon, who was also several years ABL's junior. Both were engaged in ethnological research that fit more or less neatly within the range of activities that anthropologists did during what I have called the "expedition period" of anthropological research.

The twenty-six-year-old Hocart had recently completed fieldwork in the Solomon Islands with W. H. R. Rivers on the Percy Sladen Trust Expedition to Melanesia. A. C. Haddon, at the time one of England's most influential anthropologists, had arranged a position for Hocart in Fiji as headmaster of the Lau Provincial School in Lakeba. The research for Hocart's subsequent prolific writings on Fiji was just beginning when ABL met him in Suva.

Hocart apparently made a poor impression on ABL, who misspelled Hocart's name as "Bocart" and also seems to have reacted skeptically to the young ethnologist's theories regarding African origins of Melanesians. Indeed, for ABL such migration theories seemed overly simplistic, incomplete, and often unnecessary as explanations of conditions that could be accounted for largely as the result of in situ development (Lewis 1932a, 10–14). In this theory, Hocart seems to have differed substantially from his own mentor, Rivers, who was at that very moment writing his magnum opus, *The History of Melanesian Society*. But while ABL may have thought both the young Hocart and his theories to be brash and naive, Hocart was beginning precisely the kind of intensive ethnographic research that ABL recognized was desperately needed at the time.

Near the end of his sojourn in Fiji, ABL heard that Roland Dixon of Harvard had arrived in the colony and raced down to Dixon's hotel to meet with this well-known anthropologist, who several years earlier had assisted Boas during part of the Jesup North Pacific Expedition. As one commentator has noted, "Dixon was regarded by fellow Boasians as exceptionally erudite and almost inhumanly impersonal" (Murray 1991, 149). One senses from ABL's diary that ABL witnessed Dixon's renowned arrogance and aloofness firsthand: ABL was asked to wait for Dixon to finish dining before the latter would even chat with his American colleague.

Dixon was beginning research for a book about Oceanic mythology (1916). After a few days' vacation in Fiji and a visit to New Zealand he proceeded to Sydney, where he would collect data on Australian Aborigine myths. In 1909 many anthropologists still viewed Aborigines as "survivals" of an early evolutionary stage of cultural development. Dixon would thus have expected Australians to play an important role in Pacific mythology. Intellectually, social scientists were converging on Australians because of their presumed evolutionary status. Dixon's visit was part of a much more general trend that culminated a few years later when Durkheim (1912, 1915), Freud (1913), Malinowski (1913), and Radcliffe-Brown (1913) published—in almost the same year—four important analyses about Aboriginal Australians (see also Kuper 1988 on the place Aborigines played in anthropological theory).

Although origins of customs and culture traits per se played only a minor role in Dixon's study of myth, the topic would become increasingly important in his subsequent works, *The*

Racial History of Man (1923) and *The Building of Cultures* (1928). ABL himself was less preoccupied with either the origins or the migrations of peoples, although even in 1909 he already shared Boas' interest in cultural "diffusion." Nor did ABL have a pet theory to prove in the field as did so many of the scholars he met on his travels. Nevertheless, ABL was gradually developing his own research agendas about cultural processes. These were still inchoate when he was in Fiji and would only begin to emerge as a systematic strategy a few months later in German New Guinea.

Suva, Fiji
July 4, 1909

My dear Dr. Dorsey:

I have taken the liberty of stopping over a month at Fiji, and do not think that the time has been wasted. I find that there is still a great deal to be obtained in the islands, tho the best specimens are rapidly disappearing. The natives, however, still make tapa, mats, baskets and pots in great variety and in exactly the same forms and designs as in the old time, according to the best information that I can obtain, both from the natives themselves and from the oldest settlers and those best informed in Fijian matters. Spears, certain kinds of clubs, carved and ornamented wooden dishes (plain ones very common) and certain old styles of dress and ornaments are very rare. A few very good specimens, however, are yet to be obtained, but fetch rather fancy prices, which I have not felt that I could give, even tho they seemed exceedingly rare types, and very good examples of native workmanship. Tho the Fijian rarely made any representation or drawing of man or animals, he still was noted for the great variety of his designs and his excellent workmanship. The Tongans, for example, used to get their canoes in Fiji, and Cook speaks of the Fijian as surpassing the other islanders in the variety and excellence of his implements and utensils. Tho the best are gone, a considerable number and variety remain, but very much scattered and highly prized by the natives themselves. In the short time that I have been here, I have obtained a number of specimens myself, and have also made arrangements with Mr. John W. Waters of Suva, to obtain for me a representative collection up to the value of $300.00, with full information and label, box and ship the same. Part of these I have already selected from a rather large collection he already has. A better collection, by the way, than the one he sold last year to New York, which so far as I know, is the one acquired by the American Museum. It was shipped first to England, and Mr. Waters knows that it went to New York, but does not know the final purchaser. From all that I can learn, it must be the one the Museum got, however, Mr. Waters' present collection is better than that, but has immense numbers of duplicates. I selected a type series—could not take many varieties, and passed over a few rarities, because of their high price. This up to nearly $200.00. With the other hundred he is to fill in a large number of common things, which he had not regarded of sufficient value to collect, such as a representative collection of baskets, mats, pots, fishing utensils, etc. with materials of which they are made, some in process of manufacture, etc.; also photos of stages of manufacture and uses of same. Also the fullest information he can collect with native names, etc.

Regarding Mr. Waters, I may say that he has lived in Fiji for 20 years or more, speaks the language well, is the best photographer in the island (in fact, that is really his business), and uniformly regarded as an honorable and upright man, and the one best fitted to do this work of anyone in the islands. He also takes an interest in that sort of work. He is fairly well to do, and travels around the islands in his own launch. He said he did a lot of photo work for the <u>Albatross</u> when she was down here and sold A. Agassiz about $1,000 worth of curios.

He has just left for a three to four months trip around the islands, in which he proposes to collect everything he can find. In addition to what I have bargained for, he has agreed to give me the refusal of anything else of value that he might obtain, which would serve to make our collection more complete, and seems to take pride in trying to make it as full as possible, in types, if not in specimens and varieties, for there is an immense variety in their ornamental designs and carvings.

I did not feel that I was justified in spending in Fiji any more than what would be proportional to the time I spent here, but it seems a shame to let this opportunity go, for Mr. Waters is just about cleaning out the place, and he already has purchasers for a large share of his collections. One man, in fact, had agreed to take almost every rare specimen that he got, but as I caught him the very day he returned from his collecting trip, he gave me first choice, and also refusal of any new specimens. For about $175.00 I got about 70 specimens, nearly all of them types. I also selected about 80 prints from his large collection of several hundred photo plates. As I said before, he is to get more photos as well as specimens, and as the latter are quite cheap, the number of specimens will be proportionally largely increased. I ought to have at least $500.00 more, however, to make the collection anywhere near complete, as there is great variety in their pottery, baskets, mats and tapa. I find, for example, that they still use the printing board for tapa, which is practically extinct in Samoa. They show great variety in designs, too. If you would return that $600 you took out of my appropriation, I think I would put part, at least, into Fiji. The last 10 years have caused many changes, and the next 10 will cause even more. There is now a large industrial school in operation, and even the old methods which are now so common will soon be extinct or at least the product will be no longer Fijian. Well, enough of this, but I should be glad to know what you think.

I myself have not been out of the larger island (Viti Levu), and not very far into the island. I have touched on the coast in a number of places, however, and have seen many things of interest, including the building of houses, making pots (following whole process), mats, tapa, baskets, working in their taro beds, planting yams; also seen some fish traps, crab traps and rat traps, all native Fijian. I have been so busy with this sort of thing that I have had no time for anything like social organization, etc., tho I have had some very interesting talks with two or three old settlers here, who know the Fijian as probably no other white man since Fison's death. There is really a crying need for somebody <u>just</u> <u>now</u> to work up Fiji. But, of course, there are other places in the same condition.

> Very sincerely,
> A. B. Lewis

P.S.—Expect to leave tomorrow for Sydney. Please have sent to me those photos I requested of the Fiji collections, also prints of the New Guinea photos which you promised me.

Fig. 1.1. View of Bau, showing fish trap in water. A-37597 (1609).

Fiji

||||||||||||||||||||||||||||||||||||||||||||||||||||||||||||||||||||||||||||||||||||||||||||||||||||||||||||||||||||||||||||||||

Wednesday, June 9, 1909   In morning got khaki suit and extra trousers, also 2 white trousers, mosquito net and sheet, canvas bag for clothes, etc. Had 4 £5 checks on Brown, Shipley & Co. cashed, charged 4 sh (Bank of New Zealand). Early in morning Mr. Ogilvie showed me the specimens at the town hall, the beginning of a gov. museum.

In afternoon packed up, got letter from Mr. Sutherland to native chiefs, also to Mr. Forbes, fruit inspector. Had one to Mr. Wright, Commissioner at Sigàtoca.

Went to boat at 5, but boat did not leave till 8. Had dinner on land (Steamer *Atua,* of Dunedin, Union S.S. Co. of New Zealand). Meal very good. Delay was due to loading of bananas. Slight rain at noon, only rain in daytime so far at Suva.

Thursday, June 10   Were at Momi when woke up. Bay surrounded by hills, covered with scattered trees. Beautiful morning, hardly a cloud in sight. Was quite cool during the night, even under sheet and spread.

Several boats with bananas came along side (Expect to load 5,000 bunches). Many natives came aboard with shells, etc., to sell. Took till after lunch to load the bananas, had 5,500, were more in cutters (about 6 altogether), but as one man (Chinaman) had not engaged space before, part of his had to be left. The fruit inspector would not allow more, unless Capt. took all the responsibility.

Left ship about 3 in Mr. Robertson's cutter, but as it [was] so late, and Mr. R. had business with the *buli,* the cutter ran in closer to land, and we went ashore. Low mangrove swamp, giving way to cocoanuts etc. Path to village of about 30 houses, among bread fruit and cocoanut trees. Looked around town and went to *buli*'s house, Fijian make, reed partitions slightly higher than head, mats on floor; yet in one of smaller partitioned off rooms, a sort of reed case with books and papers, and table with books, paper, ink, etc. Reminded one of sort of student camp. In main room saw some braided strands hanging on wall, prepared for the *liku,* or woman's petticoat; it is made of a reed (*kuta*) or rush. Took a piece with *buli*'s permission. Looked through cook house—some iron pots, also earthen pots, bowls, packages of native salt, etc. Had some *yagona,*[1] also took tea in *buli*'s house, table, chairs, plates, knives, forks, etc. Had cup of tea, biscuits, butter, jam, but main dish a preparation of paw-paw with cocoanut milk—quite good.

Here Mr. Ragg and Mr. _____ left us to ride to Nandi. We went back on cutter about dusk, and slept on board, I on top of cabin roof.

---

1. This is kava.

Fig. 1.2. Girdle or petticoat *(liko)* made of *terara* rush, from Nadroga. The rush is green when plaited, and considerable time is required to make a girdle. The garment is later colored. 135493 (60). A-112090.

Friday, June 11 Started off about 3 A.M. At first quiet, but later quite rough. I began to feel sick as soon as got up, so lay down again. During forenoon got worse. Finally Mr. Robertson decided to put in to Sana-Sana, where we arrived about 10 A.M. but did not go ashore till about one, as he had decided to walk to Sigatoka, and one deep inlet to cross, which he did not wish to reach at high tide (noon). About 1 Mr. R., Mr. Heard and myself went ashore to village. I left all except mackintosh, coat, brush and comb with Mr. Forbes in cutter to go on to Sigatoka, as did not care to carry much. At village Mr. R. got native to carry mail (their duty when called upon). Mr. Forbes' boy wasn't with us. The road or trail was very good part of way, about 3–4 ft. wide, but part of way was quite sandy (beach) and part of way narrow. After wading one inlet and getting boat across another, we arrived at Cuvu about 4 P.M. (about 9 miles) and stopped at Mr. North's house. Mr. North is Methodist missionary for district of Nadroga. Mr. Heard and his wife were also staying there (from Australia). Mrs. North is Mr. Heard's sister. Here Mr. Robertson got a horse to go on to Sigatoka, but Mr. and Mrs. North very kindly asked me to stay which I did, and had some interesting conversations with him.

The only churches in Fiji are the Methodist and Roman Catholic, which have separate fields, and do not interfere with each other's work, or at least very little. (Within some 6–7 years the Seventh Day Adventist have begun proselytizing.) The R.C. villages have about 10,000 inhabitants, the Methodists the rest. No pagan villages in Fiji. School and church (usually same building,—teacher = preacher) in every village. All children required to go to school up to 13 yrs.

The Methodists have divided the island into 14 districts, with a white missionary in charge of each. He examines the village schools 1–4 times a year, looks after churches, etc. Mr. North had been in Fiji 5 years, but only 9 months at Cuvu. Their house was but recently completed, finely situated on hill, with beautiful view out over harbor.

Saturday, June 12 Stayed all day at Mr. North's, talking and looking round. Visited site of old *roko*'s house, with oranges and lemons, now all deserted. *Mosquitos!* In afternoon a delegation of 70 in mountains brought offering of first fruits (yams and 2 chickens).

Sunday, June 13   In morning went to church with Mrs. North, Miss ? (girl about 15) and Mr. & Mrs. Heard,—wooden church, no seats, women and children on one side on floor, men on other.

About 60 present. Service Methodist, teacher preached. About two o'clock left on foot for Sigatoka, where had letter to Mr. Wright. Seven miles of good road, several villages, country partly bare and hilly, but road often lined with cocoanuts, bananas, etc. Got there about 4. Mrs. W. half Samoan. Her brother, Mr. Alfred Hughes, there also. Place called Lawaga. After talking a while, and looking over his collection, he went with me to Mr. Robertson's. Here found Mr. Forbes, and stayed over night.

Monday June 14   No person speaking English could be found to go with me into interior. Mr. Waters, of Suva, had also just returned from a trip up the river, where he had been unable to find a single specimen. As there was no way for me to get away for three weeks, unless I left that evening on a cutter for Navua, and there caught the steamer for Suva; I thought it best to get away.

Mr. Wright very kindly sent Mr. Hughes to show me around the neighboring villages that day. He was born in Fiji, and knows everybody around.

I saw the process of making pots and bowls. It seems that most articles are made in only a rather limited area. These villages along the lower Sigatoka make three kinds of pots, larger cooking pots *(kurú),* smaller water pots *(saga),* and rather large bowls *(dali)* of red earth.

The clay for the pots comes from the hills, is rather light in color, and is first worked over and mixed with sand. Then the women (all pot work by women) make it into balls. These are then flattened like pan cakes, one worked hollow and two others bent around and fastened on to form the body of the pot, which is then roughly shaped (by wooden paddle, with stone held on inside) and stood on rude coiled ring (bark ?).

It is then beaten into shape (with stone and paddle), and a circular piece cut out of one side and beaten onto top, which will become the bottom of the pot. A string is wrapped around them, to keep them from cracking, and they are stood out to dry for a time, till the bottom becomes fairly firm. They are then turned over, the top (old bottom) cut off, the hole covered over, and carefully beaten into shape. If they get too thin in any place, more clay is stuck on. A vessel with water is kept close at hand, into which the paddle is dipped from time to time, and the clay kept moist. When the body is formed, the neck is turned out and finished with a rather heavy, narrow paddle, with edge.

Fig. 1.3.   Earthenware dishes: cooking pot, 135546 (116); water basins, also used for cooking fish and greens *(bilo ni geli)* from Rewa, 135534 (114), 135535 (114). A-112084.

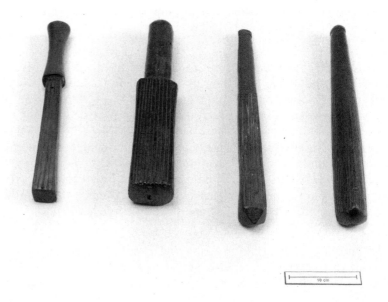

Fig. 1.4. Wooden tapa beaters *(ai iki),* probably from Sigatoka, 135460 (57); from Kadavu (Waters), 135459 (11); 135457 (52), collected by ABL at Sigatoka with four pieces of tapa in various stages; from Kadavu (Waters), 135458 (10). A-112092.

I saw the firing of the red bowls, in a village across the river. They were piled up (about a dozen) with sticks of dry wood around, which was added [to] from time to time, and burned for about an hour. While still hot they were taken out and rubbed with a sort of resin or gum. I took several photos of different stages of pot making.[2]

Also saw them making tapa. This now is made only on some special occasion, which in this case was a marriage in the village. Sticks 5–6 ft. long and about 1 in. in diameter at the butt were stripped of their bark. With a knife the man split the bark for a little distance at the base, then pulled it off by hand, holding the stick meanwhile between his toes.

The strip of bark was then rolled, and near one end bent over his finger, and the outer rough bark cut through, and then peeled off the whole length of the strip, leaving the white inner bark. This is then soaked in water, scraped (did not see this) and later beaten out to width of 1 to $1\frac{1}{2}$ ft. (from 2 in. width), then carefully folded up (from ends) and left to dry (got piece like this). Later it is soaked in fresh water and carefully separated. Also got old tapa beater from old man who said it was made when he was a boy. First saw woman using it.

In forenoon visited 3 towns on west side of river, and after dinner crossed over and visited 2 towns on other bank. Interested to see their shower baths. Water piped down from mountains. Saw bow (and arrow for shooting chickens now), stick for sewing thatch, fish spear, several kinds of baskets, including one large one used at presentations of food *(solevu).*

Met a black Carib, called himself an American, running a bake shop. Paid Mr. R. £1 for voyage to Sigatoka and lodging.

In evening about 9 P.M. skipper of cutter *Tui Navua* (Mr. Work, a half caste, father Yankee whaler in old time) sent boat for me (cutter had dropped down to mouth of river early in evening, but had to wait for right tide), with two natives. Rowed down river to his house. It was unfortunately too dark to see the scenery, but from the way the trees loomed up on each side, it must have been very interesting.

---

2. These photographs have been lost.

Fig. 1.5. Openwork basket *(sova)* in which food is carried to the chief at feasts and on ceremonial occasions, Kadavu, 135666 (86). From Waters. A-112133.

After about an hour arrived at Work's hut. He made 2 children get out (or better, off) of a bed for me. Bed only large square elevation covered with mats, and with mosquito net over whole. Told me to wake him when clock struck 2 or 3 if he did not wake.

Tuesday, June 15   Woke on strike of 3, and found Work already getting up. Boatmen had slept on floor. Went down and got in boat with the 2 boatmen, skipper and his wife, and rowed on down to cutter, about a mile. Here he gave me one side of cabin. About 3 women piled in on other.

I slept till morning, when was wakened up by boy for "coffee." Had hard biscuit, butter and strong coffee on deck. Sun just up, sea rather smooth, wind slight.

Sat around deck all day. Cutter had miscellaneous cargo,—pig, 3 turtles, chickens, grain, etc. Was going to meet the New Zealand steamer the next morning at a place about 7 miles west of the Navua river, to put some cocoanuts on board (Rovondrau Bay).

About 5 P.M. put in near shore and anchored, had supper (yams, rice, boiled corned beef, biscuits (hard), butter, tea); and then went on shore (women and most of men). Went to house of half caste where stayed till about 11 P.M., the natives all sitting around and talking, and drinking *yagona* at intervals. Got on board about 11:30. Good many mosquitos on shore, but more on boat.

Wednesday, June 16   When I woke up (called for coffee), were already nearly to Rovondrau and steamer was in sight. Here left the cutter and took steamer to Suva, where we arrived about 2 P.M., and went to Mrs. Johnston's boarding house. Visited Methodist Press to try to get Hazelton's *Fiji Dictionary*,[3] but they had just sent their copies to Sydney to be rebound (charged only 5 sh per copy). Found Rev. Small out of town. Undertook to call on Mr. David Wilkinson, but missed the house.

Spent evening at Suva Club, reading.

---

3. He means Hazlewood (1872). ABL was later able to purchase a copy for Field Museum Library.

Thursday, June 17   Rained nearly all day. Went to Waters's place in fore-noon, but found him out. He had arrived that morning from up the coast (Sigatoka, etc.). Had got no specimens on the Sigatoka river, tho he had ascended to Ft. Carnarvon, as I learned from Robertson, but had got many things from the island of Kandavu. Went again after dinner, and found him in. Spent the afternoon looking over his collection, largely clubs, bowls, hangers, and other wooden things. Not a very great variety.

Spent evening talking to Mr. Walsh.

Friday, June 18   Fine day. Spent morning with Waters, looking over collection of specimens and photos. Arranged to get a typical collection. Same part of afternoon. In evening had a talk with Mr. & Mrs. Greenland, who had spent 18 months at Herbertshohe, New Britain.

Saturday, June 19   Spent most of morning reading and looking up things on Fiji; also got 50 pounds of Brown, Shipley & Co. checks cashed, and transferred £60 to John W. Waters account. In afternoon called on him and arranged for collection and photos. Read some at Suva Club, and wrote to Miss Carrington.

Sunday, June 20   Went to native church in morning, 10 A.M.; all whites sat on platform back of preacher. Good singing. Met Mr. Hocart[4] and talked for an hour or more with him. He seemed pretty good in the language (Fijian), but had theory of Central African origin for Fijians. After dinner went to Flagstaff Hill, about 1 mile from town, also to Botanical Gardens. Evening talked.

Monday, June 21   In forenoon went to Waters's place, and took down a specimen from Lazarus's store. Found he expected to leave toward end of week. Got 1 doz. plates developed at Lu Favie's. Visited public library—not much on Fiji. One man mentioned society with Free Mason signs in the Solomons.

In afternoon called on Mr. David Wilkinson—very interesting. He is engaged in writing a book, which Sir William MacGregor is to edit, and the government publish. He is working on the legends, but is so particular that he will probably never get it done (Sir William says so, so he said).[5] Told of a Fijian's account in his possession of a week's experience or work—about 15 pages, not yet translated. He told me many things, and said he would be willing to explain what he could regarding our Fijian specimens, if we would send him specimens.

Carved tapa printing boards, native Fijian, probably were used in smaller islands. All designs seem to have had a meaning, but he could never find out what it was—nor had Mr. Fison, who prob. knew more of Fiji than any one else, ever succeeded.

Clubs probably much the same over all the islands, tho made by special men. Spears same, specially fancy ones used chiefly for dancing. Baskets more variety and better in recent times—old type pointed at bottom, also large basket for food at *solevu*s entirely native. Mats differed in different

4. Hocart had recently completed a field expedition in the Solomons with W. H. R. Rivers and on the advice of A. C. Haddon had taken a position as headmaster of the first Fijian-operated school in the colony. Hocart was a young man of twenty-six when ABL met him. He does not seem to have made much of an impression on ABL, as ABL initially spelled his name as "Bocart."

5. It seems Wilkinson never did publish this volume.

Fig. 1.6. Whales' teeth on cords *(tabua)*. Carrying cord of pandanus made into square chain with red and blue yarn decorations (left); sennit cord (right), 135504 (150), 135503 (150). Whales' teeth are used in almost every phase of Fijian life. They are presented with offerings, tribute, congratulations, sympathy, etc., also at birth, marriage, and death. They bind an agreement, serve as a request for aid, etc. A-112089.

localities, tho made of same material, yet this grew coarser some places. Edging in old time probably a fringe; many without. Now all mats without regarded as unfinished. Price say 1 sh without, 6–8 with, same size. Fineness of strip and pattern of weave different in dif. places;—natives could tell where came from.

Mr. Wilkinson agreed to meet me at Lazarus's store and tell what he could of the specimens there. Spent evening talking and reading.

Tuesday, June 22 Waited (read William's *Fiji*[6]) till 11:15 for Wilkinson, and then went down town. Found that the steamer *John Williams,* of the London Missionary Society, was in port. She makes a round of the islands twice a year, carrying missionaries and their families, provisions, etc. Headquarters at Sydney (Mr. Pratt (?) of London Missionary Soc.). Mr. Newell, who was on board, manager (title ?) for the South Pacific Islands. She visits Fiji, Tonga, Friendlies, etc., up to Gilbert and Ellice group. The next trip New Guinea. Never Solomons or New Hebrides.

Got a map of Fiji, and some other documents, from the government printer.

Mr. Wilkinson saw me as I passed Lazarus's place, and we went in and spent about 1½ hrs. over his stock. Had very fine whale tooth necklace.

A peculiar nose flute, double ended, so extra holes.

Stone axe blades in some cases were held in hand for finer work (planing or smoothing), varied from heavier ones with small cutting edge (for digging out canoe, etc.) to broader and thinner edged ones. Those remaining on handles mashed and blunted on edge by being used to break nuts, etc. as a hammer.

Wood—used as scraper to clean dirt of yams, digging sticks, etc. Some of finer make used to open the *ivi* nut.

Bamboo, wound with tapa and string, used as tapa marker or grainer, probably chiefly on smaller islands. Mr. Wilkinson did not know of any case where bamboo cut into circular grooves.

Wood pillow from Lau group, said by Roko _____, whom I met in afternoon, to be made only on island of Kabara, but traded to other islands.

6. He means Williams and Calvert (1858).

Fig. 1.7. Long bamboo headrest *(kali bitu)* with burned-in designs and wooden legs, north Viti Levu. The common type used by men, 135557 (40); wooden headrest *(kali mai tonga),* from Kambara in the Lau group, 135554 (36). From Lazarus. A-112093.

A girl's pillow, made with projections on side so no one else could lie on it at same time, for if man put head on one end, would tip up.

Bamboo pillow in store with burnt-in designs in triangles and lines, said by Wilkinson to be native, but not of best workmanship. In old days a woman (ornamented ones made especially for the young women) would not regard a pillow as a real pillow unless ornamented—would say, "Oh, that's nothing but a stick of wood."

Human or animal figures or drawings *very* rare in Fiji, if at all. Wooden pillows also had designs on them, some finely carved, but not with human or animal figures.

Walking sticks, ornamented on top, used by old men. Bought one old, heavy one, evidently a chief's, as a very fine one. Such were given to chiefs when installed in office, even tho they might have been acting chiefs before for some time. The chief was formally installed by the tribe, and (as a chief's stick was usually buried with him, tho in some places passed to his successor) a stick prepared especially for him. The chief was usually not installed till 30 yrs. or over.

Clubs—many kinds; probably at least 20 had separate names. If end hollowed out probably belonged to chief.

Coiled *yagona* strainer, when used, had placed in it a piece of the fine net-like tissue forming the sheath of the palm-leaf stalk, through which the fluid was strained.

In the afternoon met the Roko, and got considerable information on tapa. This term, he said, should be applied only to the unprinted cloth, while that colored was called *masi*.

The black color was from the soot formed by burning the kernels of a nut (_____) in a special house built for that purpose. The red was from a red earth, mixed with water. The larger black designs were first outlined, and then filled in, a piece of bamboo being placed on each side to prevent the color spreading too much, as it was applied with a piece of tapa dipped in the fluid.

46

The finer brown design were made with a stencil, cut out of the leaf of a kind of banana *(palakise)* specially cultivated for that purpose, the fruit not being regarded as fit to eat.

The stencils were often small, and the tapa folded over to get a straight edge and also prevent spreading of color.

The designs, according to Mr. Wilkinson, probably all had a meaning. The Roko said that the different parts or elements of a large pattern had each a name.

He located some designs as made in particular islands. Others might be made anywhere.

Bought several pieces of tapa. One, long, painted brown on one side, and about $1\frac{1}{2}$ ft. wide, used to wrap around body and between legs by men to cover themselves, i.e., breech-clout. (Native name *malo mali*.) Broader ones, *sulus*, those I got decorated. They also used a girdle over the *sulu*, called *aiyoro*.

Also got plain white fine *masi* turban *(aicau)*. This folded and should not be unfolded till ready to be finally mounted, as will not fold again nicely. Is wrapped around head so as to form a sort of fluted effect. Turbans usually plain white or smoked—latter most valued.

Also got large screen of tapa, made only for special occasions. Large pieces were of 2 sorts: one a screen for dividing house, or used as mosquito curtain *(tanamau)* with deep border, 2 ft. at least, all round, and general central design. The other large pieces were made to be presented at *solevus*, or for barter—and usually had a shallower border on only one or two sides, so arranged that they could later be cut into *sulus*.

Also got fine, hand painted piece from Fortuna.[7]

In afternoon visited the school of the Marist Brethren (R.C.) and got a little pamphlet on the Fijian Language—a few lessons with exercises for beginners.

Wednesday, June 23   Took to J. W. Waters books (Ellis—*Polynesian Researches*, 4 vol.; Thomson, Basil—*Fiji*; Williams and Calvert—*Fiji*;[8] Map, of Fiji, large and small; Official Gazette, several numbers) and the few specimens that I had gotten (tapa, folded together, tapa beater, and bark) from Sigatoka, as well as those from Lazarus (walking stick, flute, bamboo and Kabara wooden pillow, tapa roller, and 10–11 pieces of tapa); all to be packed and sent by Waters with his collection. Arranged with Brown to ship (£1 shipping cost, 2 dollars (?) consular fee for invoice). Waters to send me complete list of his specimens, and cost, with all expenses, up to £60. Also photos of anything extra that he thought I might want. He expects to be collecting for about 3 months.

In afternoon got $2\frac{1}{2}$ yards waterproof cloth, file to fix camera, looked over negatives (underexposed largely), went to Sutherland for letters to *Roko*s of Rewa and Bau, but he too busy to see me.

In evening called again on Mr. Wilkinson, and got some more information.

Thinks there are at least 15 dialects (as Williams says) in Fiji, more or less unintelligible, but all closely related. The Colo (word means mountains) language is the most distinct. There is Tongan influence in Nadroga (Tongans struck island opposite Cuvu) esp. Cuvu, as well as Lau.

---

7. This tapa from Futuna *(masi ni votuna)* is pictured in Leonard and Terrell (1980, 31).
8. Ellis (1859), Thomson (1908), Williams and Calvert (1858).

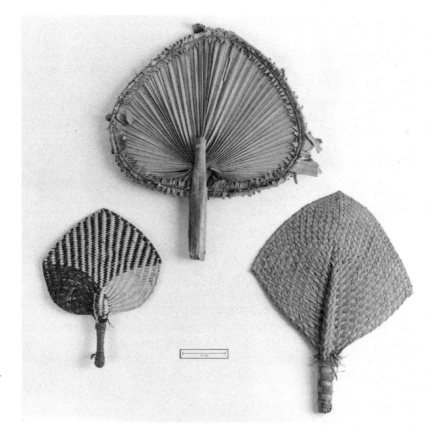

Fig. 1.8. Coconut-leaf fans used to ward off flies and mosquitoes *(nai iri):* From Rewa (left), 135521 (134); from Ra (right), 135517 (135). Palm-leaf dance fan *(iri masei)* from Kadavu (center), 135488 (137). From Waters. A-112136.

Some doctor (formerly gov. official) made a large collection of Fiji skulls, as well as thousands of measurements of heads, and came to conclusion that there were 3 distinct types in Fiji.

1. Vanua Levu
2. Viti Levu interior. Coast largely a mixture of the two.
3. Lau—Tongan largely.

His measurements he put in the hands of some one in England to be worked up.

Mention was also made of first edition of Williams's *Fiji*, which had at least 500 pages, and very full. Thought there ought to be a copy somewhere—possibly in British Museum.

Thursday, June 24   Left with boy (Somo-somo boy, in 3 yr. high school at Nausori, mission school) for the Rewa. Went to Nausori, and stopped at hotel till next morning. In afternoon looked around school grounds, met Mr. Waterhouse, agricultural director and teacher of high school, and visited sugar-mill at Nausori.

Friday, June 25   Left on launch at 8 for Rewa village, with boy. Found Mr. Chambers out, so went to *Roko* (Ratu Joni Mataitini {ten face}, *Roko Tui* Rewa). He was just going to Suva, but said I could stay at his house over night. He asked Ratu Ambrose (*Buli* of Rewa) to show me around, so we spent about 2 hrs. looking around the village, saw pots of several varieties, mat and basket making. Mats made of strips of *voivoi* (a kind of Pandanus) the wider strips from a kind said to be introduced from Tonga or Samoa (this blackens if gets wet). A finer mat, which keeps its color, made of native Fijian species. The *Buli* said that in the old days feathers of parrot were used to fringe the mats, or else the strips at edge split up to form fringe.

Fish baskets woven of strips split from sort of cane about this size, called *galo* (*veri* at Rewa); woven with 3 sets of strips, open mesh.

Flat trays for food called *sovasova*. Bowls for Fiji oil rather deep, called *tanoa*. Cocoanut is mashed up, and frequently the mashed seeds of *uci* put in with nut to give it a scent or odor (mint like). This allowed to stand a week or so, and oil comes to top, when skimmed off and bottled for use (on hair, cooking, etc.).

> *kuro* = large pot
> *sova* = food basket of *galo*
> *aisu* = rough cocoanut basket
> *sedre* = earthen bowl
> *lawa* = net (now bought, not made)

Manipusi = sort of weasel found in bush (mongoose). Introduced to kill off the rats in the sugar cane, they have increased and become a general nuisance. Kill fowls, eat eggs, etc. Have killed off many native birds, and almost all snakes (used to be some harmless varieties here). Saw one tied up by tail and hind quarters, hanging from a tree. Snarled and spat at one quite viciously.

At about 12 went to Mr. Chambers's house, found him in and he kindly invited me to stay there, but as I had already accepted invitation from the *roko* to stay at his place, said I would take my meals there, but sleep that night at the *roko*'s house. He said that on account of the numerous strangers coming to Rewa it was necessary to tell Mrs. Chambers to be very careful about taking in strangers.

In afternoon went out for a little while with the *buli*. Saw the old chief of Rewa, Tui Dreketi, an *old* man, very hard of hearing. He used to be the king of all this region, and is still probably regarded by the natives with more reverence than anyone else. The *roko* is of high family, but not so high as the *Tui*.

In evening talked with Mr. Chambers. He was missionary in New Britain for 7–8 years, but had to leave on account of his health. He showed me a number of things he had obtained there. He had once a large collection, but on leaving N.B. sold and gave nearly all away, for less than he had paid for them.

Fig. 1.9. "Native of Rewa" wearing T-shirt and hibiscus flower. A-37646 (1631).

Fig. 1.10. Earthenware dishes with highly glazed exterior: bowl, with both raised and incised designs, 135545 (2); water jar *(sauka ni wai)* from Rewa, 135532 (115). Glazed with a dark gum that is applied to the hot jar when it is finished baking. From Waters. A-112083.

49

He gave me two pieces of tapa (Fijian) one figured (from Nadroga) and one plain; also 2 carved lime spatulas from East New Guinea (Trobriands ?). He had a round coiled basket, like those in museum, said so far as he knew, they were made only at Vunagamata, Talili Bay, north coast of Gazelle Peninsula, east of Weberhafen. They are called *aim* (name of material) *rat* (basket). He also had a lower jaw, human, with band connecting ends, which he said was from the Baining, and was carried in the hand when hunting to give success. He also had peculiarly netted Baining baskets.

Slept that night at the *roko*'s house on couch covered with mats. Native house, but wood floor, wood doors (4), and glass windows. Furnished with reclining chairs, table, books, Rochester lamps, good bureau with various European articles, etc. Some nice tapa on ceiling.

Saturday, June 26   Spent most of day with boy going round the village of Rewa and neighboring towns, and took several photos. Saw mat making and material in all stages.

In afternoon went to village of Vunuku. After looking around went and looked in open door of one house. An old man near door spoke to me (had boy interpret) and we went in. I looked around and among other things saw a stone ax. By that time several people had come in, I offered to give a shilling for ax, but the old woman who apparently owned it would not sell. One man said, "Come with me and I'll get you an ax," so we went to another house, where a nice new mat was offered me to sit on. The man now got the ax, but it had no handle, so I would not take it. He then got an old handle, but that would not go, either. Another then offered an ax with an iron blade. One man offered a club for 5 sh. (not bad). I finally gave the man 6 d. for the ax, and was going to go, when the boy said to wait, that they were bringing some cocoanuts. They brought 4, and he opened one for me, which I drank. They brought a basket for the other 3, which the boy took with him when we went away.

I also bought a tapa printer *(kupete)* from an old woman in Rewa for 3 sh. She said she gave 4 for it when new. In same house saw a fine old club, but owner was away.

In one place asked about certain black designs in mat, and found they had a name.

Sunday, June 27   In morning went with Mr. Chambers to a village called Nukui about 5 miles away, where he was to hold service. The path in one place crossed a river over a single log, tho there was a hand rail on each side, rather crude, tho fairly firm.

The walk was very interesting, with cocoanut trees scattered over the landscape, taro and *via* beds at intervals, also freshly planted yams, each carefully hilled (about 1 ft. high), with a little ashes on top (one old man said it made the yams sprout quicker, and they put it on because their fathers had always done so), bananas, *yagona, voivoi* plants, *ivi* trees, etc. At the village we went into a hut, where was a chair and a table (they brought another chair) with plate and knife and fork and spoon. Soon they brought in some food and gave it to us. After we had eaten some more food was brought in and divided out into portions: one for village, one for Mr. Chambers, one for me, and one for our boys. After service our portions were taken home by the boys, but they with several of the men ate of theirs after the division had taken place. This giving of food is customary at every service and every time a man of importance visits the town. To us was given a baked chicken, very tender and good, and yams and taro, with tea.

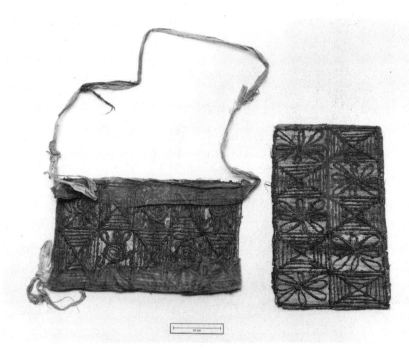

Fig. 1.11. Tapa stencils *(kupeti vui vui)*, Kadavu. Made of a mat rush *(vui vui)* on which are sewn ribs of coconut leaf, to represent the patterns to be produced on the tapa. Sewing is done with hibiscus *(vau)* bark. Used for finishing off borders in a fancy way, 135453 (97). A-112140.

If a white man visited a town, the chief, if he had food, would give him some, or if not, tell his people to get him some. It would then be set before him, and he would eat by himself. A native would always be invited to eat by any family or any one who saw him when they were ready to eat. Only a very low white man, however, would be invited to eat *with* the natives.

In afternoon (got back at 1:30 and then had dinner) rested and wrote. At supper had a Fiji pudding—boiled taro, mashed, mixed with juice of sugar cane and cocoanut milk, made into little balls, rolled up in banana leaf, and boiled again. Found it not at all bad, but rather sweet. Most white men that try it come to be very fond of it. The balls mass together in a brown sticky mass.

Monday, June 28   Intended to start for Bau in morning but found my boy sick, headache and slight fever, so decided to wait a day.

Boy showed me how to make traps for a large crayfish, of which the natives are very fond. A running noose of string (usually use cocoanut fibre, but any tough bark will do) is made over a piece of bamboo $2\frac{1}{2}$ to 4 in. in diameter (often with hole at one end in which to tie a string to carry it by).

The bamboo with noose is placed at hole, and the whole covered with mud and bamboo, then pulled out, leaving a short tunnel next [to] hole, with noose in its sides. To the end of noose (b) a bent stick (a) is fastened, and held by a trigger. This is made by passing a stick (a) through the mud into the opening left by the bamboo, so as to be along side the hole, and just beyond the noose, so that when the crayfish comes out of his hole he gets into the space left by the bamboo, passing his head or claws through the noose, and joggles the stick (a). This releases the bent stick (d), which springs up and draws the noose around the crayfish. The stick (d) is held down by a stick (e) bent so and stuck in the ground on each side of the hole, around which a loop of string (c), fastened to (d), is passed, and held by a short stick (g) passed through the loop, and resting on (a) and (e). The moving of (a) causes (g) to slip off, releasing (c) and causing (d) to pull up the noose on string (b).

The natives catch great numbers of crayfish in this way. (*dai* = name of the trap; *mana* = the crayfish they catch.)

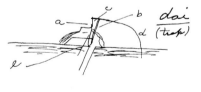

They also catch crabs in a few feet of water by means of a small square net, fastened to two sticks, to which a string is attached, by means of which it is let down in the water. To the center of the net, on top, a small crab or shrimp is fastened, and to this a long slender stick, which rises above the water. The net, weighted with a stone on each side, is let down, perhaps to bottom, and left till the shaking of the stick shows that a crab is taking the bait, when the net is pulled up quickly, and the crab secured.

The net I saw was made roughly of bark and about $1\frac{1}{2}$ feet square. Tapa patched with *yambia* root {*tou* (Bau)}, which is also used to paste the strips of tapa together into large pieces.

> *dave* = *yangona* dish
> *tabe* = basket nicely woven of *averi*

In afternoon went out with Mr. Chamber's oldest boy Harold as interpreter. He showed me a mongoose trap as natives make it. A little enclosure of sticks set in the ground is made, open on one side, and in this some cocoanut or other bait is placed. A strong elastic stick (a) is then bent over, and a string (strip of bark of _____) with running noose in middle attached, while the other end is fastened firmly in the ground (B). The stick is held down as in (C) by a trigger; a lower cross piece (b) is rested against the side sticks of the opening, and another piece (g) placed against it and another cross piece above a loop of string fastened to (a) is passed around (g) just below the upper crosspiece, which is firmly fastened to the two side pieces. Both (g) and (b) are held in place by the tension of (a); by stepping on (b), or shoving (g) to one side, the trap is sprung and the noose tightened, the end fastened in the ground holding it so.

We then went around through the village (Harold, myself and several native boys). Saw some pigs in their curious little pens. Visited the cemetery, with the graves heaped up and surrounded by stones, sometimes laid up almost like a retaining wall. In a near by village I went into a house, and after looking around finally bought an *ivi* nut opener for a 6 d. I then asked for

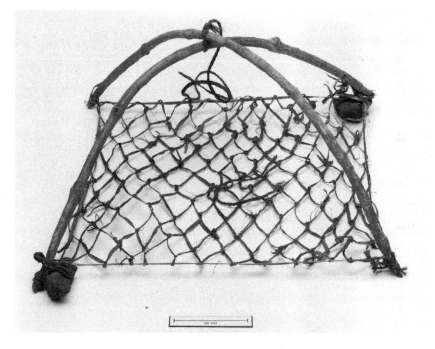

Fig. 1.12. Crab trap, Rewa, 135624 (159). Bait is placed in center of the net and trap is suspended from the bank of the river. Stone weights hold trap steady. The crab gets entangled in the mesh and is held prisoner. A-112087.

old things, as clubs, etc. and soon had quite a crowd around me, offering me various things.

I bought a club (throwing, 1 ½ sh.), ax (1 sh.), and at another place a long club (3 sh.) *kupete* (3 sh.) and kava cup. This, the man said, was brought from New Guinea by a man who had been there (place he said was called Boiwa, and was a school there). Cup had a design burnt in around edge.

Saw pot made in imitation of a cocoanut. Saw an old woman patch a piece of tapa—the torn piece was placed in position, and *yambia* root rubbed over the whole, and a piece thus pasted over the rent. The same material is used to paste the strips of tapa together, after which they are beaten to knit them still closer.

One boy offered a cup with woven handle attached for 3 sh.

In the evening I met at Mr. Chambers' house an old man, the son of the old high priest of Rewa. He said that such cups came from the interior around Namosi, and the handle did not mean anything particular, but was their way of making them. In the old days his father was not allowed to touch anything he ate with his hands, and had to eat lying on his face, with his hands clasped behind his back (he lay down on the floor and illustrated). The bottom of his kava cup was covered with mud so it would not be touched. He said the difference between the cups of the chiefs and those of the common men was that the chief's cup was blackened and polished on the outside, as well as carefully polished in the inside (put in a little water and rubbed with a piece of tapa after being used).

> *tilava* (Rewa) For splitting open *via.* (Not used in Bau, so no Bau name.)
> Rewa club, *na dromu* (Rewa and Bau)
> *nai ula* = club
> Ax = *some* (Rewa)

[Following are] Bau names. From Ratu Kandovu.

> *masi* = name of plant, and bark of same
> *seavu* = beaten out, dried and ready to put together *gatu;* when joined to-
> gether in large pieces, plain or with designs.
> *kumi* = *seavu*s joined into strips for *sulu*s
> *ketekete* = basket for carrying, made of cocoanut [leaf]. Made only near
> Cuvu, of leaf of cocoanut.
> *lalakai* = platters of cocoanut, used to put food on.
> *vilawa* = fish basket, made of *vere* (splints of)
> *sova* = large round basket for yams, etc. of *vere*
> *ibe* = mat, made of *voivoi*
> *aiseru* = comb of wood
> *coboi* = plant from which a sort of tea is made (lemon grass) by boiling
> leaves.
> nose flute [=] *bitu ni vakatagi* (bamboo) (of) (nose)

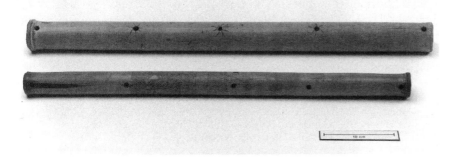

Fig. 1.13. Bamboo nose flutes *(ai vucu ni ucu),* 135616 (33), 135619 (33). Held to nose by one hand while other closes the two bottom notes. Breathing gently into end hole produce a melodious sound. Note is changed as hand is shifted over lower holes. A-112091. (For photo of Fijian boy playing one of these flutes see Lewis 1932a, plate LII-3.)

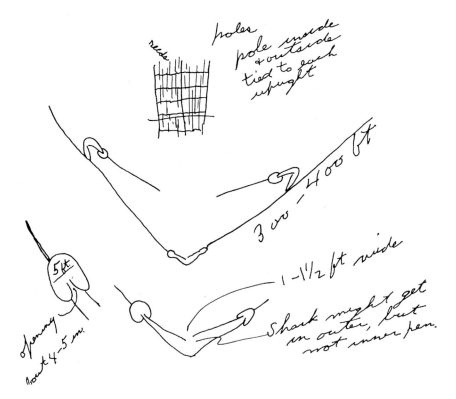

Fish trap at Bau:
Poles at intervals of 1–1½ ft. set in mud, and to them lashed a fence of reeds, fastened by turned string (vine ? called *midri*). Two sets of poles are lashed to this about 3–4 ft. apart, and these again fastened to the uprights.

Big fish trap called *uea,* made of split splints of *titi,* aerial roots (?) of *wakani titi.*

Tuesday, June 29   Boy still sick, so paid him off, and got 2 boys from Mr. Chambers to carry my luggage to Bau. Mr. Chambers gave me a note to Mr. Brown at Bau. Left about 10 and got to Bau about 1. Country flat most of way, except near Bau, where hills alternated with low lands and swamps. The natives were clearing the ground for their taro and yam patches, and burning off the debris, the canes popping like gun shots.

Bau is [a] rather small island, about ½ mile from shore. Found a boat to cross in. Mr. Brown kindly asked me to stay with him. Went to Roko to see about an interpreter. He said the men were all away on mainland that day, but he would get me one, if I would call the next morning. He seemed rather quiet, not much inclined to talk, but willing to help in any way he could. Asked him some questions about tapa, etc., and he referred to a book by Seemann,[9] which I had never heard of before. Said it was very good, and lent me his copy to read.

Looked around town a little but did not see much new. People pretty well dressed.

9. A citation from inside the front cover reads "*Viti: an account of a government mission to the Vitian or Fijian Islands in the years 1860–61.* By Berthold Seemann. Cambridge: Macmillan & Co. 1862. 447 pp." ABL acquired a copy of this volume for Field Museum Library.

Fig. 1.14. Fly whisks made of coir (fiber of coconut husk) with carved wooden handles. A necessity in many parts of the islands where mosquitoes and flies are numerous, 135527 (21), 135528 (21). A-112088.

In evening talked some to Mr. Brown, and read book. He has a fine outlook from the hill where the mission house is. Regards the climate as as fine as anywhere; never very hot, as always a breeze. Has boy of 18 and girl of 14, both away at school. For traveling in New Britain he advised wicker telescopes covered with canvas, which should be oiled with linseed oil and painted with black paint occasionally.

Wednesday, June 30 In morning got interpreter and went over to main land, to visit some of the villages there. Took Mr. Brown's boat, but owing to shallowness of water, had to wade nearly $\frac{1}{4}$ mile to shore. At first village found most of men helping to make house. Frame only up. Showed cut with iron axes.

Looked around some, when boy asked if I would take lunch at that village. Said I would, after visiting another village (then about 10:30). Took a picture of next village from the path. Set up on hill (both). Water supply piped from a large cement tank, covered, the roof of which supplies most of the water. (Same in most of neighboring villages. Bau supplied from church. But at Rewa water piped down from stream in mountains, and numerous little cement basins around through the villages.) Fine view of ocean and country from village.

Returned to 1st village, and were asked to chief's house, where sat down (on mats) and in a short time some boiled or baked yams and leg of small pig brought in. I, of course, was supposed to eat before any one else, so set to work. Pig very good and tender. Soon brought in some native tea (infusion boiled, of lemon grass). Tasted much like tea. Also brought some salt, and a little later, biscuit (crackers) to go with tea.

When I [was] done, my boy cleaned up the pig, and part of yams. Then another Bauan (Ratu _____) took a little, and joined him in taking tea.

Then looked round through village, saw fixing house with rope made by twisting vines together; rope was fastened down by wood pegs. Took picture. Also saw preparing oven—hole with stones heated by fire, then leveled down, and yams, taro and pig (3 in this oven) placed on top, covered with leaves and earth,—left 2 to 3 hrs. to bake. Took picture of oven when partly filled, when covered, and when just opened (best shows stick across bottom on which a kettle was hung, and which was in the way of the view). Also saw another oven opened, but no pigs in it.

Sort of stew and more yams were offered to me after oven opened. I took a taste, and passed the rest to the boy, who, with the assistance of a

Fig. 1.15. Thatching a house, mainland near Bau. A-37456 (1620).

couple of other Bauans, soon caused it to disappear. After watching house building etc. a little longer, we started for Bau, two other men accompanying us. At the landing we found the boat gone, so went around by hardly traceable path to main landing, where we finally managed to get a native boat to take us across. Gave the woman who owned it a shilling. Supper at Mr. Brown's. Read Seemann's *Fiji* during the evening.

Thursday, July 1 In morning got boat of Mr. Brown, and went with Johnny to fish trap out in sea, where examined the trap and saw them take out the fish. (See above for description.) Went back to Bau, and took picture of fish trap by *Roko*'s house. Saw old stone where killed victims of cannibal feasts, about 3 ft. high.

After dinner took boat and went over to mainland, and visited another village.

Friday, July 2 In morning Mr. Brown got 2 boys to carry my goods, and I left for Nausori about 7:45, and got there about 9:45, where met Mr. _____ Ross, manager of Brandyork's store, to whom Mr. Brown had recommended

Fig. 1.16. Church in Bau. A-37592 (1615).

Fig. 1.17. Boys and boys' house in Bau. A-37484 (1616).

me. The first part of the road was more or less hilly, and some interesting scenery. The last ¾ hr. was through cane fields.

Mr. Ross had heard of me from Mr. Walsh, and was expecting to see me. He is an American, but an old settler in Fiji, and had a large fund of information regarding the Fijians.

I lunched with him, and left about 2 P.M. on the launch for Viria, some 20 odd miles up the Rewa. The launch stopped at a number of places on the way up, to deliver goods. I stopped (about 8 P.M.) with the trader about a mile below Viria, and stayed there till the launch returned, about 10. We got to Nausori about 2 A.M and I rolled up in my blanket and stayed till morning in the launch.

Saturday, July 3   Left at 8 on the launch for Suva, where looked up my photos, and got the 2 doz. new ones I had developed. Talked most of afternoon with an Austrian, and wrote letter in evening.

Fig. 1.18.   Spirit houses *(bure ni kalau)* made of sennit on a wooden base. Collected by Waters in north Viti Levu, 135654 (130), 135653 (132). Used in the *lureui wai* ceremonies. At beginning of ceremony house is carried to rocky point on sea and left so that spirit of the water *lureui wai* may enter it. Carried back to town in pomp. This spirit helps them with second sight, also protects them against bullets, etc. Believe it can even open coconut shells. It also allows headmen and priests to have indiscriminate indulgence with young girls. Is now prohibited by government. A-112132.

Sunday, July 4   Wrote letters in forenoon (Dorsey, Miss Carrington, Julia Dawson, Fan[10]). In afternoon went to see Mr. Humphrey Berkeley, but found that he was moving, so could not see him till next day.

Monday, July 5   *Makura* (C.P. mail boat) came in about 8 A.M. so went down and made arrangements for berth, baggage, etc. Left photos and a number of specimens with Mr. Watson for Mr. J. W. Waters. In afternoon went aboard. Just before dinner I found out that Dixon, of Harvard, [had] come down here, and was stopping at MacDonald's Hotel, so went up there immediately, and found him at dinner. He came down after dinner, and we had a little chat. He stays at Fiji a week, and then to New Zealand for three, thence to Australia. On a "joy trip," he says, looking esp. at museums. Boat left about midnight.

Tuesday, July 6   Quiet day, read and played games.

Wednesday, July 7   Much the same.

Thursday, July 8   ditto.

10. Fannie was one of ABL's younger half-sisters, his father's daughter by his second wife; she was living in California. Miss Carrington was probably a woman he had been dating in Chicago.

The Eitape (Aitape) Coast of Kaiser Wilhelmsland

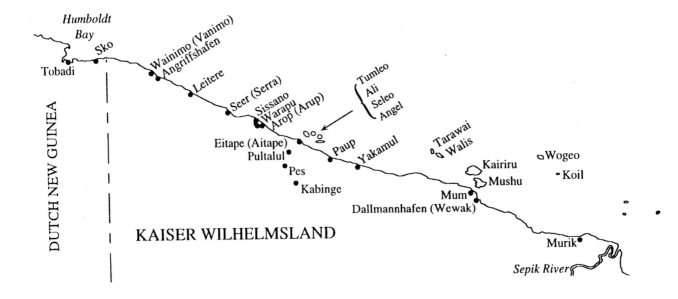

Book 2

Humboldt Bay and German New Guinea

||||||||||||||||||||||||||||||||||||||||||||||||||||||||||||||||||||||||||||||||||||||||||||||||||||||||||||||||||||||||||||||||||||||||||||||||||||||||||||||||||||

29 August 1909–11 December 1909

ABL's account of his sojourn in Fiji reads like a celebration of finally beginning a long period of fieldwork, rather than as an account of actually doing fieldwork. With delight, it recounts the kinds of mundane detail familiar to any traveler. And, while his diary offers a number of insights about Fijian life and material culture, initially it provides little beyond the account of an interested tourist. Like many tourists he tells us more about where he went and the influential people he met along the way than about the life and culture of the villagers in the places he visited. After his arrival in German New Guinea, we experience an entirely different aspect of A. B. Lewis; we witness his transformation from traveler to field researcher.

This second book is divided into three parts to highlight the subtle but important transformation ABL was undergoing. Each part of this book expresses a new facet of fieldwork and ABL's reaction to it. In each, ABL gets closer to the villagers, whose daily lives and material culture he has come to document.

In the first section, his diary for Humboldt Bay and German New Guinea, ABL is just beginning to learn the lay of the land, the environment, new place names, and a totally foreign colonial administration. Nearly always in the company of Europeans, he sees Humboldt Bay, the Sko district, and parts of German New Guinea with the eyes of German administrators. First he travels by motor launch and by small boats; then from Eitape (now spelled Aitape) he goes overland by foot into the hills to the south, all in the company of His Excellency Governor Albert Hahl. Hahl had befriended George Dorsey the previous year and was happy to assist ABL on his arrival in the colony. But one senses in the diary that ABL was relieved finally to be on his own when the governor left Eitape to return to the colonial capital at Herbertshöhe (now Kokopo) on the Gazelle Peninsula in eastern New Britain.

ABL's first short field trips on his own from Eitape—to Tumleo Island and to Malol (on the coast to the west)—were clearly both exciting and informative. But both trips illustrate how much ABL had to learn before he could begin to understand what he was seeing and experiencing. This section describes his confusion at the novelty of New Guinea, when virtually everything was new to him, and how he gradually sorted out these kaleidoscopic images for himself.

In the second section, ABL visits the Berlinhafen Islands and displays his virtuosity as an anthropologist trying to grapple with some fascinating but unexpected field data. He develops a systematic strategy for collecting and documenting his specimens. The field methods he initially adopted forced him to recognize how much intervillage trade was going on along the Eitape coast. These data led him to a more systematic method of data collection, resulting in his attaining a deeper understanding of trade relations on the coast than any other anthropologist of his day.

Finally, in the third part of the book, during a visit to Sissano Lagoon, ABL has his first opportunity to experience the village on his own. During two weeks at Sissano, he continues to collect specimens for Field Museum but spends more of his time learning about how sago is processed, how pots are made, and other details of village life. By the end of this last section ABL had spent three and a half months on the north coast of Kaiser Wilhelmsland and had assembled a sizeable collection of more than thirteen hundred specimens and 190 photographs in addition to his field notes. He had documented some of the local variation around Eitape and become an anthropologist with real fieldwork experience.

Humboldt Bay and German New Guinea

Like the first one, this second diary notebook begins in the middle of things. The first entry is dated 29 August, nearly eight weeks after the last entry in the previous book. We have very little detail about what ABL did in the weeks after leaving Fiji, but we can reconstruct some of his movements if not the precise timing of his arrivals and departures.

After leaving Fiji, ABL proceeded to Sydney, where he seems to have spent about a month buying supplies and arranging such matters as the forwarding of mail. During this visit to Sydney, ABL almost certainly saw the Australian Museum and met its curators. One suspects that it was during this initial visit that the groundwork was laid for a 1912 exchange of Melanesian material for Aboriginal Australian specimens. On subsequent visits to Sydney, ABL visited photographers, bookshops, and South Sea curio dealers, so it would hardly be out of character for him to have done so during this visit as well.

On leaving Sydney, ABL took a Nord-Deutscher Lloyd (North German Lloyd) steamer to German New Guinea, a trip that took only a few days to arrive in Herbertshöhe, the colonial seat of government. In 1909, German New Guinea was the least developed colony in the German empire. And it was on the Gazelle Peninsula of New Britain in Herbertshöhe and Simpsonhafen (changed to Rabaul in 1910) that ABL was first introduced to life in the German colony.

Administratively, German New Guinea consisted of two regions: the so-called Old Protectorate (made up of the areas formerly under charter to the New Guinea Compagnie) and the Island Territory (comprising the Mariana, the Caroline, and the Marshall islands, which Germany had purchased from Spain during the Spanish-American War). Although both regions were loosely integrated under the authority of Imperial Governor of German New Guinea Dr. Albert Hahl, only the Old Protectorate concerns us here.

The Old Protectorate of German New Guinea consisted of the Bismarck Archipelago, Bougainville and Buka in the Solomons, and the northeast quadrant of New Guinea, which the Germans named Kaiser Wilhelmsland after their emperor. European economic activity in the colony had grown very slowly in the first two decades after the German government annexed the region as a protectorate in 1884. European settlement was concentrated in the Bismarcks around Blanche Bay on the Gazelle Peninsula at the eastern end of New Britain rather than on the New Guinea mainland, which unlike the islands continued to be unhealthy because of malaria. By

1909 a number of structural changes were beginning to have a noticeable effect on conditions in the colony. These included broad changes in native administration, a major reorganization of plantation and trading firms in the colony, and an expansion of government administration into previously isolated parts of the colony.

Up to a few years before ABL's arrival in the colony, economic activities in German New Guinea had been dominated by three firms: the New Guinea Compagnie, Hernsheim & Co., and the firm of E. E. Forsayth & Co. The most flamboyant proprietor of these was "Queen Emma" Forsayth, the part-Samoan, part-American daughter of Jonas Coe, the American consul to Samoa. She settled as a planter and trader on Blanche Bay about 1878 and soon sent for a large number of her extended family and in-laws, who joined her in New Britain in the 1870s and 1880s. By the time of German annexation in 1884, Emma and her family had already established substantial plantations in New Britain and had built up a profitable trading operation that stretched across the Bismarck Archipelago. Until 1907 when Emma and her husband, Paul Kolbe, retired, her firm was the third largest in German New Guinea.

For years E. E. Forsayth's major competitor in the islands had been Hernsheim & Co., a trading firm started in the mid-1870s by Eduard Hernsheim. Hernsheim was one of the earliest European settlers in the islands, possibly arriving as early as 1870. His economic activities focused on trading with the islanders for pearl shell and trepang (sea cucumber) rather than on building plantations. By the end of the 1880s his operation included forty-two trading stations. Hernsheim's activities were centered on the firm's headquarters at Matupi (near Rabaul). These commercial activities, together with those of several of Hernsheim's protégés, appear to have been vital to the rapid growth and prominence of Simpsonhafen from its founding in 1905. By 1910 this growth led residents to push for changing the seat of government from Herbertshöhe to Simpsonhafen, changing the name to Rabaul about the same time.

From 1884 to 1899, the New Guinea Compagnie held an imperial charter to administer the protectorate. It used this authority to purchase extensive tracts of land along the coast of Kaiser Wilhelmsland. Vast tracts of the very best lands were alienated from villagers around the company's headquarters at Friedrich Wilhelmshafen (now called Madang) and Astrolabe Bay. On these lands the company established numerous plantations for copra, tobacco, and other tropical crops. It also opened a series of trading stations along the coast; some, like Seleo, were manned by a resident German trader, while others were staffed by a Chinese or Malay agent. After fifteen years of an inept, harsh (and unprofitable) administration, the emperor revoked the charter of the New Guinea Compagnie and formed a colonial administration with its headquarters at Herbertshöhe. In 1909 the company's holdings were still the largest in German New Guinea (totaling more than three hundred thousand acres), but the firm continued to be plagued by inept management and was experiencing a gradual decline in the face of growing competition.

In January 1909 the European population of the Old Protectorate numbered only 671, mostly Germans, mostly men, and mostly residing on the Gazelle Peninsula.[1] Life in Herbertshöhe and Simpsonhafen was dominated by young, single, German men, who were living for a time far from home. The few women in the colony were primarily wives and daughters of government officers, planters, and missionaries. For many years Queen Emma's family played a leading role in the lively social life that existed among the plantations and settlements strung along the shore of Blanche Bay. Nearly all of Emma's nieces married European men whom they met at parties on the Ralum or Kuradui plantations.

By 1909 changes were already under way in the Old Protectorate. Their health failing, Queen Emma and her husband decided to retire from planting and trading in 1907. They left the colony for Australia and Europe, putting Emma's business interests and plantations up for sale.

About the same time, Rudolf Wahlen, another young German trader from Hamburg, was rising to prominence in the colony. Wahlen had been in the colony for a decade, working for several years as an agent for Hernsheim, when he arranged to take an option on Hernsheim's concession in the so-called Western Islands (the Hermit, Anchorite, and Niningo groups, along with Wuvulu and Aua). Setting off for Germany, he returned to New Guinea a few months later at the head of a Hamburg syndicate with sufficient funds to buy all of the Western Islands. Almost overnight Wahlen became one of the wealthiest men in the colony; he established his headquarters at Maronn Island in the Hermit group. About the same time, Wahlen also bought two ships, including the motor schooner *Moewe,* and arranged to be appointed Swedish consul in the Old Protectorate. Although Wahlen's wife was a Swede, this appointment was probably related to his growing financial prominence.

As ABL was arriving in the colony, Wahlen was actively expanding his holdings in the islands and planning his next financial maneuver: amassing enough capital to buy out Queen Emma's holdings, a business deal he would complete in 1910 to become the wealthiest man in German New Guinea. Afterward the holdings Wahlen managed dwarfed those of all other businesses in the colony except those of the New Guinea Compagnie.

When ABL arrived in New Guinea, he planned to report to Governor Hahl as Dorsey had instructed. He hoped to be entertained and assisted by the governor much as Dorsey had been the year before. Such assistance would minimize difficulties with transportation—not to mention expenses—and would facilitate visiting a large number of areas in the colony. Such expectations were not as presumptuous as they may seem: the governor was a gregarious sort who strongly encouraged every sort of scientific research in the colony. Moreover, as part of his policy of opening up new regions to governmental control, Hahl frequently made tours of inspection and expeditions into little-known areas. Visiting scientists were often invited to accompany him on these travels. Dorsey, for example, had accompanied him on an expedition across Bougainville Island in 1908 (Dorsey 1909b; *American Anthropologist* 1908, 10:504), and the governor had given assurances that he would similarly assist Field Museum's scientific efforts when ABL arrived.

ABL also planned to call on Richard Parkinson, the noted German ethnologist and best known of Queen Emma's in-laws. For many years Parkinson had written extensively about the cultures of New Guinea and the Bismarck Archipelago. His most important work, *Dreissig Jahre in der Südsee,* had recently been published in Stuttgart. Parkinson had married Emma's sister, Phebe Coe, in Samoa in 1879, and soon afterward the couple joined Emma in New Britain. In addition to running the family's plantations, Parkinson began studying and writing about the region's indigenous peoples. For years he also sold curios from New Guinea and the Bismarcks to museums in Europe and America. He had sold two major collections to Field Museum in 1898 and 1908, and another collection was planned for 1909. As Parkinson had also assisted Dorsey in the colony in 1908, he was naturally one of the key people ABL planned to contact on his arrival in New Guinea.

But two tragic events thwarted ABL's plans and had a profound effect on the subsequent character and quality of his research. The government steamer *Seestern,* which had been in dry dock in Brisbane during May 1909, left Australia for Herbertshöhe on 3 June. But a day or two out of port, the *Seestern* sank with the loss of its entire crew of 6 Europeans, 15 Chinese, and 18 Melanesians. This disaster left the colonial administration without a ship and severely limited Governor Hahl's ability to conduct any further exploration or tours of inspection.

To those familiar with Papua New Guinea today, most of whom travel by air and conceptualize the country, or at least the mainland of New Guinea, as a vast continental island or land mass, this loss may seem relatively unimportant. But before the First World War, New Guinea was—despite its vast land area—quintessentially a maritime colony. Virtually all travel was by water; only very short patrols along the coast or into the interior were made on foot, and there were, of course, no airplanes. It is safe to say that all of the expatriates in German New Guinea appreciated the difficulties that the loss of the *Seestern* would bring to the colonial administration. Thus, when ABL arrived in Herbertshöhe in August 1909, it was clear that Governor Hahl could not send him off on the government's steamer as had been planned.

The second tragedy that befell German New Guinea was the death of Richard Parkinson on 24 July 1909. Parkinson's death meant the loss of one of the colony's earliest pioneers and leading citizens. With Queen Emma permanently in Australia, it would have a profound effect on both the social and the intellectual life of New Britain.

Even before he left Chicago, ABL had learned that Parkinson was not well, as Parkinson had written to Dorsey that poor health prevented him from sending the ethnological collection he had promised. After ABL had set off on his expedition, Parkinson's poor health worsened. It had been a bad year for the family; not only was Parkinson failing, but in February one of the Parkinson sons (Otto) had died unexpectedly in the family's home at Kuradui. When ABL arrived in the Gazelle Peninsula, the Parkinson family was again in mourning, this time for the father. It is unlikely that ABL did more than pay a polite social call on Mrs. Parkinson in August.

The situation in the colony must have seemed bleak to ABL when he first met Governor Hahl in Herbertshöhe. But as luck would have it, the governor had found some temporary solutions to the administration's long-term transportation problems. There were, of course, several ships based in the colony, such as the New Guinea Compagnie's *Siar,* Nord-Deutscher Lloyd's *Sumatra,* Forsayth's *Roland,* and Wahlen's *Moewe.* All of these privately owned cargo vessels could carry passengers or be chartered by the government if Hahl needed them. In addition, Nord-Deutscher Lloyd had regular service between the Gazelle Peninsula, Kaiser Wilhelmsland, and Europe, and government steamers and naval warships occasionally visited the protectorate. The governor made use of all of these options in administering his colony.

Despite the limitations of transportation, the governor had planned several tours of inspection in Kaiser Wilhelmsland for around the time that ABL arrived. Hahl graciously invited ABL to accompany him on a trip in the government mail steamer, *Sandakan,* along the New Guinea coast. In addition to ABL and the governor, the party included another visiting scientist, Regierungsrat Wiedenfeld, who was making zoological collections in the colony (Schlaginhaufen 1909).

The precise itinerary of the governor's party is unknown, but ABL's specimen list, together with his photo list and a summary of his collections written in the front of this diary, suggests that they stopped at Finschhafen, Stephansort (or Bogadjim), Friedrich Wilhelmshafen, Alexishafen, and Potsdamhafen (now Monumbo) on their way to Eitape. At each of these ports of call ABL bought specimens for his collection or took a few photos.

In Finschhafen he purchased a few things directly from villagers in Kambowa village; other specimens he bought from the Lutheran missionaries. In Bogadjim, a New Guinea Compagnie station, he bought the contents of one man's bag and several other items. This bag contained a decorated lime gourd, four bamboo containers, bull-roarers, a small leaf container, and the material for another. ABL noted that these items "were all carried in a bag, with other things, some European, by one man. Other men had similar bags." This was the first of several occasions on which he bought the contents of a bag to document the kinds of things people in New Guinea typically carried.

Friedrich Wilhelmshafen (Madang) was the largest and busiest station in Kaiser Wilhelmsland. Until the opening of Eitape in 1906, it had been the only government station on the mainland. It was also the main station of the New Guinea Compagnie and could boast a resident European population of about twenty.[2] Here ABL bought only a few specimens from villagers, as he was undoubtedly busy meeting government officers (*kiap*s in Pidgin) and New Guinea Compagnie personnel, on whom he would have to rely during his months in Kaiser Wilhelmsland. Dr. Scholz was district officer and station head for the government; Georg Heine was administrator and head of the Company's operations, which employed more than three thousand native and nearly two hundred Asian (mostly Chinese) laborers.

To the north of Friedrich Wilhelmshafen, the party called in at Alexishafen, a Roman Catholic station that had been opened in 1905. In the short time since its founding by the Society of the Divine Word (SVD), this station had grown rapidly and was becoming the mission's main station in German New Guinea. When it first came to New Guinea in 1896, the SVD mission had sought land near Friedrich Wilhelmshafen. When such land was denied it, the party settled far to the west on Tumleo Island in Berlinhafen (opposite Eitape) and rapidly began opening new stations nearby. By 1909 the SVD had three main stations—at Tumleo, Bogia, and Alexishafen—as well as ten other stations, three of which were opened that year; SVD missionaries in Kaiser Wilhelmsland numbered sixty-seven.[3]

At Potsdamhafen ABL bought a number of items from villagers at the station; from the New Guinea Compagnie agent he purchased another thirty-five specimens, which the agent had collected at various places along the coast. Thus, by the time ABL began his field diary in Eitape he had already obtained nearly a hundred pieces along the coast.

The governor's party disembarked from the *Sandakan* at Eitape, leaving Regierungsrat Wiedenfeld to proceed with his research there. Eitape, opened only three years earlier, was ordinarily a quiet backwater. The station itself had a resident European population of only four young German officers.[4] A few other Europeans (nearly all SVD) lived in other small settlements not far away, but Eitape station was tiny compared to Friedrich Wilhelmshafen.

When the governor and his party reached Eitape on 27 August 1909, the district might have resembled a research park more than it did a forgotten backwater of the German empire. Besides ABL and Wiedenfeld, the ethnologist Otto Schlaginhaufen from Dresden and the botanist Rudolf Schlechter from Berlin were at Eitape station, preparing to set off for the interior with Police Master Stuben and Pater Kirschbaum from the mission (Schlaginhaufen 1910a, 10–11). Prof. Dr. Richard Neuhauss, the physician and physical anthropologist from Berlin who had accompanied Schlaginhaufen and Schlechter up the Kaiserin Augusta River (the Sepik) on the *Siar,* was in Sissano by 1 September (Neuhauss 1909, 962–963). Yet another researcher, the German anthropologist and philologist Georg Friederici, would arrive in Eitape within two weeks! In addition to these researchers, the warship *Planet,* with a surveying team aboard, also called at Eitape early in September.

The scientists were not the only ones busy in the district; Governor Hahl and his party were met in Eitape by Hans Rodatz, the *kiap* and officer-in-charge of Eitape, and Rudolf Wahlen, the wealthy planter and capitalist. Wahlen had brought his schooner *Moewe* to escort the governor to Humboldt Bay inside Dutch territory, where Hahl was to meet with the Dutch resident, E. G. W. Windhouwer, to discuss plans for the forthcoming German-Dutch boundary commission.[5]

Governor Hahl, unlike Sir Hubert Murray, his counterpart in Papua, strongly encouraged scientific research in German New Guinea as a way of promoting development. But with so many researchers in the district at the same time, each collecting ethnological specimens for his home museum, one can appreciate the competitive attitude that arose among some of them. ABL and Schlaginhaufen seem to have worked more or less cooperatively, but the pompous Prof. Dr. Richard Neuhauss felt threatened by most if not all of the others. Although Neuhauss acknowledges the assistance of some government officers, resident planters, and missionaries, he writes as if he were the only researcher in a very wide and empty field. Nowhere, for example, in his account of his trip up the Sepik does Neuhauss mention the presence of either Schlaginhaufen or Schlechter on the little New Guinea Co. steamer *Siar*.

Nor is ABL's presence in and around Eitape ever mentioned by any of the other researchers except in Schlaginhaufen's unpublished diaries and in one vague allusion written by Neuhauss referring to both Dorsey and ABL. This reference was written in a letter from Sissano dated 1 September 1909 published in the *Zeitschrift für Ethnologie*:

> In the course of a few months here with an expedition outfitted with a proper little steamer one could carry out astonishing things and save wonderful ethnographic specimens that might otherwise be carried off to foreign countries. Already in 1908 the museum in Chicago sent a collector here. He made a clean sweep and now the same museum is sending a proper ship to the Augusta river. [Neuhauss 1909, 963]

It is hard to know whether ABL had made some casual comment about wanting to charter a ship up the Kaiserin Augusta or whether this statement was merely an expression of Neuhauss' own competitive fears and paranoia. Clearly, Neuhauss recognized the difficulties of transportation in German New Guinea, something ABL was only beginning to recognize in the second of his notebooks.

As this notebook opens, ABL accompanies the governor, Kiap Rodatz, and Herr Wahlen on the *Moewe* to Humboldt Bay for a meeting with Resident Windhouwer—"resident" being the Dutch term for district officer or what the Germans called *kiap* in Pidgin. It is clear from the outset that language was a tremendous problem for ABL. In graduate school at Columbia under Franz Boas, he had naturally learned German. Thus, communication with German officials presented few problems. He was less facile in Dutch but still able to communicate without much trouble. Rather, it was communication with villagers that he initially found so challenging.

In German New Guinea, Pidgin English had developed as the lingua franca, despite efforts by German authorities and missionaries to encourage and teach proper German. Pidgin's simple grammar is quickly learned in the field, but when ABL landed in Eitape he was far from fluent.

No sooner had ABL arrived in the Eitape district, where he would spend most of the next four months, than he was whisked off to Dutch New Guinea where a simple form of Malay was the lingua franca. Of this language he knew virtually nothing, and it appears that he made good use of his time aboard the *Moewe* jotting down useful words and expressions at the back of his diary notebook. Most of these words are Malay, but a few are in Pidgin. In both cases they document the kinds of vocabulary that ABL felt he needed to know. In the case of Malay—despite his idiosyncratic spelling—these notes offer an example of the kind of New Guinea Malay that was in use early in the twentieth century and may also be of some interest to linguists documenting the history of Malay and Indonesian.

As this book unfolds, readers should also note how ABL's diaries shift from references to fairly mundane topics to more systematic observations. At first he writes about the appearance of the environment; he also forgets the names of particular villages and has trouble remembering the Pidgin names for government-appointed village headmen *(luluai* and *tultul)*. But as he acquires a better grasp of Pidgin, the administrative system, the geography, and the environment, such topics fade to the background and like all anthropologists he turns his attention to more important concerns.

{Editor's note: Only part of one letter describing ABL's travels from Eitape survives. This portion—from a letter from ABL to George Dorsey—is reproduced here. Although written from what is now Madang in May 1910, it refers to events from September to December 1909. This was apparently the first letter ABL had written Dorsey since September.}

Friedrich Wilhelms Hafen
May 1, 1910

Dear Dr. Dorsey:

It has been some time since I last wrote from Eitape, but I have not had many opportunities to mail letters since, and at these times have been exceptionally busy.

After going into the bush and to Tumleo, I was laid up for some time with fever. Later I stayed in Ali, for two weeks, visiting the other islands. I collected some 400 or more specimens here, and succeeded in getting the locality for most of them. The islanders make such extensive voyages that one half of what I got proved to come from other places, from Sissano to Dallmann Hafen [now called Wewak]. I also studied, photographed, and obtained specimens of the various manufactures of the islands, in various stages, when possible.

Later I went along the coast, visiting the villages of Malol, Arop, and Sissano. This was a very interesting trip, occupying about three weeks. At Sissano I stayed with Herr Schulz for two weeks. This proved an exceedingly interesting place, quite aside from the specimens I got. As the Northwest season was on, the surf was so high that no boat could land at Sissano and I left my collection there to be brought back to Friedrich Wilhelms Hafen the following May or June. From Sissano to Arop I went by native dugout, passing on the way the old village of Warapu. This is now deserted, and the houses are nearly all in ruins. I managed to get into two or three, but my boats' crew (natives of Arop) strongly objected, and I was forced to stop before I was quite ready to.

On Dec. 2 I left Eitape for Herbertshöhe, expecting to go from there to Huon Gulf, as the winter was the dry season there, and it did not seem worth while to stay on the north coast during the rainy season.

. . .

Very sincerely,
A. B. Lewis

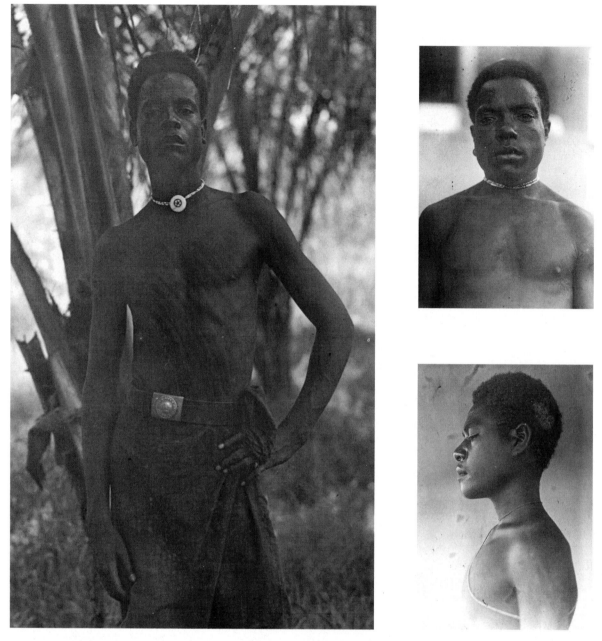

Figs. 2.1–2.3. ABL's field assistants ("boys" in Pidgin English). Marumu of Namaranga village, Warie coast, northwest New Britain (left); Kaman of Karsau Island, North Coast of New Guinea (above right); Kabai, a Buka (below right). A-31709 (16), A-31713 (20), A-31722 (29).

Humboldt Bay and German New Guinea

||||||||||||||||||||||||||||||||||||||||||||||||||||||||||||||||||||||||||||||||||||||||||||||||||||||

Sunday, August 29   Left Eitape about 9 A.M. in 60 horse-power motor schooner *Moewe,* belonging to Mr. Wahlen,[1] Swedish consul, residing on the Hermit Islands, for the German-Dutch boundary and Humboldt Bay. Gov. Hahl, Herr Rodatz, Mr. Wahlen and myself as passengers. I had my three boys, and the Government expedition, 25 police boys.

There were also 12 natives who were to be returned to their homes. 1 to Malol, 5 to Arop, and 6 to _____.[2] I went ashore with the boat at Arop, and it was very interesting to see the reception given to the boys. After the boat had been helped in through the breakers, the boys and their boxes were taken ashore, and for a while they seemed to take things rather coolly. After a time I noticed one young fellow had an old man with his arm around his neck, who was hanging to him and crying. We had to leave almost immediately, but before we got away there were several around this particular fellow, embracing him and crying. After landing the boys, we proceeded direct to Humboldt Bay.

Monday, August 30   Slept on deck, and lost hat—blew over early in morning. Arrived in Humboldt Bay about 8 A.M. Mijnheer Windhouver, the Dutch resident, came on board and after a little while he got 2 natives with a canoe to take me around the two villages near [by], as we were to remain in the bay till 4 P.M. I with 2 boys with trade, and the two natives, started out about 9 A.M. First I went to the little Malay and Chinese settlement near the residence, and managed to get a straw hat for 3 M. (tho they said the price was 1 rupee = 1.80 M.).[3] We then went to the more distant village. All the houses were on piles in the water. I got out and went into one, and soon the people gathered around, and I purchased quite a few things; ornamented gourds, carved wood pillows, bow and arrows, etc., some very nicely ornamented.[4]

Got back to ship at 12:30, and got something to eat, and then to other village, Tobadji, in which is probably the most well known men's house in all New Guinea.[5] I went in and a number of men followed. Hanging around the

---

1. Consistently misspelled as Walin.
2. Probably Leitere or Sissano.
3. He means rupiah, the currency of the Dutch East Indies, of which Dutch New Guinea was an integral part.
4. This would have been Enggros village at the mouth of Yotefa Bay opposite Tobadi.
5. He means Tobadi village opposite Metu Débi Island where the Dutch resident was stationed in 1909. Tobadi's men's house, as Lewis correctly notes, was undoubtedly the best known and most frequently pictured cult house in New Guinea. A year earlier a photo of this imposing structure had appeared in the *National Geographic* (Barbour 1908, 533–534). In 1903 under the leadership of Arthur Wichmann the Dutch New Guinea expedition established a base camp at Metu Débi and observed ceremonies and dances at the Tobadi house. The house and its ritual life figured prominently in several accounts of the expedition

Fig. 2.4. "View of houses from shore, Humboldt Bay (some on land, others over the water)." A-37447 (1558).

place were all sorts of fine feathered head dresses, many with models of birds, fish, etc., of painted cloth and feathers, on a stick some 2 feet high on top. I succeeded in buying one, but not the best, as they demanded axes, of which I had only one. These fellows were the finest got up natives I had seen,—big bushy heads of hair, with waving feathers and ornamental combs, necklaces, belts, arm and leg bands, etc. The woven bands were worn chiefly on the arm, above and below the elbow, and on wrist. Necklaces and a sort of bandolier were worn by all, but were largely of beads. The leg bands, worn chiefly below the knees, were narrow, and often covered with seeds. Their ear ornaments were chiefly tortoise-shell rings and balls of fur (cuscus).

In this building and one near by were many skulls of pigs,—also in the smaller one many skeletons of fish enclosed in a sort of frame, as well as other curious things hanging to the roof.

published before 1909 (Lorentz 1905, 37ff.; van der Sande 1907, 290ff., both of whom published several photos). Earlier Koning (1903, 280) had published a photograph of the structure. Previously the house had appeared in several sketches dating back to 1858, when von Rosenberg and van der Goes (1862, plate FF) visited Tobadi. Other renderings and descriptions can be found in Otto Finsch's *Samoafahrten* (1888a, 358) and an account by Robidé van der Aa (1879, 272). See also Wichmann (1917, 162ff.) and Greub (1992).

Fig. 2.5. Incised bamboo containers, Tobadi, Humboldt Bay, 143462, 143463, 143460 (9838); 143464, 143461 (9839). From ten Klooster. A-112032.

Boat left at 4 and crossed the bay and anchored off shore, as we were to march across to the mouth of the Sexstroh (Tami) river the next day.

Tuesday, Aug. 31 Up at 6 A.M., got packs ready, and were soon on trail with carriers and some 10 police boys. The path led first through fairly level forest, then over the mountain and finally along the beach. The forest was very interesting—ferns, palms and all sorts of trees. Only one seen in bloom, but that covered with fine red flowers.

On beach passed 4 villages, all belonging to district of Sko. The men here all had the small penis gourd. Their houses were built on piles, but on land. The best, and some were quite large and high, were so [high] one could walk under them; floor probably 8 feet from ground.

Saw some finely ornamented canoes near [by,] one of them called ———.

In the one nearest the river I stopped from about 1:30 to 4:00, the 3 men from Humboldt Bay and one Malay accompanying me. As I could not speak to any of them, I did not get on very well. They did not seem to have much or else were not willing to sell.[6]

This village was about a mile from the mouth of the river. My purchases were carried by police boys and natives to boat in mouth of river. The ship had sailed around from Humboldt Bay.

6. Despite this apparent disclaimer, ABL collected 97 specimens during the afternoon. These included 54 arrows, 2 pots, 12 ornaments, 13 carved pieces, 4 utensils, 7 lime gourds, and 5 paddles. All items seem to have been from the village of Sko Sae, now moved a bit to the west of its original location.

Fig. 2.6. Man wearing bandoliers, Humboldt Bay. A-37607 (1570).

Wednesday, Sept. 1 Up early and up the river in boat with the Gov., Mr. Wahlen and Mijnheer Windhouver, with 8 police boys to row and protect (all with guns—took turns, 4 at a time, each ½ hr. rowing) also Malay interpreter and native of Toebadi for interpreter. Rowed up the river to a small clearing

15 cm

Fig. 2.7. Canoe ornaments representing fish, Sko, 139267 (234), 139268 (235). A-112046.

Fig. 2.8. Penis gourds, Sko district, 139136 (217), 139135 (215). A-112034.

Fig. 2.9. Carved animal figures, painted black, white, and yellow, Sko, 139149 (226), 139148 (225); ornamental suspension hook, carved and painted red, white, and black, Wainimo, 139011 (380). A-112035.

Fig. 2.10. Canoe paddles, from Warapu, 139463 (3877), and from Wainimo, 139001 (391). A-112108.

where two natives lived, in hopes of being able to get guides to the interior, as the coast people had no communications with the interior, and the governor wished to establish friendly relations with the interior, in order to prepare the way for the boundary commission, which he expected to send in next May, in connection with the Dutch authorities. At the clearing one native disappeared by the time we arrived, and the other (an old man) declared he knew nothing of the people further in, or of roads thereto. While looking around, he also disappeared. We decided to go on up the river, leaving the native (Toebadi) and Malay, to try and make friends with them, if they came back. A short distance above this, we entered a tributary from the East (Mosso) and followed it for about 5 miles, in a S.E. direction, till stopped by shallow water and logs. Here we stopped, had lunch, took a swim, and then returned. No sign of the natives at the clearing, so took aboard the two men, and back to ship.

In this region there seems to be little or no connection with the interior. The Dutch resident knows nothing of it, or its people. He has only 5 Malay soldiers, so can do little.

Some Malay traders or hunters came down the river the day before (one of whom we took with us) and reported that 3 days up there were paths leading to the interior, but no towns on river (Tami).

The Mosso was a pretty little stream, rather deep near the junction, and much clearer than the main river. The banks were lined with magnificent tropical forest, with occasionally a tree covered with red flowers.

Took 12 gr. quinine at night.

Thursday, Sept. 2   Sailed all night, and arrived in Angriff's Hafen in morning.[7] All went on shore and looked around, but after a while the others went away and left me with my boys to buy what I could. I first looked into one of their large men's houses. It was quite dark, and difficult to make much out of inside. The floor was about 7 ft. high, and the entrance was overshadowed by the roof. No other opening, but a little light filtered in around the sides. It was built much the same as those of the Sko district. The men also wore the same penis gourd. Ornaments were much the same, and decoration of lime flasks, while not at all common, was the same as at Humboldt bay. They wore feathers in hair, but not so much as at Humboldt Bay. In appearance they seemed much the same. Their canoes were the same as at Sko, with ornamented bow piece, and designs of birds (?) along side. As I saw the newest canoe, as well as one in the process of construction in the Sko district, it is possible that they came from there.

Shields or drums I could not induce them to bring out. Pots are made here, of clay mixed with sand, and beaten into shape by hand from ball of clay, with paddle and stone on inside. During this process they rest on a bark ring. Those I saw ranged from 8–10 inches to 1½ ft. in height and width—all of same shape, and no decoration.

Paddles ornamented as in Humboldt bay (?), but very hard to buy; got 5 for 12 in. knife a piece. Combs and ornamented daggers I got in abundance. Pillows seemed different from those of Humboldt Bay, but I could only get two.

For trade they liked fish-hooks, matches and mirrors, no beads; iron also acceptable. Would not let me go into their houses.

With the exception of 1 hr. for lunch, I was on shore till 5 P.M. Prices seemed high. Many here spoke good Pigeon English,[8] as they had served as

---

7. Now called Vanimo. ABL usually spells the local name of the native village Wainimo.
8. ABL always used the early spelling of Pidgin.

Fig. 2.11. Wainimo pot, stone, and paddles for making pots, and leaf ring on which pot is rested while making. "This ring was taken from under a pot the woman was making." 138028 (384), 139013 (387), 139014 (385), 139015 (386), 139016 (388). A-112044.

15 cm

police boys or laborers in other parts of the colony. The Gov. assured me that the place was absolutely safe, and the fellows seemed quite friendly.

Friday, Sept. 3   Sailed all night, and most of next day. Got to Berlinhafen about 5 P.M. Packed up things for an early start to the interior the next morning.

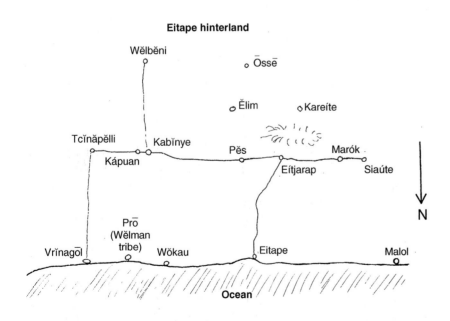

Eitape hinterland

Wĕlbĕni

○ Ōssē

○ Ĕlim   ○Kareíte

Tcĭnăpĕlli   ⎮ Kabĭnye   Pĕs   Marók
     Kápuan   Eítjarap   Siaúte

Prō
(Wĕlman
tribe)   Wŏkau   Eitape   Malol
Vrĭnagōl

N

Ocean

Fig. 2.12. "Man from Pultulul," wearing bead necklaces and nassa-shell bandoliers. A-31716 (23).

Saturday, Sept. 4   Started with my 3 boys and 3 police boys as carriers, with the Gov. and _____ police boys, the Malay hunter[9] of Regierungsrat [Wiedenfeld], the governor's boy as attendant and gunbearer, and a native of the coast village of Wokau (the *tulil*,[10] or head of a subordinate village, under a _____) as guide and interpreter, for a 3 days' trip into the interior. Herr Regierungsrat accompanied us for the first hour, to the small village of Pultalul, on a small hill, the first elevation we came to after leaving the coast. From here the path led down to a broad river bottom or plain, densely wooded but with not very heavy underbrush, over which was tramped for the next $3\frac{1}{2}$ hours. A number of men and boys from the village _____ accompanied us, as there was to be a singing at Pes. At last came the edge of the hills, and after a few ups and downs we arrived at the first village, on the crest of a ridge, where we stopped, and after a short conference with the natives, made our camp under one of the native houses. These were built on piles about $5\frac{1}{2}$ ft. high, with the roof extending out and down on all sides to about the level of the floor.

9. *Regierungsrat* was an official title given to a class of high-ranking government advisers. Wiedenfeld was in Kaiser Wilhelmsland to collect zoological specimens (Schlaginhaufen 1909), for which purpose he brought along a Malay bird hunter.

10. ABL means *tultul* under a *luluai*, both government-appointed village headmen responsible for keeping their villagers and villages in order. By 1909, the Germans had appointed a *luluai* and a *tultul* in most of the villages around Eitape. At this point in his travels ABL was somewhat overwhelmed by the intricacies of the colonial administration, Pidgin, the tropical rain forest environment, et cetera, all of which were new to him.

The houses were somewhat longer than wide, with good walls of bamboo, and floor of same. Length 15–25 ft. One house, apparently the boys' house, was enclosed all around eaves by bark slabs, painted with designs, usually the same on each slab.

house at Pes

The natives requested us to camp where we did, as they did not wish us to be very near the place where their sing-sing was held.

After we had had lunch, or dinner rather, as it was our chief meal, the natives came dancing to an open place near where we were. Only a portion took part, and the performance seemed to be in honor of a young girl some 10–12 yrs. old, who was led around by two older women, other women dancing behind and a number of men in front with drums. All were ornamented, but largely with European beads and cloth; the women especially were well clothed. It appeared to be somewhat of a family affair, but we could not find out just what. The governor and I each gave the girl a small present of beads, etc. We afterward went over to some of the next nearest houses, and talked some to a few of the natives who were there, but they did not wish us to go further. The sing-sing was now in progress, and was kept up, with hardly an interruption, till daylight the next morning. I slept first rate, however, and needed no mosquito net. In the portion of the dance that we saw, two of the women uttered a most peculiar whistle at regular intervals.

Sunday, Sept. 5   Up at daybreak, and as soon as breakfast was prepared and over, we were away on the road. At first we went to the nearest village (the real Pes) near by on a neighboring elevation, where we had to wait some time for our native guide. This day's trip was to be east, parallel with the coast, and the way was not known to our guide and interpreter from the coast. The guide had not yet had his breakfast. So we waited while he ate his meal, consisting chiefly of a sort of spinach and boiled sago. The natives also gave our men a portion, which they seemed to eat with great satisfaction.

This day's trip was about 5 hrs. long, and with many ups and downs, crossing quite a number of small streams, usually clear and apparently good to drink. Gov. Hahl drank of them without hesitation, where he saw that the natives also drank. The way seemed very little travelled, and was hardly distinguishable in most places. After many ups and downs we reached the _____ river,[11] and after crossing it, ascended a small tributary, finally coming to higher ground and reaching the village of Kabínge, near Kapuan. Here we stopped on a fine open spur of the hills, where we had a fine view to the distant mountains inland. We placed our cots under a small house, and soon had dinner. The people here seemed very friendly. There was a men's house (?) near by, with walls of bark slabs, all nicely painted in colored designs. The floor was about 3 ft high, and projected some beyond the wall, and had a fringe of grass hanging down all around, completely hiding the under portion of the house. Here were also some slabs, painted as above, but not all around. I bought 3 of these for a small mirror. The building was some 15–20 ft. square, practically empty inside, as far as we could see, as it was very dark.

There were only 5 other houses on the particular elevation we were on, tho many more were on the other side of a small valley. We did not cross till the next morning, when we passed through there on our way back to the coast. At one of the houses nearest the valley were 2 women with a small

11. Probably the Raihu River.

Fig. 2.13. Painted bark plank from lower side of sacred *tamburan* house, Kabinge. "I got these from below the floor; they were hidden by a grass fringe hanging down from edge of floor, which projected a little beyond wall. The bark planks on wall above were much the same but a little better ornamented. Two were so badly spoilt that they were thrown away." 140029 (493). A-112037.

15 cm

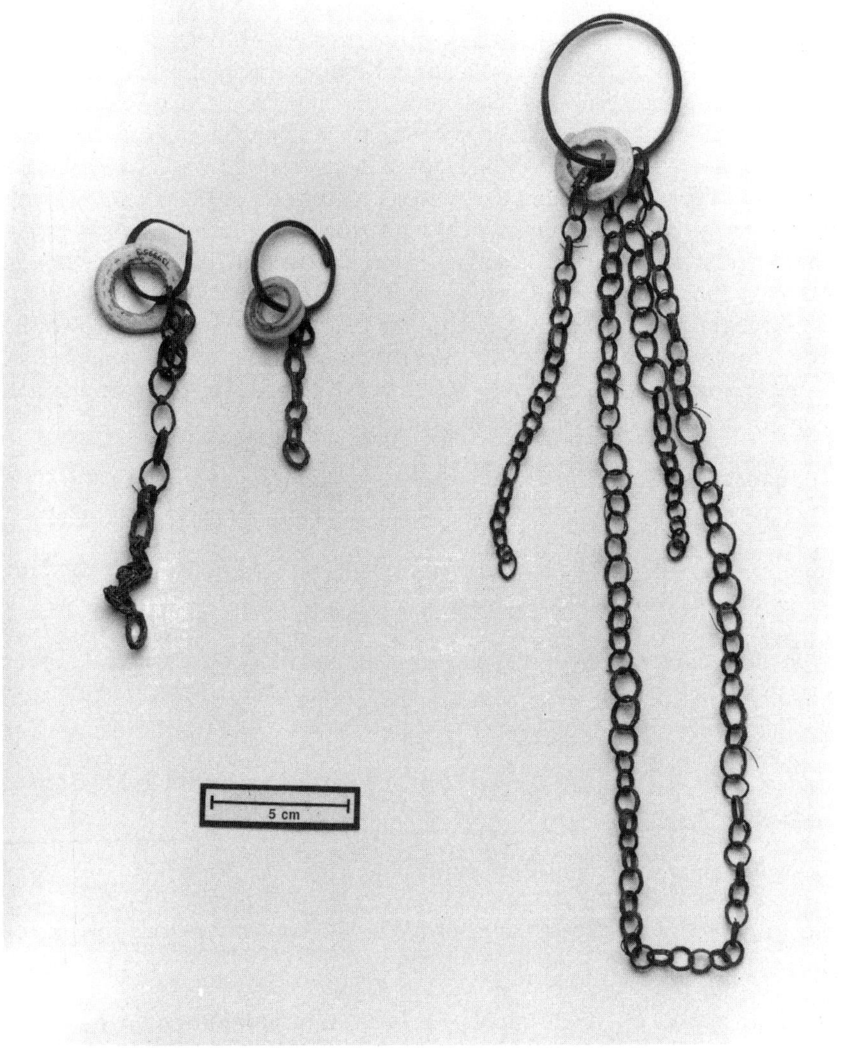

5 cm

Fig. 2.14. Earrings (pair and single ring) of tortoise shell, with small shell ring and chains of plaited fiber links attached, Kabinge, 139995 (454), 139994 (453). A-112036.

baby, who cried vigorously on my first approach, but finally became sufficiently reconciled to accept a small mirror from me. The women were preparing food, such as roasting what were apparently green bananas, and making the salad before mentioned. This was eatable, but not particularly to my taste. Later one of the men brought the baby up to the house next to where we were, and I offered him (baby) a large blue bead, which he took quite readily. I also gave the old men a stick of tobacco apiece.

After a time we asked them if they had anything they would sell us, and I got some bows, arrows and shields, with a few other things. The bows and arrows seemed the same as on the coast. Shields were different, with paintings resembling those on the slabs of men's house. Lime gourds plain, lime stick ringed, so that when rubbed up and down in hole it made a rasping sound. Arm rings chiefly woven rattan and string—not numerous. Earrings of tortoise shell, with shell rings attached, and also a woven chain of fiber. Bark loin cloths, and few leg bands. (Men only closely noticed—women were shy.)

Our purchases were tied up, and the men agreed to carry them to Eitape the next day.

Monday, Sept. 6   Started early on return to coast, with 8 natives of village to guide and show way. The village of Kapuan was quite near, but after passing that nothing more. After many ups and downs, and considerable distance on bottom lands, we reached the river again. Shortly after crossing this we came to the corner of the mission lands,[12] where was a corner stone, and a cleared way from there to the coast. This we followed most of the way, tho it necessitated crossing the river many times. On the way we saw a fine cassowary, at first not over 15 yds. off, in bush near track, which it crossed in the open ahead of us, and disappeared in bush on other side. When we last left the river part of the boys did not find the trail, and went on down the river, reaching Eitape some 2 hrs. later than we (Gov., myself, 5 natives of Kabinge, and one police boy). We stopped a short time at the mission plantation, and reached Eitape about 1 P.M.

Tuesday, Sept. 7   Vomited in night and in morning had slight fever (99), and felt very rocky. Lay down most of forenoon. In afternoon put up tent.

Wednesday, Sept. 8   Spent most of day putting up tent fly, sorting out my things, etc. Not very well yet.

Thursday, Sept. 9   Man-of-War *Cormoran* came in forenoon, and I spent a large part of the day "on top" with the visiting officers.[13] Visited the ship at 3:30, and had tea in the Captain's cabin. No time to look around.

Friday, Sept. 10   Spent the day listing and packing the things I had so far collected.

Saturday, Sept. 11   Finished cataloguing.

Sunday, Sept. 12   Rested and read (Finsch, *Samoafahrten*). Took dinner and supper with Herr Rodatz.

Monday, Sept. 13   Got some boxes from store, and took some photos in forenoon. In afternoon packed up all the small objects in boxes.

Tuesday, Sept. 14   In morning developed plates. In afternoon visited the vessel *Natuna*. Met Friederici and talked of his work, etc. He is working especially on the languages. The vessel *Natuna* has several men on board, and for several months past has been visiting the Pacific Islands, Fiji, Tahiti, Low Archipelago, Cook Islands, etc. Friederici has vocabularies of some 200 languages.

Wednesday, Sept. 15   Took photos in morning of some visiting natives from Siaute, Pes, etc. Developed in afternoon. Found in morning that it had rained some during the night, the first rain for about a week. Rain is expected during the change of the moon, and it was about one day till new moon. At full moon rain is also expected.

Fig. 2.15. *"Luluai* of Siaute." His hat serves as a badge of office. A-31719 (26).

---

12. For a discussion of the SVD plantations at Eitape and early mission economics, see Huber (1988).

13. As station head *(kiap)* of Eitape, Rodatz seems to have entertained most visitors to the station at his house. Here ABL uses the Pidgin "on top" (lit. "above") to refer to the government office and residences, which during German times were on the top of the hill behind Kiap Point. Concrete ruins of the old German jail are still plainly visible on this site.

Fig. 2.16. "*Alol* (*tamburan* house), Sapi village, Tumleo." A-31732 (39) (cf. Neuhauss 1911, 232).

Thursday, Sept. 16   Intended to start for Tumleo at 8 A.M., but was delayed some by rain, at last got away about 9:30, with my 3 boys, in a boat with 6 men kindly lent by Herr Rodatz. The boys arranged a mast and sail, so they could take advantage of the breeze. I had been eating too much in the way of meat, etc., and did not feel very well, and threw up on the way over.

On arriving at Tumleo I was met by one of the brothers, _____, and shown to the mission house, where after explaining my desire to stop a few days Pater Lohmiller[14] said I was welcome, and showed me a room where I could stop. It was then about 11:30, so we talked till dinner, which was very good (cooked beef—tinned; sausage—good; soup; peas; beans—sauce; yams—very good; omelette and canned cherries—very good; coffee and wine (no milk or sugar)). After dinner rested for an hour or so, and then Pater _____ took me around through the two villages nearest the station.

I purchased a number of objects, and tried to find out where the various things came from. There is considerable trade between the islands and the mainland. Most of the arrows come from interior villages, as Pes, Kapuan, etc. Paddles from Arup, Warupu were common. The best of their own work

---

14. ABL spelled his name Loemerle.

Fig. 2.17. "Shelf for drying pots, Tumleo." A-31731 (38).

had of course by this time disappeared. I found one old *garamut* [slit gong], finely carved, going to decay, and purchased it for 5 M., on condition that the owner deliver it in Eitape, which he agreed to do. Pillows were common, short, and but slightly carved (made in Tumleo). Ornaments were fairly common, many from a distance. Tortoise shell earrings, with shell rings attached, combs, both cut from wood, and of sticks as in Wainimo. Armrings woven and edged with nassà shells common, leg bands as at Wainimo.

The old *alol*, or men's house of Sapi, is going to decay, but still had remains of good carvings. I visited in afternoon only the two villages on end of island near mission.[15]

Supper light, and early to bed. Pater Kirschbaum came back from trip to inland in evening.

Friday, Sept. 17 Pater Kirschbaum took me round the island in forenoon, and I took a number of photos, esp. of pottery making. The clay is carried to the village in baskets of _____, and hung up under the house. After thoroughly dry it is pounded up in a trough made of a piece of an old canoe usually, then sifted through a sieve like a sago strainer, (after the larger stones are picked out).

The clay is then mixed with water and kneaded in a trough, and made into lumps about sufficient for one pot. A woman then takes a lump on her knees and with her fist and a stone makes a hole in the top—the beginning of a pot. The hole is gradually enlarged, and with stone inside, and hand or paddle outside, the clay is worked thinner and thinner, until finally it has the shape of the finished pot. It is then put up on a shelf built on one end of the

---

15. Sapi and Anopias villages.

Fig. 2.18. "Beating the pot into shape, Tumleo." A-31729 (36).

Fig. 2.19. "Woman burning pots, Tumleo." A-31753 (60).

house to dry for a day. (While working the pot, if it is at all large, the half of an old pot about the same size or a little larger is used as a support.)

The next day the pots are taken to the burning place, where a few dried leaves are burned in each pot, so that they are heated somewhat, and then the woman rubs, with her hand, fine sand over the entire outer surface, smoothing it out.

The pots are then placed, perhaps a dozen together, and palm leaf stems placed around and between, as well as over them; the burning takes a half hour or more, esp. if the pots be large, the palm leaf stems and leaves being renewed several times, the women using two sticks something like a pair of tongs. When burnt they are allowed to cool a little, and then smoked over a fire and blackened, (see Erdweg's [1902] paper for full process).

The first photos I took of the pot making were made up, by Pater Kirschbaum getting a couple of women to represent the various stages. Later I got a few photos of different stages in other parts of the village while the women were regularly pursuing their vocation.

In the afternoon a boy from the mission went with me, and I got further views.

Saturday, Sept. 18   Took several pictures in morning, and bought a number of things. Intended to leave on a native canoe, but they did not come,

Tumleo pots

"per" cooking pot

sal for preparing sago porridge

takúm for sago

sujanú for keeping sago meal

lup malangón for keeping sago meal

bowl, also covers tapel

su lapíj púak hung, bottom side up, on outside "alol" used also for sago or cooking

per atjek vol only for ornament of "alol"

"per aterapin" cooking fish, etc.

Fig. 2.20. "Sago in canoe, Tumleo." Brought to the island from mainland exchange partners. A-31737 (44).

so in afternoon the mission gave me their boat with 5 boys, and I returned to Eitape. The boys carried all my specimens up to the house, and I gave each 5 fish hooks and 3 sticks of tobacco.

The big drum was also brought over in a native canoe by 3 natives, but was so heavy they had to come up to the house to get help to get it on shore.

Sunday, Sept. 19 Developed the 3 doz. plates taken in Tumleo.

Fig. 2.21. "Making sago and distributing in breadfruit leaves, Tumleo." Her child wears a shell ring as a pendant. A-31745 (52).

Fig. 2.22. "Canoe, Ali." A-31813 (120). In 1993 the man in this photo was identified by Harry Amowe (and several others) as his father, Amowe.

Fig. 2.23. Hair ornament *(taip)* made of shell with tortoise shell inside, with bead and nassa shell in center; fastened to hair by a short stick, 139604 (522); leg band with shell rattles for dance, 139611 (534); both from Tumleo. A-112060.

5 cm

Fig. 2.24. Drum *(garamut)* on beach near outrigger canoe, Tumleo. A-31735 (42).

Monday, Sept. 20   Mail came today by mission steamer *Gabriel*—the first I had received since leaving Sydney.

In afternoon sorted over my things preparatory to new trip.

Tuesday, Sept. 21   In morning went to Mission to see captain of mission steamer *Gabriel*,[16] which came over about 9 A.M. from Tumleo, to see if I could go on it to Malol. Found he would not stop there. Wrote letters in P.M.

Wednesday, Sept. 22   Pater Kirschbaum with the mission cutter came over to Santa Anna about noon. Wrote to ask if could go to Malol with him, and received answer that he would start in short time, and could go if there. Got things together in haste and down to shore, and started along beach to mission, but saw that he had started. Went back to bridge and met Steinemann,[17] who ordered out the boat, so that I succeeded in reaching the cutter.

Got to Malol about dark and went on shore with small boat belonging to cutter—only one person could go at one time. Surf so high that left all things on board till morning.

In evening went to village with Pater Kirschbaum. He had previously lived here a month, so the people knew him well, and were quite friendly. It was very interesting to see the way the boys would cluster around him, clinging to his hands and arms as they walked along. They all seemed glad to see him and welcome him back. P. Kirschbaum wished to get the men to come in the morning with their canoes—dug outs without outrigger—and unload his stuff from the cutter. He also told them that I would come to see them and that the women and children should not run away.

Thursday, Sept. 23   The canoes came in the morning, and a great number of men and boys gathered on the beach, all interested in the proceedings, and all ready to lend a hand. Soon the things were all in the house or near there, as many had gotten wet in the surf, and must be spread out to dry.

---

16. Father Joseph Lörks, who later became bishop and moved the SVD headquarters to Kairiru Island. He was known as the "fighting bishop" (see Huber 1988).

17. This is probably the bridge over the Aitape River. Willi Steinemann was police master at Eitape.

Fig. 2.25. String bags bought in Malol: 139566 (669), 139565 (668) made in Arop or in the interior of Arop; 139563 (603) made in interior of Malol. A-112029.

Pater Kirschbaum had brought all his belongings, outfit, food, etc., for the next six months, and soon the surf became so bad that no one can land.

In the afternoon I went around through the village to the inlet, and took some pictures of houses, etc.

Friday, Sept. 24 The two missionaries spent the day getting their things. In afternoon I went to the village with my trade, and secured a number of things.

Saturday, Sept. 25 In morning went to village again, and for first time crossed the inlet to other side, where the *luluai*[18] lived. He made me quite welcome, shook hands when we met, and led me to a sheltered veranda [attached] to his house, where we sat down, and we talked a while, a couple of the older boys acting as interpreters. I gave him a present, and bought a few things, and then went on through the village with the boys as far as it extended. On returning the *luluai* himself ferried me across the inlet.

At the house I found that Prof. Neuhauss had come over from Eitape for a few days. In the afternoon we went through the villages and made some photos.

Sunday, Sept. 26 In morning went again to villages with Prof. Neuhauss and P. Kirschbaum, and photographed a number of things.

Felt very weak on return, and did not go out rest of day. Had some fever the night before, and could not eat, as my stomach was out of order.

Monday, Sept. 27 Was quite sick all night. In morning Prof. Neuhauss left for Eitape, and I sent a request to Herr Rodatz for the boat to take me back to Eitape. Could not do anything all day.[19]

P. Kirschbaum spent the day in the bush with the boys, studying the language and learning what he could, visiting the sago workings, etc.

Tuesday, Sept. 28 The boat came in forenoon, but was so heavy it could not land. P. Kirschbaum had gone to village to buy posts for his house, which he was very successful in doing, but did not get back till noon, with all the men

---

18. Government-appointed headman.
19. ABL's description of symptoms is vague, but suggests diarrheal disease, probably from drinking unprotected lagoon water. A few weeks earlier, Governor Hahl had assured him that if the natives drank the water it was safe. Even today there is higher incidence of diarrheal disease at Malol than elsewhere in the area because there are no natural sources of protected water and the lagoon is quite polluted (Mark Wijnen, personal communication, 1993).

and boys not gone to make sago in his train. After his affairs were settled, and dinner over, he got them to take my things to the inlet of the lagoon, and there get the canoes to take me out through the surf, as the natives said it was too high on the beach by the mission for the canoe to get through. The *luluai* and *tultul* went along, and on arriving at the inlet, we waited quite a while for the canoe, which finally came in the care of two boys. The things were loaded in the canoe, and we finally succeeded in passing the surf, and about 3 P.M. put up sail and got away for Eitape, where we arrived just at dark.

This visit to Malol was somewhat disappointing, in addition to the fact that on account of sickness I could not finish my work.

There did not seem to be much of the older things left at Malol. The place is near Eitape, and the missionaries have also taken much away. The mission house had been built about 2 months before, P. Kirschbaum was there for a month, and the brother had stayed six weeks by himself. They only had 10 hectares, very sandy beach soil, so that except cocoanuts, not much could be grown. P. Kirschbaum said that the villagers had already raised beans from seed given to them on their plantations in the bush, where the soil was good. They do not raise anything near the village. Their chief food is sago and fish. For sago they cross the lagoon in canoes and go an hour or so into the bush.

Fig. 2.26. "Sago platform and cocoanuts, Malol." A-31764 (71).

Fig. 2.27. "Woman shredding string from aerial roots of pandanus tree, Malol." A-31775 (82).

Each family usually has a different place. They also raise a few taro and yams in bush, but not to any extent. The sago is brought in packets to the village, and there preserved in large casks of bark for future use. This is not done to so great an extent as in Tumleo, however, as they can get sago whenever they wish from the bush. I saw very few casks, but photoed the best collection that I saw. (In this photo the cocoanuts hung up are for planting—they are hung under the eaves to sprout, sometimes they are also preserved thus as food.)

Sago is the chief export from this place, and the people from the islands come here to get sago, bringing pots from Tumleo, arm rings from Seleo, etc. Fish they catch in great numbers in the lagoon, using nets and fish traps. Cocoanuts are numerous all around the villages.

The chief industries are making nets, fish traps and baskets, all by the women. Nets are made from string made of fibre of the aerial roots of the pandanus. From these the fibre is shredded (see photo) and a bunch of fibre, perhaps 3–4 feet long, knotted in the center, and hung up to dry. This is then twisted on an old pot, in the only case that I saw of this work; the woman had the central knot fastened to her girdle, and twisted the fibres from one end on the pot—further treatment I did not find out. Got picture of woman netting net.

The men make canoes (dugouts without outrigger) but no paddles—all come from Warapu, Arop or Sissano, esp. Warapu. Many of their ornaments also come from there, though they make a few themselves. Arrows from interior, except fish arrows and spears. Bows (?), but got photo [lost] of man putting on the plaited rattan band so frequently found near the ends. He used a slender bone needle to raise the rattan to pass the other under.

As to clothing the boys, up to the time of their initiation, wear nothing. They then assume the breech clout of bark, and a girdle of leaves (cocoanut ?)[20] with rattan band, also frequently earrings of tortoise shell, with tassel

20. These appear to be of pandanus leaf.

Fig. 2.28. "Woman making net, Malol." A-78266 [A-31773] (80).

of string and seeds (see specimens). The girdle is usually not worn by the men who wear only the breech-clout. As ornaments, nose-ornament of bamboo (photo, side view [lost]), ear ring of tortoise shell, combs of bamboo (made here) rude; occasionally 3–6 small sticks tied together, but not made into good combs, as in Wainimo. Woven arm bands and breast-bands, ornamented with seeds and shells, made here, also from Warapu. Forehead bands as in Wainimo, woven with seeds. Leg bands much the same as Wainimo, said made here, but not common.

The women were so shy that I could find little out regarding them.

Houses large, the dwelling house (several families) with roof coming to ground (see Fig. 2.29). Photo of frame, and frame with women putting on *atap* roof. The boys sleep in a small house near the other. Also a small

Fig. 2.29. "House, Malol." A-31761
(68).

making atap for roof

tambaran house much like the boys' house, and a much higher *tambaran* house [men's cult house] (see photos [lost]). Could not find out about them. Photographed deserted house with grave of former owner beneath—all left to decay, with canoe and weapons of former owner also.

All the wooden bowls seen for food very rude. Water buckets made of leaf-spath of betel palm, same as to the west. Pots, of course, from Tumleo.

Saw man making *atap* for roof. Took 3 leaflets (cocoanut), from which midrib had been removed, placed them together (one reversed to other two) and bent them over stick (part of leaf-stalk), a hole was made, and another stick passed through so as to bind them to first, each succeeding set overlapping then proceding up to where stick comes out. Each piece is 5–6 ft. long.

The men, as at Wainamo, carry their possessions in a netted bag, which they said came from Warapu usually (Prof. Neuhauss said all made at a certain village inland from Warapu) tho got two small bags which they said made at a certain village in bush called Anal.[21] In these bags I did not find much, for the natives seemed pretty poor. Bone daggers and cocoanut openers were plain, also lime gourds, with very few exceptions; those decorated not like Humboldt-bay, as at Wainimo.

LANGUAGE

The language of Malol is Melanesian, Arop and Sissano are dialects of the same. Warapu is Papuan. Malol is the Tumleo name, their own name for themselves is Siau. All the coast peoples near Eitape speak Melanesian languages except Warapu and the Walman (own name) peoples.

Paup, Yakamūl, Swain all speak different dialects of same language as spoken on Angel, Seleo and Alii, which vary also dialectically. Tumleo speaks

---

21. ABL later learned that Anal was the name of a district, not a village.

Fig. 2.30. "Two men of Malol." Both wear shell arm rings and loincloths of bark cloth; one carries a cassowary-bone dagger in his armband. A-31767 (74).

a related language, about as different from that of Alii as German from Dutch.

Even the villages on Tumleo vary slightly in dialect. The north and south of Ali also have different dialects. (See paper in *Mitteilungen des Orientalischen Sprechen zu Berlin.* Jahrgang 8, Abteil 1. Ostasiatische Stud., Berlin, 1905. "Die Sprachen des Berlinhafen-Bezirks in Deutsch-Neuguinea.")[22]

Tuesday, Sept. 28 Rested most all day, as did not feel like doing much. Cleaned up room and arranged things.

Wednesday, Sept. 29 Developed photos, 2 doz. from Malol.

Thursday, Sept. 30 Rained good part of day.

---

22. Klaffl and Vormann (1905, 1–138).

Fig. 2.31. "Tumleo man chewing betel nut, ornaments from Rabuin," during a visit to Malol. A-31770 (77).

Friday, Oct. 1   Catalogued Malol collection in morning, and packed small objects in afternoon.

Saturday, Oct. 2   Read and wrote up notes, etc.

Sunday, Oct. 3–Saturday, Oct. 9   Wrote letters, report to Director Museum (Oct. 5), straightened up accounts, etc.

Sunday, Oct. 10–Sunday, Oct. 17   Sick with fever and was unable to do much beyond reading and looking over my things all that week.

To the Berlinhafen Islands

||||||||||||||||||||||||||||||||||||||||||||||||||||||||||||||||||||||||||||||||||||||||||||||||||||||||||||||||||||||||||||||||||

18 October 1909–10 November 1909

After recovering from his first incapacitating bout of malaria—first at Malol and then at Eitape—ABL made preparations for his next trip from the government station: a second sojourn to the nearby islands in Berlin Harbor (Berlinhafen). Many modern authors interpret Berlinhafen as the name used in German times for Aitape, but in fact the name referred specifically to the good anchorage that lies between Angel, Seleo, Ali, and the so-called Middle Reef. German admiralty charts designate only this small patch of water as Berlinhafen, though by extension Tumleo, the fourth island in the archipelago, is generally included also. Historically, the name Berlinhafen never referred to Aitape town, the Catholic Mission at St. Anna, or any other area on the mainland.

In September ABL had visited Tumleo, where in 1896 the missionaries from the Society of the Divine Word had established their headquarters and first station in German New Guinea. Now he planned an excursion to see the other three islands in the harbor: Ali, Seleo, and Angel.

By this time ABL had spent a total of six or eight weeks in the colony and was gradually becoming more familiar with the environment, Pidgin, the colonial administration, and local patterns of life. He was beginning to establish a series of fieldwork routines for processing the collections, information, and photos he gathered on his travels in the villages.

During the excursion to the islands detailed in the following section, ABL reveals for the first time his virtuosity as a field researcher. Left to his own devices, he quickly became aware of the importance of intervillage trade in the local island economy. While documenting his collection and studying local craft specializations, ABL became the first anthropologist to recognize the broader implications that intensive intervillage trade might have on some of the pressing anthropological questions of the day. Trade was clearly a key element in Boas' first research agenda: cultural diffusion and the cultural influence that one community might have on another. In the Berlinhafen Islands, ABL came to understand the role of trade in minimizing local variation in the material culture of different villages in the Eitape area. And yet ABL realized that trade per se did not explain all of the region's diversity.

> All the coastal region from Sissano to the neighborhood of Dallmannhafen must be regarded as of one general material culture. With many minor variations from district to district, and even from village to village. In fact, the differences frequently seem to be greater than the resemblances. The islanders are the chief traders and travelers, so the islands show the most generalized culture. Many of the coast villages are very "local." [Specimen book 2]

ABL was not the first anthropologist to recognize that the islanders were intensely involved in trade. The German ethnologist Richard Parkinson (1900) was one of the earliest to note the extensive trade relations along the Berlinhafen coast, though he offered only cursory details about it. Pater Mathias Josef Erdweg (1901a, 1902), who had lived on Tumleo, described with considerable sensitivity the character of exchange partnerships between people on Tumleo and in mainland villages. He emphasized the islanders' dependence on the mainland for sago, their chief food, all of which had to be imported from their trade partners.[6]

Each of the three anthropologists ABL met in and around Eitape in 1909—Georg Friederici (1912, 1913), Richard Neuhauss (1911a), and Otto Schlaginhaufen (1910a)—were also aware of aspects of trade relations on the Eitape coast. Each offers some description of particular trade relations, such as the pots-for-sago trade at Tumleo, but none of these writers seems to have grasped the significance of trade relations within the broader context of the entire Eitape coast. And only ABL collected data that could demonstrate on its own how pervasive and extensive trade relations were along this coast.

Half a century later, Frank Tiesler (1969–1970) would independently arrive at similar conclusions from a careful reading of more than two hundred early published accounts, together with Schlaginhaufen's unpublished field notes and collection documentation. There is good reason to believe that all four of the anthropologists working in and around Eitape in 1909 (Friederici, ABL, Neuhauss, and Schlaginhaufen) learned of the importance of trade in the region from the Catholic missionaries and government officers. But it also appears that ABL was the only one of these anthropologists to collect systematic field data about this trade network.[7]

As ABL purchased specimens from villagers on Tumleo in September 1909, he began asking where each piece was made. This strategy proved so productive that on his return to the islands in October, it had become a standard fieldwork procedure, one he would often use during the rest of the expedition. At the end of the twentieth century, this kind of data collection may seem both obvious and routine, but in 1909 it was neither. Only Schlaginhaufen collected similar kinds of data in the field and then only for a handful of specimens (see, e.g., Tiesler 1969–1970, 150, 154–165). For the entire Eitape coast, ABL collected twice as much detailed data about trade and exchange linkages as all other early authors combined.[8]

The Berlinhafen Islands consist of four small coral islands, each with its own distinctive conditions. All except Tumleo—which has a small, rocky hill at one end—are flat.[9] Angel, the smallest, was a tiny speck of land two hectares in area. It was almost entirely covered with houses for its small, but dense, population. Nearby Seleo is the largest of the islands, but in 1909 had the smallest population. A large part of Seleo was purchased for the New Guinea Compagnie in 1895 by Ludwig Kärnbach, who established a trading station on the island. The same year, the devastating smallpox epidemic that ravaged a number of mainland villages reduced Seleo's population of four hundred by at least half.

By 1909 Tumleo had become the best known of the four islands, largely because of the ethnographic writings of Erdweg (1901a, 1902), Parkinson (1900), and Schmidt (1899). In contrast, Ali was the least known, primarily because the islanders had abandoned their island following a German punitive expedition in 1896 after an Ali attack on New Guinea Compagnie personnel stationed at Seleo.[10] A decade later, Ali's population was beginning to return to the island, and Pater Jäschke had recently established a mission station on the island.

During what amounted to only two weeks in the islands, ABL was remarkably productive. He collected just over 400 specimens (328 from Ali)—roughly one-third of all the specimens he collected in the three and a half months on the Eitape coast. One might suspect from these figures that ABL was merely buying up everything in sight, but although he obtained a large number of pieces, he also collected a lot of data about particular objects, where they were made, how they were used, how common they were, et cetera. Some of these notes from his specimen lists are reproduced here as captions to the figures. In addition, he gathered considerable information about a variety of cultural topics, collected a substantial word list, and took 43 photos to illustrate his notes.

At times, ABL seems to have accepted uncritically some of the biases and views of the SVD missionaries and government officers. For example, in an extended note about intervillage trade (reproduced at the end of his diary about the Berlinhafen Islands), he described the islanders as the major traders on the coast and depicted the islands as the central places in the network of trade linkages along the coast. This view is not inaccurate per se: the islanders were active traders. Furthermore, determining which communities were the biggest traders or the central figures in the trade around Berlinhafen is a difficult matter of interpretation. But a careful reading of ABL's own field notes and collection documentation shows that the islanders were not as centrally situated in this network as some of his comments suggest. In retrospect, the centrality of the islands reported by several early authors may have emerged as a theme because for European residents on this coast, Berlinhafen was the headquarters and central place for the mission (Tumleo), the New Guinea Compagnie (Seleo), and the government (nearby at Eitape). Fortunately ABL's collection, field notes, and diaries allow us a unique opportunity to reevaluate such conclusions in ways not otherwise possible (Welsch and Terrell 1991).

In documenting and assessing the movement of goods from one community to another, ABL may have found a model in his own doctoral dissertation (1906b), which analyzed cultural influences among the Native Americans of the Washington and Oregon coasts, the most linguistically and culturally complex part of the Pacific Northwest. ABL never tells us, but he must have seen parallels in this part of New Guinea with the Chinook who lived at the mouth of the Columbia River and were also avid traders and middlemen. Such parallels, which would have raised similar questions about cultural influences on neighboring communities, probably led him to collect much richer data than the other anthropologists working around Eitape.

It is also clear that the data ABL collected in this area were far more detailed than those in Field Museum's other early New Guinea collections, such as those made by George Dorsey, Richard Parkinson, and Otto Finsch. Even the museum's catalog cards were biased against collecting data about the movement of objects from one community to another, inasmuch as they contain only a single line for recording the locality or provenience of a specimen. A single line for locality suggests that the museum's presumption was that objects were rarely traded. Certainly this format posed no problem if things were never exchanged between communities or if the collector never asked where things were made. But for ABL this was an administrative bias that he had to overcome intellectually in the field.

We will never know for certain all of the influences on ABL's research strategies, but it was clearly around the time of his visit to the Berlinhafen Islands that his field methods began to blossom.

Fig. 2.32. "Shore of Ali." A-31784 (90).

The Berlinhafen Islands

Monday, Oct. 18 Went to Ali in boat from Eitape. Had to row most of way, took about 3 hrs. Arrived about 11 A.M. and in afternoon looked through the villages of Ali.

Tuesday, Oct. 19–Wednesday, Oct. 20 Bought specimens and made photos, cloudy and rainy.

Thursday, Oct. 21 Went in native canoe to Seleo. Took ½ hr. Started about 8 A.M. and came back about 3 P.M.

Seleo has fewer inhabitants than other islands, probably less than 100. They live in small village at north end of island. The chief part of the island, including the southern portion, belongs to the N.G. Company, which has a plantation there (cocoanuts chiefly). There is also opposite Angél, a settlement of Angel people, made about 1907, of about 50 persons (10 houses). This I did not visit.

Friday, Oct. 22 Saw one large *garamut,* made in Dallmannhafen or near there. Got a few carvings, some old, and some from other places. Beyond the common articles, the people did not seem to have much.

Fig. 2.33. "House, Ali." A-31785 (92).

101

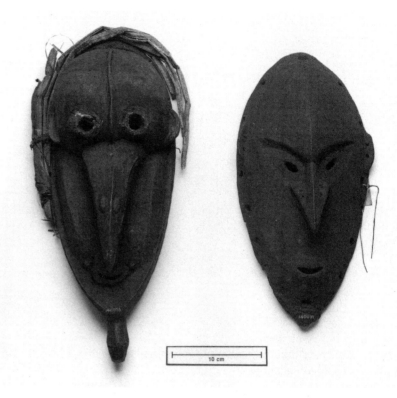

Fig. 2.34. Masks purchased in Seleo: 140038 (1043) "said to come from Murik"; 140039 (1042) "said to come from Dallmannhafen." A-112069.

Sago and fish, with other sorts of marine animals, as sea urchins, form their chief food. Pots they get chiefly from Tumleo, netted bags from the "bush," etc., and their life is about the same as in Ali. The reef lying N.W. of the island is a favorite fishing place, and for the people of Ali as well, the women going there nearly every quiet morning.

Fig. 2.35. "Canoe, Seleo," showing platform, frame for holding cargo, and carved prow. A-31804 (111).

Fig. 2.36. *"Tamburan* house, Angel." A-31810 (117).

Two men from Ali went with me and my 3 boys in canoe. I gave each 2 arm rings (porcelain).

Saturday, Oct. 23 Went to Angel in canoe with 2 men, started about 8, came back about 2. Took about 1 hr.

Angel is quite small, but has more people than Seleo. There are also several *tambaran* houses, but none very large. (Did not see the one in Seleo, as the people would not let me go near it, and I did not wish to offend them—heard afterward there were some fine carvings on it.) Saw two big drums here (from Dallmannhafen) and one made in Angel by man from Sup (Mushu), after style of Sup. (Bought this for 10 M. + 1 lava lava + 1 bush knife, and owner was to bring it to Eitape when he returned from a trip for sago, provided I did not take it earlier, or send him word to take it to Seleo.) Purchased several specimens, mostly the same as in Seleo and Ali.

{Editor's note: On October 23 or 24 ABL appears to have returned to Ali, where he continued buying specimens and taking photographs. He was so busy gathering field data about particular specimens and other cultural information that he barely kept a field diary during this trip to the islands.}

Tuesday, Oct. 26 Packed up my specimens and sent them with 2 boys (Marumu and Kabai) and four men of Ali to Eitape; also extra boxes and bags.

Fig. 2.37. "Drum *(garamut)* under house, Angel." A-31811 (118).

ANGEL SHELL RINGS

Both in Seleo and Angel the chief industry is the making of shell armrings. Large ones are made from the Tridacna shell, and with these the people purchase sago, their chief food, as well as other things, on the mainland. For one large arm ring they may get 30 bundles of sago, each of 20–30 lbs.; for a smaller ring 10 bundles. The shell is first roughly broken into rounded pieces with a stone hammer, then ground down and smoothed somewhat on both sides on a large stone or boulder, perhaps $1\frac{1}{2}$ ft. long, with sand. The edge is then bound with rattan, and the center bored out with a bamboo drill with sand. The outer edge is rubbed smooth on a smaller stone, and the inner side smoothed, now with a file, formerly with a stone. From the core a smaller ring may be made in the same way. When grinding (done only by women) the piece of shell, edged with rattan, is placed in a depression in a piece of wood, usually with some fibre below, to keep it from turning, as the drill is turned back and forth. I photographed one woman in Angel, and then purchased the outfit,—borer and stone weight, shell, and wood support (this with 3 holes, end one used for grinding, and middle one with fine sand); a cocoanut shell with water stood by (did not buy this). The

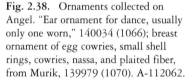

Fig. 2.38. Ornaments collected on Angel. "Ear ornament for dance, usually only one worn," 140034 (1066); breast ornament of egg cowries, small shell rings, cowries, nassa, and plaited fiber, from Murik, 139979 (1070). A-112062.

woman had around her neck the loin cloth *(māl)* of her husband (dead), which she would wear as long as it would hold together in memory of him.

Small shell rings are made from the base of the Conus shell. The base is first broken off with a stone hammer, and then ground down on a large stone, same as used for large ring, but a piece of wood is used on top of shell, as too small to hold in hand. Sand is used, and may be kept in cocoanut shell near by, and water in another, as stone is kept wet, when ground down on both sides. The center is knocked out with stone, and smoothed (now done with file) and outer edge ground smooth on small stone. Notches are sometimes made in outer edge with file, but this newly introduced [along] with [introduction of] file. These rings also made only by women and may be made in house, or outside. I saw outfit in corner of house, and got several pieces of shell, stone hammer, wood for hand, sand, and cocoanut dish, and small grindstone.

ALI

In Ali the chief industry is the making of canoes, some large, some small. These are now made entirely with iron tools, but I got a number of old stone axes and one shell adze. The side boards *(tcipatcōp)* and prows *(kālsūvīung)*

Fig. 2.39. Angel woman (in mourning) making large shell ring *(sualuong).* Boring outfit in collection. A-76551 [A-31808] (115).

Fig. 2.40. Outfit for grinding small shell rings *(reap)* from conus shells, Seleo. This kit consists of stone hammer *(tamul)* for breaking shell to get base from which ring is made; conus shell; two shell bases *(drapa);* partly ground ring; small grindstone used to finish rings (with one unfinished ring on top of it); coconut dish *(paping)* for holding sand (there should be one for water also); two pieces of wood *(ai tawing),* held in hand while grinding ring on large grindstone *(wor).* Sand *(tetang)* used to assist in grinding is from the mainland as the island is entirely coral. In old times the center was broken out and inner side finished with a pointed stone. This is now done with a file, with which the notches often seen in rings are also made. The old rings had no notches. 139955–139960, 139962 (1054–1056). A-112047.

Fig. 2.41. Bamboo borer with stone weight and boring kit for making large shell rings *(sualung),* Angel. Board has three holes; left holds shell bound in rattan, center hole for sand. Coconut shell for water. Unfinished tridacna shell (to right). (This kit used in Fig. 2.39.) 139963–139964 (1074–1075, 1077–1078). A-112048.

of some of the old ones are nicely ornamented with carved and painted designs. Took photos of several. Some had bamboo for side-boards, and no prow. The large ones *(lepīl pālē)* are made as described by Erdweg [1902] in his paper on Tumleo (names different, of course; not many canoes are made in Tumleo).

ALI CLOTHING

Of armrings the people seem to have woven bands, plain and ornamented with nassa shells (say these shells come from Warapu—some say the bands I got were made here, some say got theirs in Warapu). Also of fibre, round, black, which they say comes from the bush back of Warapu, (chiefly).

Got dance ornaments, head, ear, arm and leg, of some variety. The common combs are rude, some of wood, with carved top, some bamboo, some 4–8 sticks, with rattan (?) binding, rather rude. The red fibre used in combs, armbands, etc., is from a distance.

Breast bands as Malol, also Wainamo, woven, with shells. Necklaces of small black seeds, strings, braided; from Warapu, they say. Seeds from *bush.* Dog tooth necklaces also from Dallmannhafen region. Also shell (cowrie ?) made in Ali, rather rude. Woven armbands often with shell rings—these made here. Men's girdles of bark, broad and narrow; young men's of pandanus leaves as in Malol (meaning ?). Woven red girdles said by some to come from (Fred. Wh. Hafen ?).

Bark girdles worn by men and women, at times. All men, bark loin cloth *(mal).* Woman's *mal* broader, short, worn over girdle. Children wear nothing

Fig. 2.42. "Large outrigger canoe (from Ali), Angel." A-31812 (119).

Fig. 2.43. "Woman with child, Ali." A-31822 (129).

Fig. 2.44. Netted string bags obtained in Ali, all made in villages to the east: 139767 (780) from Matapau; 139763 (785) from interior back of Yakamul; 139771 (781) from Pelam near Sawoum. A-112030.

till 8–13 yrs. old, except ornaments, as necklace with many shell rings, etc., often representing considerable wealth from the native's standpoint.

House-hold utensils: pots, of various sizes and shapes, mostly from Tumleo, occasionally from (Komēs) *bush* inland from Yakamúl. (Got one said to be from Wāoul, 3 days inland from Yakamul, at Angel); wooden dishes, elliptical to circular, shallow or fairly deep, from 6–15 inches in diameter. Some made in Ali, but mostly bought from villages toward Dallmannhafen; water-bottles of cocoanut-shells; fish baskets, deep, rather soft, of cocoanut leaves; other rough baskets of cocoanut leaves, also platters; fish baskets, circular stiff, round bottoms; sago-sifters, wooden spoons and stirring sticks; cages for drying fish; casks for holding sago (these usually in house—in Tumleo usually outside); frames over fire, for various objects to dry on; hooks from roof to hang things on—these part of sapling, say $1\frac{1}{2}$–2 in. in diameter, with numerous branches, cut off about 6 in. from stem, reversed and hung to roof by rattan.

The men carry netted bags, usually woven in colors. There are two sorts of weaves, one coming from east of Eitape, other west, all from various villages of interior. Small bags similar to those from neighborhood of Warapu also made in Ali. Sometimes the men have a woven bag or flat basket, from Merik or neighborhood not made near Ali.[23]

The men know where most of the bags come from, and seem to distinguish them by the character and weave of the border around the mouth—also by the pattern or color design.

In the houses is usually a shelf around the wall, about 3 feet high and 1 to 2 ft. wide, the outer edge held by being suspended by stiff "bush-rope" from the roof, the inner fastened to the wall, (or also suspended ?). Also over head, or at the ends of the house, are wide shelves or places for the

---

23. These are the famous Murik baskets, which played a major role in regional integration along the north coast (see Barlow 1985). ABL consistently used this spelling when around Eitape, later writing it as Murik.

storing of all sorts of articles—pots, wood dishes, articles of food, bows, arrows, clubs, etc., etc. On hooks on side, or suspended from roof, are hung bags, buckets, baskets, water-bottles, etc. There are from one to three hearths or fire places, with drying frame or fish smoking box over them (3–4 ft. above). These are only large leaf sheaths (of betel-palm (?), same as buckets[24] are made of) covered with ashes.

ALI FOOD

The chief food is sago and fish, including shellfish, sea-urchins, etc. Yams and taro are grown to some extent, and also brought over from the mainland. Many kinds of plants and leaves are used as greens, and also as seasoning for their dishes.

Sago, "the staff of life," is purchased on the mainland, and brought over in their canoes in packets (15–25 lbs.) covered with leaves. This is then put into casks made of the lower broad part of the sago palm (wrapped with bush rope) where it is trodden down by the feet into a compact mass, and when full covered with leaves, sticks and stones. Here it remains till used. It is usually eaten after cooking with hot water. The sago from the cask *(drāpī)* is put in a large pot *(sūp)* with a little water, so that it forms a thick milky fluid, and this is strained with the sago strainer to remove sticks, stones, rubbish, etc. Then boiling water from another pot is slowly added, the sago being stirred continually, when it soon becomes thick and sticky. It is then distributed in leaves (large, as breadfruit) with the stirring sticks (2 [see Fig. 2.21]) and these tied up till eaten. In this form it will not keep longer than 2 days. The above is the common method of preparing sago, but the sago from the casks is also made into cakes, and baked between potsherds over a fire.

ALI FISHING

The customary way of catching fish is by spearing, or shooting with fish arrow (may have one or many points) by the men, and catching with nets and short spears by the women. The nets are triangular, one kind large (*r̃ā* trilled r), another sort small *(yerī)*. They are made by the women from string made of the twisted fibres of the aerial roots of a species of Pandanus *(yim)*. Long pieces (4–6 ft.) of these roots are taken, and the fibre removed and cleaned by scraping with a clam shell. The fibre is then made in small bundles, knotted in the middle, and hung up to dry. Later it is spun by being rolled on a pot or wood bowl (have seen both—some say thigh is also used), while fastened to the waist (see photo from Malol) or held between the toes (see photo from Ali). In making the nets a sort of shuttle is used, the mesh being regulated by a piece of bamboo, (see specimen). The netting is first made in rectangular sections, which are later fastened together to make the required size. In this way they are also readily patched, as a new section can be added as necessary. It is seldom, in fact, that an entirely new net is made.

In Angel a large seine *(wār),* with much larger mesh, is made. It seems a question if this is native to Angel, tho the old men say they were made long before white men came, but that the idea was possibly obtained from the Dallmannhafen region. Not made in other islands.

The natives also use a certain plant *(wālāmīél)* to poison fish. Both the roots and leaves are used for this purpose, being mashed with stones.

---

24. He is incorrect here; these continue to be made of limbum palm spathe.

Fig. 2.45. "Malakais *(tultul)* opening cocoanut, Ali." A-31816 (123).

BURIAL

The dead are usually buried near the house, and an enclosure made round the grave (seldom a small shed, as in Tumleo). This is of various kinds (see photos). Near the grave a pole is frequently placed, on which are hung various articles belonging to the deceased, the larger ones being piled up at its base. (They were willing, at times, to sell these.) These are usually broken (see dog tooth necklace from grave).

ALI MOURNING

The relatives mourn for varying lengths of time depending on the importance of the deceased. The men remove everything but the loin cloth, and smear the body and face with a clay, usually white or grey, sometimes reddish (see photo of man).

The women also rub themselves with clay, and frequently wear round the neck the loin cloth, twisted into a tight roll, (esp. widows for their husbands, and mothers for sons).

Every man has 2 souls, spirits, or shades. When alive, one is represented by his shadow, while the other lives within. These called *nenūk*. When he dies, one goes far away "long bush," and stops "long tru." This one does not come back.

The other stops near the place where the dead is buried, and the people are very unwilling for a stranger to go near a recent grave, for fear this *nenúk* might be offended (frightened away ?) by such a one. They are also unwilling to have a recent grave photographed, for fear the spirit will go away "in the box" (as the picture made is, they believe, the *nenuk*). For those who have been dead some time they do not seem to care so much, and no objection was made to photographing such graves. In my first visit to one of the villages I saw a new grave, and wished to look at it closer, but as I approached it an old man, covered all over with white clay, motioned to me very energetically to come away, and I found out later that it was the grave of his son, who had been dead only about a week. The old man (the *luluai* of Ali) would not let me go near or photograph the grave.

As for themselves, the people usually made no objection to being photographed, tho they asked me if I would take away the spirit in my camera.

Fig. 2.46. String bag from Karsau with forehead band of broken dog's teeth tied on. Bought from a man on Ali who took this and other items from a grave pole to sell to ABL. Decorated with halved coix seeds, string fringe, and three colors of string, 139779 (794). A-112033.

15 cm

ALI SICKNESS

Sickness is caused by a *pārék* (evil spirit or *tambaran*) or *nenuk* (the one that stops near the grave). To cure the man this must be driven away. Certain men (all men ?) can do this by chewing the root of a certain plant *(sāém)*, then spitting in various directions and on the hands, slapping these on the breast and armpits, and speaking to a bone (human ulna—hair also used), which causes the spirit causing the sickness to go away. It would seem, from what I could understand, that all men could use *saem,* but that only a few understood how to "speak" to the bone.

Before using medicine a "sing-sing" is held, and medicine *(saem)* used only when sing sing is not successful in curing sick.

(This whole question is very obscure. I got 3 specimens of *saem,* two with human bones.)

ALI CHILDREN'S GAMES

The children have a considerable number of games, many being played only at certain seasons of the year. When I was there they were shooting with small bows the stems of grasses. They sometimes formed sides and carried on regular miniature battles. They also had cross-bows *(ra āítc)* with which either grass stalks or small wood arrows were shot.

Another game was played with bows and small wood arrows. Two sides were formed, say 3 to 8 on a side, each boy armed with bow and arrows, and all on one side having the fruit of a certain tree. One boy of side with fruit then rolled his fruit toward other side, when all shot at it (from other side). If hit, other side retained it, and next boy rolled his fruit, and so on till all were gotten by other side (if fruit not hit, was rolled again), when they rolled the fruit, and the first side shot. (Did not see this, but it was described by P. Jäschke.)[25]

The small children also have tops, made by sticking a small stick 3–4 inches long through a certain fruit. They also have tops made of the shells of cocoanuts, but these come from the mainland. (Tops called *paitji atūng, mēl atúng,* etc. according to fruit used.) Another game is played by throwing long sticks *(aitāvél)* but I did not get a description of it.

Surf riding on rough, but specially made boards *(ai rāling)* is practiced by the boys.

They also play ball with balls made of a certain leaf, with broken leaves inside. This called *"paitc āpāng."*

A game similar to pull the rope is also played, (called *"ralōl alūp"* [*ralól* = pull; *alúp* = rattan]) with "bush rope."

A sort of buzzer *(atūr atung)* is made from a certain nut, with a strip of bark cloth for string. A hole on one side makes the noise. String figures are said to be very common and very complex, but I did not see any.

As every house on Ali was burned some 10 years ago,[26] there were few old things to be had. Most of the decorated paddles were from Warapu. I got

---

25. ABL's spelling was Joske.

26. On 14 April 1896 the German warship *Moewe* launched a punitive expedition against Ali as a show of German strength against native hostility to the New Guinea Compagnie's traders based at Seleo. The warship bombed and strafed the Ali villages, burning all the houses on the island. The entire population of about eight hundred fled to the mainland or the other Berlinhafen islands. A few people were killed during the strafing and some drowned while fleeing, but there were relatively few casualties. Many of the survivors did not return to the island but established more or less permanent settlements on the mainland. In 1909 the island's population was about 380, less than half its original total (*NKWL* 1897, 23; Schmidt 1899, 15; Tiesler 1969–1970, 129). Islanders today blame this incident on Malung village at the southern point of the island.

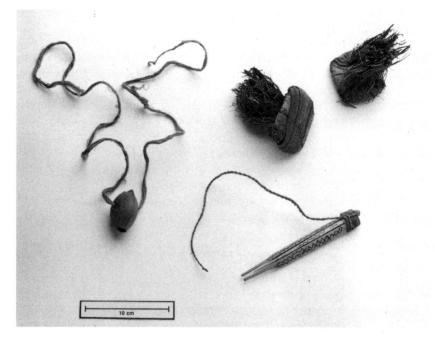

Fig. 2.47. Children's toys, Ali: boy's buzzer *(atur atung)* made of palm seed with bark-cloth string, 139811 (904); balls of leaves *(paitc apang),* 139888 (908), 139887 (907); ornamented mouth harp (910). A-112076.

one from Ali with design of 2 iguanas on each side, with scroll design said to be only for ornament. The design on a canoe prow was explained as two plants.

Every man had a lime gourd and many were ornamented; also the handles of the spatulas were carved.

pō = betel nut
annā = name of pepper plant
atung = fruit
anná atung = fruit of pepper plant eaten with betel nut
raung = leaves
anna raung = leaves of pepper plant, also chewed with betel nut
vīu = chalk or lime
víu wakēing = lime flask
pidrau = soft stone (?) sometimes chewed with betel nut

Native tobacco *(saukē)* is used by all in the form of cigarettes *(drālāng)* rolled in a piece of dry banana leaf. The leaves are taken fresh, dried over a fire, crumbled up and a small portion rolled up in the piece of leaf. Tobacco, dry banana leaves, peppers, etc. are usually kept in a leaf pouch *("rangung"*—name of *pōrīup* given for the leaf portion), with woven top *(tcīap)*.

SOME NAMES OF THINGS[27]

apūk = bamboo
yim = pandanus from which string is made
ai = tree

---

27. ABL collected a number of word lists during his four years of fieldwork. This word list from Ali is the longest and most comprehensive. Aside from short lists of a handful of special terms in indigenous languages, this is the only word list that he wrote down as an integral part of his field diaries. It alone is included here because it illustrates how intensively he was working during this short stay in the islands.

ABL was aware of a long Ali word list published by the missionaries Klaffl and Vormann (1905), but he seems to have assembled this list independently in the field, apparently

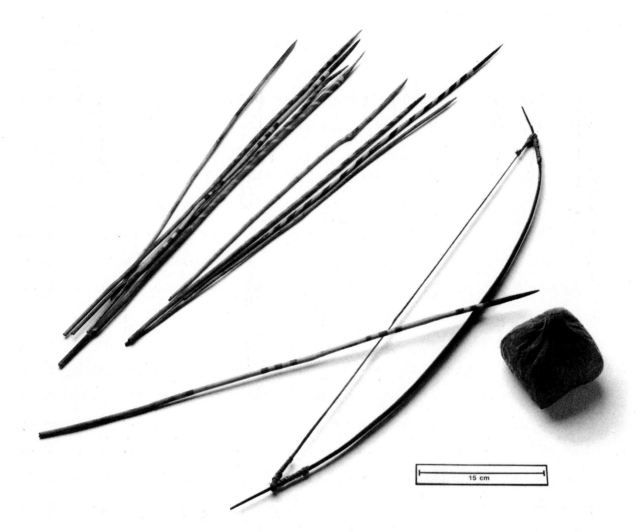

Fig. 2.48. Toy bow, ten arrows, and small wooden arrows for game using certain fruit with a square base, Ali. The arrows are wrapped with a strip of smoke-blackened bark, which is later removed. 139889 (880–891). A-112051.

kāing = bow
kāing balai = bow from interior, large
balai = (name for bush tribes)
tcāvā = fish spear with several points
māngéng = fish arrow with one point
tcāvá māng = fish spear with 2 long barbed points, and two shorter
wār = large seine (Angel)
rā = large triangular net
yerī = small triangular net
mānéng = arrow (general name)

---

from words obtained directly from villagers, although Pater Jäschke may have helped with some words. More than half of ABL's list is for terms that do not appear in Klaffl and Vormann. In addition, ABL uses the same, somewhat idiosyncratic orthography throughout his field diaries. One suspects the guiding hand of his former teacher, Franz Boas, in ABL's phonetic transcriptions. His orthography differs in a number of respects from the common German orthographies of New Guinea languages, but ABL's complex system of diacritics do show some similarities with orthographies used for languages of the Northwest Coast of North America.

tatūs = arrow for fighting, from bush

pachér = arrow with bamboo point

ni^epīl = shaft of fish arrow

pītc = white paint

pelākoúr = red paint

pīt lāng = yellow paint

acūv = palm leaf basket for betel nuts (small) or pots (large); no ends, not made in Ali

rīem = palm leaf basket

wūrīem = (different form given by another man)

sēim = woven flat basket, carried by men. Large ones made in Merik, small ones in Kabou, Put, etc.

rēēr = netted bag

tutuo = sago sieve

tāpēr = round dish

kālúk = pillow

takōl = taro masher

lau = leaf bucket for sago

waip = leaf bucket for water

tcākūl = woman's club

rās = bark cloth beater

wār = girdle for man or woman

māl = loin cloth (man or woman)

yer mail = stone axe

sowāng {swāng} = bone dagger

ati = small bamboo drum

ati áing = small bamboo drum (decorated)

drondrau = jew's harp, bamboo

fās = nose stick

lelīl = ear ring of turtle shell (= turtle really)

rê^ap = ear ornament of string

míntcīrāngē = hair ornament of small red feather

tīyuk = hair ornament of bird of paradise feathers

tcāp = arm band, leg band, etc., when woven

aur = breast band of string *(war)* with nassa shells *(tcai)*

rēp = small shell ring {*rê^a*p} {*ri ep*}

pī = shell arm band from *pi* shells

suālúóng = shell ring from tridacna (made in Seleo and Angel)

mīéng kau = cocoanut shell spoon

{*kakō*} = cocoanut shell spoon (Tumleo name)

tcérīou = drawing or ornamental design of any kind

tamūl = stone

ai lung = stick, as of firewood

līep = fire

āung = dog

wūep = rain

rāpi = sago

ais = paddle

lepīl = canoe

lepíl pale = big canoe

pale = big

tcipatcōp = side board to canoe

kālsūvīung = prow (removable)

wūyītc = poles to outrigger

sê^am = outrigger

ramiúk = mast

ramiúk raméng = top of mast (removable)

terekēau = ornament on top [of mast]

{*tārekéau*} = ornament on top [of mast] (in Tumleo)

Fig. 2.49. Carved wooden ornament for top of mast on large canoe *(terekeau)*, Ali, 139732 (986). A similar mast ornament appears at the top of the mast in Fig. 2.42. A-112075.

not = stick on top of mast through which supporting rattan *(sā kēō)* is
     passed
tcitcíl = stick to which platform is attached
ālūng = small sticks between pole and platform
wāra = sticks of platform
drāl = pitch for stopping cracks, caulking, etc. (scraping from inner bark
     (*dral* = name of tree)
tamūl = stone hammer to break shell for *reap*
drāpā = unfinished piece of base
wor = large grinding stone
tetāng = sand
aí tāwíng = chip held in hand
nau = water in cocoanut *(paping)*
rōs = to grind or rub on stone
ē'pāping = stone to break out center
mātālîeng = small grind stone
pāpíng = tridacna
drāpā = piece of tridacna
dravōl = to grind (with bamboo)
apúk = bamboo (drill)
wār = cord around edge of ring, made from imbate (vine)
alóng = core
tamūl = stone on drill
wārāpíng wārūeng = string used to tie stone on [with]
waraping = 4 (as of 4 cocoanut water vessels; 4 always used together)
warí = iguana
waa = fish
tāming = woman
rāmā = man
rūl = betel nut tree (limbum) from which *lau* and *waip* made
apuk ratcanggaur = bamboo box for paint

Wednesday, Oct. 27–Thursday, Oct. 28   Remained in Ali and got a few more specimens.

Friday, Oct. 29   Had made arrangements for a canoe to take me to Tumleo early in the morning, but as it was calm, did not leave till nearly 10 A.M.,

117

Fig. 2.50. Pair of carved wooden figures (female and male) tied together on a string, Ali, 139783 (774–775). Photo by Ralph Cowan.

and then had to press the men to go. As it was, they had to paddle part way till the breeze came up, which was favorable, and from N.E. Arrived in Tumleo about 1 P.M., and after finally persuading the men to take me to Eitape in an hour or two, if the breeze continued good, set out to get some pots. Found an interpreter in the first village visited, who went around with me, and I succeeded in purchasing 18 pots, nearly all different, and fairly representative of the Tumleo workmanship, tho not the largest, nor the finest.

Then left (about 3 P.M.) for Eitape, where arrived about 5, and brought all my things "on top," except the pots.

Saturday, Oct. 30–Wednesday, Nov. 10   Remained in Eitape, busy with developing plates, and numbering and packing my collection. It was especially difficult to get boxes and packing for the pots, but by putting not more than 2 to 4 in a box, and packing carefully with fine dry grass, I hoped they would come through without too much breakage.

{Editor's note: The villages or hamlets on Ali have been changed in some respects during the eighty years since ABL's visits to the island. There were only five recognized villages in 1990: Puyat, Turale, Etalal, Chaltaleo, and Malung. Turale appears to have replaced Alikala, while Are, Leai, and Polal seem to have been consolidated into larger settlements in the south of the island.}

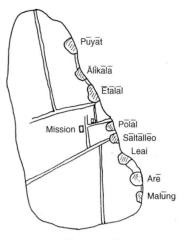

villages on Ali

NOTES ON TRADE AT TUMLEO AND THE BERLINHAFEN ISLANDS[28]

{From ABL's Specimen Lists}

Nos. 498–571 were obtained in Tumleo, but a majority of these things came from elsewhere. The same is true of the other islands of Berlinhafen, as all the islanders are great traders, having large canoes with sails. Their expeditions go as far as Sissano on the west, and Dallmannhafen on the east. Hence on the islands one finds specimens from a coast region of over 100 miles, and often further, as well as from the interior, often several days journey. They themselves manufacture only a few things, which are made in large quantities, and used in trade. When I could, I obtained from the natives the name of the place where the object was made; but this, frequently at least, indicates only the place where they obtained it, while it was made elsewhere. As, for example, netted bags said to come from Sissano (none are made there) come from the interior back of Sissano. The general locality given by the natives, if not the exact village, would seem to be correct.

All the coastal region from Sissano to the neighborhood of Dallmannhafen must be regarded as of one general material culture. With many minor variations from district to district, and even from village to village. In fact, the differences frequently seem to be greater than the resemblances. The islanders are the chief traders and travelers, so the islands show the most generalized culture. Many of the coast villages are very "local." Certain objects from the interior, however, are found in all, especially bows, arrows, and netted bags, which are the specialties of the "bush" villages, and which they trade to the coast natives for such things as salt, shell ornaments, etc.

Now, a few general statements regarding the distribution of certain classes of objects. More details will be found under the localities. Netted bags, as stated above, come almost entirely from the interior, tho a few are made in certain coast villages, and even on the islands. Two groups may be distinguished, the boundary line being about the region of Eitape. East of this the bags have an even and more open weave than to the west, where the weave is closer and ribbed. The western bags also average much smaller in size. None of the bags are ornamented with shells, as further east, but there is a great variety in color pattern. This design, and the character of the weave of the narrow band around the mouth of the bag, indicate the local place of

28. ABL wrote these notes in an ink draft of his specimen list, adding them when he copied his original pencil draft of his specimen list, probably in late November, just before sending this list to Field Museum along with his collection. The Tumleo specimens mentioned were collected in mid-September, but internal evidence suggests that these comments were based on information and field data he obtained on the islands a month later (late October 1909).

Fig. 2.51. Soft basket made of sedges and bark (the so-called Murik basket), collected Ali. The men sometimes used such baskets instead of string bags for their possessions. They are not common around Berlinhafen as they come from Murik, far to the east. 139745. A-112052.

origin. A native who is familiar with these styles can tell what village a bag came from by looking at it.

Arrows are made in almost infinite variety in this region, often nicely decorated with feathers and seeds. Aside from plain or slightly barbed wood pointed fish arrows, and plain bamboo pointed arrows, all the fancy barbed and decorated arrows come from the interior. Aside from fish arrows, most coast villages make no arrows, at least at present. As with the bags, the variety in form and decoration indicates place of origin.

Bows are also chiefly from the interior, and vary in ornamental design on back, size and making of ring holding string, and in form, color and weave of ornamental bands, also sometimes decorated with colored feathers. The more highly ornamented bows are chiefly from the interior, tho the rule does not seem to be so uniform as with the arrows.

Pots are made only locally at Tumleo, in great variety; a few at Sissano, also in the "bush" back of Sissano (here by coiling); and in a village back of Yakamul. Tumleo practically supplies the region with pots and earthen bowls. The Sissano pots are very fragile, and only used locally. The Yakamul pots are are rather small, but are occasionally found elsewhere, apparently owing to the fact that they are highly decorated. Decorated bowls from Kep, beyond Dallmannhafen, are also occasionally found.

Wooden bowls are rare, a few coming from the east, toward Dallmannhafen. A few crude ones are made locally.

120

Sissano Lagoon

||||||||||||||||||||||||||||||||||||||||||||||||||||||||||||||||||||||||||||||||||||||||||||||||||||||||||||

11 November 1909–11 December 1909

In November 1909, ABL visited Sissano on the large lagoon of the same name, about thirty-five kilometers west of Eitape. He accompanied Pater Kirschbaum as far as Malol, hiring Malol carriers to take him from there to Arop, and a new set of carriers to take him through the lagoon to Sissano. At Sissano ABL met Fritz Schulz, an independent German planter who had a small concession on the coast just west of the Sissano hamlets. Schulz agreed to let ABL stay in his house during the visit, much as he had offered such hospitality to other anthropologists, especially Dorsey, Friederici, and Neuhauss, when their respective research brought them to Sissano (see Churchill 1916, 11–18; Dorsey 1909a, 1 Oct.; Friederici 1910a; 1913, 91, 165; Neuhauss 1911a, 61–66, 157, 311).

ABL's preoccupation with material culture and collecting specimens for Field Museum may seem foreign to today's anthropologists because so few of them make systematic museum collections anymore. ABL's experiences noted in this section, however, which documents his frustrations and successes in learning to interact with villagers, will strike a more familiar chord. As most field researchers are aware, arranging even the simplest activities with informants, interpreters, guides, or carriers can be an exercise in frustration for the novice fieldworker. Such experiences, so frequently encountered, are rarely published because they tend to depict the fieldworker as impatient, naive, and out of sync with the villagers, whose way of life he or she has come to study.

Measured in the number of specimens and field data, ABL had a successful and productive visit to Sissano. In fifteen days he collected more than 250 specimens and took 58 photographs, not to mention jotting down his field notes. This sojourn in the lagoon villages was successful in another way as well. It was an opportunity to interact directly with villagers and gather data directly from the people who could answer his questions with some authority. By the time he left Sissano he had become generally familiar with Pidgin, with the tropical environment, with the German colonial administration, and with the general pace of life along the coast. He had obtained one of the largest collections ever brought back from Eitape, and his field notes were filled with data about intervillage trade and the local economy. He had also experienced village life directly.

Upon his return to Eitape, ABL readied his collections and then set off for Friedrich Wilhelmshafen and Herbertshöhe on the Nord-Deutscher Lloyd steamship *Manila*. Preparing his collections proved to be a complex series of minor frustrations. First he had to hurry to develop his negatives and pack his collections for shipment. Because only a limited number of wooden crates and boxes were available, a part of his collection was left in copra sacks at the government station until crates and boxes could be obtained. In addition, the specimens Schulz was to acquire with the money and trade goods ABL had left were not yet available; ABL would not see them until the following May. To add to the confusion, ABL had asked some men to bring a few pots from Yakamul. When the men didn't return, he packed up all his trade goods once the *Manila* arrived at Eitape. As luck would have it, the Yakamul pots arrived the next morning, just before the steamer left. So ABL quickly unpacked enough trade goods to pay for the pots. But because of the shortage of boxes, he was forced to leave these new pots with the New Guinea Compagnie's storekeeper for transshipment to Friedrich Wilhelmshafen.

ABL's difficulties over shipping did not stop there, however. His collections could not be sent on to Chicago just yet, but had to be left in Friedrich Wilhelmshafen. Some weeks earlier, in his first mail delivery since arriving in the colony, ABL received instructions from Field Museum director Skiff telling him not to ship anything to Chicago until a new freight contract had been negotiated with the railroads. As of the time he left Eitape no new instructions had been received, and ABL had little choice but to leave his collection, now numbering more than thirteen hundred pieces, with Georg Heine, the New Guinea Compagnie agent, in Friedrich Wilhelmshafen. Heine was to store the collection until shipping instructions could be sent to him, whereupon he would forward ABL's shipment to Chicago. At the time, this plan seemed like a safe and reasonable course of action, because Heine had befriended George Dorsey the previous year and had arranged to ship all of Dorsey's collection from Kaiser Wilhelmsland to Chicago. That this would not prove so would not become clear for several months—but this is another story, to which we will return in the discussion of ABL's sojourn in Friedrich Wilhelmshafen.

Toward the end of the following section about Sissano Lagoon, there is a brief reference to Otto Schlaginhaufen, the Swiss anthropologist based in Dresden. After finishing his research in the south of New Ireland, Schlaginhaufen came to Eitape for three months after a quick trip up the Sepik. We know that ABL and Schlaginhaufen had met when ABL first arrived in Eitape at the end of August, because Schlaginhaufen mentions him in his own field diaries (still at the Museum für Völkerkunde in Dresden). Although ABL makes only scant references to Schlaginhaufen, the two seem to have coordinated their studies and their collections: each went off to different field locales around Eitape for their collecting. In this respect Schlaginhaufen's attitude differs from that of Neuhauss, who ascended the Sepik on the same ship as Schlaginhaufen. Several times Neuhauss seems to have appeared out of nowhere in villages where ABL was working.

But while Neuhauss' unexpected visits to ABL's field sites must have been frustrating to ABL, it is interesting for us more than eighty years later. Neuhauss (1911a) also had a camera in the field and took photographs of some of the very same family houses, men's houses, and *haus tambaran* that ABL captured on 4-by-5-inch glass negatives. A comparison of the two sets of photos offers somewhat different views of the same structures and in some cases suggests differing interpretations. Similar differences can be seen by comparing the two sets of photos of the sunken forest and the abandoned village of Warapu. ABL's photos present a more eerie and forbidding environment than Neuhauss', a fact that may be simply a consequence of cloud cover; but the differences may also tell us something about the two researchers. In any event, of all the early anthropologists in Melanesia, Neuhauss was the only other anthropologist to take a large number of photographs in the field, although most of his photos are front and profile shots of villagers, intended as physical anthropology data.

After leaving Friedrich Wilhelmshafen, ABL had a quiet and uneventful trip to Herbertshöhe, via the French Islands (also called Vitu). He lost one of his bags between Simpsonhafen and Herbertshöhe. No sooner had ABL arrived in town than he decided to visit one of the Forsayth plantations in southwest New Britain formerly owned by Queen Emma and her son Coe Forsayth. This trip sent him scurrying around Herbertshöhe to purchase supplies, but that we shall leave until the discussion of ABL's visit to west New Britain and the Huon Gulf.

Fig. 2.52. "Dugout canoe, Malol lagoon." A-31756 (63).

Sissano Lagoon

|||||||||||||||||||||||||||||||||||||||||||||||||||||||||||||||||||||||||||||||||||||||||||

Thursday, Nov. 11   Left about 11 A.M. for Malol with my 3 boys and 3 other carriers. As P. Kirschbaum was going the same day, I waited somewhat to go with him, so as to have company. It was an interesting trip, first along the way leading to Pultalul, and then at right angles to same, by a similar broad way, to the beach west of the rocky hills around Eitape—this round-a-bout way to avoid climbing over the hills. Then along the beach through the sand for ½ hr., to the rocky promontory over which we must climb, this taking about ¾ hour. It was then all sandy beach till within ¾ hr. of Malol, when we came to a river, through which we must wade. Along the shore and at the mouth of the river were a great number of women and children (from Malol) fishing with nets and baskets in the surf for a certain kind of small fish, which they caught in great numbers, and threw into baskets hung on posts set along the beach. P. Kirschbaum said that this particular small fish was caught only *one* day in the year, depending on the moon, and that the natives could tell beforehand exactly what day it was to be. The same fish was also caught in Tumleo and Yakamul, but how much further along the coast he did not know.

After wading the river (about 3 ft. deep) we soon came to the first outlying village of Malol, where the natives were cooking and eating these fish. I tried some (boiled), and found them quite good.

"with baskets"

nat. size

Fig. 2.53. "Fishing in surf, Malol. These fish are very small and appear only on one day in the year." A-31825 (132).

125

Fig. 2.54. Plaited fish-dip basket, Malol, 139491 (1090). A-112055.

Friday, Nov. 12   Stayed in Malol over night and till noon the next day. In morning visited village with P. Kirschbaum, and also saw the Austrian bird-hunter. Pater Kirschbaum arranged for 3 carriers to Arop, and we left about 1 P.M., and about 3:30 arrived at the river before Arop. We were some time in getting a canoe, and a storm came up before we got across, so that we got somewhat wet. My carriers were also anxious to return, but I refused to pay them till we were across. The tide was also running out strongly, and it was a question whether the crazy *prōā* we had would not upset. After crossing we stopped till the rain was over in a small shed not far from the river. Then my 3 carriers returned, and Arop men carried my things along the beach and past the greatest part of the Arop settlement to the place of the *luluai,* where I expected to stay over night. As we passed along by the various houses, more and more people joined us, till finally we had quite an extended following. Many had been in service in other places, and spoke fairly good pigeon Eng. Some had returned to Arop with the *Moewe.* One had known me in Herbertshöhe, when he was with some doctor.[29]

On arriving at the *luluai*'s place, we learned that he was away in Sissano. Arrangements were finally made, however, by which I was to have a house—one that was used by the women for storage of household utensils, etc. They first offered me a man's house near the beach, but open on all sides, so that I was afraid that if it rained in the night (and it did), we would get wet. This I refused to take, and requested a better one, when the other house was offered, the women moving out most of their valuables.

29. Herbertshöhe on the Gazelle Peninsula of east New Britain was the seat of government for German New Guinea. Even in such a backwater as Arop in 1909, German New Guinea was a small world for New Guineans as well as for expatriates. Here one Arop man had seen ABL in Herbertshöhe when the man was working for a physician there. Others recognized ABL from his cruise aboard the *Moewe* to Humboldt Bay in August.

AROP HOUSE

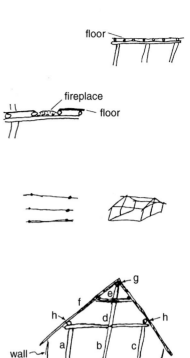

There were three fire-places, or hearths, therein, over one of which was a fish drying cage with fish. As I objected to the fire on account of the smoke, this fish cage and contents were also removed. As it was nearly 3 ft. high and 2½ ft. wide, it was a rather awkward thing to handle.

Here my cot was set up on one side, the boys sleeping on the other side.

This house was a fair representative of the average family house. The floor was of loose nipa planks, about 3 ft. from the ground, with a double set of large poles or joists, beneath the lower and larger resting on short posts set in the ground. The floor was about 10 by 16 ft.

The fire places were lower than the floor, being on planks laid on the lower set of joists. On this sand or earth was placed, on which the fire was built. This was confined to a sort of square hearth, between the upper joists and sticks at each end, so that the whole was somewhat lower than the floor above, which, of course, was cut away at this place.

The roof of the house was supported on 6 longer posts, passing through the floor, 2 in the center, and 2 on each side. The two center posts supported a ridge pole about 9 feet above the floor (g), and the side posts a plate (h), on which the rafters (f) rested, and extended over it about 3 ft. The plate rested not directly on the posts, but on a pole (d) extending across the house to the other side post, and about 4 ft. above the floor. This was lashed to the middle post (b), and about 3 feet above it another cross piece (e) was lashed, also supporting longitudinal pieces on which the rafters rested. The ends were not gable, but somewhat rounded, and sloped up to and under the top ridge.

The inside wall between the floor and the roof was about 2½ ft. high, of nipa leaf stem sheaths. This was about 1½ ft. outside the side posts (a & c). The pole (d) supported a platform of poles extending from it to the gable end, on which all sorts of utensils were placed.

This at the rear; in front the door was to one side of the center post, and the cross piece (d) was cut away on this side, giving more space to stand, the platform at this end extending only ½ across the house. The door was of the same material as the sides of the house, 4 (high) by 3 ft.—and hung by rattan loops from a pole running along the front of the house, so that it could be either pushed out and up or slid to one side on the pole.

Saturday, Nov. 13   It rained during the night and in the morning, and the boys with the canoe (for which I had bargained the night before), were a little late in coming, but finally came, with 2 *próa*s and 10 men, rather than the 4 men and 1 *proa* on which we had agreed, and for which I was to give 4 *bliong*s—one to each man.[30] After explaining that 4 men were sufficient and according to agreement, and that I would not pay over 4 *bliong*s, we finally got off about 10 A.M.

It proved to be a fine day, with sufficient cloud to temper the sun's rays. I insisted on stopping at the sunken village or island of old Warapu. The ground here is 2 to 5 feet below water, which comes up to the floor of most of the houses, but not to that of some of the men's houses and *tambaran* houses. These are still visited occasionally by the Warapu men, who now live on a river several miles away. I looked into one of the *tambaran* houses, and got a bark mask and club from it; also went into one of the men's houses,

---

30. A *bliong* is a kind of steel adze or carving tool, much prized by villagers in German times. The tools were often used as trade, and a few are still to be found around Aitape.

127

Fig. 2.55.   "Frame of small house,
Malol." A-31765 (72).

which was kept in good repair. Here I found nothing but an old shield and drum. Took a photo of this house [Fig. 2.56], also a more general view of several houses [Fig. 2.57].

From here we went on across the lagoon to the sunken forest, through which we passed slowly for nearly 2 hrs. before coming to the river leading to Sissano. This belt of dead forest is here 3–4 miles wide, and extends around a good part of the lagoon. It is quite a weird sight (see photo no. 136) to see these miles of dead trees, many more or less overgrown with epiphytes, but most only the bare trunks and branches.

In the earthquake of Nov. and Dec. of 1907, a large part of the country here sank several feet, submerging the island of Warapu and the belt of forest surrounding the lagoon. The strip of coast by Arop also sank, so that the land above high water was much lessened in extent, and as the numerous dead trees back of Arop show, there was considerable subsidence here. Many people in Warapu were killed, and the rest fled to the bush.

In Arop the people also fled to the hills (the earthquake shocks lasted for several weeks). The following winter (the Arop people had returned

Fig. 2.56. "House in Warapu," Sissano lagoon. A-31827 (134).

Fig. 2.57. "View of Warapu." A-31828 (135).

Fig. 2.58. "Sunken forest near Sissano." A-31829 (136).

in the spring, when the shocks ceased) nearly ⅔ of the narrow strip of land on which Arop stood was washed away by the waves, which during high tide broached over into the lagoon. The Arop people have built another village in the "bush," to which they have moved the most of their possessions, and where they expect to live during the winter. Herr Schulz

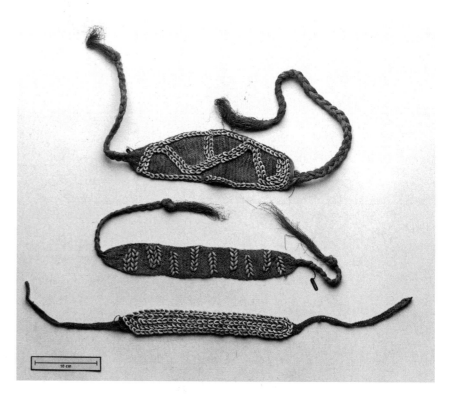

Fig. 2.59. Forehead bands made in Warapu, collected in Ali. Plaited fiber and nassa shells, 139861 (833); plaited fiber and coix seeds, 139864 (832); netted string and nassa, 139863 (826). A-112078.

Old Warapu and Sunken Forest

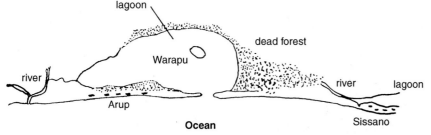

{Editor's note: The villages or hamlets of Sissano have grown considerably during the eighty years since ABL's visits to the lagoon. There were only four officially recognized villages in Sissano in 1990: Amsor, Mainar, Maindoin, and Nimas. Each of these was a hamlet in 1909 but consolidated with one of the other original hamlets. Although each now has well defined boundaries, these villages no longer have patches of bush between one another but blend seamlessly from one to the next. The shoreline on the ocean side has built out into the sea considerably since ABL's day.}

thinks that the sea will during the coming winter destroy what is left of Arop.[31]

The amount of sunken forest it is impossible to tell, but it extends nearly around the lagoon.

The contrast on entering the river leading to Sissano was striking. It was a quiet channel, 20–30 ft. wide, bordered with and overhung by cocoanuts and other trees, forming a beautiful scene, changing with every bend of the stream. Here we met 2 canoes full of cocoanuts going to Arop, as the Arop people come here to get their cocoanuts. In about 15 minutes we reached the first village of Sissano, where the shore was lined with *proa*s, the single dug-out canoe used here. Here the water also widened into a lagoon, and on each side were fish weirs and fish fences, enclosing small areas and inlets. We passed along the lagoon back of Sissano, as I wished to go to the house of the trader, Herr Schulz, who lived about a mile beyond Sissano, where he had his house, and owned a strip of coast 2,000 meters long. This was fairly well set with old cocoanut trees, but Schulz was clearing the ground, and planting all the unoccupied space with young trees.

The lagoon took us to about ¼ mile of his house, where was a little side ditch where we could go on shore, and whence a path led to Schulz's house. Here we arrived about 4, and I paid off the men with 4 *bliong*s, tho all 10 lined up and wanted something for coming along.

I agreed with Schulz to pay him 6 M. per day for myself and 3 boys. His house had two rooms, one the dining room, in which I set up my cot, and the other the bed room of Herr Schulz. The kitchen, as customary here, was a separate building.

Sunday, Nov. 14   In morning visited the village or villages of Sissano (called Eisamo by the Tumleo people) with Herr Schulz, who has lived here for about 2 yrs. and speaks the language.

We first walked along the broad sandy beach for about a mile, and then turned into a narrow path among the bushes and trees, which in a short time

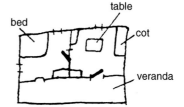

Herr Schulz's house

31. Schulz (ABL spelled his name Schultz) was mistaken. Over the past eighty years the sandy spit on which Arop sits has gradually built up from sediment moving along the shore. The mouth of the lagoon (called Otto) has gradually moved to the west, toward Sissano and the post–Second World War Warapu settlement. There is some reason to believe that the Aitape coastline generally is building out into the ocean (Terrell, personal communication 1993).

Fig. 2.60. "Men's house, Sissano." Note painted designs on walls. A-31835 (142) (cf. Neuhauss 1911, 231).

brought us to the first collection of huts, or village. Sissano has 8 "villages" with separate names: Maingdrūng, Pūrūlū, Maingār, Amsōr, Maingdrék, Raínshen, Nīmās, and Wākel.

Each village consists of a number of houses (perhaps 8 to 15—I did not count them) in an open cleared space, apparently without any special arrangement, and separated from the next village by a strip of bush. The strip of land here between the ocean and lagoon is from ⅛ to ¼ mile wide, and the villages are placed near, tho not quite on, the lagoon (with 2 exceptions) so that one cannot see them from the sea. Nearly all their boats (*proa*—a dugout) are also kept along the lagoon shore, along the shores and inlets of which the women go fishing nearly every day.

The houses in the villages are of three kinds (see photos):

(1) The men's house, usually square, with lower open and upper closed story. The lower is used during the day as a lounging and work place. These are from 12 to 18 feet square, the lower platform 3–4 ft. high, the upper 4–5 feet above this, and the room above 2–3 ft. in the eaves, and 5–7 ft. in the center. In this are kept the men's possessions, their bows and arrows, shields, bags with personal belongings, bundles with dance ornaments, etc. Here most of the men sleep.

(2) The women's or family house. This is rectangular, with one floor about 3–4 ft. high (see photos). Here the women and children stay; the girls till married, the boys till initiated as men. Usually the wives of brothers live together in the same house, so that the houses are usually occupied by several families. Only one man sleeps in the house at one time, the brothers taking turns in doing this, the others, of course, sleeping in the men's house.

Fig. 2.61. "Two types men's houses, round one (right) bush type, Sissano." A-31833 (140) (cf. Neuhauss 1911; 214–215).

Fig. 2.62. "*Tamburan* house, Sissano." A-31834 (141) (cf. Neuhauss 1911, 230).

It is not promiscuous, each man sleeping only with his own wife; but when for some reason, as frequently happens, a man cannot have intercourse with his wife, he will sleep in the men's house, and one of the other brothers in the family house. The size of the family from *one* wife is strictly limited to 5 children, tho children are never killed. One man, who had 5 girls, Schulz asked why he did not try again, and maybe it would be a boy, but the man would not.

It apparently is only a social custom, but the man would not break over it. Children were quite numerous in the village, however, and it seemed that most of the families came up to, or near, the limit.

(3) The *tamburan* house—these are somewhat varied in form. I did not see inside any, as the people would not allow it, and Schulz said that the 1 or 2 he had seen were practically empty. The women and children are not allowed to walk in front of these houses, and when they are near a path, there is a special path behind (or at a greater distance, if in front) which the women and children must use.

Monday, Nov. 15–Tuesday, Nov. 23   Visited the villages of Sissano daily, frequently twice daily, photographing and buying specimens. Through Herr Schulz I got as interpreter, a boy about 21 yrs. old from Purulu, who spoke Pigeon Eng. better than anyone else in Sissano. Very few of the Sissano had been in service, and not over 4 or 5 others spoke Pigeon Eng. at all, and then only a few words. With 2 others I was able to talk a little, but not much. I was forced to use them on two days when Mōti (my interpreter) went into the bush to make sago. I wished to see and photo the sago making, but it was some days before I succeeded. On Monday I only went to village and photographed in morning (in afternoon bought), and arranged that Tuesday morning I would come to the village and meet Móti there, and that he would take me to see the sago making in the bush. On Tuesday morning I found that he had himself gone to bush to make sago before I arrived (as it was over a mile to Schulz's house, I had not thought it necessary to have him come to the house, and then go back with me). So I could do but little, and went back to the house. In the afternoon I got from Schulz a boy from Dallmannhafen who could speak the language, so visited the village again and bought some things.

In the evening Schulz (who went to the village every evening to buy food—freshly cooked sago cakes, with greens or fish for his men) saw Moti, who said that he would go with me Wednesday morning. So Wednesday I went, and found him ready, and he with two other boys took me and one of my boys with camera in a dug-out canoe *(proa)* across the lagoon and up a small stream or narrow channel (it was tide water) for some distance into the swampy "bush." In places the water was almost too shallow to float the *proa*. Finally we stopped and took a muddy path through the bush and finally came to a single sago tree, partly worked, with contrivance for washing sago to one side. This I photoed, with boy washing. This hardly correct, as women always do the washing. I then found that this was the only place nearby where they were making sago, and that in addition nobody was working in the bush that day, so returned.

When got back to boat, photographed that with boy inside, and also a small *proa* near by. Photo looks down channel by which we came.

Both going and returning I heard a peculiar sound from a hill near the lagoon opposite the village. This, I was informed, was *tamburan*. The sound consisted of several notes, not unmusical, and the boy said these were made by pipes, blown by the men, who had a *tamburan* house on top of the hill. I tried

Fig. 2.63. Moti (ABL's interpreter) breaking out sago pith, Sissano. A-31861 (168).

to induce him to take me there, but he declared the water was then too low, and that the place could only be reached at high tide. I tried several times afterward to induce him and others to take me there, but never could succeed.

Schulz said he had never been there, but had seen the pipes (some used with water,[32] some not) but had been utterly unable to obtain a single one, tho he had offered high prices. The natives believe that if any woman, native or European sees the pipes, they (the natives) will die; so they will not sell them to Europeans, as they are sure these will let the women see them.

Prof. Neuhauss saw the pipes (I did not succeed, in the short time I was there, in seeing any), and said they were the same as those he had seen from the Kaiserin Augusta river.

The reason that the men were not in the bush making sago was that they were making *tamburan* for some special occasion.

I told Moti that I must see the people at work at the sago, and that he should take me into the bush again. He said he would the next day, but when I went next morning, he said the men were still making *tamburan,* and nobody would go to the bush that day. It appeared that a man had died the night before, and that till he was buried (which was to take place that afternoon or evening) no one dared to go into the bush. I could not find out exactly what their belief was, but they were apparently afraid of the *tam-*

---

32. These so-called water flutes are lengths of bamboo partly filled with water to control the pitch. They are still used in Warapu initiations.

buran, or evil spirit, which had caused the man's death. So I told Moti he must take me the next morning (the people seldom work in the bush much later than mid day), which he promised to do.

The next morning I found that they had made arrangements to show me the process of beating out the sago and washing it on the shore near the village, whither a section of sago-trunk some three feet long, had been brought. With this I was not entirely pleased, as it seemed not quite natural, and got up to satisfy the stranger, but Schulz said that they often brought the trunks to the village, as it saved the labor of going so far into the bush every day. So Moti broke open the trunk (photo) and pounded out the pith [Fig. 2.63], and 2 girls washed it (photos).

After this demonstration I still insisted on going to the bush, and finally Moti consented to take me. We went the same route as before, but a little further, and visited another place. The ground here was a little higher than where I had been before, and in some places there were taro patches; also some cocoanut trees. We still had to go some distance into the bush, to where a man and boy were working on a sago tree (photo); this time no one was washing, so could not photo that. On returning down the narrow channel, we found the women fishing near its mouth, and I secured 3 photos. They had built a fence, with traps (photo[33]) across the channel near the mouth, and were driving the fish down to the traps. We waited till they had finished the drive, and then they removed one of the traps, so that we could pass through. I then returned as quickly as I could to Schulz's, as it was already past noon. This boat trip was the most interesting experience that I had during my stay.

The remaining days were employed in studying the life of the people, photographing (as making pots, cooking, fire making, etc.) and getting specimens. These I packed up partly, in the few small boxes that I could get from Schulz, and left with him to send to Fr. Wh. hafen with the *Siar* next spring (May or June). I also left a list of other things that I had not gotten. For trade and board I paid him 80 M. and left with Steinmann in Eitape 2 doz. ¾ axes (value 60 M.) and 100 M. cash to pay for further specimens, and skulls, for which I agreed to give 1 M. each, as well as packing, etc. If possible, he was to get some skulls and specimens from the bush, and all the information he could.[34]

SISSANO HOUSEHOLD UTENSILS

The houses of Sissano have already been briefly described (see also photos). The household utensils are rather crude. There are large wooden bowls, for holding food, grinding paint, etc. Most are very crudely carved, but a few are better made, and ornamented (small ones in collection). These are mostly made in Sissano, and are elongated and pointed.

Many of the old sago paddles and taro mashers had carved handles. The woman's clubs were usually ornamented on side. Water was carried in buckets of Nipa leaf, similar to those in Ali, but cocoanuts were not used to hold water, tho with handle were used as dippers. There were shell and cocoanut-

---

33. See Lewis (1932a, plate XV; 1951; 66–67).

34. Schulz did in fact acquire at least 86 pieces for ABL, mostly from Arop, Warapu, and Sissano on the lagoon. These included a full-sized Sissano canoe, an Arop shield, three paddles and five wooden dishes from Warapu, a rattan cuirass from Angriffshafen, and a few smaller items. Schulz also sent ABL 68 human crania that he had purchased from villagers in Arop, Sissano, and Warapu (see Hambly 1940a). All of these collections, together with some of ABL's other specimens, were sent to Friedrich Wilhelmshafen before they were finally sent on to Chicago in 1911. ABL had asked Schulz to get information about the specimens he collected, but aside from provenience no documentation was provided.

Fig. 2.64. Carved taro mashers: stylized figure, Sissano, 139271 (1173); lizard, Sissano, 139274 (1149); male figure, Angel, 139971 (1058). A-112042.

shell spoons, but I did not see any ornamented, as in Ali. Of baskets saw fish baskets, and a sort of soft basket-bag carried by the men for their private possessions, lime, betel nut, etc. Netted bags, such as carried by the men in many other places, are very rare, and come from the interior (different places).

SISSANO POTTERY

Pots are used for cooking, boiling water, mixing sago, etc. All their best pots come from Tumleo, but they also get a crude pot or bowl from Rāmo, a village (Papuan) about 4 hrs. inland (see photo). These are crudely made, very poorly burnt, but with a crude ornament around the rim. In one village of Sissano (Maingdrúng), the women make a kind of small pot and shallow bowl.

The earth, a friable clay, is worked in water until plastic, and then rolled on a nibung platter by the hand into long rolls somewhat larger than a lead

Fig. 2.65. Detail, ends of carved wooden sago paddles, Sissano, 139282 (1159), 139281 (1168), 139284 (1170), 139285 (1163), 139292 (1160). A-112049.

pencil. These are then taken and coiled around, the pot being built up and pressed into shape with the fingers. No support, or stick for forming or beating is used (see photos [Fig. 2.66]).

These bowls are crude and not very large (6–12 in. in diameter, 3–6 in. deep). Those from the interior are larger. The people say that these are made in the same way—by coiling.

ōl (almost āl) = pot.

Fig. 2.66. "Making a pot by coiling, Sissano." A-31875 (182).

SISSANO FOOD—SAGO

The food of the people consists chiefly of sago; then fish, yams, taro, cocoanuts, greens of various kinds, and many other things. Sago remains the staple diet, however. As sago grows in swampy ground, the people must go some way into the bush to obtain it—often 2–4 hrs. journey. Each village of Sissano has, or owns, a certain region or area, whither the people go for their sago. The tree is cut down and the pith broken out by the men, and the starch washed out by the women. After the tree is cut down the outer woody shell is cut through some 3–5 ft. from the base, and then split off with a heavy wooden stick, sharpened at the end, so as to expose the pith on the top (photo made).

 to expose the pith

Nibung leaf platters are then spread along the side, to receive the pith, and the man or men, with the sago hammer *(sel),* begins mashing down the sago pith. When one section is worked out, another is begun (photo made).

The broken-down pith is then taken by the women and washed in a trough made of the stems of sago leaves, set inclined with the broad base about 4 ft. high (see photos). About $1\frac{1}{2}$ ft. from the upper end is fastened the strainer, made from the fibrous sheath of the young cocoanut leaf. Lower down is cut a hole, the channel below this being stopped by a banana leaf, or some similar material. The mashed sago pith is carried on the nibung leaf, or sago leaf stem, to the washing trough, and dumped in above the strainer, water poured in, and worked with the hands, so that the water washes out the starch, carrying it through the strainer, which holds back the fibre. The starchy water runs through the hole below into a sort of basin made of nibung leaf base. Here the sago settles to the bottom, and the water runs off over the edge. When nearly full it is allowed to settle, and the water poured off. This leaf basin may be folded up into a sort of bucket, and the sago carried to the village and kept in this; or it may be allowed to dry somewhat, and made into packets with leaves and bush rope, and so brought to the village. (Got photo of one, from which the sago is partly removed. This was so large that it was carried on a pole by two men.) In this form it is also sold, as to Ali, Tumleo, etc. [see Fig. 2.20].

In Sissano the people make the sago as needed, so have not the large casks that one finds in Tumleo and the other islands.

In the village it is kept in these packets till used, when it is either baked in thin cakes, the usual way, or made into a thick porridge. In making porridge the sago meal is mixed with a little water in a pot, and hot water added till it "jellies," which takes place in 3–5 minutes (for detailed description of process as seen in Malol see [below]). No strainers are used. This did not seem necessary, as the sago which I examined seemed perfectly clean. After it jellies it is gently worked for 2–3 minutes, and then distributed in leaves, and rolled up till used.

In the more common method of cooking the moist sago powder, as it comes from the packet, is placed in a layer $\frac{1}{4}$ to $\frac{1}{8}$ in. thick in an earthen bowl or portion of pot, placed over the fire. Another similar bowl, first heated in the fire, is placed on top, so that the layer of sago is cooked from above as well as below. While this is cooking, sago is placed in the bowl above, and when done (2–3 min.), the under bowl is removed and placed on top. The cooked sago cake, in shape like a bowl, is then removed and placed on a platter of nibung, more sago meal added, and the process repeated, and so on till a sufficient number are cooked. These cakes are usually eaten with fish or shrimp (esp. in the morning), or with a combination made of edible leaves (many different kinds used) and shredded cocoanut, boiled together.

Fig. 2.67. "Putting in hot water, Sissano." A-31837 (144).

A portion of this is placed in the cake, which is then folded over and eaten like a sandwich. This is the chief article of food in Sissano, and between 5 and 6 P.M. the women can be seen all through the village cooking these cakes and placing them on the nibung platter. A pot of cooked "greens," or the prepared shrimp, stands near, and the men come and make and eat their sandwiches, or the women may prepare them after cooking.

The principal meal is in the evening, but they also eat in the morning before going to work (6–7:30 A.M.). This is the same as their evening meal,

Fig. 2.68. "Woman with child cooking, Sissano." In 1990 villagers identified the leaves in her pot as *balbal* leaves (*Erythrina indica*) from the twigs in the foreground. A-31845 (152).

140

only more frequently they have fish with the sago cakes. The fish, small to medium size, are simply smoked over a fire in the houses, in a sort of box.

Sago is also at times cooked in a somewhat different way. Shredded cocoanut is mixed with the sago flour, this made into a thin (½ in.) cake some 6 by 10 inches, wrapped in banana leaves, and baked in the fire. This called *pīap*.

sago cakes folded like a sandwich

> *yes* = the boiled sago
> *lepī* = the sago tree, sago meal, & also sago cake's customary form

SISSANO FISHING

Fish, the article of food next in importance, are caught chiefly in hand nets and fish-traps, by the women; or speared or shot with arrow by the men (not very common). The fish traps vary from 1 to 5 or 6 ft. long, and are from 2 to 3 times as long as thick. They have an opening at the small end, stopped by a bunch of grass. They are set in the opening of enclosures, of which there are many on both sides of the lagoon. These are made of sticks, and the bottom made tight with leaves, so that at high water the fish can enter most anywhere, but toward low water can get out only at the gateway, in which the trap is set. At low water the women also go into the enclosure and drive the fish toward the trap. The women take out the traps and set them as the tide is running out. They also make temporary fences enclosing channels, with numerous traps, and drive the fish into them (as seen on trip to see sago making in bush, and photoed). The number of women (and children) employed in these drives depends on the width of the channel. On special occasions a fence may be made entirely across the lagoon where it is not too wide (in most places it is not over 3–4 ft. deep) and 200–300 women and children unite in the drive. The permanent enclosures are found on both sides, all along the lagoon. While driving, the women carry hand nets, and catch many fish as they go along.

Occasionally, in shallow water, a sort of enclosure is thrown up of mud, a trap set at the outer angle, and the fish driven into it that may happen to be caught in the enclosure. See photo.

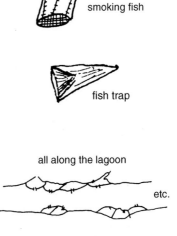

"box" for smoking fish

fish trap

all along the lagoon

etc.

> *wū* = fish trap
> *tīp* = fish net

The women also catch fish in the mud along the bottom of the shallow lagoon in their hands. Many edible snails are found there. Shrimp are caught in their nets, etc.

The men, in addition to shooting fish, occasionally get a cuscus, or a wild pig. (During my first visit to Malol, the *tultul* was suffering from severe wounds caused by a wild boar.)

Taro and yams are planted by the men, but not to any great extent.

Cocoanut trees are quite common near Sissano, but the natives seem to take very little care of them, and formerly cut down great numbers on the death of a relative or important person.

The Arop people come here quite frequently and take back boat-loads to Arop.

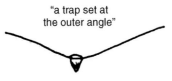

"a trap set at the outer angle"

SISSANO BOWS AND ARROWS

Bows and arrows are made in Sissano (also Arop and Malol) and are often sold to other places. The fish arrows have several points, or a single barbed point of wood.

141

The pig arrows have usually bamboo points, occasionally plain wood. Only plain unbarbed bamboo points are made in Sissano, the barbed and decorated points coming from the bush.

The shaft of the arrow is usually decorated with lines, each man (in Sissano—other places ?) having his own mark, so that, if made in Sissano, the people can tell by whom made. If from the interior, they can usually tell from which village. All the highly decorated and ornamented arrows are from the interior, just as in Ali.

The bows are frequently decorated with incised designs, woven bands, plain or colored fibre, and occasionally feathers, but these seen only on festal occasions, and I did not succeed in getting one. The nicest bows I got were said to come from Warapu, and I did not succeed in finding anything characteristic of Sissano bows. Spears seemed to be entirely lacking.

SISSANO SHIELDS

Large, finely decorated wood shields were common in the old times. There seemed to be some meaning to the decoration, but was unable to find what it was, except that some of the more realistic designs represented men or animals.

The men frequently made small shields for the small boys.

Got over a dozen shields, some showing the points of numerous arrows that had been shot into them and broken off. Shields are no longer made.

SISSANO CANOES

Many canoes (dug outs) are made in Sissano (also in Malol and Arop). These vary in size from small ones capable of carrying only a boy, to large ones capable of carrying 40–50 men. I measured one 60 ft. long in Malol, but did not see any quite so large in Sissano, tho Schulz said they had had one shortly before that was larger, so that one time he took all his things to Arop in it, and could put in his table, and sit at it and write while on the way. I returned with all my luggage, and six men, to Arop in one, and I saw several larger. These large ones are quite steady, but the small ones very liable to capsize, tho the natives show great dexterity in handling them. The large one Schulz spoke of was broken in the surf, as it was so heavy the men could not handle it quickly.

The ends of these canoes, esp. the larger, are decorated with carvings, usually a rather intricate design extending a short distance along the sides. At times these are somewhat realistic, and may represent fish, or some animal. It seemed that each man made a certain design (animal), but why, or what it meant, could not discover.

Stone hatchets and adzes are still found among the people, but no longer used.

[SISSANO BAGS]

The men carry their small personal possessions in a bag woven of cocoanut leaves, made in Sissano, or occasionally in a netted bag, bought from the interior. The women keep their small possessions in a nibung basket like the water bucket.

One is liable to find all sorts of small objects in these bags. I first saw the fire making rattan in a bush-man's bag. Now one finds iron objects, beads, matches, etc., mixed in with native things, such as bone needles, cocoanut opener and scraper, paint tubes, tobacco pouch, etc. and of course, betel nut,

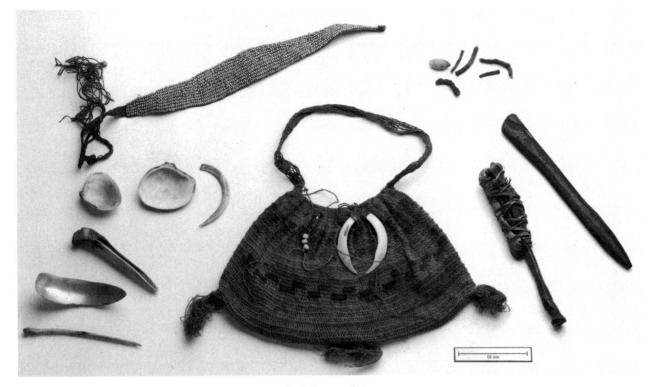

Fig. 2.69. Man's string bag and contents, Sissano. Bone awl, shell spoon, bone scraper, two shell scrapers, tusk awl or ornament, coix seed headband, areca nut and pieces of betel pepper, wood coconut-husking stick, magic bundle (similar to those in Ali). Bag old and worn, ornamented with boar's tusks and European trade beads, 139328 (3826). A-112050.

Fig. 2.70. Woman's bark container and contents, Sissano, 139334 (3827). Contents include arm bands, lime gourd and stick, areca nut and betel pepper, shell scrapers and cutting tools, comb, hairpins, bone awls, bone needles, bone scrapers and tools, human mandible, steel knife, shell ring. A-112081.

pepper, and lime gourd. The lime gourds are seldom decorated, and then but crudely. Spatulas also very crude. No decoration on bone daggers or bone cocoanut-scrapers.

As in other places in this region, they had their own tobacco, and did not care for that of the white man.

SISSANO—CLOTHING

Clothing was very simple, and quite similar to that in Ali. The men wore a loin cloth *(mal)* of bark-cloth, about 6 inches wide and 6 ft. long. This was passed between the legs, and then wrapped around the waist from behind, so that the broader end was caught in front, and hung down over the part wrapped around the body, which encircled the waist twice, and was then caught around the part coming up, between the legs behind. In addition to this, a leaf or bark girdle was usually worn. This was sometimes quite wide (foot or more), and the girdles used on festal occasions nicely decorated with incised designs.

SISSANO—ORNAMENTS

Armrings, necklaces, breast-bands, and leg bands were not so common as in Ali, and came largely from Warapu or the interior. Necklaces of black-seeds were esp. highly valued, and they refused to sell them, as they were bought from the interior at a high price. (I got one of this sort in Ali, rather cheaply.)

Narrow earrings of tortoise-shell, with pig-tail attached, were rather common, but highly valued. All the tortoise-shell rings seen were rather small and narrow. The natives said they got them from the east.

Nose ornaments of shell and bamboo (did not see any decorated, as in Ali) were common. (Shell nose sticks probably from Ali ?)

Combs rather crude, of a small number of sticks fastened together.

Feathers were frequently worn in the hair, usually single, and commonly pigeon feathers, of bluish tint. Only saw one Bird of Paradise ornament, and man said that from Ali. (Schulz said these not common, and when worn, were only for visiting or similar occasion, and not for sing-sing, as they had no complex dances, and did not dress up for the sing-sings that they had which consisted chiefly of singing, seated inside a house.) Red and green leaves and also flowers, were often worn in hair, around neck, under arm-bands, etc. See photos.

The boar's tusk breast ornament is still made, but they refuse to sell them. Saw only one, that imperfect.

The hair is cut at intervals, and one could see all stages from very short to a broad mat hanging half way down the back. When these are cut off the men are willing to sell them, but they would not cut off any for me when there, as they said they wanted them for the special "festal occasions" shortly to come. The hair when cut is rolled up and kept, in many cases at least, as I saw several, and Prof. Neuhauss bought a number.

In general they were unwilling to let another have any hair, for fear of (magic) injury to themselves, but these old heads of hair they seemed perfectly willing to sell. WHY?

The women wear a short apron of bark-cloth (also called *mal*) hung over a bark girdle. One end of this is tucked between the legs and projects behind.

Ear rings and nose rings of tortoise shell are common. (See photo.)

Children wear nothing, the same as in Malol.

No games were observed, but the boys have small bows with grass

Fig. 2.71. "Man with nose shell, Sissano." A-31874 (181).

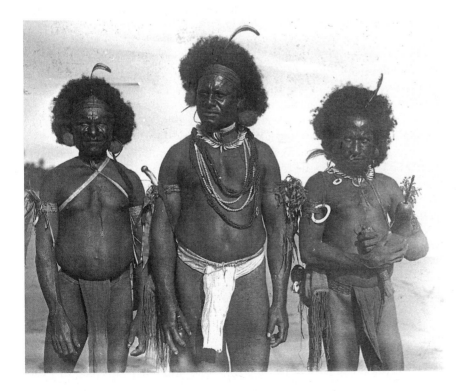

Fig. 2.72. "Three men of Sissano. Two of these were my carriers. The larger tried to kill Schulz about two years before." A-31882 (189).

arrows, and larger ones with wooden sticks for arrows, the same as in Ali. They also have a surf board, not flat, as in Ali, but cut out like one end of a canoe.

SISSANO—BURIAL (AFTER SCHULZ)

The dead are buried under the house, being first wrapped in cocoanut leaves, then in nibung, and tied with bush rope. For 1½ to 2 days before burial they are placed in a nearly upright position in the house, supported by the house ladder (or similar object). Here the people come to look and mourn (howl). The body is fitted out in best cloths and ornaments.

After a certain time, in connection with a sing-sing, the skull and radii are exhumed. The skull is (was) placed in the men's house. The radii are taken by the 2 nearest relatives (these are definitely determined for all cases) and kept as magical protectors or charms; worn on the breast shield in battle, carried on the canoes to produce wind, etc.

In Arop the dead are not buried, but wrapped up and placed over a small fire in the house. The nibung leaf wrapping is so arranged that the fluid from the body is caught in a vessel, and mixed with sago, is eaten by the nearest relatives. They remain there (with the family all around), for at least a year, till completely decayed, when the skeleton is buried, but skull and radii kept out. Very thin, old men are buried. The radii are used as charms, as in Sissano. A somewhat similar custom, according to Rodatz per Schulz, exists in Huon Gulf. (Almost 3 yrs. ago the people were made to bury many bodies, so that now the people will not let a white man see them.)

In Warapu the body is placed in a small house, perhaps 3 by 6 ft., and 2–3 ft. high, on high posts. This is outside the village.

The Walman people bury.

Between Stephansort and the Ramu river the bush people place the dead in a small house outside the village, but in a sitting posture.

Wednesday, Nov. 24   The night before Schulz made arrangements with 3 men of Nímas to take me to Malol, and to each of these I gave a "tomahawk."

In the morning they came down to the house, which we left at 7:30. At 8:25 left Nimas in *proa;* at 8:37 arrive at lagoon; at 9:20 leave dead timber; at 10:30 arrive opposite first houses of Arop, at 12 leave river, and at 3 arrive in Malol. This trip took more time than was necessary, as the canoe followed the lagoon back of Arop to the end, and then entered a small narrow stream flowing from the river into the lagoon (it was low tide), by which we reached the river, tho in places the men had to get out and pull the boat. In the river, shortly before reaching the forks, we found a timber jam, which it took some time to get through. On reaching Malol found that P. Kirschbaum with Bro. Ferdinand had just arrived with a horse from Santa Anna. Stopped with them over night.

Thursday, Nov. 25   Spent the day in Malol, bought a few things, and read Graebner [1909] on "Bogenkultur von Südsee." Saw cooking of sago.

COOKING SAGO IN MALOL

Here usually cook with hot water in pot. This is filled about ¼ full with sago meal. Then boiling water is poured in till ½ full, and stirred with stick till thoroughly mixed. Then skimmed with sago strainer, which was dipped in so that it went to bottom, but the fluid was not poured through it. In this

Fig. 2.73. Sago hammer used to break open the bark, Sissano (but stone from Dallmannhafen). From Schulz, 139392 (3823); sago pounder, used to chop out pith, Sissano, 139385 (1262). A-112070.

condition it was a rather thin, milky fluid. After about 3 min. (stirred most of time) more hot water was added, till pot nearly full, and in about 1 min. more (no stirring) it "jellied" into a thick, sticky mass, which was stirred a little more, and then with 2 small sticks a small clump was worked out and placed on leaves. This was done in 6 minutes from the time the first hot water was added.

Friday, Nov. 26 Left about 10 for Eitape, with 2 men and 2 boys as carriers. P. Kirschbaum had spoken the night before with 3 men, who promised to go with me as carriers, but they did not come in the morning, and we

Fig. 2.74. Shell adze made in Sissano. Handle and fastenings new but in old style, made of a cone shell, 139456 (1096). Gift of Pater Kirschbaum. A-112074.

147

Fig. 2.75. Pots collected around Eitape: Tumleo pot collected at Angel, 137897 (696); incised pots made in the mountains back of Yakamul: collected in Yakamul, 137954 (2984); made in Waoul (three days inland from Yakamul), collected in Angel, 137904 (697); collected in Yakamul, 137959 (2989). A-112098.

found that they had gone into bush to make sago. He finally succeeded in getting some (2) others, and 2 boys. The mission had shortly before taken away 30 young men as laborers, and as one man said, "Missionary he catch him all boy finish." Arrived in Eitape about 3 P.M., took ½ hr. to go over mountain.

Saturday, Nov. 27–Sunday, Nov. 28　Developed plates (5 doz.).

Monday, Nov. 29–Wednesday, Dec. 1　Packed up my stuff and got ready to go away by steamer *Manila* which arrived Wednesday evening.

On Saturday had sent 3 Yakamul men to Yakamul to get some pots, which I promised to pay for if they would bring them to Eitape. On Thursday morning they arrived, after my things were packed, but I got out some things, and bought some others, so paid them all off. Got 11 pots, which I had to leave with the company, the Malay storekeeper promising to look after them, and send them, with my other things, to Fr. Wh. Hafen by the *Siar*. I also left 11 packets in sacking "on top," which were to be taken down and kept by Herr Raettig[35] till spring, and sent to Fr. Wh. Hafen. He was also to crate and ship the 2 drums, box the canoe model from Ali, buy 2 nets (Seleo) and canoe (Ali) and send same to Fr. Wh. Hafen.

Thursday, Dec. 2　Was up at dawn and packed my things in a great hurry so that they could be taken down to the beach, where they stayed till 10 o'clock, when the first batch went aboard. *Manila* left about 3 P.M. Dr. Schlaginhaufen left at the same time, having finished his work in the colony, and returning by way of Herbertshöhe only to settle accounts.

Friday, Dec. 3　Spent most of the day in Potsdam-hafen. Went on shore in the morning, and looked around, but did not buy anything, as few things of interest to be seen. The houses are long, and the roof is much longer than the enclosed room beneath, the floor of which is some 4 ft. from the ground.

---

35. ABL spelled his name Rettige.

Fig. 2.76. Bark-cloth mask on a rattan frame with human hair and fringe of palm leaf, French Islands (Pitu), 137780 (_____). Red, black, and white pigments. A-112117.

This leaves a covered area before and behind, in which a platform is often built, lower than the floor. On one of these I saw the sleeping bag used in the K. A. river. The people absolutely refused to sell it. It was like a mat, checker weave, of stripes about $\frac{1}{4}$ in. wide. It was about 8 ft. long, and perhaps 3 ft. in diameter. The people said they had to pay a high price for it.

Also saw a number of pots of different shape from any seen before, pointed below with rather long, but broad necks. The missionary said they came from a place further down the coast toward Fr. Wh. Hafen.

The women wore 2 grass skirts, one before and one behind, so narrow that they did not quite meet on the sides.

Saturday, Dec. 4   Spent most of the day in Fr. Wh. Hafen, where we arrived about sunrise. Left 25 boxes of specimens here with Mr. Heine to be crated and shipped (when I sent directions) to Chicago. (Should address Die Agentur der N.G. Co.) Also he promised that the *Siar* would bring my stuff from Eitape and Sissano.

In Potsdam hafen I met a Mr. William Gramms, a planter (station Awar), who offered to take me around in his cutter along the coast west of Potsdam hafen, and as far as Dallmannhafen visiting the lagoons, inlets, etc. He said a great part of this region was untouched by the collectors. He said I should bring 6 good men along, trade, etc., and write to him when I arrived at Potsdam hafen.

Sunday, Dec. 5   Steamed all day and in evening arrived at Peterhafen, French Islands.

Monday, Dec. 6   Spent day in Peter Hafen till 3 P.M. In forenoon went in boat with 3 others to village near the station, and then walked ($\frac{3}{4}$ hr.) to another village. For about $\frac{1}{2}$ the way the path led through a large plantation of bananas and young rubber trees. All these islands belong to N.G. Co. Got a few things at the native village, as mask, float for net, basket, child's arm-rings of tortoise shell, and 2 sets pan pipes, also small basket carried by the men for small valuables.

The houses are small, low, mats for sides, ground for floor, a small covered space in front. Sometimes the floor of room is raised 3 ft. above ground. The men go absolutely naked.

Tuesday, Dec. 7   Arrived at Herbertshöhe about 10 A.M. and here went on shore, as wished to find out what the possibilities were for another trip. From Forsayth learned that the recruiting schooner *Irene* would go around New Britain about the middle of January. Heard of a gov. expedition by the *Langeoog* around New Britain and got permission to go with it to Forsayth's station on Cape Mercus, _____, and there remain till the *Irene* came, in which I could return to Herbertshöhe.

Wednesday, Dec. 8–Saturday, Dec. 11   Spent these days getting my things together, buying what I needed, writing notes, etc. The *Roland* brought my luggage from Simpsonhafen Wednesday, but one bag, with tins, small sack rice, ironing iron, 5 rucksacs, and few other things did not come, and I was unable to trace it. The men in Simpsonhafen said it went on board, that they remembered seeing it, and Forsayth's men, who unloaded said they did not find it.

Sunday, Dec. 12—   (continued in next book)

|||||||||||||||||||||||||||||||||||||||||||||||||||||||||||||||||||||||||||||||||||||||||||||||||||

New Britain and the Huon Gulf

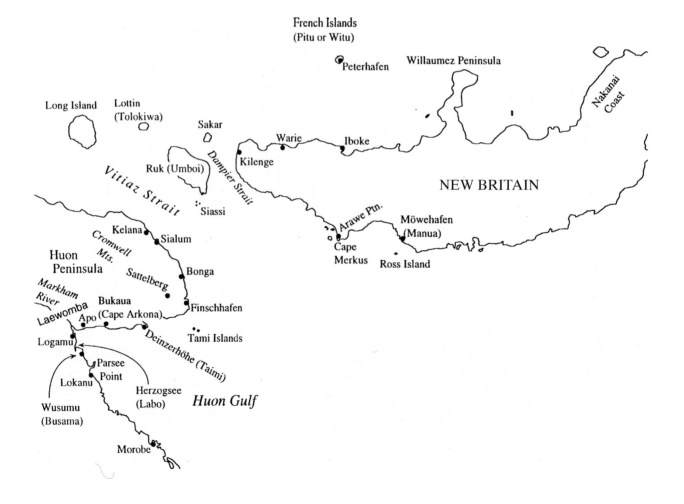

French Islands
(Pitu or Witu)

Peterhafen   Willaumez Peninsula

Nakanai Coast

Long Island   Lottin
(Tolokiwa)

Sakar

Warie   Iboke

Ruk (Umboi)

Kilenge

Vitiaz Strait

Dampier Strait

Siassi

NEW BRITAIN

Kelana   Sialum

Cromwell Mts.

Arawe Ptn.

Möwehafen
(Manua)

Huon
Peninsula

Sattelberg

Bonga

Cape
Merkus   Ross Island

Markham River

Bukaua
(Cape Arkona)

Finschhafen

Laewomba   Apo

Logamu

Deinzerhöhe (Taimi)

Tami Islands

Parsee
Point

Lokanu

Herzogsee
(Labo)

Huon Gulf

Wusumu
(Busama)

Morobe

Book 3

West New Britain and the Huon Gulf

||||||||||||||||||||||||||||||||||||||||||||||||||||||||||||||||||||||||||||||||||||||||||||||||||||||||||||||||||||||||||||||||||||||||

12 December 1909–5 April 1710

ABL left Eitape because the rainy season had begun in much of Kaiser Wilhelmsland (the New Guinea mainland) and there was little that could be done there until April because movement from one village to another would be severely curtailed by bad weather. But he did not stay put. No sooner had he arrived in Herbertshöhe than he began preparations for a new excursion, this time to the west end of New Britain.

When ABL disembarked from the *Manila,* he learned from Governor Hahl that a government expedition would soon depart on a tour of inspection around New Britain. The governor suggested that ABL accompany the official expedition as far as Arawe, Forsayth's station at Cape Merkus. There he could visit villages up and down the coast around Cape Merkus for a month and then come back to Herbertshöhe on one of Forsayth's schooners. After another excursion or two, perhaps to New Ireland or the Gazelle Peninsula, ABL could return to Kaiser Wilhelmsland for the dry season.

For its tour of inspection around New Britain, the colonial government had chartered one of Nord-Deutscher Lloyd's smaller steamers, the *Langeoog.* The expedition was headed by Dr. Arthur Osswald, who had recently arrived in the colony. Osswald was second in command in German New Guinea and was scheduled to fill in as acting governor a few months later when Hahl and his family went home on home leave. As a newcomer, Osswald had seen little of the colony, and the governor thought it best for him to get a feel for New Britain's breadth and diversity. Accompanying him was Dr. Klug, *kiap* and sometime magistrate, stationed at Herbertshöhe.

The expedition was scheduled to leave Herbertshöhe five days after ABL's arrival. After nearly four months in Kaiser Wilhelmsland, there was much for ABL to do before setting off again. He had to purchase fresh supplies and trade goods. He had to pack up and store his specimens and negatives. And there were the usual social calls to important residents of Herbertshöhe. So ABL spent the next few days feverishly arranging his affairs and preparing for a new field setting.

When ABL embarked on the *Langeoog,* he returned for a time to a world dominated by German administrators after having spent more than two months living more or less directly in native villages. Since accompanying Governor Hahl's expedition in August, ABL had become proficient in Pidgin. He now had a solid grasp of the New Guinea environment and geography and its colonial administration. He had also spent enough time with Catholic missionaries to have some feel for the pace of life around SVD mission stations. New Guinea was no longer the mystery it once had been; he had learned a great deal about material culture and social patterns in New Guinea.

After his sojourn in Sissano, ABL had become an anthropologist with some real field experience. He had already started documenting the complex pattern of variation in material culture along the Eitape coast. Soon he would recognize the extraordinary importance of trade in the local economy on both sides of the Vitiaz Strait and would begin documenting the complexity of this new economic network around Cape Merkus. ABL's awareness of the importance of trade was probably first suggested by the SVD fathers at Tumleo—if not by Paters Kirschbaum and Lohmiller then from reading Pater Erdweg's (1902) ethnography of Tumleo. But once it became clear that north coast communities were anything but isolated from their neighbors, ABL began collecting the detailed data necessary to piece together the diverse elements of this complicated economic system. Such insights would stay with him for the rest of the expedition and would motivate similar kinds of data collection on both sides of the Vitiaz Strait, which linked the west end of New Britain with the Huon Peninsula on the New Guinea mainland through an intensive trade network.

The West End of New Britain

During the cruise of the *Langeoog* ABL once again had only limited encounters with villagers. He could visit villages for a few hours at a time, but only at the places the German officers chose to visit. Despite some illness ABL seems to have enjoyed the cruise as an interesting change of pace. He was particularly pleased to call in at Lottin (Tolokiwa) Island, which, as far as was known, had been visited by only one previous expedition, the well-equipped *Peiho* Expedition led by Professor Fülleborn for the Hamburg Scientific Foundation a year earlier (Sack and Clark 1979, 294–295).

At Forsayth's station at Cape Merkus, ABL left behind the realm of colonial administrators and entered the world of the trader and plantation manager. Situated at one of the most isolated European settlements in the colony, Forsayth's manager was the only European living along the entire south coast of New Britain. Arawe was run by a Scotsman named McNicol (or possibly McNicols), who had worked for E. E. Forsayth & Co. on the Gazelle Peninsula for several years. Earlier in 1909 he had been transferred to Arawe to replace Forsayth's previous manager, a Spaniard named Roca, who had suddenly died in December 1908 (Reche 1954, 50, 57).

Despite Arawe's apparent isolation from the rest of the world, it proved a busy place to spend the holidays. As at most plantations around the colony, McNicol hosted a party for his plantation laborers and for neighboring villagers to celebrate Christmas at the station. Food and presents were provided for everyone, and traditional dances were performed by delegations from different villages. A week later McNicol hosted yet another series of dances to mark the new year. Again groups from various villages arrived to perform their dances and enjoy the feast. This repetition of dances was a fortuitous circumstance for ABL, for nearly every one of his photographic negatives of the Christmas dances had been ruined because the water for developing was too warm and so the emulsion cracked. This repeat performance gave ABL a second chance to make a visual record of the dances and costumes.

Three days before Christmas 1909, Arawe was visited by another set of guests for the holiday, Herr Schoede and his crew aboard the *Harriet and Alice,* owned by Captain Carlson and

154

Example of glass plate negative with cracked emulsion. Dance, Christmas Day, 1909, Cape Merkus. A-32085 (_____).

his partner, J. M. Rondahl. Schoede was a wealthy curio collector who had leased the schooner for more than six months. He was leisurely traveling along the coast of New Britain collecting curios, with an enormous supply of "trade" on board. The schooner solved all problems of transportation and was comfortably outfitted. Schoede even had a few luxuries, such as an expensive nickel dinner service which was carried up to McNicol's house for dinner on Christmas Eve. In the difficult months ahead, ABL would often dream of having such a set-up for himself.

Soon after New Year's, ABL borrowed McNicol's boat and set off with his two assistants and a native crew to visit the villages along the rocky coast east of Cape Merkus: Solong, Ruoto, Amklok, Manua (Moewehafen), and Ross Island. (Manua seems to have gotten its name from the local rendering of "man-of-war," the Pidgin name given to the imperial navy's warship *Möwe,* which surveyed this coast in 1894. This early warship should not be confused with Rudolf Wahlen's much smaller schooner bearing the same name.)

Once again ABL was back in the villages, sleeping in village houses and largely eating village food supplemented by a few tinned meats. At Manua he visited some hamlets a short distance in the interior. Although traders, recruiters, government officers, scientists, and curio collectors had frequently called in at virtually all the coastal villages. ABL was probably the first European to visit these inland settlements. In these bush villages ABL found the men using a long blowgun with feathered darts for hunting. He was probably the first to note the blowgun in this part of Melanesia (cf. Chinnery 1927; see also Goodale 1966), a discovery of which he was quite proud.

This discovery played a prominent role in his letters home, including a rather informal report to Field Museum director Skiff describing this journey along the coast east of Cape

155

Merkus. This report, which I edited and published with a number of photographs not reproduced here (Lewis 1988; Welsch 1988), describes this trip in somewhat more personal terms, though the details are nearly the same.

One of ABL's most important observations was the early evidence he provides for the prominent role the Siassi Islanders played in trade between the Huon Peninsula and Cape Merkus. He notes, for example, that six Siassi canoes were sold to villagers around Cape Merkus for three or four pigs each. In addition, he describes both generally and with his collection the same range of objects that Harding (1967) would later suggest as central to this regional economy. ABL's documentation of this trade, at least around Cape Merkus, appears to be the most detailed data available from before the First World War.

During this month's sojourn in New Britain, ABL collected almost six hundred objects and took 104 photographs (of which 93 survive). Photography was still new to him, and spoiled negatives were a constant frustration. ABL wrote one letter to Field Museum photographer Charles Carpenter (reproduced here). This letter details some of ABL's concerns about his photographic work as well as his frustration over having so little experience with a camera. Unfortunately, Carpenter's answer to ABL's letter has not survived, but it would seem that he was able to offer a few helpful suggestions because the photographs ABL took later are much better than the early ones. Overall, the high quality of his photographs is remarkable, given the circumstances under which they were made.

{Editor's note: Only part of one letter describing ABL's travels to Cape Merkus and the Huon Gulf survives. It continues from that portion reproduced at the beginning of book 2.}

Friedrich Wilhelms Hafen
May 1, 1910

Dear Dr. Dorsey:

. . .

On Dec. 2 I left Eitape for Herbertshöhe, expecting to go from there to Huon Gulf, as the winter was the dry season there, and it did not seem worth while to stay on the north coast during the rainy season. In Herbertshöhe I learned that a government expedition was soon to start in the <u>Langeoog</u> to go around New Britain, and I got permission to go with them to Cape Merkus on the south shore, where I could stop with the one white man on the whole south coast of N. B., and some 1½ months later be taken away by a recruiting schooner of Forsayth. The Governor said it was a good region to visit, and I decided to stop there. On the way we visited a number of places on the north coast, and also on the island of Lottin, west of N. B., only once before visited by white men (the <u>Peiho!</u>). We went to one village, however, where they had not been and I succeeded in getting some interesting things. The culture is much the same as west N. B., and this seems to be also true of the other islands, as we also stopped at Ruk [also written Rook or Umboi Island].

We were eight days to Cape Merkus (station called Arawe). From here I made boat trips along the coast for 40–50 miles, stopping at the native villages, sleeping in the native houses, etc. I also made two short trips into the interior, visiting two villages of the "bush" people never before visited by the white man. Here I found the blow pipe in use. It was of bamboo, thin and light. The length was about 15 feet, and it was formed of 5 or 6 pieces joined together. The arrows were about 2 ½ ft. long, with feathers around the base. So far as I know, the blow-gun has never before been reported east of the Indian Archipelago.

The schooner came about the middle of February, and as she was going across to Finsch Hafen, I decided to go with her, so hurriedly packed up my stuff, and went aboard, leaving my collection to be taken to Simpson Hafen by the schooner on its return. From Finsch Hafen I went by native canoe to the head of the gulf, visiting Labo in the Hertzogsee, and going south as far as Laukanu, beyond Parsi Point. This (Laukanu) is the pot making center for the whole region. In spite of the fact that the place is fairly well cleaned out (Capt. Voogdt and the missionaries together), I got some 400 specimens, many of which I had never seen or heard of before. One night I slept in the house from which Capt. Voogdt had taken the ornamented side boards—the ones we have, I think. I also visited Sattelberg (3,000 ft. high) and the natives in the vicinity (Papuans, called Kai).

In April the Manila made one of its visits to Finsch Hafen (comes only once in a month) and I came on it to Fr. Wh. Hafen, where I have been ever since, packing and shipping my specimens. . . .

Very sincerely,
A. B. Lewis

Fr. Wh. Hafen
April 19, 1910

My dear Carpenter:

I am sending my negatives back to the Museum to be "worked up." I know they are not very good; they are the best I could do, however. I hope you will get out of them all you can, as I could not duplicate most of them. The water here is so warm that I have found it extremely hard to develop and wash. Many have been spoilt by too warm water, and I often had to wait for days till we had a night cool enough; of course daytime is out of the question. Then I am traveling around so much that it is difficult to find an opportunity to develop, and water is often scarce. Most appear to be underexposed, but I hope to better my exposures in time. Often it was necessary to be as quick as possible, and I was tempted to make it too quick. The fog, I think, is due partly to age of plates, and partly to too long a time after putting in camera to development. Perhaps you can remove some of it.

Please do the best you can with the negatives, and do not destroy any. Many poor ones show things of importance. I shall also be very glad if you will write me your opinion of how I might improve them. I hope to have some new plates before long, but it is hard to get anything here.

The positives I have purchased, and I wish you would make negatives and prints for them. The prints I send please keep, but do not Paste in a book.

I should be much obliged if you could send me a <u>numbered</u> set of prints from my negatives, after you have improved them as far as possible. I wish to see how they look, and also have them for study, comparison and notes.

I enclose a list of all my negatives, also of those I purchased (these are lettered). In giving the negatives museum numbers, please <u>number</u> <u>them</u> <u>consecutively</u> <u>in</u> <u>the</u> <u>order</u> <u>of</u> <u>my</u> <u>numbers</u>. This can be easily done, and will save much useless labor later, if they are numbered in any other order. Every slide is numbered, and every box has on it the number of the slides in it; also the brown paper wrapper, so there will be no difficulty in taking the slides in their proper order, I regard this of importance.[1]

Please write me regarding the negatives, with what hints and suggestions you have to make, as soon as you can, I feel the need of more practice, and am sorry I could not have had it before I left the U.S. Many of them are out of focus, I know, but this I could not always prevent. All suggestions will be gratefully appreciated.

I hope the office will authorize the making of the prints for me, and I wish them as soon as they can be sent off. In any case, write me <u>something</u> after you have looked over the photos.

Very respectfully,
A. B. Lewis

Address: Care Agent, N. German Lloyd S.S. Co., Sydney, Australia

Fig. 3.1. Dance, New Year's Day, 1910, Cape Merkus. A-31918 (225).

West New Britain

||||||||||||||||||||||||||||||||||||||||||||||||||||||||||||||||||||||||||||||||||||

Sunday, Dec. 12, 1909 Left Herbertshöhe at 5 P.M. in the *Langeoog*, with a government expedition consisting of Dr. Oswald, regierungsrat, and to be acting governor when Dr. Hahl leaves; Dr. Klug, Herr _____.

These were making a trip around New Britain, partly for the purpose of returning laborers and police-boys, whose time had expired, to their homes, and partly to give Dr. Oswald the opportunity to see this part of the colony. They expected to be gone about 2 weeks, and visit a number of places along the coast. By permission of Dr. Hahl and Dr. Oswald, I was permitted to go with the boat as far as Araway, on the south coast, where Forsayth has a station in charge of McNicols, a Scotchman.

Monday, Dec. 13 In the forenoon arrived at Pondo, where we stayed about 2 hours, visiting the plantation of Herr Wuchert. He was so kind as to give me a Baining mask, and said that I was welcome to come and visit him anytime, but that the best time would be in May of next year. There are no native villages near, but I could go along the coast in his cutter. High up in the mountains were the Baining, but they could be easier reached from Herbertshöhe than from Pondo.

After leaving here we proceeded a few miles to the Catholic station at Tōrīū, where they have built a sawmill on the river about a mile from its mouth. They had circular and band saws, and a planing machine, all run by steam. There was a report of gold on a small tributary further up the river, and we put in about an hour looking for the place, but without success.

Tuesday, Dec. 14 After steaming all night, the next morning we anchored off the Nakanai coast. There were many reefs here, and we were so far away from the village where we were going that it took about 4 hrs. to row there in the boat. We first ascended what looked like a river, but proved to be a salt water inlet—a narrow channel in the mangrove swamp.

Later it began to rain, and by the time we reached the place where the village was I was quite cold and stiff. Here at first the natives ran away, but our interpreters soon induced two or three old men to come near enough so that we could throw them an axe and some other presents, and they soon became friendly, and invited us to their village, which lay a short distance inland. Here we stopped 15–20 minutes, but as the rain poured down, and it was getting late, we could not stay longer. Saw no women or children. The houses were low and poor affairs; the men quite naked, except a few ornaments. Saw tortoise shell nose-rings, a dozen or more in one nose, also a peculiar shell ornament on stiff thread with beads. Bought the shell ornament, (without the beads) 4–5 tortoise shell rings (could not get all), and a spear. They also had great numbers of small tortoise-shells in their ears. (A

Fig. 3.2. Nose ornaments, Nakanai coast, 137677 (1374). "Four rings of tortoise shell and one of pearl shell. This is about half of what one man had in his nose—he would not part with all. The pearl one is worn on the outside." A-112160.

161

similar custom was noted in the French Islands, and along the coast to Warie, also, along the S. coast around Cape Merkus.) It rained all the way back to the ship, and I was quite chilled when got there, but immediately stripped and rubbed down, so got up some circulation, and got into some dry clothes.

Wednesday, Dec. 15   Early in the forenoon we arrived at Peterhafen in the French Islands, and tho it looked like rain, I went with Dr. _____ to the village of Lōlē, near by. Here took some photos.[1] The men go naked, but the women wear a grass apron in front, and a somewhat similar one, but longer, behind. (Much the same at Warie, Kilinge, Lottin, and Cape Merkus.) Houses poor and degenerate.

After returning from the village took a walk through the plantation—cocoanuts, rubber, and cacao-trees.

Left Peterhafen (a fine but small harbor, apparently a volcanic crater) before noon, and at 6:30 P.M. anchored off Kapo, west of Willamez Peninsula.

Thursday, Dec. 16   In the morning went in the boat to a village (Nikivia) on the mainland about 4 hrs. distant. Was not feeling very well when we started, and by the time we got there was so sick I could hardly stand. The coast here was hilly, and the houses were built on the spurs, so that one must climb up a rather steep ascent to get to them. They seemed rather better than those seen before, and were built on piles some 4–6 ft. high. I was so sick I could do nothing but lie down, and in about 20 min. we left the place, I going back to the ship in the boat, while Dr. Oswald and Dr. Klug went in native canoes to another village. I felt a little better when got back to ship, but did not go ashore again, tho the others went to visit Kapo about 4 P.M.

Friday, Dec. 17   Did not feel well enough to go ashore today. Tho the others went ashore at Iboki, and again later in the evening when we anchored off Wārīē.

Saturday, Dec. 18   Early in the morning went ashore at Warie, where stayed till about 10 A.M. Here purchased a few things, and took some photos of the village and natives. Warie is the general name for this coast, the particular village where I went being called Mārākā, and the one next (east) Nāmāranga (Marūmu's village[2]).

The houses here are built on piles (see photos). Many of their possessions come from the west (New Guinea probably). Their earthen pots they said came from Sīkālā, an island close to New Guinea. Their carved wood bowls came from 2 small islands, called Nākārārā, close to Mandāng (?). Shell rings with ornamental design around outside, and also baskets (soft) with woven designs, they said came from a small island Rānōr, to Kilínge, where they obtained them. I got 3 spears which they said came from Pītū (French Islands), two of which were certainly St. Matthias spears.

Altogether, they seemed to have trading connections with New Guinea on the west to French Islands on east. Flat, closely woven coiled baskets, they made themselves. (Similar baskets are made in various places, from the French Islands to the west end of island, also near Cape Merkus—the design varies with the place.)

---

1. Nos. 190–193, none reproduced here.
2. One of ABL's field assistants. Two of his original three assistants were still with him.

Fig. 3.3. "Outrigger canoes from Kapo." Note man with *luluai*'s cap. A-31887 (194).

They also make a soft basket which the men carry for their small valuables, but the most ornamental of these seem to come from New Guinea or some island in that direction. The men here wear a small bark loin-cloth, the women grass aprons before and behind. Arm bands of red and yellow fibre (rattan ?) are woven here. Arm-bands of black fibre are also seen. These they say come from the interior, the fibre being found on old logs up in the mountains.

Most of the natives here spoke Pigeon Eng. and many had been in service at Kokobo[3] or elsewhere. We left here about 10 A.M., and reached Kilinge about 1 P.M. This village is just around the N.W. corner of New Britain, but as far as I could see was practically the same as those of the Warie coast.

---

3. It is uncertain whether ABL means plantation work on the nearby settlement of Kokopo or the major government center of Herbertshöhe on the Gazelle Peninsula. I suspect the former.

Fig. 3.4. Flat woven basket, collected Warie, where it had been traded from Siassi via Kilinge, 137643 (1363). A-112126.

Fig. 3.5. "Canoe from Siassi at Kilinge." A-31894 (201).

Fig. 3.6. Wooden mush paddle, Lottin Island; wooden taro spoon, collected at Cape Merkus but made in Kilinge, 137798 (1323), 137362 (1612). A-112096.

We stayed here till about 5 P.M. visiting the different villages, or house groups, each with its special name, however. I got only a few things, as the men were nearly all away at a sing-sing on some one of the islands to the westward. We left here for the small island of Lottin, which had 2 or 3 villages, and had been visited only by the *Peiho*.

Sunday, Dec. 19 Early in the morning we anchored off a village on the south coast of the island of Lottin, which rose like a single volcanic cone from the ocean.

Here we went ashore, but the natives all ran away, and we were unable to get into touch with them. After about 20 min. we left, leaving in the village two of our men, who could speak the language, with presents, so that by the time we returned from a trip around the island they could have made friends with the natives, and persuaded them of our friendly intentions. We then steamed around to the other side of the island, and anchored off the village of Tūlō, which the *Peiho* had visited before. When we first went ashore, no one was visible, but soon a couple of old men appeared, and later a few others, but not more than half a dozen. These were quite friendly, however, and we got a number of things here, esp. carvings hung on the ends of house beams, also the large poles used for platforms. Near the center of the village were 3 large carved posts, the remains of a former building, the best of which the *Peiho* had apparently taken. Dr. Klug took these as a present to the governor, tho I spoke for one. After spending a short time here, we left for the first village, where we had left the boys. (The posts mentioned above were carved toward the top to represent a crocodile on each side, head up, and connected with the head a human face. I got one rather large carving with somewhat similar design.) When we got back to the first village, (called Mbūnō), we found the natives quite friendly, many of the women also being present. Immediately on going ashore a brisk trade sprung up, the natives being very anxious for tobacco, and myself, Dr. Klug, and the captain's representative, all interested in buying specimens, while many of the police boys wanted *kundu*s [hand drums in Pidgin]. I saw only one or two small carvings, but did not succeed in getting them. Also missed the shell ornaments, with carved tortoise-shell, and cocoanut shell, inside, several of which were seen on poles near, or on top, of the houses.

Designs quite various. Here for the first time saw bows and arrows. Bow with rattan string, arrows cane shaft, wood point, round or barbed. Saw one with bone point, reminding one somewhat of those from Humboldt Bay.

Fig. 3.7. Carved wooden pendant representing fish with bird in its jaws, Lottin Island. Used as an ornament on the ends of house beams, 137790 (1345). A-112100.

After about 1½ hrs. we returned to the ship, and left for Ruk Island. We arrived off a village here late in the afternoon, and had just time to go ashore and look around before dark. Many men here could talk Pigeon Eng. and had been in service. The things here seemed similar to the Kilinge,—baskets, bowls, houses on piles, etc., but there was little of interest to be obtained. Got 2 side boards of a canoe (from Siāsi ?).[4]

Monday, Dec. 20   Steamed all night. About 12 o'clock a strong wind sprung up, and the ship rolled so I could hardly stay on my cot. At daybreak we were out of sight of land, but about 10 o'clock we arrived at Cape Merkus. Here McNicols, the planter here in charge of Forsayth's station, came on board, and I arranged to go ashore and stop with him till Forsayth's schooner, the *Irene,* came down here (prob. the last of January).

Tuesday, Dec. 21   Developed the two dozen plates I had taken on the trip. Most of them not much good.

Wednesday, Dec. 22   During the night had fever, and was not able to do anything all day. Herr Schoede,[5] the collector, arrived in his schooner (Capt. Carlson, Engineer Knight) and decided to stay till after Christmas.

Thursday, Dec. 23–Friday, Dec. 24   Still not able to do much beyond fixing up a place for my things, and numbering and packing specimens got on trip.

Saturday, Dec. 25   This was a holiday, and the natives from two or three villages near came here and gave a sing-sing, rigged out in all their paraphernalia—feathered head ornaments, painted faces, bark girdles, arm-bands and leg-bands with big bunches of leaves, etc. The women and children also came, and some assisted in some of the dances. The first to arrive were bush natives, who came before daylight. These seemed to be very poor. They were supposed to have spears in their dance, but only one was good (I bought it), two others were not so bad, but plain, while all the others were merely sticks. They had some cassowary feather ornaments, but not much else. These left about 8 o'clock, and the natives from the islands came about nine, dancing and singing as they came up the hill from their canoes. They remained till afternoon, after the dancing being entertained and fed by McNicols, who also gave them tobacco and other presents.

During the day I got a number of photos (all spoilt later by too hot water in washing)[6] and secured a few specimens, including six of the masks or feathered dancing hats. Later we went on board the schooner and had dinner, and then came back to the house, where the others played cards till 10 P.M. I might say that the evening before (Christmas eve), they all took dinner at the house, Schoede sending on shore his Malay cook and nickel service.[7] This was rather interesting, as it was all nickel, and consisted of a dozen plates, ½ soup plates, doz. knives, forks, big and little spoons, cups, kettles and bowls of various sizes, etc. all packed in two strong cases, and costing about $60.00.

4. These canoe boards are each more than twelve feet long (137857–858).
5. ABL spelled his name variously as Schrade and Schade.
6. See ABL's letter to museum photographer Charles Carpenter at the beginning of this book.
7. Such details of Schoede's nickel service seem uncharacteristic of ABL's diary and suggest that he missed being home for the holidays.

Fig. 3.8. Large wooden carving hung on end of beam in ceremonial house, Lottin Island, 137793 (1347). 161 cm long. A-112121.

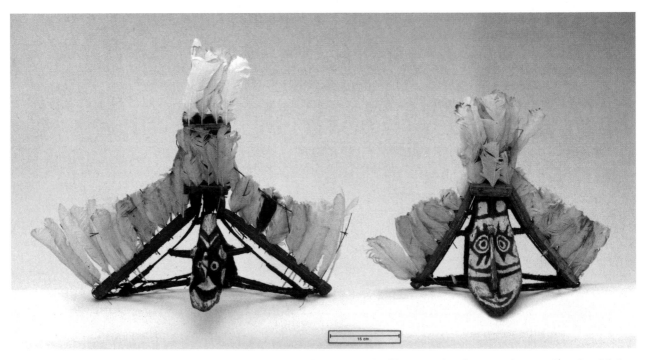

Fig. 3.9. Feathered hats or headdresses used in dance on Christmas Day, Cape Merkus, 137635 (1376), 137637 (1379). A-112107.

Sunday, Dec. 26 Schoede left in morning. He said that he had been fairly successful, having gotten about 150 specimens since he left Herbertshöhe (3 or 4 days before I did). Here he cleaned out the place of skulls (got 28), 2 wood carved masks, the last here, and other things. Unfortunately I was sick while he was here so could do little, and was not able to go to the villages. He expects to go to Fr. Wh. Hafen, then K. Aug. river, and later return along the coast to Huon gulf, then back along south shore of New Brit., and to Herbertshöhe about May 1st, when his lease on ship expires. He has over 6,000 M. worth of trade on board.

I attempted to develop the negatives I took Sat. today, but all were ruined by the water being too warm. Should have special tropical plates for this country, as no means of cooling water.

Monday, Dec. 27 Packed up the masks and other things in morning. Later it rained, so could not do much.

Tuesday, Dec. 28 In morning went over to island of Pūlīlo in McNicols' native canoe with my two boys. Did not find much here, as about all sold out, except a very few things which they would not sell. Came back about noon, and found that McNicols' boat was leaving in a short time to go to a place some 25–30 miles distant for taro, so I decided to go along. There was the crew of boys and one native as guide and interpreter. We started at 1:30 P.M. and sailed till after dark, when in attempting to find the mouth of the river to which we intended to go, we got so mixed up with the reefs that we anchored there for the night (about 9 P.M.).

The next morning [Wednesday, Dec. 29] at daylight we started again, and had considerable difficulty in keeping clear of the reefs. The river to which we had at first intended to go we left behind, as the guide did not seem able to get in, and after about 2 hrs. rowing arrived at the mouth of another river, which we entered and ascended for 4 hrs. before finding natives. We passed two places where there were taro plantations, but no natives were to be seen. At this place the interpreter finally succeeded in finding some natives, and we proceeded to fill up the boat with taro, buying some 600–800 roots. I went with the interpreter and chief to the native village, situated on a slight elevation some 20 min. walk from the river. It was a poor place, 4–5 houses in bad state of repair, and one old *tamburan* house about gone to pieces. This had formerly been ornamented on one side with painted bark boards, but some were now gone, and the others badly spoilt. This building was on piles some 5 ft. high, but in the others the ground was the floor (see photos). Here got a spear, a couple of rudely carved masks, a net, and some other things, including a shield, the pick of 4, and a poor specimen at that. The natives here were quite anxious for tobacco, one stick purchasing 10 taros.

At 4 P.M. we started down stream, reaching the mouth in $1\frac{1}{2}$ hrs. and then sailing till after dark, when we stopped on an island and camped over night.

Thursday, Dec. 30 The next morning we left at daybreak, and after sailing and rowing most all day, finally reached Araway at 3:30 P.M.

In the evening went over to Pulilo to a sing-sing, and stayed till 10 o'clock (sing-sing kept up all night). The dances and movements, dress, etc., were apparently the same as on Christmas.

Friday, Dec. 31 The night before the chief had promised to send me a man to explain some things that I wanted to find out about the dance, so this morning about 7 they came to the beach, and I went down and talked to them for about 2 hrs. Could not get much satisfaction regarding the dances, but hope to find out more later. A couple of natives from Kúmbun, who had been at the sing-sing, and were on their way home, also stopped to listen to my talk, and when I was through, I got them to take me over to their island for a short time, and then bring me back. 15–20 houses, in 2 groups, were on the island, but I got nothing here, as there was nothing new. Got back about 12, and as I was pretty tired, read and rested the rest of the day.

Saturday, Jan. 1, 1910 New Year's day, a holiday. The natives of Pelilo had promised to come over to the station and give a sing-sing, at McNicols' invitation, so about noon they arrived. The dances were the same as before, only not so many dancers, and I took some more photos. Here noticed for the first time the binding of the children's heads, with a strip of bark cloth, making them elongate. In some of the children 5–10 yrs. old the distortion was very noticeable.

Later the boys of the station also gave samples of the sing-sing of their districts, one Finsch-hafen, N.G. and one Buka. The Finsch-hafen boys danced around with drums and songs (?) much as the natives here, but the Buka boys moved more slowly, in a sort of circular mass, and blew on their pipes. These were of different sizes, and made a weird combination of sounds, not entirely unmusical. One pipe was quite deep bass.

Later there was a rope pull, and then presents for the natives.

Sunday, Jan. 2 Read and wrote most all day.

Monday, Jan. 3 Started about 10 A.M. with boat, 5 men for crew, native (of Pelilo) for guide and interpreter, and my 2 boys, for a week's trip to the

Fig. 3.10. Dancers, New Year's Day, 1910, Arawe plantation, Cape Merkus. A-31920 (227).

east of Cape Merkus.[8] After sailing about 2 hrs., stopped at a place with 2 or 3 houses, where we could get the boat to shore. The coast all along here is a rocky cliff, almost perpendicular, and in many places cut under by the sea. We went for some time before finding a landing place, passing 2 or 3 native settlements, but most on top of the cliff.

After landing I got some taro for the boys, and after dinner was over, we left with some of the natives to visit the places on top of the cliff. The place where we landed had 3 women's houses and one men's house—this at some distance from the others. Some of the women and children had also made lean-to's under the overhanging cliff. After following the shore for perhaps $\frac{1}{4}$ mile, we came to the path leading to the plateau above. It was quite steep, in some places only a foothold on the face of the cliff, but the coral rock was so weathered as to give fairly good foot and hand-holds. At top we visited 4 scattered settlements, each of 3 to 6 houses—one a men's house, the others women's houses (family). The houses were low, mostly only ground floor, tho few of women's houses were on piles. The sides were of poles, or of a sort of cocoanut mat. The people had very little; a few baskets, round coiled, and flat (of cocoanut leaves), both made here; a few Tami wood bowls; pots, said to come from far in the bush (my interpreter, from Pulilo, said that they got both the bush pots and the New Guinea pots, but that he had never been to

8. ABL also wrote a more informal account of this trip to Solong, Amklok, Ruoto, Manua (or Moewehafen), the bush village with blowguns, and Ross Island, which I edited and published in 1988 in the *Field Museum Bulletin* as "New Britain Notebook." This later account was found in a small notebook labeled "New Britain" among ABL's other papers in the Department of Anthropology archives. It was probably written as a report for Field Museum director Skiff, although none of ABL's actual reports to the director have survived.

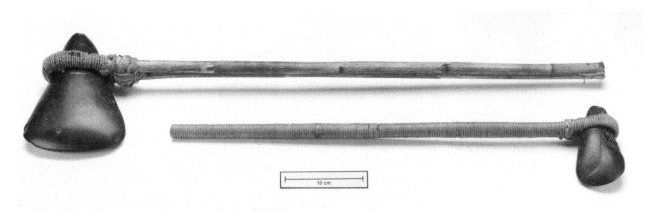

Fig. 3.11. Stone axes, Solong. Handle of split rattan doubled about stone, wrapped with string, 137423 (1680), 137420 (1685). A-112124.

Fig. 3.12. Family or woman's house, Amklok. A-31933 (240).

the place where the pots were made, as it was a long way); a few wood shields and spears; netted bags, fish and pig nets, also one for some other animal, which they said was like a dog, and had a long tail.

The men wore the customary loincloth of bark-cloth; the women the *purpur*—a sort of double apron, before and behind, of prepared fibre. This is made of some leaf, which is soaked in salt water, and the stem shredded by chewing.

The men's houses were about 12 by 20 ft. with a passage way down the middle, and a row of cots, made of sticks, either supported on a short log, or on forked sticks driven in the ground. Over head were hung the nets, and in a sort of loft were often crude wooden masks and bull-roarers. Most were plain, but I got one ornamented one said to come from Kilinge. Saw in one house a number of human and pig's skulls, hung in row, but they were *tamburan,* and could not be bought.

While at the furtherest settlement it rained, delaying us for about an hour. After this I returned with my "plunder" to the shore, as I did not care to have to go down the cliff in the dark. At the place below we got sufficient cooked taros for supper. As one of the woman's houses had a floor about 4 ft. high, we induced the people to let us sleep there for the night, and I had my cot set up, while the boys slept on the floor and three pole beds.

Tuesday, Jan. 4   Left shortly after sunrise, and rowed along the rocky coast till nearly 10 A.M. In most places was only the rocky, narrow shore and cliff, but in a few places, the shore was wide enough for vegetation, and in 3–4 places we saw a few huts. Those on top of the cliff were usually out of sight, tho in several places we saw groups of cocoanuts, and once a house. About 10 we found a place where we could land at one of the coast settlements. Here the houses, etc. were the same. I got 1 skull, 1 shield, 3 spears, and a few small things here, but they had very little. We cooked rice here, and the boys had their breakfast, after which we sailed for Rótō, as the wind was now good. We reached there about 1:30, with rather strong wind and heavy rain for the last ½ hr. Here I went ashore and purchased a few things. Very little difference from last place. About 6 houses, and 1 men's and 1

Fig. 3.13.   Outrigger canoe, Ruoto Island. A-31904 (211).

Fig. 3.14. Men of Ruoto Island, east of Cape Merkus. A-31906 (213).

boys' house, all on ground, with pole walls. About 4 left for place near by, but had to go long way around on account of reef. Here went ashore and arranged to stay all night. I had my cot set up in the boys' house, but it rather small and some of crew slept outside. As the natives here talked of attacks by "bush-men," some of the boys watched all night.

Wednesday, Jan. 5 In morning bought what I could get—not much. Then when up on plateau above cliff to see if could get some birds, Kaman shot 1 parrot and 1 cockatoo. Here saw the native's taro patch, all carefully fenced with heavy poles, to keep out wild pig. In afternoon went back to Ruoto in canoe, but got nothing but partly made fish-net. The string is made from bark of tree, and netted with only a netting needle. The one I got said to come from Kilinge. The net when first begun has loop to slip over great toe, the man sitting on the ground with leg stretched out in front. The meshes are held by the fingers, no board being used. As work progresses, it is wrapped around foot.

Stayed in same place this night (this place Wōwóskī), as found we must sail for about 8 hrs. before another good stopping place.

Thursday, Jan. 6 Left about sunrise, first had to row, then good breeze till about 9, and then had to row more or less till about 2 P.M. when reached Manua (Moewe Hafen) just before rain set in. Got things into house, and after rain (did not last long, tho looked as if would be a big storm), went out and shot a few birds.

173

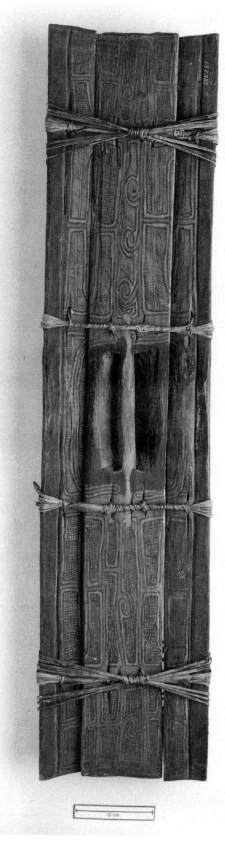

Fig. 3.15 and 3.16. Front and back of carved and painted wooden shield, collected at Manua (Moewehafen), made in the interior, 137385 (1470). A-112111, A-112114.

Friday, Jan. 7 In morning bought a few things. Very little here, as all vessels anchor off this island. The houses are scattered, and I did not see over 8 to 10, not very many natives here, and these much the same as those seen before.

About middle of forenoon left in boat for opposite promontory, where a "bush" village (? 2 houses) was said to be up on top of the high land. After about an hour's walk we reached the place. (The Manua chief went along to prevent natives running away.) We saw 4 men, no women or children. Here for the first time I saw a blow gun. It was made of several short (about 2½ ft.) pieces of bamboo, fastened together by inserting the smaller end of one piece into the larger end of another, this being split when necessary, but wrapped to prevent the split from extending too far. The joint was covered with gum, then leaves, and then wrapped with narrow rattan, blackened on outside. The arrows were 2½ to 3 ft. long, of slender pointed wood, and with feathers at the base, often brightly colored. Got a gun and 4 arrows. They had cassowary head dresses, *mal,* shell ornaments, etc. much as the other natives. After buying a few things—all I could see around the house (men's house) that they would sell—I asked for the women's house, as I might see something there to buy, but they said it was a "long way," and my guide said he did not know where it was. I asked 3 or 4 times to see the women's house, but always the same answer, or a variation of it, and finally decided to return. Just after leaving the house, one of boys said that the women's house was close by, behind some bushes at the side of the men's house. I now asked the chief-man to go with me, as I did not wish him to think that I would do anything out of the way, and started for the house, my boy going also. The roof projected at one end, leaving a covered space, and here a hot fire was blazing, with taro roasting on top, with a bushel or two lying near on the ground. (Before, when we asked, they said that they had no taro.) The doorway was at one side.

While looking around and trying to get a look inside (I did not like to go in for fear of too greatly offending them), I neglected the old chief, and when I turned to look for him, I found he had disappeared. My boy said he had gone into the other end of the house (see plan), taken out some things, and run for the bush, thrusting a present into my boy's hand, as he happened to be near. I now took a look in the other end of the house, but found nothing of interest. All the men of the place, but one, had now disappeared. I got my guide to call for them, saying we were leaving (3 were going to the boat with us) but to no purpose, so we started back. On the way our companion from the village left us for a short time, and returned with a cockatoo, which he said he had just shot with the blow-gun. He also sold me 2 more arrows. I wished very much I had seen him shoot it. I saw one man, when I bought the gun, shoot to show how it was done. He rested the far end on a tree, as the tube was not strong enough to hold in the hands. The arrow did not go very far, and seemed too heavy to be shot to any distance.

175

After returning to the boat we started for a place on the river about opposite the island where we were stopping, stopping for some taro on the way. The river was navigable only a short distance, according to the natives, who said that Dr. Klug had tried it shortly before. Near the village were some fine springs, with plenty of water. Here we washed, and filled up our bottles and tins. The village (?) consisted of 4 or 5 houses scattered along the bank,—the people, houses, etc. the same as on the island. Here I saw the painting of the *"mal"* or men's loin cloth, and got specimens. The *mal* is made from a single strip of bark taken from a relatively small sapling. This is beaten with a stone on the end of a piece of a small log, which has a projection at the other end, to set in the ground.

After the beating is finished, it is painted with a design in black and white. As near as I could make out, this design is different for each village. The black *(ewūs)* color is put on first, and is made by chewing *"edím ekékūklū,"* the bark of a certain tree [*edim* = name of tree; *ekekuklu* = bark (off tree)], with soot formed by burning the wax *(āvāngē)* of the *galip (ingip)*. The soot is deposited on a stone held over the flame, and scraped off with a clam shell when needed. A piece of bark is wrapped around some soot, and put in the mouth and chewed for a few minutes, then taken out and mixed with a little water in a cocoanut shell, a deep black fluid being the result. The black design is in narrow lines, and is put on by a piece of the bark trimmed down to a narrow edge.

The red color *(emblék)* is made by chewing a certain bark *(ekepér ekekuklu)*, leaves of a certain fern (?) *(tínggīr)*, and lime *(ekō—*as used to chew with betel nut). This, mixed with water in the same way as the other, gives a red fluid, and is put on in broader lines with a brush *"omōn"* made by chewing slightly the end of a piece of reed. While working, the *"mal"* is simply held in the hand or the knee.

In this place I found also an old blow-gun, in two parts, much smoked.

After staying here till near 5 P.M., we returned to the place where we had spent the night before. Cooked taro was all ready for the boys, and they, with the natives, put in the evening having a sing-sing.

Saturday, Jan. 8   Left early to visit the two other settlements on the islands. Got very little in either one. At last one, by much questioning, found I might be able to get guides and visit another "bush" village, and started about noon for the place, across on the mainland. It was about an hour to the coast, then came to the bush, with a path that it took better eyes than mine to see. Even our guides were not sure of the way, but after about 2 hrs. of up hill and down, but chiefly up, we reached a fence enclosing a taro patch. Here our guides went forward to investigate,—and after some time we were told to follow. We crossed the taro patch, climbed another fence, crossed a gully, into another taro patch, and soon I saw a peculiar palisade-like structure before me. For about 30 ft. the fence (of poles laid horizontally between stakes on each side), had been heightened to at least 10 ft., with stronger and larger poles, and a small door-way left in the center. Through this we went, and a few feet behind was the men's house. This was much the same as the other we had visited. As heavy rain was threatening, and it was getting late, we could not stay long, but were soon on our way back, with a native for guide, who took us over our old path, however. It poured rain on our way back, but we finally reached our stopping place on the island just as night was setting in.

Sunday, Jan. 9   Left early in the morning for Ross Island, and stayed there all day, except a visit in the afternoon to the neighboring island. Four

Fig. 3.17. "House where we slept, Ross Island." A-31909 (216).

men lived on Ross Island; one or two on the neighboring island. Got little here but 5 skulls.

Monday, Jan. 10   Left early for Cape Merkus, where arrived just before dark. Bad winds. Had to row part of the way.

Tuesday, Jan. 11–Saturday, Jan. 15   Did little beyond cataloguing and packing my specimens. Was also laid up with fever for 2–3 days.

Monday, Jan. 17   Developed plates.

Tuesday, Jan. 18   Overhauled, oiled and cleaned some of my things, wrote notes, etc.

Wednesday, Jan. 19   Made visit in boat to Kaūkūmate, had to wait there till afternoon before the men returned from work (on another island) for tho the boys had gone to tell them of my arrival, it took some time to go and come. Here bought a few things. Then a high wind arose, and we could not start back till after 4, so that it was nearly 8 P.M. by the time we reached the house. Kauukumate is on the island the furtherest out to the S.W.

Friday, Jan. 21   Went in boat to _____, a village on an island not quite so far as Kauukumate. The village is on the extreme point of the island, which is of coral rock, raised to a height of about 100 ft. The landing is back some distance on one side, as the cliffs here are inaccessible. As usual, nearly all the men were away, but I managed to get a few things. Some of the houses were built so that the back was almost over the cliff. The surface was so irregular, with masses of coral rock, that it was hard to find room for the few houses. Got back from here about 6 P.M.

Saturday, Jan. 22–Monday, Jan. 31   Rained a great deal, and I could not do much, aside from trying to find out regarding the language and customs of the natives, when I could induce my interpreter to come to me. For such purposes, however, Pidgin English is far from satisfactory and progress is slow and very uncertain as to accuracy, as there is too liable to be misunderstanding.

Tuesday, Feb. 1   Went by boat to Kamangaro, a village on island to N.W. Here also got a few things, but not many, and returned in afternoon, our return journey being rather slow, as we hoped to be able to find some fish to shoot (with dynamite).

Wednesday, Feb. 2–Thursday, Feb. 10   Labeled and packed my collections as well as I could, and tried to get more facts regarding language and customs from the people. Was also laid up several days with fever.

Friday, Feb. 11   Went early in morning with Karton and 2 other men to where they had their fields. These were about 2 miles from the village, on elevated land near the coast. They were surrounded by a good strong pole fence to keep out the wild pigs. Here they had taro, sweet potatoe, sugar cane, and a few other things. Taro was the chief. Photoed fence and man planting taro. On returning about 11 A.M. found that the *Irene,* the motor schooner of Forsayth, which was to take me from Arawe back to Simpson-hafen [had arrived], but as I found she was going across to Huon Gulf, I packed up my things hurriedly that afternoon, and went on board before dark, as the captain (Langham) wished to leave at daylight the next morning.

CAPE MERKUS—TRADE

The southern coast of New Britain, west of South Cape, is rather thinly populated. The chief settlements are around Cape Merkus, and the chief man (Liwa) of Pelilo, the most important village here, claims jurisdiction over all this region. Intermarriages take place between Pelilo and Siassi to west, and Pelilo and Moewe hafen to east, while trade and intercourse is common all along the coast. The people of Siassi often come to Pelilo, and go on to Manua (Moewe hafen), making visits and trading. They bring their canoes to sell (6 were sold—1 to Kauukumate, 2 to Kumbum, and 3 to Pelilo) while I was there, at from 3 to 4 pigs each. Siassi is also a distributing center for the regions north, west and south. From thence come pots from the New Guinea coast, wood bowls and spoons from Tami. (These were also found at Warie and probably further west on the north coast, whence they come by way of Kilinge.) Drums from Tami and Kilinge, netted bags from New

Fig. 3.18. "Siasi canoes, Cape Merkus." A-31943 (250).

Fig. 3.19. Earthen pots and a large piece of obsidian, collected around Cape Merkus, 137883 (1407), 137885 (1651), 137884 (1649), 137882 (1406); first and fourth were said to have been made in the mountains in the interior west of Solong, other two said to have come from the bush (natives in several places affirmed that pots were made in the interior); 137384 (1682) obsidian from the north coast of New Britain, used for shaving. A-112116.

Fig. 3.20. "Siasi canoe, Cape Merkus." A-31942 (249).

Guinea, as well as numerous smaller things, armbands, ornaments, etc.—also obsidian from the volcanic region of north New Britain. There is considerable local trade also. Coiled baskets are made by the interior villages, and traded along the coast; the style varying according to place of manufacture. Black fibre for armbands from the mountains at western end of New Britain. Yellow plaited fibre from coast far to east, some pots seem to be made in interior.

CAPE MERKUS—LANGUAGE

The interior villages, at least those within easy reach of the coast (say 10 miles or so) have a similar language to the coast people, in the neighborhood of Cape Merkus. The languages of Manua, Ruoto, and Cape Merkus (Solong and all the islands) are closely related, yet different. Siassi is also different. What languages may be between Cape Merkus and Siassi I do not know. Ruoto lies in the gulf about 12–15 miles N.E. of Cape Merkus, and from here to Manua there are no coast villages, and the "bush" tribes were hostile. These are probably another people. At Moewe hafen an interior tribe, having quite a different language, has 2 settlements, at least, not far from the coast. These people make the shields of the region, and also use the blow gun.

CAPE MERKUS—HOUSES

The houses, of the coast people at least, are practically the same, tho they may be a little better built in some places than in others. Each village has two kinds; the family house *(evín),* and the men's house *(um),* of which there may be one or more, according to the size of the settlement. The men's houses are uniformly built on the ground, i.e., there is no floor but the earth. There is usually a door at each end, and a central passage, on each side of which are the sleeping places of the men. These consist of some 8 to 15 small poles laid on a couple of sticks, which are supported at each end by forked stakes set in the ground. Some sleep directly on the poles, while some have leaf mats. The sides of the house are of poles, laid horizontally, and held in place by uprights on each side, lashed together with rattan.

The doors are merely places where the poles are cut away, leaving a space some 2 ft. wide by 3 ft. high, the bottom being 1½ to 2 ft. from the ground, but not so high that the pigs can easily get in. At night it may be closed with sticks, or with a mat. The roof is a rather irregular leaf thatch. There are center posts for the ridge pole, as well as side posts for the plates.

In this house sleep all the unmarried men and boys after circumcision. Strangers are also received and lodged here, and it serves as a general gathering place for the men.

The family house is sometimes built on the ground, sometimes on posts or piles 3–5 ft. high. If on piles there is a platform in front, and the door is on a level with the floor, and not over 3 ft. high, as the eaves are very low. Here lives the wife, with unmarried girls and uncircumcised boys. If a man has several wives, two, or even three, may occupy the same house, but usually there is only one to a house. The husband usually sleeps here, but may sleep in the men's house.

MEN'S HOUSE—CONTENTS

In the men's house are kept the spears, shields, and small personal articles belonging to the men, also fish, fowl, and pig nets. These latter are of

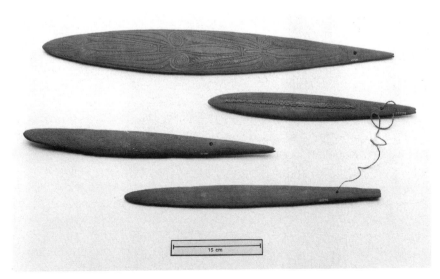

Fig. 3.21. Bull-roarers collected around Cape Merkus: *mamalo* made Kilinge, collected at Solong, 137581 (1403) top; 30 miles west of Cape Merkus, 137580 (1564) left; pair on right from Cape Merkus, 137578 and 137579 (1620 and 1621). A-112118.

181

heavy cord made from bark and may be 500–600 ft. long, by 4 ft. wide, and so heavy as to take 4–6 men to carry them. When used they are stretched partly around a dense part of the bush where the pig is known or supposed to be, and it is then driven into it, men being stationed at intervals to hold the net and keep the pig from getting away. Here are also kept the masks, usually in a small loft up near the roof in the center of the building.

WOMAN'S HOUSE—CONTENTS

In the family house are kept the woman's and children's dress and ornaments, and household utensils and reserve food. The household utensils consist chiefly of large wooden bowls and spoons (from Tami), earthen pots (from the interior or New Guinea), coiled baskets (from interior), water bottles (cocoanuts with leaf stopper), plaited baskets for taro, etc., leaf rain protectors and mats, and small odds and ends, depending on the wealth of the family.

CAPE MERKUS—DRESS

The dress of the men consists of a loin cloth of a single strip of bark cloth, often ornamented, worn around the waist and between the legs. Arm bands are common (shell, rattan and fibre, plain or decorated), leg bands rarely seen, and hair ornaments not numerous, tho a crude comb, of several sticks, or of bamboo, is often worn. Earrings are common, esp. a sort made of tortoise shell edged with small shells. Ten to twenty of these may be worn at a time in one ear. Numerous other ornaments are worn for special occasions.

The women wear a peculiar grass petticoat, formed by a large bunch of grass behind, and a smaller one in front, passed under (from above) a bark waist band. They may have few or many ornaments, consisting of shell

Fig. 3.22. Polished gold-lip pearl shell, with pendants, Cape Merkus, 137489 (5589). From Komine. A-112144 (cf. Lewis 1929: IV).

10 cm

Fig. 3.23. Carved wooden mask, Cape Merkus, 137379 (1644).
A-112101.

Fig. 3.24. Shell ornaments from the Cape Merkus area: tortoise-shell earrings with nassa shell fastened around edge, from Solong, 137551 (1414); arm band of ten incised shell rings fastened together with red fiber, from west end of New Britain, 137450 (5581); pearl-shell hair ornament on nassa-shell band; "The string is tied in the hair so that the shell hangs down to one side, Cape Merkus." 137546 (1692). A-112163.

armrings (often 20 or more together), necklaces, earrings, etc. Children up to 8–10 yrs. old wear nothing, unless it be a few ornaments.

CAPE MERKUS—FOOD

The chief food of the people consists of taro. This is usually either roasted on an open fire, or baked more carefully with hot stones. This is usually done inside the house. Small stones are first put on the ground, several layers of sticks placed cross-wise on these, and larger stones placed on top. This is then fired, and when burnt out, the coals are swept away, the stones arranged, and on them placed the taro, usually with a layer of "greens" (certain chopped up leaves enclosed in other leaves) around the outside, and the whole covered over with several layers of large green leaves, such as those of the bread fruit. This is allowed to stand for several hours, when the whole is found nicely cooked. Taro is also grated or ground up (they use several pieces of a thorny rattan, placed side by side, like a grater), mixed with a little cocoanut oil (the cocoanuts are first scraped with clam shells, mixed with a little cocoanut water, and the oil then squeezed out) wrapped up in leaves (packets as large as one's double fist) and baked with hot stones.

Tho taro is the staff of life, the people also have many others, as yams, sweet potatoes, bread fruit, cocoanuts, and many kinds of greens; they also catch many fish, the men being the chief fishers, using large seines 100 ft. or more in length, and 4–5 feet wide. They also spear fish, esp. at night by torch-light, but I did not see any bows or fish arrows. Pigs are highly valued, and reserved for feasts and special occasions.

NAMES, DANCES, TEETH

On the Liebliche Inseln near Cape Merkus are 5 villages, each on a different island: Pelilo, Kumbum, Kauukumate, _____, and Kamangaro; Pelilo being the most important. There is some intermarriage, but in Pelilo,

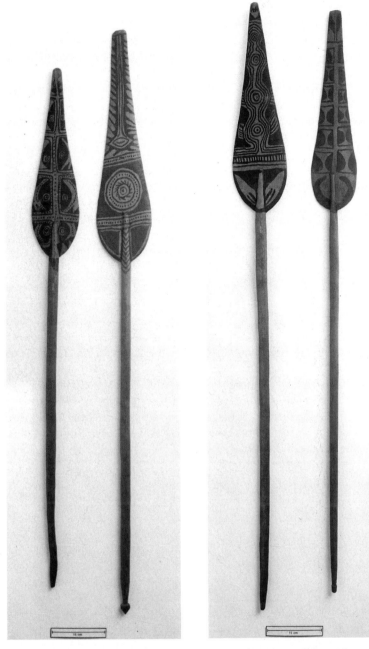

Fig. 3.25. Canoe paddles with painted designs from Pelilo: "design represents fruit and leaves of *yesan-gau*," 137306 (1603); "design represents fruit (back) and leaves (front) of *epri* tree, something like a sago-palm," 137305 (1602). A-112103. See figure, page 11.

Fig. 3.26. Canoe paddles with painted designs: "from Kumbum, design represents a kind of fish *(tit)*," 137312 (1659); "from Kauukumate, design represents roots of plant *(ate lum),* something like taro, but with larger leaves," 137314 (1661). A-112109. See figure, page 11.

at least, most of the marriages outside of the island (and these make [up] at least ½, if not more), are with other places, as Solong, Ruoto, Manua, and even Siassi. Blood relationship seems to be the only limit to marriage. The woman may come to the village of her husband, or reside in her own village, esp. if he is a frequent visitor there.

Children are given, shortly after birth, a name by their parents, which is usually that of some ancestor, esp. one who has recently died. Later they may acquire a second or even a third name, but that depends on the individual himself. A man will sometimes give his name to another, with a suitable present.

The men have a curious custom of blackening their teeth, to make themselves look handsome, they say, so that the women will like them.

There are very many dances and "sing-sings," and very often, esp. at new and full moon, the natives will keep up singing and beating the drum all night.

Most of the songs the natives declared had no meaning (i.e., the words), and two or these which I tried to take down seemed to be a constant repetition, with slight variations, of certain words or syllables.

ART

Aside from the decorative designs on the *mal* (bark loin cloth), which seemed to be characteristic of each village, and the meaning of which (if they had any) I could not ascertain (they were not made on the islands but only on the mainland), the only designs were on their canoes and paddles. The paddle designs usually represented trees (leaves or fruit) (see specimens). They said the designs belonged to certain families (men) and were inherited by a man. As the old men were dead, in many cases they could only tell in a general way what the designs were.

Finschhafen and the
Huon Gulf

‖‖

12 February 1910 – 5 April 1910

In 1910 Finschhafen (and for that matter, the entire Huon Gulf) constituted a world totally different from any that ABL had previously experienced. Aside from the occasional visit of a colonial administrator, a gold prospector, or a curio collector, the Huon Gulf was a world dominated by Lutherans from the Neuendettelsau Mission.[2] Unlike Catholic missionaries, these Lutherans brought their families with them, so their communities consisted of men, women, and children in something approaching normal proportions. Their numbers included ordained pastors as well as lay missionaries—a group that included nurses, architects, carpenters, mechanics, and farmers. There were even a few single men and women, who tended to marry one another. Although these Lutherans were nearly all German by nationality, they were far from homogeneous as a group. Yet they were a devout community, committed to evangelizing as many New Guineans as possible.

The original settlement at Finschhafen was established in 1885 by Captain Dallmann, captain of the steamer *Samoa,* together with four other Germans and thirty-seven Indonesians.[3] This well-protected harbor was to be the New Guinea Compagnie's first settlement, headquarters of a vast empire of plantations that company officials (naively) hoped would flourish in the newly annexed protectorate of German New Guinea. They dreamed of a "second Java" in Kaiser Wilhelmsland, hoping to exploit the same strategy as the Dutch in the East Indies.[4]

The settlers established a few plantations behind Finschhafen, on lands the explorer and ornithologist Otto Finsch had (incorrectly) indicated were suitable for plantation crops. But the high incidence of malaria made the station an extremely unhealthy one. Thirteen company personnel died in the early months of 1891, including the company's general manager and doctor. This led to evacuation of the remaining European inhabitants, first to Stephansort and a few months later to Friedrich Wilhelmshafen, which became the company's new headquarters (see Firth 1982, 31ff.). Finschhafen had proved a disastrous failure for the New Guinea Compagnie, and both the Huon Peninsula and Huon Gulf were subsequently abandoned by colonial administrators for the next twenty years. The German administrative presence would not return to the region until 1911, when the colonial government would open its third government station in Kaiser Wilhelmsland at Morobe.[5]

Shortly after the New Guinea Compagnie opened Finschhafen, the Neuendettelsau Mission sent out its first missionaries, Johann Flierl and Karl Tremel.[6] They soon established a station, which they called Simbang, on a coastal site five miles south of Finschhafen. Georg Bamler arrived at Simbang in 1887 and (with Tremel) established the mission's second station on the Tami Islands two years later. About the time that the company abandoned Finschhafen, the missionaries moved their station at Simbang to a new site, a bit higher up on a hill and away from the coast. They hoped that Simbang II—as the new station was called—would be healthier than the old site, but they were mistaken, and Simbang II was also eventually abandoned, about 1904. Finschhafen had proved only slightly less deadly for the mission than it had for the company. In 1892 Flierl opened a third station at Sattelberg (lit., "saddle mountain") in a mountain valley some 3,000 feet above sea level, immediately behind Simbang II. Sattelberg became the mission's healthy retreat, a cool resort that, unlike the coast, was generally free of malaria.

During the 1890s the Neuendettelsau Mission grew very slowly, the entire community consisting of only a handful of missionaries at the turn of the century. In 1899 the mission began its expansion in the region. First, Bamler opened a station at Deinzerhöhe to serve the nearby settlement of Tami islanders who had migrated to the mainland at Taimi (Taminugetu). In 1902 a station was established at Jabim; the following year another was opened at Wareo, north of Sattelberg. Simbang II was finally abandoned in 1904 for Pola, a site directly on Finschhafen's harbor. A store and guest house were built there, and Pola became the mission's headquarters, for many years under the leadership of Georg Pfalzer. About the same time, a plantation (and later a school) was opened at the nearby station of Heldsbach. These were followed by the opening of a school and printery at Logaweng in 1906. These eight stations consolidated the mission's presence on the Huon Peninsula and opened the way for expansion into the gulf.

A permanent mission presence in the gulf began in 1906 when Stefan Lehner opened Bukaua station at Cape Arkona. Bukaua was one of the largest and most important communities in the gulf, and its language was spoken in many villages beyond Cape Arkona. The station quickly became an important jumping-off place for missionaries and other travelers proceeding further into the gulf. When ABL reached Bukaua in 1910 a pair of adjacent stations, Kela and Malalo, had recently been opened at the southern end of the gulf. Another station was about to open near the present city of Lae. And while ABL was in the Huon Gulf, the Neuendettelsau missionaries were beginning their first patrols up the Markham River into and beyond the Laewomba people (Sack 1976). In less than a decade, these patrols would open up a route into the central highlands (Radford 1987). The missionaries, however, did not publicize their discoveries of large populations up the Markham or in the central highlands for fear that labor recruiters, prospectors, and Catholic missionaries would soon after arrive to disrupt their pristine mission fields.

The year 1910 was, in fact, a critical moment in the contact history of this part of New Guinea. It was a time before major gold deposits had been discovered in the nearby mountains, a time before the mission had consolidated its influence south of Bukaua, and a time before the German colonial administration had begun to reassert its authority in the Huon Gulf.

During the twenty years from 1891 to 1911, the Neuendettelsau Mission functioned very much like a government. The historian Stewart Firth (1982, 148) points out that "isolated from plantation companies and government, [the mission] became a kind of state within a state, organizing an alternative, church-based form of village government." There was minimal administrative oversight over mission activities from either Herbertshöhe or Friedrich Wilhelmshafen, although the governor and other officials would occasionally call in at Finschhafen on their way to other places. Finschhafen had more or less regular passenger, freight, and mail service from Nord-Deutscher Lloyd's steamers, but the growing community of missionaries lived in a world that was largely isolated from the rest of the colony.

The mission operated as a kind of theocracy on at least two levels: German missionaries made decisions about station openings, personnel postings, dates for baptisms, health and education services, and even punishment for crime, all based on their own ideas about the proper Christian community. Native teacher-evangelists and local church elders frequently wielded considerable authority over many aspects of village life, drawing on their own (sometimes idiosyncratic) views about proper behavior and the ideal Christian community. By most accounts the Lutheran administration was a benign one, aimed at protecting its native communities from harsh labor recruiters and large-scale alienation of productive village lands. Lutheran mission communities in the Huon Gulf differed from Catholic missions elsewhere in the colony, who also used native catechists in their evangelizing, in that Catholic communities were inevitably more directly involved with government officers, planters, and traders, simply because of their proximity to other European stations and settlements.

Hoping to protect native communities, the Neuendettelsau Mission kept certain aspects of its work secret from the outside world. One senses this secrecy here in ABL's references to the missionaries' several visits to the Laewomba; the fact of mission patrols is not concealed, but the details of what the missionaries experienced are left vague. The area around what would later become the modern city of Lae was, of course, where mission expansion was in progress as ABL entered the Huon Gulf (see, e.g., Sack 1976, 66ff). Neuhauss, whom these Lutheran missionaries saw as a supporter and patron, was allowed to accompany one of their patrols a short distance into the Markham Valley. But certain details seem to have been kept from him (or perhaps by him) as well.

What is particularly striking in the Huon Gulf is how much influence the Lutherans already had in the region, even though the mission had yet to consolidate its influence there. Virtually everyone wore European clothing of some sort, often a simple lap-lap of calico, and steel tools had become abundant in most villages. One would expect a certain sophistication in villages that, like Bukaua or Taminugetu, had resident missionaries nearby. But this influence was spread across all of the Huon Gulf villages that ABL visited, most of which had no regular European presence.

The mission's powerful influence came largely from two factors: the mission's extensive use of villagers as native teachers and evangelists and its successful evangelizing strategy (the so-called Keysser method).

After establishing its first three stations (between 1886 and 1892), the mission concentrated its efforts on training native teachers rather than opening new stations. After a certain amount of training in the Gospel and Christian living, teachers were sent out to work in assigned villages as evangelists. These native teachers were the mission's first long-term contact with most villages. In villages where the teachers had few preexisting contacts—especially in the interior—evangelizing was initially quite challenging and sometimes dangerous. But when linguistic barriers were minimal or where the evangelists already had some traditional ties with the community, it seems that the mission's backing gave them considerable prestige. Native teachers' relatively easy access to steel, clothing, and other trade goods must have made a deep impression on many less sophisticated villagers. Thus, by the time a German missionary arrived to open a new station, the host community was already familiar with the mission and its work.[7]

The Neuendettelsau Mission's success in New Guinea has largely been attributed to the evangelizing strategy or method developed by the missionary Christian Keysser. Keysser arrived in New Guinea from Germany in 1899 and served for twenty-one years at Sattelberg. He is often considered the most important Neuendettelsau missionary of his generation, primarily because he developed at Sattelberg what has come to be known as the "Keysser method" or "total method" *(Ganzheitsmethod)* of missionization.[8]

Keysser recognized the important role that village social organization played in traditional religious practices, particularly the secret men's cult, called the *balum* cult in the Huon Gulf, centered on a cult house (called *lum*). He suggested working within the traditional social organization of the village. Keysser's theory was that individual converts living in not-yet-converted villages would face tremendous social pressure to revert to non-Christian ways. But if the whole village was converted, each individual would have the support of the entire community in conforming to a Christian lifestyle. Thus, instead of trying to convert individuals, he strove to convert whole villages.

The Keysser method therefore emphasized working with entire villages rather than individuals. Integrating the church into the social life of the community became one of its chief goals. Keysser refused to baptize isolated individuals into the church, preferring to wait until an entire community was ready to join the church at once. By 1906 he had baptized some two hundred Kai people around Sattelberg, while hundreds more from surrounding villages clamored for the sacrament. At one baptismal ceremony four years later, the church at Wareo could not accommodate the crowd wanting to be baptized, though the church could seat 550 (Firth 1982, 148). Initially, these restrictions on baptisms must have enhanced the prestige of joining the church, thereby encouraging prominent village elders to seek admission. By 1910 the Keysser method had been so successful that it was becoming the standard evangelizing strategy throughout the Neuendettelsau field.

One practical effect of the Keysser method and the intensive use of native evangelists was that many villages in the Huon Gulf had moved to be closer to mission stations or to attract missionaries into their settlements. ABL reports that at least five communities had relocated their villages either out of the bush toward the coast, in the case of Apo and Logamu, or to sites more accessible to the mission, in the case of Kela, Wiakap, and Taminugetu. One senses from ABL's account that the region was in the midst of a great transformation that has not always been recognized by anthropologists subsequently.

As elsewhere in New Guinea, one of the major obstacles facing the mission was the large number of languages spoken in the region. By 1890, the Neuendettelsau missionaries recognized the need for a single language that could unify their mission field. German was too difficult for villagers to learn, and Pidgin—which was thought of as a crude plantation language—still had few speakers in the Huon Gulf region. Moreover, the Lutheran missionaries generally believed that one could reach the hearts and very being of a people only through indigenous languages. They consequently adopted two indigenous languages as their principal contact languages: Jabim (Yabim), spoken around Finschhafen, and Katê, the language of the Kai people living in the interior around Sattelberg. Jabim and Katê were used in church services, in village schools, and in general religious instruction. Over the years, both of these languages became important lingua francas on the coast and interiors, respectively (Wurm and Hattori 1981).

From their study of local languages, the missionaries recognized that there were two quite different groups of languages spoken in the region; these have come to be known as Melanesian and Papuan languages. As new communities were evangelized, Jabim teachers were sent to Melanesian-speaking communities, Katê teachers to newly contacted Papuan villages. Because all of the Melanesian languages were more or less closely related to one another, it was relatively easy for Jabim evangelists to teach Jabim to speakers of other Melanesian languages. Similarly, nearly all of the Papuan languages in the region were related to Katê, and villagers speaking these languages had an easier time learning Katê than the Melanesian Jabim.

190

By 1910 the distinction between Papuan and Melanesian languages was becoming well established by scholars.[9] ABL was already aware of the distinction when he was in Eitape, as he refers to differences between Papuan and Melanesian languages in his Humboldt Bay notebook. Because of his early Boasian training with its interest in both diffusion and culture history, such linguistic distinctions would clearly have interested ABL. In the Huon Gulf, the missionaries' concern for these linguistic differences seem to have heightened ABL's interest in language affiliation as a possible factor in cultural variation. ABL would continue to pay attention to linguistic associations throughout the rest of his fieldwork in German New Guinea, even though the Papuan/Melanesian distinction was not always a very good predictor of cultural similarity. Although ABL tells us little about the mission's view of language, throughout his diary account of his travels in the Huon Gulf region he makes repeated references to the mission's key classificatory framework: whether the people of a particular place were Papuan or Melanesian.

In addition to languages, Neuendettelsau missionaries were also keenly interested in ethnology. Like their Catholic counterparts they published many letters and articles dealing with ethnology in their mission newsletter, *Neuendettelsauer Missionsblatt,* as well as in scientific journals.[10] And as they became more proficient in local languages, missionaries also published grammars and dictionaries of several local languages (see, e.g., Bamler 1900; Keysser 1925; Vetter 1896b).

Missionary interest in ethnology and cultural details proved to be exceedingly useful for ABL. Not only could the missionaries explain details of the manufacture and use of various objects, but they also provided many insights into much more complex aspects of local life, such as the *balum* cult.[11] Both Lehner and Keysser helped ABL obtain specimens. Keysser also helped ABL develop some negatives and even allowed him to make some prints; he also sold ABL about twenty of his own prints of Kai and Hube people.

Neuhauss' visits to the gulf in 1908–1909 and in 1910 seem to have further encouraged the missionaries' interest in ethnology. Like ABL, Neuhauss got many ethnographic details from the missionaries. In 1911 Neuhauss published his three-volume *Deutsch-Neu-Guinea.* The third volume was devoted to the ethnology of the Huon Gulf region and consisted of a collection of five articles by Neuendettelsau missionaries: Keysser (1911) on the Kai, Stoltz (1911) on the people of Cape König Wilhelm, Zahn (1911) on the Jabim, Lehner (1911) on the Bukaua, and Bamler (1911) on the Tami.

Of all the people ABL met in German New Guinea, the Neuendettelsau missionaries were, as a group, among the most helpful. During his sojourn around Finschhafen and the Huon Gulf he met most of the missionaries who lived in the region. (At the front of one of his notebooks ABL made a list of many of these missionaries and their stations, reproduced below.) In addition he once again met Neuhauss, and his wife who had returned to the Huon Gulf from Eitape. Near the end of his stay ABL also ran into Regeirungsrat Wiedenfeld, whom he had met with Governor Hahl on his first trip to Eitape. At the end of March 1910, in Finschhafen, ABL also met two prospectors, Bröker and Oldörp. Nine days after ABL left Finschhafen for Friedrich Wilhelmshafen, Bröker and Oldörp set off in their boat, the *Lettie,* for the Markham River, hoping to exploit secret gold deposits discovered by the late prospector Dammköhler and his partner, Oldörp, in 1909. But as these two prospectors entered the gulf their boat was swamped in a sudden gale, and both men (and the location of their gold deposit) were lost.

While in the Huon Gulf, ABL obtained more than 750 objects. Well over 500 of these he collected himself in the villages. Others he got from Bamler (75 objects), Keysser (46), and Lehner (62), as well as 58 pieces purchased from Decker, Hertle, Meier, Raum, Stürtzenhofecker, and other (mostly unnamed) missionaries. As ABL noted in his letter to Dorsey (reproduced at the beginning of this book), the material culture of the Huon Gulf was much picked over by the

191

missionaries as well as by Captain H. Voogdt, captain of the New Guinea Compagnie's *Siar*, who had made several collecting trips to the gulf during 1906–1908. Field Museum bought a large collection from Voogdt in 1909, including ironically the carved planks and house boards from one of the men's houses where ABL happened to have spent the night.

Throughout his travels in the Huon Gulf region, ABL continued to collect information about local variation in material culture. He continued to pursue data about the movement of objects through trade. About 270 of the more than five hundred objects ABL collected in the villages were traded into the villages where he acquired them, rather than having been made there. These field data provide a remarkable amount of information about the economic networks that linked communities along the Huon Gulf and Peninsula. This information together with similar data from west New Britain adds important empirical evidence about the intensity of trade in the life of people living on both sides of the Vitiaz Strait (see Harding 1967 for a more recent view of these networks).

It is clear at the end of his Huon Gulf notebook that ABL did not ignore local social organization or religion, even though he realized that detailed understanding would require knowledge of vernacular languages that he lacked.[12] Here he provides a summary of social organization in the Huon Gulf, particularly with respect to leadership and affiliation to the *balum* men's cult. ABL describes a style of nonhereditary leadership (in contrast to chiefs) of the sort that has more recently been called "big-man leadership." Moreover, he suggests that men were not limited to membership in a single *balum* cult group, but could have membership in several simultaneously. In most of the places ABL had previously visited he had seen chiefs, but in the Huon Gulf he observed something quite different. Thus, incomplete as ABL's descriptions may now seem, he is nevertheless one of the earliest anthropologists to describe big-man-style leadership and other sorts of nonascriptive social groupings in Melanesia.

{*List of Lutheran Missionaries and their stations from the front of ABL's field notebook.*}

Lehner	Kap Arkona (Bukaua)
Schmutterer	Kap Arkona (Bukaua)
Ruppert	Kap Arkona (Bukaua)
Decker	Deinzerhöhe (Kap Gerhards)
Raum	Deinzerhöhe (Kap Gerhards)
Mailänder	Malalo=Kela (Samoahafen)
Böttger	Malalo=Kela (Samoahafen)
Oertel	Malalo=Kela (Samoahafen)
Pfalzer	[Pola, Finsch Hafen]
Meier	Logaueng, Finsch Hafen
Bamler	Logaueng, Finsch Hafen
Hertle	Logaueng, Finsch Hafen

{*In addition to these, ABL also met Keysser at Sattelberg, Stürtzen-hofecker, who was stationed at Jabim, and Miss Lindner (later Mrs. Pfalzer) at Pola.*}

Fig. 3.27. Canoe from Bukaua at Finschhafen. A-31699 (6).

Finschhafen and the Huon Gulf

||||||||||||||||||||||||||||||||||||||||||||||||||||||||||||||||||||||||||||||||||||||||||||||

Saturday, Feb. 12   Left early in the morning and sailed all day, and the following night.

Sunday, Feb. 13   Got into Finsch Hafen about noon, where the captain said he would stay till Monday morning. On my asking what he intended to do, he said he would not go into Huon Gulf to Markham river, and even if wind was good would go only short way along the coast, so, after fixing up a little, I went on shore to see what the prospect was there. Herr Pfalzer, the head (as regards business, at least) of the Neuendettelsauer Mission in New Guinea was just going to church (2:30 P.M.) so I had to wait for about 2 hrs. till it was over, before I could find out how the situation stood. While waiting I talked some with Miss Lindner, who had general charge of the domestic establishment, so to speak, at Pola (the name of the station at Finsch Hafen). About 4:30 Dr. Pfalzer returned, and the table was set for tea and cakes, to which I was kindly invited. Frau Neuhauss was also present, as she was staying at Finsch Hafen while her husband was in the gulf. He was then at Kela, the furtherest station, where he intended staying for some 3 months longer. I learned from Dr. Pfalzer that there was room for me so I went on board and got my things, also also some articles of trade,[9] as follows:

2 doz. ¾ axes	1 doz. hunter hatchets
2 doz. 16 in. knives	1 roll turkey red, 24 yds.
1 doz. 14 in. knives	1 doz. fish lines 3 oz. (never got)
1 doz. 12 in. knives	2 doz. fish lines 2 oz.
3 doz. 6 in. knives	10 lbs. small beads

    Amounting in all to about 210 M.

It was dark when I got back to shore, and some of my things were left in boat house, while others were brought up to house. The dinner in the evening was a welcome change from the fare at Arawe.

Monday, Feb. 14   Learned that one of the missionaries from Bukaua, Herr Lehner, would probably return Monday evening from Sattelberg, whither he had accompanied his wife and children, who would remain there some time, and that I could probably accompany him to Bukaua (Cape Arkona). Hence I spent all day in repacking and arranging my things for the journey, for as he was going back in a native canoe, and had his own things,

---

9. He bought this "trade" from the crew of the *Irene,* which was owned by Forsayth & Co., one of the largest trading firms in the colony. The ship was principally used to buy copra and other commodities from Forsayth's semiindependent traders. As a result, the ship was well stocked with trade goods that villagers would desire and served as a sort of general store.

I was somewhat limited in what I could take with me. I felt unwell all day, and that evening retired before dinner.

Tuesday, Feb. 15   Had some fever during the night, but felt better in the morning, tho not able to eat much. After Herr Lehner's canoe was loaded with his own things, I found that I could only take the necessary things with me, and that the others must be left to be brought by a canoe later. Our things were placed on the canoe, and then Herr Lehner and myself, with a few attendants, left to go by trail by way of the station Logaueng to Yabim, where we would join the canoe, which had to wait for a favorable breeze. The canoe people were from Bukaua.

The station at Finsch Hafen was founded in 1902, and called Pola, from the native name of the place on which the station stands. (Finsch Hafen in general is often called Madang or Matang, from a small island in the harbor.[10]) The first mission station was at Simbang, near the mouth of the Bubui river, but the place was unhealthy, and the head station was finally established at Finsch Hafen (Pola), while the Simbang station was removed to the summit of a nearby hill some 500 ft. high.

We started about 11 A.M. on our walk. The way led first for a mile or so through the young cocoanut plantations of the Mission, and then into the bush. After about an hour we reached the mouth of the Bubui, which we crossed by a native canoe. From here the station Simbang could be seen on the hills to our right. Our path was then along the shore, but soon struck into the bush and up the mountain side, which we climbed to the summit about 1,000 ft. high, and here rested and had lunch at the station of Logaueng (the name of the mountain). Here I met Missionary Bambler, but his companion Herr Meier was at Sattelberg. From here our way was down hill, and soon plunged into a river gorge, where was a saw-mill. From here on we went at a terrific pace, Herr Lehner keeping me almost at a trot, and in a little over an hour we reached Yabim (about $\frac{1}{2}$ mile, from beach), had a brief rest, and a cup of milk, and then to beach, where we found our canoe waiting for us, having arrived nearly an hour before, as soon after we left a very favorable breeze had sprung up.

We immediately went on board and proceeded on our journey. I found it a little chilly, as I was wet through with perspiration, and put on my coat and rain-coat, but still managed to catch a bad cold, as I found out later. The breeze was good and we hoped to reach Deinzerhöhe (Cape Gerhardt) that night, but had to stop about 10 P.M. at a native village on east side of Hanish bay, as the breeze entirely failed. Here we slept (?), or tried to, till 4 A.M. when we started again. (I had only 2 *zeltbahn* [ground-sheet] to soften the hard boards. We slept on the first floor of a men's house *(lum)*, and somebody was talking all the time.)

Wednesday, Feb. 16   The wind when we first started was fairly good, but after sunrise it ceased. Nevertheless, by rowing, we reached Deinzerhöhe between 7 and 8 A.M.. The station [of] Herr & Frau Decker,[11] [and] Herr Raum is on a hill about 500 ft. high, and $\frac{1}{2}$ to $\frac{3}{4}$ mile from the shore, where

10. ABL is correct here. Despite the confusion with the similar name now used for Friedrich Wilhelmshafen (at Astrolabe Bay), there is a small island in the harbor at Finschhafen that was called Madang in German times. Although the name rarely appears in more recent literature, it is well marked on an inset map of Finschhafen in the *Kolonial Atlas* (Sprigade and Moisel 1903–1912, no. 26).

11. Frau Decker and her two sons drowned near here in 1913. Their canoe capsized as they approached the Deinzerhöhe on their return from home leave in Germany.

the native village is. This village is known as Tami, as it is formed by people from that island.

We had some breakfast and rested at the station till nearly noon, when a good breeze sprung up, and we continued on our way to Bukaua (Cape Arkona), which we reached about 4 P.M. As this was Herr Lehner's station, I could go no further without making special arrangements, and must also wait for my things to come from Finsch Hafen. At this station are also stationed Herr Ruppert and Herr Schmutterer.

Thursday, Feb. 17–Sunday, March 6   The station at Bukaua is about ½ mile from the shore, on a hill between 200 and 300 ft. high, giving a fine view of the coast on either side, and of the mountains to the north, of which the hill on which the station is situated is one of the outlying foothills. The native village lies on the low land near the coast.

Early the first morning after my arrival the natives began arriving at the mission house, where I was staying, with all sorts of specimens for sale, Herr Lehner having told them that I was here to buy such things. This kept up the greater part of the day, as well as the next forenoon, by which time I had bought representative specimens of practically all that they had, and was forced to refuse most of the things offered. Later I went through the village, and I tried to find if they had anything new, but found little. I also purchased some things from Herr Lehner, including 2 carved boards from men's house, a number of charms, and several things from the Laewomba, a tribe inland on the Markham river, which Herr Lehner had visited several months previously.

Meanwhile Herr Lehner had arranged for a canoe to return to Finsch Hafen, and bring my things. This finally left Monday morning, and returned Thursday evening, when I paid them off (2 M. each, 6 men). With some of the things brought, which included large axes and knives, I was able to purchase a few more things, esp. some Tami bowls, also one of the native pig nets.[12]

BUKAUA HOUSES

The natives of Bukaua have changed their old method of life considerably. Their houses are now built better, with doors on the European style. Practically no one wears the native dress. Iron ware has displaced native implements and pottery to a large extent.

All the houses seen so far are built on piles, the lower floor of the men's house *(lum)* being about 3 ft. from the ground, and the floor of the family house about 4 ft.

The sides are made of planks, hewn out of large trees, from one to two feet wide. Two planks are made from each tree (a light and easily split wood is used), the log being split down the center. A hole is first made with the axe, and then wooden stakes are driven in, sometimes clear through, the log, by means of which it is finally split. The other side is then hewn down. Some boards are carved with raised figures but these are found chiefly, if not solely (?) on the men's houses. (Now, of course, iron is used, but in old times all this was done with stone implements).

The door is a hole in the front of the house, the bottom being rounded somewhat, and formed by the lower board, and extends to the eaves. In size

---

12. ABL bought a total of 276 objects during this short visit to Bukaua. Of these, 39 were purchased from Lehner for 200 M. More than a hundred items had been made elsewhere and obtained by Bukaua people through trade. Despite his apparent disclaimer above, ABL actually bought much more than a representative "type collection" here.

Fig. 3.28. Tami bowls collected in various places around the Huon Gulf and southwest New Britain: (top row) Cape Merkus, 137324 (1608); Siassi, 137859 (5382), from Komine; (bottom row) Manua [Moewehafen], 137339 (1486); with turtle head at one end, Wusumu [Busama], 138394 (1986); Apo, 138404 (2126). A-112326.

about $1\frac{1}{2}$–2 ft. wide by 2–3 ft. high. They are closed by a rude mat-like door made of cocoanut-leaves, usually fastened at the side so it can be swung back.

On Wednesday (Feb. 23) Herren Lehner, Raum and Ruppert started in canoes for a trip to the Lae and Laewomba, Lehner expecting to return through the villages inland on foot. On Tuesday (Feb. 29) Ruppert and Raum returned by canoe from Logamu, Lehner coming the next day, having struck inland from Apo (canoe from Logamu to Apo). Lehner and Raum made a trip into the Laewomba country, two days' march over bad trails. Raum brought back some Laewomba hats which I later purchased.

I wished to continue the trip further along the coast, but had great difficulty in getting a canoe, as the only large one was that which had brought my things from Finsch Hafen (*Madang* name of island in harbor used for place in general,[13] and *Pola,* name of place where mission station stands, both being names known along the coast) and this belonged to a man in a neighboring village. After two promises to be ready at a certain time, and failing me both times, I finally gave him up and got the canoe which brought back Ruppert and Raum from Logamu, this belonging, in part at least, to Tape, whom I engaged for 5 M. per day, to take me to Kela and Lokanu, and return, he to look out after crew. (This arrangement later led to trouble, as he had too many, and did not give them as much as they expected, for which, in native fashion, they blamed me, and I had to give them more.)

Monday, March 7 Left at 9 A.M. but soon had head winds, and stopped from 11 to 1:30. Then on to Wakangruhu,[14] where arrived at dusk, and stayed

13. See note 10.
14. This village seems to be Hogbin's Wagang (1951, xiv).

Fig. 3.29. Bark-cloth hats made in Laewomba: 138497 (1730), from Lehner; 138496 (2276), from Raum; 138490 (1962) collected by ABL at Busama; mourning hat 138500 (1734), from Lehner. A-112102.

all night. Place consisted of one house on beach, with no floor, and one back in the taro fields, with floor. Here we stayed, the women vacating it. Plenty mosquitoes.

Tuesday, March 8   Left at 6:30, had good wind but short time, then dead ahead. Pulled boat by hand along shore most of way to Apo, where arrived about 11 A.M. One tree fell just behind canoe.

Shore seemed to have sunken, as many dead trees stood in water. Stayed at Apo till morning. Waited to 3 P.M. to see if good wind would come, and then went to visit a part of the people who lived about 1 hr's journey inland. There were about 10 houses there all on piles, new and modern, yet rudely built.

Formerly (about 5 yrs.) these people lived much further inland, at foot of mountains, but about 5 yrs. before had moved to the beach and this place, apparently to be within more easy reach of the missionaries. Bought a few things here, but saw nothing new.[15] Stayed at Tape's house on the beach.

Wednesday, March 9   Left shortly after daylight, but soon stopped along shore near the native fields, where several sacs of taro, taro cuttings, and bananas were put on board to be taken to Logamu, where there was a scarcity of food.

Again head winds, and after about 2 hrs. stopped on shore and waited till 11 A.M. when the wind became favorable, and we proceeded to Logamu,[16] arriving at 2 P.M. On the way crossed the mouth of the *Wusu* river (Markham river called *Wusi*), where the sea [was] quite rough. The natives

15. ABL bought 42 objects at Apo, more than half made in other places. None were especially large, which gave him the impression that he had bought very little.

16. Logamu, situated near the Markham River, is not to be confused with Lokanu (Hogbin's Laukanu), which is far to the south of the Huon Gulf.

said many people had been drowned here. Stayed at Logamu over night, and here also purchased a few things. This place also only about 5 yrs. old, as people formerly lived further inland. Here one of the natives had built a house, of his own accord, for the missionaries, and here we stayed. (Two men expected to come here in about a month.[17])

Thursday, March 10   Left at daylight for Kela. Sea first rough, and good wind. Then wind died down and from 10–12 very little. Then good again till got to Kela about 2 P.M. Two villages here along beach, one of which I visited. Nothing to be had. These people formerly lived at Pt. Parsee, (village called Nu, which means island, as the Pt. is separated from the main land by a shallow channel). The village which I visited is called Wiakap[18] and here about 20 houses in 2–3 groups. When I returned to the landing place, at the foot of a long path to the mission house on the hill above, I found Prof. Neuhauss there, and later one of the missionaries also came down. Talked till nearly dark when put things in the boat-house, and went up to mission for supper, after which I returned and slept below to be ready to start for Lokanu during the night, as only the night wind was favorable.

Friday, March 11   Left about 1:30 A.M. for Lokanu, but as looked like rain, stopped near by for ½ hr. or more. Arrived at Lokanu about 8:30, but had to row for the last 2 hrs. Stayed here till 2:30. Large village with fine harbor.

Here bought a number of things and took photos of the pottery making, as it is at Lokanu and one or two neighboring villages that most of the pots (aside from those from the Laewomba) used in the Huon Gulf are made. The earth for the pots comes from a river about 1 day's journey to the S.E. It is first worked and kneaded, then squeezed and partly twisted into irregular thick rolls about six inches long (312) (seen in ground in photo 306). One of these is then taken and with the hands coiled on itself into a thick, heavy conical base, to which others are added (306–309 [Fig. 3.30]). The outside is smoothed somewhat with the hand, or more properly, the thumb and fore fingers. The woman then makes a hole in the ground by her side (309) in which leaves are placed, and the pot on these (310). More rolls of clay are added, the inside of the pot is smoothed and wall thinned by removing the thick projecting portions of the coils with the thumb (310, 311) and the process repeated (311–314) till nearly full size. The outside is also smoothed. The slight bending in of the pot near the rim is made with smaller rolls, formed between the hands (315) and pressed into place with the thumb (316). The rim is finally formed and smoothed between thumb and finger (317), the clay being kept slightly wet by dipping the hand occasionally in water in a shell near by. The outside is finally smoothed and the ornament added. In the pot photographed this consisted of a thin roll of clay, pressed onto the surface of the foot with the thumb and finger so as to form an irregular zigzag line below the rim (318).

After drying the pots are burned, each carefully by itself. A base [of] sticks is arranged, on which the pot is placed, and sticks set up all around and over till the pot is completely covered and hid. It is then fired and more sticks added. Before finished it is reversed and fired again. The preparation

---

17. ABL probably means native mission teachers rather than German missionaries. Such evangelists would most likely come from Yabim as this is an Austronesian-speaking area.

18. Probably Hogbin's (1951) Buakap. Point Parsee was later the site of Salamaua, a town destroyed during the Second World War.

Fig. 3.30. "Pot making, Lokanu." A-32001 (308). This photo is one of thirteen images that together comprise the most complete sequence ABL took of pot making anywhere in Melanesia. ABL published eight other images from this sequence in his monograph (Lewis 1932; pl.40 and 41; 1951; 128–131): (306), (309), (311), (312), (313), (315), (316), (318).

is not regarded as completed till taro is cooked in the pot, thus testing it and adding a sort of gluey cement, which makes it stronger for transport. The natives are very particular that the bottom of the pots do not get rained on, as they say that then they break when put on the fire.

The houses here all show the effect of European contact, and very many of the natives speak Pidgin English.

On our return we had favorable wind, and arrived at Nu about 5 P.M. where stayed over night. This place is almost deserted for Wiakap, many old houses going to ruin. I slept in the men's house, which formerly had had

Fig. 3.31. "House where slept, Wusumu [Busama]." A-32030 (337).

carved and painted planks all around, but the best had been removed and the carved figures (fish, stones, dogs, etc.) broken off (by Capt. Voogdt).[19] The supporting posts, about 5 ft. high, had heads carved on top (Capt. Voogdt had bought these also, but so far had not removed them). There was little to be obtained here.

Saturday, March 12   Left about noon for Kela, where arrived in about 2 hrs. Stayed at the mission house.

Sunday, March 13   Left about 3 P.M. for Wusumu,[20] where arrived about 4:30. Looked around some, but bought nothing, tho much pressed by natives to do so. Saw a grave hut, which is made and left over the grave for about a week after burial, when it is removed and the grave covered with stones. The hut consisted of palm-leaf roof and sides, the eaves being about 2 ft. high. It was open at one end only.

Monday, March 14   Spent most of the morning buying, as the people here had many things of interest. Also took some photos. At 11 A.M. a wind was favorable, left for Logamu, where we arrived later in the afternoon.

Tuesday, March 15   Wished to go to Labo, but as wind was not favorable had to wait till 2 P.M. In about $1\frac{1}{2}$ hrs. we reached the entrance to the Herzogsee. Here we were joined by a Labo canoe, and as we proceeded several others met us, all the natives clamorous that I should buy their stuff, mostly bags and arm rings (bags made by themselves, and arm rings[21] from interior). The *see* itself is not very large, and the channel leading to it broad.

19. Field Museum purchased these house boards from Captain Voogdt in 1908.
20. Hogbin (1951, 1963) lived in this village, which he called Busama.
21. These are woven arm bands.

Fig. 3.32. "Cooking sago. The sago flour is taken from the Tami bowl and sifted with hands into the Lokanu pot, Wusumu [Busama]." A-32029 (336).

Fig. 3.33. "House in Labo, Hertzogsee." A-32038 (345).

Fig. 3.34. "Labo (island), Herzogsee."
A-32037 (344).

There are two small villages (1 & 2 [in sketch]) on each side of the channel, and a main village on an island (3) in the lake. This is not very large, and is almost covered by houses, which make a complete circle around the outside, their backs standing in water at low tide while at high tide most of island is covered. There are a few houses and cocoanut trees in center, also church. Found the people very anxious to sell their stuff, but there was nothing new, so bought little,[22] and the people were inclined to be angry because I did not buy more. Slept in men's house.

Wednesday, March 16   Left at daylight for Logamu, where arrived about 8 A.M. but stayed all day, as Tape said wind would not be good (was good till noon).

Thursday, March 17   Was up at 2 A.M. but as it took considerable time to get all our stuff to canoe did not get off till about 3:30. Proceeded till about 9 A.M., when the wind turned contrary, and we had to go ashore (at Wakanruhu).
   Here we stayed all day, it raining several hours. At night slept in house near beach, and

Friday, March 18   Got off about 3 A.M. arriving at Bukaua about 9 A.M.

Saturday, March 19   Developed 2 dozen plates and packed my specimens the best I was able, which was not very good as boxes were rare.

Sunday, March 20   Made arrangements for a canoe, and

---

22. His collection is more representative than he suggests. He actually bought 22 items in Labo: 9 bags, 6 head ornaments, 3 stone tools, 2 arm ornaments, 3 Tami bowls, a pillow, a knife, a spear, and a bark-cloth blanket.

Fig. 3.35. "Cooking taro, Logamu." A-32044 (351).

Monday, March 21   Got off about 9 A.M., for Finsch Hafen expecting to spend the night at Deinzerhöhe, but owing to head winds had to stop about noon at Ehe, where stayed till dusk, when left for Deinzerhöhe (Taimi [or] Tami nugatu) where arrived about 9 P.M. Slept in village.

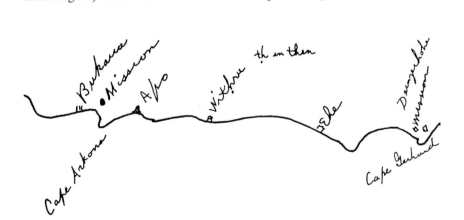

Tuesday, March 22   Early in morning went up to mission. Saw Herr Raum, bought some Laewomba hats, and got also some red cloth for trade. Then returned to the village and bought a few things from the natives. They seemed mostly to have carved cocoanuts, now. Raum said that they had heard that I would probably stop here, and that nearly everyone in the place was busy making new ones for me.[23]

---

23. ABL bought six of these carved cups; see Lewis (1925, plates XLVII–LII).

205

Fig. 3.36. Carved objects from the Huon Gulf: wooden *balum* figure, Jabim, 138440 (3933), from Georg Sturzenhofecker; wooden hook, Tami, 138428 (5460), from Komine; wooden bowl with turtle head at one end and figure of man on other, Tami, 138395 (2343) from Decker. A-112153.

Bowls did not seem to be numerous, tho possibly they kept back the good old ones. The same of pillows. Got 2 or 3 old ladles. People seemed to have very little of the old. Houses all new, and not in old style.

Returned to the mission for dinner and stayed till late in afternoon. Bought 5 Laewomba hats from Herr Raum, and some things from Herr Decker. Left Taimi about 5 P.M. and sailed [with] wind till 4 A.M. when stopped till daylight on an island, as wind was dead ahead.

Wednesday, March 23   Arrived in Finsch Hafen about 9 A.M. Stayed till afternoon, when went to Logaueng. Herr Schoede also came into port shortly after I did, from Siassi. He had been along the north coast to Dallmann Hafen,[24] and was returning by way of the south coast of New Britain to Herbertshöhe.

Thursday, March 24   Stayed in Logaueng till 4 P.M. Got some specimens from Herren Bamler, Meier and Hertle. Bamler founded the station on Tami, and from him I got chiefly Tami specimens. Some (house, M.75; photos, M.30; charms and *Barlum* sticks) were to be sent to the mission in Friedrich Wilhelms Hafen (Herr Helmich—Fragetta Island, also Herr Blum—Rheinische Mission). Herr Meier is an architect and surveyor, and has been over a good deal of the country between here and Dampier Island. From him I got a few specimens and some photos (glass celoidin positives) while some more things were to be sent to Friedrich Wilhelms Hafen. Herr Bamler showed me a number of potsherds found near there, representing a prehistoric pottery, and quite different from any at present known.

The return journey to Finsch Hafen took about 2 hrs.

---

24. ABL had met Schoede three months earlier at Cape Merkus. A large part of Schoede's collection from the north coast and a few other areas is now at the Museum für Völkerkunde in Leipzig.

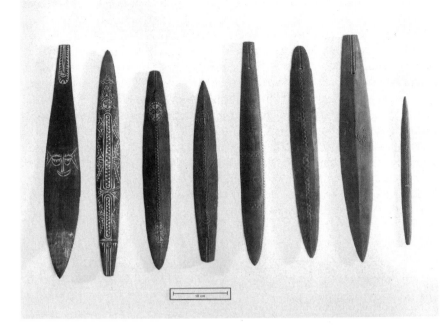

Fig. 3.37. Bull-roarers or *balum* sticks from the Huon Gulf: Finschhafen (from the Lutheran mission), 138341 (34), 138889 (32); Bukaua (from Lehner), 138221 (1744); Wusumu [Busama], 138060 (2002); Kalal, Tami Islands, 138474-3 (3920), from Bamler; Lokanu, 138089 (2053); Kalal, Tami Islands, 138477 (3921), from Bamler. Ornamented stick like a small bull-roarer *(balum)* worn under arm band by the man who makes the ceremony *(balum)* or causes it to be made (from Lehner). A-112157.

Friday, March 25   Good Friday and a holiday. Got ready for trip to Sattelberg.

Saturday, March 26   Left at 7 in boat for Heldsbach, where arrived about 9. Had my two boys and one extra rucksac. Left for Sattelberg, with native guide, at 11:45, and arrived at 3 P.M. Good path all the way, but in places on the smooth chalk rock a little slick for plain soled shoes. The way is cleared through the bush to a width of about 4 ft. Sattelberg is about 3,000 ft. high. I found I was the only visitor. The residents consist of Herr and Frau Keysser,

Fig. 3.38. "Hube (interior Papuan) men." A-32016 (323).

207

Fig. 3.39. Ornaments of the Hube people, two days' march (50–60 miles) west of Sattelberg, Papuans: hair ornament of netted string, nassa, orchid fiber (placed on a stick), 138630 (2204); "wood ornament stuck under armband so that the possessor may have good luck in buying pigs, when, for example, he goes to another village for that purpose," 138563 (2203). Red and blue pigments. Both from Keysser. A-112127.

2 children, and a missionary teacher (who is almost a hermit—saw him only once).

As this was Saturday, the natives were gathered in from all the surrounding villages, some nearly a day's journey. They come Saturday and spend the night there, and services are held early Sunday morning, so that the natives from a distance will have time to get back to their homes. Among these were a dozen or more Hube, a tribe closely related to the Kai living 3 to 4 day's journey west. I succeeded in photographing some of them and getting a few specimens. They are still cannibals. Herr Keysser has visited them and they are friendly. They came for a friendly visit, and also to get salt water. When they come to the shore they take a good drink and carry back the salt water in bamboo vessels to their home. They also take water (salt) soaked wood, esp. when decayed, dry and burn it, and then use the ashes as salt. In fact I have seen the coast natives when on their canoes eat the ashes from the fire sticks, saying it was salt.

Sunday, March 27   Read, wrote, and looked over some specimens and photos of Herr Keysser.

Monday, March 28   Started about 9 for a trip around through some of the neighboring villages lying N.E. and W. of Sattelberg. Visited first Tagi, which was only a short distance off the path to Heldsbach, almost ¾ hr. from the summit. Here was a tree-house built in the old style, but relatively new. On the way to the next village, Tembang, we passed two large trees which the natives said had in former times been occupied by tree houses. The third

Fig. 3.40.   "View of Sattelberg from tree on mountain back of station. Finschhafen in distance." A-32022 (329).

208

Fig. 3.41. "Tree house, Tagi." A-32047 (354).

village was Masangko. (These are really the names of districts, the villages are moved, divided or united every few years, and each time have a new name, while the name of the district, which belongs strictly to a certain group is permanent.) The name of the last village was Bolimbonem (*village* name). This was a full 2 hrs. west of Sattelberg. Our route was something like this:

Part of the way on the slopes below Sattelberg, the way was through dense bamboo thickets; at other times grass. West it was all primeval forest. Bolimbonem had a fine situation on a ridge of the mountains, with magnificent view over mountain and valley. Here were fine banana groves, but *new*, due to mission influence.

Got back at 6:30. Talked most of evening.

Tuesday, March 29   In morning printed pictures from Keysser's plates. In evening developed a dozen of mine. Herr Keysser did the work.

Wednesday, March 30   Labeled specimens and photos up to nearly 11 A.M. when left with my specimens (bought a number from Herr Keysser) for Heldsbach, where arrived in 2½ hrs. Here ate and talked till 4, when left for Finsch Hafen with guide, the specimens being left to come the following day. Arrived at Pola at 6 P.M.

Thursday, March 31–Saturday, April 2   Spent the time labeling and packing specimens, photo, outfit, etc. for steamer. Met Herr Bröker[25] and Herr [Rudolf Oldörp], Capt. of *Lettie*. They were bound for the Markham river, where they expected to spend nearly 2 months recruiting and looking for gold in the tributaries toward the English boundary. Bröker said the *Lettie* would return to Friedrich Wilhelms Hafen early in June, and then make a trip of about 2 months duration along the coast to Eitape or further.

Sunday, April 3   Had Herr Bröker and [Oldörp] to dinner. Herr Meier and Regierungsrat Wiedenfeld,[26] with the 4 from the plantation, were also present. Fried chicken, gravy, etc. In afternoon visited *Lettie*.

Monday, April 4   Spent most of day writing and arranging things.

Tuesday, April 5   *Manila* came about 12 M.

---

25. ABL spelled his name Brücke. A few days after ABL met Bröker and Oldörp, the *Lettie* was swamped in a gale as they entered Huon Gulf. Both Bröker and Oldörp died in the accident on 14 April 1910 (*Amtsblatt* 1910, 102).

26. ABL had met Riegerungsrat Wiedenfeld with Governor Hahl on the trip to Eitape in September 1909. His identity is unclear because some sources refer to him as Wiedenfeld, suggesting he is Kurt Wiedenfeld; others call him v. Wiedenfeld or von Wiedenfeld.

HUON GULF—LANGUAGES

All the coastal people from Bonga, some 30 miles north of Finsch Hafen to Laukanu, south of Parsee Pt. belong practically to the same group, tho divided into two linguistic groups, tho the difference is hardly more than dialectic. The Jabim extend from Bonga to Schollenbruch Pt. and the Bukaua from there to Laukanu. Beyond Laukanu there are no coast villages for nearly a day's journey, and then come the Kaiwa (Papuans), quite a different people. The Tami people also speak a related language. These are Melanesian.

In the interior, often only a few hrs. from the coast, are the various Kai tribes, with other closely related, all speaking Papuan languages, yet these all belonging to one general group (according to Herr Keysser) differing in vocabulary, but the same in syntax. The Poum (on coast north of Bonga) are of the same group. The interior people back of Kela are also known as Kai.

The Kai are all mountain tribes. On the Markham river are found another people, known as the Laewomba (Papuan).

MANUFACTURERS AND TRADE

In culture the coastal peoples (Jabim and Bukaua) are much the same. Certain industries are localized, and certain villages have much better artisans than others. In all wood work and carving the Tami people excel. They make the best carved pillows, wood spoons and ladles, tortoise shell armrings. The wooden bowls (found from west N. Britain to far south in Huon Gulf) are made by them (Tami Islands and Taminugatu or Taimi). *Only* pots for the whole region are made in Laukanu, tho the people also get pots from the Laewomba (on Markham river) and a few from the north coast (Kelana). The Kai around Sattelberg, for example, get almost all their pots from the north coast. On the gulf coast these pots are not found.

Fig. 3.42. Wooden suspension hook, Wusumu [Busama]. Incised designs filled with white, with red and black paint between, 138059 (1994). A-112135.

Fig. 3.43. Earthen pots from the Huon Gulf: from Lokanu, 137909 (2083); bought from Kai people near Sattelberg but made on the North Coast, probably Kelana, 137928 (2254); Laewomba pots collected at Apo, 137912 (2130), and at Bukaua, 137920 (1960), 137921 (1954). A-112119.

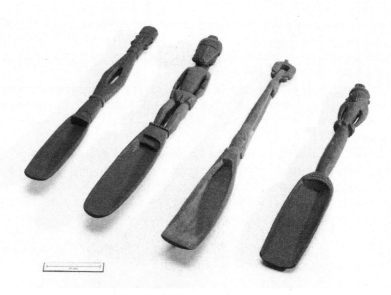

Fig. 3.44. Wooden taro ladles. From Wusumu [Busama], 138055 (2023), 138053 (1988); from Finschhafen (purchased from the Lutheran mission), 138366 (14); from Wusumu [Busama], 138054 (1986). A-112138.

BAGS, ARMBANDS

The Kai make fine netted bags, used by the women as carrying bag, also as a back ornament in many places, esp. when finely woven and nicely decorated. The Jabim make few bags, and these coarse. The Bukaua make rather coarse bags, used chiefly for carrying, tho some inland villages make finer ones, esp. Yao, where finely made and decorated bags are made (so the natives say—may come from Kai further inland, but I think not, as in Bukaua I saw the women making nicely woven ornamented bags) esp. long and narrow. The Kai south of the Markham river make arm bands of the yellow stems of a kind of orchid, which grows only high up in the mountains. The Kai armbands (of this fibre) are different for different regions, and the coast tribes also use the same fibre, but in quite a different way. The black fibre of a coarse fungus growing on decaying logs in the mountain forests is also much used, (this fibre comes chiefly from back of Sattelberg, and is usually larger than that from N. Britain).

CANOES, HOUSES

The best canoes are also made in Tami, esp. the large 2 masted sailing canoes, with one side board, in nearly all the coast villages.

In house building the Tami people also excelled, but now all the old houses are gone. Carving was more general than along the coast (for account of Bukaua house see above Feb. 17–Mar. 6) as the family house was often with carved boards, and even posts. In addition to the regular men's house *(lum)* there was a special *Barlum lum* made for this occasion only, and then allowed to decay. In Tami there was a specially decorated variety of this, with finely carved boards and posts, and wooden masks (like the masks of Rook Island) on roof, and carved figures lying under the house. The *lum* was nearly square, the longer ones such as seen at Parsee Pt. (Nu) are a recent thing.

The Kai had only a family house, no men's house. This was originally built (around Sattelberg, at least, according to Herr Keysser) square, with

Fig. 3.45.   String bag (*ba*), collected Bukaua, made in Yao. "Most of the long, ornamented bags come from the Yao, who make longer and finer bags than the Bukaua." 138155 (1814). A-112313.

one center post, and roof and sides of leaves, or of bark slab arranged horizontally on sides. Later a rectangular house was built with two end posts and a ridge pole (this was introduced from the Jabim) and at present the sides are of boards (See Keysser's photos[27] showing different stages).

---

27. ABL bought a number of photos from Keysser, twelve of which survive. None are reproduced here.

Fig. 3.46. "Woman making netted bag (138166), Bukaua." A-31989 (296).

DRESS, ORNAMENTS

The dress of the men was usually in two parts (of bark) on a girdle, and the other a piece passed under the girdle and between the legs. This was sometimes painted, but most of the painted bark cloth came from the north coast or Siassi, whence also came the long painted *mal*s used in N. Britain.

The women's dress was a short skirt, broken on the sides (i.e., not continuous all around) made of fibre. On the coast it was usually made from the leaves of the sago palm; among the Kai from the leaves of the cocoanut. Further inland from string, and still further from grass. Ornamental extra pieces were added for dances, etc.

Ornaments are numerous, but at the present time there are many introduced from elsewhere by returned laborers. Carved bamboo combs, feather head ornaments, forehead bands, round breast ornaments of shells, other breast ornaments, also carried in mouth in fighting, armbands, etc. for men. For women netted hoods of string, ornamental bags on back (many such are seen in a Sunday service at Bukaua), arm bands, etc. Both men and women now wear the hair short, tho formerly the men wore it long and hanging down the back in sort of curls.

The men usually carry a bag with lime flask, betel and fruit or leaves of some other plant,—also many other small personal possessions. In Bukaua

Fig. 3.47. Model of two-masted Tami canoe, Tami Islands, 138430 (37). From the Lutheran mission, Finschhafen. A-112146.

these bags were small and of a special weave, and were made by the men. The Laewomba bags were small, but more like the ordinary netted bag. In most places an ordinary bag not too large, and of fine mesh, is at present used. Also the Labo bags are used.

The lime flask is seldom decorated, but always has a shell ring at mouth, and usually 1, 2 or more rows of nassa shells stuck with gum around neck at mouth. Spatula frequently has bone handle, with pendants.

WEAPONS

Weapons are now rare, but formerly consisted of spears and wood club, with shield. Stone clubs, when used, were probably obtained from the Kai who still have them. These are usually disk shaped, with edge, occasionally star shaped, and rarely pointed or spherical. The shape also varied with the locality, but all these were found near Sattelberg.

Bows and arrows came from the afar interior, at least the ornamented arrows, fish arrows, and possibly bows, were made on the coast. Spears were of wood, with plain or barbed point, sometimes carved and ornamented with feathers, shells, etc. Details varied with most every village.

PILLOWS, BOWLS, FOOD

Wooden pillows have been mentioned. The finest were made in Tami, and widely distributed. The most common Tami designs were an animal, a kneeling man, often with snake behind, and 2 kneeling men, one at each end. Some of these (esp. 2 kneeling men) are imitated in other places, but not very well. The Tami bowls had the trade mark of the family in the center below.

215

Fig. 3.48. *"Tago* mask, bamboo frame covered with painted bark, with fringe of white feathers and bunch of cassowary feathers on top *(kalug)*, Tami," 138433). From Bamler. A-112328.

Fig. 3.49. Large carved female figure, Huon Gulf style, west end of New Britain. Red, black, and white pigment, 137383 (5469). From Komine. A-112303.

Fig. 3.50. Stone-headed clubs from the Huon Peninsula: disc-shaped head with bunch of feathers at end, Girogat, Cromwell Mountains near Cape Konig Wilhelm (from Hans Meier), 138590 (2281); disc-shaped head with ring of nassa, Kai people near Sattelberg (ABL), 138586 (2263); star-shaped head with cassowary feathers at handle, Hube people, two days' march (50–60 miles) west of Sattelberg (from Keysser), 138582 (2208). A-112185.

Fine carved drums, with faces; mortar for mashing taro, with pestle, were also made by the Tami.

Taro, usually boiled in the Laukanu pots, is here the chief food of the natives, tho they have many others, esp. sweet potato and banana, with many kinds of greens, fish, snails, etc.

NETS

They have pig net *(hū)*, tho not of the size found in New Britain. Rectangular small nets (say 8 by 12 ft.), nets for catching birds (seen among Kai), long nets for birds; nets for some forest animal, both long and small round, used on end of stick. Of fish nets the Bukaua had at least 4 varieties:

> *apū*, a large net held by 4 men (it is let down on one side) and then a number of men drive the fish toward and into the net, when this side is raised, and the fish thus enclosed (about 10 by 15 to 20 ft.). It is made from *tu*.
>
> *kātā*, a small dip net used on the end of a pole, made from *tu*;
>
> *pūtingāsang*, net held by 2 poles, with crosspiece, made from *tu*;

217

gwa (kwa), a round net with circular opening used by women, by hand; made from *tu* or *aúhō*.

FIBRES AND OBJECTS FOR WHICH USED, BUKAUA

The ornamental bags *(ābūmbē)* are made chiefly from *īsēlē*, also *sūālū*. The large carrying bags *(abrū)* from *auho, kwati (gati)* or *suálu.*

Fibres — *tu (du)* used for fish nets.

auho [for] large bags, sometimes canoe rope.

kwati — large bags, making house bindings, and canoe ropes.

ísele — ornamental bags.

sualu (large forest tree) [for] netted bags of all kinds, [and] pig nets.

wain — canoe binding.

pi (tumbi) — used for armbands (fine, black).

Leaf of *auho* is used for cigarettes.

FIBRES AND OBJECTS FOR WHICH USED, KAI

[Fibres]   [Objects]

sähe — he

wede — siwi, he

pipisa gbagbaue (ming-gbabga) — he, singsing [whitish] *— ufi lepane*

pipisa babalong (ming-barlong) — he, singsing, ufi lepane [reddish]

gāle — he, ufi, singsing

gäpi — simengeng (also *kata* of Jabim)

geuggong — ufi, siwi

muzuc — he

wäwe — ufi, also fastening stone axes   {cultivated}

gäubo — ufi-glängeng, singsing   {cultivated}

bäläng — ufi

{explanations of objects above}

he = netted bag
siwi = fish net
singsing = woman's skirt
ufi = pig net   *{lepane* = cord at top}
simengeng = crab net

COLORS FOR STRING, ETC. KAI

Būge—plant used to color strings for bags, etc., black. The leaves are chewed, and the chewed mass held in the hand while the strings are drawn through it. This is done after string twisted, and before weaving. The color is a dark bluish green.

Gbondäng—a grass, chewed and used in same way as *Būge*. Gives light green color.

Barlong (= red)—To color the string red it is boiled in a mixture of the following: (a) a red insect (*gaile gisi* = insect boiled with sago); (b) a red herb (*gili);* (c) the young reddish leaves of sago (*gai-gaza* = sago leaf which is red); (d) the red leaves of a tree *(gbozäli)*, the old leaves when ready to fall off turn red. This is made by women only, the men must not be present.

[SOCIAL ORGANIZATION]

The social organization is very loose. There are no true chiefs, and the villages are practically independent. The *Barlum* organization seems to be the chief center of power and authority. There is one in every village, tho each has also many members scattered in other villages. The badge of membership is the *barlum* stick or bullroarer. When a man is made a member he receives one of these. A man of another village may be made a member as an honor. He then becomes, as it were, a member of that village, is regarded as such when he visits them, and in turn must entertain in his own village all visitors from there. Every member must be elected, so to speak, but a man has a right to demand membership in his *mother's* village. A man may be a member in several villages, but is not recognized as a man till he has passed through the *barlum* ceremony. As these are often over 20 yrs. apart, he may be a married man before he is a member, but he still has only a boy's privileges, is forbidden to eat certain foods (as the boys), has no voice in public matters, is not allowed in the *lum* or men's house, etc.

The ceremony is theoretically the initiation to manhood, and practically a test of endurance and instruction in the men's secrets, with circumcision (the prepuce is slit, according to Bamler, varies in different localities) as a mark of membership.

The word *barlum (balum)* has several meanings: (a) the spirit of a dead person (all become *barlum*s, and are feared; the people also recognize the

Fig. 3.51. Headrests or wooden pillows with designs: collected Apo ("from Logamu"), 138095 (2103); collected Lokanu ("from Tami"), 138426 (2052); collected Taminugetu ("from Ehe"), 138381 (2193); Finschhafen, 138355 (8); collected Apo ("from Logamu"), 138094 (2103); collected Bukaua ("from Tami"), 138424 (1791); collected Wusumu [Busama], ("from Tami"), 138418 (1998). A-112167.

spirits, who give help and good luck). (b) the *balum* stick. One or two in each village have names, of important persons, occasionally of a living person. (c) a monster without arms and legs, who is supposed to swallow the candidates, and later (when appeased by hogs) to throw them up. They then become stronger and larger. He is represented by a specially constructed house *(lum),* into which the candidates go (before circumcision, having first passed under the village *balum* sticks, each on the long bamboo pole (15 ft. long ornamented with cassowary feathers—the chief one covered, the others in places). The string is just long enough that when held upright the *balum* stick touches the ground. It is with these poles that the *balum*s are swung, but when so used a duplicate is substituted, to prevent loss of the regular *balum* stick. (For details of the ceremony, see "Der Balumskultus bai den Einge-boren Neu-Guineas," by Missionary Vetter [1896b]).

The candidates must undergo preparation in their own village (in a specially constructed *lum*) for several weeks before coming to the village where the ceremony is held, and afterward must remain concealed for a time. They are often severely tested by whipping, and receive much good council, and are given rules of good conduct, as: Do not steal, strike the children, or another's dog or hog, bewitch people, etc.

The Sepik Coast of Kaiser Wilhelmsland

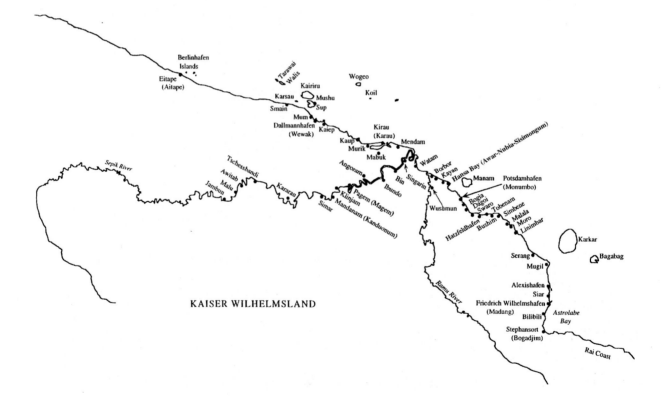

KAISER WILHELMSLAND

Book

Friedrich Wilhelmshafen and the North Coast

||||||||||||||||||||||||||||||||||||||||||||||||||||||||||||||||||||||||||||||||||||||||||||||||||||||||||||||||||||||||||||||||||||||||

5 April 1910–24 September 1910

By the time of his return to Friedrich Wilhelmshafen in the spring of 1910, ABL had been away from Chicago for eleven months. His field experiences were now extensive enough for him to have a growing sense of self-confidence in his research. And he was beginning to fashion something of a systematic research strategy. This strategy was not a research plan devised in Chicago, but one developed in the field in much the same way that, in Fiji, he developed his own working definition of what constitutes a systematic collection.

Sitting in Chicago, ABL could never have anticipated the cultural diversity he found in New Guinea; empirically, there was simply too little known about cultural variation. Nor would he have expected the variation from one community to another that was all too apparent in the field. Nearly every village he visited in New Guinea differed in unexpected and unpredictable ways from its neighbors, even though neighboring villages nearly always had a great deal in common. In this respect, ABL was the first—and for many years, the only—American anthropologist to recognize Melanesia's remarkable diversity, a fact that would continue to confound most anthropologists who would follow him to New Guinea for the rest of the century.[1]

His observations during eight months in New Guinea clearly showed that cultural variation, though poorly documented, was a characteristic feature of Melanesia. Diversity was not a special trait of only the Eitape coast, southwest New Britain, or the Huon Gulf; it was prominent in all three areas and could be expected along the entire north coast of Kaiser Wilhelmsland. With this realization, ABL arrived in Friedrich Wilhelmshafen preparing to make a systematic tour along the rest of the north coast to document how these communities both resembled and differed from one another.

In 1910, documenting cultural variation was one of the chief tasks of ethnology. Without more or less detailed data it was impossible either to describe or to explain observed distributions of particular cultural features, nor was it possible to account for complex configurations of traits. ABL's (1906b) doctoral dissertation had dealt with cultural diversity among the American Indian tribes along the Washington and Oregon coasts. Drawing exclusively on published sources, he had attempted to delineate the cultural influences that had shaped these diverse

Indian communities. During this earlier research, he had repeatedly faced the problem of explaining distributions that were poorly documented in the literature. Now, on the north coast of Kaiser Wilhelmsland, he was in a position to document for himself a kind of diversity similar to that which he had confronted in the literature on Washington and Oregon. Indeed, one might argue that of the many parts of North America ABL might have studied for his dissertation, he chose the one region that would most resemble what he would find in German New Guinea.

ABL's strategy in Kaiser Wilhelmsland was now to collect sizeable samples of material culture in as many villages as possible. These objects would—he hoped—illuminate both cultural similarities and cultural differences. As before, nearly everywhere he traveled during his next two months around Friedrich Wilhelmshafen and Potsdamhafen he found striking cultural similarities. And just as in Eitape, nearly every community was linked by trade to communities speaking different languages. In his fourth notebook, observations of what was similar and what was different along the coast became part of ABL's standard research protocol. These were not, of course, the only field notes he wrote, but his continual reference to similarities and differences in material culture was a strategic part of his research program.

When possible he regularly tried to collect examples of both commonplace and unusual objects. He was, of course, dependent in his collecting on the desires of the villagers: he could purchase only those items that villagers would sell him. To guide the interaction, he might ask for specific kinds of items to be brought out for sale, but ultimately the villagers both set prices and determined what he could collect. In this sense ABL's situation was much as O'Hanlon (1993) has discussed for his own museum collecting for the British Museum in the Wahgi Valley.[2] As O'Hanlon suggests, without coercion field collecting is never as one-sided as recent critics have suggested, but is always a complex matter of negotiation between villager and collector.

Yet while the villagers may have determined what was offered for sale, it was ABL who decided whether or not to buy what was offered, and these decisions illustrate both his biases and his research goals.

ABL had come to Melanesia to study traditional culture. Ironically, although he was a student of culture change and how one culture influenced another, he had very little interest in how Melanesian cultures were being influenced by Europeans and the colonial experience. He cared little about changes resulting from contact with the modern world. As a result, during four years in the field ABL bought very few examples of objects decorated with beads, cloth, or paper, even though his diaries confirm that in many communities such items were common.[3]

For example, on 12 April 1910 he wrote the following about his visit to Panim village several hours inland from what is now Madang.

> After that I made some photos, and bought a few things. Not much here. Pots from Bilibili. Also a few from the interior, thin coiled ware. Got 4 of these. Bowls (wood) from Rai coast; a few old shields, and spears, ornaments not many (compared to islands), and a tendency to mix in beads. Saw one dance mask or headdress, shaped like a house, with a long pole on top, covered with feathers and cloth. The house was of painted bark, also paper and cloth, so that it was of no worth. Had been made for the Christmas dances.

He bought 18 items (4 pots, 6 bull-roarers, 2 bamboo tubes, 1 comb, 1 string bag, 1 bow, 2 arrows, and 1 spear), but apparently the villagers were not willing to part with their wooden bowls and old shields, items that ABL would almost certainly have collected. At the same time,

224

ABL bought none of the ornaments with beads on them, and he makes it clear that the headdress of a house made for the Christmas dances was of no value for his research because it contained cloth and paper. In other cases, ABL bought string bags or carrying baskets together with all of their contents to illustrate the people's ordinary daily possessions, but he gave back without even noting what was returned all the iron and European goods. Such items seemed (to him) somehow illegitimate because they were examples of a corrupted or tainted traditional culture.

Before the Great War and for several decades afterward, virtually all anthropologists were concerned primarily with traditional societies and cultures in much the same way that ABL was. British functionalists like E. E. Evans-Pritchard (1940) or Raymond Firth (1936) were just as biased, excluding evidence of how the communities they studied had been influenced by pacification, the colonial administration, and European contact generally. In their monographs, both anthropologists described the communities as if they were isolated societies that were still unchanged, despite what we know to have been decades of foreign contact. Even Malinowski (1922) wrote of the Trobriand Islanders in the "ethnographic present" as if they had been only vaguely aware of the Methodist missionaries, the resident magistrates (one of whom lived in the Trobriands), and several hundred miners working on Woodlark Island to the east. While ABL was clearly biased against collecting material that blatantly displayed the effects of European contact, he did not completely ignore such materials in his notes and diary.

One of ABL's other collecting biases should also be mentioned here because it bears directly on his broader research goals. At several villages in the Huon Gulf and later on the north coast he writes in his diary that there was nothing new in a particular village and that he thus bought little there. To the casual reader, it may seem that ABL was biasing his collection to emphasize the differences between villages, but this was not the case. His diary is often understated in such instances, and he nearly always bought more than his dismissive text may suggest.

Moreover, as he visited a series of adjacent villages he inevitably saw numerous examples of the same kinds of plain, undecorated, and nondescript everyday items—such objects as lime gourds, bark buckets, and bone tools.[4] A few examples of these items obtained in one village was (in ABL's mind) sufficient to represent these things in the entire series of villages. Because they had no distinctive designs or motifs, these plain and extremely commonplace objects had, for him, little importance for distinguishing one material culture assemblage from another.

Today, we may wish ABL had obtained examples of the same undecorated items from every village, because such a collection would provide strong empirical evidence of the underlying similarity among these villages. Such similarities, however, were not as important for him as the similarities and differences in more decorated objects; only the latter offered much hope of helping him sort out the cultural influences that had been operating along the coast to shape and create the communities he observed. This field strategy was a bias in his collecting philosophy, but it was a systematic practice that became part of his basic research plan; and, of course, as he acquired things he steadily depleted his stores of trade goods. In each new village visited he became more reluctant to waste his supply of fish hooks, beads, cloth, and steel on items that had little importance for his research.

When ABL left Finschhafen for Friedrich Wilhelmshafen he had successfully surveyed three key areas in the colony—Eitape, west New Britain, and the Huon Gulf—and had found important trade linkages between at least two of them. Now, on his return to the north coast of Kaiser Wilhelmsland, he hoped to survey other areas that were also linked, both to Eitape on the west and New Britain and the Huon Peninsula on the east.

225

Concerns at Friedrich Wilhelmshafen

On arriving in Friedrich Wilhelmshafen, ABL had much to do and much to think about before setting off on his next excursion along the coast. As yet *none* of his collection had been shipped back to Chicago. Soon after he arrived in German New Guinea, ABL received instructions from Field Museum recorder D. C. Davies[5] that no specimens should be shipped until new shipping instructions were forwarded; the museum was negotiating more advantageous terms for freight charges with the railroads and naturally wanted ABL to hold off for a month or two until the parties agreed upon a new arrangement. Unfortunately, the new instructions did not arrive in New Guinea for another six months, and by this time ABL had long since left one-third of his collection in Eitape to be sent on to Friedrich Wilhelmshafen later. Another part of the collection had been left at Cape Merkus to be sent on to Herbertshöhe, and the rest he took with him from Finschhafen to Friedrich Wilhelmshafen. By that time ABL had collected more than twenty-five hundred objects, of which some four hundred pieces were in Rabaul; the rest were in Friedrich Wilhelmshafen or Eitape. A daunting task of packing and shipping awaited him.

In addition to the more mundane matter of packing and shipping specimens, ABL was trying to plan his fieldwork for the next six months. As before he had to arrange transportation, which was not always an easy task in New Guinea. Motorized vessels were in short supply and expensive, and even sailing vessels were hard to come by. Then, too, ABL had to get his supplies of trade goods. He would have to ask around to find out what kinds of goods were desired in different parts because local preferences for imported goods were often as varied as local cultures.

He wanted to make a systematic sweep westward along the coast from Friedrich Wilhelmshafen as far as Dallmannhafen. A tour along this stretch would link up with his earlier work around Eitape, providing data about communities along four hundred miles of the north coast. ABL also seems to have hoped for a quick trip to the east along the Rai coast to link up with his work out of Finschhafen, though this tour never materialized.[6]

In addition, ABL desperately wanted to visit the Kaiserin Augusta River, which already had a worldwide reputation for its fine carvings. But traveling upriver for any distance required a steamer or motor schooner, and such ships were hard to find in German New Guinea. Even when one was available, chartering a schooner or steamer was expensive. Planning for a trip up the river required certain guarantees of funds from the museum, a luxury ABL had heretofore not enjoyed.

When ABL landed at Friedrich Wilhelmshafen, he soon learned about something that would materially affect his work on the north coast: George A. Dorsey's articles in the *Chicago Daily Tribune*. Indeed, these articles threatened everything ABL had planned and much of what had already been accomplished.

Dorsey's *Tribune* Articles

Three months after ABL left Chicago, Field Museum curator Dorsey (1909a) began publishing a series of articles in the *Chicago Daily Tribune* describing his trip around the world in 1908. At the time, the *Tribune* was filled with scandalmongering and sensational stories. Dorsey's articles consisted of a hundred popularly written columns—purported to be transcripts from his field diary. The original diary is now lost, but one suspects that Dorsey enhanced his diary entries to make them more appealing to a general audience whose tastes ran toward the salacious. These columns are filled with unflattering descriptions of the many people he met along the way. Often Dorsey seems to have self-consciously played on typical American stereotypes of peoples in foreign parts to add excitement to his columns.

The columns started running in mid-August, dealing first with a visit to Egypt where Dorsey arranged for Field Museum to acquire an ancient Egyptian tomb, several mummies, and other artifacts that Chicago philanthropist Edward E. Ayer had purchased.[7] Dorsey then visited India, the Dutch East Indies, and Australia before arriving in the remote colony of German New Guinea. He spent two months in the colony being wined, dined, and well looked after by his German hosts, who included the governor as well as New Guinea Compagnie officials Georg Heine and Capt. H. Voogdt. His columns about New Guinea ran from 18 September to 6 October—the very time that ABL, Dorsey's assistant curator, was beginning serious work in the colony.

Several of Dorsey's columns contained insulting references to German staff of the New Guinea Compagnie who had assisted him in New Guinea. Among the most incendiary of these was a passage in the column of 6 October 1909, describing—perhaps too publicly—Dorsey's thoughts the evening before his departure from Friedrich Wilhelmshafen and German New Guinea:

> The steamer will surely arrive tomorrow. I think I could not wait another day. With one's work finished, it is not pleasant to tarry here, with the malaria demon hovering over you day and night, with the sordidness of the life of the Germans, the routine of indolent, lazy days broken only by shaking dice for beer at the public house, the intolerance of the whites for the natives, their violent language and often brutal treatment of these children of nature and the constant talk against the new tariff and the overpopulation of the colony by missionaries and officials.

A German living in Chicago sent these columns to Heine, the chief administrator of the New Guinea Compagnie in Kaiser Wilhelmsland. Heine took particular umbrage at this passage; he was specifically mentioned earlier in this particular column and therefore thought (probably correctly) that these remarks referred specifically to him.

Heine had in fact been more than accommodating—as Dorsey noted elsewhere in the same column. Voogdt, too, skipper of the company's steamer *Siar,* was stunned by Dorsey's comments, so much so that in a letter to Dorsey he asked rhetorically why Dorsey did such a thing.[8]

Heine was so infuriated by the columns that he sent a formal letter of protest (reproduced below) to several German and American newspapers. This notice, signed just before Christmas 1909 by sixty-one Germans living in the colony, was published several months later.

Ironically, ABL seems to have left Rabaul for Cape Merkus just before word of the Dorsey columns arrived and inflamed German reaction against him. Thus, for three months ABL went about his work at Cape Merkus and in the Huon Gulf apparently unaware of the anger and resentment that was building up against Dorsey, against Field Museum, and against ABL himself. Both Cape Merkus and Finschhafen were, in their different ways, isolated from the social life and contentions of Herbertshöhe and Friedrich Wilhelmshafen. The Lutherans at Finschhafen would probably have shared many of Dorsey's sentiments about the New Guinea Compagnie and the lifestyle it fostered. The mission clearly did not hinder ABL's work at Finschhafen, and they do not seem to have warned ABL about the reaction he should expect from the company either. But almost as soon as ABL disembarked at Friedrich Wilhelmshafen, he learned directly of Heine's anger over the Dorsey columns.[9]

Heine and virtually all of the New Guinea Compagnie's employees refused to help Field Museum in any way. The company would not allow ABL to travel on its steamer or use its facilities. Company officials grudgingly agreed to transport ABL's specimens, but at much higher freight charges than they had previously offered. And the company absolutely refused to pack his specimens or to provide him with lumber, boxes, and other packing materials. As ABL soon found out, many of his specimens were still in Eitape, and the company would do nothing to help him retrieve them. His growing enthusiasm for his research was quickly dampened as he learned of Dorsey's newspaper columns and the profound effect these would have on his own research.

ABL never mentions this unsettling state of affairs in his field diaries. He did, however, describe the disruptive conditions within which he was forced to operate in three surviving letters, each written about two months apart.[10] Each is reproduced here (following the introductions to his diaries from Friedrich Wilhelmshafen, the north coast, and the Kaiserin Augusta River, respectively) because they provide somewhat different personal insights into how these conditions influenced ABL's research.

These three letters detail the severe difficulties ABL had in moving around on the north coast of Kaiser Wilhelmsland. They also document the anger he repeatedly faced and had to deal with in Friedrich Wilhelmshafen. ABL wrote in his letters that he was socially ostracized by nearly all the Germans. Governor Hahl told him personally that Dorsey had "killed the Museum" in the colony.

There can be no doubt that the company made life difficult for ABL in countless ways, but hostility was not invariably the attitude of the *kiaps*, the missionaries (both Catholic and Lutheran), and a handful of independent planters and traders. Even two company agents—Richter and Blesser—helped ABL during his travels. One can only conclude that ABL wrote to Dorsey with some hyperbole, probably in a state of frustration and incredulity over what ABL must have felt was Dorsey's stupidity. In practical terms, such insensitive remarks by Dorsey about his former hosts were foolish at best, especially when his own assistant curator was still in the field relying on the goodwill of these same men.[11]

This episode illustrates how dependent anthropologists in the field have always been upon the goodwill of residents, both villagers and expatriates. Without this goodwill it is virtually impossible to conduct any kind of careful and systematic fieldwork.

Fieldwork on the North Coast

Despite the obstacles put in his way, ABL was surprisingly successful in making a systematic survey of the coast. He made several trips to the interior behind Friedrich Wilhelmshafen with Police Master Stuben—whom ABL had met in Eitape—and to Ragetta and Siar, where he was assisted by Rhenisch Lutheran missionaries Blum and Helmich.[12] At Alexishafen, Bogia, and Monumbo he was helped once again by SVD missionaries. Richter and Blesser of the New Guinea Compagnie assisted him in Potsdamhafen and occasionally in other places. But most of all during these five months on the coast he was aided by Wilhelm Gramms of Awar plantation at Hansa Bay. ABL had met Gramms in Potsdamhafen in early December after leaving Eitape for Friedrich Wilhelmshafen and Herbertshöhe; Gramms had invited him to visit Awar during the dry season and made good on his offer of assistance.[13]

Around Friedrich Wilhelmshafen ABL visited communities that were among the most profoundly influenced by contact with Germans. These villages had been evangelized by the Lutherans; large tracts of their lands had been alienated by the company; and they were being administered harshly by German *kiaps* (see, e.g., Hempenstall 1978). To prevent all the village land from being transformed into New Guinea Compagnie plantations, the administration had

228

even been forced to establish reserves or reservations around Friedrich Wilhelmshafen (see, e.g., Sprigade and Moisel 1903–1912, No. 26, inset K1). ABL seems to have enjoyed good relations with people in these villages, but only a few years earlier Friedrich Wilhelmshafen had been the site of an armed insurrection (Hempenstall 1978, 188–190).

Conditions were considerably different on the coast to the west. Compared with Friedrich Wilhelmshafen, the coast from Hatzfeldhafen and Potsdamhafen to Hansa Bay and Kayan was virtually undeveloped. There were few Europeans living on this part of the coast, and the material culture was considerably less well known to the outside world. Once ABL made Awar plantation his base camp, his fieldwork again resembled his earlier research at Sissano. The villages were far from uncontacted, but they were virtually unevangelized, and only insignificant amounts of land had been alienated for European plantations.

Transportation was the only major problem along this stretch of coast, but ABL was able to charter a cutter from Gramms, captained by a New Ireland man named Laias. Based at Awar, ABL could avoid most of the company's unpleasantness, and he began what appears to have been a very cordial relationship with Gramms, probably the warmest relationship ABL established with any of the Germans in the colony.

To help him with his work around Awar, ABL still had two of his original assistants, Kaman (from Karsau Island near Wewak) and Kabai (from Buka). Marumu, his third assistant, seems to have left ABL's employ and may have returned to his home village in the Warie district of west New Britain some months earlier. In addition to his regular staff, ABL hired at different times four men from Hansa Bay as interpreters: Tarep and Bogasu from Awar village, Saii from Sisimongum, and Baa from Nubia. Elsewhere he took on other interpreters and field assistants. From these various interpreters and assistants ABL obtained a number of word lists, none of which is reproduced here.

Unlike his sojourn in the Huon Gulf, where he was principally in the very European world of the Lutheran mission, ABL was now in a world peopled principally by New Guineans. He dined from time to time with Gramms, Richter, one of the Catholic priests, or even one of the Chinese traders, but most of his time was spent with villagers, interpreters, and assistants.

{Editor's note: This concludes the letter ABL wrote to Dorsey soon after his arrival in Friedrich Wilhelmshafen in April 1910. ABL wrote two other letters discussing the effect of Dorsey's Tribune articles on his work; these letters, to Field Museum director Skiff and to assistant curator S. C. Simms, are reproduced later.}

Friedrich Wilhelms Hafen
May 1, 1910

Dear Dr. Dorsey:

. . .

In April the <u>Manila</u> made one of its visits to Finsch Hafen (comes only once in a month) and I came on it to Fr. Wh. Hafen, where I have been ever since, packing and shipping my specimens, (only part, most are still in other places. I could not ship before, as the shipping directions you told me to wait for did not reach me till the middle of February, sent to Arawe by the recruiting schooner), developing plates, visiting the neighboring villages, etc.

The steamer comes tomorrow from Hongkong, and also the mission steamer Gabriel, by which I hope to be able to go to Potsdam Hafen, and from there get boats or cutter to go further along the coast. And here I must mention a thing which has materially changed the aspect of things here, has made me change my plans, and may make me leave German Territory sooner than I expected. Some one in Chicago sent to Mr. Heine a copy of your articles on New Guinea, and at some of the things you wrote, especially just when leaving here, Mr. Heine, as well as others, took serious offense. Mr. Heine declared that if you were here he would have you arrested for slander.[14] They said that you had been received into their homes, had eaten, so to speak, of their salt, had received every kindness and help in your work, and had basely betrayed their confidence. Of me personally, they know nothing, but as coming from the same institution, and sent by you, they would have nothing to do with me. From the [New Guinea] company I cannot get permission to go on the Siar; I cannot even get a boat here to go to a neighboring island. They refuse to do me any favors whatever. There has been no change in Governor Hahl's attitude, but he has now left for a year's vacation. He told me, however, (I saw him here about a week ago on the steamer when he passed through), that it had killed me and my work here in the colony, as well as seriously affected his reputation, as all men here regard him as your special supporter. The government officials have been uniformly helpful. I am now staying with the police-master [i.e., Stuben], and the new Kiap[15] here (Dr. Scholz is also away) has given me the use of a government boat, but I know that considerable pressure is being brought to bear on them to "cut" me as the others have done. No one will have anything to do with me socially.

The trouble comes chiefly from the company. Most of the missionaries are more or less friendly. I depend on them and one or two independent traders for assistance; if they fail me, I must leave. I fear I shall not be able to get to the Kaiserin Augusta river, under the circumstances. It would be necessary to charter a steamer, and that is almost too expensive, even if one could get one. That the situation is exceedingly unpleasant for me you can imagine, to say nothing of my personal feelings. I have stayed here during the rainy season, and the dry season, when work is possible along the coast is just now beginning. Besides I have left two large collections in other places, expecting to return on the Siar, make a trip along the whole coast, and gather them in. At the time I was told that I could do this. Now permission is refused. Whether the company will deign to bring to Fr. Wh. Hafen my collections as freight, I do not know, but they certainly will not pack them, so I must either stay here or lose them.

I hope, when I get away from Fr. Wh. Hafen things will go better. I do not know how it is in Herbertshöhe, as I left there before they knew of your article, but from what Gov. Hahl said it is probably no better than here. I wish I could get a ship and half a dozen assistants, and come down here and clean out the place, in spite of the company. Well, you know I have wished for that before. I hope (and expect, from what I hear) that things will go much better in English New Guinea.

I could have made arrangements last September for a motor schooner (of Herr Rud. Wahlen) to go up the K.A. river this summer, but then I did not dare, as the cost would have been at least $1,000, and I did not know how long I could stay here, or what money I could have. By last mail I got a check for $3,000, but no further information, though Davies said that the Director had or would write. I suppose I shall get the rest of this year's appropriation. I cannot work to advantage unless I know a considerable time in advance what I am to receive. If the next year's appropriation is granted, I wish to know as soon as I possibly can, and would also ask that my leave of absence be extended to four years, so that I may be able to finish my work here, and see something of the East Indies, India and Europe on my return. As transportation is the great difficulty here, I can do better if I have a little longer time, or else, a little more money, so I can have a boat of my own.

I have had the fever a few times, but not a touch for the last three months. How long my good luck will continue, I do not know. Going round with the natives, and in the native villages, is extremely interesting. Beyond material things, however, "pidgin" English does not reach, and it is impossible to get much information regarding the beliefs of the natives. One must learn the language to do that. Outside of the missionaries, there are no interpreters. Some of them take an interest, however, in these things, and I expect that within the next two or three years some books and articles will come out giving much fuller information on New Guinea than we have had before. Culturally (i.e., material) I have studied rather thoroughly three different regions. I had hoped to be able to get a connected view of the whole coast, as well as the river. How far I shall succeed remains to be seen. It looks rather hopeless. After three months here I expected to go to the Admiralties and New Ireland, but I fear, under the circumstances, I shall find it to my advantage to go elsewhere. However, that remains to be seen.

Since writing the above I have been to see the new <u>kiap</u>, who, I understood, wished to know what I intended to do. I could only say, that depended. In the course of the conversation your article came up again, with an additional cause of reproach, that you were a mere collector, that such collections were practically lost to science, and that if he had his way they would not be allowed. The implication as to the Museum and myself was pretty evident.

Very sincerely,
A. B. Lewis

P.S. May 2.—I have seen Pater Lörks, the captain of the <u>Gabriel</u>, and he has given me permission to go with him as far as Potsdam Hafen.

{Text of a notice published 28 May 1910 in the Deutsche Kolonialzeitung *(1910; 27:363).}*

A Word of Caution

We have received the following statement from German New Guinea with a request that we publish it:

"The curator of Field Museum in Chicago, George R. [*sic*] Dorsey arrived in Herbertshöhe in July 1908. There he was allowed to travel on behalf of his museum, to conduct ethnological research, and to make collections. Everywhere he was very hospitably received and enjoyed much additional assistance. The Governor took him along on a trip through the Solomon islands; he took part in the first crossing of Bougainville island; the Administrator of the New Guinea Compagnie at Friedrich Wilhelmshafen gave him a trip and also the opportunity to go up the Kaiserin Augusta river for the purpose of collecting. Dorsey himself reported the richness of his sojourn in boastful words as he left with an important collection of over 2,000 pieces. The exaggeration of his descriptions cause, no doubt require, one to be irritated. His whinings about being deprived of fresh provisions, about getting a frigid reception, and about tight living quarters on the small recruiting ship, all show a feeble-minded lack of comprehension for the conditions of such a journey and a confused man wandering in the wilderness.

In the *Daily Tribune* of 6 October 1909, Dorsey now betrays his gratitude to the colony and its inhabitants in a very specific manner. He says the lifestyle of the Germans is dirty, labels us as lazy, calls us drunkards, and claims we display intolerance and cruelty toward the natives. We are bracing ourselves against the bitterly cold remarks of our former guest.

It is pointless to try to rectify this matter with him personally from this great distance.

The success of his trip has encouraged Mr. Dorsey to send his assistant who, just like his boss, would like to exploit both the private and the official cooperation for the advantage of his museum. We are locking our doors to such friends!

Herbertshöhe, 23 Dec. 1909."

Warnecke, Stuebel, Schober, Ketzner, Kriebel, Katzner, W. Stosch, W. Blankenhagen, Dr. Paul Preuss, Director of the new New Guinea Co., A. Dowaldt, Fritz Ehemann, M. Thiel, E. Timm, R. Spangenberg, Conrad, M. Pfuhle, Carl, Regala, Walter Wichmanm, Philipps, Hochenleitner, Georg Wittrock, L Kohl, Werner, Oskar Haefner, H. Dierske, F. Ritter, Aug. Roscher, T. Rinck, Stolle, Mahleer, Klug, Wahlers, H. J. Liversay, Scholz, E. Krockenberger, Wilhelm Haeberle, Bruechner, H. Geisler, Kempter, Spiegelfeldt, Helmich, Blum, P. Ahr, Schmid-Burgk, J. Elmies, A. Blesse, W. F. Brinkmann, M. Strezinski, Rud. Schreger, Mikulicz, F. Merseburger, Rhades, Glitz, W. Throne, Schamann, Fr. Schaefer, Richter, G. Glasmann, F. Glahn, G. Heine.

{Note: Among the sixty-one signatories of this notice are the Rheinish missionaries Helmich and Blum as well as company agents Blesse and Richter, all of whom later helped ABL on the north coast. The names of two officials, Klug and Scholtz, are also among those individuals ABL mentioned in his diaries. It appears that company administrator Georg Heine, whose name is last on the list, initiated this published notice.}

Fig. 4.1. "Man with spear thrower and spears, Awar." A-33359 (419).

To Friedrich Wilhelmshafen

||||||||||||||||||||||||||||||||||||||||||||||||||||||||||||||||||||||||||||||||||||||||||||||||

Tuesday, April 5, 1910   Left Finsch hafen in *Manila* about 10 P.M.

Wednesday, April 6   Arrived at Stephansort about 2 P.M. Did not go ashore. Arrived at Fr. Wh. Hafen about 5:30. Found Herr Stuben, formerly police-master at Eitape, was now at Fr. Wh. Hafen, and as there seemed to be no other place to which I could go, he invited me to stay with him.[1] Went on shore with my room luggage about 10 P.M. Heavy rain.

Thursday, April 7–Sunday, April 10   Overhauled my stuff, wrote letters, visited Fragetta[2] and mission, etc. Hongkong steamer arrived Sunday morning and left at noon.

Tuesday, April 12   Left at 2 P.M. with Herr Stuben and police force, with my two boys for a village (Panim) about 4 hrs. in interior. Arrived at 5 P.M. Path pretty muddy part of way. Slept at night in a native house, as I had no cot with me. Next morning Herr Stuben made a complete census of the village.

After that I made some photos, and bought a few things. Not much here. Pots from Bilibili. Also a few from the interior, thin coiled ware. Got 4 of these. Bowls (wood) from Rai coast; a few old shields, and spears, ornaments not many (compared to islands), and a tendency to mix in beads. Saw one dance mask or headdress, shaped like a house, with a long pole on top, covered with feathers and cloth. The house was of painted bark, also paper and cloth, so that it was of no worth. Had been made for the Christmas dances (see photo).

Clothing *mal,* and grass (?) petticoats for women, open at sides. Some reached below knees, others very short (esp. girls—children wore no clothes, only ornaments). Men's house had no floor, others floor about 3 ft. high. Saw cooking of taro in pot, which was covered tightly with leaves, but no leaves were put in pot, to assist in removing taro at bottom, as in Huon Gulf.

Arrows, except plain fish arrows, they said from Rai coast. Bows from Rai coast or interior. Also saw 2 small wood shields carried over shoulder in net sac. Sac much broken.

Left Panim at 1 P.M. and got back by 4:30. Took another path in part, and visited another village,[3] but all the people were away. On this trip it took about 1 hr. and 10 minutes to pass through the cocoanut (on higher ground) and rubber (on low and swampy ground) plantations of the N.G. Co., and reach the bush. On return struck a broad road about 6 miles out, and followed this for almost 3 miles, when reached the plantation road. In one place had to wade a river, where was an unfinished bridge, with one abut-

---

1. This was undoubtedly due to the reaction in town against the Dorsey columns.
2. ABL means Ragetta Island.
3. This would be Foran village, a three-hour walk from Friedrich Wilhelmshafen.

Fig. 4.2. "Magic sticks (bull-roarers ?) collected in Panim, tho said to come from further inland," 140095 (2334), 140093 (2338), 140094 (2335). A-112316.

ment finished, and many timbers lying rotting on the ground; as so often in this colony, had begun to build, and were not able to finish.

Thursday, April 14–Tuesday, April 26 Packed and prepared specimens for shipment, developed 4 doz. plates, wrote letters and reports, cast up accounts, and in general straightened up my books and correspondence for the last six months.

Wednesday, April 27 Found it was impossible to get a boat from the New Guinea Co., at least for more than a day, and that uncertain. I got one from the government for the day, and went over to Ragetta, where I visited Missionary Helmich, and looked through the village. The houses are large—men's house no floor, other houses on piles 3–4 ft. high. In men's houses saw bows (from inland), arrows (from inland and Rai—also fish arrows home made), spears (native and from inland), 1 shield, 1 broken figure (post ?) with snake and frog, and feet of human image broken off. Canoe with one side board very rudely ornamented. End piece bent (made from side flat roots, bent, of large forest tree) and ornamented.

In men's house saw drums *(kundus)* some from Dampier [Karkar Island], some from Tami and Bukaua; dance head dresses as in Pelilo (Cape Merkus) and Panim. Ornamented combs, bowls from Tami and Rai. Pots from Bilibili. Saw the men making waist bands, arm bands, and broad leg bands (worn above ankle) of plain and red fibre; also grinding down shell for nose ornament (see photos).

Man's dress *mal;* women's fibre skirts, open on sides, made of sago-palm leaves.

236

Fig. 4.3. Earthen pots from inland Friedrich Wilhelmshafen. "Collected Foran (3 hours from Fr. Wh. Hafen), Bili-bili and Yabop type, where most of the pots of this type are made," 137929 (3222); "coiled pots obtained at Panim, made at place 2–3 days inland from Panim," 137933 (3230), 137932 (3229). A-112319.

Thursday, April 28   Spent most of day in overhauling and repairing boxes and kit, and packing stuff for Potsdam Hafen.

Friday, April 29   Went in boat from gov. in morning to Siar, visited Missionary Blum, who kindly accompanied me around the village. Made photos

Fig. 4.4. "Weaving leg band in place, Ragetta Island." A-33323 (382).

Fig. 4.5. "Girl of Siar." A-33334 (393).

and bought a few things. In afternoon went back, visiting on the way the island of _____ with a small village. Here traded for some things, esp. Rai bowls. Houses, dress, etc. the same as at Ragetta.

Saturday, April 30–Friday, May 6   As the Hongkong steamer and the *Gabriel* (on which I hoped to get permission to go to Potsdam Hafen) were expected most any day, I could not go far away. Developed my plates, packed up my things, and waited.

Saturday, May 7   Steamer came at noon, left at 10 P.M. *Gabriel* loaded on 50 casks of cement, and left for Alexis Hafen at 2 A.M. The Captain (Pater Lörks) kindly gave me permission to go along.

Sunday, May 8   Spent day in Alexis Hafen. Over 200 laborers. Saw them given rice and meat (salt beef). Looked around the place some.

Monday, May 9   In morning went to village of Sek, but spent so much time looking at fish and coral reef that had not much time there. Place, house, etc. much as at Siar and Ragetta. Saw nothing new.
    Left at 2 P.M. At 4 stopped at mission station of _____ where stayed till 6. As no village here, and surf high, did not go ashore.

Tuesday, May 10   Arrived early in morning at Potsdam Hafen, before daylight, but Capt. decided to go back to Bogia, a mission station about 7 miles east. From here I walked to Potsdam Hafen, arriving about noon. On way passed through 6 villages. Had dinner with Herr Richter, the [N.G.] Co. manager, and arranged to stay with him (at his invitation). *Gabriel* came about 1 P.M. and my things were put in store.

Fig. 4.6. "Men, Siar." A-33327 (386).

Wednesday, May 11–Thursday, May 12 Visited village of Monumbo, but found little new. Men wore the *mal,* women the petticoat of fibre, here usually red or reddish. Men had hair shaved in front, and behind long, confined by a woven band, in some cases. Netted bags, or woven soft baskets (from Murik) carried by men; bags also sometimes by women.

Saw two kinds of wood bowls in houses, one said to come from coast (tho made in interior) east of Hatzfeld Hafen (Tukumu etc.) and other from interior of Hansa bay.

Of pots there were three kinds, one from coast beyond (East) Hatzfeld Hafen; one from interior (Waimbóm) from Bogia, and one from Kaiyán, near the Ramu. I saw one of these latter that was at least 2 ft. high and nearly as wide. Saw little else of interest. The men's lime gourds were plain gourds, often nearly round, spatulas plain wood or bone. Ornaments relatively few, mostly beads, and plain woven arm or leg bands.

Friday, May 13 Left with Herr Richter about 9 A.M. in whale boat for Manam (Vulcan Island) where arrived at 3 P.M. Here was a small Chinese trader, and we stayed all night at his house. Before dark visited a native village near by, where got a few things.

Saturday, May 14 In morning went along coast on foot to another village, and then by boat to still another. This latter was nearly 2 miles inland, and at quite a little elevation. Here we stayed an hour or more and then returned to shore, and left for Mombuan (name of N.G. Co. place on mainland) a little after noon, reaching Mombuan about 5 P.M.

Manam is an active volcano, and smoking nearly all the time. The last outbreak of lava was in 1902, and while the lower parts of the flow are covered now with vegetation, the upper parts are still bare. The soil and rocks are volcanic solely, the outline of the island forming a typic volcanic cone.

The vegetation in many places is open, and reminds one of Australia. The native villages are all inland, on the lower slopes of the mountain. The settlements consist chiefly of several groups at a short distance apart, of 2 to 8 houses each. The houses resemble those of Monumbo, but are smaller and

239

Fig. 4.7. "Vulcan Island from house at Potsdamhafen." A-33350 (410).

not so well made. Have men's house and *tamburan* house (both without floor; others have floor about 4 ft. high).

Culture seemed practically the same as on mainland. Their wooden shields, however, are characteristic.[4] The men also seemed more given to long hair bands than in Monumbo, and if not this, at least a band of twisted hair string (said was made of man's own hair, which was cut when got too long). Practically all the old things were gone. No bows or arrows seen, tho saw several varieties of spears. Pots, bowls, etc. as in Monumbo. The language, however, is different from that on mainland.

The cause of this visit to Manam is interesting. On the *Gabriel* with me there came, from Fr. Wh. Hafen a native police boy,—an *"unter-officier,"* with a letter from the *kiap* to Herr Richter[5] that he should assist him to get a certain native woman (hardly more than girl) as wife. This woman had formerly been the wife (!) of Herr Fabricius, the N.G. Co.'s Agent at Potsdam Hafen. Fabricius had left about a month before, and the woman had returned to her native village. Before this, however, the police-boy had given the woman 10 marks to become his wife. This she had taken with that understanding, but later had apparently repented of the bargain, and had given the 10 Marks to another boy to return to the police-boy, but he had not yet received it. The cook in the house at Mombuān (Potsdam Hafen) was also an applicant for the hand of the maiden, and had given her father some dog's teeth (here money).

So, esp. on account of the *kiap*'s letter, Herr Richter decided to go over to the island and find the woman, and see how the case stood. It took us some time to find where she was, but the last village we visited was not far from her father's village, where she was staying, so we sent for her and her father. The reason why we had been directed to the wrong village we found to lie in the fact that she had a *native* husband in this village, but that the

4. For photos of three of these Manam shields collected by ABL, see Tiesler (1970, Abb. 15–17).
5. The *kiap* was probably G. Berghausen. Herr Richter appears to have replaced Fabricius as New Guinea Compagnie agent at Potsdamhafen earlier in 1910.

people of the village, for some reason we could not find out, did not approve of this and had driven her out, so she had returned to her parents' village. It appeared that this marriage was one arranged in youth by the parents.

On her arrival a "palaver" was held, but it appeared that she would have neither the police-boy nor the cook. The people of her husband's village, however, would not have her, and they, as well as her father, said she should take the cook, as she would then not be far away. None favored the police-boy,—said Madang (Fr. Wh. H.) was too far away. The husband, who was hardly grown, was afraid to come near, would not say a word, and finally disappeared. The thing was rather complicated, esp. as Herr Richter did not wish his cook to have a wife. He finally decided that as the 10 marks, as well as the dog's teeth, had not yet been returned, she must return with him and see that the police-boy got his money back. Then her father should come over Monday and return the dog's teeth, when she could return to her village with him. He secretly hoped that between times she could be persuaded to take the police-boy.

Sunday, May 15 Herr Gramms and Herr Blesser came to dinner, and spent the afternoon and night with Herr Richter.

Monday, May 16 Went back with Gramms to Awar, I went in whale boat with my things, but Gramms returned by horse along shore. Boat took about 2 hrs. Spent the morning getting my things ready and left at 1 P.M.

Fig. 4.8. Betel-nut mortars from various North Coast communities: Murik, 140914 (3409); Mendam, 140674 (3184), 140673 (3185), 140675 (3186); Manam (Vulcan Island), 140276 (79); Kayan, 140480 (2501); Bushim, 140211 (3094). A-112211.

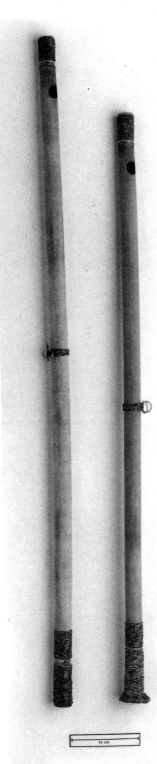

Tuesday, May 17 In morning went with Herr Gramms [to] village (Awar) in boat. Lagoon opening about 2 miles from house. Village lies on lagoon. Looked around, visited house where *tamburan* was present, and in general tried to make friends of the natives.

Wednesday, May 18 Went to village with one of Gramms' boys and my two, in boat prepared to buy what I could find. Did not find much of interest, aside from everyday objects, was dark with rather heavy sea when got back.

Thursday, May 19 Found that there was sago making near the village before, and today went early, hoping to get a chance to photograph process, but either no one was working, or they did not wish me there, as I could not hear or see anyone at work. Also had learned that pots were made in the village, but my endeavors to photo the process were not very successful. When first came to Awar (to cross the lagoon I sent over my two boys to get the natives to bring a native canoe for me) the interpreter "Tārep" had said that in afternoon I could see the process in the small village of Awar. So I spent the morning till 2 P.M. in Sissimongun and Nūbīa, seeing what I could, sampling foods, etc. On returning to Awar we went to the place where the woman was to do the work, but she was in the shade, so I tried to persuade her to come where the light was better. One photo I got [discarded], but then she retreated into the shade, saying (so Tarep said) that the sun would dry the clay too fast. I tried to get Tarep to tell her to come back, but for some reason things did not go well, and she went away, and would not return. The men also got suspicious, and I could do nothing more, so returned. On speaking with Gramms he said that he would go with me the next day and see that I got to photograph what I wished.

Friday, May 20 Sent Kaman about 8 A.M. to get natives to bring over canoe, and shortly after went myself with Kabai. On arriving at lagoon found no canoe, and waited till after nine before Kaman came with 2 canoes and men from Nubía, who had been at Awar, and were returning to Nubia. Gramms had said he would come later on horse-back. Went first to Sissimongun, but tho Saiī [the interpreter there, see Fig. 4.11] had said that they would work sago that day, found all there busy having a big feast and resting ("all same Sunday"), as "Tamburan" had "gone long bush" the evening before. The men were putting their pipes in order, and getting ready to stow them away, while all the women were banished from the place. As I thought that Gramms would be along by this time, I returned to Awar, and found him there, and also the Chinese trader (formerly Gramms' cook) for the N.G. Co. at Nubia. He spoke the language fluently, and it was soon arranged that some of the men should cut a sago tree, and break out and wash the sago, so I could photo the process.

Then we went to the small village of Awar, where I had tried to get photo of pot making the day before, and here a woman (not the same) made the beginning of a small pot (photo nos. 430, 431) as there was only a little clay in the place, it could not be finished. What there was I took as a specimen.

Then I also wished to photo the women fishing, and through the Chinaman's wife (a native of the place) six women were induced to go into the lagoon near by and fish, while I took some photos. As it was then fairly late, we returned to the house.

Fig. 4.9. *Tambaran* pipes *(mrep),* of bamboo and rattan, Awar. "These pipes are blown in connection with certain ceremonies, and are supposed to represent the voices of the spirits, one male and one female (one pipe is pitched higher than the other)." 140363 (2471 and 2472). A-112113.

Saturday, May 21   Developed photos and listed my specimens.

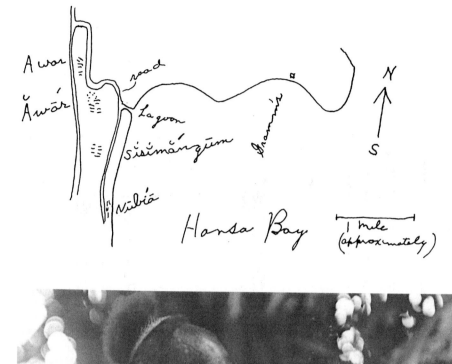

Fig. 4.10.   "Blowing *tamburan* pipes, Awar." A-33362 (422).

243

Sunday, May 22   Developed some photos and wrote up notes.

There was in former years a large village called Gumaiá extending along the lagoon (see sketch map on opposite page) from Awar to Nubia. These were hostile, and the village was attacked and destroyed, and the natives driven into the bush. Many were killed or died, but they finally made peace, and the villages were rebuilt as now named. A portion of the people, however, went to Ramu, and there formed a large village noted for its hostility. Another small group also live a short distance in the interior.

The houses of these villages are large, and often quite long. They are usually built so that the end faces a sort of central way or road, but are not at all regular. The floors are 5 to 6 ft. from the ground, and under the house are often platforms or racks for dishes, pots, etc.; stores of firewood; canoes, and other objects. Each family has its own house, and usually a man has only one wife. There are no men's houses, aside from the lounging or rest houses used by the men by day. These are open on the sides, but often have a small cupboard or enclosed place under the roof for the various *tamburan* objects (pipes, masks, etc.), and men's ornaments. The floor of these houses is about 3 ft. high, and they are not so long as the others. Each village has also a small house to one side, where the women go for childbirth (see Fig. 4.12).

The size of the family house varies, but may be 40–60 ft. long, 15–18 high and nearly as wide. There is a platform in front, about 3 ft. high, and from this a notched log (ladder) (see specimen) enables one to ascend to floor. There is also a platform behind, usually the same level as house floor. These end platforms are from 6–10 ft. wide.

The houses are substantially built, the central posts being large and massive, often 1½ ft. in diameter. The gable ends project far over platform (see photos). The roof is supported by a heavy centre plate and side plates, on these are rafters, then again longitudinal smaller poles, and again still smaller poles as rafters, to which the sago-leaf roofing is attached. To make this the leaflets on one side are turned over the midrib, and woven with those of the other side into a sort of mat. These are fastened, overlapping, at

Fig. 4.11. "Saii, my interpreter at Sisimongum, boy about seventeen." A-33369 (429).

Fig. 4.12. "Small house where women must go for childbirth, Awar." A-33365 (425).

Fig. 4.13. "House of Tapi, Awar." Note sleeping bag *(ndi)* in center of room. A-33496 (555).

intervals of 2 to 3 inches, making a very thick roof. (See photos of end of house.) The two sets of rafters toward the ends of the house gradually slope out more and more, thus making the gable. All are firmly bound together with "bush-rope." The large posts are of a variety of iron-wood (*Afcelia viejuga*). The plates are of logs, the outer rafters of bamboo bent over ridge pole. The outer longitudinal of bamboo; the inner rafters of wood or bamboo. The floor is of nibung plank. The door is a square or rectangular opening, closed by a nicely woven door proper, stiff and strongly made, and hung from above so that it is swung out and up from below. The front of the house is usually nicely decorated with strips or mat-like arrangement (see photo).

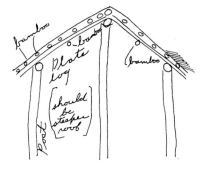

Inside there is one large room, with shelves often along the wall for various objects, and hanging hooks from the center above. These have a square piece of bark on the rope (rattan) above to keep the rats from coming down.

Household utensils are carved wood bowls, *tuⁿ*, made here, also occasionally bowls of another form from further east, also pots *tāndē*, made here from a black, stiff clay, somewhat sandy, but very fine—apparently an alluvial deposit. The pots are made by coiling (see photo), the clay being rolled out on a piece of bark (or nibung leaf-sheath). The outside and inside are smoothed by the hand. Water stands near by in a vessel of nibung leaf sheath. The pots are plain, but often quite large, pointed somewhat below. They are esp. used for cooking sago.

The dress of the men consists of a waist band of woven rattan, red, and wound many times around the waist. Over this is often a black woven band (obtained from Manam), the two being so arranged as to show alternately red and black. The black band is not so wide. A bark loin cloth is then passed under this, the broad end hanging over it and down half way to the knees (see photos); then between the legs and the smaller end also passed around

Fig. 4.14. Hair baskets from various villages on the North Coast: *kaut,* Kayan, 140429 (2490); Borbor, 140557 (2571); Bure, 140409 (2686); Manam, 140262 (2395); *kot,* Awar, 140340 (2464); collected Sissano, but made in Rabuin, 141052 (1211). A-112205.

the waist and caught under behind, much the same as where no waist band is used.

The other things worn are ornaments. Around the hair a hair basket, held in place with bone pins. This is only put on for special occasions, as it pulls the hair so tight it would make the hair come out if worn all the time. To put it on, the hair is tightly wound with a strip of bark, one end projecting behind, and the basket slipped over this, when the bark strip is pulled out behind.

Ear ornaments are various, a few dog's teeth on a string being most common. There are numerous holes around the border of the ear, so that when all these have something in them the ear is invisible. Narrow tortoise shell rings were seen, but not many.

The nose has a hole in each side, as well as the central one. In the side holes are stuck feathers, bits of grass, etc.; in the other a shell rod or shell ornaments, thin. Necklaces of dog's teeth and nassa shells, also with many small rings hung around of shell (tridacna ?). Woven arm bands, with nassa shells and lappets; also plain. Plain wrist bands, rather wide. Diagonal shoulder bands of strings with nassa shells were fairly common. Leg bands not seen.

The woman's dress was a skirt of shredded sago leaves, often colored red or reddish. There was a very narrow opening on the sides.

The food consists chiefly of sago, which is easily obtained, as there are sago swamps all around the villages. The tree is cut down, and the outer rind cut across, so as to make sections some 4 or 5 ft. long. The rind is then removed with a heavy stick [photo lost] for about $\frac{2}{3}$ of the way around. The man then sits on the log at one end, and begins breaking the sago pith with the sago hammer (here of wood, hollowed out below), holding the broken pith in place with his feet. When a mass of this is broken, it is put in the baskets for washing. These are made of strips of the sago leaf, nicely woven, but at the bottom open, the strips of leaf extending for a foot or

Fig. 4.15. "Driving fish in along shore, Awar." A-33383 (443).

so, however, so that they can be turned in and firmly tied together with a strip of rattan.

This is for convenience in cleaning the basket. When full, the baskets are taken to a place where a water hole has been dug. By this is a frame, on which the basket is placed, and under this is a nibung leaf receptacle for the sago. Water is dipped out of the hole with a cocoanut dipper with long bamboo handle (see specimen) and poured into the basket (see photo 438). The basket is then turned and pressed, so that the sago flour is washed out into receptacle below. Here it stands till it settles to the bottom. Is then taken out, made into packages, and taken to the village. It will keep several days, but not indefinitely. To cook, some of this flour is sifted into water, in a nibung bucket, and stirred in. Water is boiled in a pot, and this sago flour poured in. The whole is stirred rapidly, and in a few minutes it thickens into a reddish sticky mass. This is distributed with a cocoanut cup to a number of wooden dishes, in which it is served. At the same time fish, crabs, shrimp, pork, or something of the sort is also cooked, and served on top of the sago in the bowl. All this is done by the women, and the prepared dishes are then taken to the men to eat.

Fig. 4.16. "Bogasu, my Awar interpreter." A-33470 (529).

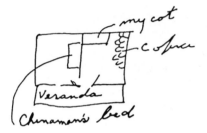

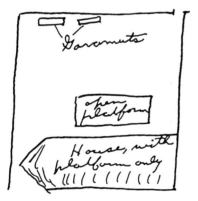

The women spend much of their time fishing, as fish of some kind form the chief addition to the sago. The nets are a sort of dip net, and the women, in the shallow lagoon or on the sea front, wade out and surround a portion of water, and then all come together with their nets, so that the fish are driven into them. They also drive to the shore. (See photos.)

Other food consists of yams, bananas, bread fruit, greens of various kinds, etc., but these are exceptional rather than the rule.

The dead are buried near the house, and over the grave a small house or shed is erected (photos 414–417). In this, food is often placed in bowls, for the spirit. (Photo 417 shows bowls.)

The bones are not dug up, and the skulls formerly found in the resting houses were of slain enemies.

The occasion when the *tamburan* pipes are blown seems to be that of a feast. One is male and one female, and the two are blown at one time. *Garamut*s are also beaten. This is kept up for two or three days (in some house) while the men lie around and feast on the food which the women must prepare for the *tamburan*.

Monday, May 23   Spent most of morning writing notes, packing up, etc. and left about 11:30 in boat with my 2 boys, Bōgāsū (interpreter from Awar) and 4 men to pull, for Kaián, where we arrived about 5 P.M. The village of Kaian lies a short distance back from the shore, but a Chinese trader has a house on the shore, and here I landed my things, and made arrangements to stay with him for a week. His house had two rooms, one of which he occupied himself with 2 native girls, and the other, which also had a loft, was used by the boys, and was a store house for copra, etc. I set up my cot in one corner of the copra room, and the boys took to the loft.

Tuesday, May 24   In morning the natives came with all sorts of things to sell, and I bought quite a little. Then went to village and got some more things. The men were having a *tamburan* with pipes and *garamut*s, in an enclosure of cocoanut leaves, on one side of which was a men's lounging house. The fence was about 8–10 ft. high. I succeeded in getting a photo of the men blowing pipes, beating drums, and also of some of the men.

The first village was rather small, but further back was a larger one. I got permission to enter several of the houses. The natives were very friendly, tho the women and children were visible only at a distance. About 2 P.M. I returned, and spent the rest of the day listing my specimens.

Fig. 4.17. "Beating the *garamut*s inside the *tamburan* enclosure, Kaian. (These may be beaten with or without the accompaniment of the pipes.)" A-33394 (454).

Wednesday, May 25   Went to Bórbor, on a small river a little to the west, and spent part of the forenoon here; then up the river about 2 miles to another small village, called Gúmī. Got a few things at each place.

Thursday, May 26   Rained part of the day, but I again visited Kaian, got a few photos, and a few things.

Friday, May 27   Went along beach to mouth of Kwā river, and then by canoe to Būrē, about 4 miles up the river. Here got a considerable number of masks. I had tried to get a man or two from Kaian to go with me, but they would not, and all reports were that the Buré natives were afraid, and would all run away. With Bogasu and my boys I went in the Chinaman's canoe (which was a wretched affair, and had to be repaired before we could use it), and found not the least difficulty. Some time before there had been some trouble with the Chinaman, and part of the natives were living in the bush. Also many of their best things were there, and most of the women and children. The village itself showed many houses in a state of decay. The time was about 1¼ hrs. along the beach, and the same up the river.

Fig. 4.18. "Dance in *tamburan* enclosure, Kaian." A-33397 (457).

Fig. 4.19. String bags ornamented with coix seeds: Mabuk, 140826 (3272); Kayan, 140448 (2483), 140449 (2484). A-112028.

Saturday, May 28 As there was another village further up, which I had not time to visit the day before, I went there today, but got very few things. The trip was interesting, as beyond Bure the river (or lagoon) was not so deep, and was in places almost filled with fish traps or enclosures. These were built on both sides of the river, and were made of bamboo stakes set side by side, and bound together with rattan. At the lower end was a wide opening, which could be closed. During the rising tide this was left open, so that the fish could enter, and at high tide was closed. The enclosures were quite large, 50–80 ft. wide by 100 to 300 long, and in one corner was a smaller enclosure, apparently so that the fish could be driven into it. At low water the enclosure would be almost dry, so there would not be much difficulty in catching the fish.

Fig. 4.20. "Man of Borbor." A-33413 (473).

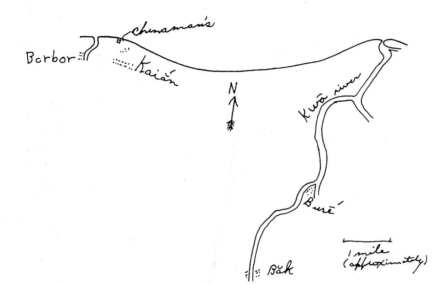

The houses in Kaian and Bure are practically as in Awar. The frame is built in the same manner. I estimated one in Bak (really a part of Bure, the language is the same as Kaian) approximately at 100 ft. long, with projecting verandas at ends, each of which approx. 20 ft., so 60 ft. for house proper, 20–25 ft. wide. Floor 8 ft. from ground. Roof 3 ft. high at sides, and 10 ft. in center. This house was larger than usual. One difference between Kaian and Awar is that the veranda in Kaian is level with the floor, while in Awar it was lower, only about 3–4 ft. high.

Household utensils here the same as in Awar. The pots they said came from Wūsūmūn on the Ramū, but they were the same as made in Awar (Wúsumun is really a division of the Awar people).

Dress and ornaments apparently same as Awar. Canoes too, as far as I could see. The body is dug out, carved at both ends and on the sides. The ends represent a face (human) then an ornament, then crocodile head, with something in mouth. Below is a crocodile. There is a platform built on the outrigger poles on one side, but it does not extend over body of canoe. 3 longitudinal poles, then short knee pieces (b), and on these narrow nibung strips. The mast is set in a basal block, and is lashed to middle pole to outrigger, the lashing being strengthened by an extra piece bound to pole on side. Above it is held in place by 4 sticks lashed to mast above and to platform (or, better, to a special stick lashed to platform). These sticks are forked below.

A shorter platform, surrounded on 3 sides by carved boards, extends over the body of the canoe and out a foot or more on the other side, inside it is continuous with the longer platform. It rests on a long pole (b) binding

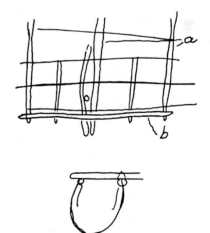

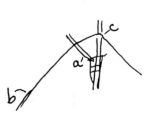

251

Fig. 4.21. Boy's surfboard *(ter)*, Kayan. Made of very light softwood, crocodile head at front, 140506 (2532). See also Linton and Wingert (1946; 122). A-112348.

the ends of the outrigger poles (a) together, shorter poles (c) support the long platform. The outrigger poles rest (sometimes) on a strip of nibung placed on the edge of the canoe for protection, and are lashed to the sides of the canoe with rattan. The mast is held in place by rattan (b) fastened to each end of the long platform, and at top running through or lashed to a piece (a) over which passes the rope to the sail. It is then fastened to the mast at (c). When (a) is behind, the outrigger (usually at least) is to the left. The top of the mast is frequently ornamented with fringes of grass, cross pieces of wood, etc.

In addition to the round dip nets, rectangular nets, with pole at each end, were seen.

Sago is here washed in a trough of stem of leaf at base of which is fastened a piece of cocoanut leaf-sheath fibre. This is supported on a frame, so that water with sago runs out and is caught in receptacle below.

Sunday, May 29 Bogasu, returned to Awar, with a note to Herr Gramms. The Chinaman reported that there was to be a sing-sing in Borbor tonight, so in the afternoon we went there.

The *tamburan* pipes were going and the men were evidently preparing for a big feast. One of the men's houses was especially decorated with leaves and red and yellow fruits of some tree (*not* good to eat), and in one end was a large pile of taro, yams, bananas and sugar cane. There was a fringe of split leaves all around the floor (about 3 ft. high) so that men with *tamburan* pipes could sit below. Here I saw a new kind of noise maker *(tamburan)*. It was merely a tube of bamboo, about 2 ft. long, and $1\frac{1}{4}$ in. in diameter, which was cracked all around about $\frac{1}{3}$ from the lower end. This when talked into (the end should be entirely closed in the mouth) gave a peculiar vibrating hum to the sounds, almost uncanny. These, as well as the pipes proper, were going nearly all the time, either under the floor of this house, or in a closed man's house near by.

The pile of vegetables was divided soon after we arrived, each receiving a certain share, even the visitors, two very large taro and a stick of sugar-cane falling to me. The women took the food away and prepared it (see photo). About five o'clock the feast was served, the women bringing wooden bowls with boiled sago and other things by the dozen to the men's houses. I was also kindly invited to partake, but boiled sago is not particularly to my taste. As I had heard that the men would have special dance costumes, I tried to get some of them to don them before dark, so I could photograph them, but without success. About dusk some came with spears and leaf ornaments, and went through certain evolutions, something like those at Arawe. What it meant I could not find out. My boys said it was only "play," and I had a suspicion that the real performance did not come off till the moon arose, about midnight, but I was tired and sleepy, and the Chinaman was anxious to go back, so, as I had his canoe, I did not stay much after 9.

Monday, May 30 The next morning I returned to Borbor. *Tamburan* pipes and feasting were in full force, but no dancing. I stayed an hour or two, and then returned, after buying a few things, including 3 of the new *tamburan* tubes, which no woman or child was allowed to see.

About noon Gramms' cutter arrived, and my things were loaded on board, and about 3 P.M. we started on our return to Awar. This cutter I had agreed to charter for a few weeks for 25 Marks per day. The carrying capacity is not very great, and made it necessary to make several journeys

Fig. 4.22. "Men's lounging house, especially decorated, Borbor; women bringing food for the men, in wood bowls." A-33402 (462).

back and forth later. The crew numbers 4 natives, but the captain (a New Ireland boy) is quite skillful, and perfectly familiar with the entire coast.

As the current was against us, and the wind ceased shortly after dark we anchored off the Kwa river, and waited for the land breeze, with which we continued our journey, and arrived at Awar about 3 A.M. but did not go ashore till morning.

Tuesday, May 31 As the *Gabriel* was expected back from Eitape, with my boxes,[6] Tuesday night or Wed. morning, I started for Monbuán about noon, or as soon as the wind seemed favorable, and got there about 5 P.M., unfortunately, too late, as the *Gabriel* passed us on the way, and was gone on to Bogia (the mission station about 8 miles further east) where the captain said he would remain over night.

Eight (out of 10) of my boxes he had brought, and also most of my specimens from Eitape. I stayed over night with Herr Richter.

Wednesday, June 1 The next morning got my boxes on board, bought some more trade, and returned to Awar.

Thursday, June 2 In morning went by boat to Nubia, as Herr Gramms had said that a number of the "bush" natives were come to the beach there to burn drift wood for salt. I landed on the beach, but did not succeed in coming in contact with the natives, as they all ran away at my approach. So I went on to Nubia, bought a few things, and then returned to the beach, but with no better success. The Nubia people said that the salt makers were staying at Sisimangum, so I went back to that place (from the beach) and finally through an interpreter or two there, succeeded in getting a nearer view of the "bush" men, buying some things, and even getting a photo of some of them (No. 477).

---

6. These were ABL's crates of specimens, left at Eitape in December 1909.

Fig. 4.23. "Burning wood for salt on beach near Nubia. This is done by natives from the interior who come to the coast for that purpose. They were staying for the time at Sisimongum." A-33416 (476).

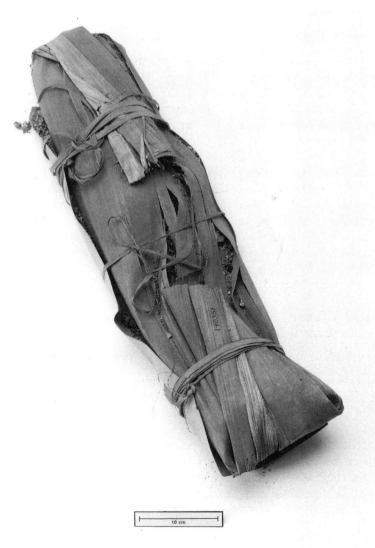

10 cm

Fig. 4.24. "Package of ashes used as salt (*muis*) by inland natives." Purchased at Sisimongum from inland people of Mingum, 140351 (2782). A-112387.

I also bought a package of ashes (salt) all prepared ready for transport to their place (Fig. 4.24, Sp. 2782). The outside of drift logs on the beach is cut away, piled up and burnt (Fig. 4.23), and the ashes used as salt. When wanted to use, the ashes are boiled (?) in a small pot, and the salty water dipped out and poured over the cooked sago, or whatever it may be which they wish to salten, after it is cooked and placed in the wooden dishes or plates.

Friday, June 3   Developed plates, labeled specimens, etc.

Saturday, June 4   Shortly after breakfast the boys reported that the *Siar* had entered Potsdam Hafen, so Herr Gramms and I went over in the cutter. Got there about dark. I stayed on the *Siar* till about nine, then went up to the house. The others (Gramms and Richter) did not come till midnight, when the *Siar* left.

On the North Coast

|||||||||||||||||||||||||||||||||||||||||||||||||||||||||||||||||||||||||||||||||||||||||||||||||||||||||||||||||||||||

5 June 1910–2 August 1910

By the beginning of June 1910, ABL had had two excursions since his return to the North Coast. He had visited a number of places around Friedrich Wilhelmshafen and later, while based at Awar plantation, he had completed a more or less systematic survey of the coast to the west of Awar almost as far as the Kaiserin Augusta River. At the end of May ABL had arranged to charter Herr Gramms' cutter, and now he had more mobility and flexibility than he had previously enjoyed in the German colony.

In the next two months ABL made several more excursions from Awar. He sailed once more to the west visiting Watam (east of the Sepik mouth) and Kirau (on the Murik lakes, west of the Sepik). Then he surveyed the villages to the east from Eitel Friedrichhafen and Kronprinzhafen (Moro and Malala), visiting most of the villages between these points and Potsdamhafen. On his return from these eastern villages, he went back to Kirau, proceeding inland across the lagoon to Mabuk. Although ABL would make another trip along the coast from Awar, by the beginning of August he had collected about a thousand specimens since arriving in Friedrich Wilhelmshafen, and he had a fairly good idea of how these coastal communities differed from one another.

During his repeated visits to the four villages at Awar—Big Awar, Little Awar, Nubia, and Sisimongum—ABL got to see quite a bit of village life. He saw sago making, potting, fishing, and feasting, including nearly a complete round of ceremonies and dances associated with the *tambaran*. Although he had still not figured out a way of making a trip up the Kaiserin Augusta River, he had by now successfully overcome most of the obstacles that had confronted him since hearing about Dorsey's *Tribune* articles. But on his return to Awar on 1 July 1910, he received yet another blow with his mail, this time from a most unexpected quarter: Field Museum director F. J. V. Skiff.

Early in February, Skiff had written to ABL questioning several aspects of his assistant curator's work in New Guinea. Skiff's original letter is lost, but he seems to have been most concerned that although ABL had been away from the museum for ten months, no specimens had as yet been sent to Chicago. Skiff criticized ABL for having deviated substantially from his original fieldwork plan, meaning that ABL had spent too much time in German New Guinea. At precisely the moment when ABL was coming into his own—becoming productive and overcoming unavoidable difficulties—Skiff suggested that he shorten his fieldwork by a year!

ABL was stunned. How was it possible that his success in the field could be so greatly misunderstood and misinterpreted at the museum?

Four days later he wrote a lengthy reply to Skiff, detailing the many problems he had encountered. Ironically, most of the difficulties he had faced were themselves caused by the museum. The first shipment of specimens had had to be delayed until April because new shipping instructions had not arrived until February. Dorsey's articles had, of course, made everything more complicated and expensive. Further, ABL had not been informed whether or not his allocation for the following year had been approved; when the allocation did come, it came as a lump sum, causing further difficulty and expense.

Although Skiff's attack seems anything but just, it forced ABL to explain some of the goals of his fieldwork. ABL's reply to Skiff (reproduced below)—together with a second letter five months later (5 December 1910, reproduced with the Gazelle Peninsula material)—provides ABL's only formal statement explaining what he was trying to accomplish. The first letter offers a general statement that ABL wanted to build as complete a collection as possible. His collection was to be a research collection as much as it was to be a collection for exhibition. ABL also told Skiff that he intended to write a series of papers about his collection. Most important, perhaps, ABL suggests that he hoped to describe (and to explain) the diversity he found on the coast of New Guinea. For these ends he wanted the most complete collection possible.

ABL's diary is filled with the day-to-day details of fieldwork; immersed as he was in such attention to detail, he never had the opportunity to step back and reflect upon why he was building the particular collection he was assembling. These letters to Skiff, though offering only a general overview of what he was hoping to accomplish, suggest that ABL had specific objectives in mind.

As he traveled from village to village, ABL was planning future exhibits at the museum. He was also trying to do something far more significant for anthropology: he was building an important research collection. At the time, ABL could not have foreseen that he was to assemble as large and important a collection as he did, but he knew that he could be proud of what he had already obtained. That Skiff could question his achievements to date seemed incredible.

Continuing Work along the North Coast

After posting his seventeen-page, handwritten reply to the director, ABL set off to add to his collection and visit parts of the coast he had not yet seen. He returned to Kirau on the Murik lakes to visit Mabuk, one of the "bush" villages at the back of the lagoon that traded sago for fish from the coastal Kirau and Mendam peoples. As had happened so often before, ABL was practically forced to recognize the importance of trade on the coast. His collections continued to bear witness to the volume of such transactions, and he began to see canoe-loads of villagers taking their products to their trade partners.

After filling the cutter with specimens from Mabuk, ABL returned to Awar, planning to set off once more for another trip along the coast. At this point, however, he learned of a series of *tambaran* ceremonies[16] at Hansa Bay (Awar, Nubia, and Sisimongum). He had heard of these in May and had even seen some related ceremonies at Kayan and Borbor, a few miles to the west. For the next month most of ABL's activities were centered on these ceremonies.

Throughout his four years in the field, these were the only *tambaran* rituals that ABL observed in more than bits and pieces. Most *tambaran* ceremonies in Melanesia went on for weeks or months at a time, and ABL rarely stayed long enough in most places to see very much. Here at Awar, ABL witnessed the preparations of the ceremonies, particularly the large, feathered masks that embodied particular *tambaran* spirits. On several occasions he watched these masks emerge from the *tambaran* enclosure. Repeatedly he saw men blowing on pairs of long, sacred bamboo flutes, which he regularly called "*tamburan* pipes." During this time he often saw the men playing the large *garamut*s (the large wooden slit gongs) and witnessed the feasts associated with these ceremonies.

Many anthropologists will find ABL's account of these ceremonies strikingly familiar. His confusion about what was happening and what these ceremonies meant resembles the feelings of many anthropologists who have followed his pioneering work in Melanesia. Few of us who have observed *haus tambaran* rituals in Papua New Guinea or other Melanesian countries have been spared the frustrations of delays and the changing schedule of these events. That ABL understood only the most general outline of these ceremonies goes without saying, but his descriptions and his vivid photos are unparalleled for this part of the New Guinea coast before the First World War. Similar masks are still used in and around Hansa Bay, and ABL offers one of the earliest observations of these performances.

For many readers, one of the most startling observations to emerge from that part of ABL's diary recounting his trip along the North Coast will be the prominent role Chinese traders played there. ABL mentions Chinese traders living in Manam, Nubia, Kayan, and Watam, and there were undoubtedly others in the region that he did not mention. This little-known group of individuals had a profound effect on the communities they inhabited, seen here indirectly in their collaboration (and at times collusion) with local villagers.[17]

Many of these Chinese traders were brought to the colony as laborers to work for Ah Tam, the leading Chinese resident in the colony, who was based at Matupi on the Gazelle Peninsula. After a few years of service with Ah Tam, these men often became agents for Hernsheim or Forsayth in the Bismarck Archipelago or for the New Guinea Compagnie in Kaiser Wilhelmshafen. They usually established trading stations on the coast and primarily sold copra to the company's steamer on its periodic calls at the coastal trading stations. These Chinese men usually married local women (sometimes more than one woman) and played an extraordinarily important role in village affairs often overlooked by historians and anthropologists alike.

As in each of the other regions of German New Guinea he visited, this part of the colony had its own distinctive character. Here we enter a world at the periphery of colonial development and administration. It was a mix of independent planters and semiindependent agents of the company, with a handful of SVD missionaries tossed in. But villagers on this coast had only tenuous ties with European life; their lives in 1910 were as little influenced by colonization as those villagers around Friedrich Wilhelmshafen were directly affected by it. Here ABL's diary shows quite vividly how varied the contact experience was for different villages along the New Guinea coast.

Awar, Potsdam Hafen
July 4, 1910

The Director
Field Museum
Chicago

Dear Sir:

Your letter of Feb. 4th, 1910 was received four days ago, and I take the occasion to make an informal report and statement regarding certain things, some of which were suggested by your letter.

Your statement that the course I have taken has been altered from the itinerary outlined by Dr. Dorsey I do not quite understand, as in his letter of instructions, dated May 5, 1909, he expressly states that I am to proceed first to German New Guinea, and report to Gov. Hahl, which you know from my reports was the course I pursued. Approximately one year was to be devoted to the German Colony, one year to English New Guinea and the islands (Solomons, New Hebrides, New Caledonia) and one year to Dutch New Guinea and the islands to the west (i.e., the East Indies). At the same time I was at liberty to pursue any course I might think best, under the circumstances.

Circumstances are a controlling factor here, I find. At first I expected, and Dr. Hahl said that he would have been glad to give me the opportunity to visit the various parts of the colony in the government ship, the Seestern. But the Seestern was lost at sea, with all hands, shortly before I arrived in the colony. Then I expected to be able to visit parts of the New Guinea coast in the New Guinea Co's steamer Siar, but the Siar ran on the rocks, and had to proceed to Sydney for repairs shortly after I arrived. Still I hoped later to be able to go around in her, but now comes the final blow. Dr. Dorsey's articles on German New Guinea, especially that of Oct. 6, 1909 (Chicago Tribune) gave serious offense to the colony. Some of the men were especially bitter against him, as he had been given every assistance here in the colony (far more than any German investigator had received) and they regarded some of his statements as a base slander as well as a betrayal of the most generous hospitality. As I was known to be sent out through him, and by the same institution, I came in for a full share of suspicion. Everything goes by favor here, as there are no public means of transportation; one must travel with a government boat, a mission boat, or that of some private firm. The result has been that a large number refuse to have anything to do with me. I am not even allowed to travel on the Siar as a passenger, tho she will carry my specimens for heavy freight charges (she carried Dr. Dorsey's for nothing, he paying merely for himself as passenger).

All this makes it exceedingly difficult to do what I wished to do, and very hard to get from place to place, as well as very unpleasant for me personally, as most treat me as a questionable character. I would have left the colony before this, only last fall and winter made two important collections in places from which I could not remove them at the time, owing to lack of transportation during the rainy season. If I left, these were lost, as no one would pack them in my absence. So I have remained here, and done what I could. Dr. Albert Hahl is at present in Europe on leave of absence. He is the governor of the colony, and he himself told me that Dr.

Dorsey had "killed the museum" in this colony. Dr. Hahl is still friendly, and willing to help, but he is almost the only one. I have understood that a protest against Dr. Dorsey's article, signed by most of the influential men of the colony, has been published in both German and American papers.[18] Dr. Hahl would doubtless be able to give further information regarding this matter.

Though this has made my work difficult and unpleasant, I still think that I have been fairly successful, and there are a few men who are still friendly. With one of these [Gramms] I am now staying, and have chartered from him a small cutter, with native crew, to enable me to visit various places along the coast. It makes progress exceedingly slow, but much more thorough, and what is lost in one way is gain[ed] in another. This part of the coast is very interesting and I would have regretted exceedingly being forced to leave New Guinea without seeing it. The natives here are practically untouched by European civilization, aside from a few iron implements. Either today or tomorrow I expect to leave in the cutter for the mouth of the Kaiserin Augusta River, and there to visit some villages lying on the interior lagoons never before visited by white men. I hope some interesting specimens may be obtained on this trip.

As soon as I can get my specimens together, I shall pack them and send them home, and then probably leave for English territory. I should like very much to visit certain other parts of the colony for a month or so, and will see what the feeling is before finally leaving.

Packing is also one of my difficult problems. Suitable lumber and packing material it is impossible to obtain. I must pack the things locally in what boxes I can obtain, and then ship to Fr. Wh. Hafen. There I must repack in special boxes made to order, at heavy expense, or ship the boxes as they are, trusting that they are sufficiently strong to bear the journey, or at least that loss by breakage will not equal the extra expense of new boxes and repacking. In the last shipment I had the smaller boxes fastened together as crates, and I think I shall do the same again, only make them still stronger. I shall await with anxiety the report on this shipment, as I have requested Mr. Simms to have part of the shipment unpacked. I hope that my pots, at least, came through in better shape than Dr. Dorsey's and Mr. Voogdt's shipments.

Regarding the duration of my stay in Melanesia, I hardly know how to answer your request that I shorten the time. Three years, to say nothing of two is altogether too short for the work as I should like to do it. At the same time I may be forced on account of my health to leave before three years are completed. I feel now that I cannot stand my present mode of living very many years—traveling for weeks in a small cutter or native canoe, sleeping in native houses, living on native food or poorly cooked tins, etc. In British territory, however, I hope to be able to change my method of work and get over the ground much faster. That depends on conditions, however. I hoped to get around here faster than I am succeeding in doing. Possibly it would be well for me to do what I can in say two years and a half, and then with more experience and a better understanding of the work return for a year or two at a later period. For one thing, I wish to make a rather complete study of the New Guinea coast and that will take fully another year, probably much more, if I do what I should like to do, unless I find the means of transportation much more favorable than here. I hope to make my studies and collections complete enough so that I shall have something worthy of publication on my return. Then all the other islands—Solomons, New

Hebrides, etc. should be visited! I hope you will leave the matter open for the present, at least till I can find out something of the condition there.

I fear this communication is already too long, but there is another thing I should like to mention. Your letter regarding shipment of specimens was six months in reaching me; the one I am now answering five months; none reach me in less than three. The draft on Sydney came in about 3 months, but it might have been six. I have not yet been able to realize on it as I must have it sent to Sydney, and pay a heavy rate of exchange on the whole, before I can get a cent. At the best it takes six weeks to hear from Sydney. Here it will probably take 3 months. There are also many chances that it gets lost. If all drafts were sent me in duplicate, about a month apart, so as to be in different mails, it would be much safer. If the drafts could also be smaller, it would simplify matters, especially when I am traveling from place to place. Now I must pay an exchange rate of between 1 and 2 percent on the whole $3100.00, while if it had been in smaller amounts, I could have used here only what was necessary, and kept the other till my return to Sydney, or English territory. If duplicate drafts for £100 each could be sent me, I am satisfied it would simplify matters, and be cheaper, as well as much safer for me.

Another thing might be done. The Lloyd checks have proved very satisfactory, and are far cheaper than the draft, considering the rate of exchange I must pay. Additional checks can be made out in Chicago, and sent out here to be delivered to me through any agent. It is now too late to send here, and I suppose when this reaches you, the remainder of $2500 will have been sent. If there is occasion to send me more money, as I hope there will be, I trust these suggestions will be borne in mind.

I also wish to thank you for the personal interest you have shown, and the kind wishes you have expressed, in your last letter.

One more thing I am tempted to speak of. As long as I have anything to do with the Melanesian collections, it will be my ambition to make them as complete and interesting as possible. Of models, etc. I shall say nothing now, but I have now the opportunity to do something which I cannot do later, i.e., interest certain men in making and sending collections of specimens to the Museum. Dr. Dorsey had interested Capt. Voogdt. I am staying with the man who sold Capt. Voogdt many of his best specimens, including the large feather mask and the two large canoes. This man, Herr Gramms, I have every reason to believe is a perfectly honorable and upright man. He has lived in the colony for years, and now owns one of the few independent (from the New Guinea Co.) plantations in New Guinea. He has been of much help to me, and has shown an interest in my work, and has expressed a willingness to collect specimens for the Museum, not as a business but incidentally, as he has many opportunities, in his travels here and there, to get many rare and interesting specimens, especially from the interior. He is almost the only man whom I have met in the colony whom I would care to trust with such a commission. Of course all things must be conditional, but I should like to know if the Museum would look with favor on such means of extending our collections. I might also in English New Guinea meet men who could help us in this way. For my own reputation, as well as that of the Museum, I do not care to suggest such things to responsible business men when there is a probability of the Museum turning the whole thing down. The special collections from such sources might be small, but they would be select, and all together would make an important collection. Certainly the help of local men has been often obtained in America, where it is even less important than here, owing to the great distance, difficulty of communication, etc. but especially as this is a new region, now exceptionally rich, but in a few years probably stripped bare.

It might interest you to know that within the last ten minutes a native hunter (of birds of paradise) of Mr. Gramms has returned from near the mouth of the Kaiserin Augusta River, and reported that an unknown steamer has recently ascended the river. It cannot be the N. G. Co's steamer, nor the mission steamer, for we know that both these are elsewhere. So it must be an outside steamer, probably also bound on making ethnological collections.[19] I had hoped to get up the river myself, but fear I cannot. Oh! for a steamer for three weeks!!

Please pardon the length of this communication. I hope you understand, however, that I shall do my best to help put the Museum in the front rank, and make its collections as perfect as possible.

Very respectfully,
A. B. Lewis

I have already directed that till further notice letters should be sent to Sydney, care N. German Lloyd, as when I first came out.

Fig. 4.25. "The procession coming out of the *tamburan* enclosure, Sisimongum, Hansa Bay." A-33515 (574).

On the North Coast

||||||||||||||||||||||||||||||||||||||||||||||||||||||||||||||||||||||||||||||||||||||||||||||||||||||||

Sunday, June 5   About 4 P.M. went back in cutter to Awar.

Monday, June 6   Packed up my stuff and got away about 11 A.M. for Watam, dropping on the way the Kaian Chinaman. It was nearly 8 P.M. when we anchored off Watam, so did not go ashore till morning.

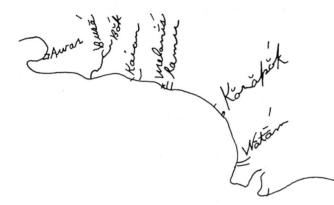

Tuesday, June 7   Went ashore early, had some breakfast, left my things at the Chinaman's (where expected to stay over night), and then to the village

Fig. 4.26.   Small wooden figures from communities on the North Coast: Sup, 141069 (3448); Murik, 140901 (3356), 140900 (3354), 140904 (3358), 140693 (3357); male, Kirau, 140698 (3151); Mabuk, 140879 (3265); Watam, 140633 (2822); Kayan, 140497 (2504); Bure, 140369 (2693), 140368 (2692); Borbor, 140536 (2592); Monumbo (Potsdamhafen), 140243 (2389). A-112315.

near by. There were no natives here who could talk, so took the Chinaman along. Language and customs here much the same as at Kaian. Bought a number of things, esp. wooden images. There were small ones (4–6 in.) and larger ones (1½–2½ ft.). One name for all, but could not find out what they meant. Also a few masks, but almost nothing old.

Herr Gramms had said that the *tamburan* house here was one of the finest on the coast, and that Rodatz had tried formerly to buy it, but would not give the price asked. I thought maybe I could get the house, but found it had been burnt shortly before. The ashes were quite fresh, and had not been rained on. When I asked to see the house, the natives and Chinaman all declared there was none in the place. The Chinaman denied all knowledge of any. It was evident they all wished to deceive me (the Chinaman here, as at Kaian, had a native woman for wife, and spoke the native language). The captain of the cutter knew where they (there were 2) were (not in the village, but in the bush not far away) and led me to their ashes. It seemed as tho they had been burnt on purpose, as everyone denied all knowledge of them. The natives make baskets, wooden bowls (similar to Kaian), *garamut*s (much similar to Kaian), masks and wooden images. *Kundu*s (at least the best) come from the Schouten Islands. Sleeping-bags from Kirau. Houses the same as in Kaian. Canoes both sea-going, with outrigger, and plain dug outs, for river and lagoon.

Wednesday, June 8   In morning loaded my things into cutter, and left for Kīrau, where arrived about 4:30. Kirau lies some 15 miles west of the main mouth of the K. A. river. There are two villages, called by the inhabitants Utum and Djepóp. Méndām (native name Djerāmūt) is on the beach a few miles east, but is now nearly deserted, owing to the fact that the sea has washed away most all the cocoanuts there. The coast here is low and narrow, and back of it is a network of lagoons and streams.

We anchored off Utum, nearly ½ mile out, as the water was very shallow. I went on shore with the boat, and got the natives to give me use of a house (*kómesan*, or men's house), where I arranged to sleep.

The natives seemed quite friendly, but I found only one who could speak fairly good Pidgin English. One of them stole Kabai's pipe from the boat when landing, and I was afraid there was going to be trouble, but after 10 or 15 minutes they succeeded in "finding" it. Luckily I saw the man take it, so knew it was not lost.

Thursday, June 9   Bought a number of things, esp. sleeping bags, which are made here in great numbers. Got a doz. for Herr Gramms. In afternoon went to Djepop, and got a few more things.

Went into several houses, and 2 *tamburan* houses *(tāv* or *tābu)*. In the family house *(īdān),* which were usually open, or had a door, only in front, was an elevated platform at the rear, enclosed except for an opening (a) in the center, which was closed by a curtain, so to speak, of fine leaf fringe. In this enclosure were the *tamburan* masks and figures. In one I saw 3 full figures, about 2 ft. high, and 4 masks, 1½ to 2 ft. long, and finely made, leaning against the back wall, and 3 masks lying in front of them on the floor.

Fig. 4.27. Large wooden figure, Watam. Decorated with nassa shells and bark cloth, 140648 (2850). A-112366.

Fig. 4.28. "Old wooden mask, rattan band around top, Watam," 140628 (2884). A-112382.

Fig. 4.29. "Man of Watam, with hair ornament no. 140657 (2881)." A-33418 (478). See Fig. 4.30.

Fig. 4.30. Hair ornament, Watam. Bone pin with double figure, decorated with nassa shell, hair string, feathers, 140657 (2881). A-112356.

I could buy none of them, and only as a favor was I allowed to see them. The interpreter said such masks came from Panam, in the "bush."

The *tamburan* house in Djepop was similarly constructed, tho I was not allowed to see behind the curtain. The main room had a couple of *garamut*s and a sleeping sac or two. The only noticeable thing was a carved wooden figure, higher than a man, fastened back to against the central house post. The natives objected to my going very close to it.

In Utum the main room was the same, but had a large, finely carved mask, instead of the large figure, fastened to the house post. Here I was allowed to look behind the curtain, and saw some finely carved masks. The arrangement was the same as in the house, only the carvings were better. In the center of the house, close under the roof, was a small loft, which the natives said could be only looked into by old, *gray* haired men who had lost their teeth (i.e., very old men) and that there was no one in the village at present who knew what was therein. The meaning of the masks and figures I could not discover, but was led to think, from what one man said, that the small figures (1–2 ft. high) had some connection with the initiation and circumcision ceremonies. The wall in front of the platform was all painted with various designs.

The *tamburan* house in Borbor had the front central post ornamented, and to this was fastened the large mask *(murūk)*. I did not find out if there was a secret hoard of masks in the rear or not.

In Kirau the chief industry was the making of baskets and sleeping bags. These are made of *kīran* {*Scirpus* sp. (Standley)}, a sedge about 6–8 ft. high (see July 9) growing in shallow water.

It is pulled up in bunches by twisting the tops around a stick *(brīt)*, and taken to the village and spread out on the ground to dry. When dry it is tied in bundles and kept in the house till ready to use. I saw large stores in some of the houses. To prepare it small bundles are beaten with a club *(kīorbrīt)* on a log to flatten the stems, and it is then either split, or woven without splitting into the baskets and bags. In the bags are also woven strips of bark *(nūnavīkōn)* from a certain tree, reddened by boiling it in a decoction of the bark of another tree *(tong)*.

Wooden bowls did not seem to be made here (my interpreters lied so much I could believe hardly anything they said, as if they had an idea I would value a thing more if it came from a certain place, they always said it came from there). Of those I saw, some were of the Kaian type, some from Mum (round or nearly so).

Pots were partly from the Mum region, partly from Wusumum, and partly from the "bush." These were the largest, with crude incised patterns around the top.

Small shell rings were also made here. They were ground down on a piece of sand-stone (said to come from Sup) and bored with a pump drill with short bamboo (?) points slipped over the wood point. The piece of shell is wrapped with strips of "bush rope" and held between the woman's feet. The grindings from the sandstone are used with the bamboo to assist in the cutting, with a little water placed near by in a cocoanut cup. Only small rings seem to be made, from tridacna and a sort of cone shell.

*Garamut*s were of the same type as Watam and Kaian. *Kundu*s and paddles said to come from the Schouten Islands. A few netted sacs were seen, either Kaup type or the "bush" type, same as at Awar and Kaian, with seeds. Hand spears, and spears for throwing sticks common, same types as to east. One bow seen, from far to west (same as from the interior at Berlin Hafen). Shields mostly gone.

Fig. 4.31. "Interior of *tamburan* house, showing wooden image, sleeping bags, fireplace, etc. A canoe sail is put up in front of door at end, Kirau." A-33448 (508).

Fig. 4.32. Large, soft basket of sedges *(larkom),* decorated with fringe (originally) colored red, yellow, white, and black (now dark brown, brown, tan, and natural sedge), Kayan, 140446 (2478). A-112256.

Fig. 4.33. "Making basket, Kirau." A-33422 (482).

Fig. 4.34. "Woman drilling shell with pump drill (specimen no. 140729 [2918, 2923]), Kirau." A-33423 (483) (cf. Lewis 1932; pl. 39-2; 1951; 121).

Fig. 4.35. Small wooden maskettes, often attached to string bags: Mushu, 141055 (3469); Rabuin, 141044 (3472); Watam, 140620 (2870); Mabuk, 140844 (3219); Gariess near the Ramu, 138694 (_____) from Gramms; Kayan, 140494 (2509), 140491 (2510); Bure, 140374 (2705); Awar, 140334 (2459); Monumbo, Potsdamhafen, 140244 (2381). A-112306.

Sago chief food, washed as in Kaian and Watam (see photos 480–481). After beaten out by men, taken by women in baskets to the washing trough, set up (made of stem of sago leaf, large end down) near the water. The end of the sago stem trough is closed with a piece of cocoanut leaf sheath fibre, held in place by sticks stuck into base of sago leaf (see photo). The water is dipped up with a half cocoanut on end of long handle. After settling, the water is poured off, the sago rolled into balls as large as one's head, these wrapped in leaves and taken to the village, and so kept till used. The sago meal is either boiled or baked in thin cakes, (apparently much the same as at Sissano, but the cakes are flat—I did not see the baking).

The houses are smaller and more poorly made than in Watam, but constructed in much the same way. In fact, the houses at Awar and Kaian are the largest and best along this stretch of the coast, the houses decreasing in size, and becoming poorer in construction, both to east and west.

Friday, June 10 In morning sent my things and purchases on board cutter, and about 11 A.M. got away for Awar, the wind, however, was not very good.

Saturday, June 11 All night and day under sail. Crossed the K.A. river, the current of which took us far out to sea. The boundary between the river and sea current from east was quite marked, even when almost out of sight of land. The sea was quite choppy where the two came together.

Sunday, June 12 Got to Awar about sunrise. Rested during the day.

Monday, June 13 Developed photos and catalogued specimens.

Tuesday, June 14 Wrote up notes and loaded cutter with specimens for Potsdam Hafen, for which place left about noon.

271

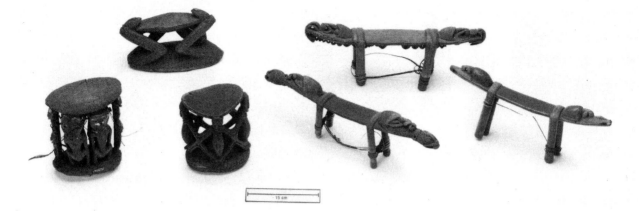

Fig. 4.36. Headrests or pillows from the North Coast made of carved wood or wood with rattan legs: (wood) painted red and blue, Sup, 140072 (3454); collected Awar, made Mingum in interior, 140352 (3294); Kirau, 140716 (2934); (rattan legs) Bushim, 140209 (3098); Swaro, 140225 (3108); Tobenam, 140188 (3038). A-112384.

Wednesday, June 15 As sea was so rough, did not land my specimens till this morning. Then sent the cutter back for the remainder of the specimens left at Awar, and packed.

Thursday, June 16 Cutter returned, packed.

Friday, June 17 Packed.

Saturday, June 18 Finished all that I could do, but had not boxes enough for all. Had 31 boxes and 49 bundles.

Sunday, June 19–Monday, June 20 Rested and waited for *Siar*.

Tuesday, June 21 As *Siar* did not come, I concluded not to go to Fr. Wh. Hafen as I had intended (get the *Siar* to tow the cutter, if I could), but to send my specimens to be stored there. About noon I left on foot for Bogia, sending the cutter on beforehand. Stopped at the mission station over night. The missionary (P. Girards) reported that little was to be found inland, short of 3–4 day's journey. The inland tribes were poor. No more stone axes or shields were to be found in the neighborhood. He said he had previously obtained 3 small stone images (now in Europe), so far as he knew, the only ones from New Guinea.

Wednesday, June 22 Rained early in morning, but left about 9 for Dāgoíi, where hoped to obtain the *tultul* (Bōngemālā) to go with me further along the coast, and act as interpreter. Reached Dagoii about 2 P.M., and arranged with Bongemála to go with me. Bought a few things, and then as the sea was rough went over to the lee of an island lying off the coast to stay over night. Here shot several pigeons.

Thursday, June 23 Left early in the morning, and ran most of the day, arriving late in the afternoon at Dūgūmūr, (Hatzfeld Haf.). Went on shore

Fig. 4.37. Fish traps of rattan: Linimbar (Eitel Friedrichhafen), 140126 (3070); Moro (east of Kronprinzhafen), 140131 (3058); Linimbar, 140125 (3069). A-112332.

and looked around, but did not buy anything, as told the natives to get out their things and would buy in the morning.

Friday, June 24 Bought a few things but the natives did not have much, and left in forenoon for further east. Soon ran under the shelter of a peninsula, and visited a small settlement near by (Tōbenām). Got a few things here. Left about 3 P.M. and ran all night to east. Rain.

Saturday, June 25 Arrived in morning at Eitel Fr. Hafen, and anchored off the village of Línimbār. Here bought a few things, and then with guide started west along the coast to visit some other villages near by. (To the east no more villages on the coast for a day's journey.) The cutter was to sail along the coast, but there was no wind, so after visiting three villages and waiting at the last some time, I decided to go back to where the cutter was. The cutter had proceeded some distance from the harbor, but the coast was all coral rock, and made it impossible for a boat to land in the surf. Hence I walked clear back to the harbor, the boat, which had come off from the cutter, following. The cutter also turned about, and made for the harbor with what little wind there was. Finally I searched [for] a place where I could get into the boat, and the boys got a native canoe from the village near by, so we reached the cutter, and returned to the harbor for the night.

Sunday, June 26 Left in morning with land breeze, and ran west to a village (Mórō) a little east of Kronprinze Hafen, where landed. Bought some things, and sent them by boat to cutter, while walked around the harbor to Mālālā, on the west side. Here did not get much, but as it was not yet late, decided to walk on to the next village, where was a fairly good harbor, so that the cutter could anchor there over night. Reached this village (Símbenē, a short distance east of Cape Gourdon) about 4 P.M. Had barely arrived here, when the whole interest of the place was centered in the arrival of 4 large canoes from Manam (Vulcan Isl.) with baskets of *galíp* nuts, which they wished to exchange for pots. It was an interesting sight seeing the large canoes come on shore, and 20 or more men drag them up on the beach out of the reach of the tide. The Manam men were a little wild and afraid of me, so that my interpreter asked me to go back into the village. Some of the men were hanging on to their spears in a suspicious manner. I stayed in the village

Fig. 4.38. Two baskets of canarium (*galip*) nuts, collected at Simbine. "These are traded in this form by the Manam people to various places along the coast" 140258 (_____), 140256 (_____).
A-112281.

till nearly dusk, buying 2 baskets of nuts through my interpreter, and then went out to the cutter, which had meanwhile arrived. Stayed here over night.

Monday, June 27   Left early in morning. On west side of Cape Gourdon a canoe came out to the cutter from the village there (Būshim) with 3 good shields and some other things.

Stopped at the village of Eídābāl (in Hatzfeld Hafen). Here the natives had previously had some trouble with the *kiap*, and had threatened to kill the first white man they could. So we took a couple of guns along, but the natives (outwardly, at least) were very friendly. Leaving here we ran to Swāro, where we stopped over night.

Tuesday, June 28   In forenoon arrived at Dagoii. I had long been trying to find out where pots were made, and the missionary at Bogia had said that they were made at Kināmbum, inland from Dagoii. So after landing I got my interpreter to lead me to the village. After an hour's journey we reached a village on a hill, where we found a few men (all the women had run away). Here the natives declared no pots were made. That they had came from a place called Tanggūmū, 3–4 day's journey in the interior. They said that at Bānāpūtū, further east along the coast, pots were made. This was 5 or 6 miles away, and I decided to stay at Dagoii over night, and proceed to Banapútu the next day. Cutter to anchor off the island.

Wednesday, June 29   Left for Banaputu early, with two guides and inter-preters (see photo). About 9 we arrived at a deserted village on the beach, Banaputu, the guide said, but there was another Banaputu a little further on, still another part way up the hill toward the interior, and the main Banaputu on top of the coast range, nearly 1,000 ft. high. I decided to make for the first one toward the bush, where the guides said the young men stayed. The old folks all stopped in the village on top. The people had attempted to close or conceal the path by felling trees across it, and filling it with brush, in several places—but my guides found a way around these places. In a short time we came in sight of the place, perched on the side of the hill above us. Three or four men were visible at first, but they disappeared, and when we arrived no one was to be found. The houses were small, with ground for floor, 8 or 10 all together. The path led on up the hill, and one or two men were to be seen

Fig. 4.39. "View in village of Banaputu." A-33429 (489).

further up. I sent on one of our guides to talk to them and explain who we were—while we followed later. On our arrival at the top we found the men waiting for us, and ready to have one of the women make a pot for my benefit. This was done, and I photoed the process—beating out of a single lump of clay. We also learned that the clay was obtained on the hillside lower down in a side ravine, and this we determined to visit on our way back. The village was situated on the very summit of the range, here a sort of ridge, with fine views around in all directions, when one got out from the trees and brush, which covered the top. There were many very old cocoanut trees. The sides of the range, except in some side ravines, were covered with *alang* grass.

After going down about ¾ of the way, the guides said that the place where the clay came from was off on one side, near the foot of a very steep slope. Down we went, however, sliding a good part of the way, and found a mere hole in the hill-side, some 4 or 5 ft. deep. The clay was nearly black. They said that before using it was mixed with white sand. After photographing the hole, we climbed back to the path and returned to Dagoii, where we arrived about 1:30 P.M. and immediately sent our things on board the cutter, and got off as soon as we could for Potsdam Hafen, where we arrived about 5 P.M.

Thursday, June 30   In morning my things were put in the store house, and after loading on some things for Awar, we left about 9 A.M., but owing to light and contrary winds, did not reach Awar till nearly dark.

Friday, July 1–Saturday, July 2   Developed plates, wrote up notes, etc.

In making this trip to the coast lying between Potsdam Hafen and Fr. Wh. Hafen, I had hoped to find something rather different from that at Pots. Haf. There was very little to be found, however. The people are all Papuans, and according to the missionaries, the language, or languages, are related to that of the Monumbo (Potsdam Hafen). Beyond Linimbar (in Eitel Fr. Hafen) there are no villages on the coast till one comes to Serang and Megear, Melanesian settlements of Karkar people. The people live some distance in the interior, but from this region comes the heavy pots with rather long, wide neck, and rectangular wooden bowls. The natives said they were also made in some of the eastern coast villages we visited (?), most come from interior. In several we saw netted sacs being made, very similar, if not the same, as those from back of Awar and Watam.

Bows and arrows were found, somewhat varying in type, but always said to come from the interior.

No wood shields were found east of Moro, and those from here had no fringe. Small wood shields, ornamented with a face near center, come from interior back of Dagoii. Spears, both with plain bamboo and barbed wood points, were found everywhere, and often said to come from the bush.

Bowls somewhat resembling the Kaian type were also found in places, and said to be made there.

Only three types of pottery, the same as those seen in Potsdam Hafen, were seen. One type thin, small and rounded, the type of Banaputu (apparently also made by neighboring villages, as the natives, when at the clay hole, pointed to some neighboring hills, and said the people from there got clay for pots from the same place). This is made by beating out the pot from a single lump of clay, with a wood paddle, and a stone, or only the hand, inside. The rim is trimmed with a bamboo splinter.

Another type, already spoken of, is from the coast (?) to the east.

The third type is from the interior, 3–4 days' journey. The Dagoii people called the place Tanggúmu. Those seen were slightly pointed below, and the rim showed rings, as if coiled. The natives also said they were made by coiling. The boys at Bogia also said that these pots came from 3–4 days' inland.

The dress is the same as all along the coast to K.A. river,—bark loin cloth for men, and fibre skirt for women. In places to east this is of bark of some tree, also in places of grass.

Very few ornaments were seen, beyond woven arm bands, of plain or reddened rattan (reddened by boiling with leaves of a certain tree), or of the Manam type (probably purchased from Manam).

A few *kundu*s were seen, rather crude,—some carved pillows. *Garamut*s were seen at Malala and east of a quite different type from that of Bure and Kaian, plain and heavy, with a hole at one end.

Fish nets, seines and with 2 long poles, were common, also fish traps of bamboo, of varying sizes up to 4 ft. diameter and 6–8 ft. long. These large ones are fastened to a sort of platform, weighted with stones, and sunk in

Fig. 4.40. "View south over Hansa Bay from Mr. Gramms' house, Awar." A-33445 (505).

deep water (often at least 100 ft.), being fastened to a strong rattan rope with bamboo float at end. These floats were frequently seen during our trip (from ¼ to ½ mile out to sea), and several were pulled up, but no fish found.

Pig nets are also used.

The houses become poorer and smaller as one goes east or inland. Many, if not most of them, have only the ground for floor, tho I think in all villages visited there were some with raised floor. Inland, as well as in some places to the east, the roof is of *alang* grass.

Taro is the chief food, with yams, sweet potatoes, cocoanuts, etc. No sago was seen, tho it is doubtless used in some places.

There are no *tamburan* houses, and the people do not make masks or carved images, so far as I could find out.

Sunday, July 3   Rested and wrote.

Monday, July 4   Wrote letters.

Tuesday, July 5   Left with cutter about noon for Kirau, where expected to visit one or two villages in bush. On passing mouth of K.A. river saw large steamer anchored in mouth. Natives said that 2–4 days previously it had come to mouth of river, and that a smaller one had gone up the river.[7] Arrived off Kirau about nine, and anchored for night.

Wednesday, July 6   In morning captain took boat and sounded mouth of lagoon, to see if we could enter. On return waited for wind and about 11 went in. It was shallow, barely deep enough for cutter, ½ mile out, but nearer mouth deepened. The tide was nearly out, but was still some current, so had some difficulty in coming to anchorage place. Did not finish till 2 P.M.

---

7. These steamers were probably associated with the the Dutch-German boundary commission. See Schultze (1910–11, 1914).

Fig. 4.41. "My two guides and interpreters (Bas and Namun) from Kirau." A-33456 (515).

Then visited village near entrance (Yérpūāp), and stayed till 5 P.M. While there saw a new *"tamburan"* enclosure, which the natives would not allow me to enter. Later a peculiar masked figure appeared, with wooden mask face, and head and body all covered with bark cloth, a sort of cape being over the head. The figure was represented with a long, prominent penis. This was about 3:30. The natives said that at noon a female masked figure had appeared for a time. This (the male) seemed to delight in chasing the young boys.

Made arrangements with Bās and Nāmūn to leave with me early next morning for Mābūk.

Thursday, July 7 Left shortly after six with 2 boys, 1 boat's crew, Bas, Namún, and another native. We first followed the lagoon, ½–¾ mile wide, to the east till past exit by Kirau, and then turned. The lagoon seemed to have many branches. The one we turned into gradually narrowed, and finally we turned into a narrow winding channel, barely wide enough for the boat. All the land here seemed barely, if any, above water level (high tide). The banks were lined with mangroves. The narrow way was pursued for about 20 minutes, and then we came out (about 2 hrs. after leaving) in a wide river, or narrow lagoon. This we followed for between 3 and 4 hrs., before reaching our destination, on a narrow side branch. Here we were very friendly received, with cocoanuts, food, etc. I visited first a number of houses, including 2 *tamburan* houses. Here, in a covered platform behind, were a number of masks, and several (in one 4, other 2) large figures, apparently representing crocodiles, some 4 feet long. Some of the masks were small, some larger, up to 2–2½ ft. long. Some were very old and decayed, but others were still in good condition, and as fine as any I had seen. Some had carved birds on the foreheads, similar to what I had seen in Kirau.

I then returned to the house where my things were, and trade began. The men brought some masks and other things, but the best masks and carvings they would not bring. Finally I decided to take some of my trade and go to the *tamburan* house, and see if I could not there buy some of the better things, esp. the carved crocodiles. The instant I said I would go to the *tamburan* house to buy something there, the old men began to slip out, and I heard much talking and running about outside. I took a dozen 16 in. knives and some hatchets and immediately went to the house from which I heard men slipping out behind as I entered. Several of the natives came with me, and I found the place practically deserted. I noticed a fine mask lying on a platform to one side, but almost immediately an old man grabbed it and made off. No further attempt was made to remove anything. I now asked to buy one of the crocodiles. They said they would not sell one. I finally spread out a dozen large knives and 2 hatchets on the floor, and said I would give that for one, only I was to pick it out. After some talk they seemed to agree to it, and let me go up to the platform (about 8 ft. from the floor) and look at the figures. I then found that all the best masks had been removed. I selected the crocodile I wanted, and the men agreed to its sale. Two rather inferior masks I also succeeded in buying. Another crocodile they would not sell.

These crocodiles were very crudely carved out of a log and but faintly resembled that animal. The head and tail projected at each end of a sort of inverted trough, carved on the sides, and with some rudely carved small figures on top.

These carved crocodiles each had a special name, or perhaps better, represented a spirit of that name. These were very powerful *tamburan,* and had the form of crocodiles, or lived in certain crocodiles. It was customary to make the young boys sleep under the image, to "make them strong." (Apparently in connection with certain ceremonies, but I was unable to find out more.) Women or children must not see the images. The natives seemed to stand in considerable fear of them, as well as my own men, who repeatedly assured me that "*tamburan* he no good, he make boat capsize," and declared I must not take the things back in the boat. My interpreter settled the difficulty by getting the natives to promise to take image, as well as the other things, back to the cutter in their canoes. I later succeeded in buying a second image (older and not so good), from the chief man of the place, who was away in the bush looking after his yam and taro patch today. My interpreter said this was the only village where such crocodile *tamburan*s were found, and it would seem that these crocodile spirits were especially honored or feared in this village.

Fig. 4.42. Detail of carved wooden spear point, Mabuk. Fastening of plaited cord and fur string, 140821 (3286). A-112254.

279

As it was necessary to leave very early in the morning, in order to get through the narrow creek at high tide, I decided to stay over one day.

Friday, July 8 Rained during the night and morning. The natives left the house to me and my men, and in the morning the chief came while I was getting breakfast ready, but of his own accord then called out to the other men not to come now, and shortly withdrew himself, and did not reappear till breakfast was over—an example of native politeness. I bought a few more things this morning, and then photographed the making of sago.

MABUK—SAGO

The sago grows at some distance from the village, and the sago trunks are cut into sections about 4 ft. long and floated to the bank of the stream near the village. They are then split on top, and the rind pried apart with a sharpened stick, and propped open with small sticks. The man then stands to one side and breaks down the pith (photos 525 & 526) much as in Sissano. The sago is then taken in baskets to place near by where the women wash it. The stem of a sago leaf is set up, and at its base a strainer of the cocoanut sheath fibre fastened with sticks. In this trough the sago

Fig. 4.43. "House which we occupied in Mabuk, a men's house." A-33455 (514).

pith is dumped, and water for washing dipped up out of a hole near by with a half cocoanut shell on a long handle, and poured into the trough. The mass of pith is then worked by hand, and the water with sago flour runs out into a spread out base of nibung palm leaf, which often drains into a second. After settling, the sago meal is made into balls nearly as big as one's head, and this form (not wrapped in leaves) is kept till used. Sago here is both cooked with hot water, and baked in thin cakes. Much is traded to the coast (Kirau and Mendam), two canoes with sago accompanying us on our return.

MABUK—DISHES, CANOES, POTS

Round or nearly round flat wood dishes are also made here, as I saw some in different stages of manufacture. Also many canoes. The canoe of all this region is peculiar, in that the rear is cut so low that it must usually be further closed with a dam of earth. The rear tongue itself is usually ornamented.

The prow is often elaborately carved, with crocodile heads, birds, etc.

The pots here were all said to come from Spīk (K.A. river), usually from a village called Angōram. Large pots and bowls were ornamented with sharply incised lines in a broad band around the rim. There were also pots, or rather bowls, of the type coming from back of Mum, with broad incised grooves representing faces, etc., covering most of outer surface. The interpreters said these also came from Spik, but as I had already found out that they lied whenever they thought it to their advantage, I put no faith in this statement. It is possible these pots may have come through the bush, however, and not by the coast.

Neither bows and arrows, nor shields were seen here. The natives declared shields were not used in the interior. Spears were of many designs, often elaborately barbed.

Dress and ornaments the same as at Kirau.

Fig. 4.44. Ornament set in front of war canoe, with mask attached, Mabuk, 140840 (3247). A-112191.

10 cm

Fig. 4.45.   Small wooden charms or images (batlike figures): Murik, 140919 (3408); Kirau, 140712 (3157); Rabuin, 141041 (3475), 141039 (3478). A-112305.

The houses were not so good as at Kirau, both roof and sides being of the plaited sago leaf. All were on piles, 4–5 ft. high; the largest was perhaps 15 by 20 ft. There were not over 20 houses all told.

Some of the masks and larger images had special names. One image about 1 ¼ ft. high represented a spirit which helped dogs to catch pigs. The back and cheeks of the image were scraped with a clam shell, and the scrapings put in the dog's food. Then the next day when hunting the spirit rode on the dog's neck, guided him, and made him able to run and catch and hold the pigs.

Most of the smaller images seemed to be love charms. When a man wanted a woman he made an image. Then the spirit of the image went into the woman and caused her to like him. (The explanation was not clear, and when I tried to get details, they could not, or would not, understand me.) Sometimes these images were hung up during [the] night over the sleeping bag where the woman slept.

The figures of bats were also love charms, as betel nut was put in the hole on top, and pepper fruit under the wings. These were later given to the woman, and caused, when chewed, her to like him.

Most of the masks were used as part of a masked figure in the dances and ceremonies. Some at least seemed to represent particular spirits, as they had special names, but of what nature I could not discover.

Saturday, July 9   Was up at peep of day and got away before sun rise. Two canoes carried my extra purchases, as the natives had agreed to take them to the cutter. There was a fog over the water when we started, so that one could hardly see 100 ft. away.

About 9 we reached the narrow channel. Close to this channel there were flats covered with reeds, where the natives from Kirau came to get reeds (sedges) for their baskets and sleeping bags (see June 9). The place was swampy, but not under water, even at high tide, tho it was so far from the channel that probably the tide had no effect there. The sedge (a species of *Scirpus* Standley) was about 6 ft. high (see photo 511).

We reached the cutter about noon, and I immediately went over to Yerpuap to see if I could get the dress of the masked figure, seen before I went away. This I bought (tho with a different mask from that shown in the photograph (510)[8]) as well as some other things. On returning I got something to eat, and then went to Kirau, by boat. It was longer than I expected. Got but little there, and returned on foot.

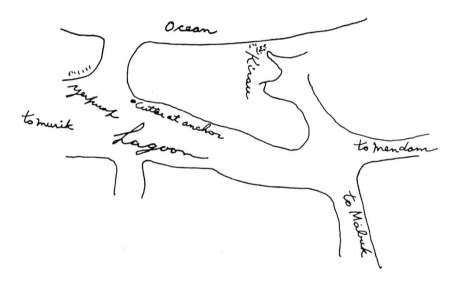

Fig. 4.46. Old wooden image *(kandingbang)*, Kirau. Black face, red eyes and body, 140709 (3159). A-112349.

Sunday, July 10   Left early in morning for Awar. Rained most of forenoon, and little wind. Off Mendam I decided to go ashore, and here got a number of shields and pots.

This, as many other places along this coast, is gradually being overwhelmed by the sea. Many of the houses were in ruins, and back of the narrow strip of beach was swamp, showing in many places the posts of former houses. Apparently the land is sinking.

Monday, July 11   Sailed all night. About noon arrived in channel opposite Awar, but wind failed, and was dusk before we came to anchor.

Tuesday, July 12   Developed my photographs. Did not feel well in morning, and by noon was too sick to do anything more. Apparently a combination of fever and stomach trouble.

Wednesday, July 13–Monday, July 18   Too unwell to do anything but read and write a little. Laias (capt. [of the] cutter) also sick, so could not have sailed had I been well.

---

8. See Fig. 4.47.

Fig. 4.47. "Fibre covering with wooden mask for masked figure, Kirau. The man's head, except the face, is covered with pieces of palm leaf sheath sewed together, and the ornamented mask is in front of the face." 140885 (3160). A-112386.

Tuesday, July 19 Packed and wrapped up my specimens, after numbering same.

Wednesday, July 20 Intended to start in evening for a trip along the coast, but heard shortly after noon that there was to be a big "sing-sing" in Sisimangum, with large masks, so went immediately with my boys and two of the women, who had reported the thing, to Sisimangum. Here found the natives had erected, around the front of a house, a high fence of sago leaves (photo 557, back of house shows to right). Inside the enclosure, hung up under the front of the house, were two large frames covered with feathers of various colors, arranged in regular rows and patterns. Below on the frame was a wooden mask, and above this there were 4 wings, so to speak, each covered with feathers, the one in front, over the mask, only came about half way down. The masks as they stood were about 15 ft. high [Fig. 4.48], extending from the ground to the comb of the projecting gable. They were not completed, however, and we were told that the dance would come off the next day. So after looking around a little, we returned.

Thursday, July 21 In morning finished wrapping up specimens, and in afternoon again went to Sisimangum. Here found little progress, and was told that the dance would not come off for 2 or 3 days (by Saii). Heard the drums in Nubia, however, and learned that a sing-sing was in progress there,

Fig. 4.48. "Large feather masks inside *tamburan* enclosure, Sisimongum." A-33499 (558).

so went to see what it was. The ordinary sing-sing, with 2 *tamburan* pipes and drums in house, where plenty [of] food was brought in bowls for the men to eat. Tried to photo the interior of the house, but without success—too dark.[9]

Friday, July 22   In morning developed photos, and in afternoon went to Awar. In morning Gramms had sent his shooting boy, Yāban, to go by way of Awar and tell Bogasu to come to the house, so that he might act as interpreter for me. About 11 he came, and after talking with him a while, I arranged to return in the afternoon to Awar, where he was to have a canoe ready to take me across the river. It was nearly 4 P.M. when I got there, and I spent all the time I had to spare in photographing. I tried to photo the interior and under side of the houses (but only one (552) proved worth keeping), and then, with much persuasion, succeeded in getting 4 men to be

9. This very dark image has, however, survived, but is not reproduced here.

Fig. 4.49. "Men's house in Sisimongum, with drums." A-33505 (564).

photographed (531–538).[10] Most of the men, and all the women, were afraid, and would not allow me to get near them with the camera.

Saturday, July 23 In morning developed photos and then went to Awar. Found most of inhabitants, including Bogasu, were away fishing. Got Tapi to act as interpreter, and again photographed two interiors (553–554 & 555–556 [Fig. 4.13]), giving exposures of 1 to 1½ minutes. Then went to Sisimangum. Found that now the masks were hung under a special shed roof built to protect them, but otherwise little changed. Photoed a (no. 543) bundle of sago, ornamented with reddish-yellow fruits and green and greenish-yellow leaves and strips of sago leaves. Such a bundle was in front of nearly every house, preparatory to the feast.

Under Saii's house the women were cooking sago in a large pot. This I also photographed, as well as the distribution of the cooked sago with a cocoanut shell in the numerous wood bowls set on the platform behind (546 [lost]). These the women then carried to the men in another house (547).

The water is first heated and the sago, mixed with a little water in a limbum-leaf bucket, is then poured into the boiling water, and stirred till cooked in a thick gluey mass.

10. Nos. 531–538, 552; not reproduced here.

Sunday, July 24 Developed photos. Richter and Blesser here.

Monday, July 25 In morning Bogasu came to house, and I got a short vocabulary from him, with much work. In afternoon packed my pots.

Tuesday, July 26 Wrote and read in morning. Rained. In afternoon went to Awar. Bogasu was not there, and no canoe. Finally got the natives to carry me across the river. Went to Sisimangum, but found little progress. Said the dance would come off in 2 or 3 days. This was the old story, tho Monday Bogasu had said it would not come off for 4–5 days.

Wednesday, July 27 To Awar about 11 A.M. felt sick when got there, and lay on platform in front of house the whole afternoon. Got back all right, but temperature 105°. Had not taken quinine for 15 days, as it had made me so sick the last time. Took some in evening.

Thursday, July 28 Shortly after sunrise Bogasu came, saying that the "*tamburan*" would "come up" this morning. Already the *garamut*s could be heard. I was still pretty weak, but went in the boat, to Sisimangum, and succeeded in seeing some of the performance. As was not well, returned shortly after it was over, and rested in afternoon.

Friday, July 29 Rain in morning. In afternoon went to Sisimangum, and again saw a part of the afternoon performance, but left (5:30) before it finished.

Saturday, July 30 In morning got together trade (14 large axes, 30 toma-hawks, 4 claw hatchets, 1 doz. 16 in. knives, 1 doz. 12 in. knives, 1 doz. 6 in. knives and sheaths, 2 doz. planing irons, $\frac{1}{2}$ doz. razors, and some red cloth) to value of about M. 160, and started in boat for Sisimangum, to see if I could buy one of the masks. On way stopped on cutter, and found that the crew had neglected to pump out the water for the last 2 days, so that the water had risen inside nearly to the bunks in the cabin. Most everything was wet, and much destroyed. Spent $\frac{3}{4}$ hr. here getting things to rights a little, and then left Kaman and went on with boat to Sisimangum, but arrived too late to see dance. Took my trade into village and spread it out for the natives to look at, but they declared the masks were not for sale, as they (Awar, Sisimangum and Nubia together) had only two, and did not know how to make more, as the old men had died. Herr Gramms had about 2 yrs. pre-viously obtained two masks from the natives, who had made them specially for him, as they were then in fear of a fight, and wished to please him. He had before often tried to obtain one, but they had always firmly refused to sell one. Herr Gramms declares these two are the only ones that have ever left the place.[11]

As I wished to look after my things on the cutter, I did not stay long, but returned in a boat about 11 A.M.

In morning had seen a smoke (of steamer) at Potsdam hafen, and now learned that the *Siar* had come, and would anchor off Awar in the evening. Gramms went over to Protokulo, where it then was, and I got some of my things in order. About dark the *Siar* arrived, and I went on board. The Capt.

---

11. These masks are two of the four now at Field Museum. These two were obtained from Captain Voogdt; the other two ABL later bought from Gramms. All four are on exhibit in Stanley Field Hall.

said he should be back in 2–3 weeks, and I finally decided to go up the coast and meet him in Mum, whither he would return in not less than 10 days. He said he would then probably make a short trip up the K. A. river.

On return to shore about 7 P.M. with Herr Richter, the boat was upset in surf, I lost nothing of value but my glasses.

Sunday, July 31   Rained all day.

Monday, August 1   Went to Sisimangum in boat in morning, but was again too late to see the morning performance. Had only my two boys and Tarep (man from Awar) with me, and the tide was out, and strong current coming out of lagoon, with water so low that the boys had to drag the boat for some distance.

Decided to stay all day and wait for the afternoon performance, when they said the *"tamburan"* would "go along bush."

Fig. 4.50.   "One of the small masks, Sisimongum." A-33523 (582).

Fig. 4.51. "Killing pig for feast, Sisimongum. Pig is bound to pole and offered to the *tamburan* and a small arrow thrust into heart from behind foreleg. No external bleeding."
A-33529 (588).

During the day photographed some more drums, and got quite a little information regarding ornamentation, tho with much difficulty.

In afternoon went to Nubia to look up Bā, who Gramms said understood pidgin English better than any other. On return was too late to see the beginning of the dance, but waited till it was all over, and the *tamburan*s had returned to their watery home.

The meaning of this dance I could not find out. Gramms said it was supposed to represent the cassowary, but the natives refused to talk about it. I got a little information, however. There are two small masked figures (photos 575–576 [see Fig. 4.53], 581–582 [see Fig. 4.50]), representing women, named Kanggai and Gímör, and the two larger, one of which, Gwémbē, is the son of Kánggai, and the other, Kōrai, the son of Gimor. These have their home in a fine house in the bottom of the lagoon near Nubia, whither they return after the dance is over (when the masks are immediately demolished, all the women and children being required to leave the village till this is all finished).

The immediate occasion of the performance seems to be a big feast, extending over several days, the dancing taking place once or twice a day (morning 7–9, and evening 4:30–6) for 1 to 2 hrs., when hogs, usually 4 (this time six, as they had so many), are offered to the spirits (*tamburans*) or masks, one to each; and also numerous baskets of taro, yams, cocoanuts, sago, etc. This is then eaten, but not all that is eaten is so offered.

All the three villages (Awar, Sisimangum, and Nubia) unite in a performance, which takes place, according to Herr Gramms, not oftener than once a year, being held in the different villages in succession. For a week or more before the performance all the people are busy collecting provisions. Several days are spent in washing out sago, one or two in a big fishing expedition, either along the beach, or in the interior lagoons. Then there is a big pig hunt, and they often make a voyage to Manam or other places to buy pigs or other provisions.

Shortly before the feast the sago is made up into ornamented packets, and hung up before the houses (photo 543). On the first day or days of the feast, yams and taro are set out on frames in wood bowls, and also many bundles of sago hung up on a frame (photo 570). The pigs are firmly bound and fastened to a pole [Fig. 4.51] and over this ornamental leaves and woven sago leaf mats are thrown (photo 572 [lost]). The pole is hung up on supports near the house, and the pig may remain so for a day or more. It is killed by thrusting a sharp wood arrow into the heart (?) from just behind the fore leg. This may be repeated two or three times before the pig dies. There is no external bleeding.

For the masks a high enclosure of sago leaves is made (557),[12] enclosing the front of a house. (There are no special *tamburan* houses in Awar.) Here the large frames are hung up under the projecting gable and the feathers arranged thereon [Fig. 4.48]. Later these are set up on supports, over which they sit, under a high shed roof (573). The smaller masks consist only of a frame, with wood mask (face), and covered with split young cocoanut leaves and other leaves.

On this occasion the *tamburan* "came up" in the morning. The procession is arranged inside the enclosure, an opening then made (the drums going all the time), when the dancers can be seen, and they come slowly out.

In front 2–4 men with their finest ornaments, then a large mask, then 2–3 more men; the same repeated for the second mask, and last the 2 small masks side by side. In the afternoon performances which I saw, these were lacking. The number of dancers varied from time to time, and women often joined in the dance (see photos) sometimes taking a position in front, sometimes along side of the men. The men carried *kundu*s, or some of them beat two cocoanut shells together. The movement was slow, 4/4 time. (1) One foot to side and slightly forward, (2) then the other foot tapped the ground along side, (3) then down firmly, (4) rest; then the same repeated with the other foot. Meanwhile all, including many of men around, sang. All whom I asked declared it was merely "sing-sing," and that they did not know what the words meant. Those in front often turned round and faced, or nearly so, the masks. During the singing of a particular stanza (?!) there was very little forward movement. Then they would advance a little and sing another, etc., thus going from one end of the village to the other. The whole performance might last from one to two hrs. On presentation of pigs, baskets of food, etc. they were carried and held a short time directly in front of mask. I could not tell whether anything special was said or sung at the time or not. When over, the procession retreated into the enclosure with all formality, and the masks were set or hung up till the next time, while the dancers removed their special ornaments. The bodies of the

12. See Fig. 4.17.

Fig. 4.52. "Man adorned for dance, Sisi-mongum." A-33508 (567).

Fig. 4.53. "The rear of the procession, Sisimongum." A-33517 (576).

masked dancers were shiny with oil and red paint (dark red earth). Some of the other dancers painted their faces, and all had more or less red paint.

Between the main performances one or both of the small masks would come out with sticks (see photo 581–2 [see Fig. 4.50]) and run around the village. All the young men and boys took to their heels, and if was caught anywhere near by, a stick was thrown at him. These masks did not seem to have any special honor, as during the performance the women could often talk to them and even slap them in the face.

During one performance (afternoon of 2nd day) which I saw, a woman dancer indulged in a special fit of scolding (to the spectators, apparently) and was answered by 2 old men, who apparently were among the spectators. This continued for ten minutes or more. The woman would come out and talk excitedly for some time, stamping the ground with her feet and swinging her arms, and then the men (one or both) would answer, running around the dancers in an excited manner. I was told the woman was scolding the men for killing so many pigs, and using up so much taro, etc. Said that they had already had enough, and should not kill any more. The real meaning I could not discover.

Fig. 4.54. "Man partially adorned for dance, Sisimongum." A-33509 (568).

Shortly after, a man came with a bunch of bananas, and made an excited speech, while he ran around the procession and beat the bunch on the ground, scattering the bananas in all directions—this was apparently an offering to the masks.

The performance closed on the evening of the 5th day (Aug. 1, 1910). After a short performance 3:30–4:30, the masks retreated to the enclosure. Then all the women and children disappeared from the village. After 10 or 15 minutes the shell trumpets were heard giving a peculiar wailing sound, and the procession again came out and proceeded, with trumpets, to the end of the village. Here they stopped and the trumpets proceeded on slowly down to the lagoon. Meanwhile a number of men with spears took their places near the masks, and at a certain signal the spears were thrown into the masks, which then fell down (killing the masks). (The meaning I could not find, as the men would not talk about such things.) The trumpets gradually got weaker (to make the women and children think the *tamburan*s were going back to their house in the lagoon, so my interpreter said). The masks were then immediately dismantled, and the feathers, etc., put away for future use. I left, and as I passed the enclosure, there was still one man therein, blowing away on a shell trumpet. No women or children were to be seen in or around the village.

The ornamental designs of the Awar people nearly all have names. Some of these names do not seem to have any other meaning, but of that I could not be sure, as many others are the names of plants or animals, also sun and stars were found. (See other note book for details.)

The Awar people bury the dead, and so far as Gramms knew, the bones in whole or part, were not dug up. The numerous skulls kept in the village were those of enemies. When a man was buried, the old men swung a sort of *(schwirholtz)* made of a piece of bamboo (about 2 ft. long) with handle 2–3 ft. long, and string of similar length.

When enemies were killed, it was customary to cut out pieces of flesh from different parts of the body. These were made into a bundle, and hung up in house. The drippings were caught and mixed with their food. Thus they partook of the strength of their enemies. (All skulls from Kaian, Watam, Bure, Kirau, and Mabuk were also skulls of enemies.)

Tuesday, Aug. 2   Wrote up notes and photos in morning, in afternoon packed up and sent stuff on cutter.

Up the Kaiserin Augusta River

||||||||||||||||||||||||||||||||||||||||||||||||||||||||||||||||||||||||||||||||||||||||||||||||||||||||||

3 August 1910–24 September 1910

After the feather masks appeared for the last time at Sisimongum, ABL turned his attention to further investigations along the coast. Using Gramms' cutter, he set off once again to the west intending to visit the Dallmannhafen area. During this sojourn along the coast, ABL stumbled upon good fortune: he found a way to ascend the Kaiserin Augusta River.

The Kaiserin Augusta River was one of the earliest discoveries made by the Germans around the time of annexation: Otto Finsch came upon it in 1885 during his famous cruise in the *Samoa* and explored it by whale boat for a distance of about thirty miles (Finsch 1888a, 297). In each of the next few years, one or two groups of German explorers visited the river, gradually reaching farther and farther from the mouth. In 1886 the *Samoa* reached a point about seventy six kilometers upriver (*NKWL* 1885, 67). The same year, the steamer *Ottilie,* under the leadership of Baron von Schleintz, also ascended the river (*NKWL* 1886, 123), traveling about three hundred miles. A year later both the *Samoa* and the *Ottilie* returned to the river in the service of the New Guinea Compagnie, reaching about 380 miles from the mouth (*NKWL* 1887, 152, 189; 1888, 23). For a survey of these early ascents of the river see Bonaparte (1887) and Hellwig (1911).

For the next twenty one years no Europeans are known to have ascended the mighty Kaiserin Augusta River any significant distance[20] (Firth 1982, 96; Hellwig 1911; Schlaginhaufen 1910a, 7), but the situation changed dramatically in August 1908, when the New Guinea Compagnie made its first attempt to recruit plantation laborers from the heavily populated villages on the river. After 1908, visits to the river became regular and routine.

Ironically, despite the intensity of activity by German scholars conducting expeditions in the colony, it was not a German but an American, George Dorsey, who inaugurated this new era of scientific research on the Kaiserin Augusta. Together with Captain Voogdt and Georg Heine (New Guinea Compagnie administrator), Dorsey ascended the river in the *Siar* as far as Pagem, which lay 100–120 kilometers from the mouth. From Kopar village near the mouth, they visited the villages of Singrin, Bin, Ibundo, Wolem, and finally Pagem.

After this, a steady stream of researchers made the arduous trip upriver. Virtually every

295

significant expedition to Kaiser Wilhelmsland came to the river, which was just opening up its remarkable carvings and art to the world. These ascents of the river, together with a handful of visits attempting to recruit laborers, provided a growing number of steel tools for villagers on the middle course of the river, among the peoples now called Iatmul and Sawosh.

When ABL ascended the river, he was fortunate in being able to reach some of the villages that were home to those now distinguished as upper Sepik peoples. At least one of these villages, which ABL later called Jambun, appears not to have been visited previously, although the *Peiho* reached some villages not very far from this community, and Leonard Schultze and the Dutch-German boundary commission had sent two launches much farther, to nearly a thousand kilometers from the mouth. The fact that people in ABL's Jambun did not recognize steel tools suggests how little the commission's expeditions influenced villages where they did not stop.

Although labor recruiting was one of the primary motivations for opening up the Kaiserin Augusta, it would appear that during the German period labor recruiting on the Sepik was minimal at best. ABL recounts the various tricks and strategies attempted by the unnamed captain of the *Siar* to encourage young men to become laborers. Yet it appears that not a single recruit was obtained on this particular trip. After no success, the captain decided to collect ethnological curios and allowed ABL to do the same. Sale of these curios would provide the captain at least some return for his efforts.

Except for the boundary commission's expedition upriver, nearly all ascents of the Sepik before 1911 closely resembled the one described here. They were ordinarily only quick trips upstream of no more than a week or two. In many villages the parties did not even go ashore, and never did they explore the countryside away from the river. By comparison with today's fieldwork in village communities, such a trip upriver was hardly more than a tourist junket.

Early Twentieth-Century Excursions up the Kaiserin Augusta (Sepik) River

Year	Vessel	Farthest Point Reached	Participants	References
1908	*Siar*	ca. 120 km	George A. Dorsey	(1909a)
			Capt. H. Voogdt	*DKB* (1909, 741)
			Georg Heine	
1908	*Langeoog*	ca. 335 km	Georg Friederici	(1909)
			Bezirksassessor Full	(1909a)
			Captain Roscher	*DKB* (1909, 739–745)
1909	*Peiho*	ca. 436 km	Professor Fülleborn	
			Otto Reche	(1910, 285–286)
			W. Müller	
			F. C. Hellwig	(1927)
			Capt. Richard Vahsel	(1909)
1909	*Siar*	ca. 347 km	Otto Schlaginhaufen	(1910a)
			Richard Neuhauss	(1911a, 61)
			Rudolf Schlechter	Steenis-Kruseman (1950, 470–472)
			Georg Heine	
			Dr. Scholz	
1909[a]	*Cormoran*	ca. 339 km	Albert Hahl	Pfarrius (1909)
1910	*Edi*	ca. 370 km	Leonard Schultze	Schultze (1910–1911)
	Java			Penck (1911)
	Pelikan			Schultze (1914)
1910	*Siar*	ca. 465 km	A. B. Lewis	

[a]These three were all with the Dutch-German boundary commission; 2 launches reached 960 kilometers.

Indeed, ABL's trip has many parallels with the kinds of excursions now enjoyed by hundreds of international tourists each year. But before anthropologists and other travelers denigrate ABL's experiences on the river as trivial, it is important to remember that this was only the fourteenth Western ascent of the Sepik ever, and ABL reached what was at the time the second-highest point ever visited by any expedition.

Steamer <u>Coblenz</u> off New Britain
Sept. 7, 1910

Mr. S. C. Simms
Field Museum
Chicago

My dear Simms,

I was very glad to get your letter of June 20th, which arrived a few days ago. I am sorry that the specimens did not arrive before you wrote, but they were delayed in Hong Kong, as you probably know by this time. I wanted especially to hear about them before sending another shipment, but I cannot wait longer. I suppose that before you receive this you will have written to me regarding them. I am sending a new shipment, by this steamer, and others will follow later. I have collected approximately 4,000 specimens in the last year, and they take up a considerable amount of space, and are causing me no end of trouble, as I could not, in all New Guinea, get boxes or timber to make them, and was forced to go to Simpson Hafen for this material. Then owing to Dr. Dorsey's articles on New Guinea, especially the one in the <u>Tribune</u> of Oct. 6th, 1909, the Germans here are up in arms, and most of them refuse to aid me in any way. He has certainly given the Museum a black eye in this region, and the governor himself told me that he (Dorsey) had "killed the Museum" in the colony. Dorsey was entertained everywhere. I am cut by every-body, since his articles came out. My collection could have been one half better and cost less money, to say nothing of the trouble and worry, if Dorsey had never seen this region. He would find it a warm spot if he came back here—but enough of this.

Since last writing I have visited the coast villages from Hatzfeld Hafen to Dallmann Hafen; that is for a hundred miles or more on both sides of the Kaiserin Augusta river. I saw, for example, the dance where the big feather masks that Voogdt sent were used. I have at least 150 carved wooden masks of all sorts, but time is too short to go into details now. I had a small cutter chartered for about two months, and with this and a native crew I went from place to place along the coast and occasionally a short distance inland. For several reasons I did not think it advisable to make an extensive trip inland. In most places the inland tribes are hostile and that, of course, makes it dangerous, even if this were not so, the difficulties of transportation are great and little could be brought out. Then there is not much to bring out, as the culture of the mountain tribes is poor according to all the reports that we have. Then my time was too short to do everything and I thought it better to get a good general ideal of the whole coast. Even for that my time was too short.

By a lucky chance I was able to get up the K.A. river. The head of the New Guinea Co. [Heine] had refused me permission to go in their steamer, the Siar. (This was after Dorsey's article came out, before that I had been invited to go.) I got up the coast in a mission boat and then chartered the small cutter of the only independent planter in New Guinea. I was beginning to wonder how under the shining heavens I was going to get back to Fr. Wh. Hafen, when along came the Siar with a new captain. (Voogdt had gone home sick.) He had apparently received no instructions regarding me, so I tackled him for a ride back to Fr. Wh. Hafen. I had heard that he intended to go up the river on his return from up coast, so I said I would meet him with the cutter at a certain place (on the other side of the river.) Thus, on my way to Fr. Wh. Hafen I took in the river too. The captain was trying to get native laborers, and on the way up would not allow me to buy anything, but on the way down he concluded to buy himself, and gave me permission to do likewise. I got nearly 300 specimens on the river all together, many of them very interesting. The captain got about 1,000 but he made the whole crew work for him, and I had only my two native boys. Still he allowed me to go ashore in the boats with the others, and that was better than nothing.

We went up much further than Dorsey and Capt. Voogdt had been, so far that we got into quite a different and more primitive culture. At the highest village we visited they seemed to have very little. They apparently do not know the use of iron as they preferred a few beads to a good knife, in fact would not take knives in trade at all. They were absolutely naked. I got a hide (boy's) shield here—the only one I ever heard of in New Guinea. The captain would not go on shore, so I could find out very little about the people. Further down we went ashore, but here the culture was different, and much higher than above. Still lower down we found some very interesting things. Pots 2 to $2\frac{1}{2}$ ft. high, with modeled designs around the neck (sometimes human faces) painted all over; big earthen bowls, with raised designs around rim, etc., etc. Also large wood carvings, painted all over with designs. I never saw or heard of anything like them before. Also skulls with faces modeled in clay, and painted—really excellent work. I saw one complete head, from the shoulders up, modeled in clay but could not get it.

Well, I hope to get a few of these things home without breaking, but I fear greatly for the pots—they are very fragile.

All this, of course, was higher up than Dorsey was. The captain promised to sell me some of his best specimens, but the poor man died a few days after our return, and as everyone else is hostile to me and the Museum, I have no hopes of being able to get anything more. I have had so much trouble trying to pack up what I have, that I am not very anxious to get more anyway.

I think it best that these shipments remain in the boxes till I return, but please let me know if the boxes are broken, or if the crated boxes have come apart.

Regarding Jones' material, I know of no manuscripts.[21]

I was very sorry to hear that you were suffering from the effects of your trip. So far, since I last wrote, I have had slight attacks of rheumatism, esp. when on cutter.

Very sincerely yours,
A. B. Lewis

Address: c/o Lohmann & Co., Sydney

{Simms' response to ABL's predicament came in two letters, parts of which are reproduced below. On June 21, 1910, Simms wrote:}

My dear Dr. Lewis:

I was more than glad to get your very welcome letter of April 19. I am extremely sorry that any published opinions of Dr. Dorsey of the people with whom you are thrown should be considered by you as obstacles in your work and contentment. It seems that, in your case, the sins of the Curator are visited on the Assistant Curator. . . .

{A few months later on November 1, 1910, he wrote:}

My dear Lewis:

I was very glad indeed to get your newsy letter of September 7th, which was awaiting me at the office after an absence of several days, due to an attack of threatened typhoid. . . .

I fully appreciate the handicaps under which you are working and earnestly hope that you have overcome them and are thoroughly satisfied with your investigations. You must have derived considerable pleasure in penetrating localities untouched by Dr. Dorsey and Capt. Voogdt, for the reason that it will give you greater knowledge upon a greater territory. I could not help chuckling to myself when I read how you managed to get on the enemy's boat. Let's hope that this little incident may be the turning point in your favor. . . .

Should an opportunity present itself, I wish you would procure for me, at as low a price as possible either in beads, wire or money, some feathers of the birds of Paradise and Crown Pigeon.

{Months later—21 June 1912—Simms wrote to ABL alluding jocularly to Simms' own earlier characterization of the Germans as "enemies":}

I have not the slightest idea in what territory you are working and do sincerely hope you will make a good clean up, leaving scarcely anything for our friends the enemies.

Fig. 4.55. "Canoes, middle Kaiserin Augusta River." A-33551 (610).

Up the Kaiserin Augusta River

Wednesday, Aug. 3   Left at 3 A.M. for Potsdam Hafen, with all my property; arrived about noon. Spent the afternoon in packing my collection. Evening with Herr Richter. Bought a black bird of Paradise (27 M.) and 3 king birds of Paradise (1 M. each) and 1 blue bird (2 M.).[13]

Thursday, Aug. 4   In forenoon finished packing, and left about 1 P.M. for Murik. A native of Murik also went along.

Friday, Aug. 5   Arrived at Murik about 8 A.M. The native went ashore in the cutter's boat, and sent out a canoe, on which I and 4 boys, with all my trade, went ashore. There are here really 3 places: Kālēlān, Wākūn, and Murik proper. As the native was from Kálelan, he got the canoe from there, and we went ashore there. Bought a number of specimens, and then went to Murik proper, while canoe took my specimens to cutter. After finishing at Murik, I tried to get the canoe again, but found that someone had broken the fastenings of one of the outrigger poles. Just who I could not make out, but it was evidently through jealousy that I had first gone to Kalelan. A canoe without outrigger took some of my things, and I went in the boat on return. As morning had been calm, the surf was not *very* bad. Murik has one of the worst surfs on the whole coast.

In the culture here is not very different from Kirau. The houses are much poorer. Bags, without fringe, but with ribs, or raised ridges, and a few sleeping bags, are made here. All the pots I saw they said come from "bush." The hair basket was still common, and some rather long. Did not see many ornaments.

In two *tamburan* houses saw a number of masks on a sort of platform or shelf running along the wall. Only 3 or 4 were better than what I had bought. The *tamburan* houses were entered by a ladder from below, so to speak, and there was no platform in front, only some planks on the ground.

All the houses had a sort of neglected appearance.

Left about noon for Sup, as decided not to try to visit other places along the coast on account of the heavy sea.

Saturday, Aug. 6   Arrived at Mum, where 2 native hunters for birds of Paradise for Herr Gramms were to go ashore, about 9, and at Sup about 1 A.M. In morning numbered my Murik specimens before going ashore. Here got only a few specimens, but succeeded in getting some carved out-

---

13. Some of these were accessioned at Field Museum in the zoology collections; others were sent to Curator S. C. Simms, who had requested them in a letter.

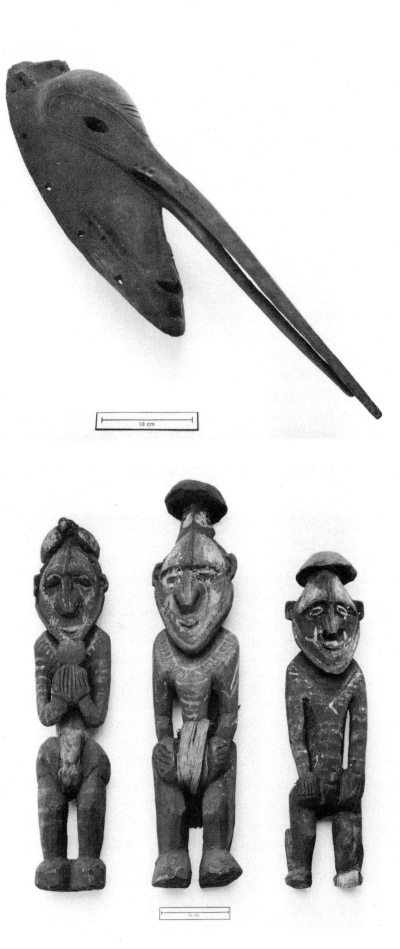

Fig. 4.56. "Wooden mask with long beak-like nose, Murik," 140949 (3367). A-112373.

Fig. 4.57. Carved wooden images, Sup, 141078 (3461), 141076 (3466), 141077 (3465). A-122192.

Fig. 4.58. "End of new *tamburan* house, Sup (Mushu Island)." A-33536 (595).

side corners from the old *tamburan* house. This is now rapidly falling in decay. There are two new ones, one better than the old one. In this the entire outside is painted, and on the ends are many carvings, carved boards, etc. Inside the posts and some of the rafters, as well as the comb plate, are carved from end to end. Inside house I saw only 5 or 6 old masks and images, none good. The houses here are much better than in Murik. Most of them have a covered and enclosed room or veranda in front of the main room proper. All on piles. *Garamut*s are made here; all the various designs have names, much as in Awar, and are not very different.

About noon left for Mushu, on the same island, but further west, where arrived about 9:30. Here found all old men away at work, and got but 1 good mask (from Kaip.[14]) As the return voyage to Rabuin was difficult, owing to wind and current, decided not to wait till night, when the men would return, and I might buy something, but to proceed immediately for Rabuin. This cost

14. He means Kaiep village, the major pottery center east of Wewak. Despite the complex spelling it is pronounced Kep (with short e).

Fig. 4.59. "Mask with long pointed
nose, Mom (on coast)," 141011 (3491).
A-112368.

almost the whole night, and it was nearly morning when we anchored off
Rabuin.[15]

Sunday, Aug. 7   In morning went ashore and to the village, but found
almost nothing. The natives declared that they had sold everything, and that
the "bush" people had burnt their *tamburan* house long before. The women
and children here showed little or no fear, even when I went in the houses.
European *lava-lava*s and beads were everywhere, however. Houses here
similar to Sup, but not so good or so large, and with no separate veranda or
fore-room, as there, (in those I entered). The houses were more or less
scattered along the beach for ⅓ mile or so.

Left about 11 A.M. for Mum, where arrived about 8 P.M. Anchored and
slept on board.

Monday, Aug. 8   Early in morning went ashore. The houses here were
scattered in the "bush" in small groups of 1 to 6 or 8, at some distance
apart—none on the beach. Here also found practically nothing. In one place
a small *tamburan* house, but only one mask; of sago (?) rind over a frame,
and painted. This the people would not sell for any price. In another place
saw old frame covered with sago (?) rind, but not good, and the painting
more or less obliterated. Got the men to renew the feathers in two, and
photoed them. The arms go through holes on the sides, and there is no
purpur (grass or leaf fringes, etc.) added so the people said. There was also
another frame, long with band near middle. Did not see this put on, so not
sure how worn. Houses here as in Rabuin.

Got some pots here. They come from the "bush," about one day's
journey or more inland. There are two kinds, a common pot, burnt and
unornamented, and a bowl, ornamented with engraved designs on outside.
This is not burnt, but only sun-dried, so the people said, and used only to put
the food in—not for cooking, as the other. Only old men make pots in this
interior region, not the women, as in all other places which I know. The pots
are made by coiling.

15. This is the small (now uninhabited) island just west of Wewak, easily visible from
Wewak town hill. The next bay to the west of Rabuin—not the harbor at Wewak town market—was called Dallmannhafen in German times.

Fig. 4.60. Man wearing mask at Mum (Mom) on the North Coast. A-33543 (602).

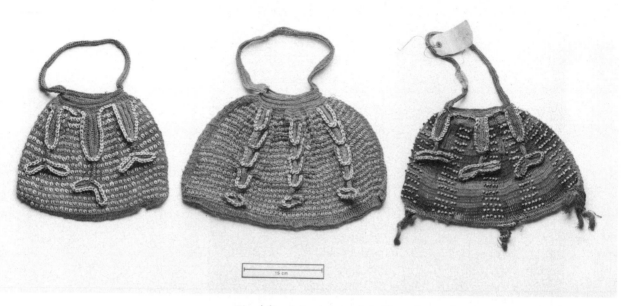

Fig. 4.61. String bags made in Kaup, decorated with nassa shells and flaps: 141033 (_____); collected Rabuin, 141047 (3484); collected Ali, 139776 (796). A-112027.

From Kirau to Mun I found similar bowls, and in each place they declared they came from the "bush," so it would seem there are numerous or at least several, places in the mountains where these are made. The designs are very similar except that from Kirau come pots with simpler designs, and cruder, which the people declared were made at Angōram (see July 8). At Kaip large cooking pots are also made, but plain, as a rule, tho sometimes with simple pattern around rim.[16] These are made by beating, as in Tumleo, so Kamān (my boy) said. Saw some in Sup nearly 2 ft. high. Got two masks here which the people said come from "bush," very similar to one from Mushu which was said to come from back of Kaip (not very far from Mum).

In Sup, Mushu, Rabuin, and Mum bows and arrows common. Bows with braided ring at end usually. Arrows often of type from interior of Eitape.

Spears mostly plain, often with cassowary feathers near center. In Sup saw some with a short stick projecting on one side near center, which the people said was held against the finger in throwing the spear, so as to give a better grip. No throwing sticks.

The *garamut*s seen (Dallmann Hafen region) were of the Sup type, and were not very numerous. *Kundu*s also rare, and only simple ones seen. Netted bags of Kaup type, with shells; of interior type back of Awar to Kirau—loosely woven with bands of seeds, and of type of interior west of Rabuin (i.e., Smain, etc.—see Tumleo) loosely netted with colored designs; not very numerous of any any type. A few Murik soft baskets seen, but rare—the natives wanted to buy some I had. Wood bowls apparently from the islands (esp. Köil).

No shields, tho in Sup I saw some apparently of Potsdam Hafen region type, but without hand-holds; perhaps only imitations.

Canoes relatively small, almost without ornament. A few with sail, with outrigger.

---

16. As at Tumleo, this is still a thriving industry. Kaiep women now decorate their pots with elaborate applique designs.

About 9 returned to coast, to find the *Siar* coming, and not far away. Started immediately for the *Siar* with small boat, and told the cutter crew to make sail. I thought for a while that the *Siar* would pass by without stopping, but Herr Proiker went on board, and told the Captain that it was I, as he had thought that the cutter was the Company cutter, and did not know that I was here. So after steaming out a little, he returned to coast and anchored; the cutter came up, and I got my things on board as quickly as I could, and we were soon under way.

The *Siar* stopped at Kaip to return some laborers, but I did not go ashore. Late in afternoon stopped at Murik, and stayed here all night.

Tuesday, Aug. 9   About 10 A.M. entered the K. A. river. About 12 the boat went ashore at _____ [Singarin], but the captain would not let me go, as he was afraid that too many white men would make the natives run away. At 4 P.M. arrived off Bin, and here went ashore. No laborers. I had promised the captain that if I could go ashore, I would not buy anything till the men were through with trying to get laborers. So waited here for 1½ hrs. while they (the 1st and 2nd mates) tried to get men through a young man who had been taken to Fr. Wh. Hafen the year before. He was not a laborer, and had been treated as a guest, and many things given him, including a suit of white duck, and cap. He had a chest, and bag of old beer bottles. No laborers volunteered, however. The boy was to go with us up the river, and translate, but after returning to ship, he slipped away back to village in a native canoe. So the company got nothing for their trouble.

The houses, canoes, *garamut*s, fish traps, clothing, etc. that I saw here were practically as in Mabuk. The natives at first brought a few things to sell, but nothing of value. So I bought nothing in the place.

Stayed here all night. Quite cool.

Wednesday, Aug. 10   Steamed up river all forenoon, about 11 stopped at Pagem. Here also a native was landed, who had been entertained as the

Fig. 4.62. "Pagem on the Kaiserin Augusta River." A-33547 (606).

307

other, but with equally fruitless results. This place was quite large. Houses large, floors 8–10 ft. above ground, roofs well built. Did not stop long enough to look around village. Saw no good things in carvings, except one the natives brought to ship while I was on shore, and which the captain bought. Here the type of ornamented lime gourd, several of which I had bought on the coast. The carvings the natives brought were new, or old and broken. Dress of men simple—a narrow waist band, and bunch of leaves hanging down in front.

Saw also 3 little clay faces about 2 in. long. Succeeded in getting one. The face was modeled and painted.

Continued on up river, and about 5 arrived at Mandanam, where stopped over night. Here bought a number of things, including 6 skulls with modeled faces, but not good. Did not go on shore, but this seemed to represent another culture. Canoes much the same, also dress of men, as in village below, but carvings different.

Fig. 4.63. Shield of pigskin, Jambun. Edges of skin lashed with rattan to a heavy rattan ring, 141363 (3558). Carved plank, with open fretwork, Simar, 141179 (3782). A-112314.

Thursday, Aug. 11   Steamed nearly all day up river. Culture much [the] same. In one place they brought out magnificent carvings, but the captain would not let me buy, as he wanted to get boys. Some of the houses seen were very large with high ends, with figures on top.

Friday, Aug. 12   Steamed most of day, stopped for short time in one place, but bought only 2 specimens. Capt. could get no boys. Culture much as day before, but apparently not so good. Many native fields along banks, often with good fences around.

About 5 anchored off village Malu, the furtherest point reached by *Peiho.* Capt. would not send boat ashore, and I was dependent on him. Here bought a few things before dark. Most of men naked, some with belts, woven, and with shell rings on them. Woven arm rings numerous, some with shell rings; also woven bands covered with small shells over top of head; a few simple feather ornaments. Some men painted red, in patterns, esp. on face. Others black, or with white around eyes, etc. Hair short. Small weak bows seen.

Women wore grass skirts, rather short, often red. Saw but few carvings, and these not esp. good. Sago washing by river. Many fish traps and nets.

Saturday, Aug. 13   In morning steamed up river for 2 hrs. to next village. Here many natives came out in canoes, eager to trade, but with nothing of value. Got one wood shield, one hide shield (pig skin), spears (very rude), small woven string bags for men, and arm and waist bands. Saw no carvings. Men naked, women with short skirts. Houses apparently crude, (could not go ashore), mostly built on small hill. Stopped here ½ hr., but very little turned up. Saw two small woven baskets and rattan armrings, which did not get. Men had almost no ornaments, and no clothing. Culture here evidently quite primitive,—very different from that lower down river, and more primitive than at last village.[17]

This was the furtherest point reached, and about 8:30 we started on our return trip. Did not stop at Malu, and first stop was at Awitab. Here got but few things, as the stop was very short, and the natives did not bring much. Culture seemed a little higher than higher up river. All houses on piles. Was in one house. Have sleeping sacs, wood stools, drying frames, pots up to moderate size, ornamented around rim with circles, etc. Also a most curious fire place, a sort of large earthen bowl, set sloping, with notched and ornamented rim. These were as much as 2 feet across, but rather shallow. These stood on each side of house near the rear. Fish nets and traps, and baskets.

Stopped here only about 20 min. Lower down we stopped for a few minutes at 2 villages, and anchored at a 3rd, where the culture was practically identical. Skulls with modeled faces, carved figure hooks, long wood faces, woven breast ornaments, etc.[18]

The men mostly naked, but a few with a sort of apron, held in place by string around waist. Women grass skirt. Houses on piles, fairly well built. Fine pottery, some jars 2½ ft. high, with rather broad necks, on which faces or other patterns modeled, others more open, with circles and beaks around rim, also large bowls 2 ft. across, with ornaments around rim. The large pots

Fig. 4.64. Suspension hook (human figure standing on head of a catfish), below Tschessbandi, 141296 (3596). A-112309.

17. ABL later identified this village as Jambun.
18. This cluster of villages ABL identified as "below Tschessbandi."

309

Fig. 4.65. Masks, from below Tschessbandi: wooden mask painted white and red, carved parrot's head below chin, with boar's tusks in nose, 141305 (3612); painted white and red, 141308 (3646); woven mask (paint gone), eyes represented by woven discs on pegs, 141315 (3618). A-112347.

stood in the houses, with a small bowl as cover, on a woven ring; but all I saw were empty.

Sunday, Aug. 14 As heavy fog, did not start till 8, but capt. would not let me go ashore, and natives would not come out. Here a man "pulled" from village got away the night before. After about 2 hrs. reached another village, where stopped and got a few things but culture here apparently poor. Did not have much time. Dress, ornaments and houses much as above. About noon stopped at a village a little above another village, where we had seen on our way up many canoes with carved figures, etc. Here and at the village below got about 115 specimens (3649(?)–3765). The carvings here were similar to what we saw the day before, but larger. Pottery also the same, but with a mixture of the incised clay bowls, same as made back of Mum. As the place lies almost directly inland from Mum, they probably come from the mountain region between. They showed much

15 cm

Fig. 4.66. "Large wooden mask for front of ceremonial house, Kararau," 141238 (3650). A-112340.

Fig. 4.67. Carved and painted wooden trumpets, Kararau: red and white, 141227 (3698); red, white, and black, 141228 (3697). A-112282.

variety, and some were very good. Also got here 3 dance masks, wicker work, with grass fringe below and wood face on side, also a woven mask of much interest.[19]

Men here wore a sort of apron, as above, women a fibre skirt, very well made, like the skirts worn by women in dance at Awar, which they said came from "bush."

About 5 anchored off Simar where remained for the might. Here went on shore and got a number of things. In this, as well as the last places, the women and children remained at some little distance, and took great interest in the bargaining. The men were quite bold, almost impudent, in the way in which they pressed their things upon one. They were also given to thieving, and stole my note book of specimens, which I had carelessly left in my pocket when I left the ship.[20] They would not let us into their houses, nor even approach what was apparently their *tamburan* house.

Culture here as in villages above.

Monday, Aug. 15   Continued on down river most of morning. Stopped short time at village Anum. Very little to be gotten here, apparently sold out, but also evidently somewhat different from the villages above. No such carvings as found above, nor modeled skulls. What few carvings seem like

---

19. ABL identified this as Kararau.

20. In a 1928 letter to Clark Wissler regarding an exchange with the American Museum of Natural History that had been arranged by Margaret Mead, ABL wrote that "two are wooden masks from New Guinea, and I suffered the great misfortune of having my detailed notes of specimens from this particular region stolen." ABL was able to reconstruct some of his detailed notes from his specimen tags, many of which survive.

Fig. 4.68. Large earthen pot with face at neck, painted red and white, Kararau, 138014 (3764). [We now know this to be an example of an Aibom pot.] A-112290.

Fig. 4.69. "Small flat wooden dish, handles represent head and tail of turtle (?), Simar," 141161 (3773). A-112371.

Fig. 4.70. Small wooden carving, Anum (Klinjam or Amnim), 141138 (3799). A-112357.

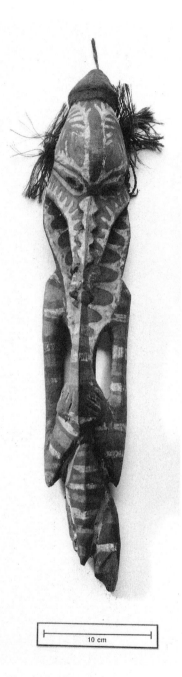

Fig. 4.71. "Wood carving of peculiar type, apparently representing human figure with long nose, arms and legs all connected, Pagem," 141109 (3518). A-112361.

Our next stop was at Pagem, where we had left a native on way up. Did not go ashore, but bought a few things from canoes, including a shield of different type from both those above and those on the coast. Here the natives brought out great numbers of freshly modeled heads and faces in clay (nearly black). Some were well done. No skulls were seen, possibly all had been sold.

Anchored for night off Bin, but did not go ashore, and natives brought out nothing.

Tuesday, Aug. 16   Early in morning the boat again went ashore, but no boys were forthcoming. After two short stops, due to something wrong with engine, left river about 11:30, bound for Potsdam Hafen.

Culturally the river, as far as we went, shows 3 or possibly 4 regions:

1. The lower river to Bin or above is the same as on coast on either side of river.

2. Above this comes a sort of intermediate region, with peculiar carvings, distinct shield, fine houses, as represented by Pagem, and other places visited by Dr. Dorsey. A *garamut* was heard in Pagem. *Kundu*s common. Finely carved canoe prows. Men no bark loin cloth, but bunch [of] grass.

3. Above Mandanam we come to places where carved and painted figures and faces are common; fine shields, skulls with modeled clay faces; also modeled clay faces done (all painted). Woven masks of different kinds, a peculiar and highly developed type of pottery, often with painted designs on larger pots. Peculiar apron (?) for men, or naked. A few very rude *garamut* (?) about 2 feet long was seen, but none were heard in this part of the river. *Kundu*s also were not seen, but still may have been present. Canoes much as below, but not so nicely carved at prow. Paddles same as below, but more with notched lower end. All with long handles, as the men always paddle standing.

4. At Malu, and esp. at the village visited above, the culture was very poor. Bows and arrows, hide shield, wood shield primitive and crude. Houses much poorer than below; all men naked. Pottery simple. No carv-

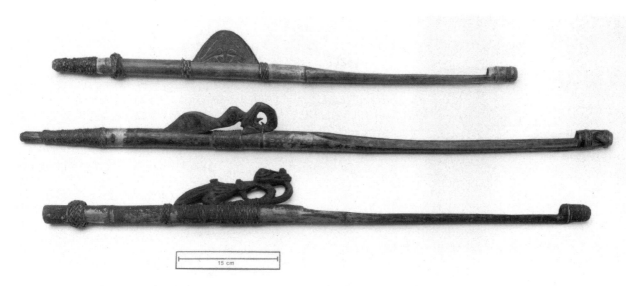

Fig. 4.72. Spear throwers, bamboo with rattan binding and carved wooden ornament: from below Tschessbandi, 141335 (3648); Kararau, 141217 (3701); Gumi (inland Kayan), 140523.1 (2621). A-112396.

Fig. 4.73. "Brinkman's hotel, Friedrich Wilhelms Hafen." 33570 (629).

ings or skulls seen. Houses poorly built,—apparently a type of culture very similar to that found in the mountains back of Eitape (by the Schlecter expedition).

Got to Potsdam Hafen about 3 P.M. Got my things on board, said adieu to Herr Gramms and Richter, and was away by 9 P.M.

Wednesday, Aug. 17 Arrived in Fr. Wh. Hafen about noon. My things were the first put out on wharf, and the last to go in, so I had to spend the whole of the afternoon doing nothing but watching to see that no one ran off with them. It was dark before they were in.

Thursday, Aug. 18 Got a little order in the chaos I found in the shed, as Sissano, Huon Gulf, Potsdam Hafen, and other specimens were mixed up in a fearful mess.

Friday, Aug. 19–Tuesday, Aug. 23 Packed.

Wednesday, Aug. 24 Cleaned up and waited for steamer. Could get no boxes from Co. and lumber out, so had to leave part of specimens unpacked, and finally decided to go to Simpson Hafen by steamer, get boxes etc. and return with same. This would also give me a chance to find out the situation there, wind up my affairs and get everything ready for the next steamer.

Thursday, Aug. 25 Waited for steamer.

Friday, Aug. 26 Left for Rabaul in *Prinz Walden*. On board met 2 members of Capt. Scott's Antarctic expedition who were taking Siberian ponies to New Zealand to meet the expedition.[21]

Sunday, Aug. 28 Arrived in Rabaul. Stayed on steamer.

---

21. These were Lt. Wilfred Bruce and Cecil Meares.

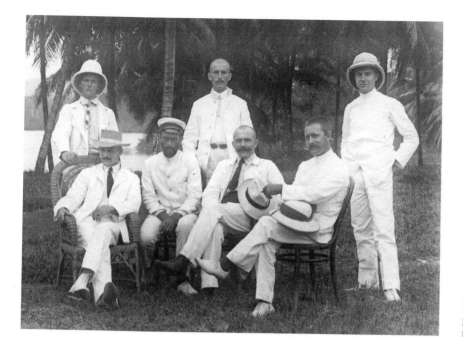

Fig. 4.74. "Group, Friedrich Wilhelms Hafen." A-33571 (630). [This photo probably includes Bruce and Meares from the Scott expedition.]

Fig. 4.75. "Government house and post office, Friedrich Wilhelmshafen." A-33563 (622).

Monday, Aug. 29   In afternoon went with Forsayth's pinace to Herbertshöhe.

Tuesday, Aug. 30–Friday, Sept. 2   Packed up my specimens sent from Arawe to Herbertshöhe by *Irene*. On Thursday visited Mrs. Parkinson, and spent a very pleasant forenoon. She promised to visit the Sulka country and see what could be got in the way of specimens. Sent her cart for me.

Friday afternoon returned to Rabaul in pinace (chartered).

Saturday, Sept. 3   Collected boxes, straw and packing material, and lumber for Fr. Wh. Hafen.

Tuesday, Sept. 6   Steamer came Sunday evening, but took nearly 2 days and nights to unload the lumber, etc. Left about 8 P.M.

Thursday, Sept. 8   Arrived about noon at Fr. Wh. Hafen, but could do nothing till next day.

Friday, Sept. 9–Saturday, Sept. 10   Packed. Got 17 boxes from Missionary Blum in Ragetta.

Fig. 4.76.   "Laborers before the New Guinea Co. offices in Friedrich Wilhelms Hafen." A-33569 (628).

318

Monday, Sept. 12–Saturday, Sept. 17   Spent the week packing. Got 2 carpenters from Monday to Friday. Saturday labeled boxes, but did not quite finish. Bought 5 wooden figures from Mr. Hellmich from Dampier Isl. (M.250) and one from Rich Isl. (M.40).

Monday, Sept. 19   Marked and numbered boxes 62–99, 38 in all, including 2 garamuts crated and 2 canoes (1 crate).

Tuesday, Sept. 20   Sold a few thing to Missionary Blum (tent M.40, *zelt-bahn*, rucksac). In afternoon went to Yabop, an island about 4 miles from Fr. Wh. Hafen. The island is about ¼ mile from the shore, which here is high, so that the station house (Herr Schmidt here) has a fine outlook.

Some natives were at Herr Schmidt's when I arrived, and he induced them to take me over in their canoe. This place, together with Bili-Bili (whose people now all live on the coast opposite the island, about 2 hrs. walk from Yabop) is the chief source of pots for the coast for many a mile.

The clay comes from inland. It is kneaded in water, and mixed with river sand when worked into pot. (See photos 611–613 [see Fig 4.78], where the woman is working sand into a ball of clay for a pot. The bucket contains sand, and there is a considerable quantity on the leaf.) Both came from a "long way," so the natives said. The ball of clay, after being kneaded, is formed into an egg-shaped mass, and the pointed end carefully rounded and smoothed with a little water (kept in cocoanut near by). It is then held in the right hand, and the thumb of the left hand used to work a hole into the mass as it is turned around (photo 614).

This hole is the beginning of the pot cavity. If the sides are not even, more clay is added in places (photo 615) and the opening widened and smoothed with one hand, as the mass is turned with the other (photos 616–617). As the clay used is soft and contains much water, at this stage the operation is discontinued till the next day, and the clay is stiffer. The hollow is then deepened with the hand (photo 618), and after the pot is roughly outlined, the walls are beaten thin and into shape with a wooden paddle, a rounded stone being held inside (photo 619). The rim finally is rounded and smoothed with the hand. After drying, a number are burnt together. A few are slightly ornamented around the rim, either with a stick, or the finger nail, with narrow incised lines or dots. Practically the only variation is in size, and the small amount of ornament. The pots seen ranged from 6 to 20 inches in height.

The unworked clay was light in color, but when worked reddish, and the burnt pots bright brick red, where not blackened.

The houses, canoes, dress, ornaments, household utensils, etc. were as in Siar and Ragetta. Photoed a group (photo 620), the hair is all worked up with dark red paint into fine frizzy curls. The two middle men were my canoe paddlers over and back. I gave each a 35 pf. knife and 3 fish hooks for his work.

Wednesday, Sept. 21–Thursday, Sept. 22   Spent most of time making prints of some of photos.

Friday, Sept. 23   Waited for steamer.

Saturday, Sept. 24   Left in evening for Rabaul.

Fig. 4.77. "Ancestral image, large head; painted red with some black and white, old and faded, Rich Island," 140120 (4000). From Helmich. A-112325.

319

Fig. 4.78. "Pot making in Yabop (same in Bili-bili), working the clay into a lump with river sand, suitable for one pot." A-33553 (612).

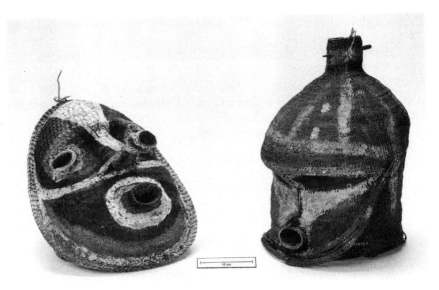

Fig. 4.79. Woven masks from near Ramu mouth: painted red, white, black, and yellow, 138708 (_____); painted reddish and yellowish white, 138709 (_____). Both from Gramms. [Two of roughly a hundred specimens obtained from Herr Gramms of Awar Plantation, Hansa Bay.] A-112345.

The Gazelle Peninsula in East New Britain

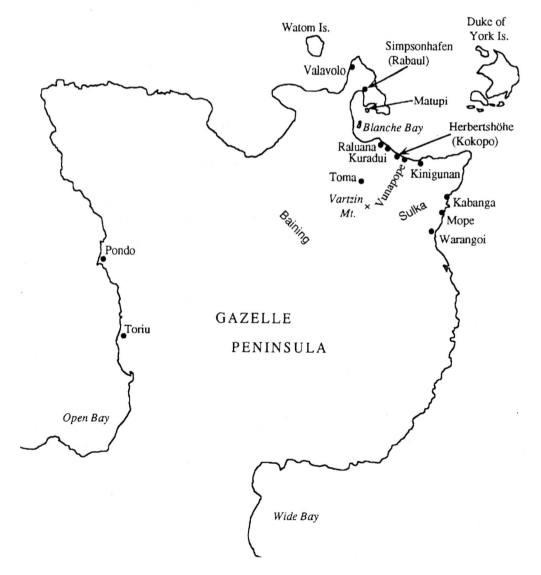

Watom Is.

Duke of
York Is.

Simpsonhafen
(Rabaul)

Valavolo

Matupi

Blanche Bay

Herbertshöhe
(Kokopo)

Raluana
Kuradui

Vunapope

Kinigunan

Toma

*Vartzin
Mt.* ×

Sulka

Kabanga

Mope

Warangoi

Baining

Pondo

Toriu

GAZELLE

PENINSULA

Open Bay

Wide Bay

Book 5

The Gazelle Peninsula and Solomon Islands

||||||||||||||||||||||||||||||||||||||||||||||||||||||||||||||||||||||||||||||||||||||||

26 September 1910–6 January 1911

By the end of August 1910, ABL was more than ready to leave German New Guinea. Despite persecution by many German residents, he had surveyed the New Guinea coast from Humboldt Bay (in Dutch territory) to Lokanu (at the southern end of the Huon Gulf), except for a stretch of about a hundred miles of the Rai coast east of Bogadjim, and by chance had even managed a trip up the Kaiserin Augusta River. ABL had now collected more than four thousand objects in the colony; it was time to move on to other territories where the expatriates would be more friendly and helpful.

Before he could leave German New Guinea, ABL still had to deal with his collections. His first shipment of thirty boxes—sent in April—was just arriving in Chicago, though he would not receive word of its condition until the end of November. He could not leave Friedrich Wilhelmshafen until he had readied a second shipment. Anyone who has shipped even a small number of boxes home from the field can appreciate what a daunting task it was to pack more than a hundred boxes and crates for shipment overseas. As usual, boxes, packing material, and lumber were in short supply. Thus, the months of September and October were largely occupied with packing.

In his eternal quest for boxes, lumber, and packing material, ABL had been forced to make a brief visit to Simpsonhafen and Herbertshöhe on the Gazelle Peninsula as there were no supplies to be had in Friedrich Wilhelmshafen. He gathered together and packed the specimens he had left at Cape Merkus the previous winter. While on the Gazelle Peninsula ABL also had got to test the social climate in and around the colonial capital; the situation had not improved appreciably. Returning to Friedrich Wilhelmshafen, he packed his specimens and by the end of September was able to leave Kaiser Wilhelmsland once and for all. He returned to the Gazelle Peninsula to see if anything useful could be accomplished before setting off for one of the English-speaking territories.

A number of changes had occurred while ABL was working in west New Britain, in the Huon Gulf, and on the North Coast. Simpsonhafen had grown rapidly, and residents of the colony had chosen to change the name of the town back to its original name, Rabaul. About the same time, leading citizens had successfully lobbied to have the colony's administration officially moved from Herbertshöhe to Rabaul, where there was more room for development. Governor Hahl had left for Europe in April, and the *Regierungsrat,* Dr. Osswald, was acting imperial governor in his absence. Back in Hamburg, Rudolf Wahlen had formed a new syndicate specifically to buy out the vast trading empire of E. E. Forsayth & Co. Now the governor could proudly write in his annual report that all the major economic interests in the colony were in German hands. The colony's expatriate residents had even constructed a monument to Otto von Bismarck at Toma, celebrating the twenty-fifth anniversary of the annexation of the old protectorate of German New Guinea.[1]

But some things had not changed in ABL's absence. As we read in his letter to Dorsey of 30 October, the majority of German residents who lived along the shores of Blanche Bay still refused to have anything to do with ABL, his specimens, or his museum. This meant that ABL's contacts with German officers, planters, and traders would continue to be limited. The Gazelle Peninsula was the most cosmopolitan part of the colony, however, and many of its expatriate residents were not German.[2] It was primarily around these residents, together with a few German missionaries and officials who remained unconcerned about Dorsey's articles, that ABL's life now revolved.

Among the most important of this cosmopolitan group of settlers was Phebe Parkinson. When ABL first arrived in German New Guinea, the Parkinson family was in mourning over the death of Richard Parkinson, Phebe's husband, and it is uncertain whether he met the widow during this visit to Herbertshöhe. Conditions were quite different a year later, and when ABL arrived in Herbertshöhe on 28 August, he made his way to the Parkinson homestead the following day.

The part-Samoan, part-American Mrs. Parkinson and her late husband had helped Field Museum several times in the past, sending a collection of ethnological specimens and another collection of skulls some months before Parkinson's death. Dorsey had visited Parkinson in 1908 and had asked him to make another collection for the museum, but Parkinson's ill health prevented this collection from ever being assembled. Late in August, therefore, Mrs. Parkinson offered to visit the Sulka country specifically to make a collection for ABL.

It was with this same cooperative spirit that Phebe Parkinson would befriend Margaret Mead nearly twenty years later. In a biographical sketch written long after Mrs. Parkinson's death, Mead (1964) described her friendship with Mrs. Parkinson and many aspects of the latter's life. As a pioneer settler of New Britain, Phebe Parkinson had seen and experienced firsthand much of the island's colonial history. The Parkinsons and their relatives the Kolbes had been central figures in the diverse mélange of people who made up the vibrant society that developed on the shores of Blanche Bay.[3]

On the day after ABL returned to Herbertshöhe in September, he was invited to lunch at Mrs. Parkinson's home. In the weeks that followed, she seems to have taken ABL under her wing. During the five weeks he spent on the Gazelle Peninsula, ABL made six visits to see Mrs. Parkinson at her home in Kuradui, these in addition to his first visit in August. One senses from ABL's letters that Mrs. Parkinson took some satisfaction in getting the best of her German neighbors by helping a fellow American with his collections.

In the month after ABL first met Mrs. Parkinson, whom he often writes of as Mrs. P., she obtained more than seventy-five items for him, including at least two canoes, twenty large masks, and many other bulky items. These she sold for a total of M. 1,700 or roughly $340. This sum was substantial—more than ABL's salary for three months—and Mrs. Parkinson undoubtedly made a tidy profit on the transaction. But these specimens were large, nearly covering Mrs. P.'s lawn at Kuradui (see Figs. 5.2 and 5.7). They represented areas ABL had not visited and were among the largest and (as curios) among the most valuable pieces he had yet acquired.

Mrs. P.'s assistance was not limited to selling curios to Field Museum. She introduced ABL to Methodist missionaries Fellmann and Cox and arranged for ABL to visit Mope in the Sulka country, where he met Father Joseph Meier. Mrs. P. organized a trip for ABL to the tablelands behind Kuradui, where he met Auguste Hertzer, a retired nursing sister who for many years had run a small hospital at Friedrich Wilhelmshafen for the New Guinea Compagnie; ABL also bought a few large Sulka pieces from Sister Auguste. Later Mrs. Parkinson helped ABL make a trip to Toma in the interior. There he met Father Kleintitschen and visited the Vartzin, Repui, and Viviren districts. Another day Mrs. Parkinson sent word for ABL to come to Kuradui to meet a group of Baining men who had brought some masks and other specimens from their village behind the Taulil country (back of the Toma). All in all Mrs. Parkinson provided considerable assistance to ABL's work and helped him acquire a remarkable volume of specimens in a very short time.

Of course, all of these specimens had to be packed and shipped. Most of the larger items seem to have been packed (at Mrs. P.'s request) by Hernsheim, though the Sacred Heart Mission (at Vunapope) appears to have crated the large Raluana canoe for him. Other specimens, which he bought at Matupi village or from the Rabaul trading firms S. A. Whiteman and Forsayth & Co., were packed and sent on to Chicago by Stephen A. Whiteman, an Australian businessman living in Rabaul.

Finally, on Halloween day in 1910, ABL saw the last of his 132 boxes of specimens loaded aboard one of Nord-Deutscher Lloyd's steamers for Hong Kong. In all ABL had sent more than forty-two hundred specimens, more than seven hundred glass plate negatives, some bird of paradise pelts, and several boxes of books, pamphlets, and maps. This substantial collection, whose documentation was far better than most Melanesian collections from the period, had all been assembled in fourteen months.

ABL's collection from the Gazelle Peninsula, however, differs significantly from his collections made in other parts of the colony. Busy with packing, he had little time for or interest in acquiring a great deal more until his earlier acquisitions were finally taken care of. His expenses rose dramatically during this month as he made large purchases of specimens from Mrs. Parkinson and prepaid freight as far as Hong Kong, so his financial position was in some doubt until all his boxes got off.

ABL did make two visits to the inland communities of Mope and Toma, though he collected very little in either area. As he explained in his letters and diary, these communities had little to sell. He did buy a sample of what was available, including slings, arm bands, skirts, loincloths, pan pipes, dance caps, paddles, a belt, some paints, and a lime container. These complemented the eight Mope masks he had obtained from Mrs. P., but it is clear that for ABL this was not a systematic collection. His other Sulka and Baining collections contain some exquisite masks, but are otherwise quite limited.

During these two brief sojourns from Rabaul, however, ABL did take a number of photographs, and his diaries offer considerably more detailed notes about the two areas, particularly about houses, than he wrote about almost any other community he visited so briefly. It would appear that what was lost in potential collections was gained in more detailed notes.

After shipping his boxes, ABL visited Father Esser at Valavolo on the north coast of the Gazelle Peninsula. Here he saw some old stone figures and learned about some unusual prehistoric pottery found on Watom Island. This pottery, which has subsequently been called Lapita pottery, has become some of the best known prehistoric material in the entire Pacific (Meyer 1909, 1910; Kirch and Hunt 1988; Terrell 1989). Unfortunately for Field Museum's collections, ABL was not able to bring back even a single sherd among his specimens.

Readers should remember when reading this part of his diary that ABL was not living within the usual expatriate community during this productive month on the Gazelle Peninsula. He operated around the periphery of the German colonial society, interacting principally with missionaries and non-German settlers. At the center of this world was Phebe Parkinson and her large extended family. To help him sort out the family's many connections in the colony, ABL listed the members of the Coe and Parkinson families at the back of this diary notebook (reproduced here). It was an impressive circle in which to operate during his last days in German New Guinea before setting off for British territory.

                                                            Rabaul
                                                            Oct. 30, 1910

My dear Dr. Dorsey:

Since last writing I have spent a good share of my time packing, I saw Mrs. Parkinson, and have purchased 13 Sulka masks, 2 Dukduks, 2 Tubuans and one ceremonial canoe with finely carved prow and stern as well as a number of other things, from her. She went down into the Sulka country herself and got the masks, I heard that the "Kiap" had ordered the Sulkas to keep all masks for him, but she has more influence than the government. I also visited the Sulka country and saw a few others, but no good ones.

I told Mrs. Parkinson I wished she would have the things packed, as I did not wish to be bothered with it, so she said she would get Hernsheim's to pack them. I said that would be all right as I thought that Hernsheim's would know more about packing than I. The cases are tremendous and I do not know if they will go through all right or not. The Lloyd men say they won't. It makes the freight charges high, esp. as I have to prepay freight to Hongkong. I am sending 32 boxes with this steamer (in port now) and while I have not got the bill yet, the freight to Hongkong will be about $250.00; I am going to ask the museum to return me the money. Packing and local freight charges is already a very heavy item, and you said I was not to pay freight out of the appropriation. The Lloyd agent here refused absolutely to ship over the lines the Director instructed me to ship over, and bill the goods through, so I have to pay freight to Hongkong, and have the goods shipped from there. Luckily the agent in Fr. Wh. Hafen billed through, so I had no freight to pay from there, or I fear my cash would have been pretty well used up.

As I have found that all the photo plates I got here are bad, I am going to ask the museum to take part of this money (due me for freight) and order sent to me some fresh plates from the factory (Seed's <u>tropical</u> I think would be best here), soldered in tins. Best put 2 doz. in a tin, soldering a strip around so it can be caught with a pair of forceps and ripped off. Sydney, care Burns, Philp & Co. I should like 4 gross to begin with, and then after about 4 months as many more.

For the last 2½ months I have not done much else but pack and look after boxes and collections, till I am almost sick of them. I hope in English N. G. I can get some one to do <u>something</u> of that sort of work, but here it seems impossible to get any one whom one can trust. Then it is almost impossible to get good boxes, or even lumber to make them, unless I buy New Zealand pine, and that costs tremendously. I thought I would sooner have a few things smashed up, than get new boxes, so I have used all sorts of makeshifts, and am waiting anxiously to hear how they come through. I have not yet heard of my first shipment in April. It might be well to have the large boxes of masks (nos. 25, 26, 27, 29) unpacked, but don't let them throw away the grass and leaf dresses worn below the masks. These are necessary for the full masked figure. I am a little afraid of Hernsheim's packing, but <u>hope</u> that they come through all right.

There is very little change in the situation here. I go my own way and have little to do with most of the people here. Mrs. Parkinson has helped with advice, guides and carriers in my trip up to the Sulka region, and also to the country around Mt. Vartzin. It was interesting to see the places, but there is practically nothing to be gotten. I intended to take a trip into the Baining country, but packing took up too much of my time. From what I hear, however, there is nothing to be found unless one goes far into the interior. This is not the right season for masks. Mrs. P. has promised to get the museum some. I think we would be safe in commissioning her to get us a few things—and <u>she</u> can get them, if any one can. She also seems anxious and ready to help the museum, which other people are not. As one man said to me, the prevailing sentiment here is, "Nothing for the American." By the way I forgot to say that if the masks in no. 29 show any injury from water, the Lloyds ought to be made to pay. They let 3 boxes stand out on the wharf for 3 days—<u>outside</u> the shed, in spite of my protests. The boxes had been sent to the wharf (from Hernsheim's Matupi and Forsayth's Ralum) to be ready for shipment. It rained heavily one day at noon. I went out to see what I could do, and with a few boys got one box in, partly wet (no. 19) and covered the big box (29) with a rotten tarpaulin, full of holes—the box was too heavy for us. Of course the men whose business it was to see to things never came near the place till the rain was over. They wouldn't deign to get their clothes wet! (or take that much time over my boxes!?) One night it also rained but not much. Boxes 19, 25, and 29 were out then. You might examine them all. This is only a little sample of the trouble I have had here. It's enough to turn a man's hair gray. You asked once what you could do to better things. I think I have mentioned all that is necessary, but you <u>might</u> (?) see that my salary is put on the same basis as that of the other assistant curators by the time I get back.

I wonder if you have seen Dr. Hahl while he and you were in Europe. If it was not asking too much, I'd tackle him for a ride around the colony in his new yacht. I understand Capt. Moeller is to come out with it in the spring. I think the colony owes me a pleasure trip for the way I have been treated, and I suspect some folks connected with the museum think I have sent in about enough boxes from this corner of heathendom!

Well, I must stop, or I'll not finish my correspondence before the mail closes. Luckily I have had no fever for the last six months. I think I'll feel fairly well when I once get out of this hole.

Very sincerely,
A. B. Lewis

{List of Coe and Parkinson families, written inside the back cover of Book 4.}

Coe Family:	Mrs. Kolbe		
	Mrs. Parkinson	(Kuradui)	
	Mrs. Horgren		
	Mrs. Rondahl	(Kabakaul)	
	Mr. Coe	(Kabanga)	
	Mr. Coe	(Guam)	{Mrs. Kaumann
			{Mrs. Schultze
	Mr. Coe (dead)		
	et al.		
Parkinson Family:	Mrs. Diercke	(Bougainville)	
	Mrs. Wrightson		
	Frank	(Borneo)	
	Edward	(Vunapope)	
	Paul	(boy at home)	

Fig. 5.1. Sulka masks *(sisiu)*, as worn in dance. At Mrs. Parkinson's house, Kuradui.
A-33576 (635).

The Gazelle Peninsula, New Britain

Monday, Sept. 26   Arrived in Rabaul in forenoon. Went to Herbertshöhe in afternoon.

Tuesday, Sept. 27   Visited Mrs. Parkinson and took lunch there. Found she had gotten from the Sulkas some rare masks, and agreed to take 4 large masks *(hémlaut)* and 9 smaller ones *(sīsīu)* for M.1000.; two *duk-duk* and 2 *tubuan* from Raluana, for M.200.; one dancing belt *(vīpīt)* from Raluana (no. 4001); 3 feather dancing caps *(avērok)* from Sulka, and 1 fine long feather mask (?) from Baining, very rare. (This was the first one Mrs. Parkinson had seen) for M.50; a number of miscellaneous objects (nos. 4002–4044,

Fig. 5.2. "Sulka masks on lawn of Mrs. Parkinson's house, Kuradui." A-33575 (634).

Fig. 5.3. Sulka masks *(hemlaut)*, as worn in dance. A-33582 (641).

Fig. 5.4. Sulka mask *(sisiu),* as worn in dance. At Mrs. Parkinson's house, Kuradui. A-33580 (639).

4048–4053) for M.200; and a finely ornamented ceremonial canoe from Raluana for M.250.

Wednesday, Sept. 28–Thursday, Sept. 29 Went out to Mrs. Parkinson's Wed. morning and stayed till next afternoon. She had sent for the chief from whom the canoe was obtained, and also 2–3 others, to come and explain it to me. Also to the Sulkas for a chief and some others to come and explain the masks. This took most of the afternoon and evening. The next morning I photoed the masks and canoe, and numbered and listed the miscellaneous specimens. After lunch I visited and had a pleasant talk with Missionary Fellmann.[1] Mrs. Parkinson sent me back to Herbertshöhe at 4 P.M. in cart. I visited Catholic Mission and they agreed to pack canoe, which Mrs. P. sent down by water the next morning.

---

1. ABL spelled his name Feldman.

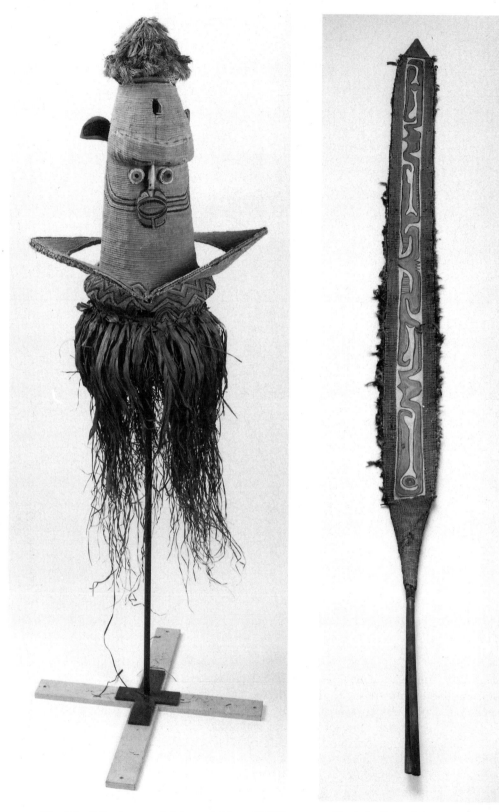

Fig. 5.5. Sulka dance mask *(yituwung),* Mope, 138902 (4117). From Auguste Hertzer. A-112398.

Fig. 5.6. Painted dance wand, Sulka. Green and light brown pigments, 138874 (4119). From either Auguste Hertzer or S. A. Whiteman. A-112359.

Fig. 5.7. Ceremonial canoe (Gazelle Peninsula type from Raluana, purchased), in front of Mrs. Parkinson's house, Kuradui. A-33606 (665).

Friday, Sept. 30   In forenoon went out to Mrs. P. for lunch with Assessor Weber, in his cart, and after lunch up onto the table-land (about 1 hr.) to Sister Augusta's[2] (nursing sister, for many years active in Africa and South Seas, now retired, and has taken up land here). I stayed here while Mrs. P. and Herr Weber went on to look at Mrs. P.'s new place on hills beyond. Bought from Sister Augusta, 2 Sulka masks *(yītūwūng)* and two dancing wands (_____) for M.120.

Saturday, October 1   Chartered Forsayth's coal pinnace to go to Rabaul and get my things (M.40). Left at 10, arrived 12:15. After attending to business, wind so heavy that thought best not to return.

Sunday, Oct. 2   Returned to Herbertshöhe in morning.

---

2. This is Auguste Hertzer.

Fig. 5.8. "Old man, Mope." A-33597 (656).

Monday, Oct. 3   Went to Mrs. Parkinson's in morning, and brought back the 2 dancing wands, which after dinner took to Mission (Winapopo) to be packed in canoe. Then packed up my things and got ready to go to Mope, as Mrs. Parkinson had promised me a Sulka boy as guide to my 2 boys, and that I myself could go the next morning in the carriage to Kabakaul, and there meet the boys. She could not go, however, as had not yet arranged for packing the Sulka masks, for which Hernsheim's cutter was to come.

Tuesday, Oct. 4   Again had to put off the trip, as it rained.

Wednesday, Oct. 5   One Sulka as guide and a boy with carriage arrived about 7 A.M., and I set off for Mōpe. Rode to Kabakaul, and from there walked, stopping only to drink cocoanuts and rest at Kabāngā (Mr. Coe).[3] Arrived at Mōpe about 3 P.M. and Father Meier kindly agreed to put me up for my stay. He is somewhat of a student of native languages and customs, and has published several papers,[4] so the time passed very quickly till bed time. He has been in Mope (the first Sulka village) only about 5 months, still had several kinds of fresh vegetables for the table. In fact, outside of bread, butter and coffee, tea and sugar, everything we had was from the neighborhood—quite a contrast to the way many other people live in N. Guinea. Pigeon and soup, taro, yams, cabbage, kohlrabbi, lettuce, and eggs (bought off the natives, as one can not very well keep fowl and a garden at the same time—as, for example, Herr Gramms, who found his chickens spoilt his garden every time) gave considerable variety.

Thursday, Oct. 6   Visited village with P. Meier in morning. He acted as interpreter, and showed me what he knew. I bought a few things, and took some photos of houses, natives, drum, canoe, etc. After visiting the village on the other side of mission, we returned about 11 A.M. As it was very warm, did not go out again till nearly 4, when visited a couple of villages on the hills near by. Spent the evening till nearly 12 talking, partly on religion.

Friday, Oct. 7   In forenoon took a round of the Sulka villages, going along the coast to Warangoi, and then back over the hills, or rather, on the high plateau back from the coast. Visited in all 8–10 villages, some of them rather small. Mope is about the largest, having over 100 inhabitants. There are in all about 1,000 natives, mostly Sulka, but a few O-Mengen. They formerly lived on the south coast, but owing to repeated attacks from the Baining, they removed, with assistance of the government, to this region, a sort of no-man's land, lying between the Baining country and that of the Gazelle Peninsula natives. The Warangoi river is the boundary of the Baining territory, tho none are found for a long distance inland. Only a portion of the Sulka have removed here, however, many still remaining on the south coast.

The Sulka and Oméngen are closely associated, intermarrying with each other, and having practically the same habits and customs, tho a different language. The Sulka, Taulil and Baining have non-Melanesian languages (P. Meier said Papuan); the Omengen a Melanesian speech, and from native reports this extends nearly or quite to South Cape. Many of the Sulka

3. This was Henry Coe.

4. Pater Josef Meier was the most prolific of all the prewar Sacred Heart missionaries, publishing more than sixty articles, monographs, and letters; see especially Meier (1904, 1907, 1909, 1911, 1913, 1929). For a more complete listing of his publications see ANU (1:164–175) and Sack (1980; 183–187).

Fig. 5.9. "Frame of Sulka house," Mope area. A-33594 (653).

customs are strikingly similar to those of Möwe hafen (Manua). They use a bamboo tube when smoking a cigarette, holding it at the far end; they have the blow gun; they make black and red paint in the same way as the Möwe hafen, and with these paint a bark loin cloth very similar to that there; have pan pipes.

In leaving their former and old home they left many of their best things behind them, and I found very little in the villages. The houses are built in a more or less irregular fashion surrounding a central cleared space. The usual house is elongated, or ovate, rounded at the ends (or at least behind, the front is sometimes left unfinished) about 8–10 ft. wide, 6–10 ft. high, (often much higher in front than behind) and 15–25 ft. long. This is the family, or woman's house (usually one to each wife, when several). The construction is relatively simple. Forked or notched posts (about $3\frac{1}{2}$ ft. high) are set around in an ellipse, where the sides of the house are to come. On this a pole or poles (3–4 in. dia.) are placed, extending clear around the ellipse. Then long poles are set on the ground reaching to the comb from each side, and supported by the side poles. At the comb there is often a supporting beam, in its turn supported by a central post.

(This beam is sometimes omitted, especially in the men's houses, which are built in the same way.) While building the house this beam is supported by end posts, which are removed when finished, as the numerous rafters hold the beam in place. These rafter poles, from $\frac{1}{2}$–2 in. in diameter are placed very close together (can hardly put your finger between them), and held in place by small poles bound underneath to each rafter with rattan and extending round and round the house at intervals of 8–20 inches, so that the whole roof framework is very firmly bound together. To this are bound layers of grass thatch with 6–8 in. lap, $1\frac{1}{2}$–2 ft. long, butts down.

337

In front is an opening nearly the width of the house, about 3 ft. high. Here at the lower end of the rafters is a woven roll 3–5 in. in diameter, from which hangs a fringe 1–2 ft. long, nearly closing the view. Inside, in the woman's house, is a partition, the space in front of this being used for the pigs, a special log pen being often built on each side of a narrow passage-way.

The house is sometimes built without the front vestibule, in which case the posts and poles do not run clear around, and the straight front is only rudely closed with palm leaves or palm leaf mats.

In this case there are also usually two posts to the comb beam, and often the rafters do not extend to the ground, but rest on the side pole or plate, and a wall of logs or posts or more carefully woven wicker work is made from this to the ground. The front vestibule may be added later. The family house is called *rīk.*

Of men's houses there are several kinds. A rich man may have one for himself, to entertain his friends. This is often circular, with conical roof and central post, usually nicely built and thatched to the ground. This is called *a wūṅgūlūm.*

The usual men's house *(a ṅaúlū)* is built with or without central post, elliptical in form, and nicely finished inside. Sometimes there is a nicely woven wall, but usually the rafters extend to the ground. In one I saw the entire inside was covered with a layer of splints (split vine ?) bound to the rafters, and entirely concealing them.

Sometimes the men's house is open all around, the rafters being supported by the side poles or plate, and ending about 2½–3 ft. from the ground in the same sort of woven roll as found over the door. In this case logs 4–6 ft. long and 1½–2½ ft. thick are placed around under the eaves, to sit on and keep out the pigs. These are rather assembly houses than sleeping houses. The central post, when present, is often carved and painted, and then is quite large, 1½–2 ft. thick. All designs seen were very similar conventional curved bands, hooks, etc. To keep the sides of the roof apart small beams are set across from one side to the other, 2–3 ft. under the comb.

All three houses have only the ground as floor, but one type of men's house *(ṅaútūgūl)* is built with a high floor where the men sleep. In one photoed this was fully 8 ft. high. (This house not finished. They were waiting till they could get a good supply of taro and pig for a feast before putting on the finishing touches. As there was a drought when I was there, and taro was scarce, everything was at a standstill.)

One type of house seen, with high, pointed ends, they said was an imitation of the house of the natives of the Gazelle peninsula.

Of household utensils and furniture there is very little. The Sulka have no earthen or wooden bowls, no pots. They cook with hot stones, (or if only a little, over open fire), usually *in* the woman's house. The cocoanut (occasionally bamboo) is their water vessel. The nibung leaf supplies a sort of platter. They make netted bags, but very few were seen. Things to be protected from rats, etc. are put in a bowl shaped basket hung from the roof by rattan, on which is a half cocoanut shell to prevent vermin from descending the line. Very rude baskets for taro and yams are made from the cocoanut leaf.

The most noticeable thing in the house is the sleeping frame, about a dozen round sticks laid on a pole at each end, it in turn supported on two forked sticks set in the ground—the whole about 1½ ft. high, 1½–2 ft. wide and 4–5 ft. long. There seems to be no regularity in their arrangement inside the house, and in the men's house they often take up most of the floor.

In the men's houses I saw also spears (mere rude pointed poles), clubs (not good), partly finished shields.

338

Fig. 5.10. Men's house with floor (called *nautugul*), unfinished, Mope. A-33589 (648).

No bows or arrows seen. Slings are also used in fighting. The string on one side has a loop, which is passed over the first finger, while the other string is held between the side of the finger and the thumb.

The men's dress consists of a band of bark cloth, 6–9 in. wide, and 10–20 ft. long. It is passed several times around the waist, one end being passed between the legs and under the band in front, so that the free end hangs down. This end, and often the whole, is sometimes ornamented with designs in black, or red and black. The black paint *(kāvāin)* is made by chewing the bark of a certain tree with the soot from burnt *galip* wax. (Compare Möwe hafen.) The red *(swel)* paint is made by chewing the bark of a certain plant *(a ham)* with the leaf of a fern *(a gērāp)*.

Ornaments were not numerous. Combs of sticks fastened together. Earrings of many small discs of tortoise-shell said to be worn, but did not see any. Arm bands of woven fibre, with yellow decorative designs, reminded one of Arawe and Huon gulf. In dances a sort of netted cap, with cassowary or other feathers attached, is worn.

The woman's dress consists solely of a girdle *(a kūrpin)* of a bunch of string, and a bunch of grass (wild ginger ?) passed over this in front. The tops are caught under the girdle while the stems hang over, and if long enough, are often passed between the legs and caught under the girdle behind. The string for the girdle was first twisted from the fibre of a certain vine *(a nepan),* and then over this string a narrow band of fibre from another vine *(a wunmāt)* is wound. The cord thus formed is coiled round and round like a coil of rope, and tied together on each side, these forming the ends of the girdle.

Ornaments for women seemed lacking. Both men and women wore hair cut short.

In the men's houses were seen pig nets, similar to those of Arawe, but not so large.

Their canoe *(dortmai)* are dug outs, with outrigger. The walls are made very thin, and strengthened with bows. Sometimes an extra plank is fastened on the side. The prow and stern are also separate pieces, and an extra height

339

is obtained at the ends by another side piece, often decorated. In one seen the end was like this.

This canoe must have been 35–40 ft. long, and 3 ft. deep, tho not over 2 ft. wide at the top. They also have quite short canoes, 5–6 ft. long, used by a single man. These are quite thin and light, and relatively broad (1½ ft. or so).

Paddles are short, with narrow blade, often ornamented with black or red designs.

SULKA—BURIAL

In the men's houses saw also 2 long bundles done up in leaves. One hung up under a cover of cocoanut leaves, and the other stood on end at the end of the house. These contain the bones of a single person. The body is first buried, and later the bones are dug up and kept in this bundle in the house till a special feast is held, after which they are either finally buried or thrown away.

SULKA

The Sulka have the *kundu, garamut,* and pan-pipes (also jew's harp of bamboo, but did not see this). The only *kundu*s seen were large and plain.

The *garamut*s were different from anything seen before. They are often a dozen feet or more long, but only one end is hollowed out. The cavity is not very large, and is hollowed out more on one side than the other, except in the center where struck or beaten (with the end of a heavy stick). At the other end is a hole in the side, said to be made for transport.

Three different varieties of dance masks were obtained: the *hemlaut,* very large, with flat umbrella like part above, and various figures below; the *sísiu,* conical shaped above, and more simple below, and the *yituwúng,* like a helmet, with face on one side. The two former appear only singly. The *yituwung* appear in numbers on the occasion of more popular sing-sings. (For example, the natives are preparing for a great feast and sing-sing at Mrs. Parkinson's on Christmas, but are making only *yituwung* for this occasion.)

Apparently the masks are only used but once, and are then put in the house and later destroyed. Saw 6 *sisiu* in one men's house.

The making of these masks takes a long time, and is carried on in the bush. The large masks take a year or so to make. They are painted only the day before use, tho the other part may have been completed weeks before. While being made food must be cooked at a distance, and when needed a man puts on a netted cap *(vérok),* with body hid by leaves, and goes out to the plantations and takes what he wants. Any person (man, woman or child) getting in his way is killed.

The construction of these masks is rather complicated. First a frame is made of the desired shape. The *yituwung* and under parts of the other masks are covered with the pith of a vine *(ṅaírōp).* This pith is shoved out in pieces 6–10 in. long, beaten flat, and fastened on the surface with the fibres from the aerial roots of the pandanus. The under side of the *hemlaut* umbrella is made of split pieces of the pith of a kind of grass *(káteeṅ)* like corn. Cockatoo feathers (white & yellow) and others are used.

Colors used to paint the masks are red, white, black and green (blue ?). Red paint *(sewél)* is made by grinding up a red stone, and mixing it with water.

Also (red) made from bark of a certain plant *(ham).* This is chewed with leaf of a fern *(gérap).* Another said it was chewed and put into the half of a

340

wild orange—the juices then squeezed out into a leaf, when it is ready for use.

White paint *(kūvō)* is made from a white clay, washed, and mixed with water (found in Mope).

Black paint *(kāwaín)* is made from the soot of burnt *gālīp* gum. This is caught on a stone over fire, and chewed with the bark of a certain tree.

Blue paint *(mᵃtóm)* is made from a blue clay, dried, and mixed with water from a young cocoanut. (Said from a substance found in standing water.)

Saturday, Oct. 8   Left Mope at 7:45 A.M. and got to Herbertshöhe about 2 P.M.

Sunday, Oct. 9   In afternoon visited Mrs. Parkinson, and arranged to get boy the following afternoon to go to Toma (Vartzin).

Monday, Oct. 10   Developed plates. In afternoon sent boys to Toma, but as carriage did not come for me, waited till next morning.

Tuesday, Oct. 11   Went up to Toma, where arrived about noon, very dusty ride, as I was behind. In afternoon took a short trip to a few small villages near by, in district of Repūī.

Wednesday, Oct. 12   Started about 8 for an all day's trip around the Vartzin. On way met P. Kleintitschen, who was just returning from an overnight visit at some villages, and got from him some information regarding road and places.

For about an hour had a very good path, down hill most of the way. We then crossed a deep ravine, where was a natural rock bridge, about 20 ft. wide and as many high. From then the path wound around the ravines and mountain side, up and down, passing from time to time the small native villages, first through the district of Vīvīren, and then that of Dāmānaírīkī. Stopped in several of these to photo and drink cocoanuts. My guides came from Damanairiki, and the *lūlūai* then made me a present of a cockatoo and a rooster (which refused to be caught, however, so my guide had to go back for him the next morning. They tried to catch him with a string, one end of which was fastened to a post (of fence), and the other end to a stick held in hand. Near the post a running loop was made, and lightly pegged down, about 1 foot wide. The chicken was then enticed into this with some food, and when inside, a sudden throw back of the stick drew the loop, and caught him by the feet. At the first attempt the string broke, and Mr. rooster refused to enter a second time.)

Got back to Toma about 6 P.M.

Thursday, Oct. 13   In morning went down a neighboring ravine and photoed a large tree with outstanding roots.

Friday, Oct. 14   Visited the top of Vartzin in morning.

Saturday, Oct. 15   Returned to Herbertshöhe in forenoon. Packed in afternoon.

The natives of the Vartzin region are probably the wildest of the Gazelle Peninsula natives at present. They live in small groups, 3–8 houses in a place, usually on the tops of ridges or hills. Each village is surrounded by a light fence. Between others lie the fields of taro, yams, bananas, cane, etc., while in and around the villages are cocoanuts. The district is fairly populous, and there is very little original forest standing. The fields are also fenced, but not so strongly as at Arawe. The fences around the villages, in old times, were made very high and rather light, so that any attempt to get over or through would cause so much noise as to alarm the villagers. The houses are simple and rather small (see photos). Of specimens I saw none of interest, and bought nothing.

In the neighborhood have been found interesting carved stone figures, of men and animals. Dr. Thurnwald got some, and the missionaries also. P. Meier said that the natives were divided into 2 totem groups, exogamous, each with bird totem which could not be killed or eaten. (The carved figures the natives keep hidden, and they are very hard to get, are of both soft and hard stone. Saw one head of dog of a rather soft volcanic tuff.)

Sunday, Oct. 16 Developed photos.

Monday, Oct 17 Went to Mrs. Parkinson's, as she sent word that a number of Baining from back of the Taulil country had come to visit her with some specimens. Got these (M.30)—4 masks and 7 pieces of bark cloth, used to cover the tamburan pipes (bamboo) held in the mouth and blown when dancing. These masks come out only at night, and appear to be something like the *tubuan*.

Photoed the Baining also a Taulil chief, who acted as guide and interpreter. Most of the Baining had never been out of their own country before.

Tuesday, Oct. 18 Packed up masks and other specimens (Boxes 30 & 31).

Wednesday, Oct. 19 Developed photos and wrote notes.

Thursday, Oct. 20 Went to Rabaul in forenoon in Forsayth's pinnace. Arranged to leave some of my stuff with Mr. Whiteman at his store, and spent the next day in overhauling it.

Saturday, Oct. 21–Saturday, Oct. 29 Spent most of time making boxes and packing. Took two trips to Matupi—bought 2 fish traps. Bought large Admiralty drum from Forsayth. All my boxes had to be got together, two broken ones repaired, several marked and measured, etc., etc. Got 32 boxes for shipment. Listed as follows:

1–20, 30	with 512 specimens, including 31 skulls. Box 30 chiefly shields, also Sulka, and small specimens from Mrs. Parkinson.
21	Nissan canoe, 4 Sulka masks, 2 fish traps.
22, 23, 28	Ceremonial canoe and posts, 2 Sulka.
24	Large Admiralty drum.
25	2 *tubuan*s, 2 *duk-duk*s.
26, 27, 29	15 Sulka masks, (29 the large one).
31	1 Nissan mask, 4 Baining masks.
32	Plates 376–701. 17 pamphlets, 4 books, personal (Parkinson, Surgery, 2 lit.);

Fig. 5.11. "Fish traps in Matupi" near Rabaul. A-37250 (703).

Bonwick—*Daily Life of Tasmanians.*
            —*Wild White Men.*
Wilson—*Pelew Islands*
Seemann—*Viti*
3 reports on N.G.
Reprint Cambridge, Lang.
1 Yellow Bird Paradise[5]
2 Black
3 King
1 Blue bird
1 bag Kaip
3 clay for pots.

5. The books mentioned by title were later accessioned by Field Museum Library. Six of the birds of paradise were accessioned and are still in the museum's zoology collection. At least one of these birds was given to anthropology curator S. C. Simms, who had repeatedly requested birds of paradise in his letters to ABL in the field.

Fig. 5.12. Stone figures from the north coast of Gazelle Peninsula opposite Rabaul. At Pater Esser's. A-37270 (705).

Monday, Oct. 31　Wrote reports and saw my boxes off for Hongkong.

Tuesday, Nov. 1　Went across to Pater Jos. Esser, at Valavolo, on the north shore, about one hrs. walk from Rabaul. On way the road led through a tunnel about 500 ft. long. At P. Esser's saw a number of carved stone figures, mostly broken. Some were of animals (dog & pig), but most human. According to the old men, they were used in connection with the initiation into the *inguet* society. These are all broken, and P. Esser found them by digging over one of their secret places, whither they were thrown after being used.

Got two baskets of split cocoanut leaves of style made by natives of region. The elongated baskets, with rounded bottoms, and strongly woven (as in Mus.) are made by the Baining.

On the island of Watom broken pottery is found, with ornamental patterns of fine incised lines and dots.[6] This is different from anything I have seen. (Saw some at Vuna Pope.)

Wednesday, Nov. 2　Got my stuff in order and on board *Sumatra,* which was leaving early the next morning.

Thursday, Nov. 3　Left at 6 A.M. for Matupi. Here saw a collection of a Japanese [Komine][7] who had been in the Admiralty Isl. for some 15 yrs. It apparently was very good but he wanted a big price for it. What I saw largely N. Ireland, including a number of *ulu*s. About 10 went to Herbertshöhe. I left there in evening.

6. This is the famous Lapita pottery of Watom Island; it was first noted here by Father Otto Meyer (1909, 1910).

7. ABL purchased Komine's collection the following year in October 1911. See the section on ABL's return to German New Guinea.

Fig. 5.13. View from hotel veranda, looking down on New Guinea Compagnie store, Rabaul. A-33626 (685).

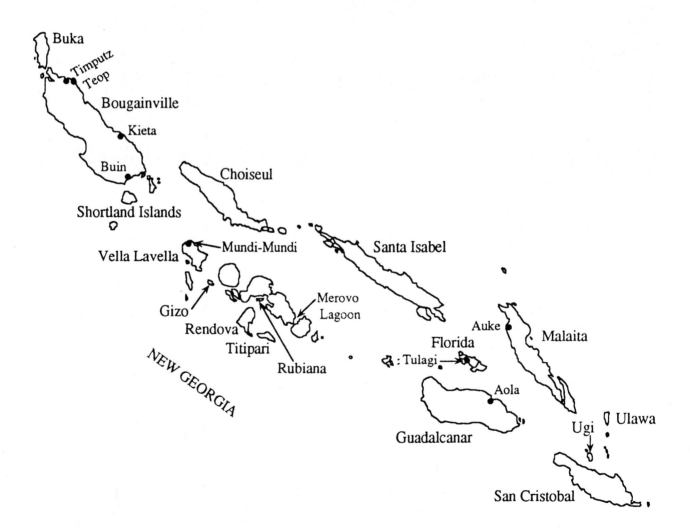

The Solomon Islands

Buka

Timputz
Teop

Bougainville

Kieta

Buin

Shortland Islands

Choiseul

Vella Lavella   Mundi-Mundi

Santa Isabel

Gizo

Rendova

Merovo
Lagoon

Titipari

Rubiana

NEW GEORGIA

Auke

Florida

: Tulagi

Malaita

Aola

Guadalcanar

Ugi

Ulawa

San Cristobal

The Solomon Islands

||||||||||||||||||||||||||||||||||||||||||||||||||||||||||||||||||||||||||||||||||||||||||||||||||||||||||||||||||||||||||||||

4 November 1910–6 January 1911

When ABL bid farewell to Herbertshöhe aboard Nord-Deutscher Lloyd's steamer *Sumatra,* he did not immediately leave German territory. He was off for the Solomon Islands, the northernmost of which—Buka and Bougainville—were part of German New Guinea. His next difficulty would come in trying to get from the German Solomons to the British protectorate. Only a narrow strait between Bougainville and the Shortland Islands separated these two colonies, but neither German nor British steamers regularly crossed this international boundary.

The German Solomons were a sleepy backwater of the Old Protectorate. Bougainville had only three major settlements on the *Sumatra*'s regularly scheduled route. Mrs. Parkinson's daughter and son-in-law (Diercke family) had established a plantation at Timputs on the north end of Bougainville. Kieta on the east coast was the largest settlement on the island, complete with a small government station (opened five years earlier), a Hernsheim agent, and a few independent plantations. And at Buin in the south, the flamboyant "King Peter" Hansen, formerly of Peterhafen in the French Islands (Vitu), had recently established a new plantation. Besides settlers at these stations there were fewer than two dozen other Europeans in all of Bougainville.[4]

ABL left the *Sumatra* at Kieta, arranging for Hernsheim's motor pinnace to take him across to Faisi in the Shortlands. There he could catch a British steamer for other parts of the Solomon Islands Protectorate. After calling briefly at Buin to deliver mail, the pinnace set sail for the Shortlands. But the wind died down and the captain could not get the engine to start; they had to return to Buin, towed behind the *Sumatra*. ABL would have been forced to stay here for some time except, by chance, a British pinnace arrived bringing two travelers from British territory. ABL boarded this second pinnace on its return and was taken to the Australian steamer *Moresby.* After sixteen months in German New Guinea, ABL was finally in the British Solomons.

The British Solomon Islands

As ABL supposed, he could rely more readily on the cooperation of expatriates in the Solomon Islands than was possible in New Guinea. As he would soon learn, however, the

Solomons presented more logistical difficulties for his research than the New Guinea Compagnie had.

The Solomon Islands were notorious for their vicious headhunters and cannibals. Because vast stretches of the larger islands remained unpacified, ABL could visit only those villages adjacent to European settlements. Imported trade goods had long been among the daily household goods in many of these communities, and traders had largely bought up all of the older curios. All of this meant that ABL found few "traditional" specimens in the villages, and those he did see were usually expensive.

The general lack of development in the British protectorate also meant that there were almost no regular steamers running among the islands. To get from island to island ABL had to rely on ships belonging to one of the traders or the Methodist mission. A Burns Philp steamer did, however, link the protectorate with Australia, though this steamer called only every six to eight weeks.

The Solomon Islands Protectorate was the last Melanesian territory to be annexed by a European power.[5] European and American whalers, traders, and blackbirders had regularly visited the Solomons since the early nineteenth century. Prompted by the growing need to police labor recruiters and traders—many of whom were all too eager to import firearms—the British Colonial Office reluctantly declared a protectorate over the Solomons in 1893. The reluctance of the Colonial Office was largely financial, since no one could imagine how a Solomon Islands protectorate could ever be self-supporting. No funds were provided for its newly appointed resident commissioner, the naturalist Charles Woodford, to actually visit the island until 1896. The protectorate administration grew slowly; the few officers added to the administration were mostly needed for dealing with hostile native communities. When ABL arrived, fourteen years after Woodford had established his administration, the entire staff consisted of only five men based at four stations. This skeleton staff faced the enormous task of pacifying the native population while simultaneously policing the traders and planters.[6]

To fund his tiny administration, Woodford needed all sorts of (taxable) expatriate development. He encouraged the operations of independent traders, several of whom were already established in the Solomons. These included such men as Norman Wheatley, who arrived in the New Georgia group in 1892, married local women, and exerted considerable influence in this part of the protectorate.

Woodford also encouraged missionaries to establish stations in the protectorate because he (correctly) believed that missions would help with pacification. As long as missionaries did not compete with expatriate traders, private business interests in the protectorate also encouraged and assisted the missions. For ABL, the most important missionaries in the Solomons were the Methodists, sent by the Methodist Missionary Society of Australasia in Sydney. Previously, of course, ABL had met many other missionaries from this same society in New Britain and Fiji.

The Solomons were the Methodists' newest mission district in the Pacific islands, established in 1902 under the leadership of the Reverend J. F. Goldie. By 1910 there were three ordained missionaries and one lay worker in the Solomons, based at three stations in the northern part of the protectorate: Rubiana (Roviana) and Vella Lavella in the New Georgia group and another station on Choiseul.

The government had its headquarters at Tulagi, in the Florida group. Tulagi was a small island situated in a protected harbor and thus was relatively safe from attack by hostile natives and reasonably well protected from storms. In the same protected harbor were settlements of two large private firms that Woodford had also attracted to the protectorate: Lever Pacific Plantations at Guvutu and Burns Philp at Makambo.[7] Both of these firms were acquiring vast tracts of plantation land in the islands and would play leading roles in the protectorate's economic

348

development between the two world wars. At the end of 1910, however, both firms were just starting their commercial empires, actively planting coconuts on their new plantations. Each firm had a small white staff, rather thinly distributed among their stations in the Solomons. The most famous of these men was W. H. Lucas, who played a major role in shaping Burns Philp's investments in the Solomons before the First World War; after the war Lucas achieved considerable notoriety as chairman of the expropriations board in the Mandated Territory of New Guinea.

At Guadalcanar (better known today as Guadalcanal) another firm had recently begun acquiring land for plantations when ABL visited in 1910. This was the Malayta Company, whose leading shareholders were the Young and Deck families, associated with the South Sea Evangelical Mission (Bennett 1987, 144). Here at Aola, ABL would wait nearly two weeks for the Sydney steamer.

Although ABL spent a total of seven weeks in the Solomons, this would be his least productive sojourn in any part of Melanesia. He collected only eighty specimens, more than half of them from a single community on Vella Lavella. Even his photography would be far less productive than previously; ABL sent only twenty negatives back to Chicago (and only nine of these images have survived). It was a disappointing and frustrating trip for him.

But although the Solomons proved a disappointing field for his research, ABL's diary contains some interesting notes about the protectorate. He offers some brief but informative observations about the people living at Vella Lavella and on Malaita, and he provides some details about the European settlements at Tulagi, Makambo, and Gavutu. ABL seems to have appreciated some of the incongruities of colonial life in this remote corner of the British empire. In a parenthetical comment he notes, for example, that the government office at Tulagi—a settlement of two Europeans and a few native workers—kept regular office hours, 8:00 A.M. to 11:00 and 1:00 P.M. to 4:00. Tulagi may have been far from London, but it remained an outpost of the empire.

Shaping a Collecting Philosophy in the Field

After three or four weeks in the Solomon Islands Protectorate, ABL received another biting letter from Field Museum director Skiff. ABL's April shipment had arrived in Chicago in early September, and Skiff had had the shipment opened in one of the museum's back rooms so he could have a look at what he must have expected would be an amazing assortment of large and wonderful pieces. The first shipment contained only smaller pieces; these included a large group of pots, twenty of which had arrived badly broken.

Skiff was apparently most upset at what seemed to him an extraordinary cost for an apparently worthless collection. He was even more concerned that the collection had few large, showy pieces in it, not to mention the sad state of ABL's pots. Skiff also seems to have wanted to know why no shipments had as yet been received from John Waters, ABL's agent in Fiji.

This letter must have come as quite a blow to ABL, who had only recently spent weeks packing up specimens in Friedrich Wilhelmshafen and Herbertshöhe, followed by a frustrating month in the Solomons for which he had virtually nothing to show. In his response explaining the strengths of his collection to Director Skiff (reproduced below), ABL provided the most direct statement describing his overall collecting strategy. He clearly explained why his collection did not consist exclusively of large, showy carvings and masks. His collection was an attempt to make a representative collection that would illustrate the sum total of the life and achievements of the many different peoples he had visited in New Guinea.

The letter is explicit; ABL viewed his photographs and field notes as integral parts of his collection, such that the whole of what he collected (in specimens, photos, and information) was much greater than the sum of its parts. Throughout his travels he had specifically collected raw materials that could illustrate the manufacturing process of many items in the collection. Where possible he had taken photographs of the same objects as they were being made. All of these were conscious decisions on ABL's part. One suspects that he was planning exhibit cases while he was collecting particular groups of specimens in the field. ABL was especially keen to point out that his collection was far more useful for illustrating New Guinea life than earlier collections (for example, those assembled by Dorsey and Voogdt) had been because he had systematically tried to understand how the objects were made and used.

Here ABL offers his view that a great natural history museum has responsibilities beyond its exhibits. One of these obligations was to build great research collections that would withstand the test of time. From ABL's other letters it is clear that he expected his collection to be a major research collection. Here, he goes beyond the value of his collection to suggest that knowledgeable research staff were also important: as an "Assistant Curator of a great museum, 'in charge of Melanesian Ethnology'" he has an obligation to obtain as much knowledge of the field as possible.

ABL emphatically states that Skiff should not expect field collections to yield all their results immediately. A good field collection, he argues, should provide results. But "some very valuable results may only *materialize* later."

ABL knew that his first forty-five hundred specimens were already valuable as "curios" and would only appreciate in monetary value in the coming years. He also knew that he could mount new and innovative exhibits with his collections. In addition, he was in a position to understand and make use of the Dorsey, Voogdt, and Parkinson collections because he now knew more about the material culture of the Melanesian region than any other American. Finally, ABL expected that the value of his collection as a research collection would also appreciate with time. Like most fieldworkers whose work is rooted in the present, ABL may not have imagined how valuable his collection and field notes would be as historical record of New Guinea life, but he clearly understood that his work would be valuable for future generations who would use Field Museum as an educational and scholarly resource.

Makambo, British Solomon Islands
Dec. 5, 1910

The Director
Field Museum
Chicago

Dear Sir:

Your letter of September 9th is at hand and contents carefully noted. As by the time this reaches you my other shipments from the German territory should have arrived, it is perhaps unnecessary to mention that the shipment under consideration represented only about half of the collections made up to that time, and render certain conclusions regarding cost, absence of certain objects, etc.,

350

premature. I fail to understand why this fact was not noted, as a complete catalogue of about 2,400 specimens was sent in the box with the photo negatives, and should have been in the hands of the Department at the time. This embodied careful notes as to use, material, distribution, etc., of the articles concerned, covering over 100 pages, and absolutely necessary in order to properly appreciate the value of the specimens, many of which are games, toys, medicines, material in various stages of manufacture, etc. All of which, of course, look in themselves worthless, but with proper explanation and photos should make very interesting exhibition specimens.

A large percentage of the photographs were taken especially to illustrate the collection, the use of different articles in the native's daily life, the stages and methods of manufacture, etc. These certainly should not be ignored, and taken with the collection, surely make the whole, for exhibition purposes, very much more valuable. Many of these apparently common things have a deep interest when shown up in connection with the native's daily life. I fear that the possibilities of making exceedingly interesting and valuable exhibits from many of my apparently worthless specimens have not been duly considered; but it can only be done by one who has studied native life, and never from such collections as Voogdt's or even Dorsey's. Pardon me if I say that my studies also increase the value of such collections to the Museum when I have had time to properly classify and label them. I am sure Dr. Dorsey agrees with me in the above statement, as we have spoken of such things frequently.

I do not take it that even a museum should limit itself to show specimens, but should make its exhibit illustrate that sum total of the life and achievements of a people, whether showy or not. I have made a careful study of the whole of New Guinea already explored, in addition to visiting a few places practically unknown. I have talked with most of the men who have been in regions not personally visited, and I can safely say that few men know more about the subject. My collection, together with what the Museum already had, which I have not intentionally duplicated, is fairly representative, though not by any means complete—to make it so would take years. There are many things in it from the interior, and some very rare and valuable, though not very showy. It is only from the big river valleys, as the Kaiserin Augusta river, that one gets large and showy specimens; the mountain peoples, and most of the interior is mountainous, are relatively low in culture. All of these regions are represented in the collection, and I trust that my collection as a whole will be sufficient to satisfy the demand for material for exhibition purposes.

Some of my specimens are also dismantled, so to speak; as for example a very large and rare feather dancing mask. This must be put together to be understood. I have photographs and full descriptions in my possessions, but did not send directions, as Dr. Dorsey had told me my boxes would not be unpacked without my directions. The same is true of my other things in my later shipments.

I might also say something as to the actual cash value of my collection merely as curios. Prices here are continually advancing, as specimens become rarer. However, I prefer to leave such estimation to Dr. Dorsey.

Regarding the packing, it is useless to say more. Before passing final judgment, however, especially regarding the percentage of pottery broken, I hope you will consult with Dr. Dorsey.

I am in constant communication with our agent in Fiji. The collection is nearly as complete as it can at present be made, and I have directed him to pack and ship it as soon as possible. It is not very large, but representative and well worth the price. Mr. Waters had a fairly large collection, and I had first choice, but could not buy as much as I wished, as I wrote Dr. Dorsey at the time. I had secured an option on the whole, however, or any part I wished, for several months, when I wrote. After waiting nearly a year, he declined to wait longer, and sold the remainder of the collection to the Government of Fiji for $2,000.00 for the local museum. That shows what they thought of the collection. Your extra allowance of $600.00 came just too late. Mr. Waters thought he might collect further to the extent of $100.00, however, and I sent him that amount. The rest I have turned into the general fund. This collection includes many photographs, and is to be fully catalogued and described by Mr. Waters himself. In addition to many rare old specimens, it is particularly rich in photographs and specimens representing industries and native life. I told Mr. Waters to take his time and make it good and as complete as he could. Also I saw no advantage in having the collection [opened] much before my return, as I wished to unpack it myself. Unless you regard its unpacking as necessary in order to judge of my results, I hope it may await my return unopened.

I do not forget that I am in the field as a collector; but, as Assistant Curator of a great Museum, "in charge of Melanesian Ethnology," I deem it my duty as well as privilege to obtain a knowledge of the whole field, and as a <u>collector</u>, I labor under the disadvantages that a part of that field is already nearly exhausted, and from other parts the Museum already has large collections. Of course, sufficient results must be shown to justify cost, but what constitutes results? Some very valuable results may only <u>materialize</u> later, even to the advantage of the Museum, which suggestions I very respectfully submit to your consideration.

I have written to Dr. Dorsey regarding my latter shipments, especially the one from Rabaul (Simpson Hafen). Many of the things in this collection are extremely rare and valuable, and much sought after. Some of the things had never been seen by the oldest residents. Of the larger things, I would mention the ceremonial canoe, and the large Sulka masks. Even the Government itself has never been able to obtain such masks. The natives take about a year to make one of them. I hope they arrive in good order.

I thank you for your kind wishes for my success.

Very respectfully,
A. B. Lewis

352

Fig. 5.14. "House, Rendova." A-37050 (717).

The Solomon Islands

||||||||||||||||||||||||||||||||||||||||||||||||||||||||||||||||||||||||||||||||||||||||||||||||||||||||||||||||||

Friday, Nov. 4　In afternoon about three in Corona Harbor, on N. end of Buka. Did not get a chance to go ashore. Here saw some fine canoes, made of a number of planks, with high prow and stern. One was rowed by 12 paddlers, 6 on a side. Both ends were carved and painted.

Saturday, Nov. 5　In morning at 6 A.M. arrived at Taínpos (Tímputs), the place of Mr. Diercke[8] (Parkinson's son-in-law). Here went on shore and visited a couple of native villages near by. The houses are low, 5–6 ft. high, 6–7 wide, with often 15–25 ft. long. The ground is the only floor. The bed a number of sticks (or nibung planks) on poles on ground. The house has a center-comb pole, and supporting poles on each side. The rafters are small and close together, and to them are found longitudinal poles outside. To these the palm-leaf thatch is fastened. On top a second pole is laid over the ends of the rafters, and over this an inverted hollow rind of nibung or other palm. The sides of the house are not over 2 ft. high, of nibung plank held in place by uprights on each side. At the ends is usually a small platform outside, and a very small door, about $1\frac{1}{2}$ by $2\frac{1}{2}$ ft. The end is closed by poles, planks or woven palm leaves.

Saw pots, up to a foot high and 9 in. wide, plain black, or very slightly ornamented around rim; large wood mortars, with rounded stones.

*Garamut*s, plain, with narrow slit and large plain ends. Men naked. Women with waist band and grass in front and behind. Little was to be seen in the houses, outside of crude palm-leaf baskets and bundles bound in palm leaves.

Canoes with out-riggers, dug-outs with narrow platform of poles extending to outrigger.

Took breakfast with Mrs. Diercke, and about 9 A.M. boat left. Stopped at one place between here and Kieta for short time, but had no time to go ashore. (Here Mr. Carter was starting a new plantation, and Mr. _____ was stopping here to look after it.) Reached Kieta after dark.

Sunday, Nov. 6　Arranged with the Hernsheim agent here (Mr. Glas[9]) to go in their pinnace to Faise, which place I would probably reach in time to get the English steamer *Moresby* to any place I might wish to go further in the Solomons. Left at noon.

Monday, Nov. 7　About 2 in morning stopped at Peter Hansen's[10] place to give him the mail. Left at 4, but motor would not go, and as very little

---

8. Carl Diercke and his wife Nellie Diercke nee Parkinson. ABL spelled their name Dierke.

9. This is probably Herr Class, whom Dorsey met on Bougainville in 1908.

10. This is the eccentric "King Peter" Hansen, who built and lost his fortune on Vitu (the French Islands), whereupon he opened a new plantation on Bougainville.

Fig. 5.15. Lime gourd with stopper decorated with orchid fiber, and coconut water bottle, Buin, south Bougainville, 136108 (5303), 136104 (5603), from Komine. Lime coconut, Timputs, 136124 (P-14), from Mrs. Parkinson. A-112129.

Fig. 5.16. Canoe at Timputs. A-37238 (708).

Fig. 5.17. Young men's initiation caps, Buka: 136126 (P-16), from Mrs. Parkinson; 136045 (5041), from Komine. A-112399. Outer cover at left partly removed to reveal intricate designs of cut palm leaves underneath.

wind, and current against us, made little progress. About 10 the *Sumatra* arrived, and took us in tow to Buin, where we arrived at nearly dark. Here Mr. Hansen was stationed, and invited me to stop, but I decided to go on, as an English pinnace came over that same night with 2 passengers for *Sumatra* (North & Kelley[11]), and agreed to tow us on to Faise, which place we reached some time before morning.

Tuesday, Nov. 8   In morning got my things taken on board the *Moresby*, and about 10 they left, stopping for the afternoon at a cocoanut plantation on small island not far away.

Wednesday, Nov. 9   Arrived in Gizo in morning. After seeing Mr. Goldie, the head of Methodist mission and captain of their schooner, who offered me a trip with them; and Mr. Norman Wheatly, who said I might go around with one of their trading schooners, with native captain, I decided to go with the mission boat.

Thursday, Nov. 10   Got what things I wanted, and some provisions, and left with the mission boat about 4 for Vela Lavella. Spent the night at mission station (Mr. Nickelson) on south end.

Friday, Nov. 11   Left early in morning, calling at Mr. Martin's place (island [of] Renard) to deliver some lumber, and near evening arrived at Mundi-mundi, where Mr. Williams was to build a store for the mission. Here there was a Tongan and a Rubiana teacher. We stayed in the Tongan's house. Spent night on schooner.

Saturday, Nov. 12   Got my things on shore, and looked around a little. In afternoon went over to a small island to shoot pigeons. Here found 2 stone cairns (?) about 3 ft. high, 3 ft. wide, and 4–5 ft. long. On these in a little

11. The identities of these two travelers are not known. They were probably Australians.

enclosure were a number of skulls, some ornamented with shell rings bound on, but could not see much of them without disturbing them, which I did not like to do then, as the natives were with me.

Sunday, Nov. 13   Rained all day.

Monday, Nov. 14   Got my things ready for trip to bush as understood there were two villages in the interior.

Tuesday, Nov. 15   Rained all forenoon, but about 1 P.M. left with 5 carriers (Simíone, a Fijian teacher for Rubiana, Shotokānā Līkōnī, Ṅgāringāri, and Mōlā), and in about an hr. reached the first village, Kūmbōkānā. Here stopped a short time to rest, and then on for about 1½ hrs., when reached the furtherest village, Mbākkōwārā. These two villages my men declared were the only villages they knew of in the interior. Stayed here over night. The natives were getting ready for a feast, and cooked that afternoon a pig, cut up, and other things, in a south-sea oven. The heated stones were covered with leaves, on which the food was placed, and over all large leaves laid till all thoroughly covered. Left about 1½ hr. In the evening the food was distributed, the natives giving me and my men each some.

Wednesday, Nov. 16   In morning bought some things, and left about 11 for return. Stopped on way at other village, and got few things more. Reached Mundi-mundi about 5 P.M.

Thursday, Nov. 17   Catalogued my things and got a few more. In afternoon packed up and sent things on cutter, ready to start for Rubiana, as Mr. Williams had now finished store. (The mission cutter had also come from Gizo to Mundi-mundi, to take us to Rubiana, for which place the schooner had left Saturday morning.)

The natives of Mundi-mundi, Kumbokána and Mbakowára, as well as one or two other villages at some distance along the coast, all belong to the same group; with one chief, who goes from place to place.

The villages are very small. In Mundi-mundi are 2 houses, one large, in which a number of people live. There are 3 canoes in center, and on each side several platforms, which are occupied by the different people.

The two bush villages are on hill tops, and consist of 2 parts—an earthen platform about 3 ft. high (faced with stones in part) on which are 2 sheds, facing each other, for the men, and the woman's or family houses to one side. Mbakowara had 3 family houses, and one open shed outside, and the other place 6–8 family houses, but most of them in very bad repair. These average about 5 by 10 ft. with floor about 3–4 ft. high (under part often used for pigs). The sheds on the platform are 10–25 ft. long, and about 8 ft. deep, with floor about 4 ft. high, or built out from platform. In each place I should say there were not over 4 families.

The people have an abundance of sweet potatoes, taro, and bananas, with some cocoanuts. In the interior an important article of diet and trade is the nut of a tree, called *nēnī*. The kernels are partly mashed and packed in packages, of leaves, carefully tied up with bush rope. These packages weigh from 10 to 100 lbs. or more, and are often 3 ft. long and 1 ft. in diameter.

They claim such a package is worth nearly a pound, and will buy a shield in Rubiana. When eaten these nuts are usually mixed with mashed taro,

Fig. 5.18. Package of *neni* nuts, mashed and packed for trade, 135827 (S-21); loose *neni* nuts, 135829 (S-22); hammer for breaking *neni* nuts, 135830 (S-23); mortar used to mash taro and *neni* nuts, with stick for pestle, 135834 (S-13). All from Mundi-Mundi, Vella Lavella. A-112199.

wrapped in leaves and baked over hot stones—their only way of cooking,—they have no pots.

Bananas, taro, yams, meat, etc. are also baked in the same way. For mashing taro they use a hollowed log some 5 ft. long by 6–10 wide and deep. They also have round mortars, often covered with woven rattan, from 3–12 in. in diameter. Have no wooden dishes. Make rough palm-leaf baskets, and also a fairly good soft basket of split cocoanut leaf, from 3–15 in. diameter. These are usually carried by the men for their small valuables, betel-nuts, lime bamboos and gourds (all gourds seen plain, bamboo often ornamented) etc.

The women also make a netted bag, which they carry on their backs, suspended from the head. Shields come chiefly from Rubiana. All I saw were the same. Spears from Bougainville. Saw only 2 bows—one a boy's plaything, the other larger possibly used to shoot fish. Saw no arrows.

They make a rather coarse bark-cloth from the inner bark of various trees (Beater a shell on stick). This is used as the dress of both men and women. The men wear a strip like the *mal* of New Guinea, but no flap in front. The women wear a broad piece caught under the belt behind, and passed between the legs and again caught under the belt in front. Behind it is as broad as the body, and apparently of several thicknesses, as when they stand it stands out like a bustle. Ornaments now are very rare, about the only ones being a few rattan and fibre arm bands. Formerly they had shell ear and breast ornaments. The canoes are built up of planks, and some old ones seen ornamented with inlaid shell, and shells on prow and stern.

Paddles.

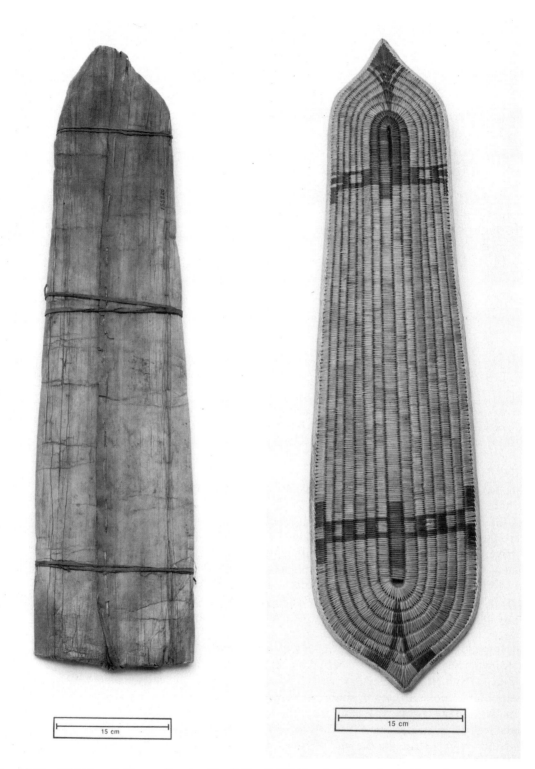

15 cm

15 cm

Figs. 5.19 and 5.20. Shield from Rubiana, collected at Mundi-Mundi, Vella Lavella. Wrapped in leaf for trading to other groups and un-wrapped to reveal the intricate plaiting and design. "Shields are not made in Vella Lavella, but bought from the natives of Rubiana and other islands. They pay for them with a large package (about 3 feet long and ¾ to 1 foot in diameter) of mashed taro and nuts (called *neni*). They claimed such a package was worth £1 sterling. (shield = *mbako*)." 135826 (S-1). A-112307, A-112408.

Friday, Nov. 18 Left early in cutter. I went in small boat to island to get some skulls before seen, (gave chief man 30 sticks tobacco for same) but found natives had taken away all the ornamented ones, leaving only 2 plain ones. Had no time to go back and ask what they meant by this.

Sailed all day and night.

Saturday, Nov. 19 Wind practically nil all day. Put in part of morning studying fine coral reef, with its various colored corals, sponges, fish of brilliant hues, etc.

Sunday, Nov. 20 Arrived about 7 A.M. at Ruviana mission station. Went ashore to service, and spent afternoon and evening with Mr. & Mrs. Goldie. Mr. Rooney was also there. There were about 100 natives at the church, all sitting cross-legged on the mat floor; the men dressed in white loin cloth and singlet or shirt, many with a neck tie; all women and girls in dresses, all very neat, and no loud colors. In the evening most of them assembled again on the house veranda for evening song and prayer. This took place every evening. Several songs were sung, usually quite well, with parts. Some of the men had quite good voices, and were often singing on board the cutter and schooner. I slept on the schooner.

Monday, Nov. 21–Wednesday, Nov. 23 Made several visits to the villages along shore, as well as [to] Norman Wheatley, whose place was about a mile from the mission.

This region is the most famous in the Rubiana lagoon, and in former times much noted for their fine carvings, canoes, and inlaid work. Now there is little left. Saw several canoes, a few inlaid to some extent. Baskets are made still, of split cocoanut leaf (the young, unfolded leaf is taken), often

Fig. 5.21. Wooden bowl inlaid with mother-of-pearl, Rubiana lagoon, 135878 (S-74). Inlaid dancing club, Ulawa Island (from Huggett), 135893 (H-5). A-112141.

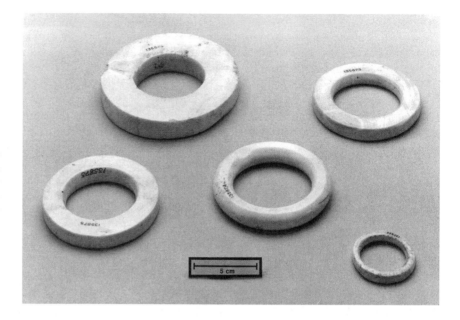

Fig. 5.22. Shell rings from various islands in the Solomon group: "Shell money *(pota)*, made of tridacna shell, Rubiana. This specimen is rather old, 135870 (S-52) from Wheatley; shell money rings from Choiseul, 135873 (S-54), 135874 (S-55) from Wheatley; large shell ring used as money *(tacula)*, Mundi-Mundi, Vella Lavella 135875 (S-37); small shell arm ring for child, Mundi-Mundi, Vella Lavella, 135843 (S-29). A-112246.

with red fibre interwoven. The fibre is first soaked in water with certain leaves for about 2 weeks, and then boiled with the roots of a certain tree. A string handle is often added to the basket.

Tridacna shell rings are also made, both arm rings and money. The latter are about an inch wide, nearly as thick, and 2–3 inch inside diameter. Now they are sawn out of the shell with an iron band and sand and water. They are then ground down on stones to smooth round discs. These stones are often quite regularly squared, and stand near the house, about the height of a good stool. The disc is then drilled with a pump drill, tipped with iron nail (formerly shell), near where inner side of ring would come. Through this hole a wire fastened to a bow is passed, and with this the inner circle is sawn out. In old time a strong vine or rattan was used for this purpose, with water and sand. The inner side is finished with a cylindrical stone (or file now). The finished ring is worth 5–20 shillings, depending on finish and character of shell, yellow translucent being the most valuable.

Most of the houses now are more or less modified, and all wear European cloth. Few of the old things are to be seen, tho one occasionally sees a shell breast ornament, carved in sort of fret work.

Thursday, Nov. 24   Left about eleven with Wheatley for Tulagi. We went down the lagoon, winding around the islands and reefs by a very tortuous passage, and about 10 miles away emerged into the open, and ran over to Rendova, and anchored about 1:30.

I took boat and went on shore to visit some villages. Stayed till nearly sun down but did not find much. Larger baskets than in Rubiana are made here, also bark cloth and shell rings. Houses simple, beds some sticks or mats on ground.

Friday, Nov. 25   Left in morning for plantation on Titipari, where spent most of day waiting for Mr. Lucas, the island manager of Burns Philp & Co. In afternoon went to Merovo lagoon, but owing to darkness had to anchor before reaching station.

Saturday, Nov. 26   Arrived early at station. Visited a few houses opposite, but found little—a few colored baskets, arm rings, a stone mortar, and few other things.

This region is one of the most troublesome in the group, and many murders have occurred here, one only about 6 months before. The interior is practically unknown, and decidedly dangerous.

Left in afternoon for Makambo, and sailed most of night, as engine got too hot.

Sunday, Nov. 27–Sunday, Dec. 4   Arrived at Makambo about noon. This is the name of a small island on which B. P. & Co. have their store. The government station of Tulagi is across the harbor about a mile off, while Lever Pacific Plant. Co.'s place, Gavutu, is another island about 2 miles away.

In this region spent the next week, hoping each day to get away, while Norman Wheatley, _____ Bennett and Jack Ellis, the men on our launch, the *Roviana* (correct form for Rubiana), tried to get the engine into shape.

There are no settlements in the Solomons. Tulagi is the seat of government, and consists of 2 houses on the hill, where Gov. Woodford and Mr. Barnett, his deputy (postmaster, etc.) live, and an office (hrs. 8–11, 1–4) on the beach, with 2 small tool and work houses, and boys house. No soldiers are to be seen. There is a small government steamer, which is often anchored off the station.

B. P. & Co.'s place (Makambo) also has 2 houses on hill (for store keeper, assistant and 1 or 2 white skilled workmen) with store and sheds on beach. Gavutu is more ambitious, has doctor's house on hill, and large dwelling and office house near beach, with large store, shed, store houses, shops, etc. There are several white men here.

It was the morning of Friday, Dec. 9 before we finally succeeded in getting away, and then another ship was hired to take the boys back to Malaita. Norman Wheatley had left on the *Lily* (Hernsheim's boat) for Rubiana several days before. The engine of the *Roviana* refused to go, so at last another boat was hired, and we left for Malaita, where we arrived the next day.

Saturday, Dec. 10   Mr. T. W. Edge-Partington (son of the famous writer on south sea curios), sub-commissioner at the gov. station near Auke, kindly allowed me to stay with him for a few days. He had been there for about a year (was formerly at Gizo), and had a comfortable house on the hill, but was the only white man in the place, and while I was there [he] was laid up with an ulcer on his ankle. I visited the village of the "salt-water" people near by. Many of the bush natives were at the coast, catching crabs and preparing for a big dance shortly to come off on Auke. One day about 80 bush people came up to see the house. Many of them had not seen a white man before. At home the men go naked, but here most of them had a strip of cloth on, wrapped around the waist and drawn between the legs. They had almost nothing with them—a few combs, ear sticks, belts, and shell ornaments being all of interest. The combs and ear sticks were nicely ornamented with colored fibre woven in patterns,[12] also the belts (of rattan) in places.

---

12. Production of these combs had nearly ceased by the 1960s but was started up again in the early 1980s at the encouragement of David Akin (1993) and Kathleen Gillogly, then American Peace Corps volunteers, now anthropologists, who spent about three years among the inland Kwaio, best known to anthropologists from the work of Roger Keesing.

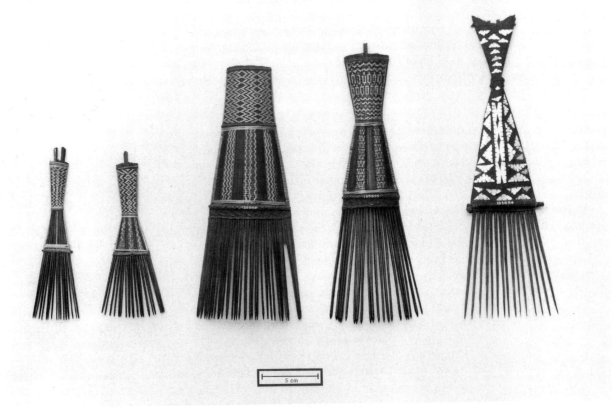

Fig. 5.23. Combs from Malaita made of palm wood laths and decorated with yellow orchid fiber and red rattan: 135901 (S-88); 135900 (S-88); 135898 (H-13), from Huggett; 135899 (S-88). Ulawa comb inlaid with mother-of-pearl, 135894 (H-14), from Huggett. A-112128.

The shell ornament most valued was circular, about 2–2½ in. in diameter, with black incised lines representing birds, etc. One to several were worn on a string around the neck. All these are made by the bush people, and that is about all of interest which they have. They live scattered in small settlements, constantly at war with the coast ("salt-water") people, and more or less with each other, except when forced by the white man to refrain from hostilities.

The "salt-water" people live on islands, often built up so as to increase the height and surface (so-called fortified islands), and even then much crowded. Their houses are low (4–6 ft. at comb), small, and crowded together, so that only narrow passages wind in among them. The floor is the ground, and the only bed a sort of leaf mat (the sleeping place is sometimes surrounded with sticks), forming a rectangle, laid on the ground. The house walls are of bamboo, set upright, and bound together with rattan. Household implements consist of crude baskets, deep bowls of wood for food (6–20 in. long), a sort of flat wooden plate (very rude), and crude pestles and stirring sticks for mashed taro, cooked with hot stones. No pottery, practically no carvings. Make shell rings about 2 in. diameter (for ears) and shell money. This is of 3 kinds, white, red, and black. Certain shells are used for each and the places where these are found are owned by certain individuals. The shells are broken into pieces about the right size, ground down on a flat stone (several pieces are rubbed on the stone at once by means

364

Fig. 5.24. "Cocoanut shell with pieces of white shell, some drilled and some not, for shell money, Auki, Malaita, 135904 (——). (The money is made from a bivalve, about the same thickness as money or a little thicker. The pieces are first roughly chipped out with a stone and then ground on a flat grinding stone. Several are ground at one time, being held on stone by a piece of rather soft wood, so that the pieces do not slip. When ground to proper thickness, they are placed around in the cocoanut shell, and drilled with a pump drill, tipped with quartz. Fly string laid on a piece of wood, and smoothed and rounded by being rubbed longitudinally with a stone, which often is deeply ground to fit the roll. Shells for money are both red and white, but red are rarer, and much more valuable.)" A-112245.

of a rather soft piece of wood) on both sides, bored with a pump drill tipped with flint (this is sharpened with a shell) in a cocoanut shell (with water only). They are then strung, and finally ground down to a uniform circular size. To do this the string is placed on a piece of wood, and a stone rubbed along it length-wise. The stone finally comes to be deeply grooved like the roll of money.

The red money is the most valuable, being worth about a shilling a foot. It is usually put up in fathom lengths (as long as a man can reach). The making of this money is the chief industry of Auke.

There is one important chief, who has considerable honor shown him. No one can enter his house (the largest in the place) except at certain times, and only a chosen few are allowed to come near him.

In an enclosure at one side of the village are several small houses (about 6 ft. long, 4 wide, and 3 high) in which the women must stay while having their flow. No man will go near the place, as a drop of the flow on him would cause his death. During and for 3–4 months after child-birth they must live

Fig. 5.25. Loom with partly woven fabric, Santa Cruz, 133485 (_____). From Huggett. A-112400.

in a small hut especially built in another enclosed (by stone fence) place, which after use is thrown bodily into the sea.

In the interior of Malaita the people are everywhere dangerous, and in many places have a price out for a white man's head. If a person dies, no matter how, they think some one is to blame, and they must have a head to pay for it. If a laborer dies in Queensland the white man is to blame, and they must have a white man's head. Before Mr. Partington established the station, almost nothing had been done to put a stop to this condition of affairs, but a beginning has now been made. It is still unsafe, however, for a white man to go into the bush, except a few miles from the station.

Friday, Dec. 16   Left Auke with the *Jubilee,* a sailing schooner of the Malaita Co., for their station at Aola, on Guadalcanar, where arrived the next day. On Monday and Tuesday visited a number of villages along the coast, but found little of interest—nothing really worth buying.[13] The only household utensils seen were very crude wooden bowls and baskets. The houses seemed a little better made than in Malaita and larger, usually nibung planks, 2–3 in. wide, arranged horizontally, and tightly bound together and to uprights on each side. Roof quite thick, of leaves of ivory nut palm.

Stayed at Aola till Wednesday, Dec. 28 when left on *Moresby* for Sydney. Due Friday morning, January 6, [1911]. Had fever Monday after Christmas, and was several days before well.

Not many things to be gotten in Solomons at present, and prices for these very high, even when natives can be induced to part with them. The interior of San Christoval is as yet unexplored, but has been visited in places. Very little there. Partington said he saw nothing of interest on a visit to a large interior village.

Isabel now is largely Christian or missionary. Very few natives in the interior. Culture similar to Rubiana, by which natives it was conquered before white influence. Here the incised lime bamboos are made.

---

13. The villagers here must have offered ABL very little indeed, as he had bought hardly anything in the previous month.

‖‖

The New Hebrides and New Caledonia

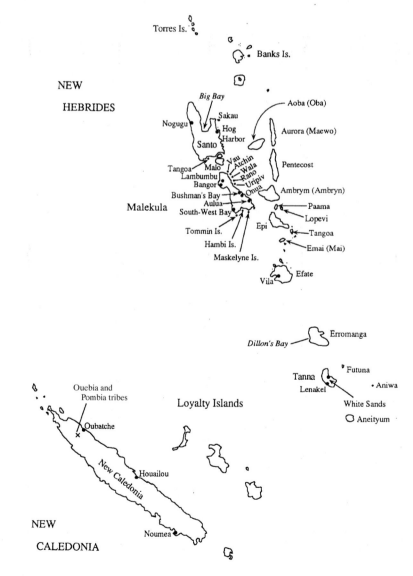

Torres Is.

Banks Is.

NEW

HEBRIDES

Big Bay

Aoba (Oba)

Sakau

Nogugu

Hog
Harbor

Aurora (Maewo)

Santo

Yau
Atchin
Wala

Tangoa
Malo
Lambumbu
Bangor

Rano
Uripiv
Onua

Pentecost

Ambrym (Ambryn)

Bushman's Bay

Paama

Malekula

Aulua
South-West Bay

Lopevi

Tangoa

Tommin Is.

Epi

Emai (Mai)

Hambi Is.

Maskelyne Is.

Vila

Efate

Dillon's Bay

Erromanga

Ouebia and
Pombia tribes

Loyalty Islands

Futuna

Tanna
Lenakel

Aniwa

Oubatche

White Sands

Aneityum

New Caledonia

Houailou

NEW

CALEDONIA

Noumea

Book 6

To New Zealand, the New Hebrides, and New Caledonia, with a Return to German New Guinea

6 January 1911 – 25 December 1911

On New Year's Day 1911, ABL found himself aboard a Burns Philp steamer bound for Sydney. When he arrived in Australia a week later, he had been in the tropics for seventeen months. Sydney's hotels, shopping facilities, and urban environment must have seemed like luxuries to the now well-seasoned anthropologist returning for a field break. Before setting off for other parts of Melanesia, ABL had an opportunity to rest up, replenish his field gear, visit the Australian Museum, prowl the book shops, and even visit some curio dealers.

A few days after his arrival, the Australian Association for the Advancement of Science opened its annual meeting in Sydney. ABL attended this convention and met a number of Australians with interests in ethnology, natural history, and other sciences. Even George Dorsey turned up in Sydney for the AAAS meeting, fitting it in during another one of his overseas junkets.[1]

ABL spent several days with Dorsey, during which time he appears to have discussed in some detail the successes and difficulties he had experienced in the field. No documents survive describing how Dorsey responded to the German reaction to his *Tribune* columns. The indirect evidence in Field Museum's correspondence files, however, suggests that Dorsey exhibited his characteristic insensitivity, apparently dismissing the significance of reactions to the columns and showing no particular concern for the museum's tarnished image. Dorsey would have enthusiastically turned the conversation to exciting prospects of future research in other territories. ABL also expressed to Dorsey his concerns over Skiff's recent letter, the significance of which Dorsey seems to have minimized. With his usual flamboyance, Dorsey voiced his opinions about which places and islands ABL should visit in the New Hebrides (and other colonies) and the kinds of wonderful specimens ABL would undoubtedly find in each of these places. Because Dorsey had no firsthand experience in these territories, many of these suggestions proved to be wishful thinking. Nevertheless, it must have been satisfying for ABL to be able to talk about his research with interested colleagues like Dorsey and a few others he met in Sydney.

After twenty-five days in Sydney, ABL was off again to begin a new round of research. Compared with his months of ostracism in German New Guinea, the first half of 1911 was a

369

time of sociable contacts. He met dozens of people on these travels, many of whom would later achieve considerable prominence in their particular fields. Nearly everywhere he went he encountered people who seem to have been eager to help him with his research.

To Fiji, Samoa, Tonga, and New Zealand

ABL's first trip from Sydney was to New Zealand, with stops at Fiji, Samoa, and Tonga en route. He justified this excursion to Director Skiff as a side trip while waiting out the dangers of the hurricane season in the New Hebrides. But I suspect that after so many months in difficult field conditions, ABL wanted a month or two away from the tropics to rest up and recuperate from the effects of malaria *and* his quinine. He undoubtedly wanted a chance to see other parts of the South Pacific in relative ease. That the New Zealand steamer would stop in Fiji may also have helped shape his decision, for he could meet once more with John Waters to discuss his Fiji collection, which, according to Skiff, had not yet arrived in Chicago.

On 22 February ABL arrived in Auckland. Although he spent most of his month in New Zealand traveling from place to place, mostly visiting tourist attractions and resort areas, such as the baths at Rotorua, he did spend a few days at the Auckland Museum and a week at the Dominion Museum in Wellington. At both museums ABL spent time looking over Maori collections and photographs. Here he met several important individuals: T. F. Cheeseman, director of the Auckland Museum; Augustus Hamilton, of the Dominion Museum; and the photographer Josiah Martin (from whom he bought a number of photos). At the back of one of his notebooks he listed the prices of various kinds of specimens from curio catalogs. It would appear that although ABL purchased only photos and books in New Zealand, he contemplated acquisition of some Maori material later on, probably after he had returned to Sydney.

After a trip to South Island, where he visited the museums in Christchurch and Dunedin, ABL returned to Sydney via Hobart, Tasmania, and Melbourne, Victoria. In the few hours he spent in Hobart, ABL met photographer John Beattie, from whom he purchased some photos taken in the Melanesian islands. In Melbourne ABL visited the museum, where he met a fellow curator, R. Henry Walcott; later he called on Prof. Baldwin Spencer of Melbourne University, who had written two important volumes about Aboriginal tribes in central Australia. In Melbourne ABL also had an opportunity to meet the influential Atlee Hunt, secretary of the Department of External Affairs, who provided letters of introduction for the New Hebrides and Papua.

Immediately on his arrival in Sydney, ABL made preparations for his next expedition to the Melanesian islands, departing two days later for the New Hebrides on the Burns Philp steamer *Malaita*. He would spend the next three and a half months in the New Hebrides.

The New Hebrides

Of all the colonies and protected territories in the South Pacific, the New Hebrides (now Vanuatu), which had been administered jointly by the British and the French since 1887,[2] had the most peculiar form of government. Neither the French nor the British saw much economic potential in the New Hebrides, and it was clear that these islands were not suitable for large-scale European settlement as New Caledonia and New Zealand had been. Because they wanted to preserve the balance of power in Europe, neither the British nor the French dared annex the New

Hebrides; because both had interests in these islands, neither wanted to surrender the group to the other.

For many years the Queensland sugar industry had been dependent on laborers recruited from Melanesia, a large portion of whom were recruited from the New Hebrides. Some British subjects had acquired land in the islands, and a growing number of French nationals had large holdings; among the most prominent French landowners was the New Caledonian–born Nicholas Hagen, who began acquiring land from about 1900.

After a series of Anglo-French conventions and agreements in 1887, 1904, and 1906, the New Hebrides, together with the Banks and Torres Islands, were formally recognized as "a region of joint influence," such that the British and French retained jurisdiction over their own subjects and citizens, and neither power was to exercise exclusive control over the entire group (Scarr 1967, 227). The convention of 1906 established a Joint Court consisting of British and French judges and a court president appointed by the king of Spain. Each power had its own bureaucracy, constabulatory, and magistrates for administering its own nationals and certain issues involving natives. Issues involving both British subjects and French citizens were to be handled by the Joint Court.

Following the formal establishment of the Anglo-French Condominium, Britain's high commissioner for the western Pacific appointed Merton King as British resident commissioner, making him the first civilian resident commissioner in the islands. King appears to have been extremely helpful to visitors to the New Hebrides, including ABL, but was disliked for his political ineptness by Atlee Hunt and many other Australian officials and businessmen.

ABL had relatively little contact with either British or French officials, largely because he spent little time in Vila. Away from Vila, which seems to have always been alive with political intrigue and international diplomacy, the New Hebrides was a colonial territory dominated by a growing number of independent traders and missionaries. Both groups provided ABL with considerable assistance, without which it would have been impossible to do anything in the condominium.

Like the Solomons, the New Hebrides consisted of many widely scattered islands that were not connected by any regularly scheduled public transportation. The Melanesian Mission (Anglican), however, operated a steamer (the *Southern Cross*) and regularly took passengers and freight to most parts of the archipelago. The Melanesian Mission had stations principally in the northern part of the New Hebrides, the Banks and Santa Cruz groups, and parts of the Solomons. ABL met both Bishop Cecil Wilson and Rev. J. Blencowe, but they played only a minor role in his work in the New Hebrides.

Much more important for ABL were the Presbyterians with the New Hebrides Mission, of whom he is known to have met at least twenty while in the archipelago. The New Hebrides Mission was supported by Presbyterian congregations in Australia, Scotland, Canada, and New Zealand.

For ABL, one of the most important of the Presbyterians was the Reverend Fred Paton, son of pioneer New Hebrides missionary John G. Paton. The younger Paton was born in the New Hebrides and lived nearly his entire life in the islands. ABL met Paton, at the time a widower, on Malekula, and the missionary took the anthropologist with him on his various travels around the island. Inspired by ABL's visit, Paton visited Chicago the following year while on leave in Canada and the United States. During this visit he called on anthropology curators at Field Museum to see the Pacific ethnology collections. Paton gave and sold ABL a few specimens (about twenty). Five or six other Presbyterians also sold him small collections, the largest numbers coming from Dr. Annand at Tangoa and Dr. Taylor at Nogugu (both on Santo). ABL's cordial relations with the many Presbyterian missionaries may have been enhanced by the fact that he was himself a Presbyterian. And it should be remembered that ABL's aunt (Harriet Lewis) was still a Presbyterian missionary in Canton, China, where she had been based since 1883.

In addition to missionaries and bureaucrats, ABL encountered a surprisingly large number of independent traders or planters in the islands. He mentions at least seventeen traders, planters, and businessmen in his diaries—as well as a few others, whom he may not have actually met, in his other notes. The most important of these traders was Thomas C. Stephens, who lived on Ambrym (which ABL spelled Ambryn). Stephens helped ABL in and around Ambrym and southeastern Malekula and helped him ship his collections back to Chicago. Later ABL enlisted the support of Stephens as an agent, much as he had enlisted John Waters' support in Fiji. In all, Stephens acquired more than two hundred pieces for Field Museum, including a large number of elaborately decorated masks, modeled skulls, and a variety of other objects. McAfee, another trader, who lived at Southwest Bay, Malekula, sold ABL about seventy five pieces.

Throughout his months in the New Hebrides, ABL was forced to rely heavily on the goodwill of traders, missionaries, and government officers for getting around from village to village and from island to island. The New Hebrides was, of course, an island territory. It was clearly a maritime environment, even though many of the larger islands had vast hilly and mountainous regions in the interior. What is perhaps most striking is how dependent all expatriates seem to have been on water transportation, even when they wanted to go to an adjacent settlement along the coast.

While in the New Hebrides ABL met the noted German ethnologist Felix Speiser, who had already been in the condominium for about a year. Speiser's work there was far more comprehensive than ABL's, and his major ethnographic study is still one of the best summaries of cultural variation in the archipelago (Speiser 1923; see also the recent English translation by D. Q. Stephenson 1991). Clearly, ABL did not expect to be as systematic in his research as he had been along the coasts of New Guinea, and his stay of less than four months in the New Hebrides could hardly yield results to rival Speiser's research. Apparently there was no professional jealousy; anthropologists seem to have been friendly and cooperative with one another in the field; Speiser even seems to have helped ABL acquire several tree fern figures and carved poles from dance grounds.

During this trip to the New Hebrides ABL took 160 photos. He also tried something new with his photographs. In Sydney just before he left for Vila, ABL bought a new type of Kodak film that he decided to use together with the glass negatives he had used in 1909 and 1910. This was an early nitrate sheet film (measuring roughly 2.5 by 3.5 inches), which he developed in the field much as he did his glass negatives. More than fifty of his photographs from the New Hebrides were on this Kodak film. Although the original negatives seem to have been nearly as good in quality as his glass plate negatives, the nitrate in the Kodak film is unstable and gradually destroys the emulsion through oxidation. Over the years, there has been some damage—mostly minor—to the emulsion in many of these film negatives.[3]

Compared with his experiences in the Solomons, ABL found the New Hebrides a personally satisfying and productive stint of fieldwork. Although ethnological specimens were expensive in the New Hebrides, much as they had been in the Solomon Islands, ABL was able to assemble a substantial collection of more than twelve hundred specimens, a collection still larger than any other New Hebrides collection in North America.

372

Sydney
Sept. 21, 1911

My dear Simms:

I enclose full lists of contents of boxes 50–63 of present shipment. List of boxes 1–34 sent in from Vila (or Noumea) (skipped numbers 35–49, as some more stuff to follow these from New Hebrides, which it was impossible for me to get as ship would not stop for it). Please file these lists away carefully, as I send them to you for safe keeping.

It is not necessary to unpack the boxes, unless the Director wishes. I do not care for prints of the negatives sent.

There is not much in the New Hebrides or New Caledonia, but I got a fairly representative collection. Prices are very high, even in the islands. Look up Webster's catalogue and you will find that his prices are too! For example, the natives themselves are willing to pay from $75.00 to $150.00 for a shell-band armlet like one I have in collection. A dealer in Sydney asked £50 for a similar one. The natives have plenty of money, and value their old things highly.

The Dominion museum of Wellington, N.Z. should have sent some photos to the department, perhaps also some other things. Also some books, etc. for me, from Mr. Hamilton with whom I spent a very pleasant and profitable week. One dozen photos from New Zealand Tourist Dept. should have been received for which I paid. Also some from Beattie, of Hobart, Tasmania. Please let me know of all things that come in. Box of specimens from Mrs. Parkinson should have arrived. Kindly let me know of that, also of the Fiji collection. Some Santa Cruz things should come in soon, also from other islands. Please keep me informed of all such arrivals. It is impossible for me, in the short time I am in the different islands, to get all I want, so I have to leave it to others, and trust that from all of them we will get enough to make it worth while. Mañana is as favorite a term in the south seas as in other tropical lands, I find.

I am leaving for New Guinea today. Have been nearly three weeks in Sydney, and yet find it impossible to get through all my business. Have been up till midnight or after every night, writing up notes, reports, letters, overhauling outfit, etc. etc., and my days are full too. Well, I must stop, hope you can read this.

Most sincerely,
A. B. Lewis

Care Lohmann & Co.

S.S. <u>Prinz Waldemar</u>

Sept. 30, 1911

The Director

Field Museum

Chicago, U.S.A.

Dear Sir:

Since making my last formal report from Rabaul, I wrote again from the Solomon Islands, and wish to thank you for your kind reply to this letter.

I spent only six weeks in the British Solomon Islands; stopping over between steamers, which run only every six weeks. During this time I visited several of the different islands, and got quite a number of specimens. From the museum standpoint there is not very much left in most of the islands, except in the most inaccessible parts. I found it would take a year or so to visit the different islands, and make a representative collection, and so deemed it inadvisable to stay longer. One of the residents of the island, however, who has already done considerable collecting, especially for the governor and the British Museum, agreed to try and get together a collection for the Museum within the next year. While not an ideal collector, he seemed to be the best man in the islands for this purpose. He has occasion to visit most of the islands on business during the year, and so can pick up many things without going to special expense.

I returned to Sydney in the early part of January, intending to visit the New Hebrides and New Caledonia next. (It is impossible to get from the Solomons to these other groups directly.) February and March is the hurricane and rainy season in all these islands, and as I was much run down from malaria, I thought it wisest to postpone my visit till April, and meanwhile took a trip to New Zealand by way of Fiji, Samoa and Tonga. In Fiji I got a few things, and arranged for our agent there, Mr. Waters, to get any further specimens that he could. In the other islands I got a number of photographs. At Auckland I was fortunate enough to meet the former captain of the Melanesian Mission steamer, and from him got a few very rare and valuable specimens, chiefly from the Solomon Islands.[4] After spending a week or more in the geyser district, I proceeded to Wellington, and spent a week there studying the collections in the Dominion Museum. Mr. Hamilton, the director of the museum, agreed to send to the Field Museum a collection of photographs and some other things in return for some things which I was to send him from the field. I trust that you have already received what he sent. A dozen photos, purchased from the New Zealand government, were also to be forwarded to the Museum. The same also applies to some island photos purchased from Beattie, in Hobart, Tasmania.

From Wellington I decided to return to Sydney by way of the South Island and Melbourne, as I wished to visit the museums at Dunedin, Christchurch, and Melbourne, and get letters from the Commonwealth officials at Melbourne to the officials in British New Guinea and the New Hebrides. These letters were kindly given and I returned to Sydney just in time to catch the steamer for the New Hebrides, April 1st.

It takes six weeks to make the round trip of the islands and return to Vila, the chief port. In addition to taking this trip I spent two months in Malekula and

Ambrym, the most interesting of the New Hebrides group. Here I succeeded in getting a number of very rare specimens, including some of the large drums and carved wood figures. Most of these have been already forwarded to the Museum; but unfortunately owing to bad weather, the steamer was not able to stop at one place where I had a number of specimens, so I arranged for these to be sent on later. I also arranged for the missionary in the Santa Cruz group[5] to send a collection to the Museum, as it would have taken too much time for me to have gone there. I hope you will receive both of these special shipments safely. Santa Cruz can only be reached by the missionary boat twice a year, and the collection should be very interesting.

After packing my collection at Vila, I proceeded to New Caledonia, and spent a month there visiting the wildest portion of the north end of the island, and getting a very interesting, tho not very large, collection.

I then returned to Sydney, and there purchased a few rare specimens which I had not been able to get in the islands. These and some books that I had purchased for study were packed and forwarded with the boxes from New Caledonia. I have already written concerning this shipment.

I have also arranged for a further collection from New Caledonia, which will probably not be ready for some months yet, as it will take some time to get it together. The man who is doing this had done quite a little collecting and made the collection for the Paris Exposition, among others.[6] As I have said before, I cannot, in the time I have, either make these collections myself or wait for others to make them—the region is too vast. Specimens are getting scarce in these islands, now, and unless we get the things soon, there will be nothing left. There is quite a demand for "island curios," and the prices are rising rapidly, as the objects become scarcer. The curio dealers in Sydney will give good prices for things from the islands. The specimens from these islands may not be as showy as those from New Guinea, but they are rare, and worth much more than they cost, if one can judge by Sydney or London (Webster Catalogue) prices.

I am now on my way to Simpson Hafen, where I hope to buy a collection which will nicely fill out our collections from the German colony, it being from just those islands I was unable to visit myself. If I succeed, I shall write more fully concerning it later. From there I shall proceed to British New Guinea as soon as possible.

Very respectfully,
A. B. Lewis

Care Lohmann and Co., Sydney.

Am sending report of expenses under separate cover.

Fig. 6.1. Man with two types of drums, north Ambrym. A-37628 (782a).

New Zealand and
the New Hebrides

||||||||||||||||||||||||||||||||||||||||||||||||||||||||||||||||||||||||||||||||||||

Arrived in Sydney Jan. 6. Next week attended the meetings of the Australian Ass'n. for Advancement of Science, and spent the two following weeks in looking up literature and getting things fixed up generally.

Wednesday, Feb. 1, 1911   Left for N. Zealand on *Tofua*, by way of Fiji, Samoa and Tonga. In Suva saw Waters, and as was still something over on what I had advanced him, asked him to continue to collect what he could. Got some photos from Tattersall, in Apia, also from W. F. Dufty, Nukalofa, Tonga.[1] Arrived at Auckland Feb. 22. Stayed till Saturday, Feb. 25. Got number of photos from Martin, of Maoris, and Maori art and specimens. Had pleasant visit with Mr. Cheeseman of Auckland Museum.

On Sat. [Feb. 25,] left for Rotorua, where stopped at Brent's Bathgate House.

Sunday [Feb. 26] to spring and Oreke.

Monday [Feb. 27] with _____ on lake.

Tuesday [Feb. 28] lake.

Wed. [March 1] to Wakarewarewa.

Thurs. [March 2] to Warmangu and Waiatapu.

Fri. [March 3] to Wanakei [Wairakei?] and Rupua.

Sat. [March 4] at Wanakei [Wairakei?] and to Spa.

Sund. [March 5] at Spa.

Mond. [March 6] on Lake Taupo and to Taumani.

Tues. [March 7] to Pipiriki.

Wed. [March 8] to Wellington, where stopped with Mr. Hamilton till following Thursday [March 16]. Spent most of time studying photos and collections in Museum.

Friday [March 17] in Christchurch,

Sat. [March 18] in Dunedin and

Sunday [March 19] (in part) at port.

Monday [March 20] at Bluff.

Arrived at Hobart on Friday [March 24], and spent most of day there, and at Melbourne on Sunday [March 26].

Sunday, March 26   Visited Museum, on Monday, met Mr. [Walcott], in charge of ethnology (and geology).

Tuesday, March 28   Morning to University to see Prof. Spencer, and then to office of External Affairs to see Mr. Atlee Hunt, and get letters to men in N. Hebrides and N. Guinea. For these waited till following day, and spent time in museum.

---

1. Most of these Tattersall and Dufty prints appear to have been lost. Many of the Josiah Martin prints have survived.

Fig. 6.2. "Tanna house and volcano."
A-38081 (3f).

Thursday, March 29 Left by night express for Sydney, where arrived before noon next day. Found N. Hebrides boat left at noon, April 1st, so hurried to get things ready to leave by her *(Malaita)*.

Stopped at Lord Howe short time, also at Norfolk Isl., where got carriage to go to Melanesian Mission.

Tuesday, April 11 Arrived in Vila. On 12th visited Judge Roseby, and Mr. Merton King, British Resident.[2] Lunched with Judge Roseby. In afternoon to Mr. King's place and then to steamer.

Thursday, April 13 Stopped at Erromanga (Dillon's Bay, Mr. [Hugh] Robertson) and to Tanna (Dr. Nickelson's and Mr. Worthington, at Lenakel). Stayed at Mr. Worthington's all night, and left about 9 next morning to walk across island to White Sands (Mr. McMillan). Track fairly good, but much up and down. Arrived about 3 P.M. Crossed with Capt. Edwin Harrowell. In evening went up volcano, with about a doz. natives. Mr. McMillan lent me horse to foot of volcano.

Next day, Saturday, April 15 left on steamer about noon on return trip to Vila, where arrived Sunday (16th) morning. Spent day with Capt. Harrowell, and in evening went out to *Southern Cross*. Here met Bishop Wilson and others of [Anglican] mission. Rev. J. W. Blencowe, of Santa Cruz Islands, agreed to collect some things for me. Gave him eleven pounds (£11) for that purpose.[3] He would be in the islands about 6 weeks before the *Southern Cross* returned from the Solomons, and during this time expected to travel considerably around the group. The things were to be sent down by *S.C.* to Vila (B.P. store—Mr. McKenzie). The *Southern Cross* expected to leave at midnight, so about 9:30 the *S.C.* launch took me back to the steamer.

Monday, April 17 Spent forenoon on shore, got some letters of introduction from [L. S.] Woolcott (solicitor, looking after the lands of the mission). Left a few specimens at B.P. store. Spent afternoon on board.

---

2. ABL spelled his first name "Morton."

3. Blencowe was not able to collect these promised specimens. Soon after arriving in the Santa Cruz islands, Blencowe was confined to his house by hostile villagers for several months. He left the condominium late in 1911.

Tuesday, April 18   Stopped at several places on way north. Spent night at Tongoa, where [lived] Rev. O. Michelson, who promised to get me a model of canoe, with side boards.

Wednesday, April 19   Stopped at number of places in Epi, night at Kingdove Bay.

Thursday, April 20   To Paama, where Rev. [Maurice] Frater, and Mr. Grube (trader) [live]. Here met Dr. Felix Speiser who had been in the Group for nearly a year, collecting specimens and anthropological data. He expected to remain nearly a year longer. Had been over most of northern islands except south Malakula and north Ambryn.

Next west of Ambryn, where at _____ went ashore,[4] and the trader there, Mr. Spencer, agreed to get me some things. Here saw one carved figure (tree fern trunk).

Arrived at Tesman Bay[5] (Mr. W. Lang) in evening, and accepted Mr. Lang's invitation to stop there. So got my goods on shore.

Friday, April 21   Morning in launch to Aulua (Rev. Jas. S. Jaffray[6]) in afternoon took some photos.

Saturday, April 22   Developed photos. Water too hot, so spoilt. So damp that plates did not dry in next two days.

Sunday, April 23   Service at Pangkumu, about 20 minutes walk across point. Rev. Fred Paton preached. Afternoon visited some villages.

Monday, April 24   Overhauled things and made new bag for bed.

Tuesday, April 25   In morning Mr. Jaffray came in launch, and took me and some of my things to Uripiv. On way stopped at Onua, and took lunch with Mr. Fred Paton. Then continued to Uripiv (Rev. Jas. Gillan), Mr. Watson, a trader from South Santo, also came along.

Wednesday, April 26   Went in morning and visited two villages on mainland—rained most of time. Villages poor, got 3 spears. Not safe to go inland, as bush people hostile. Had even threatened to kill Mr. Gillan, if he went inland; a thing they had never done before. This condition due largely to injudicious action by capt. of man-of-war (British). The tribes in the bush were fighting, and one or more men were killed. The captain came and declared that war must stop. He sent word to bush for all to come down to beach and make peace. Some who wished peace came. Others sent defiant messages. The cap't ignored these, but told the others they should not retaliate, but leave punishment to the government. The result was that as soon as the ship went away the warlike party immediately killed two more men, and several more since, while the cap't of man-of-war has done nothing

---

4. Probably on Malekula.
5. South Malekula.
6. ABL spelled his name Jeffries.

to stop it. Now the hostile party think they can do anything, and threaten all white men as well as the other natives.

Thursday, April 27   Left about 10 A.M. in Cap't Henam's launch for Lambumbu, on other side of island, with Mr. Gillan and son (Whitecross, age 8) and daughter (Nellie, age 15).

Arrived about 7 P.M. Here is a mission station with resident native teacher, and mission house and church.

Friday, April 28   Many of the bush natives were down at beach to trade, sell copra and yams to Mr. Henam, and buy goods. In afternoon went down coast at Bangor.

Saturday, April 29   Returned in morning to Bangor, as natives had promised day before to bring yams for trade. Got a number of things here, esp. women's head-dresses. In after noon went up to a village near coast. Here saw an old dance ground, with row of 10 carved and painted figures set up on one side, covered by rude roof. About half a dozen drums were set up in center, but all old and rotten. The carved figures were 4 to 6 ft. high, and on top were two different posts or figures, each double, i.e. one figure carved over another. On returning to beach (all men were on beach trading), I succeeded in buying these from chief at 5 shillings each, also one of uprights. Most of uprights were too large, being over a foot in diameter. None of the local natives, even Christians, would carry them down, but I finally got one of the teachers (from another place) to bring them to the beach. On inquiring into their history, I found that the 2 double figures came from Bangor, and were made by men from S.W. Bay. One of the chief men of Bangor had lived in S.W. Bay many years before, and had been struck with the type of figures there. One he had bought, and had got some men from S.W. Bay to come to Bangor and make 9 others. For these about 20 pigs had been given, which the men took back to S.W. Bay. A feast of many pigs was also held at Bangor when the figures were set up.

Only two of these figures were of hard wood, and after the others had decayed these two were given (sold ?) to village where I got them (about 1 yr. before).

Sunday, April 30   Attended service here in morning. In afternoon walked with Mr. Gillan to village about 1 hr. distant. Left at 10 P.M. for Uripiv.

Monday, May 1   Got back to Uripiv about 7 A.M. just before rain began. Rained hard all day.

Tuesday, May 2   Rained and blew all night and most of day. Almost a hurricane. Mr. Henam's cutter was driven ashore at Bushman's bay and badly damaged. Steamer *Malaita* passed into bay (Port Stanley) about noon, but did not stop.

Wednesday, May 3   Steamer called in morning. Later went through the villages on island (Uripiv), but was not successful in getting much.

Thursday, May 4   Left early in morning in Mr. Gillan's launch for islands to north. Called first at Pīnállum, then Rano (where trader Jimmy Wright)

Fig. 6.3. "Two figures with sheds, somewhat decayed," Atchin. A-38090 (16f).

where had about one hr. to look through village. Tried to buy drum or carving, but natives would not sell.

Dinner at Mr. Wright's, then to Wala and Atchin. Took a few photos at Atchin of *manke* grounds, but could buy nothing. Here one of the grounds had new figures erected, with winged birds (trees with wide roots) on top, each covered with small bamboo shed. These had not yet had pigs killed to them, so of course were not for sale.

On return to Wala (3 P.M.) Mr. Gillan said I could have 1½ hr. to look around before he must leave, but could stay till next afternoon if I wished. I went around villages, and as in one place a man agreed to sell me an image *(démitc)*, I concluded to stay. But had to hurry back to tell Mr. Gillan. Then was so late concluded to go for *demitc* next morning.

Fig. 6.4. Club used to kill pigs, Wala, northeast Malekula. The pigs are knocked on the head with this, usually with considerable ceremony on the dance ground before the wood images *(demitc)*. Two faces carved on this pig killer, 132774 (1084). A-112297.

Wala was formerly Dr. Crombie's station, but now was left in charge of a native teacher, who agreed to look after me, while I stayed in the mission house. His wife cooked me some yams, and these with tinned meat did very well.

Friday, May 5 Next morning the teacher and a couple of others went with me back to the place where I had bought (by agreement) the figure, with saw prepared to cut it down. When man saw us at work, however, he got afraid, and refused to let the image go. I then tried to get others, but no good one could be bought. Managed to get a few other things, but all very high, and natives not at all anxious to sell.

About 3 P.M. Mr. Gillan returned, and we left, calling at Rano on way, where I succeeded in getting Mr. Wright to try to get me some images and drums.

On reaching Uripiv found Mr. Paton had come for me.

Saturday, May 6 Left for Onua, stopping at Bushman's Bay and visiting a village a short way inland. Mr. Flemming accompanied us to Onua (also Mr. Watson).

Sunday, May 7 In morning Mr. Paton went to Pangkumu for service there. Afternoon service at Onua, about 120 attendance, mostly fairly well dressed. Very few here wear lava-lavas as in N. Guinea, and even in Solomons. Church native structure, no floor, but rude benches.

Monday, May 8 Visit villages north of mission house and buy a number of things.

Tuesday, May 9 In morning visit villages south of station, but find almost no men in—all at work or away. In afternoon try again, and find a few, but darkness coming on, could not stay.

Wednesday, May 10 Again in morning to villages, and find a few men at school (Christian) [in] village. Here bought a tree fern *(demitc)* and few other things, and the men agreed to inquire about drums, and see if any one would sell.

Thursday, May 11 Rained all day, wrote up notes.

The islands Rano, Wala, Atchin and Vau represent the most advanced of the Malakulan peoples, and in general the bush tribes are much poorer than the coast peoples. Nicely woven baskets and belts are made in the interior, tho the coast peoples also make belts, but not so good baskets. Most arrows also seem to come from the interior. On the islands above mentioned one finds the best wood carvings, seen in drums, carved figures, wood bowls (saw one with head at one end, but could not buy it) and masks. Owing to religious ideas associated with figures and drums, they would not part with these.

Friday, May 12 Mr. Jaffray came in launch in morning. Packed my things for trip around S. coast. Left after dinner, and called at Tesman to take rest of things from Mr. Lang to Aulua, so could get them on return, and bring them to Onua. Stayed at Aulua over night.

Fig. 6.5. "Drum in village near Onua," Malekula. It is one of those in Fig. 6.6. A-38124 (7f).

Fig. 6.6. Drums in village near Onua. A-38092 (9f).

Fig. 6.7. "Model of canoe with outrigger, Mai Island. Made by natives, and
out of proportion, as the body is too
wide and high for the length," 133305
(1544). From Reverend Michelsen.
A-112341.

Fig. 6.8. Carved wooden masks from northeast Malekula: from Vau, 132997 (from Stephens), and from Wala *(livil),* 132762 (1080), 132763 (1081). A-112145.

Fig. 6.9. Men from interior back of Onua with Mr. Paton, Onua. A-37632 (783).

Saturday, May 13 Left at 4 A.M. for S.W. Bay, calling in at the Maskelynes, Hohai (where got some things), Hambi (island), Loperu (opposite Hambi, where arranged with trader, L. Bird, Esq., to get some specimens for me if he could—He is purchaser of Holcroft), where had dinner. Then on to S.W. Bay, stopping at one place on way. Arrived about 5:30. Day showery, but no heavy rain. Mr. Watson and 3 native boys went along, one or two others coming in from the Maskelynes. In evening the trader, Mr. McAfee, came up to mission house. The missionary stationed here, Mr. Boyd, was away for a few months, and that is why Mr. Paton came around to look after station.

Sunday, May 14 Mr. Paton left at dawn for a trip around through the villages, getting back about 1 P.M. The paths are very bad in this region, esp. after heavy rains.

In afternoon had service at church near house, near which a small mission village had been established. Many also came from the heathen villages. Four babies were baptized at this service. Probably 50 people were present. There was a native teacher here, as indeed at all the places where we stopped on the way.

Monday, May 15 In morning left in launch for trip to some coast villages further north, also returning some of the natives. At only one place did we try to go up to villages, which are set high up on the ridges back from the coast about a mile or so. Here bought some things, and saw a sacred or men's house (*gamal, hamal,* etc., in dif. languages) in which were a number of peculiar hollow cones of wood, used to make the "spirit" or mysterious noises, after a man dies. They said that the men blew into these through bamboos, but could get no very clear idea of the performance. They were afraid to have us touch them even.

The posts of the house were carved, so as to represent persons, but only in relief. There were also a number of carved sticks in the roof, but they would not allow us to touch these either. In fact, most of the natives had got out when we went up to these things to inspect them, and the two old men

Fig. 6.10. "Women at South-West Bay, showing dress and ornaments." A-38080 (4f).

who remained were trembling with fear, and beginning to scowl, so we thought it time to leave. Outside there was a high scaffold of bamboo on which yams and pigs are placed at the feasts or *manke*s. The dance ground was surrounded by upright stones, often brought from a great distance. These stones, in fact, were noted at almost every village visited in Malekula. There were also a few old drums here (see photos).

Here we also bought a few things, as women's skirts of string, woven arm bands, arrows, wrist guards. The people did not seem to have much. No spears but plain wood shafts were seen. Bows and arrows as all around coast. Men's dress same as elsewhere on Malekula, but women's different, being a skirt of string. Women also had nose shells, some curved, and others straight, up to six inches long. Would not sell the long ones. Has also woven string and shell arm bands. Men had tortoise shell ear-rings, and wood wristlets, also coiled. Houses much as elsewhere, but so perched on sides of ridge among trees that could get no good photo.

These people were coast people, the bush people being at least 4–6 hrs. hard walking inland.

On return took back some copra for Mr. McAfee, and stopped at his place for couple of hours, during heavy rain. He had a few specimens, esp. clubs and masks, which I bought.

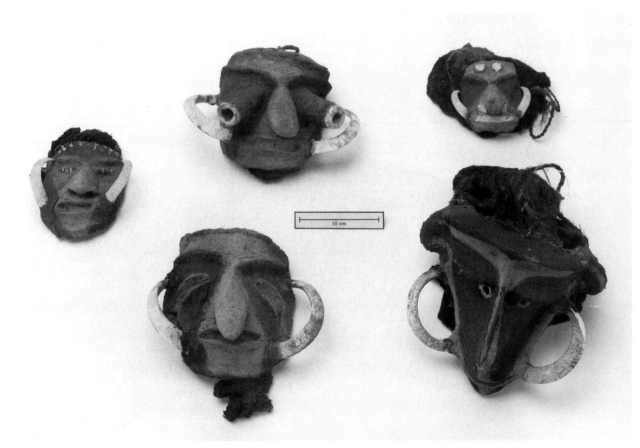

Fig. 6.11. Dance masks, South-West Bay. Grotesque human faces with boars tusks. Coconut fiber stuck together with gummy sap. Hood of cobweb at back to cover head. Masks of this type come from the interior back of South-West Bay and are characteristic of most of south Malekula, especially the southwest. Top row: 133053 (_____), 133042 (_____), 133050 (_____). Bottom row: 133043 (_____); 133058 (S-62), from Stephens. A-112385.

Fig. 6.12. Dance masks, South-West Bay. Coconut fiber and gummy-sap on a conical framework of bamboo strips and leaves. Each mask has two brightly painted faces: 133081 (_____), cobwebs on cone at top of head, 133084 (_____). From McAfee. A-112280.

Tuesday, May 16   Left about 7 A.M. on return trip. Heavy seas with S.E. wind, and squally. Put in at Hombi about noon to escape rain, but as it let up later, left and ran down to Hohai, where arrived just as heavy storm came on. Stayed here over night, sleeping in church (or school-house), built like native house, only higher, with sides of upright poles, so as to let in the air. Here got 5 skulls, some deformed. For this purpose they said that the children were made to wear a sort of hat, which could be taken off or put on at pleasure (of parents). Was unable to get or see one.

Fig. 6.13. "Drum, Maskelynes, Malekula." A-37358 (728).

Wednesday, May 17   Left at dawn, as sea had gone down some, and proceeded to Maskelynes. Here Mr. Paton had a marriage to perform, after which we went around through the villages, and I succeeded in getting a few wooden figures. Here, as also at Hombi, all the drums were more or less decayed. Only one *gamal* remained on the island, but it was interesting, as containing a figure with human skull. The body was of wood, but legs and arms were sticks covered and filled out with fibre (cocoanut, or from some tree bark ?) covered and held together with juice from breadfruit. In this particular figure there were faces modeled on shoulders and elbows; pigs tusks as hands; head a real skull, with face modeled; whole figure painted. This was probably the same as the so-called mummies of S. Malekula. These are all (?) male figures, but some times made over the actual skeleton, as well as skull. This cult extends from S.W. Bay to about Pt. Sandwich. Very few mummies (!) were made, even in old times, probably only one for village. This was probably for a very important man. In a case like that seen, the body was probably buried (burial was common there) and head later taken up and prepared for figure. The spirit of the man was supposed to live in or near the skull.

Mr. Paton says that there were probably never over 20 mummies in region, and most of these were looted by men-of-war (under excuse of punishment). Sometimes skulls were kept and covered with false face and painted, and preserved in *gamal*. These of course were more numerous than the complete figures. (Now they are often so prepared to sell), but even this was only done for important men.

Found mourning (funeral rites) was performed for the dead on various intervals after death, depending on place. Such rites, however, were never performed for men below a certain rank.

A considerable number of the natives on Maskelyne Isl. are Christian, and among the others the old customs are being given up.

About 2 P.M. left for Aulua, half a doz. men coming off with us to push the launch through the passage in the reef, as it was now low tide.

Arrived at Aulua at 4:20, and stayed here over night. Took back with us all the arrow-root we could carry. All the Christian natives are at this time collecting arrow root for the mission. This is prepared on the stations, (ground up, strained through cloth into tubs, and washed 3–4 times to remove poison—each time stirred up, then allowed to settle, and water poured off—then powder dried and packed in bags) and sent to agents in Australia and Scotland to be sold for the mission, J. G. Paton Fund (price 1 sh per pound). It is said to be as good as, if not better than, the best Bermuda arrow-root.

Thursday, May 18   Got my things on board launch and left for Onua about 9:30. On arrival found Dr. Speiser, who had been at Mr. Paton's house since Monday, when Stephens (trader) had brought him over from Ambrym. As Mr. Jaffray was going down to the Maskelynes after the steamer (next Tuesday) Dr. Speiser decided to go with him, and left for Aulua about 3 P.M.

Friday, May 19   Spent most of day developing plates and films.

Saturday, May 20   Packed up, as expected steamer at any time, and had concluded to take a trip around group.

Sunday, May 21   In morning Mr. Paton went to Pangkumu, returned about 1:30 P.M. Later had service in church here,—about 140 in atten-

Fig. 6.14. Wooden clubs: face on each side, said to represent particular individuals, with carrying sling, north Ambrym, 133236 (1382); Erromanga, star club *(telughomti)*, 133409 (—); Epi or Ambrym, 133210 (—), from Stephens. A-112295.

dance,—one baptism of baby. Read Dr. Steel's book on N. Hebrides, and Dr. H. A. Robertson's book on Erromanga, both chiefly missions, but with few points on ethnology.[7] In evening a few natives gathered for worship at house—mostly singing.

7. Robertson (1902); Steel (1880).

Fig. 6.15 and 6.16. Male and female effigies, South-West Bay. Painted red, white, and blue, 133103 (_____); painted red and black, 133104 (_____). From McAfee. A-112318, A-112317.

Monday, May 22　Expected steamer at any time, so could not do much but write up notes.

According to Mr. F. Paton, there are at least 20 distinct languages in Malekula, most if not all, with numerous dialects. Most of these are as follows (general region):

Pt. Sandwich

Aulua

Bush, Pt. Sandwich to Aulua

Pangkumu and Rukumbu

Pangkumu bush

Uripiv

Letcletc, (coast opposite Uripiv)

Lālip, (bush opposite Uripiv)

Metcnevat (N. Malekula)

Big busbus (N.W. Malekula)

Lambumbu

S.W. Bay (Three languages here)

Ahom and Maskelynes

S. coast opposite Ahom

　Others in bush

Houses are much the same over the whole island. Usually they are low with no sides, the roof coming down to the ground on each side. The floor is the ground, cocoanut-leaf mats serving to sleep on. The usual roof is of leaf of ivory-palm, tho cocoanut-leaf and cane grass are also used. The roof is quite thick, as the layers of leaves are lashed on quite close together (can be seen in photo of end of house). The ends are usually closed, except a small square hole in front, just about big enough to crawl through. The woman's or family house is the ordinary one, but in each village there is also one or more men's houses, one of which also serves for the secret or sacred objects. This is more noticeable on the south end of the island, where carved figures, sacred objects, skulls, etc. are more common. There does not seem to be any sharp distinction between this and the other men's houses, and one name is used for all (*gamal, amil*, etc.).

The usual weapons are the bow and arrow. The bows are of various woods, one much prized being of the arched roots of the mangrove, taken of such size that when split the half is about right size for bow. The old fighting arrows were of cane, with wooden heads and bone points, poisoned; at least all the natives believe so, and are much afraid of them. Bow-string guard of wood.

Spears are not much used for fighting, except by the islanders (north esp.), but were much used in *manke*s and to kill pigs. The spear of the south was of plain hard wood. That of the north often had cane shaft, with wood point, sometimes tipped with bone. The wood shaft sometimes had faces on each side. Such were said to be esp. used by the "great busbuses" of N.W. Malekula.

Shields do not seem to be known, except a sort of small ceremonial one used shortly after birth of boy (30 days). The boy shoots with small bow and arrow (he is held and arrow drawn and directed by a relative (uncle ?)) at one of his relatives (uncle ?), who protects himself with this small shield (sometimes only a stick). If hit, it indicates boy will be a great warrior.

Fig. 6.17. Wooden clubs (some have a carrying sling attached). Type 1 *(ndembangor* or *nowa-nira)*: north Malekula, 132930 (_____), from Stephens; Rano, 132862 (1279). Type 2 *(nagit* or *nahit)*: Wala, 132864 (1074); Onua, 132865 (1128) ("This club has killed a man.") Ambrym, 133218 (_____). Type 3 *(buonk)*: Uripiv, 132859 (1299); South-West Bay, 132881 (_____), from McAfee. A-112293.

The common weapon is the club, which even now is probably the cause of as many deaths as the musket. These use many different kinds of clubs, at least seven being known on Malekula, each with a separate name. As these differ in the different languages and even dialects, it is hardly worth giving names, tho I will give them in the Onua language. Even here the villages pronounce the words slightly differently.

1. *ndembángor*—This club is highly valued, and may be regarded as typically Malekulan, every chief being expected to carry one at certain ceremonies.
2. *nāgīt (nahit)*—One of the most common of all clubs, with 4 rounded knobs slightly back of a rounded end. Malekula and Ambryn.
3. *būonk* (= taro)—A rather short plain club, very common, all over Malekula.
4. *xrūmera* (= tongue)—A flattened club, with raised ridge on each side. E. Coast Malekula.
5. *nauvu*—Rare; rounded or conical point. Really a Pentacost club, but sometimes copied here.
6. *némberi*—Broad and flattened, not common. From bush back of Onua.

Fig. 6.18. Wooden clubs. Type 4 *(xrumera)*: northwest Malekula, 132856 (1555), from Mr. Tanna; Vau, north, Malekula, 132925 (S-5), from Stephens. Type 5 *(roman buonk)*: Onua, 132860 (1130). Type 6 *(nemberisnamul)*: Wala, 132858 (1075). Type 9 *(sangut)* with iron axe at one end: New Hebrides, 133406 (1251), from Annand. A-112294.

    7. *míntcetc* (= swallow)—Rare club with 4 projecting sharp points at
       end, and 4 back of these.
    8. *simsam* (Wala language)—Like [no.] 4, but large, 6–7 ft. long. Bush of
       north Malekula.

Also since Cook's time the tomahawk *(sāngut)* on handle with carved end. Clubs often (esp. [nos.] 2 & 3) had a woven rope at handle, by which the club was slung from the shoulder.

The dress of the men consists of a band of bark or cocoanut-leaf sheath, over which a narrow woven band is usually worn (now a leather belt is used) tied tight to keep bark band in place; also a strip of leaf or short woven band, wrapped around the penis and brought up and tucked under belt. Shore men bring it straight up in front; bush-men diagonally to one side.

The woman's dress is in most places a string belt, with a woven band or mat some 8–12 in. wide brought around the hips, and the fringe on upper side of ends tucked under belt in front to hold it in place. Behind this, band often hangs down almost to knees. On west side from Lambumbu to S.W. Bay a sort of petticoat or skirt, made of twisted strings about 12–15 in. long, is worn. These are fastened to a band, from 6–12 ft. long. Also woven in bush in center of isl.

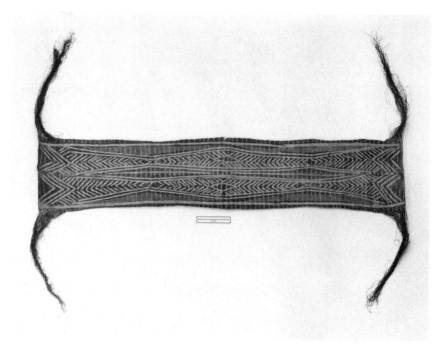

Fig. 6.19. "Woman's waistband or mat, red designs, Onua. Colored ones such as this one are worn only by women of rank. Made of pandanus leaf," 132690 (1122). A-112369.

Ornaments are not very numerous. In S.W. Bay saw women with shell nose sticks, woven arm bands of string. Men with tortoise shell ear-rings, and wrist bands of coiled wood. In Lumbumbu a peculiar woven head-dress is worn.

Household utensils are rare. Cooking is with hot stones (oven) or open fire. Wood dishes are found in north, but not very common. Food is often cooked in bamboos. Pottery is a lost art, but potsherds are found in old village sites, and 20 yrs. ago the old men remembered when earthenware was used, one man at least mentioned that it was made at a certain bush village (Mr. Paton authority). Baskets are woven in different places, esp. in the bush. The women also make (Onua at least) a long woven mat, used to carry burdens strung on the back, the mat being passed around the stuff and over the shoulder.

From Onua north, a mat somewhat similar to the last is used as money, and great numbers of these may be seen hanging up in the houses, more or less blackened with smoke. They are used to buy pigs (3 or more for pig) and many of them are distributed with yams, etc., at their *mánke*s.

Tuesday, May 23 Steamer arrived about noon, and left in evening for Pentacost.

Wednesday, May 24 Stopped at one place in S. Pentacost, and then to N. Ambryn. Left in evening for Aoba.

Thursday, May 25 Called at several places on Aoba. Spent a few hrs. ashore at Duin-Dui, Mr. _____ Purdy, missionary (and trader, an independent missionary). Found little of interest. Mostly new houses, not of old style. A few drums from $2\frac{1}{2}$ to 6 or 8 ft. long, but plain. A few rather plain wood dishes, woven baskets and mats. Mr. Purdy promised to try and get me some things for next steamer.

Fig. 6.20. "Weaving mats, Aoba" (probably at Duin-Dui). A-38112 (28f).

Friday, May 26   Arrived at Hog Harbor, Santo in morning, and stayed till 10 A.M. Here visited Rev. & Mrs. MacKinzie. Spent afternoon and next day taking in copra on S.E. coast of Santo.

Sunday, May 28   Spent day anchored in Gargon Channel.

Monday, May 29   Worked S. Santo and Tangoa. Here Dr. Annand gave me a few things.

Tuesday, May 30   Visited Nogugu and Big Bay. Both Dr. Taylor and Mr. Fish said they would try to get me a few things. Was on shore at Nogugu, but saw little. Houses new. Drums as in Aoba, dishes, and earthen bowls and pots. These are made in several places from near Nogugu south to Wus. At Nogugu they are made by coiling, but to south they are worked out from a single lump of clay, worked by the hands over the knees, as near as I could understand.

Wednesday, May 31   At Banks. Spent forenoon at Frank Whitmore's place where Mrs. Frank Whitmore gave me a few things. About 3 P.M. went to Ruldar Co's place, and here Mr. Choyer had a few things for me, and said he would try to get me some more to be sent to Vila by the *Southern Cross*.

Thursday, June 1   S.W. Santo and Malo, copra stations.

Friday, June 2   Malo and Tangoa to Vau.

397

Fig. 6.21.   "Village, Santo." Note megaliths. A-38133 (27f).

Fig. 6.22.   "Wooden knives for cutting pudding, Banks group. The native 'pudding,' as called by the whites, is made of mashed or grated yams, mixed with juice from cocoanut (squeezed out, wrapped in leaves, and baked with hot stones in oven)." 133464 (1260); 133465 (_____); handle inlaid with shell, 133466 (_____). The last two from Captain Huggett. A-112289.

398

Saturday, June 3   Atchin (6–9 A.M.) did not go ashore, as supercargo said would stop only ¾ hr. At Malo from 10 to 12:30, while steamer went on to Rano. Then all afternoon opposite Wala. In night to S.W. Bay.

Sunday, June 4   S.W. Bay all day. In afternoon went ashore to McAfee's place, and with him to old deserted village, where he said he had seen some skulls and old pieces of pottery. Got some old skulls, but could not find pottery. Place was on a spur of the hills, overlooking the sea, and all buried in bush.

Monday, June 5   Left about 2 A.M. (loaded copra from 12 Midnight), to Uripiv, where landed. Had fever rest of day, Mr. Gillan went to Wala, and on return started for Ambryn (with Jimmy Wright) stopping over night at Onua.

Tuesday, June 6   Spent part of day in villages, buying a few things. Visited dance at night. Not much to it, as about a dozen and half of men and boys, in irregular group, sang and stamped the ground for a few minutes, and then ran part way around central group of drums, when stopped and stamped again, and so on. Each man beat together two sticks or pieces of bamboo which he held in each hand. Could not get them to tell me what the words meant.

Wednesday, June 7   A more important performance was held today lasting from middle of forenoon till about 1:30 P.M. A considerable number of yams were tied to poles (bamboo) and leaned up on a support near by [Fig. 6.24]. Many more were brought in from 9 to 11 by women, also a considerable number of pigs, lead by rope to fore-leg (photo 773). These were tied to stakes and stones around the dance ground. 40 to 50 were brought on all together. Ten of these were killed later. Before many of these were brought, most of the people had assembled and the men leading the pigs were often received with thumping of the drums and singing.

Fig. 6.23. "House, Uripiv." A-38111 (13f).

Fig. 6.24. "Yams, tied to bamboos and leaned up on supports—to be given away at dance, Uripiv." A-37570 (772).

When all the pigs were brought on, there was more singing and dancing (photo 776), and then the pigs were killed with a certain amount of ceremony over each one. They were simply knocked in the head with the killing club, the smaller ones being held up by one man while another struck it on the head. After this the yams and pigs were laid out on the ground (photo 777), and an old man (chief ?) made a sort of oration over them while he walked back and forth (photo 778). They were then distributed, and the people dispersed, each with their share. Each village got a pig or two, which was cut up, and cooked over night (with "pudding"—mashed yam and cocoanut—etc.). This dance was the first for a *manke* which was expected to continue for 3–4 yrs.

Mr. Gillan returned in evening from Ambryn.

Thursday, June 8 [Mr. Gillan] Left for Lumbumbu, taking me to Rano, Mr. Wright also returning at same time. I arranged to stay with Mr. Wright, and in afternoon visited the villages.

Friday, June 9 Visited the villages and bought a few things. In afternoon a dance at one village (Lōūnī), but it was the same, only not so formal, as dancers not ornamented, as that held the next day, which was the great day of the feast.

Saturday, June 10 Went to the dance grounds about 10 A.M. and found a few men from the local village (Lóuni) there, but it was not yet time for the dance. About 10:30 the drums beat the signal, and the women and men (not dancing) began coming in till some old man (local) then danced and sang (photo 755). There were 200–300 present. At last the dancers arrived on the scene, coming running onto the grounds, one behind the other, and about 100–200 ft. apart, and forming up in 5 rows, 5 in each row, facing the women and children (photo 756). Each had on his head an ornament of rooster feathers, fastened on a bamboo set upright, the whole about 3 ft. high. Their faces were painted black, and bodies yellow (with root—tumeric ?—see specimen), with darker bands and spots, and in one or two cases rather elaborate designs. On each ankle was a seed rattle, and around the loins

Fig. 6.25. Dance at Rano. Second position, one performer is dancing around each rank. A-37690 (758).

400

handkerchiefs were tied. (This, of course, was something different from usual.) Each had also a woven band around the waist, the two fringed ends hanging down behind. They were nearly all young fellows. There was also a man who carried two sticks and beat time, who took his place in the center. After forming in line they stomped back and forth a little, singing.

Then they faced at right angles, and there appeared on the scene an extra dancer, specially painted, who danced around and between the ranks with arms extended (photos 757–758 [see Fig. 6.25]). He represented a pigeon, and the dance was called the pigeon dance. Then the formation changed, and they danced around in circles, two rows (photos 759–760), the pigeon leading, dancing backward. Later they formed in rows again, and the pigeon again danced around them (photo 761). Finally he disappeared, and another performer arrived, armed with bow and arrow, who danced around, and back and forth, pretending to be looking for something, the regular performers all the time stamping and singing, often advancing a few steps and halting suddenly with loud stomping, and then back again. This kept up for some time, and then the man with the bow and arrow disappeared, the formation suddenly broke up, and all the dancers ran away. This was the end of their performance.

After a little time the drums again beat, and a few old men took up the dance and song, while some men led on some pigs. These were sung over, and one by one thumped on the head with the pig-killer, but not killed. Then the yams were laid out on the grounds preparatory to distribution, some tied to bamboos, and others taken from the yam house built on the grounds. When this was finished each group took its yams and mats (a great number of these were also laid out with the yams—some of the women had brought great loads of mats to the grounds), and the assembly broke up.

This performance was, of course, only a small part of a *manke*. The whole thing often extending over 3 or 4 yrs. Hundreds of pigs were often killed during one of these *manke*s. A man's rank depended on the number of pigs (esp. boars with coiled tusks) that he had killed, and at each ceremony a number of pigs would be killed by those anxious to advance in rank. The number of ranks varies in different parts of Malekula, but there are at least 4 or 5, and often many subordinate stages in each rank, through each of which the man must advance by killing pigs, the higher the rank the greater the number.

The occasions of *manke*s are various—the mourning for the dead, the dedication of new drums or canoes, or the erection of carved figures *(demitc)* to their ancestors. (For a good canoe 10–20 pigs and as many fowls would be killed, the figure-head being the specially sacred part of a canoe. If this should be broken by any one, the whole value of all pigs was claimed in compensation.) The costumed dances taking place on these occasions were usually pantomime (with descriptive songs) performances, representing all sorts of occurrences.

The carved figures *(demitc)* represent ancestors. They belonged to individual men, and one or several might be erected at one time. As far as I could find out, they did not represent any particular person or ancestor. During the *manke* the ancestral spirits were supposed to hover around them or abide in them, and receive the benefits of the pigs killed (a man's rank in the future as well as the present world, depended on the number of pigs killed).

The drums belong to several individuals, so it was almost impossible to buy one.

The performances at present are very much degenerated from the old time, as the younger men are losing their belief in the old things. They all are very fond of the dancing, however, but at present the dances, esp. those continuing during the night, are the means of exciting their passions, the darkness and neighboring bush rendering more easy the gratification of these.[8] Sometimes this is winked at, but it is often the cause of all sorts of troubles. The mission (Pres.) has absolutely prohibited attendance at these dances.

Monday, June 12   Rowed over to Wala, but got nothing.

Tuesday, June 13   Took some photos and got a few things.

Wednesday, June 14   Mr. Gillan arrived about 3 P.M. and I returned to Uripiv.

Thursday, June 15   In morning went up in launch to Suaori, to see if could get a drum. One of the natives (Lungaula) said he had a drum on a small island near Suaori, which he had bought from the Bush people, who formerly lived on the island. When we arrived it was gone. On going to Suaori Mr. Collet (the trader there) said that he had heard of the talk of selling the drum, and had taken it away, as he had bought the land and all on it from the natives. He kindly said he would give the drum to me.
     Returned to Uripiv for lunch, and then to Onua.

Friday, June 16   Developed photos.

Saturday, June 17   Packed specimens.

Monday, June 19   Packed specimens.

Tuesday, June 20   Mr. Paton took me over to Mr. T. C. Stephen's place on Ambryn, in morning. In afternoon went to Dr. Bowie's place, about four miles, to see about getting up to North Ambryn. Said he would come down to Stephen's place on Thursday (after steamer) and go north on Friday (in each case visiting mission stations), and would take me with him.

Wednesday, June 21   Started to walk around in morning, but soon heard steamer whistle, and returned to shore. Steamer stopped till 3 P.M.

Thursday, June 22   In morning went around some villages (got one of mission men as guide), returning at 2 P.M. Did not get much. Left with Dr. Bowie about 3 P.M. and stayed at his house over night.

Friday, June 23   Went to north Ambryn in morning, and arranged to stop with Mr. Decent. Went around a little in afternoon.

Saturday, June 24   Started early with guide, and put in day going around villages. Bought a number of things, but did not find much.

Monday, June 26   Rained and stormy.

Tuesday, June 27   Stormy, but got around a little.

---

8. Here ABL is reporting the views of the conservative Presbyterian missionaries rather than his own observations.

Fig. 6.26. "Wife of chief, north Ambrym." A-37191 (809).

Wednesday, June 28 Returned to Dr. Bowie's with him.

Thursday, June 29 Spent forenoon at Dr. Bowie's. In afternoon went to Mr. Stephen's place with him.

Friday, June 30–Saturday, July 1 Spent time packing.

Monday, July 3 Went with Mr. Stephens and Fraser for trip along coast to a sub-station of Mr. Stephens. Did not see much new.

Tuesday, July 4 Overhauled stuff and finished packing.

Fig. 6.27. Old man by his hut, west Ambrym. A-37625 (778a).

Fig. 6.28. "Men's house, west Ambrym." A-38176 (52f).

Fig. 6.29. Stephen's house, west Ambrym. A-37186 (801).

Wednesday, July 5   As steamer expected any moment, did not dare go away.

Thursday, July 6   Ditto. Took some photos.

Friday, July 7   Steamer about noon, left for S.W. Bay.

Saturday, July 8   At S.W. Bay and Ahom. McAfee put on board one box and one crate with 2 large masks—badly packed.

Sunday, July 9   At Maskelynes.

Monday, July 10   At Tesman and Onua. Got all my specimens here. (Steamer had left those at N. Ambryn, as just finished their copra when dark and too low tide.)

Tuesday, July 11   Paama, loading copra.

Wednesday, July 12   Epi; saw a few specimens at Hagen's place, also at A. D. Fraser's, who said he would try to get some Malekula masks and skulls.[9]

Thursday, July 13   Tongoa, etc.

9. Some of Fraser's material may have been included in Stephens' later shipment.

Fig. 6.30. "Drums, west Ambrym." A-37409 (796).

Fig. 6.31. "Old man repairing nose of tree fern figure, north Ambrym." A-37404 (810).

Fig. 6.32. Tree fern figure, north Ambrym. A-37650 (790),
A-37545 (789).

Friday, July 14 Arrived at Vila early. Got my things ashore in forenoon. Today holiday, French celebration of taking of Bastille. Spent afternoon at seeing show—races, tug-of-war, greased pole, etc. Dinner with Judge Roseby. Evening at grand ball, till 3 A.M. Met very interesting man in Capt. of French man-of-war *Kersaint*.

Saturday, July 15 Rain. Saw several people and arranged for packing. Went to Mr. Merton King, British resident, who kindly invited me to stay with him while in Vila.

Sunday, July 16 Rain; read.

Monday, July 17–Friday, July 21 Packing.

Saturday, July 22 Developed photos.

Monday, July 24 Rain.

Tuesday, July 25 Developed photos.

Wednesday, July 26–Friday, July 28 Wrote up notes, letters, etc. Also packed two more boxes of things Mr. King gave me, esp. some fine Santo pots.

Fig. 6.33. "Image of lizard used in ceremonies, Ambrym. 'The men all advance and shoot arrows into the ground all around it.' (Stephens). Made of trunk of tree-fern covered with clay and painted with white lines and little red ones," 133268 (S-61). From Stephens. A-112283.

407

Saturday, July 29   Left in evening on steamer *St. Louis* for Noumea.

The natives of the New Hebrides vary much in the different islands, both in stature, color, and general appearance. There are none so dark, however, as in the western Solomons, and few as light as the Malaita people. The Malekula natives are quite dark, and those from the interior rather short. Mr. Paton said there was no difference between the coast and interior native on the whole, and instanced interior tribes who had come to the coast, and could not now be distinguished from coast tribes. He thought the shorter stature due to food, and suggested lack of salt as a possible cause of stunted growth.[10] Some very small people are reported from the interior of Santo, but this has probably been investigated by Dr. Speiser.

The languages are numerous, and dialects much more so, almost every village or group of villages having a separate dialect, at least.

According to the missionaries the following distinct languages may be recognized.

Polynesian	Aniwa, Fortuna, part of Emae, and Mele and Fila islands (Efate)
Melanesian	
Tanna	3
Aneityum	1
Erromanga	1
Efate to Tangoa, Central group	1
Epi	3
Paama	1
Ambryn	3
Malekula	20+
Malo	1
Tangoa	1
Santo	7+
Oba	3
Pentecost	3
Maewo	?

One may safely say at least 50 separate languages, and probably many more. One or two languages of N.E. Santo are reported to be quite peculiar (Hog Harbor, Sakau) and possibly not Melanesian.

These islands have been visited by white men, traders and recruiters, for many years, and the missions are also not recent. The southern islands have lost almost all of their old culture, and there is little to be got from them.[11] The central group is also practically exhausted, and these islands are more settled by the whites. Ambryn preserves some of its old life, but the natives are quite well-to-do, and refuse to part with their good things. I found it impossible to buy a good drum, and they also refused to show me any masks, tho known to have many. Money is no object to them. Large *wood* carvings are very rare, but they are known to have a few. Fern tree figures are more common, almost every village having one or more, but not so many as in Malekula. The making of these figures is said to be a recent importation from Malekula, and the style is very similar.

10. These comments are forerunners of ABL's thoughts on the so-called pygmy question—that is, the origin of short-statured folk in the interior of New Guinea and other islands—published in his monograph (1932a, 10ff.).

11. Another example of ABL's bias toward objects uninfluenced by Europeans.

Fig. 6.34. "Mission family, west Ambrym." A-37546 (781a).

At each village dance ground are two drums (N. Ambryn), a large and a small—or 2–4 (W. Ambryn). (See photos.)

The fern tree figures are usually set up near these. They are first cut out (one I saw very nicely done) and then covered with clay, so as to smooth the surface and round out the figure and features, as nose. This is then covered with the sap of the bread fruit tree, laid on with a small brush. This is something like rubber, and binds it together, turning black on drying. The figure is also often painted.

There is also a men's house near the dance grounds. (Same also in parts of Malekula.) Often the chief's (?) house is not far off, and this is frequently surrounded by a high stone wall, even when there are no other stone walls in the village. Stone walls or fences were more common in Malekula, apparently to keep out pigs.

The plantations[12] in Ambryn were surrounded by sticks set upright and close together. These usually took root and grew, making a living fence. Between the fences passage-ways were left 4–6 ft. wide, as roads.

The yam and breadfruit form the chief foods. This seems generally true over the whole group. Taro is cultivated in places, but never so extensively as to occupy chief place.

Cooking is by open fire or the earth oven. In Ambryn a few large wooden plates or shallow bowls were seen, but do not seem to be much used now. The yams are grated (thorny bark of vine) to make the so-called puddings, not pounded, as in Santo. The roasted bread fruit is often peeled with a clam shell and beaten into a long soft roll with a wood paddle, while held in the hand. A number of such rolls are placed on the plate before dinner is served.

The bows and arrows seen were as in S. Malekula. Spears not seen. The common club, made in island; also the round and pointed Pentacost clubs were common, carried by chief men. Others very rare.

Ornaments were not very numerous. Woven arm-bands covered with shell beads were the most highly prized, and impossible to buy.

---

12. He means food gardens.

Fig. 6.35. Carved wooden post, Ambrym, 133515 (_____). Painted red, green, black, and white, length 211 cm. Probably obtained with the help of Felix Speiser. A-112342.

Fig. 6.36. "Group of women, north Ambrym." A-37461 (792).

Canoes, paddles, etc., all very crude. All seen in the islands had outriggers.

Malekula mats and baskets have been spoken of, and those of Ambryn are much the same. The best are made in Aoba. These mats are frequently painted in various designs, tho sometimes the designs are woven in.

Some very nice clubs were found in Epi in old times. I saw two, one shaped something like a double bladed battle axe. Both raised on sides.

The social organization varies much in different islands, even in different parts of the same island. In Santo, Malekula and Ambryn, possibly elsewhere also, there are many ranks, and a man rises from one to another by killing pigs (only those whose tusks make a complete circle count), and it may take hundreds to reach the highest rank. (One said 300 in Santo.) Few, and only the richest in very old age, ever reach the highest rank. In parts of Malekula one rank may not eat with another, nor of food cooked on same fire, nor may the food be handled by a man of lower rank.

In certain islands there seem to be totems—at least certain animals are tabu and sacred. Did not hear of exogamous groups. In Malekula the limits of forbidden marriage seemed purely those of relationship. In Aneityum, according to Dr. Gunn, marriage of children of brothers, or those of sisters, was forbidden for 2–3 generations, or as long as the relation was remembered, but cousins by brother and sister were regarded as potential man and wife, and the man had a right to the girl, so much so that if another man wanted to marry her, the cousin's consent must be obtained and a present given him.[13]

In the southern islands sacred stones are very common for all sorts of purposes, such as making yams, breadfruit, etc. grow, increasing pigs, making rain, safety in war, etc., etc.

In most cases the shape of the stones (natural) seemed to suggest its use. I saw a box full at Mr. Macmillan's, which the natives had given him.

In Malekula and Ambrym the war charm was the only one I came across.

13. These comments about cross-cousin marriage and earlier comments about rank show that ABL was not disinterested in social organization.

New Caledonia

||||||||||||||||||||||||||||||||||||||||||||||||||||||||||||||||||||||||||||||||||||||||||||||||||||||||||||||||||||||||||||||||||||||||||

31 July 1911–30 August 1911

Nearly everywhere in the New Hebrides, ABL visited the villages and bought specimens for his collection directly from the villagers. He watched them dancing and feasting in some places and in most communities took photos of village life and dance grounds with their large slit gongs. He even went to Sunday church services in the villages. Generally, however, his involvement with villagers in the New Hebrides was more attenuated than in New Guinea.

For the most part, ABL's world during his travels in the New Hebrides was dominated by the many European settlers he met along the way. He stayed with missionaries, traders, planters, and officials. He dined with expatriates, traveled from place to place on boats or ships owned by resident Europeans, and often bought ethnological specimens from his expatriate hosts, in a few instances deputizing these Europeans to collect for him.

Overall, ABL's research and collecting in the New Hebrides was successful, but it seems far more typical of late-nineteenth-century ethnological expeditions in Melanesia than of the more intensive kinds of field research that were just beginning to become fashionable among professional anthropologists (see Stocking 1983): Speiser in the New Hebrides, Sarasin in New Caledonia, Rivers in the Solomons, Hocart in Fiji, Seligman in Papua, Schlaginhaufen in New Ireland, Neuhauss in the Huon Gulf, and ABL himself in German New Guinea. Each of these anthropologists had different fieldwork strategies and were interested in different research questions. But despite these differences and their varying success in the field, each was a pioneer in developing new patterns of fieldwork. ABL's successful but relatively unintensive research in the New Hebrides sets his earlier work in New Guinea in much sharper relief.

Now, in the French colony of New Caledonia, the intensive nature of his New Guinea research becomes even more apparent. When ABL took a French steamer from Vila to Noumea, New Caledonia's capital and largest town, he left behind a Melanesian society of more or less traditional villages with scattered European settlements. In New Caledonia he found a European society where the Melanesian population had been in steady decline for more than a quarter century.[7] Here Melanesian communities were appendages to French economic interests; more or less traditional villages could be found only at the periphery of the French community.

New Caledonia was economically much more developed than any colony ABL had visited since Fiji. The economy benefited from the island's temperate climate, which encouraged European settlers even before France annexed the islands in 1853. Nickel deposits were discovered near Noumea about 1875, and mining became a major industry soon afterward, encouraging substantial investments from France and prompting further European settlement.[8]

From 1864 to 1897 the French had used New Caledonia as a penal colony, much as the British had used their Australian colonies during the preceding century. Many convicts returned to France after serving their sentences, but a substantial number of freed convicts stayed on in New Caledonia, where they and their descendants played prominent roles in the colony's social and economic life. By 1911 the convict population had fallen to 5,671 (Sarasin 1917, 4); it continued to decline until the Second World War.

From the beginning of European settlement, New Caledonian commerce was dominated by a mélange of free settlers who had established themselves as traders for sandalwood, bêche-de-mer, copra, shell, and other products from island Melanesia. During his brief sojourn in New Caledonia ABL met members of several of these families, such as the Bougarde, Engler, and Henry families at Oubatche and Nicholas Hagen in Noumea. Many of the prominent New Caledonian families had economic interests in the New Hebrides and other South Pacific territories. The most notable of these is Hagen, whose trading operations ABL had already encountered in the New Hebrides.

Not all of these families had a strictly French background, and whatever their origins, most families were involved both commercially and socially with Australia. The founder of the Henry family, for example, was probably of Australian origins and settled on the island in the 1860s. The Australian-born businessman Thomas Johnston, who later became British consul in Noumea, was in many ways more Caledonian than Australian and lived in the French colony from 1883. The Engler family, originally of Swiss descent, made periodic visits to Sydney. In sum, New Caledonia was a cosmopolitan place.

When ABL arrived in Noumea, planning to visit the native villages, he soon learned that most of the island was already developed. In many respects the colony was much more European than Melanesian. There were only a few "primitive" areas left, most of them set aside as native reserves. In these reserves, people told him, one might see indigenous New Caledonians in something approximating their traditional way of life. The peoples around Oubatche up the rugged east coast were the among the last groups to be pacified. There he might find the kind of traditional material he was looking for. But as ABL soon found out, even in these communities, villagers had long before adopted European clothing and ceased producing many of their traditional objects.

The cosmopolitan residents of Noumea seem to have sent all of their visiting anthropologists to Oubatche. When the Swiss anthropologist Fritz Sarasin (1917), who was a cousin of Felix Speiser's, arrived in Noumea five months earlier than ABL, he too was first sent to study the people around Oubatche. Like ABL, Sarasin met the Englers and the Bougardes. He even made a patrol into the hills in the interior visiting the Diahot River valley (ABL's Dihot). Sarasin went on to spend more than a year in New Caledonia, visiting a number of other parts of the island. (He was still conducting his research in the French colony when ABL arrived for the month of August.)

ABL refers to the two groups living in the Diahot valley as the Ouebia and Pombia tribes; Sarasin calls them the Ouébia and the Pamboa. Both Sarasin and ABL took photos in some of the same small villages, including one particularly stately Pombia house in a hamlet that Sarasin identifies as Tchambouenne (Sarasin 1917, Fig. 15; Sarasin and Roux 1929: Tafel 29; Lewis 1932a, plate IX; 1951, 61; see Fig. 6.37). Both anthropologists also took strikingly similar photos of another house in the same village (Sarasin and Roux 1929: Tafel 31-1; Fig. 6.47).

412

Considering the small populations in the interior[9] and the long period of intimate contact with Europeans in New Caledonia, ABL was surprisingly successful in collecting a total of 233 objects (130 specimens) during his month in New Caledonia.[10] These items include a pair of very large carved posts weighing more than a hundred pounds each. As so often before, packing again became a problem. All his specimens had to be left with Hagen in Noumea to be sent to Sydney from there. While Hagen's men were packing his boxes in Noumea, ABL boarded a French steamer to return to Sydney.

Fig. 6.37. House in Pombia village, near Oubatche, New Caledonia. A-38152 (68f).

New Caledonia

||||||||||||||||||||||||||||||||||||||||||||||||||||||||||||||||||||||||||||||||||||

Monday, July 31, 1911   Arrived in Noumea late in afternoon. Saw Mr. [Thomas] Johnston, who kindly agreed to store my things and helped me to hotel, etc. Went to Hotel Constants.

Tuesday, Aug. 1   Got my things ashore in morning. Visited Museum. Some good things, but all mixed up, and no labels. Have 2 fine Malekula mummies, out on wall. Two N. Cal. dancing masks in cases. Many carved N. Caledonia figures, boards, and faces, some clubs, spears, and misc. objects.

Wednesday, Aug. 2   Saw Governor, and he promised to see the officials were informed of my coming (in north) and to help. Made some purchases and calls.

Thursday, Aug. 3   Made some more purchases and calls.

Friday, Aug. 4   Wrote and saw people.

Saturday, Aug. 5   Wrote and saw people.

Sunday, Aug. 6   Left on *St. Pierre* for trip up east coast to Oubatche, where most of people seemed to think there was a better chance of getting things, as the Oubia tribe were about the last to be subdued. Here also lived Mr. Engler, formerly for 30 yrs. chief of topographic survey, and who knew

Fig. 6.38. Wooden clubs, all called *buat*, from Ouebia: *tewain*, 132606 (1822); *mumpusii*, 132605 (1821); *buap*, 132604 (1820). A-112120.

415

the island and natives better than most any body else. His wife was English, and he spoke English well.

Steamer left at 7 A.M. Rained all day.

Monday, Aug. 7   Clear and sunshine. Coast as we passed high and mountainous. Many torrents came pouring down the sides of mountains. Very little vegetation, and no trees of any size.

Tuesday, Aug. 8   Country much the same. Steamer stopped at several places to take off cargos, and always anchored over night, as many reefs. Passed one place where could see big mining operations, dumps, etc. Seem to be surface workings, nickel.

Wednesday, Aug. 9   Much the same, tho country not so barren, and coast not so precipitous. Shore in many places fringed with palm trees, but nothing that could be called a coastal plain.

Thursday, Aug. 10   Arrived at Oubatche at 9 A.M. Met Mr. Engler, who lives about 2 miles from Oubatche; also his son and Mr. Bougarde, who as partners keep the store, and own the land near by, and with Mr. Bougarde's sister, Mrs. Henry, make up the population of Oubatche, tho there is a gendarme station (2 men) about ½ mile down the coast.

Young Mr. Engler went with me to station to see if could get carriers for a trip to interior, but they said it would be 4–5 days before they could get them. (When called upon by the government, the natives are required to work, but it must be done through the chief. In this case it was necessary to get Oubia men, as I was going to their country, and the chief was in the interior.) Mr. Engler said he thought he could get men to go with me in less time, so did not ask gendarme to get them.

Friday, Aug. 11   Could get no men, as feast on, so visited settlement of Pombias on coast about a mile to north.

Saturday, Aug. 12   Visited villages of Pombias to south, but near noon was taken with fever, and had to return and go to bed.

Sunday, Aug. 13   Spent afternoon at old Mr. Engler's.

Fig. 6.39. Men at lunch by stream at divide between Ouebia and Pombia country. A-38095 (76f).

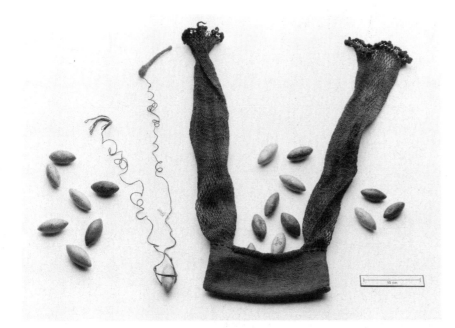

Fig. 6.40. "Bag with sling and sling stones. Bag *(ken paik)* and sling *(windat)* made of bark of *hang*. When used, as in war, it is tied around the waist so bag hangs in front." Extra stones put in the side pieces, Pombia tribe, 132609 (1824). A-112123.

Fig. 6.41. "Man ready to use sling, with bag of stones around waist," Wabanu, Ouebia country. A-38094 (72f).

Fig. 6.43.   House near Oubatche. A-38180 (62f).

Fig. 6.42.   Rounded post set on top of house (same house as in Fig. 6.44), Pombia tribe, 132667 (1854). A-112106.

418

Monday, Aug. 14   Tho they promised to come, men did not turn up. So in afternoon visited some old huts up on hill, and got a few things.

Tuesday, Aug. 15   Men turned up late, and finally got away about 10 A.M. I got horse from Mr. Bougarde. My guide also had a horse.

It was 27 kilometers over the divide to first village on Dihot river. The path (made by convicts in earlier days) wound along the sides of the hills, and rapidly rose toward the divide, giving some fine views over coast and ocean, with the numerous reefs showing light green against the dark blues of the deeper water. At about 600 meters the forest began. The divide was about 900 m. high, and we were soon out of the forest on the other side, with fine views of the interior valleys and even the ocean on the west.

Reached the village, Pirémbōnū, about 5:30 after a very steep descent to the river. There were many orange-trees about the village, and the natives gave us all we could eat. At first I was in doubt as to where I was to sleep, but the natives invited me to sleep in one of their houses, which had 2 doors, and was fairly airy. They themselves slept in a smaller one near by.

Fig. 6.44. Four carved boards, set on each side of door of house, small ones outside, Pombia tribe, 132660.1–.4 (1850–1853). A-112104.

Wednesday, Aug. 16   Could not induce my men to start early, but got away about 8 A.M. As the path would allow it, I rode the horse for about an hour, and then left it with my guide's horse loose to graze at a place not far from his village. From here the path was up over the divide at the head of the Dihot, and down into the Oubia country. Reached the first village (Wain) about 4:30 P.M. There were only a few houses, and only one family lived there. Had shelter made, and slept outside.

Thursday, Aug. 17   Left at 8 A.M., and during day visited several (3) Oubia villages, all small, but hard traveling to get to them. Slept at a village, Pan(g)u, about an hour from Wain.

Found very little of interest. Some of the door boards were better than seen on coast, but were far too large to carry away. Everything was the same as on the coast, as in fact most of the tribe lived on the coast. The whole tribe numbered less than 80, so the interior villages consisted of only a family or two, in the largest place not over 10 persons.

Friday, Aug. 18   Returned over divide, but stopped where left horses for the night.

Saturday, Aug. 19   Back to Oubatche, where arrived about 6 P.M.

Monday, Aug. 21   Went with Mr. Engler to Tao, about 25 kilometers south along coast. Passed several native villages. At place where had lunch

Fig. 6.45. Carved top from house, Pombia tribe, 132669 (1894). A-112112.

Fig. 6.46. Wooden mask, Pombia tribe, 132659 (1834).
A-112139.

saw 2 fine old axes, quite large. Reached Tao about 3 P.M. Here putting in electric water power for smelting works.

Tuesday, Aug. 22   Returned to Oubatche. On way back purchased some large carved posts.

Wednesday, Aug. 23   Catalogued specimens.

Thursday, Aug. 24   Visited villages to south, and bought some more things. Had great difficulty in getting one house-top *(hūp)* I wanted. When I finally found the owner, he agreed to price I had offered for it, *delivered,* but after much discussion it came out that the house was tabu, and the owner too sick to climb up and remove the *hup,* and no one else would. Finally a young man said he would, but of course I had to pay him extra, and the owner wanted the same as I had promised for the thing *delivered,* and seemed to think I had promised that much, but at last took loss, and I got the thing the next day.

Fig. 6.47. Another house in Pombia village, near Oubatche. A-38179 (61f).

Friday, Aug. 25 Packed.

Saturday, Aug. 26 Packed. Steamer called in morning on way up, and returned at 3:30. I had 10 boxes & cases, and one was not finished, but sufficiently good to take to Noumea, where we arrived Tuesday afternoon. Mr. N. Hagen agreed to look after boxes, and I left them in his care, as the steamer *(Pacifique)* left the next day, and would take no more cargo, as they were full of copra from N. Hebrides.

Wednesday, Aug. 30 Left at 4 P.M. for Sydney.

On the way to Noumea I met a Mr. Bozon, of Houailou, an old settler, who agreed to make a collection for me, and I left £40 with Mr. Hagen for him, and 4 for Mr. Hagen for packing, etc.

New Caledonia has a very uniform culture, which shows only slight variation in different parts of the island. The objects to be found are nearly all described by Pere Lambut in his book. I could add little to it, and many of the things are not to be found now. For example, no hats or men's clothing (only a penis wrapper, with sometimes a piece of bamboo in which penis was stuck). Good clubs were rare. The people all wore European clothes. A few old pots were left, but no longer made. The houses were falling into decay, and the new ones were of different style.

The old men's esp. chief's, house was large and high, (not so high in north as central N. Cal.) with center post and row of wall posts. Center post had many short poles bound to it at top, which received and supported the rafters. The roof was of bundles of grass, the sides of bark (of *naouli*) held in place with strips running round, and sometimes covered with grass. Sometimes roof had a layer of bark under grass.

The Bismarck Archipelago, German New Guinea

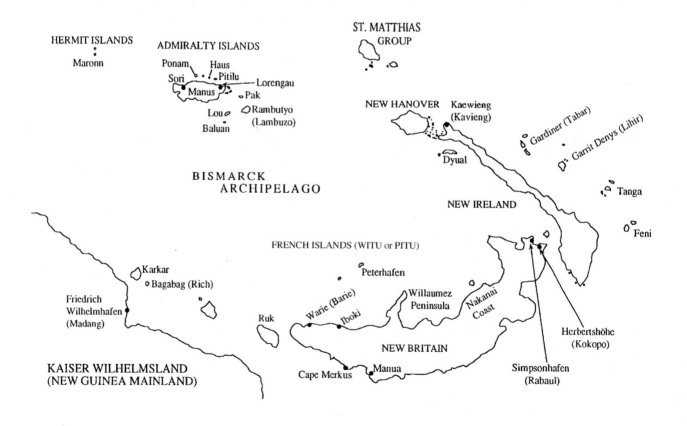

Return to German
New Guinea:
The Admiralty Islands

||||||||||||||||||||||||||||||||||||||||||||||||||||||||||||||||||||||||||||||||||||||

3 September 1911–25 December 1911

On his return to Sydney from New Caledonia early in September 1911, ABL began preparations to return to German New Guinea. He was not planning to collect specimens in the villages as before, but intended to buy an ethnological collection belonging to the Japanese trader Komine. Formerly an agent for Hernsheim, Komine had established himself as an independent trader based in the Admiralties. Over the previous decade he had built up a substantial network of trading stations on Manus and many of the smaller islands. When there was no copra or trochus shell to buy, he had his men trade for curios from the villagers. Komine was having financial difficulties and wanted to sell his collection for 10,000 marks (= $2,000) to an overseas buyer, preferably a museum in Europe, Australia, or America.

In 1910, on his last day in Rabaul before leaving for the Solomons, ABL had seen part of Komine's collection at Matupi, and had been impressed by it, particularly some large *uli* figures from New Ireland (Fig. 6.54). But he was in no position to purchase the collection; he had not received his allocation for the following year's research and had no money with which to buy the material.

On board the *Sumatra,* ABL undoubtedly heard more about the collection from Captain Nauer, whom Komine had appointed as his agent. Komine had also enlisted the assistance of Belgian-born businessman Octave Mouton to help him find a buyer for the collection.[11] When ABL ran into Mouton in Sydney in March 1911, the collection was still available. As ABL had by this time received his next year's allocation and therefore had money available, he authorized Mouton to purchase the collection on his return to German New Guinea. Mouton told Komine he had an American buyer, but as the cost was high Mouton did not risk making the purchase for ABL until the latter had seen a list of the collection's contents. Mouton duly sent ABL the specimen list, but did nothing further in the matter; when ABL arrived in Rabaul at the beginning of October, he purchased the collection from Komine directly, visiting Komine's main station in the Admiralty Islands to number and pack the collection.

In the meantime Captain Nauer of the *Sumatra* and other men working for Hernsheim—all of whom were eager to earn a commission on the sale—continued to seek potential buyers in

Germany. In the end, these efforts to sell the Komine collection nearly prompted an international incident.

One of Hernsheim's people had contacted Professor Karl Weule, director of the Museum für Völkerkunde in Leipzig, about the collection. After considering the matter, Weule also made an offer to buy the material for his museum, but his offer did not arrive in German New Guinea until after ABL had paid for the collection and was packing the specimens for shipment.

Believing that Field Museum had improperly obtained the collection out from under him, Weule wrote to Field Museum director Skiff, threatening a lawsuit. ABL did not hear of the matter until the following June, when Skiff sent along a copy of Weule's letter, demanding an explanation (this correspondence is reproduced below).

The whole affair illustrates several major points about museums and the international curio trade before the Great War: (1) the sometimes intense competition among museums for collections and the ethnological significance such collections had for museums; (2) the important role played by traders like Komine, Hernsheim, Voogdt, Richard Parkinson (later Mrs. Parkinson), and Gramms in procuring curios from native peoples; (3) the complex relationships that linked traders, sea captains, businessmen, and potential buyers in Europe, Australia, and America; and (4) the important role this international curio market had on the production of museum specimens, even in areas as remote as German New Guinea.

This is not, of course, the first time we have come across any of these points in ABL's travels during the Joseph N. Field Expedition; they have been the backdrop against which ABL had worked since he first arrived in Fiji in June 1909. But here we see the texture of this complex global network of economic relations played out as ABL sails among the islands, villages, and trading stations in the Bismarcks and the Admiralties.

At the time anthropologists and ethnologists were well aware of the effects this curio market was having on the local production of objects. This awareness explains ABL's interest in obtaining older pieces representing what we may call the "ethnographic past," a time before the curio market—not to mention pacification, plantations, labor recruiting, and missions—had affected "traditional" life and "customary" crafts. Older pieces were presumed to be freer of the contaminating influences of the global commoditization of objects. Thus, old objects were thought to tell us more about customary relationships between and among communities in these primitive places.

Today it is clear from the accounts of Cook's voyages that objects were being made for sale to foreigners almost as soon as these outsiders set foot on South Pacific shores,[12] the "ethnographic past" was as important to ABL and his generation of anthropologists as the "ethnographic present" would become for the generation of anthropologists that would follow. The ethnological purity of both the "ethnographic past" and the "ethnographic present" are, of course, illusory, and we are correct in being cautious about accepting either as social facts about the way things were. But in both ethnographic tenses, field researchers collected real data about real human communities and the context in which people lived. And in both cases, the data written in notebooks and packed up in shipping crates are far more complex data sets than most field researchers probably assumed at the time. For all their limitations as representations of the past, the masses of objects collected during the expedition period in anthropology remain valuable empirical data about communities that were linked in complex ways to one another as well as to the broader global community.

The Komine Collection

The Komine collection consisted of more than three thousand items, almost two-thirds of it from the Admiralty Islands, where Komine's operations were centered. Ironically, although the

424

collection contained some material from nearly every part of German New Guinea, it was especially rich in material from the very places ABL had previously been unable to visit. The collection had already achieved a reputation within the colony. The *kiap* Berghausen (1910, 36), for example, visited the Admiralties in 1909 and was surprised to see such a large private collection at Komine's place on Ponam, calling it "a small ethnological museum."

The material from New Ireland included a number of carved funerary posts called *malaggan*s, large *uli* figures, chalk figures, and masks. The Admiralty Islands material contained large numbers of specimens of several object types: wood bowls, beds, carvings, obsidian-bladed spears and daggers, shell breast ornaments (*kap-kap*s), nose shells, etcetera. Each of these types of object is represented by dozens of examples illustrating many varieties. Some of these could be thought of as "duplicates," though ABL makes it clear that he did not view most of the Komine collection in this way. He did not, however, dismiss the possibility of using some of the Komine collection for exchanges with other museums.

There were very few fine old pieces in the Komine collection. Most of the pieces had never been used, and much of the Admiralty Islands material seems to have been freshly made when Komine acquired it. Many pieces, such as most of the obsidian daggers, appear to have been made specifically for sale to Komine and his agents, or perhaps to other foreigners. These daggers—and thus possibly other objects—may even have been mass produced for the foreign market (Torrence 1989, 1993).[13]

The major weaknesses of the Komine collection are its minimal documentation about use, methods of manufacture, and materials; and the absence of a specific, reliable, village-level provenience. Despite these limitations, the Komine material filled in many gaps both in the Lewis Collection and in Field Museum's other Melanesian collections.

Preparations at Sydney

On his arrival in Sydney from New Caledonia, ABL had much to do before setting off for Rabaul to send the Komine collection back to Chicago. ABL's crates and boxes from the New Hebrides and New Caledonia had arrived in Sydney and had to be prepared for shipment to Chicago. While in Sydney ABL made his rounds of bookshops, curio dealers, and photography studios. He bought a few pieces from Tost and Rohu[14] and a few more photographs from two of Sydney's leading photographers, Charles Kerry and Henry King. He readied his negatives and prepared copies of specimen lists to accompany his shipment.

While in Sydney, ABL once more visited the Australian Museum, where he met one of the assistant curators, Charles Hedley. The two curators discussed the possibility of an exchange between their two museums. ABL would provide duplicate Melanesian specimens from his material and Hedley would assemble a collection of Aboriginal Australian objects. ABL planned to use some of the Komine collection for this exchange, which took place a few months later on ABL's return from Rabaul. The Australian material consisted of 167 specimens representing many parts of Australia. For these specimens ABL gave the Australian Museum a collection of 402 specimens principally from the Admiralty Islands.[15]

Back to New Guinea

On the way to German New Guinea, ABL spent a few days in Brisbane, where he visited the Queensland Museum and met Sir William MacGregor, who was then governor of Queensland

and chancellor of the University of Queensland. MacGregor had formerly served as chief medical officer in Fiji and as administrator and lieutenant governor of Papua and was thus well acquainted with the Southwest Pacific. At the Queensland Museum ABL had an opportunity to see the extensive ethnological collection Sir William had made during his years in Papua (Joyce 1971, 368).[16]

After three days in Brisbane, ABL once again boarded a Nord-Deutscher Lloyd steamer for Rabaul, where he landed on 1 October 1911. ABL's arrival in German New Guinea was noted in the *Amtsblatt für das Schutzgebiet Deutsch-Neuguinea* (1911, 224), the official newsletter for the colony, in its listing of arrivals at and departures from Rabaul.

ABL soon learned that Octave Mouton was in Sydney; thus, ABL would have to arrange the Komine purchase himself. He also learned that the climate among Germans in the colony had not appreciably changed since his last visit, so he chartered the schooner *Harriet and Alice* from Captains Carlson and Rondahl and set off to find Komine, who was presently at one of his stations in the Admiralty Islands. (ABL was already familiar with this schooner, having seen it when he met Herr Schoede, the German collector who had chartered the same schooner during his expedition in 1909 and 1910.) In preparation for what he knew would be another difficult job of packing yet another large collection, ABL loaded the schooner with lumber for making more boxes. He also brought along more "trade," which he planned to use for collecting on the trip to Pitilu Island, Komine's current headquarters in the Admiralties.

Between Rabaul and Pitilu, ABL stopped at New Hanover, St. Matthias, Rambuzo (Lambuzo or Rambutyo), Pak, and Manus (the main island in the Admiralties). In each of these communities he did some collecting on his own. In the Admiralties, ABL also visited Sori, Haus, Ponam, and other unnamed villages on the main island. On this excursion ABL took 154 photographs using both glass plates and Kodak film. It was a busy time for him.

During his travels in the Admiralties, ABL experienced a complex economic network of trading stations. Some of these stations had been associated with Hernsheim, but Komine was gradually expanding his economic interests and had become the dominant foreign influence in the group. He was not, however, an all-powerful authority in the Admiralties; on more than one occasion he had been attacked by hostile villagers. Relationships between islanders and foreigners were in a constant state of flux. And while ABL was packing up the Komine collection, the German government was opening its first station in the Admiralties, at Lorengau.

After packing up his collections at Pitilu, ABL returned to Rabaul. The remainder of Komine's collection had been left at Matupi with Ah Tam, the leading Chinese citizen in the German colony. With Ah Tam's help, ABL again tackled the task of packing and shipping a large collection back to Chicago. When his packing was complete, he took his leave from German New Guinea, returning to Sydney on yet another Nord-Deutscher Lloyd steamer.

On Christmas day 1911 ABL returned once more to Sydney, having spent another two and one half months in the islands. It had been a successful trip. The Komine collection had been sent off together with a few pieces purchased from S. A. Whiteman and the five hundred specimens ABL himself had collected in New Hanover, St. Matthias, and the Admiralties. He had also enjoyed the luxury of chartering a schooner for travel around the islands, something he had dreamed of since Christmas two years before, when he had first seen the *Harriet and Alice* at Cape Merkus. With the schooner it was possible to collect a large number of specimens in a short time. Ironically, because of the schooner, these collections turned out to be less well documented than those he made when he had chartered Gramms' cutter or in the days when he had been forced to take a dugout canoe through the lagoons at Sissano or Malol.

FIELD MUSEUM OF NATURAL HISTORY
CHICAGO

April 18, 1912

Dr. A. B. Lewis
Care of North German Lloyd
Sydney, N.S.W., Australia

Dear Sir:

I enclose herewith a copy of a communication received from the Director of the Museum für Völkerkunde at Leipzig, Germany.

Please provide at the earliest possible moment a narrative of this transaction, setting forth all the details relating to the acquisition of this material and the conditions surrounding the purchase.

Yours very truly,
Director

{Copy of Translation}

MUSEUM FÜR VÖLKERKUNDE

Leipzig
March 26, 1912

Field Columbian Museum of Natural History
Jackson Park, Chicago

Dear Sirs:

In the autumn of 1911 we purchased by telegraph the ethnographical collection of the Japanese Komine of the Admiralty Islands, and also we had already paid half the purchase price to a Hamburg firm. Recently we hear by letter that the Japanese, in spite of our payment, has handed over the collection to your representative Lewis who has carried this [collection] to America. You can imagine that this communication is not very pleasing to us, and in case our demand fails to be made right in some other way, we must reserve the right to recover from him. We do not doubt for a moment that a law suit would be very costly and wish to settle this in a peaceable manner. The proper way seems to me to be as follows: The Komine collection contains, according to their catalogue which we have, many duplicates of which the greater part are desirable for any museum. I ask you if you would be willing to deliver up the designated part of the collection in exchange to the Leipzig Museum für Völkerkunde. In response we can offer a very valuable and complete collection from East and West Africa, or a designated part by the Mediterranean Sea. I desire to know your stand in this matter and satisfactory arrangements to both sides can be made when I hear your decision in the matter.

> Museum für Vöelkerkunde
> Prof. dr. Weule
> Director

Port Moresby, Papua
June 19, 1912

The Director
Field Museum
Chicago

Dear Sir:

Your letter of April 18 has just been received, and I note your request for details concerning the purchase of the Komine collection.

I first heard of this collection in October 1910, before I left German New Guinea for the Solomon Islands. Captain Nauer, captain of the Norddeutscher Lloyd island steamer <u>Sumatra</u>, which runs from Rabaul to the Admiralty and other islands, asked me if I would not like to buy it, and said Komine had requested him to try and sell it. I saw part of the collection then, but had no money at the time to purchase. While in Sydney in March [1911] (after I had received word of further appropriation for my work) I met a business man, Mr. Mouton, from the German territory, and requested him to act as my agent and purchase the collection if still complete and in good order. He got a list of specimens and a price of the collection, from Komine (the owner), but did not care to risk buying the collection till I had seen it. From this list, and what I had already seen of the collection, I was satisfied it was a good thing, and sent him word to buy, and I would come up in a month or two and pack it. (I was then in the New Hebrides.)

When I arrived at Rabaul, I found that Mr. Mouton had been away in Sydney and had done nothing further in the matter. I then saw Captain Nauer and asked him about the collection. He said he had been trying to get some people in Germany to buy it for a long time, but it seemed as if they were unwilling to do anything, and if I wanted to buy it, to go ahead. I never understood Captain Nauer to imply that he had an option on the collection, and I also had, through Mr. Mouton, a price and list of the collection direct from Komine, the owner. As Komine was in the Admiralty Islands, I chartered a boat and took a trip out to the Admiralty Isl., collecting on the way. There I saw Mr. Komine and the remainder of his collection (part of which I had seen at Matupi nearly a year before), and offered him 450 pounds for it, part cash, and rest check on Sydney. This was about $200.00 less than the price he had set on the collection, namely 10,000 marks. He accepted the offer, however, and I packed and shipped the collection, as given in my report.

Such are the facts relating to my purchase of the collection. About a week after closing the deal, when 100 pounds had been paid and accepted, and part of the collection sent to Friedrich Wilhelmshafen, I heard that Hernsheim & Co. had sent word to their agent in the Admiralty Isl. to buy Komine's collection at his own figure, 10,000. I was not aware before that Hernsheim & Co. were interested in the collection, though I knew that Captain Nauer had been trying to get some one to buy it, as he had told me about it and in fact tried to get me to buy it nearly a year before. Komine had been trying to sell the collection for a long time, and had asked several people if they would not get some one to buy it, but had finally given up hope of getting any offer from Germany. So far as I could find out, he had given no one an exclusive option to sell; but even if he had, my purchase was in good faith and entirely ignorant of any such, and bitter as the Germans in New Guinea were against the Field Museum, and sorry as they were to see the collection go there, I never heard any of them express any question as to my right to the collection.

I fear that Director Weule has misunderstood the conditions of the (his) deal, which was an offer, and not a purchase till Komine accepted it. Certainly Komine did not "hand over the collection" to me "in spite of" his payment, as he says, since he [Komine] never received even word of the offer till afterward.

As the Leipzig Museum has absolutely no claim on the collection, the Museum should certainly <u>not</u> "deliver up the <u>designated</u> part of the collection in exchange," though an exchange might later be arranged, as there are a great many pieces which are more or less duplicated.

I think the implied threat of a law suit can be ignored. If there had been any hold on me at all, I certainly would never have gotten the collection out of German territory. It is quite possible that Prof. Weule has a case against Hernsheim & Co., but that is another matter.

I think I have said sufficient regarding this transaction. Komine simply accepted the first definite offer he received. I mentioned the later offer in my report, but as no one in German New Guinea ever questioned my right in the purchase, I did not think it necessary to say anything more about it.

Very respectfully,
A. B. Lewis

FIELD MUSEUM OF NATURAL HISTORY
CHICAGO

August 16, 1912

The Director
Das Museum fur Voelkerkunde
Leipzig, Germany

Dear Sir:

Referring to your communication of March 26: I have received a report from Dr. Lewis, in the field, and have also been in conference with Dr. Dorsey, the Curator of the Department of Anthropology, and there does not seem to be any justification for acceding to your demands with relation to the material from the Admiralty Islands.

Very respectfully,
F. J. V. Skiff
Director

Fig. 6.48. "Houses built on piles in the sea, Rambuzo Island." A-38138 (86f).

Return to German New Guinea: The Admiralty Islands

||||||||||||||||||||||||||||||||||||||||||||||||||||||||||||||||||||||||||||||||||||||||||||||||

Sunday, Sept. 3, 1911 Arrived Sydney about 11 A.M. Got room at Grosvenor Hotel.

Monday, Sept. 4–Thursday, Sept. 21 Spent in Sydney. Got photos from King and from Kerry, and a number of specimens from Tost & Rohu. These with odd books and plates packed and sent by Union Co. New Zealand (Com-Aust) to Tacoma.

Boxes 1–34	from New Hebrides
Boxes 31–60	from New Caledonia
Box 61	from Capt. [Huggett] Auckland
Box 62	from Tost & Rohu, and some Solomon Isl.
Box 63	books, photos, etc.

Thursday evening (21st) left for Brisbane.

Friday, Sept. 22 Arrived in Brisbane 9 P.M.

Saturday, Sept. 23 Visited Museum, and in afternoon Sir William MacGregor.

Monday, Sept. 25 Left on *Prinz Waldemar* about 6 P.M.

Sunday, Oct. 1 Arrived at Rabaul.

Monday, Oct. 2–Saturday, Oct. 14 Stayed at Rabaul, bought specimens from S. A. Whiteman and packed same.
  Arranged to charter motor schooner for 50 Marks per day. 5 Marks per day for food, and all benzine used. *Harriet & Alice*, Capt. [Carlson], Capt. Rondahl,[14] half owner, and laid in supply of lumber for boxes and trade.

Sunday, Oct. 15 Left 8 A.M. for Kabakaul, where Capt. got some more supplies, and left at 2 P.M. for New Hanover.

Tuesday, Oct. 17 About 4 P.M. arrived at Capt. _____ place.

---

14. ABL had met Carlson over Christmas 1909 at Cape Merkus, when the *Harriet and Alice* was under lease to Herr Schoede. Rondahl had married Mrs. Parkinson's sister.

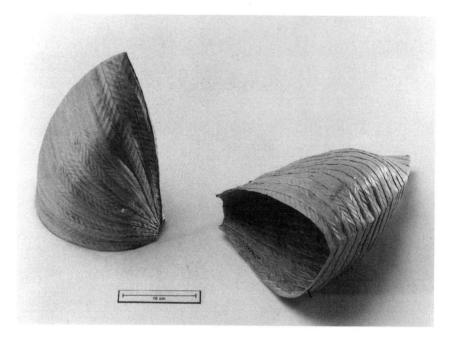

Fig. 6.49. Sun hats of pandanus leaves, worn by women, New Hanover. Ends go to the back, 137028 (4211), 137029 (4212). A-112182.

Wednesday, Oct. 18 Bought a few things. Men here formerly went naked. Women wore a grass apron in front and similar one behind. Often wore a peculiar cap of pandanus leaf; also rain hood, larger than those of Buka. A kind of shell money is made here of reddish bivalve. Pieces chipped out, rubbed down on stone, each piece held on end of stick. Bored with hand drill, strung on string, and then roll rubbed on stone while held in hand.

Left about noon.

Thursday, Oct. 19 Arrived at St. Matthias about 9 A.M. Only one good anchorage, in behind small island. There were several other islands off the main island. Went over to one of these, but did not find much. A trader has been stationed on one of the islands for about 9 months, and few things are left. A number of canoes came off to the vessel, and brought a few things.

Friday, Oct. 20 In morning went over to some places on main island, and spent forenoon there.

Most of houses are scattered, not grouped in large villages. Houses simple, sides and roofs of sago leaf, floor ground. Chief food taro; not many cocoanuts.

First visited place on shore, and bought few things,[15] then went further on around point and up river. Here carried ashore. Village on high bank of river. Stopped here short time, and then sent back boys (except one) with specimens to boat, to take it around to first landing place, while I walked across—took about ½ hr., several scattered houses on way. Crossed river and swamp on way. Got away from St. Matthias about 4 P.M.

Saturday, Oct. 21–Sunday, Oct. 22 On sea.

---

15. ABL bought 195 specimens at St. Matthias.

Monday, Oct. 23   Off Rambuzo in morning. Some canoes came out, and bought a few things before getting to anchorage. In afternoon went ashore at a village, built out on piles in sea. Took photos and bought some things,[16] esp. drums and large oil vessels. The drums are made in this island (also in other places). Oil vessels come from Manus. These large pitched baskets are set up in houses, usually in pairs, and filled with oil for feasts. The cocoanut is first scraped, and the oil squeezed out by twisting it in fibre from leaf-sheath. This fluid is boiled, the oil ladled off into cocoanuts, and finally stored in these large vessels.

The large wood bowls are used to mash up taro, etc. in. The oil is poured over this as condiment. Smaller baskets and bowls for food and eating. The houses are fairly well built, and floored with strips of trunk of a small palm. Saw (and smelt) remains of man. When man dies body kept in house till decayed. After few days skin removed, and after flesh falls away bones washed and cleaned.

Tuesday, Oct. 24   In forenoon visited some villages near shore. None of these large. Houses on ground (see photos). Nothing new. Altogether got very little—no carvings. Schoede[17] 2 yrs. before filled the ship at this island with all sorts of good things.

Left in afternoon for Pak. Arrived too late to go ashore.

Wednesday, Oct. 25   Visited villages on island. Little here.[18] A station of Hernsheim & Co. for some time.

Left for Manus, when arrived about noon, and anchored in _____ bay, for short time, but as no villages near, left for further up coast, and anchored for night off village.

Here went ashore and bought a few things. Houses larger than previously seen, and mostly on piles, at least the women's houses. Men's houses on ground.

Thursday, Oct. 26   In morning again went ashore to see process of sago manufacture. Much like Sissano. The upper half of trunk removed with stakes. Hammer with bamboo end. Put in baskets to carry to washing place. Here arrangement differs from what seen before.

There is a frame supporting below 2 bases of sago leaves, large ends fastened together, to receive the washings. Over this is a single leaf stem, with cocoanut-leaf sheath strainer fastened at end. The piece is rather long, and bottom pegged fast all around inside of base of leaf. The other end is held in the hand, and the sago worked back and forth in this.

Left about 9 A.M. and arrived in afternoon at Pitilu, Komine's place. Here went ashore, saw his collection, and arranged to purchase it for £450. Sent all timber ashore.

Friday, Oct. 27   Catalogued collection.

Saturday, Oct. 28–Wednesday, Nov. 1   Packed and loaded up the *Harriet & Alice* with all she could hold. Necessary to send her to Fr. Wh. Hafen,

Fig. 6.50. Detail, woven belt, St. Matthias. "Worn by men on special occasions; ordinarily go naked," 137096 (4266). A-112388.

---

16. ABL bought 237 specimens at Rambuzo.

17. This was Herr Schoede, the collector. Here ABL spelled his name Shrader.

18. This was Pak Island, where ABL bought 28 specimens. On Manus, the main island, he bought 44 objects.

Fig. 6.51. "Men's house, St. Matthias."
A-37525 (823).

Fig. 6.52. Containers from Rambuzo
(Lambuzo) Island: wooden bowls,
133695 (4444), 134011 (4451); oil vessel (rattan covered with pitch), 133674
(4413); food bowls (coiled baskets covered with pitch), 134015 (4456),
134020 (4461). A-112392.

Fig. 6.53. Obsidian-bladed daggers, Admiralty Islands: double blade, 134727 (6191), 134726 (6190); single blade, 134766 (6230), 134775 (6239), 134733 (6197), 134712 (6176), 134720 (6184). Komine collection. A-112395.

as benzine ordered sent there. Now I must go back to Matupi to pack rest of collection.

Thursday, Nov. 2   Capt. Carlson left in morning. I had to wait till Komine could take me and the rest of collection to Rabaul.

    Comet (gov. steamer) arrived about noon. Komine busy with them rest of day.

Friday, Nov. 3   Could do nothing, as Komine with gov. people. They were founding a new station on mainland about six miles west of Pitilu.[19] *Kiap*, doctor, police master, and 50 police boys.

Saturday, Nov. 4   Komine loaded up the skull and some bones of a whale stranded on south coast, which he was going to give to the governor, and we went down with them in Komine's boat *(Manuela* formerly *La Caroline)* to the *Comet*, where arrived about sunset. I spent the evening with Capt. Müller. Left about 10 P.M., and ran down to one of Komine's stations, where anchored for night.

Sunday, Nov. 5   Next morning stopped here short time, and then went over to Ponam, an island on which Komine was formerly settled. Here spent some time looking around, and seeing the process of making shell money. The shells used are small univalves. The shell is first stuck in a short stick, base out, and this ground down on a stone. Then a piece of midrib of palm leaflet is stuck in hole, and the other end of shell broken off with a large shell as hammer, leaving a ring rough on one side. These pieces are then set in the

---

19. This station was called Manus station, now Lorengau. It was the government's seventh station outside east New Britain.

Fig. 6.54. *Uli* figure, interior behind Katedin and Pinikindu, New Ireland, 138790 (5472). Komine collection. A-112374.

Fig. 6.55. *Malagan,* New Ireland, 138799 (6083). Komine collection. A-112376.

Fig. 6.56 and 6.57. "Making shell money, Ponam." A-37658 (912), A-38162 (102f).

Fig. 6.58. "Building with lookout at Komine's station on the north coast of Manus, opposite small island of Haus." A-38099 (111f).

end of a short soft stick and ground down smooth. The rings are then strung on a piece of rattan forming long piece. This is fastened on a plank, tied at each end, and the roll as a whole smoothed by rubbing lengthwise with a piece of coral rock. This is continued till the whole roll is nicely smoothed and rounded.

Left in evening and anchored for night off Sori, on main land. Here Komine had founded a station shortly before, not far from a native village. This village was hard pressed by the bush natives, and within the last year at least 40 had been killed and eaten.

Monday, Nov. 6 Went on shore in morning. The natives looked like wild fellows with long hair bound up in bark.

Later in forenoon left for Haus (Hus), an island where pottery made. So far as I could find out, pottery made only on this island and on Bugi, island on south coast. The method is said to be the same in both places, and is practically identical with that in Tumleo.

The clay is from the mainland (said from river). It is softened with a little water, and mixed with coral sand. An amount about right for a pot is then taken, and on a leaf platter this is worked and mixed with the fingers. With a stone it is then pounded a little, flattened and worked into a disk, hollowed, placed over one hand, with stone, and with paddle worked into shape. Two paddles, a broad and a narrow, are used, nothing else but the hand and round stone, with a woven ring on which to rest the partly formed pot. Burning did not see.

Fig. 6.59. Men dancing, Pitilu. A-37679 (894).

Tuesday, Nov. 7 Most of day put in loading my collection on Komine's ship.

Wednesday, Nov. 8 Komine busy, so had to wait.

Thursday, Nov. 9–Wednesday, Nov. 29 Left afternoon Nov. 9 and arrived next afternoon at Hernsheim's station on _____, where Mr. Stehr left us. The next morning to Lambuzo, and that evening Nov. 11 left for French Islands, where arrived the 13th. Here we stayed for a few days as Komine wished to recruit. Visited one village in interior. Took nearly two weeks to get to Rabaul, because of calms and contrary winds (engine broke down).

Thursday, Nov. 30 Unloaded boxes on wharf.

Friday, Dec. 1 Got timber and boxes on board, and went to Ah Tam's place in Matupi, to pack up rest of collection.

Saturday, Dec. 2　Listed the things with Komine, and packed up a few things.

Monday, Dec. 4–Wednesday, Dec. 13　Spent time packing up, first on Wharf, and then at Matupi.

Thursday, Dec. 14–Friday, Dec. 15　Arranged to have things brought over by Ah Tam, got out bills of lading, etc.

Saturday, Dec. 16　Steamer arrived.

Sunday, Dec. 17–Saturday, Dec. 23　On way to Brisbane, arrived Sat. morning. Left Sat. evening for Sydney.

Sunday, Dec. 24　At sea.

Monday, Dec. 25　Arrived Sydney Noon.

{The Komine collection contained the following material:}

Summary of objects from the Admiralty Islands:

obsidian spears	187
other spears	76
obsidian daggers	169
other daggers	13
wooden bowls	110
basket bowls	38
coconut water bottles	72
carvings	57
ladders	19
beds	31
belts	30
beaded aprons	28
shell armlets	138
woven arm bands	19
breast ornaments (*kap-kap*)	267
nose ornaments	55
combs	53
canoe prow ornaments	14
canoe paddles	32
canoe bailers	14
lime gourds/sticks	62
axes/adzes	17
fishhooks	24
shark hooks	62
wood spikes for pitfall	73

slit gongs	4
canoe models	20
other objects	91
Number of objects from other places:	
Dutch New Guinea	6
Kaiser Wilhelmsland	32
Western Islands	10
Ruk Island	10
Siassi	20
New Britain	205
Pitu (French Islands)	9
St. Matthias	7
New Hanover	24
New Ireland	264
Tabar, Lihir, Tanga	72
Nissan	81
Buka	59
Bougainville (mostly arrows)	618
Total	3,192

The Papuan Gulf

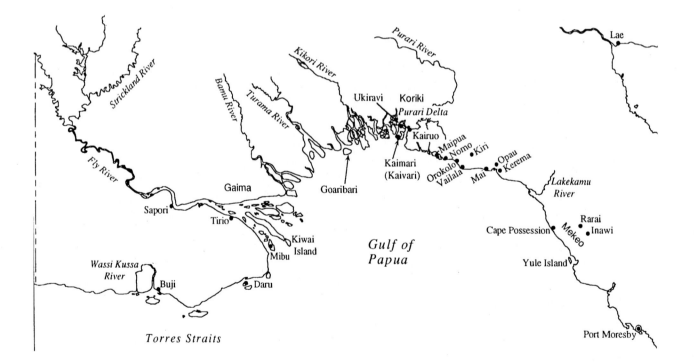

Strickland River

Bamu River

Turama River

Kikori River

Purari River

Ukiravi Koriki

Purari Delta

Kairuo

Maipua

Nomo Kiri

Kaimari Opau
(Kaivari) Kerema

Orokolo

Vailala

Mai

Fly River

Gaima

Goaribari

Sapori

Lakekamu River

Tirio

Gulf of Papua

Rarai

Kiwai Island

Cape Possession Inawi

Mibu

Mekeo

Wassi Kussa River

Yule Island

Buji

Daru

Lae

Torres Straits

Port Moresby

Book

Papua, Dutch New Guinea, and Home

||||||||||||||||||||||||||||||||||||||||||||||||||||||||||||||||||||||||||||||||||||||||||||||||||||||||||||||||||||||||||||||||

25 December 1911–June 1913

After his return from Rabaul, ABL spent about six weeks in Sydney. This was his third Christmas away from home, and it would be his last field break in Sydney before returning to Chicago. Aside from making arrangements for his exchange with the Australian Museum, it is not clear how he spent his time during these weeks. But two and a half years in Melanesia and the frequent bouts of malaria had taken their toll, and ABL was clearly entitled to a well-deserved respite in town before setting off for the hardships of New Guinea once more.

During part of this time in Sydney ABL was waiting to hear whether or not his next year's allocation had been approved. If not approved he would be forced to return to Chicago almost at once. As it turned out, the allocation came through, he received his bank drafts, and he was able to make two more excursions to New Guinea, first visiting Papua and then Dutch New Guinea.

Port Moresby, his first destination, could be easily reached by steamer from Australia. Burns Philp operated a regular shipping service between Australia and Papua. On a six-week cycle BP steamers left from Brisbane, calling at Cairns (in northern Queensland), Port Moresby, and either Daru in the west or Samarai and Woodlark Island in the east. Samarai and Daru were the two largest towns and most important government stations after Port Moresby. Woodlark Island in the eastern Massim region was a thriving gold-mining district opened in 1895. In 1912 the Woodlark goldfield had about ninety white miners and more than four hundred Papuan laborers, mostly working for three major mining companies. Gold was one of Papua's most important exports, and this regular steamer service was essential for keeping the field supplied and providing the miners with regular transport to and from the goldfield.

ABL left Sydney for Brisbane and from there set off for Port Moresby on the Burns Philp steamer *Matunga*. When the steamer stopped at Cairns, ABL took the train up to Barron Falls, the local tourist stop, and the same afternoon continued onward to Papua. ABL offers few details about this journey, but we know something about the voyage and his fellow passengers because travel writer Mary Hall was among them. Hall (1914) described in some detail the otherwise uneventful passage to Port Moresby. She mentions ABL and many of the other passengers, which seem to have included, among others, Papuan police master George H. Nicholls, Father Claussen, Dr. Hamilton of Sydney, a bank manager, a lay missionary, and a number of "rough-and-ready" miners bound for Woodlark. In describing her fellow passengers on the *Matunga* she wrote:

> On my left was a young doctor from Sydney [Hamilton], going up country in Papua under contract for a year. . . . His *vis-à-vis* was a learned American anthropologist, who after spending some months in the Solomon Islands and German New Guinea was now going to extend his field of study to the Territory of Papua. He had a very congenial neighbour in Father Claussen, a bearded French Roman Catholic missionary, educated, intelligent, and broad-minded. One overheard scraps of conversation between them on science, art, or some classic work. [Hall 1914, 203]

This reference to ABL together with her description of a visit to the Motu village of Hanuabada at Port Moresby represents one of the few independently published accounts of ABL in the field.[1]

After arriving in Port Moresby, ABL spent the next five months traveling around Papua. He then set off for Dutch New Guinea, which was administered as an unimportant part of the Moluccas or "spice islands." Although the Dutch New Guinea border was about 150 miles west of Daru, Dutch immigration regulations forced ABL to enter the colony formally at Batavia, Java, some 2,500 miles farther west. From Batavia (now called Jakarta), the capital of the Dutch East Indies, he could then catch a Royal Dutch steamer for the eastern islands and New Guinea. After six months in Dutch territory he returned to Batavia and finally set sail for Singapore in January 1913. From there he returned to Chicago late that spring.

Papua or British New Guinea

In 1912, Papua had been an Australian colony for six years. Like German New Guinea, it had been independent of European control until 1884. Queenslanders had long urged the British government to annex part of New Guinea because, on the one hand, they feared foreign annexation of this large, adjacent land mass, and, on the other hand, they hoped eventually to use New Guinea as a source of inexpensive plantation labor. In 1883 Thursday Island police magistrate H. M. Chester was even sent by the premier of Queensland to annex New Guinea for the British Crown. But the British government repudiated Queensland's actions, and the territory remained independent until the following year. By then Britain and Germany had arranged a partition of African territories; this settlement included an agreement to divide New Guinea into British and German protectorates. Thus, on 6 November 1884 Commodore Erskine of the Royal Navy raised the British flag at Port Moresby, formally annexing the southeast quadrant of New Guinea.[2]

This action completed the partition of New Guinea. Some weeks earlier Otto Finsch had hoisted the German flag on the New Guinea mainland (henceforth Kaiser Wilhelmsland) and in the Bismarck Archipelago, formally proclaiming these areas as a protectorate of Germany. A half century earlier, the Dutch had officially claimed the western half of New Guinea, up to the 141st meridian east longitude. After receiving (inaccurate) reports that the British planned to establish a station in southwest New Guinea, the Dutch feared intrusion into their monopoly over the spice trade in the Moluccas (principally cloves, nutmeg, and mace). To preempt this possibility, the Dutch in 1828 had established their own fortified settlement on Triton Bay on the south coast of New Guinea and annexed the territory as part of the East Indies. Twelve years later this settlement was abandoned when more than seventy of the colonists had died of malaria and other diseases, but it established Dutch claims to western New Guinea.[3]

British New Guinea had been administered as a British protectorate for four years when the British government formally annexed the territory as a colony, installing William MacGregor as its first lieutenant-governor (1888–1898). In 1901, when the six Australian colonies achieved independence as the Commonwealth of Australia, the British government—keen to be spared the colonial expenses—made preparations to transfer its colony in New Guinea to Australia. In 1906 Australia finally accepted responsibility for the colony and officially changed the territory's name from British New Guinea to Papua. Two years later, Hubert Murray was promoted from chief judicial officer to lieutenant-governor, a post he would hold until 1940.

Papua was divided into a number of administrative regions called divisions, each headed by a government officer called a resident magistrate. The number of divisions changed almost every year as new stations, new goldfields, and new territory were opened up. In each division the resident magistrate (R.M.) was assisted by one or more assistant resident magistrates (A.R.M.s), a clerk, and a few other civil servants.[4] Native administration in Papua was thus roughly analogous to that in German New Guinea, except that the administration in Papua was much more developed than its counterpart in Kaiser Wilhelmsland.

During the Murray administration, the government staff grew gradually but substantially as new areas were explored, new mineral deposits found, and new stations opened to administer a growing number of controlled villages. In 1912 the fifteenth government station was opened on the Kikori River. In all, there were nine divisions in Papua with eleven R.M.s and thirteen A.R.M.s; the entire Papuan civil service consisted of about 110 officers. ABL must have met a large number of these officers during his travels.[5]

An Excursion to the East and Another to the West

On his arrival in Papua, ABL called on Lieutenant-Governor Murray at Government House. After receiving ABL's letters of introduction and hearing about his research plans, Murray invited ABL to accompany him on a trip to the Western Division in about three weeks. While waiting for this trip to begin, Murray suggested ABL accompany him to the eastern part of the colony aboard the government's steamer *Merrie England*.[6] Murray was sending two of his officers (Massey-Baker[7] and Cardew) to Samarai and Buna to recruit carriers for an expedition up the Kikori River in the Western Division. While the two officers were recruiting carriers, ABL had a chance to visit some of the villages at Buna Bay and Gona. At Samarai, ABL met Frederick Ramsay (an Anglican priest), who agreed to collect a few specimens for him.

On their return to Port Moresby, ABL was honored with an invitation to stay at Government House as the guest of the lieutenant-governor. Previously he had stayed at Ryan's hotel, which many visitors to Port Moresby will know as the Papua Hotel.[8] Two days later the government expedition left for Goaribari Island, where a decade earlier Chalmers and Tompkins, two missionaries from the London Missionary Society, had been ambushed, killed, and eaten by the people of Dopima village.

Murray's tour of inspection to Goaribari and the recently established Kikori station was prompted by a government-sponsored expedition sent up the Kikori River to investigate some coal deposits. A prominent Papuan businessman named William Little had visited the Kikori in 1908 on the Mackay expedition when a coal seam was sighted (see Clune 1942a, 179–210). Three years later Little (1911) returned to the Kikori to investigate these deposits and discovered a new seam. Always keen to develop the colony's mineral resources, Murray sent Little back to the Kikori accompanied by A.R.M. Massey-Baker and Joseph Carne, the government geologist of New South Wales.

Accompanying ABL and the lieutenant-governor on the *Merrie England* were two other American visitors to Papua: Prof. and Mrs. William Patten of Dartmouth College. Patten, a noted biologist, was taking a year-long sabbatical. He had come to Papua specifically to look for a certain species of nautilus. After arriving at Goaribari, ABL and the Pattens were left to their own devices for several days to collect ethnological and zoological specimens as they wished. Here ABL collected 142 specimens (including 46 arrows), one of the largest collections he made from any community in Papua. The Pattens also collected ethnological specimens on Goaribari; of these, 190 specimens (including 117 arrows) found their way into the collections of the Hood Museum of Art at Dartmouth College.[9] Together, the Lewis and Patten collections represent one of the most important collections ever made among the Kerewa people.

After this visit to Goaribari, the Pattens proceeded to Java via Daru and Thursday Island. ABL and the lieutenant-governor stopped briefly in Daru and then proceeded on a tour of inspection up the Fly River in the ketch *Ada*. On their return to Daru, Murray returned to Port Moresby, while ABL stayed on for a few days to pack his specimens. He met virtually all the resident expatriates in Daru and bought specimens from most of them. He obtained collections from the traders L. Luff and Hughie Beach, from R.M. Wilfred N. Beaver, from A.R.M. Massey-Baker, and from the Reverend E. Baxter Riley of the London Missionary Society. Each of these men had considerable experience in various parts of the division and provided a selection of specimens from places ABL was not able to visit. As so often before, when ABL purchased collections from resident expatriates, he was rarely able to obtain any significant documentation aside perhaps from the name of the village or district where it was collected. One exception to this is a small collection of figures and masks from the Gaima district, obtained from E. B. Riley who, at ABL's request, wrote up some notes about these objects and their use in the *muguru* ceremonies in a letter to ABL (reproduced below).

Back to the Papuan Gulf

On his return to Port Moresby, Murray invited ABL to go with him once more into the Papuan Gulf. Murray left ABL and the *Merrie England* to visit the Lakekamu goldfield, which had been opened in 1909. ABL was taken as far as Kerema, where he left the government party. At Kerema and elsewhere in the Papuan Gulf, ABL visited the surrounding villages and was captivated by their enormous longhouses, which he at first refers to using the Papuan lingua franca (Police Motu) term *dubu,* later with the vernacular term *davi*. In nearly every village he visited he found one or more of these communal houses with its tall gable in front. Inside were cubicles for hearths around which were hung carved and painted ancestor boards, masks, and carved figures.

From Kerema he proceeded farther into the swampy country of the Purari Delta, where he spent nearly a month. Here ABL made several large collections in Maipua, Koriki, and Kaimari (Kaivari), as well as around Kerema. Once again ABL was living in the villages and traveling from place to place by dugout canoe.

Ironically, although the Purari Delta was one of the most remote parts of coastal Papua, he was seldom away from European officers, traders, prospectors, planters, and missionaries. Nearly every large village had a European trader or planter living nearby.[10] The London Missionary

Society had been active in the gulf for some time, and, of course, the resident magistrates were constantly visiting villages on their patrols.

Besides the traders, government officers, and missionaries, in 1912 while ABL was in the Gulf Division, the area was alive with prospectors and geologists looking for oil and other minerals. Government geologist E. R. Stanley was just beginning a major petroleum survey of the division. These initial patrols had been initiated after Lewis Lett discovered some oil vents up Kiri Creek a few months earlier. The possibility of profiting from the discovery of a commercially viable petroleum deposit seems to have encouraged a group of men who resided in the division to help Stanley with his surveys; these included Talbot, Hill, MacDonell, Cowley, and MacGowan, several of whom had also assisted Carne with his own petroleum investigations. The lure of mineral deposits thus made this a very busy time in the Papuan Gulf, and ABL's observations call into question long-standing stereotypes of the region as an extraordinarily remote, economic backwater. They also challenge recent characterizations of this coastal world as one where "contact with outsiders was sparse and sporadic in many areas well into the twentieth century" as a result of "politicoeconomic disinterest" (Knauft 1993, 28).

For ABL, all this activity made the region seem heavily worked over, especially compared to some of the regions he had visited in Kaiser Wilhelmsland.[11] Such intense activity, of course, meant that transportation was somewhat easier here in Papua than it had been in remote parts of the north coast of German New Guinea. But despite ABL's remarkable collection of ancestor boards, masks, drums, belts, and other items, the region appeared to him to be profoundly affected by European contact, a fact that would become obvious less than a decade later with the eruption of New Guinea's most famous cargo cult, the so-called Vailala madness (Williams 1923, 1977), in which villages destroyed most of their traditional masks plus ritual paraphernalia and even fell into fits of shaking in an (unsuccessful) attempt to bring modernity and modern goods—the cargo—to their village.

Port Moresby, Papua
July 21, 1912

My dear Simms:

I hope you will not think that I have forgotten you, but I have been wandering up and down in New Guinea, and it has not been easy to write. I received some little time ago your letters of May 5th and April 2nd and also that of Sept 28th, 1911, which had gone astray. It looks as if the Museum never would get a permanent abiding place. I had hoped that the new building would be completed before I got back, but now it looks as if it might not even be begun. I don't see how I can work if I should get back now.

Regarding shipments, I have sent three from British N.G., which may already have arrived, and one from Port Moresby will follow shortly. I have not yet heard whether three boxes, nos. 61, 62, and 63 sent from Sydney at the same time as the collections from Vila, N.H., and from New Caledonia, arrived safely. These three boxes are rather valuable, and I should be glad to know that they arrived safely. Box 63 had books and photos. The three together are worth at least $500, and should be traced if they have not turned up. I had them and their contents listed on the consular invoice sent in from Sydney.

I have been in British N.G. since the early part of February. It is not as interesting as German N.G., as the country has been longer settled, and also contains many more persons. The white population is estimated at about 1,000, and nearly every man is, or has been on the lookout for "curios." With very few exceptions, these have all been sent away to Australia or England, so there is little to be seen here.

Native things are high now; stone clubs bring from $5 to $20 or more. I have known $15.00 paid for a medium sized stone ax blade, chipped at that. Shell arm bands the natives themselves will buy at $20 to $50 apiece. Shell money is worth up to $5.00 a foot. Feather ornaments are also very valuable. Moreover, the government absolutely prohibits any white man to buy feathers of a bird of paradise from the natives. In some places the natives have fine feather head-dresses, but they will not part with them at any price. I have managed to get about 1,500 specimens, and have arranged for a few more to be collected and sent in later.

It is nearly midnight, and I must pack about 20 pots tomorrow, besides getting my baggage ready for the steamer, which arrives the following day. I expect to go from here to Java, and then return to Dutch N.G. for several months.

Very sincerely,
A. B. Lewis

P.S.—I found enclosed bill in one of the letters you sent me. If the book has arrived, I would be very much obliged if you would pay the bill, and explain the delay. I shall repay you when I get back.

You might also recommend the purchase of the book, the notice of which you sent me.

A. B. L.

Daru, Papua
June 4, 1912

Dr. A. B. Lewis
Port Moresby

Dear Sir,

Enclosed you will find receipt for the amount of your cheque, for which I thank you.

Re the wooden figures [Fig. 7.15]. They are objects of reverence and women are not allowed to see them. They play an important part in the muguru. This

<u>muguru</u> is really a religious ceremony. There are two different ceremonies, the sago <u>muguru</u> and the garden or yam <u>muguru</u>.

At the sago festival all the images are decorated with grass and different croton leaves, mud, red, white and black is painted on the figures. These are then placed in little cages made from the midrib of the sago palm. These cages or rather cotes are enclosed in cocoanut leaves and put on the top of bamboo piles in the sacred house. For any woman to see these means instant death, which would be caused by the evil spirit in the bush.

A wild pig is then caught. It must not be shot but taken alive. The pig is slain. The ceremony of killing is called <u>maruu</u>. The flesh of this pig is eaten by a certain number of the oldest women in the village. A portion is reserved for the sorcerer. When these have eaten to the full the remainder of the pig is thrown into the new sago garden, as an offering to the spirit which causes the sago to grow. The young sago trees are planted and the following words are uttered as each separate tree is planted: "Nabodi, Sabodi, nigoto pari arotoribo, nimo pai narodurumo." The translation is as follows: Nabodi Sabodi, you two plant this garden, we do not plant. Nabodi and Sabodi may be the names of the wooden figures. The natives differ so much in their attempts to explain these names that it is difficult to know what is really true.

The figure of the head is said to be the representative of the spirit which presides over the yam garden. When the yams are planted the same words are used, the natives turning their eyes towards the East when planting. The name of the head is Meauro [see Newton 1961, 43].

Re masks. These masks are used both at the <u>muguru</u> ceremonies when they are worn by dancers. They are also worn as a sign of mourning. If a man's wife dies he will wear a mask, also a woman for her husband or child. They also wear pigs tusks and other native ornaments in addition to the masks. The sorcerer has a large mask the grass often covering the whole of his body down to his feet. He looks a terrible object and frightens all the women and children. The masks from Gaima with the feathers in them are used simply as dancing ornaments [Fig. 7.15]. The men often carry the head of some near relative under their arm whilst dancing.

I trust this is what you wanted, if not kindly let me know and I will try to supply you with any information you require.

> With kind regards,
> Yours sincerely,
> E. Baxter Riley

I do not know any thing about the Goaribari masks. The above remarks apply to Gaima and the delta of the Fly River.

Fig. 7.1. *Semesi* masks at dance, Kerema, Papuan Gulf. A-37933 (1095).

Papua

||||||||||||||||||||||||||||||||||||||||||||||||||||||||||||||||||||||||||||||||||||||||||||||||||||||||||||||||||||||||||||||||||||

Monday, Dec. 25, 1911   Arrived in Sydney from German New Guinea, and stayed there till Feb. 9 [1912] when left on steamer for British N.G. Stopped Feb. 16 at Cairns, where visited the Barron falls, and got a few postcards of same, which sent to my name at Museum. Left at 3 P.M. and arrived at Port Moresby on Feb. 18 about 6 P.M.

Monday, Feb. 19, 1912   Visited the native villages with Mr. Bell. Miss Hall, the African traveler, also went along.[1] Spent some time in village, and took some pictures. Also visited the Missionary, Mr. Lawrence, the head of the London Mission.

There are two villages near together, built on piles over the sea, but so one can reach the platforms of the front row of houses from the shore. Very few pots being made. Natives have a few wood bowls, nets of various kinds. Saw some bark cloth, painted, but said to be made elsewhere. Many houses show European influence, some with tin roofs.

The natives seem rather more slender, and smaller than most of the coast natives of German N.G. The skin is also often a lighter (yellowish brown) color than ever seen there. Some also have straight hair, and one boy's hair was irregularly streaked with light brown.

Settled at hotel (Ryan's) in afternoon, Mr. Bell lending me boys to get my things ashore.

Tuesday, Feb. 20   Visited Governor Murray in afternoon.

Wednesday, Feb. 21   Visited Mr. Lawrence in afternoon.

Thursday, Feb. 22   Saw several people and discussed plans for future.

Friday, Feb. 23   Developed negatives.

Saturday, Feb. 24   In afternoon took walk with Mr. Ross (postmaster) to see run of bower-bird. It was only about a foot long, and ornamented with some kind of green berry in branches. Tried to get picture with Kodak.

---

1. Mary Hall (1914) described this voyage from Australia to Port Moresby, as well as the excursion to Hanuabada and Elevala villages together with ABL, Leslie Bell, and Dr. Hamilton.

Fig. 7.2. "Port Moresby, looking north from Ryan's hotel, showing native village (Hanobada) and mission station on other side of bay." A-37125 (930).

Fig. 7.3. "Port Moresby, looking south from Ryan's hotel." A-37127 (931).

Fig. 7.4. "Elevala from hill, Port Moresby." A-37884 (958).

Monday, Feb. 26 Visited villages and took number of photos.

Tuesday, Feb. 27 Developed photos.

Wednesday, Feb. 28 Got ready to leave next morning on the government boat *(Merrie England)* for a trip to the east end of N.G., as the Lieutenant-Governor (Judge Murray) had kindly invited me to go along. They were going to try to get boys for carriers for the coal expedition (with Mr. Carne, gov. geologist of N.S.W.). After returning from the east they were going up to the Papuan Gulf, and here I also wished to go.

Thursday, Feb. 29 Left at 10 A.M. and stopped a little after lunch at Rigo, where took some photos (Kodak) and got Mr. English to agree to try and get me specimens. The native village here was at least 1,000 ft. out in the sea.

Fig. 7.5. "Canoe on beach at Samarai." A-38039 (142f).

Friday, March 1–Saturday, March 2   On way to Samarai.

Sunday, March 3   At Samarai.

Monday, March 4   Back to _____, to pick up one of the officials who had been instructed to try to get some carriers.

Tuesday, March 5   In morning arrived at Samarai again. Visited Mr. Ramsay and saw collection he had. Stone implements valued at £300. He also agreed to try and get me some specimens. Gave him £10 for this purpose. Left for Buna, a government station some 40 miles south of Mambare river in evening.

Thursday, March 7   Arrived in evening at Buna.

Friday, March 8   In morning Mr. Cardew was going in launch a few miles up the coast to try to get some more carriers, and I went with him. After going a few miles we landed, and then walked about 10 miles along the coast to Gona, where we again took the launch and returned. (The launch could not get in shore between.) Passed through several villages on way, and had to wade across a number of small creeks and small rivers.
  The villages were rather small. Houses also small, floor about 3 ft. high,

Fig. 7.6. "Group welcoming boy who has been away three years, Gona. He is reclining in center, and the women are crying around him. They kept this up for two hours." A-37334 (965).

with roof and sides of cocoanut leaf mats. Took about 30 photos.[2] Natives did not have much, a few thick heavy pots, a few crude wood bowls. Painted bark loin cloths were worn by men, also a wider piece, like a lava-lava by women. At Gona a dance was just over, so many men had feather headdresses and ornaments on (see photo). Got several plain and slightly barbed wooden spears. Got back to *Merrie England* toward dark.

Saturday, March 9 Left early in morning and arrived at Samarai on Sunday, March 10.

Monday, March 11 Left about noon for Pt. Moresby, where arrived in morning.

Wednesday, March 13 Lieut.-Gov. Murray asked me to stop at government house, so stayed on shore while in Port. Spent most of Wed. and Thursday getting ready things for trip to west with *Merrie England*.

Friday, March 15 Left Pt. Moresby about 10 A.M. for Kerama and Goari Bari (near mouth of Kiori river[3]). On board had also Prof. Wm. Patten, of Dartmouth College, and Mrs. Patten, who were in S. Seas looking for zoological material, esp. young pearly Nautilus. Prof. Patten had a year off, and was on his way to Java.

Saturday, March 16 Arrived at Kerama in afternoon, and went ashore (about 4 P.M.) at gov. station. Nicely situated on hill. This place very hard to

2. Thirty of these thirty-one photos survive.
3. He means the Kikori.

Fig. 7.7. "Men ornamented for dancing, Gona." Both men wear painted bark cloth and many ornaments. A-37340 (971).

get to in S.E. season, owing to surf on bar. Here we were to pick up Mr. Little, the leader of the coal expedition, and Mr. [Carne], geologist from N.S.W., and take them on to Goari Bari.

I got a guide at station, and went down to village on beach. Here saw several masks and carvings, but unfortunately had no trade with which to buy. I got only two small masks, that one native brought up to house. The masks most common, quite a number of which they were making at the time, were of frame work covered with painted bark cloth, about 5 ft. by 2, flat, with crocodile (?) head projecting from front [Fig. 7.1]. Left a letter at the station for Mr. Max Assmann, to see if he could not get some for me, with Mr. Henderson (G. Magistrate).

Got out to vessel about 8 P.M., just shortly before squall came up.

Fig. 7.8. Pile of skulls and carved figure at Peltumula, Goaribari. A-37223 (1004).

Houses here large, esp. the men's house where masks kept. Entrance covered (compare some on north coast).

Sunday, March 17   Arrived in evening at Goari Bari.

Monday, March 18   The governor with launch and 3 boats in tow left in morning for gov. station up the Kiori river, from where they were to see the coal hunting expedition safely off. This consisted of 3 white men (Little, Baker,[4] Carne), and about 35 carriers. They expected to be gone about 6 weeks.

The governor said we (Mr. & Mrs. Patten and myself) could have the *Nivani*, a motor (broken) schooner, with her crew and small dinghy, to visit native villages near where we were anchored. There were very few native villages up river, and none near new gov. station, so I did not go up, but spent next few days visiting villages near by.

Monday afternoon went in boat to Dopima.

---

4. Massey-Baker.

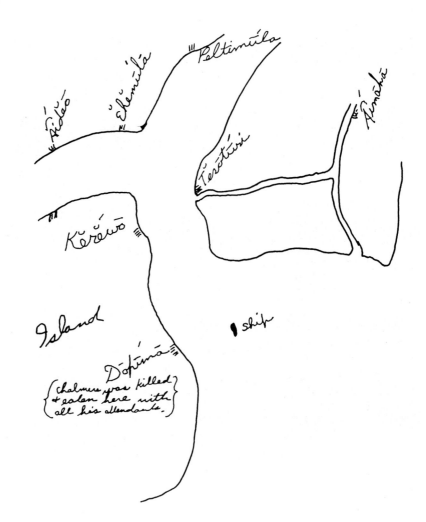

Fig. 7.9. "Carved and painted board (from curved outer part of palm trunk) on which are hung bones and skulls of various animals (crocodile, fish, hornbill, etc.), Goari Bari. This hung on wall of men's house just inside door." 142712 (7843). A-112269.

460

Tuesday, March 19 Up river to Peltūmula, left at 9, got there at 12. Had to go up with tide, and come back with same, as currents very strong. Stopped at Kerewo on way down.

Wednesday, March 20 Went to Ehemula and Terōtūri. Wed. evening gov. Murray returned in whale boat, but left launch and other boats to take expedition 1 day's journey up river to landing place from whence they started on their march. Launch got back Friday evening.

Thursday, March 21 Went with gov. to Aímāhā in whale boat. This the most interesting village visited, but had very little time to buy things.

Friday, March 22 Visited Dopima again, but did not get much.

These villages consist as a rule of one or more long men's houses, with several smaller women's houses. The men's houses may be from 200 to 400 ft. long, with passage way down center, door at each end, and doors at intervals on sides. On piles about 5 ft. high. The level of the ground is very little above high tide. The houses are 20–25 ft. wide, or sometimes even more. The central passage as much as ten feet wide, while the sides are divided into compartments for the different men. Sometimes there are some sticks or poles between, but often nothing. Each man has his sleeping mat and pillow

Fig. 7.10. "Prof. Patten at Dopima." A-37704 (1020).

Fig. 7.11. "Mrs. Prof. Patten on shore at Dopima." A-37240 (998).

Fig. 7.12. Two boys from Dopima. A-37627 (997). Professor Patten also took a photo of these two boys at the same time and from virtually the same spot.

(a crude stick, as a rule), and various possessions hung up in baskets, bags or bark bundles. There is also often, esp. in the women's houses a sort of loft or platform under the roof over the compartment, where fire wood, food, and various other things are kept. The women's houses, tho smaller, are built on much the same plan, and apparently contain a number of families. At the side the eaves are about 4 ft. above the floor, while the comb is 8–12 ft., varying with the size of house. The floor is fairly close, of planks of rind of palm, same as on north coast.

In men's houses were seen several shrines (?) of skulls [see Fig. 7.8]. At the back was a carved board representing head and body of man, and in front of this, on a sort of table about 3 ft. high, were piled from 10 to 50 skulls. These were usually carved, with lower jaw bound on with rattan, artificial nose (often long) and more or less modeled about face. A rattan (with loop at end) about 1½–2 ft. long was attached, the loop of which was hooked over a part of the image.

In one house I saw as many as 5 of these piles of skulls. In the men's houses were also seen bows (palm wood, *no* bamboo) and arrows, a few bags, baskets and fishnets. Also at a few of the side entrances were small boards (images) with fish and bird skulls attached. A few carved boards (*gōpe*) were set up along the wall or partition, or on front of house outside door.

A few wooden bowls were seen, but they were nearly all broken. A few stone axes, which are said to come down the river from the interior. Got several woven rattan masks of different kinds, bark belts (narrow), feather ornaments, clothing, etc.

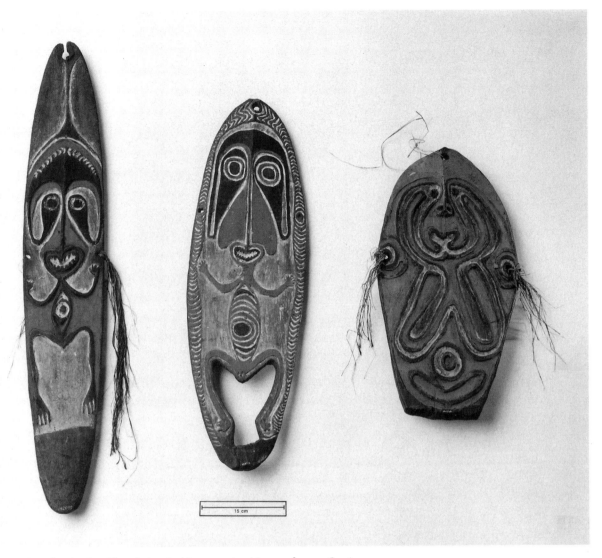

Fig. 7.13. "Carved and painted boards *(gope)* with conventional human figures, Goari Bari," 142695 (7871), 142710 (8020), 142709 (7874). A-112188.

Saturday, March 23   Left in morning for Daru.

Sunday, March 24   Arrived [Daru] in forenoon. Here went ashore, and stopped with Mr. Walter Maidment.

Tuesday, March 26   Started with Mr. Murray in *Ada* for a trip up the Fly river.

Wednesday, March 27   Stopped at Sui, nearly opposite Parama Isl. Here all natives wear clothes, and saw nothing of interest. In evening stopped near Mībū, where Mr. Cowling lived up a very muddy creek.

Sailed all night, and in forenoon of Thursday stopped at Tirio, above Kiwai Island.

Fig. 7.14. Ornaments from Goaribari: cassowary-feather headdress, cowries in center, 142686 (7835); small string bags decorated with coix seeds, usually worn on breast by men for their small possessions, 142683 (7821), 142680 (7839). A-112169.

Friday, March 29   Went up river in night to Sapori, above which there are no villages for nearly 100 miles. Coming down stopped at Bārāmura, up a creek. Then anchored off Mādīrī (new plantation of _____ Co.[5]).

Saturday, March 30   Got away about 10 A.M. and started for Gaima, on opposite side of river, but as tide was against us, and no wind, decided to give it up, and return to Daru.

There are very few villages on lower Fly river, and these not large. The houses are much the same as at Goari Bari, but in men's house each apartment has a door (on side) of its own, making a row of doors along the side of house. No masks or house boards seen. Carved board used on bow of canoe. Bows here of bamboo. Very few things to be gotten.

Tides in river 6–8 ft. and approaches to villages at low tide very bad and muddy.

No wood dishes or pots seen. All things seemed very crude.

Sago making was seen at Goari Bari. Both here and on Fly hammer was a hollowed stick. Washed in woven bag fastened in sago leaf stem.

Sago usually cooked in sago or nipa leaf. The meal is put in leaf, which is bent over and pinned together and the sago then roasted over fire.

Pots were rare in old times, but some were traded this far. Saw some at Goari Bari.

Sunday, March 31   Got to Daru late in evening.

Monday, April 1   Got things ashore. Arranged to get boxes of Rev. E. B. Riley, and pack at the resident Magistrate's (Wilfred Beaver) house, or underneath it. Stopped at house of Walter Maidment, who was a carpenter, and agreed to make boxes for me.

Tuesday, April 2–Friday, April 5   Developed negatives and packed boxes, nos. 167–173. Put negatives in box 169 (nos. 965–1034). Boxes were left with Mr. Beaver to be forwarded later to Thursday Island.

---

5. He probably means Papuan Industries, an industrial mission established in Papua in 1904.

Fig. 7.15. From east of the Fly River. Turama River: bone dagger with coix seeds, 142754 (8039) from Beaver. Bamu River: carved wooden heads on handles, used during the *muguru* or initiation ceremony, 142741 (8025), 142742 (8023), both from Beach; "carved wood figure (from Gaima) used in *muguru* ceremonies, in connection with the planting of sago; at these ceremonies the images are painted and ornamented with grass and colored leaves and placed in little cages," 142784 (8171), from Rev. E. B. Riley; "carved and painted board, similar to those found further east and probably has much the same meaning," 142749 (8149). Girara district: "mask or head ornament of light soft wood, with feathers around edge," 142779 (8105), "circular painted board with shell in center," 142764 (8099), both from Massey-Baker; "painted stick set up at entrance to the village when a man dies," 142776 (8119), from Beaver. A-112367.

Saturday, April 6 Left in *Mindoro* (B.P.'s coastal boat) for Port Moresby, where arrived Sunday evening.

Monday, April 8 Visited Governor, and he invited me to go on *Merrie England* up into Gulf. Spent most of day with Mr. Nicholls,[6] the police master, who came up on *Matunga* from Sydney with me.

Tuesday, April 9–Wednesday, April 10 Not much to do but lay in supplies, and get ready for trip to Gulf.

Thursday, April 11 Left in evening by *Merrie England*.

Friday, April 12 Arrived in morning at Yule Island. Went ashore with Governor, Mr. Ian _____, Mr. Hen____, and Mr. Stanley (gov. geologist). Visited Gov. station first, and then the mission. This is the head station of

6. ABL spelled his name Nicols.

465

Fig. 7.16. Drums from the Western Division, painted with red ochre and with lizard-skin heads, except as noted: (back) hide drumhead, Buji, 142965 (8013), from Beach at Daru; Buji hinterland, 142971 (8058), from Massey-Baker at Daru; blue paint is used in part of design, 142972 (8018), from Beach; Buji, 142967 (8017), from Beach; (front) white paint, Dembeli village near Dutch border, 142969 (8012), from Beach; Tirio, Fly River, 142954 (7916), ABL; Tugeri people, Buji hinterland, 142957 (8009), from Luff at Daru. A-112268.

Catholic Mission, and quite a large place, with many buildings. One of the fathers (Mr. _____ Van _____)[7] promised to try to get me some things. His station is about 25 miles in interior.

Left about 11 A.M. and in evening arrived off the mouth of the Lakekamu river.

Saturday, April 13   Governor and gov. secretary, with Mr. Bensted (gov. store keeper) left with launch and whale boat in tow about 6:30 for Lakekamu. We then left for Kerema, where arrived about 10 A.M. Spent day

7. Probably Edward van Goethem, stationed at Veifa'a, but possibly Henri van Neck, who was based at Vanamai.

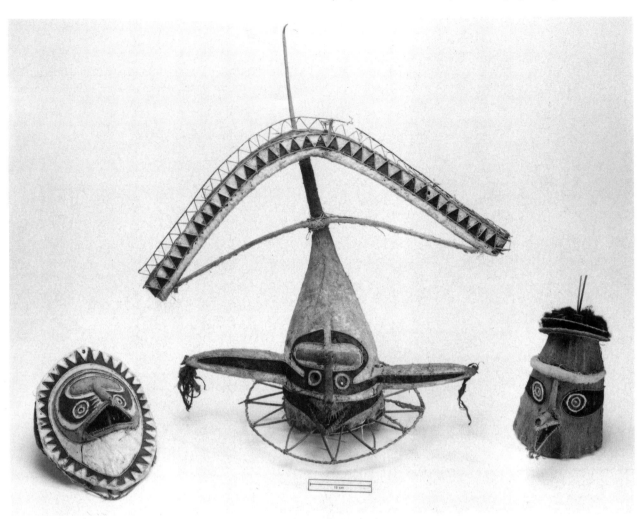

Fig. 7.17. Bark-cloth masks from Papuan Gulf: *eharo* mask, Semeni village, Kerema, 142108 (8304); *eharo* mask, Opau district, 142115 (8310); *imunu* mask, Maipua, Purari Delta (hair at top; corresponds to the *kowabi* of Orokolo), 142439 (8427). A-112267.

in getting things ashore, as only our boat from steamer. This was loaded and sent ashore, and on return also brought station boat out, so that all things were ashore by night. Anchored far out, for fear of S.E. blow.

Monday, April 15   Arranged my things. In afternoon visited village near station, Kalaaita (or Cōrāaíta). Saw a number of very large masks *(sēwési)* in process of manufacture.

Tuesday, April 16   Went up a river to west of station to Ōpaú, a general term for several villages scattered along a clear flowing creek, which rose in hills not far behind. Rowed up river for about 2 hrs. and then landed and walked nearly an hour to first village (Puōlāfīlū). Vīnākīna about 15 minutes higher, and Hāvibūhu 5 min. further, on opposite side of creek. The *dōbus,* or men's houses, were of fair size (see photos). Got several masks *(ēhārō)* here, but mostly in dilapidated condition.

Wednesday, April 17   Went in boat to Wārīpī, opposite Kerema on coast. Spent the day there, and got quite a number of things. Developed photos morning.

467

Thursday, April 18 Went to Mēī (Mai) about a mile further along coast from Warípi.

Friday, April 19 Went up river to Uripi, a rather poor village (photos) on small hill overlooking river (film photo [lost]). Here took several photos, but got very few specimens.

Saturday, April 20 Developed photos and labeled specimens.

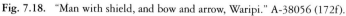

Fig. 7.18. "Man with shield, and bow and arrow, Waripi." A-38056 (172f).

All villages around Kerema station much the same. Saw bows and arrows, very few spears, a few shields (see photo with man with shield shooting bow). Many pots from Port Moresby region, wood bowls very rare, if any. Knitted bags made in some of villages, but not numerous.

In men's house in several villages they were making the large *sewesi* masks for a future festival, which they said would not come off for nearly a year yet. Some of these masks were at least 15 ft. high, of frame (flat) covered with bark, on which small strips are sewn, forming patterns. They are then painted in various colors. The figure of head of some animal (usually crocodile) is fastened on in front. This is set over head, and a sort of frame covered with split young sago leaves is used to cover body. Bands of similar material are fastened above ankles.

A few planks (set up as mementos of the departed) were seen in the *dóbu*s, esp. at Mei, but they refused to part with most of them. A sort of fish trap, a large round dip net, and a portable woven fish fence, set in tidal inlets at high tide, so as to enclose fish when tide ran out ([got] photo of one in village) were common in villages. Fish were also caught with a line fastened to one end of painted wood float. There is a double noose at end of line.

Sago is also made in quantities being strained through cocoanut fibre (see photos). The chief way of cooking sago is roasting on fire, either in chunks, wrapped up in long palm leaf, or in bamboos (see photo).

Monday, April 22   Left in morning in whale boat for Vailala river. Mr. J. P. F. Hennelly (Resident Magistrate at Kerema) and E. R. Stanley (gov. geologist) were leaving on a trip to the west, and I took the opportunity to go that way also. Mr. Stanley was going to explore the newly discovered oil field on the Vailala, and Mr. Hennelly to help Mr. Stanley, and also to visit the Purari on official business because of some trouble reported from that region. Owing to the heavy load we had, we landed at Mai, and got carriers for a part of our stuff. It was well we did, for it was rough over the bar, and the boat (a new one) did not prove a very good sea boat.

Got to Vailala about 5:30 and ran in over the bar safely, only shipping a little water. Here landed and stopped in the government rest house, one of which is found at intervals all along coast. In evening visited the local trader, Mr. [S. G.] MacDonell.[8] Here met Mr. C. F. Talbot, manager of British New G. Co. for this region; also R. Hill.

Tuesday, April 23   As Mr. Stanley was not very well decided to wait till next day. Mr. Hennelly had also to wait for carriers, which arrived shortly before noon. The pay here is 3 sticks of tobacco per day, or two sticks between villages if not over ½ day. The natives will seldom carry beyond the nearest village.

Visited the village near rest house. Quite a large village (estimated at 1,600). In *dúbu*s many unfinished *hevéhi* masks, as at Kerema, and a few carved planks. Saw also 3 carved figures, crude, about 3 ft. high. They would not sell them nor most of the planks. Only got 4 and had to pay 4 shillings for best. Culture same, and language nearly same, as at Kerema.

Wednesday, April 24   Left in morning for Kiri, 4 to 5 hrs. up river, with Mr. Stanley, Talbot and Hill, who were going about a day's journey further

---

8. ABL spelled his name McDonald, but this is almost certainly S. G. MacDonell, a trader who lived for some years at Orokolo.

Fig. 7.19. "Hennelly (Resident Magistrate, Gulf Division), Henderson (Patrol Officer), and Stanley (Government Geologist) at Kerema." A-37717 (1092).

up to Akaúda to look at an oil outflow. Mōrō, the son of the chief of the Kiri villages, had promised, through Mr. MacDonell, to look after me while there.

We landed at the mouth of Kiri creek, where the Kiri people had a few garden houses, and some of them were stopping. These and Móro got my things ashore, and into the gov. rest house, one of which was at this place. Then Moro got some carriers, and all my things were taken about 1½ mile up the creek to the house, on a new plantation which had just been started,

Fig. 7.20. "Prisoners at Kerema." A-37733 (1087).

Fig. 7.21. "Carved planks set up in men's houses, in which protecting spirits dwell, Vailala," 142124 (8326); 142127 (8325). A-112278.

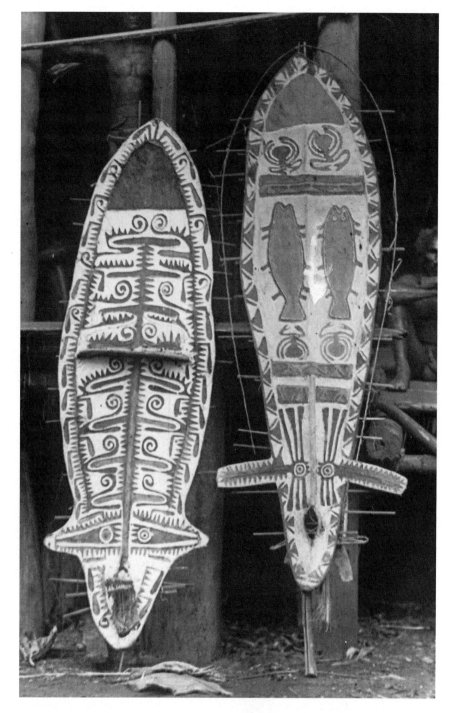

Fig. 7.22. *"Semesi* masks, Kiri."
A-37915 (1104).

the white men being absent at the time.[9] Here the native care-taker opened the house while the house boys got my meals. Moro also stayed to interpret and look after me. Watermelons were plenty in the new plantations, but not very good. For every meal had pumpkin and sweet potato.

Thursday, April 25   Left next morning with Moro, Ewari (who promised to go with me for 2–3 weeks, but later backed out, as his family ob-

9. This white man was Lewis Lett, the noted Papuan writer.

Fig. 7.23. "Boys with some purchases, Kiri." A-37936 (1111).

jected) and others for the Kiri villages, 3 of which I visited, about half hr. from the house, and ¼ hr. from each other. Much like Vailala. Here saw several barks of *hevehe* masks, and got 3 (see also photo) also one curious mask with watering pot on top, made by boy returned from Port Moresby, (see photo).

The villages visited were Ōpā, Āpūrādīā, and Idīkāhū. Spent most of day here, but did not get very many things, some shields, planks, charms (of young cocoanuts, these are not made west of Orokola), fighting sticks (see photo). Bows and arrows common, but most made in bush, esp. the good bows. The people have also a few spears. No wood dishes. All the things were brought back to house.

Friday, April 26 Got a canoe to take specimens to Vailala, care Mr. MacDonell, while I went to river bank with luggage, and waited for boat, which came along about noon, on return to Vailala, where arrived about dark.

Fig. 7.24. "Masked boy out in village, Vailala." A-37380 (1126).

Saturday, April 27 In forenoon visited village near Vailala, passing the place where they were working sago on the way. Here the sago was beaten with sticks while washing (see photos). At village the natives were having a dance with *kowābe* masks, but the masks were all in house at that time, tho two went out while I was there (see photos). These masks they would not

Fig. 7.25. "Women and girls, three with ornaments ready for marriage, Orokolo." A-37384 (1138).

sell, and said that after ceremonies were over (in month or more) they were all taken to house in bush and left there.

In afternoon labeled and packed some of my things.

Sunday, April 28 Packed up and went up beach to Orokōla, where stopped at Mr. Talbot's place.

Monday, April 29 Mr. Talbot got a boy (Mārkō) to go with me for the next 2 or 3 weeks; also a cook boy who could not speak English. Said he had been cook at mission. Visited number of men's houses with Márko, but they would not sell their good things. In afternoon moved to Mr. Hay's place, as Stanley and Talbot left for Moru.

Tuesday, April 30 Visited Erīhaúva about a mile beyond Orokóla and got a few more things. In afternoon tried again to buy some of the good planks and carved figures in Orokola, but all refused to sell, as they said they were made by their fathers, who were now dead, and no one now could make

Fig. 7.26. "Interior of men's house, Orokolo." A-37310 (1131).

475

so good ones. One figure esp. had the best modeled face I had seen in New Guinea.

Wednesday, May 1   Developed photos in morning. Took some in afternoon of interiors, showing carved boards, and wood figures.

Thursday, May 2   Developed plates.

Friday, May 3   Marko came in morning with about 18 others from Erehavo, to carry my things to Nomo. Got off about 10, and stopped at Erehavo till 12:30 to wait for low tide to cross river. Arrived at Nomo in about 1 hr. from Erehavo. Here was a station of B.N.G. Co., and found Mr. Sullivan and _____ at place. Stayed here over night. Both men had formerly been in W. Africa (Liberia, Sierra Leone, and Gold Coast) and regarded it as much better in all ways, than New Guinea.

Saturday, May 4   Rained part of forenoon, and most of preceding night. Mr. Talbot returned in morning, the launch *Rambler* having returned from up river. She left about noon, and with her the 3 men who had been at the station. All were sick of N. Guinea, and wanted to leave.

Marko came about noon, and reported that canoe he was to get for me to go round Delta in (his own) was too old and leaked. So he said he would go to Maipūa, and bring canoe with paddlers, from there, and would return next day. Gave him 15 sticks of tobacco for traveling expenses, etc. Developed films in afternoon.

Sunday, May 5   Rained most of night and stormy, with heavy rain during the day.

Monday, May 6   Rained all forenoon. About 1:30 Marko returned from Maipúa with big canoe and crew, and I got my things together and off about 2. He certainly brought crew enough, for with 18 paddlers in canoe, 8 others had to return in another canoe, as there was no room for them with all my stuff, myself, Marko, and old Mama, the chief of Nomo and part of Erehavo, who had great influence in all this region, and went along to look after me. On starting, my cook (Mārūpi) said he was sick, so paid him off, and one of crew (Awaí) was installed as cook, and did very well for rest of trip. Trip to Maipua took about 3 hours, and we crossed two large rivers near their mouths, narrow channels connecting the different larger branches of the Purari. These were usually lined with Nipa and Mangrove (see photos).

On reaching Maipua stopped at the B.N.G. Co.'s house. They have rest houses in all the big villages of the delta, so with one exception (Ukiravi), I always stopped at these houses. Was welcomed by a crowd of natives, but did not go out into village.

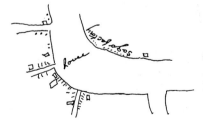

Tuesday, May 7   Spent day at Maipua. In forenoon visited *dubu*s (here called *dāvi*), took photos, and purchased specimens. Maipua is spread out along the banks of a branch of the river and up several small creeks, down one of which we came on our arrival at the village.

The population is supposed to be about 2,000. There were several men's houses *(dávi),* and a great number of smaller houses for the women and children, tho the men often stay there too. The *davi* have no front (see photo) and the interior is divided into a great number of sections, each allotted to certain men, and having on the partition the *kōhe* (carved board)

Fig. 7.27. "View of last *davi,* with other houses, from across river, Maipua." A-37793 (1151).

belonging to these. In each section was a fire place, drying platform, mats, etc., for the occupants.

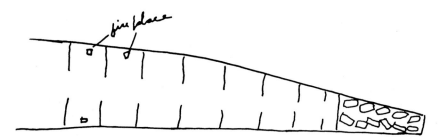

At the rear was a section curtained off for the sacred woven figures *(Kaiímenu),* which no woman or uninitiated man is allowed to see. The partitions between the sections are 3 to 4 ft. high, and on these are hung the carved boards *(kóhe).* One man may own several of these, which at his death descend to his son. They absolutely refused to sell any in the *davi,* but brought me new ones, and some old ones, from the private houses. They said that if those in the *davi* were sold, the *Kaiímenu* would make them die. Could not find that the designs represent anyone or thing in particular (main design a person). They were set up or consecrated in connection with certain

477

Fig. 7.28. "View up creek, from bridge over creek, Maipua." A-37817 (1145).

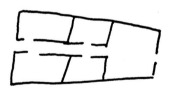

ceremonies and feasting, and the whole was supposed to give success in war, or hunts, or good harvests, etc.

The women's houses were occupied by more than one family as a rule, and divided into several small rooms. One I was in was as follows: The separate rooms were each entered by a small opening, about 2 ft. wide by 3 high; otherwise completely enclosed, and quite small and dark; filled up with family possessions—mats, baskets, bags, nets, reserve food, etc. All the houses decrease in height and width from front to rear (see photos).

The creeks were crossed by pole bridges, and the pathways were of the same material, or logs, as considerable part of the village area on river was more or less under water at high tide.

All the delta villages manufacture much sago, which at Maipua was worked chiefly on the other side of the river. The sago logs were cut into sections 4 to 10 ft. long, and floated down to this place, and drawn ashore or lashed to stakes. The woman washed out the sago, filled her basket, and took it to her washing trough near by, and washed it. Then pounded out some more, etc. When first put in the trough it was pounded with a stick (as at Vailala). The straining was done through a woven basket, as at Goari Bari, and differing from Orokolo and east, where fibre from base of cocoanut leaf used. There must have been 50 to 70 of these washing troughs along the bank of the river.

Wednesday, May 8 Left early, (about 7) for Kaivari (or Kaimari) on west side of delta, crossing three rather large branches of rivers on way, the first being the Purari proper. Along the channel between this and the next branch is the mission station of Mr. Holmes (now absent). Arrived at Kaivari about 2:30, and after unloading at house, went to nearest *davi* to photograph and buy a few specimens. Language and culture here as at Maipua.

Thursday, May 9 In morning bought a few more things, and about 10 left for Ukiravi (or Ukirābi), the first of the Kōrīkī villages. This was somewhat to the east, and further up in the delta. The mangrove and nipa palm gradually gave way to forest trees, sago swamps, and later many cocoanuts, particularly the channel (see photo) just before reaching Ukirávi. Here we put up in a *davi*, as the rest house was in bad condition. I occupied the outer section, just back of the front screen (this consisted of split and dried sago leaves hung from a pole about 5 ft. high, extending across the whole front of the *davi*). In some other *davi*s there was a sloping screen of cocoanut mats set up in front.

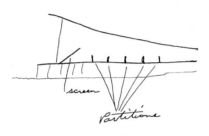

Friday, May 10 Loaded up in morning, and visited another *davi*, but did not get much. Then left for Korepenaiu, which was only about an hour away,

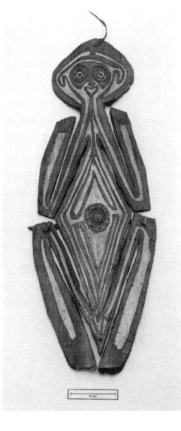

Fig. 7.29. "Carved and painted *a-a* on base of palm leaf, Koriki, Purari Delta," 142428 (8635). A-112124.

Fig. 7.30. "Interior of *davi*, Kaivari." A-37162 (1163).

479

Fig. 7.31. "Interior of *davi,* Kaivari." A-37815 (1159).

Fig. 7.32. "Looking down creek toward river, Ukiravi." A-37165 (1166).

on the next large branch, and reached by a narrow channel. This passed for a considerable distance through pandanus swamp (see photo). Did not stop long at Korepenaiu, as place small, but visited *davi*, and bought a few things. Then we went on to Kairuo, passing up the branch of river to where it united with (or separated from) another branch, down which we passed to Kairuo. The banks of the river here were higher than lower down, and cocoanuts, sago, and large forest trees lined the banks.

Reached Kairuo about 3 P.M. and after unloading, visited two *davi*s, and bought a few things.

Saturday, May 11   In morning did a rushing business in stone axes with fish-hooks (2–5 apiece). Also got some sticks, said to be spears, tho not like any others I had seen.

About 9 all things were loaded up, and we were off to Maipua. First down the river, then by narrow channel to next branch to east, then down to near mouth, and across to Maipua, where arrived about 3 P.M. Here unloaded and listed all my specimens.

Sunday, May 12   Loaded up all my stuff (part in a second canoe), including what I had left at Maipua (all purchased there on first visit). This had been left at the rest-house in charge of the chief on whose land the house stood, and to him I had to give a present (tobacco & cloth). Reached Nomo about 1:30, where landed all things at B.N.G. Co's place (Mr. Charles Talbot, manager).

On the way the boys (had 16 canoe boys for whole trip) caught an eel. They saw it go in hole in mud at side of channel. The entrance was enlarged so one could look down hole a little, then our man with bow and arrow watched at entrance, while one or two more drove down sticks in mud 3–5 ft. deep at 4–8 ft. distance, working round, nearer to entrance, till the eel appeared at entrance, and was promptly shot with arrow by man watching. Then they dug down and caught him with their hands.

Monday, May 13   Developed 2 doz. plates and 2 rolls films. In afternoon took some photos of women fishing in creek in front of house. There must have been 60–80 women and children, nearly all with nets, some triangular, some circular. Some stationed themselves at intervals along creek with nets in water, while others worked down towards them. Some fine fish were caught. The boys ran around with the conical traps for small fish and crabs.

Figs. 7.33 and 7.34.   "Fishing at Nomo." A-37873 (1185), A-37871 (1188).

Tuesday, May 14   Developed photos.

Wednesday, May 15   Labeled photos and packed up specimens.

Thursday, May 16   Wrote up lists and notes.

Friday, May 17–Saturday, May 25   Could do little but wait for a boat, as did not know when one might call. Stormy nearly all the time, and very little sunshine. Often rained during the day, and heavy rain at night. The S.E. [season] is undoubtedly the rainy season in this region.

Visited the small village Nomo (Orokolo people) near the B.N.G. Co's house, where I am staying, and took some photos, of making nets, etc. The string for nets is made of bark (Hibiscus ?) of a large-leaved tree common on the beach. The outer bark is stripped from the bast, and this is put to soak in the lagoon for a month, when taken out, washed and dried, and is ready for use. The thin layer of bast is carefully split into narrow strips. Two of these are taken, and with a movement of the hand one way they are twisted (on the thigh), and with the movement the other way are twisted together into thread. The women use two kinds of nets here, a circular, from 4½ to 8 ft. in diameter, and a triangular, fastened to two poles, with a cross piece for a handle to lift with, and crossed below to rest on the thigh, to assist in raising. Both kinds are netted with a much closer mesh at the center pocket or bottom than at the edges.

The channel opening to the sea below Nomo runs up the coast nearly to Ereava, and is much used for fishing, sometimes 100–300 women and children fishing at once, some driving the fish down, and others stationed below across the channel in second places, gradually working down stream and driving into each other's nets. (See photos.)

The people from Nomo to Cape Possession (except two small villages) all speak dialects of the same language. The same or related languages are also spoken at Kiri, up the Vailala for at least 60 miles, and even on the Purari above the delta. The delta people, however, speak an entirely different language, related to the languages further west. Goari Bari is not so very different from Baimuru, and this in turn quite similar to Maipua. It would

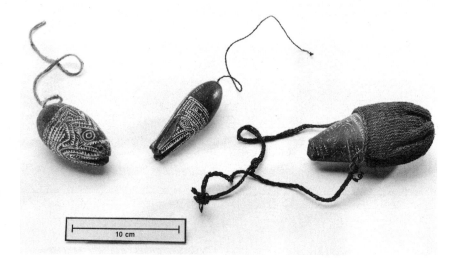

Fig. 7.35. Charms made of small coconut, Orokolo: 142183 (8381), 142184 (8380); "charm in a small tightly woven string bag in which such charms are often carried. The bag is hung about the neck." 142189 (8382). A-112202.

Fig. 7.36. Carved objects from the Papuan Gulf: carved figure *(idikape)* of palm wood, Kaivari ("The owner kept this very carefully wrapped up, and valued it highly."), 142431 (8804); bull-roarer, Maipua, 142365 (8448); painted wood image, 142726 (8021) (from Beach, Daru); wooden comb, Kaivari, 142445 (8687); coconut charm, Orokolo, 142186 (8377). A-112201.

seem that the delta people are a relatively recent incursion from the west, who have driven out the Orokolo people. These in their turn, moving east, have driven out the earlier inhabitants, of which the two villages mentioned are remnants.

The customs of these two groups are also quite different. The western are cannibals and head-hunters. In Maipua (less at Kaimari), they use somewhat similar masks to the Orokolo people, but the meaning seems to be quite different. Both groups seem to have totems, or at least a sacred animal which they may not kill or eat. This seems to be less important toward Cape Possession than farther west.

The guardian spirits of the men's house abide in certain carved planks and figures at Orokolo, but in the wicker work animals (crocodiles ?) in the delta, while the planks, tho sacred to them, have a different meaning.

At Orokolo there are 3 (at least) different kinds of masks (used in different ceremonies): *kōwābī, ēhārō,* and *hevehe* (this is known as *semési* or *sewesi* from Kerema east). The meaning of these ceremonies could not be ascertained, but *kowábi* seems to be connected with the initiation of boys. The boys are confined to the *elábo* for a year (?) or so, "till their hair is grown." Toward the end (probably also at other times), they put on these *kowabi* masks, and appear in the village, and often spend considerable part of the morning, or even day, running about on the beach. The Ereava *kowabi* finished May 24th, and for a week or more previously I often saw them at Nomo on the beach, usually 2 to 4 together. When at Orokolo May 1st the *kowabi* appeared, and when they came out first early in the morning, each one was escorted through the village by 3 or 4 men, got up in their best ornaments and paint, who ran along side with them and called or sang out something from time to time (apparently the same thing each time). In connection with these ceremonies there are special performances in the bush, which no white man has seen, nor is allowed to see. Formerly they would have killed anyone happening on such a performance, and some think this may have been the cause of the death of Chalmers.

483

Fig. 7.37. "Masked figure and carvings, Kairuo." A-37158 (1174).

The *hevehe* masks are large, and said to take a year to make. They were being made at Kerema and Vailala. Marko said this dance was held every two years, but could get nothing as to its meaning.

The *eháro* masks are small, and may be seen by women and children.

Sunday, May 26   In afternoon *Wakefield* (B.N.G.D. Co. steamer) arrived, loaded up about 2 tons of sago, and finally about 8 P.M. got my specimens and luggage aboard. Mr. Massey Baker kindly sent some carriers to get my stuff to boat.

Monday, May 27   Left early, and got out Purari mouth. Got to mouth of Vailala about noon, but as tide going out, Captain Knutson would not enter over bar, so anchored out all night.

Tuesday, May 28   Entered early in morning, took Mr. Cowley, Carne, MacDonell, Talbot, Hill, and MacGowan on board, and went up river for Akanda. A few miles below Akanda ran on ledge of rock near bank, and stuck. Stayed here 3 days, till rain in hills caused river to rise and float us off.

Friday, May 31   Got off in forenoon, and party who had gone up river in boat 2 days before met us soon after started on. Anchored at mouth of river that night.

Saturday, June 1   Out of river about 11 A.M. but stuck on bar for nearly an hour. Finally bumped over, and off for Pt. Moresby.

Southeast Papua

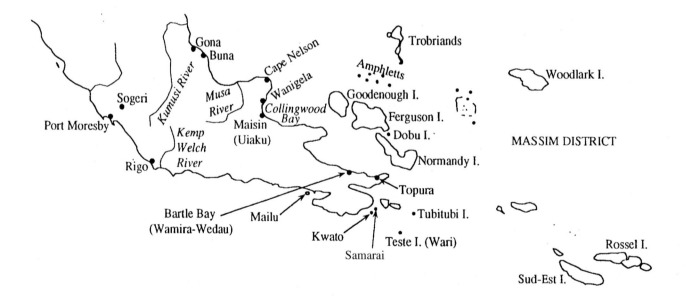

Port Moresby

Sogeri

Gona
Buna

Kumusi River

Cape Nelson

Wanigela

Musa River

Collingwood Bay

Maisin
(Uiaku)

Kemp Welch River

Rigo

Bartle Bay
(Wamira-Wedau)

Mailu

Kwato

Samarai

Teste I. (Wari)

Topura

Tubitubi I.

Trobriands

Amphletts

Goodenough I.

Ferguson I.

Dobu I.

Normandy I.

Woodlark I.

MASSIM DISTRICT

Rossel I.

Sud-Est I.

Eastern Papua and the Massim

||||||||||||||||||||||||||||||||||||||||||||||||||||||||||||||||||||||||||||||||||||||||||||||||||||||||||||||||

2 June 1912–25 July 1912

ABL began his last two months in Papua with a trip by steamer to Samarai and the Massim district. Unlike his travels in the Purari Delta and Papuan Gulf—where ABL often took dugout canoes and stayed overnight in government rest houses—here he traveled by steamer and usually slept on the ship or in the homes of expatriates.

On the way east and on his return to Moresby, ABL once again visited with the pioneer settler A. C. English, whom he had first met in February soon after his arrival. English had assembled a large collection of stone clubs, which he offered to ABL for the tidy sum of £400 (roughly 40 percent of ABL's annual allocation). ABL apparently thought the price far too high; he declined this offer. In Papua, ABL generally found all the stone tools offered for sale by expatriates too expensive. These expatriate prices contrasted sharply with his earlier experiences on the Purari, where one morning he conducted a "rushing business in stone axes with fish-hooks (2–5 apiece)."

At Samarai he once again visited Reverend Ramsay of the Anglican mission, who had also assembled a collection of about two hundred pieces for him. These specimens were from Wanigera and Maisin (Uiaku) in Collingwood Bay, Wedau in Bartle Bay, and Ferguson Island, all places where the Anglicans had mission stations.[12] (In addition, Ramsay had assembled an assortment of 181 potsherds, mostly decorative rimsherds, from a prehistoric kitchen midden in Wanigera.) Later Ramsay also sent ABL another collection, which had been collected by his fellow Anglican missionaries at Wanigera, Bartle Bay (Wamira and Wedau), Goodenough Island, and Teste Island.

From Samarai, ABL made an excursion around the islands, calling briefly at Woodlark, where he saw the mining operations, and the Trobriands, where he bought some specimens from the villagers. After a stop at Buna, where he bought a few more things, ABL returned to Samarai. Then, following a visit to the LMS mission station of Kwato, ABL returned to Port Moresby, calling in at Mailu and Kapa-Kapa on the way. Thus, in 1912 ABL visited both Mailu and the Trobriands, two and three years earlier than Bronislaw Malinowski, who would make both communities famous in anthropological circles. (ABL collected some carved lime spatulas and a few other items in the Trobriands and one Mailu pot, but otherwise did little in either place.)

From Port Moresby ABL set off for the pot-making center of Yule Island. As he had done so many times before, he bought some pots, took notes on pot making, and made some photos of women working on their pots. He then set off on his last excursion into the villages in Papua, this time to the Mekeo and Roro districts on the mainland opposite Yule Island. On his return to Port Moresby, ABL visited the Motu village Tanobada, where he collected still more pots.

In Moresby, ABL set about packing his Papuan specimens, which now numbered nearly two thousand. Half of these he had collected in the villages himself, the others he had bought from helpful expatriates. The trip to the east had been disappointing, for he had seen little and obtained almost nothing while aboard the steamer, but he had arranged to buy an important collection from Ramsay. Now in Port Moresby he again ran into Captain Griffin, who sold him a collection of more than a hundred pieces.

ABL had now been in the field for more than three years. One senses during these last weeks in Papua that he was starting to tire from the sheer strain of fieldwork. Constantly on the move over arduous country, confronted by tropical heat and malaria, ABL's health was in fact worsening. And traveling by steamer along routes that linked government stations, missions, and mining centers was hardly the most productive way for an anthropologist to experience village life.

He took more than 480 photographs and made substantial collections; but his field notes were becoming more abbreviated, and collecting was itself becoming more difficult. Most of the places he visited in eastern Papua had been picked over by a generation of Europeans eager to collect curios that might fetch a profit in England or Australia. Even the fine carvings for which places like the Trobriands are now known were already much influenced by European contact; they were far removed from the pristine conditions suggested by so many of Malinowski's writings.

ABL finished his packing and set off for Dutch territory at the end of July 1912. After five months in Papua, he left Port Moresby to complete the final leg of his long odyssey in Melanesia.

Fig. 7.38. "Men's house, Aipeana, Mekeo district." A-37028 (1259).

Eastern Papua and the Massim

‖‖

Sunday, June 2   Got into Pt. Moresby in evening.

Monday, June 3–Saturday, June 8   Packed up most of specimens, except some large masks, and spears. Specimens from Kerema, Vailala and Orokolo came in by the *Lahui,* of Max Assmann, and were stored with Whitten Bros. One box from Orokolo was missing, and not to be found.[10] Ten boxes (174–183) were turned over to Whitten Bros. to be sent on by first steamer to N. York.

Sunday, June 9   *Mataran* in. Got mail and wrote letters.

Monday, June 10   Packed luggage and got it on *Mindoro,* for trip to east.

Tuesday, June 11   Left in morning. About 11 A.M. arrived at Kapa Kapa. In afternoon went ashore, and Mr. English took me, Mr. Carne, and Captain _____, in carriage up to his place. Saw the preparation of sisal hemp. Later saw English's collection of stone axes and clubs, but not much time to look at them. Got him to name some photos I had got from King, Sydney.

Wednesday, June 12   Stopped at 3 places but no time to go ashore.

Thursday, June 13   Arrived at Samarai in morning. Found Rev. F. W. Ramsay had got a number of things for me, including about 40 pots from Collingwood Bay, and a great number of pieces of the old pottery there. Spent the afternoon listing specimens and packing.

Friday, June 14   Packed.

Saturday, June 15   Finished packing 4 boxes (184–187) in morning, and arranged to have them shipped via Sydney. 184–185 contain 24 pots; 186, 7 pots and some other things; 187 potsherds and specimens from Collingwood bay. Left at 2 P.M. for Woodlark Island.

Sunday, June 16   Arrived at Woodlark in afternoon.

Monday, June 17   Went ashore in morning, and up to settlement, which is about 2 miles from landing. Two mines working, with shafts 300–500 ft. deep. Gold ore is a decayed white rock. No native villages anywhere near. Left about 3 P.M. for Trobriand Isl.

---

10. This probably contained two feather headdresses and a few other small items from Kerema.

Fig. 7.39. Carved wooden objects with human figures and peculiar ornament above head, Wamira, Bartle Bay. Wooden image, 141685 (R-72); suspension hook, 141683 (R-73), painted red, black, and white. Both from Ramsay. A-112043.

Tuesday, June 18 Arrived at Trobriands about 9 A.M. Ship anchored about 4 miles from shore, so was nearly noon when got ashore. Took dinner with Dr. Bellamy, gov. magistrate.

In afternoon visited village near by. Several hundred people. Houses small, on ground, but many yam houses on posts. These are even more numerous than the dwellings (only one kind) and about 4 by 6 or 7 feet, and 3 to 4 feet to eaves. Front often ornamented. This has some relation to totem. Got some lime sticks and gourds here. According to Mr. English, they make

Fig. 7.40. Selection of carved and ornamental objects obtained from Rev. F. W. Ramsay, Samarai: wooden bowls, Wedau, Bartle Bay, 141590 (R-25), 141588 (9138); carved wooden club, Topura, east coast mainland, 141691 (R-68); fine carved axe handle, Waningera, Collingwood Bay, 141451 (R-42); carved suspension hooks, Wamira, Bartle Bay, 141681 (R-76), 141682 (R-75); tortoise-shell earrings, ornamented with red beads (left) and shell discs (right), Ferguson Island, 141705 (9147), 141703 (9145). A-112321.

very nice ornamented pottery,[11] but did not see any. Left about 8 P.M. for mouth of Mambare river.

Wednesday, June 19   Arrived at Mambare about 7 P.M. and anchored all night.

Thursday, June 20   Left at daylight for Buna Bay, where arrived about 2 P.M. Visited the magistrate, Mr. Oelrichs, and got a boy from Mr. Cardew to guide to village. Here took some photos and purchased 4 pots, and few other things. Pots from interior. Pottery is made at many places, both on coast and inland, on N.E. side of Papua, from the German border down to Collingwood bay. The process is always described as coiling. Made by women, tho one man (Mat Crow[12]) said he once saw 3 old men making a bowl in the interior. Flat-bottomed pots and dishes are also made in the interior. According to Mr. English, the natives do not live in the mountains above about 3,000 ft., so that the higher interior watershed is uninhabited. Pots are made only on the N.E. side of the range. On the south side they are made only by the Motu-motu people (Kapa Kapa the last village to the east), at Aroma, Mailu, Fife bay, and many of the islands to the east, at Teste Island, Tubitubi (Engineers Group), and several villages on Normanby, Fergison, and Goodenough Islands. Everywhere from Mailu east by coiling or building up process. (Aroma ?).

Took supper with Mr. Oelrichs, who kindly gave me a pointed wood club from interior, and a pig net. He has a great variety of colored bark cloth around his dining-room.

---

11. These would be Amphlett pots.
12. He means the prospector Matt Crowe.

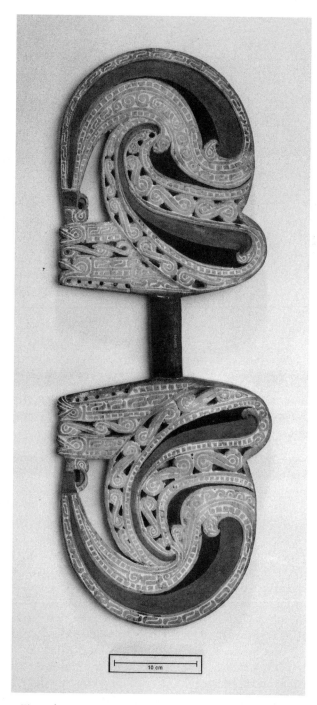

Fig. 7.41. Dance shield, designs in red, white, and black, Trobriand Islands, 135741 (G-14). A-112365.

Friday, June 21 Left in morning, and arrived about 2 P.M. at Cape Nelson. Mr. Henderson magistrate here. Mr. Chignell and 2 women got aboard here for mission conference at Bartle Bay.

Saturday, June 22 Left in morning, picked up two missionaries and arrived at Bartle Bay in evening.

Fig. 7.42. "Cooking, Buna Bay." A-37846 (1199).

Sunday, June 23   Left about midnight and arrived at Samarai about 9 A.M.

Monday, June 24   Holiday,—read.

Tuesday, June 25   Packed.

Wednesday, June 26   Packed in morning, and in afternoon visited L.M.S. station near Samarai, where Rev. Mr. Abel has his industrial mission. Unfortunately he was away, and all the boys belonging to the mission were off at a plantation. A younger missionary, who had been in country 3 years, received me, and as the launch did not return, entertained me for the night.[13]

This mission, tho established about 20 years, has only about 35 boys, many of whom have grown up on the station from children (orphans). Only young children, or those over which the mission is given complete control, are received. Often approved boys from the other stations are received. While they are connected with the mission they are under complete control, are not allowed to leave island without permission, to sell any of their things (I was not allowed to buy a pot from one of the boys) or to receive presents or pay from any white man for service. Their position is literally that of children of the mission.

Thursday, June 27   Got back to Samarai in small boat in which boy took over milk to Samarai. *Matunga* arrived about 8 A.M. Could do nothing but read.

---

13. The identity of this young missionary is unknown; he is not listed in Langmore (1989).

Friday, June 28   Read. Got away about 4 P.M.

Saturday, June 29   Called at Mailu few minutes, anchored for night.

Sunday, June 30   Steamed for Kapa-Kapa but too late to get inside reef, as passage very narrow (reef 4 miles from land). We struck reef in attempt, and stuck fast for about 20 minutes, but finally got off without damage, and stayed out all night.

Monday, July 1   Got in soon after day, and anchored off Kapa-Kapa till nearly noon, taking cargo.
Arrived at Pt. Moresby about 5 P.M.
Mr. A. C. English came aboard at Kapa Kapa, and I got some information from him. He has been in N.G. for nearly 30 years, for a long time in gov. service. Was with Dr. Finsch in *Samoa* during part of his voyage along south coast. Had seen 3 methods of making fire in N.G. With rattan way in interior. By twirling stick motion in hands near base of ranges on south side, and rubbing along coast.
Has a very fine collection of stone axes and clubs, for which wants £400. Stone clubs in different stages of manufacture. Do it by pecking with pointed stone. Said got one man to make a pick axe club, and took him 2 years to only roughly finish it. Told him he was in a hurry for it, too. Knows of one place on Mt. Suckling, where jade boulders are found, tho not plentiful. Once had two small stone betel nut mortars. Spoke of selling few stone clubs in London for £42. (Mr. Ramsay said that natives offered him £5 for most any stone club.) Stone clubs made in many localities in interior.

Tuesday, July 2   Left Pt. Moresby about 4 P.M. for Yule Island.

Wednesday, July 3   Arrived at Yule Isl. in morning. Got things ashore, and fathers gave me room. Got things ready to start on trip to Mekeo district in afternoon, but just after starting found I had forgotten my cot, so put my things ashore and returned. Two of the sisters were going over in the mission boat, and as they had about 2 hrs. walk after landing, could not make them wait any longer.

Thursday, July 4   Went to village in forenoon, also in afternoon. Took some pictures and bought a few things.

Friday, July 5   Went to village in afternoon with Marūki, the native interpreter at the magistrate's. More photos and pots.
The clay for the pots is gotten near the village on the flat. They use only a layer about 4 in. thick, which lies under about a foot of surface soil, and over a much lighter, clay subsoil. The layer they use is quite black and somewhat gummy. It is taken to the village, dried and pounded up, and when ready to use mixed with a black sand from the coast of the mainland, just enough water being used to make it easy to work. The clay, when thoroughly worked and mixed, is kneaded into masses, each sufficient to make a pot, and formed roughly into a rounded mass with a depression in the center. These are let stand a little time, and then partly worked up into a vessel. Usually several are made at one time, and the first is ready to work by the time the others are finished. The clay on the sides of this ring is simply pulled up by the hands (see photos), and gradually worked into a deep rounded bowl. The top of this is then widened and smoothed to form the top of the

bowl. (I did not see a pot made.) The whole is left to dry for some time, when the bottom is worked into shape with a wood paddle, and the whole nicely smoothed by hand.

The pots are dried for a day or more, and then burnt by piling sticks, in, around, and over them, when the whole is fired.

They distinguish 5 kinds of pots:

1. *ūrō*, the ordinary family cooking pot which may be over a foot high, and 1 ½ ft. or more wide.
2. *ē'ē*, similar in shape, but much smaller, used for one or two persons, also a cooking pot.
3. *nāosu*, a small pot, slightly drawn in at the top, but no rim, used to cook bananas, esp. for a sick person, when the juice is given him to drink. (When cooking bananas in quantity, the large *úro* is used.)
4. *ōrōrō*, a wide shallow bowl, in which the food is placed for eating.
5. *pūo*, a small or medium sized, narrow-mouthed vessel, in which water is kept.

This pottery is plain and unornamented, though occasionally a few incised lines are seen on or near the rim.

Pottery is also made in two villages on the mainland opposite Yule Island, but nowhere else in the neighborhood. This district is the most western pottery center in Papua, and pottery is traded from here both along the coast and into the interior.

In Siria (Yule Isl.) I also saw the only purely ornamental pottery so far seen. In front of the *marea,* or men's house, under the projecting gable end, were hung numerous ornaments, including 3 inverted bowl-like pieces, each with a round opening with slight rim in top, through which the suspending lines passed. There were also projecting ornaments on the sides and rim, those on the rim being pierced, and shredded sago-leaf tied in them. (See photo). They were hung over a sort of rattan frame, from which hung great bunches of split sago leaves.

Pottery is the chief industry of Siria, and a number of women could nearly always be seen at this work.

Fig. 7.44. Carved ornaments, Mekeo district: carved piece of wood worn on breast or back during dance, 141958 (9260); charm made of scented wood, 141957 (9308). A-112334.

497

Fig. 7.45. "Front of men's house *(marea), Yule Island.*" A-37786 (1207).

Very few wood bowls were seen, and these were similar to those at Port Moresby. A few bags, water gourds and cocoanuts were the only other things noted in houses.

Saturday, July 6 Expected Marúki to come in morning with canoe to take me across to the mainland, as he had agreed to take me around for two or three days, esp. to Mō and Rāpa. He did not come, however, and I found out later that it was because the others wanted money, while I had told him I would give them tobacco.

Sunday, July 7 In afternoon Mr. Simpson, government bridge builder, came over to mission, and invited me to go back with him in his canoe. We went as far as Mr. H. L. C. Johnston's place, where we stopped for the night. As Mr. Johnston was going across in the whale boat in the morning, and then on to his place in Mekeo, and had plenty of carriers, I agreed to go with him.

Monday, July 8 Left about 8 A.M. and arrived at Pīnapāka, the village on coast, about 9, and at Mo about 10. Here stopped some time at the mission.

Fig. 7.46. "Mission building, Yule Island." A-37129 (1274).

Then on for about 3½ hrs. walk to the plantation, passing and stopping at Mr. Simpson's camp on the way, as it rained quite heavily while there. About 5 when arrived.

Tuesday, July 9 Left about 9 for Ināwi, about 1¼ hr. off. Here stopped some time, and bought a number of things. Mr. Johnston, who had come with me that far, then went back, and I continued on to Rāraí. First we had dinner with the missionary, who had also helped me much in looking around and buying. Leaving Ināwi with two boys lent me by Mr. Johnston, I came first (40 min.) to Aipēana, then (10 min.) Bēpa, a large village, (20 min.) Awōewo, and (70 min.) Rarai. Here Father Ed. van Goethem received me kindly, and put me up for the night. He also let me have a few bags and feather ornaments which he had.

Wednesday, July 10 In morning Father van Goethem went with me to village, and I got a few things, but not very much. I then took a number of photos, and later got Father van Goethem to give me the names of the ornamental designs on the bags. He has given most of this in a paper, which he has sent to *Anthropos* [1912]. The designs have names, but many of them

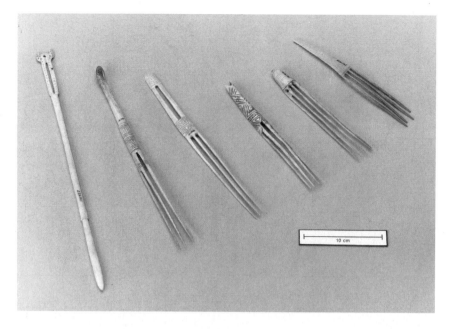

Fig. 7.47. Carved bone ornaments, Mekeo district: lime spatula, Mekeo, 141927 (9295); fork, Siria village, Yule Island, 141902 (9248); forks, Mekeo, 141916 (9299), 141917 (9304), 141919 (9306), 141918 (9305). A-112232.

are the names of districts, others of objects, such as mountains, hooks, etc. The bags from the mountains are much valued, as, tho all the designs are in black, it is a permanent color, and will wash, while their own colors will not stand washing.

Left about 11:30 on return, buying a few things at Bepa and Inawi on return. Got back to Mr. Johnston's about dusk.

Thursday, July 11   Expected to leave in boat for Yule Island in morning, but it did not arrive till Thursday evening. So spent most of day reading. Mosquitos very bad, so lay under net most of time.

Friday, July 12   Left about 8 A.M. Stopped about ¾ hr. at Mo where bought some fish nets. Below there saw working of sago by some natives of Biōto. Sago hammer very crude—a piece of bamboo fastened to handle. Washing through fibre from base of cocoanut leaf, and pan of leaf sheathing base, as at Sissano.

Arrived at Yule Island about dark.

The Mekeo district, at least as far as visited, lies in the flood plain of the St. Joseph river, and is largely under water in the rainy season. The villages are numerous, but not very large, varying from 50 inhabitants up to 350. The houses are usually on posts, with floor 3 to 5 or 6 ft. high. They are arranged, more or less irregularly, on each side of a central street, fairly wide, and kept quite clear of vegetation. The houses are not very large, and only occupied by one family. They are often open in front, or they may have a sort of sloping roof covering the front completely (see photos). The posts of the men's houses are occasionally carved in geometrical designs, similar to those on boards in front of *marea* at Siria. At Aipéana only were two or three boards with designs of human face or form. The carved designs are of the same type as those on the bags. Those painted on bark cloth were also geometrical. The woven or knitted work seems to have set the fashion for the whole.

Household utensils are not numerous. Pots come only from the coast. Wood bowls very few, and those very crude. Water gourds common. Co-

Fig. 7.48. "The village policeman and wife, Rarai, Mekeo district. She has on a special dress worn only for dress occasions, as dances, etc." A-37039 (1226).

coanuts do not seem to be used for water. String bags and net making chief industry. Large nets used for pigs; smaller for wallaby; several kinds of fish nets, etc. Here for first time in N.G. got a considerable number of bone forks.

Saturday, July 13   Packed in morning. Early in afternoon *Wakefield* arrived, and I got aboard, bound for Port Moresby.

Sunday, July 14   Arrived at Port Moresby about 5 P.M.

Monday, July 15   Spent most of day arranging business matters. Expected to go to Sogeri to see Capt. Griffin the next day, but about 4 P.M. learned that he had just arrived in town, so visited him, and found that he had brought in a number of more specimens. Had agreed to take 17 stone

Fig. 7.49. "Woman and baby, Bepa. This is the ordinary way of keeping the baby." A-37093 (1230).

clubs before, and now got 12 more, some Trobriand lime sticks, 4 stone adzes, and few other things. For these, together with some more things at his house (Sogeri), paid £35. He also agreed to collect for the Museum what he could get, and send the Sogeri things in with his collection. For this gave him £10 more. Also my medicine chest, and a few other things.

Tuesday, July 16–Thursday, July 18 Developed plates and films. Capt. Griffin kindly let me use his house and water, which was quite an item, as water was very scarce in Port.

Friday, July 19–Saturday, July 20 Packed my specimens and over-hauled luggage for trip to Java.

Monday, July 22 In morning bought 27 pots from Tanobada natives, who brought them over to me in morning. Sunday afternoon I had been over to the village, and picked out a number that I wanted, promising to pay them a certain price.

I got 9 different kinds of pots and bowls, as distinguished by different names:

1. *ūro*—ordinary cooking pot, sometimes quite large, 1 ½ feet in diameter or more.
2. *kēikei*—a small *ūro*, 5–8 in. in diameter.

502

Fig. 7.50. "Men of Rapa on a visit to Mo, Roro district." A-37710 (1253).

3. *nā'u*—large food bowl, or dish, for cooked food for several persons; may be over two feet in diameter and 1 foot or more deep.
4. *kībō*—small *nā'u*, for one or two persons.
5. *ōbūrō*—to contain cooked food, medium or small sized deep bowl, no rim.
6. *hōdu*—water vessel and cooler, small mouth.
7. *dīhū*—flattened and somewhat elongated dish or plate for food.
8. *tōhe*—large pot for keeping sago, may be two feet or more high.
   These are often taken with them in the *lakatoi*s when going for sago.
9. *ītūli*—small bowl or dish used to contain the black coloring used in tatooing; often with sort of base or ornaments.

This set of pots was packed by noon. Spent afternoon in arranging business matters.

Tuesday, July 23   Expected Dutch boat for Java, but she did not arrive. Arranged with Mr. Alom, of B.P. & Co. to forward my boxes; also any others

Fig. 7.51. String bags from Mekeo district: black bands (below) and red bands (above), 141936 (9277); collected Mekeo, "said to come from the Kobio district, in mountains near Mt. Yule," 141930 (9279); designs in light blue, dark blue, and red, "upper part of design called *kiyu* (hornbill), lower part called *vuau*," 141938 (9269). A-112229.

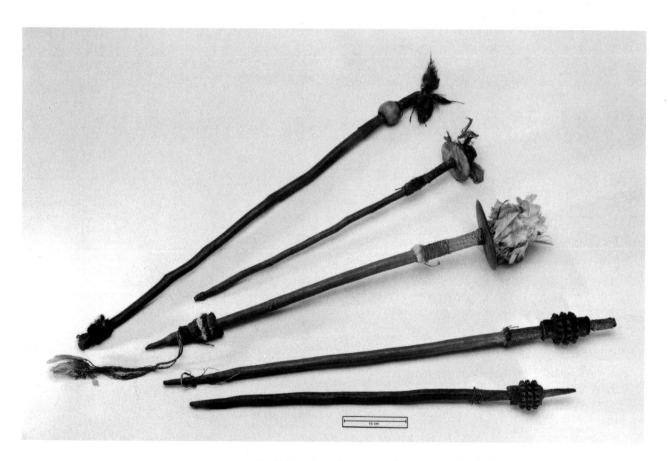

Fig. 7.52. Clubs from eastern Papua: round head of light quartzite, Dobudura village, about 12 miles south of Buna Bay, 141825 (9360); disc head of light quartzite, Kumusi River, 141826 (9357); disc head with feather ornaments, Kokoda, about 40 miles inland of Buna Bay, 141835 (9363); knobbed head, Buna Bay, 141819 (8148), ABL; knobbed head, Dinadele tribe, Mambare River, 141845 (9333). All from Griffin (except 8148). A-112208.

Fig. 7.53. "Tanobada and Elevala, from mission station." A-38052 (128f).

that Johnston, Griffin, or anyone else might give them; also to pack anything for the Museum delivered into their care.

Boxes 190–204 left to be sent on:

190–191	Pots & misc. sp. Yule Isl. and Mekeo.
192	Nets.
193–194	Stone clubs, 1 drum.
195	Pots (Pt. Moresby) bowl and lime spat.
196	Pot (Pt. Moresby).
197	Masks (6) from Kerema (3) & Kiri (3).
198	Large Sago pot & 3 small ones.
199	Camera, negatives & books.
200–203	Pots, Port Moresby.
204	Bundle spears (7) Buna Bay.

Thursday, July 25   Steamer *(van Warwijck)* arrived in forenoon. Left about 10 P.M.

Dutch New Guinea and the Moluccas

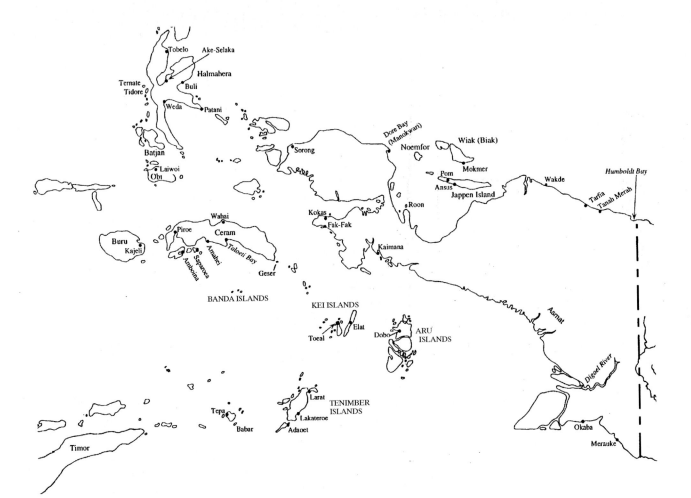

Dutch New Guinea

||||||||||||||||||||||||||||||||||||||||||||||||||||||||||||||||||||||||||||||||||||||||||||||||||||||||||||||||||||||||||||

27 July 1912–25 January 1913

By the time ABL left Papua for the Dutch East Indies, the stresses and strains of fieldwork had already begun to overtake him. Sickness, not research and collecting, would dominate his last six months in the field. At Thursday Island in the Torres Straits on the first day of his voyage to Java he came down with fever. This bout of malaria lasted only two or three days, but it was a precursor to a much more serious attack six weeks later.

After traveling through Java and visiting some of the Moluccas, the so-called Spice Islands, ABL became deathly ill with blackwater fever, a condition that in those days was typically fatal. He was taken ashore at Merauke on the south coast of Dutch New Guinea. There he was nursed back to health by Catholic missionaries (Sacred Heart Mission), especially by one of the mission brothers, Brother Hamers, who had been in Merauke since 1905 after previously serving with the Sacred Heart Mission in New Britain.[13] Had it not been for the attention and care of Brother Hamers and the other missionaries, ABL would almost certainly have died in the field.

Blackwater fever is rarely seen today, but it was formerly a leading tropical killer. It is essentially a complication of malaria, specifically falciparum malaria, in which the red pigment (hemoglobin) from large numbers of infected blood cells is excreted in the urine, causing the urine to turn dark—hence the name. It is now generally thought that this condition is associated with the regular use of quinine (Ewers and Jeffrey 1971, 60). By this time, of course, ABL had taken quinine routinely and often for three and a half years.

The Netherlands East Indies, of which Dutch New Guinea was a remote and economically insignificant part, was a colony unlike any other ABL had visited during the expedition. It was enormous, stretching more than three thousand miles from Sabang (off the western tip of Sumatra) to Merauke near the Papuan border. The colony's population was well over forty million, but three-quarters of these people lived on Java and Bali; other parts of the colony—particularly the Moluccas and New Guinea—were sparsely populated. And the colony was a very old one; parts of the archipelago had been under Dutch control for more than three centuries, 175 years earlier than the first European settlement in Australia.

The East Indies was an Asian colony, made up of hundreds of ethnic communities that had long been in contact with other parts of Asia. Most communities in the archipelago had been linked for centuries by trade involving spices, textiles, gold, silver, and iron, as well as pearl shell, bêche-de-mer, bird of paradise plumes, and other island products that ABL had frequently seen elsewhere in Melanesia. Until the Dutch imposed their own monopolies in the seventeenth century, the archipelago's commerce had largely been in the hands of Makassarese, Buginese, Javanese, Moluccan, Chinese, Malay, and Arab traders. Early in the twentieth century, these traders continued to play an important role in the colony's commerce, but principally as small interisland traders rather than as major importers and exporters as they once had (Alatas 1977).

Most parts of the archipelago were socially stratified, with elaborate hierarchies of local sultans, kings, princes, and nobles outranking various tiers of commoners and slaves. For centuries the governor-general and his army of civil service administrators, called residents, assistant residents, and controleurs, had governed the colony through a complex system of indirect rule. Ranking sultans or princes were allowed to maintain their (now strengthened) traditional authority over the native peoples living in their realms, provided they carried out the colonial administration's instructions. In the Moluccas, this system generally required only that native rulers enforce the Dutch monopoly on international trade. But in Java local potentates had to administer a command economy—somewhat inaccurately called the culture system—that involved forced production of specified cash crops, for which villagers were paid fixed (usually low) prices (Furnivall 1944; Multatuli 1982).

This pattern was less true in Dutch New Guinea, where in some places, such as at Merauke, indirect rule was impossible because there were no established local elites. But in other parts of the island, such as at Sorong, Fak-Fak, and Kaimana, local princes and nobility—on what we might tend to think of as the Indonesian model—were well established.

Most of the Indies had converted to Islam, beginning in the tenth or eleventh centuries. Islam and its association with international trade had been instrumental in the rise of many powerful kingdoms and empires that controlled much of the region when the Portuguese, Dutch, and English colonizers arrived in Southeast Asia. Only in the interior of some of the larger islands such as Sumatra, Borneo, Sulawesi, and New Guinea were there few Muslims. As in German New Guinea and Papua, the majority of the coastal villages in Dutch New Guinea practiced traditional religions or were recent converts to Christianity (following European missionization). But even this pattern was not universal in Dutch New Guinea, where many Muslim New Guineans lived in communities on the Bird's Head and the west end of the island.

This part of western New Guinea and eastern Indonesia has long been an interactive zone between Asian and Oceanic communities. Influences seem to have swept through this zone from both the east and the west for many centuries.[14] It would be a mistake to discount all influences from the Indies on these New Guinea communities as the result of recent contact. Unlike the European influences ABL observed in Papua and German New Guinea, which largely date to the 1880s and 1890s, on the west end of Dutch New Guinea and along parts of the north coast and Schouten Islands these influences are very old indeed.

So-called Malay and Chinese traders, by which ABL and other early observers usually meant traders from Ternate, Tidore, Sulawesi, Timor, and other parts of eastern Indonesia, could be found in nearly every community that ABL visited. In some places they were so numerous that they dominated the local economy. At Merauke, for example, which was a part of Dutch New Guinea that was little influenced by colonization before 1905, the Malay-Chinese trading community numbered many hundreds (ABL suggests a thousand). Such influences would have existed with or without the Dutch, and the imposition of a Dutch monopoly in the seventeenth century probably had little effect on interaction between New Guinea and the Moluccas.

508

Nowhere in his diaries and letters does ABL discuss in detail the continuities he perceived between parts of Dutch New Guinea and parts of the Moluccas. But in a number of places he noted that there were similarities in certain aspects of the material culture from these two areas, and his collections from various places suggest how profound some of these continuities were.

The most striking specimens are some iron-tipped spears made on Wiak (Biak) Island. Such metal work, made by itinerant Biak blacksmiths, could be found on many of the Schouten Islands, as well as on parts of the mainland coast (see Held 1957). ABL collected other examples of iron-tipped spears on Halmahera, Tenimber, and Kei in the Moluccas (Fig. 7.76). Similarly, ABL collected a number of sago ovens or sago toasters made of stone or earthenware in many Moluccan communities as well as in some New Guinea communities (Fig. 7.57). Some pottery from Kokas on the west end of New Guinea also resembles that in several Moluccan communities. Perhaps most striking of all is the carved openwork found along much of the north coast and Schouten Islands, which shows many similarities with styles found throughout the Moluccas (Fig. 7.81).

These influences, commonalties, and continuities were not one-sided: Moluccan communities also had items of material culture that made use of shells, beads, and bands typical of Melanesia. From Tenimber, for example, ABL brought back many brass and ivory bangles and bracelets that seem typical of the Indies, but he also collected some shell bracelets or arm bands that are common in many parts of New Guinea.

These linkages do not merely reflect late-nineteenth- and early-twentieth-century contact but are evidence of much older relationships within the region. When the Dutch officially claimed New Guinea in 1828, they annexed those parts of New Guinea up to the 141st meridian, excluding areas already claimed by the sultan of Tidore. Since 1671 the Dutch had formally recognized that the sultan had at least tributary rights over parts of what is now Irian Jaya (see van der Veur 1966, 6–13). During the 1950s, of course, Indonesians made much of Tidore rights when asserting their claims over the province as an integral part of Indonesia. Before dismissing these claims out of hand, we should not forget that it was only for a brief period of a dozen years (1949–1962) that Dutch New Guinea had a political existence separate from the rest of the archipelago (see e.g., Bone 1958; Lijphart 1966). At all other periods since the sixteenth century the western part of New Guinea was connected with the Moluccas in complex economic, political, and cultural ways.

In sum, ABL gives us ample reason to assume that in his day there was no important and meaningful separation between what is now Irian Jaya and the Moluccan islands. Dutch New Guinea was administered in two parts, as subdivisions of the two residencies in the northern and southern Moluccas, respectively. Even the two missions operating in Dutch New Guinea—the Protestant Utrechtsche Zendings-vereeniging (UZV) in the north[15] and the Sacred Heart in the south—had established bases in the Moluccas. With such bases both missions could then turn their attention to evangelizing the non-Muslim communities in New Guinea. These political ties corresponded with what appeared to ABL as rather striking (and at first surprising) social, religious, economic, and artistic continuities between western New Guinea and the islands.

Such ties between New Guineans and the Malay world did not, of course, stop at the 141st meridian, which formed the border between Dutch and German territories. Even after the Dutch-German boundary commission of 1910, contacts persisted between the Dutch communities of Humboldt Bay and Sko and the German communities of Vanimo, Leitere, and Eitape. These ties are most noticeable in the glass beads and rings that were used in bride-price payments in all the communities from Tanah Merah and Humboldt Bay to Vanimo and Leitere. Such beads of diverse Asian and European origins had apparently been brought to the region by Malay traders several centuries before (van der Sande 1907; Thomas 1941–1942). They were central to the brisk regional economy within this area and are still in use.

When ABL visited Humboldt Bay in 1909, his first excursion was to buy a hat at the so-called Malay village near Metu Debi. Although ABL was unaware of it, German New Guinea villagers from as far away as Warapu, Sissano, and even the Berlinhafen Islands frequently traveled to Metu Debi and later Hollandia in this early colonial period. Later, when ABL was in German New Guinea, he met a few other Malays, mostly local traders or employees of European firms. Still other Malays continued to cross the border for birds of paradise, for the most part in violation of German laws (see Rodatz 1908, 1909a, 1909b). These individuals, surreptitiously crossing the border in both directions, were all that was left of a much more intensive involvement in the mid- and late-nineteenth century, during which time Malay traders came as far to the east as Walis and Tarawai, possibly as far as Wewak, to buy plumes and trochus shell with iron, beads, and other products. These Malay contacts at Walis had long preceded the Germans and were probably typical of many parts of the north coast.[16]

With the opening of Eitape station in 1906, these contacts were sharply curtailed by German (and later Australian) authorities eager to protect their own monopolies from these Dutch subjects. Both administrations subsequently minimized the importance of early contacts across this border. As a consequence, what amounts to government propaganda has turned the attention of anthropologists and historians away from these important early cultural contacts.

Through Java

When ABL arrived in Batavia, the capital of the Dutch East Indies, he began making arrangements for a trip to New Guinea. He visited the curio shops in Batavia and called on the American consul (the businessman Bradstreet Rairden). He also had a look at the colonial museum and visited the botanical gardens at Buitenzorg.

Batavia was a city of more than two hundred thousand people. Aside from Sydney, it was the largest city ABL had visited since leaving the United States. And Java, with roughly a hundred thousand European settlers, had far more European residents than all of the Melanesian colonies combined. In addition, Java was much more developed, having an elaborate rail network that connected most of the island's towns. For travel to places not served by trains, there were horse-drawn carts called *sado*. Java even had a well-developed tourist industry, complete with a tourist bureau subsidized by the colonial government.

When he learned that it would be a week till the next Batavia steamer for New Guinea, ABL decided to spend the time seeing something of Java. He first went to Garoet, a cool resort area in a volcanic part of west Java. From there he took a train to Jogja in central Java. Like most tourists today he visited the ruins of the ancient temples of Borobudur, Mendut, and Prambanan. Then ABL took another train to Soerabaya, the large port in eastern Java, where he caught up with his steamer and luggage.

ABL did not attempt to make a systematic collection in Java, but when he visited some of the batik factories and shops he did buy examples of this resist-dyed cloth. He also bought a set of *tjanting,* the tool used to paint melted wax onto the batik (see fig. 7.55) and obtained a set of batik samples showing the various stages in making batik.

On to the East

From Soerabaya he sailed on the Royal Shipping Line (Koninklijke Paketvaart Maatschappij) to the Moluccas, calling on Resident Raedt van Oldenbarnevelt at Amboina, his assistant resident at Amahei (Ceram), and another assistant resident at Kokas on the west end of New Guinea. On his return to Amboina ABL met another well-known traveler to the Indies, A. F. R. Wollaston, who had returned to New Guinea as leader of the Second British Expedition to Dutch New Guinea.

Setting off again from Ambon, ABL called in at Banda, the Kei Islands, Dobo (Aru Islands), and the Tenimber Islands before sailing to Merauke. ABL spent too little time at any of these ports of call to be able to make a systematic collection on his own. Had he stayed on, he would probably have had to stay a month or more until the next steamer arrived, but he did leave money with some of the Catholic missionaries from the Sacred Heart Mission at Tenimber and Kei to make collections for him. Brother Dominic's collection from the Kei group and Father Cappers' collection from Tenimber are probably the largest and best early collections in the United States from these islands.

ABL's next port of call was Merauke, where the colonial government had opened a station in 1902 in an effort to suppress headhunting among the troublesome Tugeri (or Marind-Anim), a group notorious for making raids into the Western Division of Papua.[17] The assistant resident invited the Sacred Heart Mission to establish a station at Merauke as well, which they did in 1905. Working closely with the mission's other stations in the Kei and Tenimber islands, the Sacred Heart sent at least four priests and two or three brothers to Merauke by 1912. Besides the main station at Merauke, they opened three other stations nearby at Okapa, Jobar, and Wendoe. Most of these missionaries had previously seen service with the Sacred Heart Mission in New Britain.

In addition to their headhunting, the Marind people were notable for their highly stratified system of age grades among both men and women. These grades were marked by elaborate sets of ornaments, worn on the body and in the hair as hair extenders. ABL learned about these age grades from the missionaries and especially from a paper published in *Anthropos* by the father superior, H. Nollen (1909). ABL was sick when he arrived in Merauke, so he was unable to collect on his own. He did, however, take more than 150 photographs, including many portrait shots of Marind people, illustrating the variety of ornaments and coiffures associated with different statuses or age grades. ABL also arranged with the missionaries to put together a collection to represent the Merauke area; these pieces included many objects from Merauke as well as from communities in the interior and other areas along the coast as far as the Asmat.

ABL left Merauke on 14 November and returned by steamer to Ambon by way of the Kei Islands, where he picked up the collection Brother Dominic had made for him. Then he set off to the north, visiting Ternate, the capital of a once powerful Islamic sultanate, situated on a small island off the coast of Halmahera. From here he visited several communities on Halmahera, including Tobelo, where he met the protestant missionary A. Hueting of the UZV. Like the Catholic missionaries in the south, Hueting agreed to make a collection for him. A few days later, ABL arrived at Manokwari on the east coast of the Bird's Head, where he met missionary F. J. F. van Hasselt, who also agreed to make a collection for him.

From Manokwari, ABL made a series of brief stops at Roon, Ansus, and Wakde, collecting specimens and taking photos at each port of call. Then on 18 December ABL arrived in Humboldt Bay, which he had visited three and a half years earlier after his arrival in Eitape, German New Guinea. Since his previous visit, a station had been established at Hollandia, the current site of Jayapura. Hollandia was still a remote government post, administered by a controleur (J. A. Wasterval), the lowest tier in the civil administration. After collecting a few more specimens, ABL left with the same steamer to return to Manokwari, stopping at Biak and Jappen in the Schouten Islands.

Back in Manokwari, ABL obtained a collection from Captain ten Klooster of the Dutch military expedition to north New Guinea. At Weda (Halmahera) on Christmas day he obtained some hats from trader G. E. Vincent, who agreed to pack and ship ABL's specimens and to forward shipments from Hueting and the other UZV missionaries on to Chicago. From Halmahera and Ternate, ABL returned to Ambon. At Piroe (Ceram) he visited Kraijer van Aalst, another UZV missionary, who also agreed to make a collection for Field Museum.

From Ambon, ABL began the long journey home, spending the first two weeks of 1913 on an interisland steamer bound for Java. After settling his affairs in Batavia, he left for Singapore to begin his return to Chicago.

This excursion by steamer through the Moluccas and Dutch New Guinea closely resembled his trip through eastern Papua and the Massim. He saw many ports but spent so little time in most of them that it was impossible to collect systematically. It was even more difficult to get any sense at all of native life, subsistence practices, and methods of manufacturing local goods. Moreover, through most of this sojourn in Dutch territory ABL was either sick or physically run down and weak. In this respect it is amazing that he was able to collect some 550 specimens on his own and to take nearly 300 photos. We should forgive him if this last part of his diary offers rather little more than an itinerary.

But while ABL himself was not able to collect systematically as he traveled from place to place, he authorized others to make collections for him. In some cases he bought collections directly from missionaries, traders, and military explorers; in other instances he left money, arranging for them to assemble collections and send them directly to Chicago. In all, these collections purchased from others totaled more than thirteen hundred pieces.

It had been an arduous trip through the East Indies, but he had survived and, having recovered from a nearly fatal tropical illness, was able to start the long trip home.

Ambon, Dutch East Indies
Nov. 30, 1912

Dear Dr. Dorsey:

I think I wrote you last when on the way to Java. I had to wait a week for the New Guinea boat, so took a trip through Java by rail, taking in the ruins of Burabudur and some other places on the way. The New Guinea boat went first to west N.G., but from what I could find out there, it did not seem worth while to stop there, so I went on to Merauke, passing the Kei, Aru & Tenimber Islands on the way. None of these promised much, and at the Tenimber Islands I could not have gotten away for two months, so I decided not to stop. I got some things from the Mission at Kei, (sent in boxes 206–210); and the mission in Tenimber promised to make a representative collection and send it in later, as it would take some time. This may arrive before I get back. Just before reaching Merauke I was taken sick with black-water fever, and was carried ashore to the Mission (R.C.), where they very kindly took care of me for two months; only the last two weeks was I able to get about. If it had not been for the mission I doubt if I could have pulled through. The last two weeks I was able to get around the native villages, and took a considerable number of photos (they are in box 212) but could get very few things, as the natives are very unwilling to sell. They care little for European stuff, and get all they want for a few cocoanuts from the Malay and Chinese traders, who swarm over the place. They are about the largest natives I have seen in New Guinea, and rather dark, but not so black as the Fly River natives. Huts very simple—not much more than shed—no floor; and they have not much in the way of household utensils.

The mission agreed to get me a representative collection—with time. I left the few things I had to be forwarded by them, except a box of skulls and prepared heads (box 205). It was impossible to do much at Merauke, so I am going to North New Guinea.

Mr. T. C. Stephens is getting some things for me in the New Hebrides, and reports that he has already sent in a shipment, and will later send more. He is trying his best to get some of the Malekula prepared heads and mummies, as well as some large wood drums and figures and carvings. New Hebrides things are expensive, and if he succeeds in getting some good things, it may be that the value will be much more than I have allowed him. If he writes to the Museum about it please see to it.

Very respectfully,
A. B. Lewis

Fig. 7.54. "Boys painted in preparation for ceremony initiating entrance into next class, Merauke." A-37831 (1499).

Dutch New Guinea

||||||||||||||||||||||||||||||||||||||||||||||||||||||||||||||||||||||||||||||||||||||||||||

Saturday, July 27 Arrived at Thursday Island in morning. Went ashore and mailed financial report to Museum. Felt so sick returned on board and went to bed. Fever.

Sunday, July 28 Fever.

Monday, July 29 Fever over, weak.

Friday, August 2 Arrived in morning at Mackassar. Spent most of fore-noon looking about the place. In afternoon took an hour's drive in motor car with 3 fellow passengers. Country level; good roads. Native houses on piles, set in banana groves.

Monday, Aug. 5 Arrived Surabaya. Spent part of day ashore.

Tuesday, Aug. 6 Left about 9 A.M.

Wednesday, Aug. 7 Arrived Samarang in morning.

Thursday, Aug. 8 Arrived Cheribon in morning. Left about 1 P.M.

Friday, Aug. 9 Arrived at Batavia about 8:30. Got landing permit, sent some of my luggage to Hotel des Indes,[14] and then went to Batavia to look up American Consul (B. S. Rairden, Esq.). Found he no longer had an office down town, so took a *sado* to go out to his place, which after some inquiries succeeded in finding. Here got a letter from the Museum and a general letter of recommendation from the government of Ned. Ind. Then went to K. Pak. Mat.[15] to inquire about ticket, etc.

After lunch went to Bank to deposit money and arrange for checks, etc. Returned up town and visited Tourist Bureau to arrange trip through Java.

Saturday, Aug. 10 Visited steamship agency, then went to Priok to get things off *van Warwijck*. Found she had left wharf, so had to get sampan. Got all cabin luggage ashore, and left with Steamship Co. to put on *Duymaer van Twist*, the next boat to N.G. for Soerabaia, where I would join the ship.

In afternoon visited museum for a little while, then got steamer trip finally arranged, with letter to captains, and deposited 2,000 guilders with

---

14. This hotel, like all the major hotels in Batavia, was actually in Weltvreden, the upper and more modern part of Batavia township (Official Tourist Bureau 1922, 48, 95–110). Arrival was always at Tanjung Priok, which remains the modern port of Jakarta.

15. This is the Koninklijke Paketvaart Maatschappij, the royal shipping company.

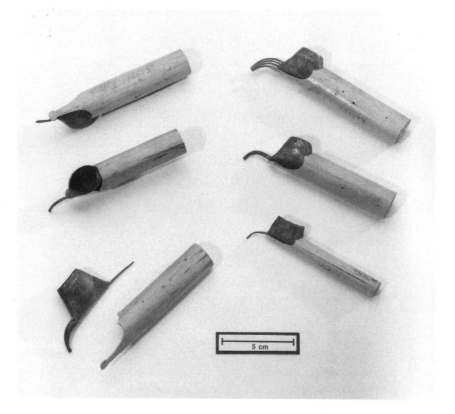

Fig. 7.55. Tjanting, Djokjakarta, Java. Pieces of reed to which copper bowls are fastened. These have from one to six tubes leading from them through which molten wax runs. Used to make batik, 132553 (_____). A-112179.

Co., which I could draw on from the different agencies and captains. Visited consul again, and then a curio shop "Ost & West," where saw a few interesting old brasses from Atjeh (Sumatra), also sarongs and clothing from Sumatra and Java.

Sunday, Aug. 11   Left at 7:25 for Buitenzorg, arrived 9:25 and went to Hotel Belle Vue. Then took walk for 3 hrs. through botanical gardens. Very pretty, but not representative of real tropical forest or jungle. Afternoon at hotel.

Monday, Aug. 12   Left for Garoet at 6:34, arrived 1:37. On way met Englishman. Hotel Papandajan, Haack, proprietor. In afternoon went out to some lakes.

Tuesday, Aug. 13   Left at 5 A.M. in cart for old volcanic crater, where mud springs. About 1½ hr. by cart, then horse to top, about 2 hrs. Old guide to take us around, nothing but hot springs and bubbling mud. Got back little after 1. Fine country. In afternoon saw making of tapioca in Chinese factory. Then hotel runner took us around to see manufacture of batik, but only one woman working, as a man had died day before, and all were off. Went to native shop and bought some batik (12 sarongs, 2 *slendang*s [sashes], and 2 head-cloths) pieces from different places.

Wednesday, Aug. 14   Left on 6:22 train for Djodja,[16] where arrived about 1:30. In afternoon saw batik working. Visited old "water castle," and later

16. He means Djokjakarta, now spelled Yogyakarta but pronounced Jogja.

so-called Museum. Bought 3 fine batik pieces (1 *kain* [lengths of cloth], 1 sarong, and 1 head cloth) and 2 common stamped pieces. Ordered a set of samples showing batik in different stages.

Thursday, Aug. 15   Left for Moetilan 5 A.M. and thence by carriage (met 2 teachers from the Chinese technical college in Shanghai, and went with them in carriage) to Borabudur. Had about 3 hrs. there, visiting Mendut on way. Late in afternoon walked about town.

Friday, Aug. 16   In forenoon visited market, very interesting. Afternoon went to Prambanan, and walked out to ruins, with small boy for guide. On return saw some village theatricals.

Saturday, Aug. 17   Left 6:30 for Soerabaya, where arrived 1:20 (Goebang St.) and took cart to landing, and thence to steamer *(Duymaer van Twist)*. Found luggage aboard all right. Steamer left about 5.

Sunday, Aug. 18   In morning at Boeleleng (Bali), where spent forenoon. Went ashore with a Mr. Freiman, agent Kon. Pak. Matj., at Pasoearum, who got a cart to drive me around for about 2 hrs. In nearly every village a Hindu temple, village about every ½ mile near town. Arrived at Ampenan (Lombok) late that evening, but did not go ashore, at daybreak were off for Maccassar.

Tuesday, Aug. 20   Arrived at Maccassar in evening.

Wednesday, Aug. 21–Thursday, Aug. 22   At Maccassar, looked about town some. Not much to see. Left in night.

Sunday, Aug. 25   Arrived at Amboina in morning. In forenoon I went up on hills back of town. Quite a pretty place.

Monday, Aug. 26   Visited Resident's office,[17] and he asked me to come to house at 5 P.M. to see his collection. Had many interesting things. Gave me letter to Assistant Resident at Amahei, and wrote to Fak-Fak also.

Tuesday, Aug. 27   Left in morning. Afternoon at Saparoea, nothing of much interest here. Took on board many pots for Banda. The large bowls were glazed inside with dammar gum.

Wednesday, Aug. 28   Early morning at Amahei, where stayed about 2½ hrs. Here visited Assistant Resident and gave him letter. An army lieutenant from Wahai had just arrived (Crossed island in 4 days), and returned to Wahai by steamer. He promised to try to get some things for me.

About 1 P.M. arrived at Taloeti-bay, where stayed till midnight. Here spent afternoon ashore. Saw sago working. Hammer of bamboo. (Sometimes with stone in end.) Strained through fibre from cocoanut tree, but caught in bases of sago leaves, 2 or 3 fastened together as trough.

Saw also fish traps made by Timor men.

Left in night for Banda.

17. The resident was H. J. A. Raedt van Oldenbarnevelt.

Fig. 7.56. "Men of Kaimana in village near settlement, Kaimana, Dutch New Guinea." A-37852 (1319).

Thursday, Aug. 29 Spent day at Banda. In morning walked around town. Have seen canoes with double outrigger everywhere east from Lombock (first seen). Double outriggers were also seen at Daru.

Friday, Aug. 30 Arrived at Geser in morning, but did not stop long, and did not go ashore.

Saturday, Aug. 31 At Kaimana most of day. Settlement of Malays and Chinese only. One small native village about 2 miles away, where went in afternoon in launch. Nothing of interest. Natives had nothing Papuan, unless (?) a stone for cooking sago cakes, cut out like the baked clay ones. Said it came from mountains in interior.

Sunday, Sept. 1 Most of day at Fak-Fak. No native village within reach.

Monday, Sept. 2 Most of day at Kokas. Here met Assistant-Resident. In forenoon visited native village about ½ hr. distant. Resident told "raja" to take me there. Built on shore and partly over water, with plank to shore. Natives gave me few things, would take no pay. Evidently resident had told "raja" not to take anything. Saw some good Ceram drums.

In afternoon went with Mr. Schmid to another village, and bought a few things. Pots with covers they said from large village about day's journey away. Natives not pure Papuan type, but apparently much mixed with Malays.

Fig. 7.57. Sago ovens. Kei Islands: "made of coarse reddish clay," 143674 (9510), "cut out of soft, light-colored stone (volcanic tufa?)," 143670 (9506), both from Brother Dominic; *sniere,* made of very soft sandstone, Tenimber Islands (below), 143559 (3-V), from Father Cappers; Kokas, west end, Dutch New Guinea, 143291 (9687). A-112217.

Tuesday, Sept. 3   Arrived at Wahai about 11 A.M. I spent rest of day there. Walked to village of inland people (Alfur) about 3 miles away, but found nothing there. New village, well built.

Wednesday, Sept. 4   Arrived at Piroe about 2 P.M. Visited village and got boy to show where sago made. Took some photos. Same as at Taloeti-Bay. Heard a German trader (Oelhoff) near had a good Ceram collection, but he was not close enough to allow of a visit.

Thursday, Sept. 5–Saturday, Sept. 7   Arrived in Amboina in morning. As this was end of this trip, had to stop at hotel for 3 days. Went to Hotel Esplanade (Hotel des Arte) with Mr. Conrad Schmid, of the firm A. Schmid, Maccassar, who had helped me in many ways on trip.

Saturday evening visited the Resident, and at the Club met Mr. Wollaston and Gosse,[18] of the English expedition. Also saw the book Mr. Wollaston [1912] had written of his last trip.

Sunday, Sept. 8   Left at 5 P.M. Had fever in afternoon, so went aboard and to bed.

Monday, Sept. 9   Spent day at Banda. Not well yet.

Tuesday, Sept. 10   Arrived at Toeal, Kei Islands in morning. No natives to be seen here. Here gave Bro. Dominic[19] of Catholic Mission, 50 G.[20] for specimens to be delivered to steamer in Nov.

Left at 2 P.M. for Elat, where arrived about 4:30, and stayed over night. Missionary to get 5–15 pots, and leave in Controleur's office, Toeal.

Wednesday, Sept. 11   Left in morning for Dobo, where arrived about 3 P.M. All town on a sand-spit, as in Wallace's time. Saw a few natives here, as they came in to meet some of their "rajas," who had been to Ambon on a

18. He means C. Boden Kloss of the Federated Malay States Museum in Kuala Lumpur.
19. This appears to be Brother Dominic van Roessel, MSC.
20. ABL generally abbreviates guilders as "G." rather than the more accepted "ƒ."

Fig. 7.58. Earthenware from the Kei Islands. Back row: large earthen jar with cover, 107871 (MC-52), small earthen stand or shallow dish, 107876 (—), large heavy bowl, 107873 (—), small red vessel, 143857 (—), large painted pot (uncataloged). Front row: large pot, painted designs in red and white, 143859 (—), teapot, 143856 (9464), bottle with floral designs below neck, painted red and white, 143648 (—), pitcher, painted, 143662 (9476), shallow dish with pedestal, 107874 (—). All from Brother Dominic. A-112227.

visit, and were returning on ship. These were dressed in white suit, straw hat, white shoes, etc. and I had not noticed them before.

The Dobo people seemed rather slender, and smaller than the average Papuan, but as dark as the Papuan Gulf natives, and features of the Papuan type, in general, but still different from any I had seen.

Met here a Mr. O'brien,[21] from Boston, who was traveling in the east, writing a tourist book, so he said.

Met also Mr. A. S. Clark, brother of Mr. Clark of Ceram.

Thursday, Sept. 12   Stayed at Dobo till 3 P.M. when left for Tenimber Islands.

Friday, Sept. 13   Arrived about 8:30 A.M. at Larat, a small island just north of the large Tenimber. Here went ashore, and found the usual assortment of Malay, Arab, Chinese, etc. with a few natives. These are much lighter than the Papuans. Lighter even than most of the Malays,—a yellowish brown, with wavy to curly hair, colored reddish to flaxen color with lime. This is cut short or worn long (1–2 ft.) wrapped up in cloth. The men are good size, larger than the Kei Islanders, and a quite different type, in color, features, and build. They seem not unlike Polynesians.

_____

21. It is not clear who this writer may have been. The popular travel writer Frederick O'Brien (1919, 1921) wrote somewhat later and primarily about Polynesia.

520

Fig. 7.59. "Natives of Adaoet on board ship, Tenimber Islands." A-37839 (1488).

Saturday, Sept. 14 In morning at Lakateroe, where stayed an hour or so, (gave Father Cappers G.400 for specimens), then to Adaoet. Here a number of canoes came out to meet us, and paddled around the ship with beat of drums and singing. Afterwards they came aboard, and I took some photos of them. Later went ashore and got some more photos. The peculiar head ornament of the men is now made of European cloth only, this often of different colors, yellow and red predominating. Got a few specimens only. All the natives near had been removed to the new village near the landing, and the houses were like the usual Malay type, and no carvings to be seen.

Sunday, Sept. 15 In morning at Tepa, where stayed but a short time, and then left for Dobo. Here left G.50 with a missionary to get some specimens, to be put on board steamer in 2 months.[22]

22. These specimens seem to have been sent by Father Cappers and commingled with ABL's collection.

Fig. 7.60. "A woman weaving, Adaoet, Tenimber Islands." A-37644 (1496).

Monday, Sept. 16   Arrived in Dobo in forenoon, where stopped but hour or so, and then left for Merauke, where arrived Sept. 18. The day before I was taken sick with black-water fever, and when arrived was unable to go ashore. The next day the Captain spoke to the Cath. Mission, who agreed to take me in, and I was taken ashore to the mission and put to bed, where remained for nearly two months before was able to get about much.

(Capt. H. Huijkman, Steamer *Duymaer van Twist*.)

Wednesday, Sept. 18–Wednesday, Nov. 13   Stayed at Merauke. For the first month was hardly able to get out of bed. Bro. Hamers of the mission, took care of me. After about 5 weeks was able to get out a little, and take a short walk in morning with Father Viegen.

First went to native village about 1 hr. distant on Nov. 1st. On Nov. 2nd went again and took a few photos. From this till end of my stay visited villages several times, and took and developed a considerable (about 150) number of photos. Also bought a few large drums (from Malays).

Owing to the great number of Malays and Chinese (about 1,000) in and around Merauke, who trade for cocoanuts, the natives have all the European things they wish, and will not sell their things, so it is very difficult to get anything near Merauke, or indeed anywhere where it is safe to go. There is a mission station about 15 hrs. west of Merauke, and it is regarded as safe some ten hours further. One can only go a few hours inland, or to the east, when one quickly reaches regions regarded as unsafe. The government has very little influence a few days' march away from Merauke. They have not enough soldiers to properly police the region, and at present no ship. From the English border to 100 miles or more west of Merauke, the language is much the same, also for some days inland. The differences are only dialectic. The natives sometimes come from as far as the English area to visit the villages here, on occasion of special ceremonies, but immediately return, as they fear any longer stay.

522

Fig. 7.61. Native loom with partly woven band, brown, yellow red, and white, Ceram, 143921 (K-6). From Kraijer van Aalst, Piroe, Ceram. A-112257.

These natives are dark in color, nearly black, varying to a yellowish brown. The color seems about the same as in the Papuan Gulf, not so black, perhaps, as at mouth of Fly. The men are large, mostly as tall or taller than I am (5 ft. 9 in.). Some of the women even as tall as I. In general, they are the largest people I have seen in New Guinea. Types, dress, and general appearance may be seen in photos. They have extensive plantations of cocoanuts, sago, yams, taro, etc. extending for miles inland and almost continuously along the coast, and are well supplied with food. These plantations demand much care, as the land must be raised above high water of the rainy season, when the country is practically flooded, and there is an extensive system of ditches 3–4 ft. deep. The villages of the coastal tribes are

523

Fig. 7.62. "Mission house, Merauke."
For six weeks ABL was nursed back to
health here. A-37069 (1462).

all built on the sand ridge thrown up just above high water mark, and form
a single irregular line of houses, surrounded by fences (see photos). Inland
all is swamp.

The houses are low, wretched sheds, made of pole frame and sides of
sago or cocoanut leaf-stalks and mats, roof of same. In these there is a
sleeping platform about 3 ft. high. The men live together in one house, and
women in another. These are usually not very large, so that every village
contains many houses. Boys after a certain age (or class) must live in separate house outside of village, and must not be seen by the women. (For
classes, and dress & ornaments of same see *Anthropos,* [Nollen] 1909.)

Fig. 7.63. "Yasuk, Nori, and Poti (all
kivazum-iwag group), Merauke."
A-37318 (1393).

524

Fig. 7.64. Sau (*ewati* group), left; Monai (*amnangib* group), right, Merauke. A-37354 (1416).

Cooking chiefly by baking with hot stones—sometimes over open fire. Food is fairly varied, tho sago forms the staple, often made into cakes with scraped cocoanut and cocoanut milk. No pottery. The simplest shallow wood platters rare. (Usually use leaves.) Some rather crude baskets are also made. The only carving seen was on the posts of some of the men's houses.

Some of the villages are quite large, up to 2,000.

Thursday, Nov. 14   Left Merauke in evening with steamer *Van Riemsdijk*. The Captain was 1st mate in K.P. steamer whose 3 officials were killed at Merauke about 1898 (at village where most of my pictures were taken), and was badly wounded [at the] time.

Sunday, Nov. 17   Dobo.

Monday, Nov. 18   Elat (Great Kei).

Tuesday, Nov. 19   Toeal. Here Bro. Dominic had 5 boxes of Kei specimens (224 nos.), for which I paid him 400 G. in addition to the 50 I had before given him. These were taken to Ambon, from where 3 were sent on with box of skulls from Merauke (Nos. 205–208), and 2 taken ashore to repack at Ambon.

Wednesday, Nov. 20   Returned to Great Kei to load timber which took nearly all day. Then to Geser.

Thursday, Nov. 21   Banda.

Fig. 7.65. "Kukan (*a patur* group), Merauke." A-37284 (1339).

525

Fig. 7.66. "Borom (*ewati* group), Merauke." A-37372 (1351).

Fig. 7.67. Soft, woven baskets from the South Coast: baby cradle (*kabu*), used to carry the baby, 143010 (28); bag from Jei (*Jei wad*), 143005 (31); Mayo bag (*majo wad*), 143009 (32). From the Catholic Mission, Merauke. A-112220.

Fig. 7.68. Baskets from the Moluccas: (left) two large carrying baskets and a small one, Kei Islands, 143772 (9426), 143774 (9430), 143782 (9434); open-work rattan basket with cover and open-work pot support, Kei Islands, 143715 (9517), 143714 (9519); small woven jar and round basket, both coiled, Kei Islands, 143800 (9121), 143789 (_____); woven food covers, Kei Islands, 143751 (9513), 143753 (9511); (top center) Ceram, 143915 (K-11); large coiled basket *(trifu)* with cover, used for valuables in house, Tenimber Islands, 143547 (13-IV); two ornate baskets with covers, "used to contain articles used in betel-nut chewing, Tenimber Islands," 143539 (5-II), 143538 (4-II). Kei baskets from Brother Dominic, Ceram basket from Kraijer van Aalst, Tenimber baskets from Cappers. A-112273.

Friday, Nov. 22   Ceram and Saparoea.

Saturday, Nov. 23   Amboina. Here left steamer and stopped till one for North Coast of New Guinea arrived.

Sunday, Nov. 24–Monday, Dec. 2   At Ambon. Packed up specimens from West N.G. left here in boxes 209–210, which had some stuff in from Great Kei. Also 211 and 212 with books, batik, and negatives.

Tuesday, Dec. 3   Left Amboina in evening. Kajeli (Buru Isl.).

Wednesday, Dec. 4   Laiwoi (Obi Isl.), and Batjan.

Thursday, Dec. 5   Ternate.

Friday, Dec. 6   Ternate.

527

Saturday, Dec. 7   Left Ternate in evening.

Sunday, Dec. 8   Tobelo. Here the missionary[23] said he would try to get me a few things from Halmaheira, or rather, from the particular tribe around Tobelo. Said about 25 separate tribes and languages in Halmaheira. In evening stopped at Ake-Selaka.

Monday, Dec. 9   Buli and Weda.

Tuesday, Dec. 10   Putani. Here many nice hats and boxes, covered with yellow stems of orchids, are made. Sometimes mica plates are also used, under an open net or lattice work. The Chinese and Malay traders on the steamer had bought out everything before I got ashore, so got but one hat.

Wednesday, Dec. 11   Sorong, W. New Guinea.

Thursday, Dec. 12   Manokwari in evening.

Friday, Dec. 13   Day at Manokwari. Saw Rev. Van Hasselt, and he promised to get a collection of North New Guinea specimens for the Museum. He thought he could get good collection for G. 1000. Gave him 500 G. Left at 5 P.M.

Saturday, Dec. 14   At Roon in forenoon. Stopped but 2 hrs. then to Wooi bay, where arrived after dark, and left early in morning. Did not go ashore at either place. Natives at Roon seemed rather small, with more primitive type of face (progn. jaws, deep sunken bridge of nose, etc.) than usual in N.G. Settlement where we stopped all Malays, Chinese, Arabs, etc. Native village at some distance to one side, on piles in water. Houses much as seen before.

Sunday, Dec. 15   Arrived at Ansus about 8 A.M. Harbour well protected. Settlement and large native village all on piles, as country seemed to be all swamp. Went to native village in canoe with Chief Engineer, but natives would not let us in houses. Some of these were very long. All seemed to have a central open passage way, with closed rooms on each side so that the large houses contained many families. Passage about $\frac{1}{3}$ width of house. The roof of front veranda sloped *down* and narrowed. Said they had no pots. Saw no good things. A few round wood bowls, with raised rim around base. Bows and arrows, some with bone points,—not very long. Bows mostly palm wood (saw one bamboo) with rattan string.

Monday, Dec. 16   Left Ansus about 9 A.M. Before this I went over to village in canoe and took a few pictures. Developed after starting, 3 doz. negatives.

Tuesday, Dec. 17   In morning arrived at Wakde, where stayed till 5 P.M. Wakde an island about 2 miles from mainland, whither the settlement from Jamna was moved in April (on account of lack of water). Natives not many,—about a doz. houses. These all on shore, but on posts about 4 ft. high. One house (sacred house ?) was larger than others, with painted boards placed edge to edge on front and back, perpendicular (see photo). Inside

---

23. Missionary A. Hueting.

Fig. 7.69. "View of Malay and Chinese settlement, Ansus, Jappen Island." A-37429 (1529).

Fig. 7.70. "Prow end of a canoe, Wakde." A-37423 (1537).

Fig. 7.71. Wooden headrests: with scroll work, Wakde, 143411 (9822); scroll work with a double-headed figure at base and string of blue and black beads, east coast of Geelvink Bay, 143309 (9831); Mokmer, Wiak [Biak] Island, 143397 (9784). A-112222.

empty, but several fire places. End of beams in front nicely carved. Natives here fairly good at carving. Large harpoon, carved at one end. Carvings on ends of canoes. No images seen. Pots from Humboldt's bay. Bows (palm) and arrows (rather long, often points much carved in blunt bark, some bone points. Much larger than seen at Roön or Ansus).

Wednesday, Dec. 18 In morning at Humboldt Bay, or rather at Hollandia Bay, a small bay at western end of Humboldt Bay proper, where the gov. station has been established about two years. The settlement is on the

Fig. 7.72. "Back of sacred or *tamburan* house, Wakde. The only difference between this and the front was that the ends of the beams were covered in front, but not at back." A-37418 (1552).

530

15 cm

Fig. 7.73. Painted earthenware pot, Humboldt Bay, 148030 (9772). A-112095.

Fig. 7.74. "View of houses in Hollandia Bay from the sea, Humboldt Bay." A-37449 (1556).

Fig. 7.75. "Man in canoe, Humboldt Bay." A-37476 (1572).

main land, but the native village is on a small island (see photo from ship at anchor).

First visited the controleur, Mr. Westerveld,[24] and he gave me a few specimens. Then I went with native canoe to the village, where took some photos and bought a few things, mostly lime gourds. The natives did not seem to have much or were unwilling to sell. They also objected to my looking in the houses much. The houses are nearly square, with 4 sided pyramidal roof, which is steep, and extends rather low down (see photos) covering a sort of front veranda before the interior of the house proper, which is 2–4 feet above the ground. They all seemed to be family houses.

Got back to ship about 11 A.M., just as it began to rain, which continued most of rest of day.

Thursday, Dec. 19 Was also rainy. Many natives came aboard. Took some photos and got some things, but did not go to village.

Left about 5 P.M. Several men went with ship to Wakde with many pots, and I got 8 painted ones from them.

Friday, Dec. 20 At Wakde in morning. Here with the assistance of the chief, I got a small canoe, 7 harpoons, drum, and few other things. Mr. Alexander helped me in talking to chief and bargaining for canoe. Left about 10 A.M.

Saturday, Dec. 21 Arrived at Mokmer (Biak or Wiak Island) in morning. Here the natives have a rather bad reputation, and had several years before shot at steamer people. I was advised not to go to village. Here Lieut. Eland[25] and gov. exploring expedition, who had been in island for a month

24. He means Controleur J. A. Wasterval.
25. This seems to be Lt. G. A. Ilgen.

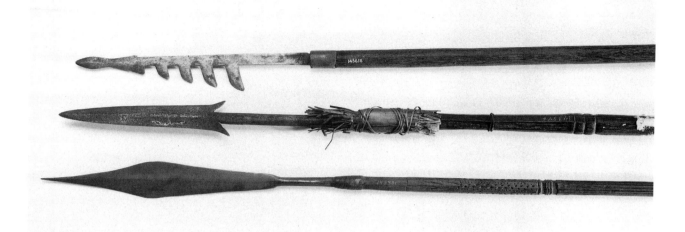

Fig. 7.76. Iron-bladed spears: "Mokmer, Wiak Island (the iron heads are made on Wiak [Biak] by the natives)," 143381 (9794); Halmahera, 143896 (_____), from Hueting, Tobelo; barbed-iron head, Tenimber Islands, 143618 (_____), from Cappers, Lakateroe. A-112253.

or more, came aboard, to return to Manakwari. He said it was perfectly safe now. As the village was a long way off, and the natives brought the things to ship (also was rainy) did not go to village. Here got some spears and shield (rare). Iron points of spears are made here, so Lieut. E. said. Also said houses were same as on Jappen Island (Ansus and Pom). Canoes here with double outrigger, more of Malay style, often with carved and painted ends. Settlement consisted of only 3 houses, but had cargo to keep us all day.

Sunday, Dec. 22   In morning at Pom (Jappen Island). Here went to village in boat with Lieut. E. and took some photos. Natives would not let us on or in houses. All these on piles, none on shore. Many traders at settlement, about ½ mile from village. Left in afternoon and arrived at Manakwari in night.

Monday, Dec. 23   Stayed at Manakwari till about 2 P.M. Here Capt. ten Klooster gave me a box of very interesting specimens. I gave missionary van Hasselt some of my old outfit, in exchange for specimens (to be sent later).

Pottery is made at Manakwari, and in few other places on north coast. So far as I could learn, it is always worked by hand into shape, from a single mass of clay. Is usually simple. Only simple pots, plain, are made at Saparoea, and these are traded far and wide. Many were taken to Banda on ship when I went there, and transhipped there to prows for other islands. No pots are made on Ceram, or in Halmaheira, so far as I could learn.

At Kei Islands the makers came originally from Banda, and settled at Kei. No pots made at Tenimber or Aru Islands, or on south coast of New Guinea, as far as I could find. On West end made near Kokas, prob. in several places.

At Saparoea made by hand of one piece of clay. While still hot are often given a sort of glaze by rubbing over with damar. (Compare Fiji.)

533

Fig. 7.77. Carved drums: *tibal* with lizard-skin head, Tenimber Islands, 143612 (IV-1), from Cappers; with lizard-skin head, Wakde, 143412 (9821); with lizard-skin head, Pom, Jappen Island, 143337 (9823); with head of hide, Mokmer, Wiak [Biak] Island, 143396 (9820). A-112224.

Tuesday, Dec. 24   Sorong in morning for few hours. This only a trading settlement on small island.

Wednesday, Dec. 25   Morning at Weda. Here Mr. G. E. Vincent (of Molluca Trading Co.) came aboard for Ternate, and brought me some hats of native make. That evening we called at Patani, but as after dark, did not go ashore.

Thursday, Dec. 26   At Boeli in morning. Here visited missionaries house, but not much to see. Got one drum.

Friday, Dec. 27   In morning at Ake-Selaka (plantation of Herr Duivenbode [?]), only a plantation—no native settlement. Left at 9. About noon arrived at Tobelo. Here visited Mr. A. Hueting, the missionary. He sold me 2 native women's dresses, of painted bark cloth. Said he would try and get me some things, so left him 110 guldens for this, with instructions to send to Mr. Vincent at Ternate to be forwarded.

Fig. 7.78. Ornamented bamboo lime containers, incised designs: east coast of Geelvink Bay, 143323 (9856), from ten Klooster; collected Ansus, Jappen Island, 143326 (9723) (with stopper, design unfinished), 143327 (9722). A-112230.

Fig. 7.79. "Carved wooden images *(karwar),* made on the death of some important person, and supposed to abide in the image. Food is offered at feasts to this, and its help is sought for various purposes, Wiak [Biak] Island." 143379 (9834), 143378 (9834). From ten Klooster. A-112221.

535

Fig. 7.80. Carved male figure, Jamna; red and black pigments, 143433 (9835). From ten Klooster. A-112231.

Most of the people of Halmaheira now live on the coast, and live as the Malays, etc. in rest of archipelago. The principal thing still made peculiar to Halmaheira are the hats and food covers, also boxes.

Saturday, Dec. 28　At Ternate in morning. Left my specimens with Mr. G. E. Vincent to pack and forward to Museum.

Sunday, Dec. 29　Stopped a few hrs. at Batjan.

Monday, Dec. 30　Ditto Lawoei.

Wednesday, Jan. 1, 1913　Arrived in morning at Ambon.

Thursday, Jan. 2　Visited Mr. H. Kraijer van Aalst, missionary at Piroe, Ceram, and he promised to get for the Museum a collection from Ceram, and forward it later. Gave him 450 guldens for same, which he said he thought would be sufficient for all that could at present be obtained.

In afternoon called on Resident Herr Raedt van Oldenbarneveld. Left about 12 midnight.

Friday, Jan. 3　Arrived at Banda shortly after noon.

Saturday, Jan. 4　Left at 8 A.M. for Peroe (Buru Isl.).

Sunday, Jan. 5　Arrived at Peroe in morning. Anchored outside of harbor, which is small, with narrow entrance, so if weather good, ships do not go in. Small settlement of usual character. Left at 9 A.M.

Monday, Jan. 6　At Boeton. Fine harbour, and many villages around.

Tuesday, Jan. 7　Arrived Maccassar.

Wednesday, Jan. 8　Left Maccassar.

Thursday, Jan. 9　Arrived Lombok, went ashore and visited old sultan's place, where fine pond and Hindu temple.

Saw woman weaving sarongs with gold thread patterns. Asked ƒ75 for one.

Saturday, Jan. 11　Bali.

Sunday, Jan. 12　Soerabaja.

Monday, Jan. 13　Left Soerabaja in afternoon.

Tuesday, Jan. 14　Samarang all day. Pekalongen in night.

Wednesday, Jan. 15　Morning at Tegal, afternoon Cheribon.

At all these places on north coast of Java had to anchor far out in ocean—no harbour, so did not go ashore.

Thursday, Jan. 16　Arrived at Batavia, and went to Hotel den Nederlanden. Visited Consul Rairden.

536

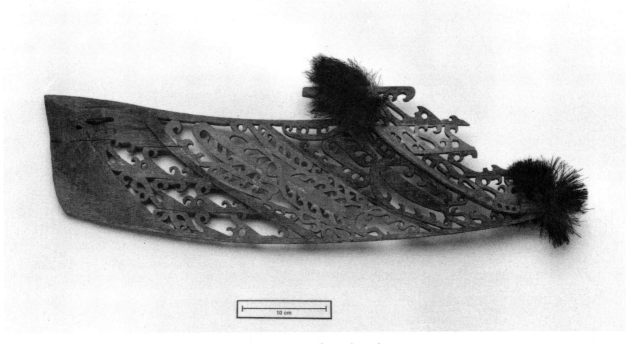

Fig. 7.81. "Canoe prow ornament with rather thin band cut in open fretwork, Mokmer, Wiak [Biak] Island." Ornamented with two bunches of black fiber, 143394 (9797). A-112311.

Friday, Jan. 17–Friday, Jan. 24 Spent time at Museum, and looking over new and old books, of which I got a few at Kolff & Co. They also helped pack 2 boxes, and agreed to forward same to Chicago for me. Settled account with K.P.M., who agreed to notify all ships' officers and agents to forward freight for Museum charges collect in New York.

Saturday, Jan. 25 Left in *Rumphius* at 3:45 for Singapore.

The Long Road Home:
From Batavia to Chicago

||||||||||||||||||||||||||||||||||||||||||||||||||||||||||||||||||||||||||||||||||||||||||||||||||||||||||||||||||||||||||||

Once ABL left Batavia for Singapore he stopped writing in his diary, but he described the rest of his expedition in correspondence. Only two letters to Dorsey survive, one written 25 January 1913 aboard the *Rumphius* and another written near Naples three months later aboard the *Prinz-Regent Luitpold*. Dorsey's response to each of these letters has also survived and offers some sense of how ABL's work—not to mention his crates—was being received back home. ABL's letter from the *Rumphius* was the first word anyone at Field Museum had heard from him in two months, when he had informed Dorsey of his bout with blackwater fever. These letters describe the complex world of tourist attractions, museum visits, curio dealers, and visits with professional colleagues into which he had now emerged after forty-five months in the South Seas. They also document the conditions that he would soon confront back in the museum.

ABL's trip home was a mix of business and pleasure. He took in a number of tourist attractions in India, Egypt, and Europe, but he spent nearly as much time visiting museums and curio dealers. It is not clear from surviving documents which anthropologists he met in Europe, but one presumes he visited with Haddon and probably several German or Dutch scholars in Hamburg, Berlin, and Leiden.

One of most significant aspects of this correspondence is Dorsey's unrestrained satisfaction and delight with the results of ABL's work. Here he writes that Skiff and other administrators had by now revised their earlier opinions of ABL's collections. Dorsey delicately alludes to the sharp letter Skiff had written three years earlier (4 February 1910, discussed in book 4), which ABL received while at Friedrich Wilhelmshafen. The "petty spirit" of 1910 had been transformed into elation with the growing mountain of boxes and packing crates that were still arriving at the museum.

One can well imagine ABL's pleasure at reading these encouraging words about how his expedition was being received. And he must have been delighted to hear Dorsey say about his work what he already knew: "Your trip [has] been one of marvelous success, in fact, one of the most remarkable trips ever made by any ethnologist, yielding results far beyond our expectations." ABL was ready to go home to Chicago.

KONINKLIJKE PAKETVAART MAATSCHAPPIJ

S.S. <u>Rumphius</u>
26th Jan. 1913

Dear Dr. Dorsey:

I am now on my way to Singapore and have left the Dutch Indies. My trip to North Coast of N.G. was not very fruitful, as the country has been pretty well raked over for years. I got some things, and had some very nice things given me by the Capt. of the Dutch Exploring Expedition of the north coast. It is now the rainy season, and not much doing. Rev. van Hasselt, of Manakwari, has agreed to get what he can after the rains are over. He travels along the whole coast east to Humboldt Bay, and knows the region better than anyone else. From Halmahera I hope also to get a few things, but they are very rare there now. The Rev. Mr. Hueting has said he would do what he could to get some things, and he can if any one can. Also from Ceram I hope to get a few things, as these people were wild up to a few years ago. The things I got are to be packed and forwarded by J. E. Vincent (head of the Molluka Co.) of Ternate, as the ship did not stop long enough for me to get them packed myself, and to have brought the things loose to Batavia would have cost much more, and been dangerous for the specimens too.

Father Cappers writes me that he has a fine collection from the Tenimber Islands all ready to ship, but that it is held up by the company demanding freight prepaid. I have smoothed this out now with the head office, so hope there will be no further delay in shipping. He is to send a full list to the Museum, which you may have already received.

From Burns Philp & Co. I hear that Thos. Stephens of Ambryn has sent in a dozen or more cases from the New Hebrides. I suppose you have received full lists of these.

Rev. J. W. Blencowe, of Santa Cruz Group, writes that he was confined to his house by hostile natives for some months, and then left the Islands. Much of his property was destroyed. He hopes to go back soon, however, and has promised to do what he can for us. It is just as well I did not go to the Santa Cruz group, as you suggested at Sydney!

I am sending from Batavia two boxes with camera and a few other things of outfit, (most of my stuff I traded off for specimens) together with some books and negatives.

I enclose list of some books which I should like ordered. Possibly the library already has two or three of the latter ones, but I put them down to be sure.

The government "Pandhuis" has promised to send a copy of their publications, with atlas of illustrations, including all the rare batik patterns. This is a special book, not on the market and not to be bought. I might add that I can read Dutch now almost as readily as German.

I will send under separate cover a list of specimens and of negatives from Dutch territory. On the last page is a list of correspondents from whom specimens may be expected sooner or later, though I have told them to be in no haste, but be sure and get good things.

Have you heard from Herr William Gramms, Awar, German New Guinea? I hope he will continue to collect for the Museum, as he is most favorably situated for that purpose—about the nearest settler to the most interesting part of <u>all</u> <u>New Guinea</u>.

Address: Care Thos. Cook & Son, Cairo, Egypt, up to the first of April or a little later. Have not worked out my full program yet.

Very sincerely yours,
A. B. Lewis

FIELD MUSEUM OF NATURAL HISTORY
CHICAGO

March 4, 1913

Dr. A. B. Lewis
c/o Thomas Cook and Son
Cairo, Egypt

My dear Lewis:

Your letter of January 26, written on the steamer between Java and Singapore, is just now received. I am very glad indeed to know that you have escaped New Guinea and the perils of Melanesia with a whole skin, even though it may be a little scarred by the battles you have fought. I don't mind telling you that your letter telling me of your attack of black water fever worried me a great deal. It is a very serious trouble. I congratulate you on having pulled through. I would have acknowledged receipt of that letter, but you gave me no address.

I hope very very much that your trip between Singapore and Cairo has been all that you could wish. I am sure you will have enjoyed India, and trust that that visit was one of unalloyed joy and pleasure. Egypt, too, will appeal strongly to you, I am sure. You will of course, go to Berlin and Hamburg. They have a new building in Hamburg now and more of the <u>Peiho</u> stuff is put up. They are a pretty mean lot there, at least so I found them last month, and will want to keep you from seeing much. Don't let that deter you, but find your way about. Haddon will be much pleased to entertain you in Cambridge. Before you go over to London write him,—3 Cranmer Road,—giving him a London address so that, if he sees fit, he will invite you to his house during your visit in Cambridge; and above all, rest assured that you will find a warm welcome for you back home, with everybody glad to see you. Meanwhile, I am doing what I can to get things in working order so that on your return you can proceed to the work of unboxing, etc. with as little inconvenience as possible.

I will not bother you with details concerning collections, etc., suggested in your letter. These will be taken care of in due time. I had a long talk with Mr. Stanley Field the other day, who, naturally, takes great interest in your work and who was much delighted and gratified when I told him that your trip had been one of marvelous success, in fact, one of the most remarkable trips ever made by any ethnologist, yielding results far beyond our expectations. To put it another way, even though I venture on rather delicate ground: the petty spirit which prompted a certain letter a few years ago has entirely disappeared, for, although authorities have seen very little of the inside of your boxes, yet, from the number and size of them, conviction is driven home to them that you have made good, and they are correspondingly elated.

We are all well here and all here except Owen, who has been spending a couple of months among the Hopi. I expect him home within a week or two. [Berthold] Laufer and [Fay-Cooper] Cole are both busy on their collections, and there is a good deal of installation work going on, due to the fact that we have, at last, what amounts to an unlimited supply of cases.

The list of books that you sent in will be at once transferred to the proper course, and I will urge their immediate purchase so that as many as possible may find you on your return.

We have heard nothing of Gramms of Awar.

Now, again with best wishes for your health and happiness and safe return home, and my best congratulations for the completion of your wonderful trip, believe me

Sincerely yours,
Geo. A. Dorsey

NORDDEUTSCHER LLOYD, BREMEN
DAMPFER *PRINZ-REGENT LUITPOLD*

Near Naples
April 19, 1913

Dear Dr. Dorsey:

Your letter of Mar. 4th I received at Cairo. I was there just five days—altogether too few! The museum itself is worth a week. I followed your program very closely.

From Singapore I went to Calcutta instead of Colombo, which gave me three days at Rangoon. I visited all the places you gave me in the outline, except Johalpur, and in addition Lahore, Hyderabad, and the Seven pagodas south of Madras (very easily reached from Chinbepat [?] station). Darjeeling was grand. The day I went up it was raining, and very little could be seen on the way; but the next day was bright and clear in the morning, with not a cloud to obscure the whole range of the Himalayas. I was very chilly, tho, and I wished I had that overcoat. Also caught a bad cold, which nearly laid me up for a few days. It was cold and <u>raining</u> in northern India; but central and south India were hot enough.

I have not yet decided on what date I shall sail, but shall probably get back about the first of June. There is the museum at Leiden I want to see, as well as all the other places we talked about in Sydney. I also know of some other New Guinea collections, which I should like to visit if I have time.

At Hamburg and London I wish to see what the dealers have also, and get prices. You said in Sydney I should buy any [that are] good. By your letter you have been in Hamburg recently. Do you still wish me to buy? I have no more money, not enough for myself.

Please ask Mr. Davies to send me $100.00 care Thos. Cook & Son, London. A wire to Thos. Cook & Son, Berlin will reach me if necessary.

Sincerely yours,
A. B. Lewis

FIELD MUSEUM OF NATURAL HISTORY
CHICAGO

May 3, 1913

Dr. A. B. Lewis
c/o Thomas Cook and Son
London, England

Dear Lewis:

I am delighted and at the same time greatly relieved to have your letter of April 19 written before your arrival in Naples. Ever since you had the fever in New Guinea I have been more or less worried about you. But now that you are safely out of the Tropics I trust that we can count on your living long enough to bring some order out of the vast chaos in which the South Pacific collection now exist. I am very glad, indeed, that you had the opportunity to see something of India, especially Darjeeling, Lahore, etc. The mere reading of your letter makes me quite hungry to get back there again.

There is not much to add. While we shall be very glad to see you home and while there is plenty for you to do, take your time about the European end of you journey. Davies is today sending you draft for £, c/o Cook, London. You could have had more had you wanted it.

Yes, I visited Europe this winter, and wired Umlauff about a collection of masks from Baining and Sulka, and Voogdt's material from New Guinea. These collections have arrived and are held for your hands. I should be very glad if you would inquire into any collections from New Guinea or otherwise Melanesian, and while, if your money is exhausted, you cannot buy, at least get a 60[-day] option on them, and then, on your arrival here, we will take the matter up with Mr. Field, whose father, as you know, backed up your expedition and who still maintains his interest in South Pacific work to the extent, at least, of having put up the money for the purchase of the material which I selected at Umlauff's. I understand that Boas is to spend some time in Europe soon. Perhaps you can get in touch with him. I don't know just when he is leaving, but am sending him a note to the effect that you will be there till the middle of May, in case he is sailing soon. You will, of course, visit Haddon, and you will see in Hamburg some of the <u>Peiho</u> plunder. I hope that everything will go well and satisfactorily with you while on the continent and that we may very soon have the pleasure of having you with us again.

With best wishes,

Sincerely yours,
(Geo. A. Dorsey)

Fig. 8.1. Large feather masks, Awar (Hansa Bay), mounted on manikins and installed at the south end of Stanley Field Hall, Field Museum, 132571, 132572. From Gramms, Hansa Bay. A-58765.

Return from the Field

||||||||||||||||||||||||||||||||||||||||||||||||||||||||||||||||||||||||||||||||||||||||||||||||||||||||||||||||||||||||||||||||||||||||||

ABL returned to Chicago in June 1913, just in time to celebrate his forty-sixth birthday. He had been away from Field Museum for more than four years and had much to celebrate. Most of his collection, which numbered nearly fifteen thousand items, had already arrived. But the collection was in great disorder, nearly all of it still in its original crates. More than a year earlier Simms had written that the accumulation of ABL's boxes "reminds one very much of a freight house on a busy line of railway traffic" (Simms 1912). And ABL's boxes continued to arrive. The Department of Anthropology had been forced to close off one exhibit hall just to store his more than three hundred crates and wooden boxes. One can only imagine the thoughts that ran through ABL's mind after seeing the piles of his boxes and crates stacked to the ceiling in no particular order. On the one hand, he was undoubtedly proud of his vast collection; on the other hand, he could hardly have forgotten what a headache packing these mountains of specimens had been. The prospect of unpacking, numbering, and cataloging his specimens must have given him more than a moment's pause.

Director Skiff was no longer critical of the size and quality of ABL's collection, having long ago forgotten some of his less than charitable comments written to ABL in 1910. Skiff could write of the collection with great pride in his annual report for 1912 that

> the collection forms one of the largest, most important, and most interesting ever acquired by the Museum through field work. Practically every region of Melanesia is represented. Dr. Lewis has supplemented his specimens by numerous photographs, anthropometric measurements, and photographic records. To date 277 cases have arrived at the Museum as a result of the expedition. Of these 91 have been received this year, and it is known that at least 21 cases additional are on the way. A great many of these cases exceed 10 feet in length, with other dimensions to correspond. [*FMNH Annual Report* 1913, 4:207]

Skiff was, of course, still impressed by large, showy specimens, and the large number of oversize crates must have made a deep impression on him. But while the director was pleased with the collection, he was now all the more eager that ABL quickly dispose of the great mass of boxes that for more than a year had threatened to take over the anthropology department.

Upon his arrival in Chicago, ABL seems to have suffered from "returned fieldworker's syndrome," a situation that most anthropologists experience after nearly every period of fieldwork, whether of two months' or four years' duration. Everyone seems to have wanted to hear all about his expedition—for about fifteen minutes; then they turned to more interesting topics, particularly local affairs. One major topic of interest to all at Field Museum was the site of the museum's new building.

When Field Museum founder Marshall Field died in 1906, he left the museum a substantial sum for construction of a permanent building.[1] The old building in Jackson Park had been erected for the World's Fair in 1892 and had never been intended as a permanent structure. The building was already showing its age when ABL left in 1909, and most people expected the new building would be completed before ABL returned from the South Seas. In March 1911 the museum signed an agreement with Chicago's park commissioners to build in Jackson Park on a site immediately north of the original building. For a few months in 1911 and 1912, the museum's west annex was even vacated in preparation for construction to begin.

But plans for the proposed site in Jackson Park began to unravel in 1912. The annex was reopened, and installation of new cases proceeded in anticipation of eventually having a new building. By 1914 the museum tendered an offer for another site, this time at the museum's present location on reclaimed land at the south end of Grant Park. Construction on the new building commenced in 1915 and was completed five years later.

In one way or another, the new building seems to have preoccupied nearly everyone at Field Museum for the next eight years, that is, until the museum opened its doors to the public 2 May 1921, when the present building and its exhibits were finally complete. And so, shortly after returning to the museum, with discussion about the new building very much in the air, ABL took a much needed vacation and left the city for a few weeks to visit his family in California.

Crates continued to arrive at the museum while ABL was away. In addition to those ABL himself had sent from the field, shipments were also arriving from his various agents in Melanesia. Many of these, like Waters in Fiji, Gramms in German New Guinea, and Stephens in the New Hebrides, had regularly corresponded with him while he was in the field. All three of these men, in fact, had assembled additional collections on ABL's request, and these specimens arrived at the museum during the summer of 1913.

The number of shipments that ABL anticipated from the far-flung corners of Melanesia had increased so much that he was concerned he might forget all of those with whom he had left money in the field. And the steamer tour of the East Indies and Dutch New Guinea added to the separate shipments he expected. As he left the Dutch East Indies on his way home, ABL jotted down the following note at the back of one of his specimen list notebooks:

> Shipment to be expected sooner or later
>   From Catholic Mission, Merauke
>   From Father Ed. Cappers, Tenimber
>   From van Hasselt, Manokwari
>   From J. E. Vincent (& Hueting) representing Tobelo, Halmahera
>   From Kraijer van Aalst, Piroe, Ceram
> Also from the following
>   H. L. C. Johnston, Yule Island
>   Capt. H. L. Griffin, Port Moresby
>   F. W. Ramsay, Samarai
>   T. C. Stephens, Ambrym, N. Hebrides
>   J. W. Blencowe, Santa Cruz Isl.
>   R. W. Bouchier, Ravatu, Solomons
>   Mrs. Phoebe Parkinson, Rabaul

Herr William Gramms, Hansa Bucht, Kaiser Wilhelmsland
John W. Waters, Suva, Fiji
Australian Museum, Sydney

It appears that shipments were received from all of the agents mentioned above except Blencowe and Bouchier.[2] By the end of August 1913, nearly everything had arrived, and ABL began the long process of cataloging.

In the four years ABL had been away, George Dorsey had also been busy buying still other collections from Melanesia. These purchases included a collection from the ethnologist Richard Parkinson and two collections from Captain Voogdt of the New Guinea Compagnie, all of which were bought in 1909 and 1910 out of the Joseph N. Field South Sea Islands Fund. In 1912 Dorsey had also drawn on this fund to purchase a sizeable collection from curio dealer J. F. G. Umlauff in Hamburg. This collection largely contained material Umlauff had obtained from Captain Voogdt.

None of these collections had been cataloged in ABL's absence. Even Dorsey's own German New Guinea collection, which had been in Chicago since early 1909, was still uncataloged. All of this material was waiting for ABL's attention as assistant curator of African and Melanesian ethnology. Together, all of these other collections numbered more than 10,000 items, which when added to the material ABL had brought back, meant that he now faced cataloging 25,000 specimens.[3]

ABL did not unpack, number, and catalog these collections by himself: he had preparators and assistants to help him, though he supervised every aspect of the process. But these were not his only labors; he was also expected to prepare exhibit cases for the museum's exhibition halls, selecting specimens and writing explanatory label copy. ABL had been planning to put together such exhibits for four years, but these first months back were hardly the most conducive context for mounting the grand exhibition he had long hoped for, facing, as he did, the monumental task of organizing, sorting, and cataloging all of the new Melanesian collections, a task that would occupy him for the next six years.

ABL also had to settle the expedition's financial accounts and finish itemizing all of his expenses for the four years he was away. From time to time ABL had sent in financial reports from the field, but he still had to list the rest of his expenses for the previous year or so. There were also the various new shipments from Gramms, Waters, and Stephens that had to be added to his accounts. He did not finish his expense account until two days before Christmas 1913. Then he could write Dorsey a memo announcing that he had formally closed the account of the Joseph N. Field South Pacific Islands Expedition (reproduced below).

According to ABL's expense report (reproduced below), the entire expedition had a direct cost of $19,573.95, to which ABL's salary for fifty months ($5,000) and the cost of international freight and shipping charges should be added. In all the expedition had cost well over $30,000, which if translated into today's dollars amounted to more than three-quarters of a million dollars, probably very close to one million. The expedition had been an expensive proposition from the beginning, but as the crates were unpacked one by one, it became increasingly clear to all that the quality of ABL's collections had more than justified their costs.

Cataloging and Exhibiting the Collection: 1913–1921

ABL had many burdensome responsibilities at the museum when he returned from Melanesia. Processing his thousands of specimens took up nearly all his time and seems to have prevented him from analyzing his material. In this respect, his experience was quite different from what we usually expect of anthropologists today when they return from an extended period of field research. Most anthropologists are now expected to write up their research in the form of conference papers, articles, and books. Time for analysis and writing may have to be fitted in around teaching or other responsibilities, but writing is a normal part of nearly every anthropologist's work load.

For ABL, there was no time for writing. His time was committed to curating the Melanesian collections that were now his primary responsibility. For the next eight years he had no opportunity to write up his research; there was simply too much unpacking, cataloging, and labeling to be done.

By the end of 1913 ABL had written his first three thousand catalog cards. He had also brought some organization to his negatives and had even arranged for museum photographer Charles Carpenter to make lantern slides from some of these images.[4] In November the same year he gave a public lecture at the museum illustrated with some of these slides. ABL would undoubtedly have given a number of other lectures at the museum in the next few years except that as plans for the new building materialized, the museum had been forced to discontinue its public lecture series for lack of space (*FMNH Annual Report* 1915, 4:369).

During the following years, ABL was an active member of several professional societies and organizations. From 1914 on, he was active in the American Anthropological Association; in 1919 he was elected to its council. About 1914, he also became a member of the Geographic Society of Chicago, the American Ethnological Society, Sigma Xi, and a fellow of the American Association for the Advancement of Science.

In November 1914 he gave a lecture at the Geographic Society of Chicago entitled "Life in New Guinea," which was illustrated with "many excellent colored slides of the natives and the country." A month later, he and Fay-Cooper Cole gave members of the society a tour of Field Museum's exhibits, which included the first thirty-seven cases of ABL's material from Fiji, the New Hebrides, and the Admiralty Islands.

The opening of this new Melanesian exhibit came about only after Acting Curator Berthold Laufer had urged Skiff to find space for exhibiting at least a part of ABL's collection.

> More than a year has now elapsed since Dr. Lewis's return from the field, and the public has not yet been given an opportunity of forming a correct estimation as to the wide scope and high character and quality of his work. In justice to Mr. Joseph N. Field, under whose auspices his expedition was carried on, and in justice to our cause, to the public, and to Dr. Lewis himself, I am of the opinion that at least a selection of his material should be placed on permanent exhibition, and made accessible to both students and all interested parties at the earliest possible moment. [Laufer 1914]

Skiff acceded to Laufer's request, and after Joseph N. Field's death the same year, the hall in which the collection was exhibited was named in honor of the collection's late benefactor (*FMNH Annual Report* 1915, 4:364, 370).

Each year ABL worked steadily on cataloging his collection. He completed 1,400 catalog cards in 1914 and another 8,100 cards the following year—more than half of these being the Umlauff, Voogdt, and Dorsey collections. In 1917 he finished more than 4,000 cards, and by January 1919 Skiff could announce in his annual report that with the last 984 catalog cards, all of the material from the Joseph N. Field Expedition had finally been cataloged (*FMNH Annual Report* 1919, 5:233). It had taken ABL five years to catalog all of the new collections from Melanesia, but the job was now complete.

During the period from 1913 to 1919, ABL had cataloged 25,000 objects, installed 50 cases for exhibits, and written more than 3,000 labels. But he had published nothing whatsoever about his research. His only known publications during this period are two book reviews that appeared in the *American Anthropologist* (Lewis 1916, 1919).

In 1919, with all of ABL's cataloging complete, Field Museum prepared to move into its new building in Grant Park. The new building had been nearing completion in 1918 when the United States government initiated negotiations with the museum to use the building as a military hospital during the war. Following the European armistice in November 1918, the hospital was no longer necessary, and the museum's plans changed abruptly. Skiff and the board of trustees now wanted to move into the new building as soon as possible. The entire staff turned their attention to packing up specimens, cases, and equipment for the big move.

Ironically for ABL, no sooner had he finished unpacking his mountains of crates than he had to repack everything so it could be moved by rail to the new building in May 1920. After everything was in the Grant Park building, he had twelve months in which to complete installation of the new Joseph N. Field Hall of Melanesian Ethnology (Hall A) on the ground floor. During this year, ABL installed 103 cases in the hall. It appears that he completely reorganized the exhibit, renovating all of the cases that had been on exhibit in Jackson Park. During this period of installation, ABL introduced a number of innovative exhibit cases combining photographs, raw materials, and specimens in new and interesting ways intended to illustrate the lives of Melanesian peoples rather than simply display objects. Here he put into practice some of the ideas for exhibits he had developed in the field.

Only after the new exhibit was opened to the public on 2 May 1921 could ABL feel that he had finally finished working on his collection. Only then, at the age of fifty-four, twelve years after he had set off for the South Seas, could he begin to write up the results of his research in the field.

In July 1919, after ABL had completed cataloging his collection and was busy packing up his collection for the move, one more shipment of his collection unexpectedly arrived at the museum. The Reverend van Hasselt of Manokwari, Dutch New Guinea, had made a collection for ABL as requested, sending it either just before or shortly after the outbreak of war in Europe. Long delayed by the war, van Hasselt's collection finally found its way to Chicago to join the rest of the collection of which it was a part. After more than a decade, ABL could finally put down his catalog cards; he had completed the A. B. Lewis Collection.

FIELD MUSEUM OF NATURAL HISTORY
CHICAGO

December 23, 1913

Dr. George A. Dorsey
Curator, Department of Anthropology

Dear Sir:

I have today closed the account of the Joseph N. Field South Pacific Expedition, and am asking the office to forward the balance—$97.94—to William Gramms, of Awar, German New Guinea. This is not sufficient to pay for the collection which he has sent in to the Museum, and I recommend that a further amount of $200.00 be appropriated for that purpose. The collection is worth more, and I trust that, in justice to Mr. Gramms, this amount will be forwarded to him as soon as possible.

Respectfully yours,
A. B. Lewis
Assistant Curator
Department of Anthropology

{Editor's note: The following expense report suggests that Dorsey was able to find a bit more money ($77.64) in the department's budget to send to Gramms, but not as much as ABL requested.}

List of Expenses of A. B. Lewis
JOSEPH N. FIELD SOUTH PACIFIC ISLANDS EXPEDITION, 1909–1913

Outfit, Photographic materials, etc.		691.60
Transportation—Steamer & Railroad Fares, etc.		2,270.47
Hotels, Rooms and Board, etc.	965.40	
Personal Expenses—meals, tips, washing	539.75	
Food Supplies purchased en route	344.23	1,849.38
Collections purchased [itemized below]	7,526.70	
Specimens, Books, Photographs, etc.	697.66	
Goods purchased for trade with natives	2,682.25	10,906.61
Charges for freight	1,217.97	
Hire of steamer, etc.	1,131.78	
Cost of materials and labor used in packing specimens	469.85	
Hire of carriers & transportation of same	138.24	2,957.84
Amount paid for exchange of money	105.35	
Loss on exchange (estimated)	300.00	405.35
Funds deposited with certain persons for collection of specimens		243.50
		19,314.75

Included in the above figures is the amount of Dr. Lewis' European expenses, viz., $199.14, but this amount covers nothing for transportation.

{Addendum to the bottom of this list}

March 13, 1913	John W. Waters	Fiji Islands Material	16.35
July 22, 1913	Mr. T. C. Stephens	Malekulan Skulls	67.27
Decr. 29, 1913	Wm. Gramms	New Guinea Material	175.58
			259.20

Collections Purchased by Dr. Lewis

JOSEPH N. FIELD SOUTH PACIFIC ISLANDS EXPEDITION, 1909–1913

J. W. Waters, Suva, Fiji	292.20
H. Helmich	112.50
J. W. Waters, Suva, Fiji	102.50
W. Gramms	108.75
Mrs. Parkinson	725.00
Mrs. Parkinson	261.36
Natives, New Hebrides	188.81
Natives, New Caledonia	115.01
Hagen	214.28
Tost & Rohu	246.90
Whiteman	375.00
Komine	2,269.50
W. Beaver	175.00
Riley	210.00
Ramsay	100.00
H. L. C. Johnston	100.00
H. L. Griffin	225.00
Specimens	280.00
Brother Dominic, Kei Islands	180.00
Van Hasselt	200.00
Krayer van Aalst	180.00
Sundries	864.89
	7,526.70

{Editor's note: Several of these entries seem to combine purchases made from more than one individual. For example, the entry for Brother Dominic almost certainly includes the money sent to Father Eduard Cappers, who was from the same mission. Similarly, the amount advanced to the Protestant missionary Krayer van Aalst almost certainly includes money for the collection from Tobelo, Halmahera, made by Hueting of the same mission.}

FIELD MUSEUM OF NATURAL HISTORY
CHICAGO

July 8, 1919

Dr. B. Laufer
Curator, Department of Anthropology

Dear Dr. Laufer:

While in Manokwari, Dutch New Guinea, in December, 1912, I left *f* 500 ($200.00) and some of my old equipment with Missionary F. J. F. van Hasselt, to be used in obtaining specimens from the north coast of Dutch New Guinea. He was in the habit of making trips every year to various parts of the coast, and said that in the course of two or three years he could easily make a fairly representative collection. I heard nothing from him till 1915, when I received a card saying that some material would be sent by the following steamer. Nothing further was heard till the shipment arrived a few days ago, having, apparently, been held up by the war.

The collection comprises over three hundred specimens from various places along the north coast of Dutch New Guinea, including some fine large wooden figures, house ornaments, and about twenty-five ancestral images (korwar). These are rare and valuable. Weapons, implements, household utensils, clothing and ornaments are all well represented. This part of New Guinea has been more or less visited by Europeans for many years, and very little of original native workmanship is at present to be had. The numerous Chinese and Malays settled along the coast have also tended to destroy or modify the native industries. Hence, but little from this region can be obtained, and that often betrays foreign influence. Good specimens cannot be secured in a day and this is why it took so long to bring this collection together.

Some of the specimens have suffered considerably from the long delay and rough handling, but on the whole the material was well packed and is in fairly good condition. The collection as it stands is worth much more than the cost.

Yours respectfully,
A. B. Lewis
Assistant Curator
Melanesian and African Ethnology

Fig. 8.2. *Korwar* figures, North Coast of Dutch New Guinea, 151176, 151170, 151169, 151162, 151159. From van Hasselt. A-112405.

PART

THREE

Conclusion

A. B. Lewis and
the Discipline of Anthropology
before the Great War

||||||||||||||||||||||||||||||||||||||||||||||||||||||||||||||||||||||||||||||||||||||||||||||||||||||||||

During his lifetime, A. B. Lewis was best known for four achievements: his expedition, his collection, his monograph *(The Ethnology of Melanesia)*, and the large Melanesian exhibit he installed in the Joseph N. Field Hall. Of these he was best known to the general public for his exhibit, which Field Museum visitors viewed for sixty-five years. From its opening in 1921 the Joseph N. Field Hall (Hall A) remained much as Lewis had designed it until the hall was closed for renovation in 1986.[1] For nearly all of this period it was the largest and best known Melanesian exhibit in the United States. Without doubt, this exhibit did more to inform the public about the southwest Pacific than any other museum exhibition, book, or film until at least the 1950s.

For Field Museum, the Lewis Collection has been his most lasting and important contribution. To be sure, conserving, storing, and maintaining such a collection has been for eight decades a constant reminder to museum staff of the size and importance of the collection. Willard L. Boyd, former Field Museum president, described the museum's Pacific collections—of which the Lewis Collection is the centerpiece—as one of Chicago's two great museum collections, the other being the Art Institute's world-renowned collection of impressionist paintings.

Ironically, although Lewis was proud of his collection and clearly felt it would have lasting value both for exhibition and for research, in later years it was not his collection but his expedition that he personally thought was his greatest achievement.[2] A. B. Lewis was a true bibliophile, a man much more at home in a library than in the tropical rain forests and swamps of New Guinea. And given his quiet, scholarly temperament and self-deprecating style, his expedition was—as his friend and colleague Wilfrid Hambly (1941) suggested—"a remarkable achievement of endurance." At the purely personal level, it is thus not surprising that Lewis would take such satisfaction at having successfully completed four grueling years of fieldwork in one of the world's most difficult and dangerous regions. Professionally, it would have seemed increasingly important, too, because by the 1930s American anthropologists had begun to view fieldwork as the crucial rite of passage that made one an anthropologist.

At the time of his death in 1940, however, most anthropologists would have seen his monograph, *The Ethnology of Melanesia* (1932a), as his most important contribution to the discipline. Originally written as a catalog or guide to the Joseph N. Field Hall, Lewis' only book-length publication was the first anthropological work in English that attempted to deal with all of Melanesia and its many local cultural variations. This book, like his exhibit and many of his shorter publications, was written for a general, popular audience rather than for professional anthropologists. By the 1970s and early 1980s, his pioneering book, like his other popular writings, seemed out of date, far too general, and quite out of step with modern research on Melanesia. He may have been a pioneer in Melanesian anthropology and ethnology, but he was an unrecognized and virtually unknown pioneer to younger anthropologists trained in the 1960s and 1970s.

When Lewis had finished installing his exhibit in 1921, few men or women alive knew as much as he did about the material culture of Melanesia. No anthropologist—even today—has ever visited so much of Melanesia or seen so much of its material culture in use. And no one, either before or since, has assembled such a large and diverse museum collection from this part of the Pacific.

The Joseph N. Field South Pacific Expedition was nearly the last and certainly one of the most extensive expeditions of its kind in Melanesia.[3] From its collections alone, it was unquestionably one of the most significant museum-sponsored expeditions ever to visit the southwestern Pacific, and Lewis was the leader of the only ethnological expedition that reached all of the Melanesian colonies. In these respects, his fieldwork represents the culmination of the "expedition period" of ethnological research in Melanesia. He had seen, photographed, and collected more than any other anthropologist before the Great War.

With all of these achievements behind him, A. B. Lewis should have become a major figure in Melanesian ethnology. But instead of becoming a revered founding father of anthropology in New Guinea, Lewis and his research have largely been forgotten, and for seventy years the vast collection he assembled has been ignored as younger scholars turned their attention away from comparative studies of museum collections to intensive local studies of particular villages or a single ethnic group in this region of diverse cultures.

What happened? Why didn't A. B. Lewis become the prominent anthropological figure he seemed destined to become when he returned to Chicago in the spring of 1913?

The simple answer, of course, is that anthropology changed. While Lewis was busy cataloging and installing his collection, a different style of anthropology was developing. Anthropologists started investigating quite different problems from those that had interested Lewis and his contemporaries before the war. Only one of the many diverse field strategies being tested before the Great War emerged in the 1920s as the dominant field method. With these changes in problem, field strategy, and method, Lewis' place in the discipline changed too.

Functionalism and the Demise of Museum Anthropology

While Lewis was busy cataloging his collection and installing it in Field Museum's new building in Grant Park, a new style of anthropology was being born. As Lewis unpacked his crates during the first years of the Great War in Europe, a young Polish anthropologist in the Trobriand Islands was reshaping the goals of anthropological fieldwork, in the process developing what would become known as the "ethnographic method." And a few years later, while Chicagoans enjoyed the opening of the new Joseph N. Field Hall and Field Museum's new building, functionalism, in the guise of British social anthropology, was about to be born as the seminal manuscripts of Bronislaw Malinowski (1922) and A. R. Brown (later A. R. Radcliffe-Brown 1922) neared completion.

The ethnographic method has long been associated with Malinowski, who repeatedly claimed credit for its invention. But while Malinowski—through his many students—was clearly responsible for establishing local, village-based research as the anthropological norm in Britain, claims that he single-handedly developed the ethnographic method during his fieldwork in the Trobriands are exaggerated. As Stocking (1983) has shown, Malinowski was at best only one of a number of fieldworkers who had been experimenting with systematic village-based research for several years; he was certainly not the first. But as a prolific and talented writer, who was equally adept at self-promotion, he transformed the discipline in Britain within a single generation.

Tied as the ethnographic method was to synchronic studies in a single community or ethnic group, no wonder in the 1920s and 1930s functionalism brought about a major revolution within the discipline in the British empire: acceptance of the ethnographic method marked an abrupt shift from the historical and evolutionary studies that it replaced. When Radcliffe-Brown weighed in on the side of synchronic, functionalist studies of customs, practices, and institutions in particular societies, the death knell tolled for extensive, regional studies concerned with such global processes as culture change, diffusion, evolution, and culture history. In the process, comparative ethnology using museum collections nearly ceased. Those anthropologists who persisted in addressing processual or historical questions and those who continued their comparative studies of museum collections were branded as old-fashioned and behind the times.

It was not that these earlier problems and research questions had been exhaustively studied, much less solved. Nor had museum collections been so thoroughly examined that they had yielded all they could to our understanding of how communities were related to one another or the extent to which they had interacted in the past. Victory came about largely because functional studies were presented as rigorous science in an age when anthropologists were self-consciously trying to make their discipline as systematic and scientific as physics, chemistry, and biology. Functionalists prided themselves on the accuracy of their data drawn from direct observations made by trained observers in primitive societies. They contrasted their direct observations with what they branded as "speculative" reconstructions of an unobserved past or as the unsystematic gathering of oddities and "queer occurrences."

Malinowski, for example, used his introduction to Reo Fortune's functionalist monograph, *The Sorcerers of Dobu,* to define functional ethnography as more rigorous than the "fact-worshipping, theory-dreading, curiosity hunting" anthropology that he claimed had preceded it.

> The first point concerns the definition of *fact.* As long as the anthropologist was supposed to do no more than report what was striking or sensational in a native community, he could move about just collecting observations of queer occurrences. Now that the functional method commands him to give a full picture of primitive culture, he has to analyse the forces of social cohesion, the sanctions of law, custom, and morality, the principles of primitive economic systems, and the structure of native ideas and beliefs. Nowadays, the anthropologist can no longer spread his nets far and wide to allow the queer fish of strange custom to float in, at his and their leisure. He has to investigate the relations between custom, institution, and type of behaviour. For we are now more and more interested in the connections between the component parts of an institution in the relations of institution to institution and of aspect to aspect. We are interested, that is, rather in meaning and function than in form and detail. Only an inductive generalization or a functional relation is to the modern anthropologist a real scientific fact.
>
> The functional anthropologist has constantly to make inductive generalizations from what he sees, he has to construct theories, and draw up the charters of native institutions. In short, he has constantly to theorize in the field, theorize on what he sees, hears, and experiences. [Malinowski 1932, xxiv–xxv]

Here, with one stroke of the brush, Malinowski dismissed virtually all previous anthropological studies as unsystematic, sensationalist, and nontheoretical. Clearly, Malinowski exaggerated what

559

he depicted as the unsystematic nature of ethnological research in Melanesia before the Great War; Lewis and nearly all of the other anthropologists working in Melanesia at the time were each conducting systematic surveys and studies. Even such scholars as W. H. R. Rivers, whose theoretical conclusions were fanciful even to such loyal and devoted students as Hocart (1915), had collected systematic and accurate data on kinship and social organization that is still highly respected. To be sure, these diverse ethnological surveys had different goals from those of the functionalist ethnographers (and often from one another's as well). But such differences in goals did not make that research unsystematic. As Lewis' diaries show, he was disinterested in the strange or the peculiar; for four years he focused his attention almost monotonously on mundane, empirical facts about variation in Melanesian material culture as he observed it directly in the field. Similar comments could be made about nearly every other anthropologist Lewis met during his expedition. Most ethnologists before the Great War were no more interested in recording observations of "queer occurrences" than was Malinowski. They were carefully attempting to find patterns and meaningful generalizations from direct field observations.

Anthropologists today have heard this functionalist litany rehearsed so frequently that most of us have come to accept Malinowski's claims as fact and to view the ethnographic method as the natural kind of fieldwork that anthropologists should conduct. The local problems that Malinowski and his students confronted now seem, commonsensically, to be the only sorts of problems that anthropologists should investigate.

Of course, there is nothing inherent in either functionalism or the ethnographic method that would make local ethnographic studies more rigorous and scientific than the processual and regional studies they replaced. Even as Malinowski himself described the ethnographic method, functionalist field data were subject to all of the same observational biases as data gathered during the expedition period, since data gathering was continually informed by theoretical considerations. A functional analysis was just as subject to suspect conclusions as analyses written in a culture history, evolutionary, or diffusionist mode.

Scholars from the historical school made unsubstantiated (and often inaccurate) assumptions that certain aspects of culture had persisted (essentially) unchanged as "cultural survivals." A. B. Lewis assumed that the process of culture change was more complex, that variation in material culture and other culture traits offered evidence of the combined effects of diffusion, local in situ development, and inherited traditions. Some functionalists assumed that virtually all customs, practices, and institutions interacted to inhibit cultural change, so that culture functioned to maintain stability. Other functionalists assumed that the origins of particular customs and institutions were rooted in their ability to satisfy certain basic psychological or social needs. All anthropologists made assumptions about the world, and these assumptions influenced both the data that were gathered and the conclusions that were drawn from the data.

Compared with the highly suspect analyses of the British historical school (e.g., Rivers 1914; Perry 1923; Smith 1928), the functionalists seemed—because they had more detailed data about particular communities—more able to produce new, interesting, and reliable analyses. But few of the startling associations among customs and institutions discerned in the 1920s and 1930s are now accepted as having nomothetic status as "natural laws" of society. Nevertheless, in the end British ethnography won out over ethnology, positioning itself as a more scientific fieldwork strategy (see Radcliffe-Brown 1952, 1957, 1958; see also Kuklick 1984, 1991; Stocking 1984).

Back in the United States however, functionalism was much slower to emerge as the dominant style of research. (In fact, functionalism did not really flourish in Britain until the mid to late 1930s.) In America, Franz Boas had set the agenda for anthropological research before the Great War. Not surprisingly, after the war it was again Boas who set a new agenda for the next two decades. With his first batch of students at Columbia—Kroeber, Jones, Lewis, Lowie, Speck, Sapir, Goldenweiser, and Cole—Boas had stressed the need to understand in detail the histories, linkages, and shared pasts of different communities in particular culture areas. He and his students had carried forward the banner of diffusionism (and local particularism) in their battle with naive evolutionary models (à la Lewis Henry Morgan). Toward this end Boas had stressed the need to gather careful, systematic data that could elucidate the cultural processes by which communities and societies changed.

But after the war, Boas decided that diffusionist studies had been successful; with his new batch of students he turned to a different set of problems, the most important being the threat of eugenics. These new problems generally demanded detailed local knowledge of communities rather than ethnological surveys. When in 1923 Margaret Mead began her studies with Boas, the question of "nature versus nurture" rather than evolution versus diffusion would inform her studies at Columbia, her reading, and ultimately her fieldwork.[4] Thus, by a somewhat different route, American anthropology gradually shifted to more intensive kinds of local fieldwork.

The long years of war in Europe (1914–1918) together with the period of reconstruction that followed the armistice created an effective break that served to distinguish anthropology before and after the war. Anthropology never actually ceased during the war: some researchers, like Malinowski and Thurnwald, were actually in the field during hostilities.[5] But so many scholars were involved in the war effort in one capacity or another that for several years the discipline was practically in hiatus.

When anthropological research started up again at the beginning of the new decade, great transformations were under way in both Europe and America. New social processes and philosophies were emerging, new questions and concerns had arisen, and new sources of funding for research were being established (see Stocking 1985b). The effect was to create the impression that there was a great difference between anthropology as practiced before and after the war. In this new formulation of the discipline, younger scholars sought a clean break with the old-fashioned and outmoded practices and problems that had attracted the attentions of older scholars before the war. Increasingly, these new formulations of the discipline came to focus on individual societies, leaving little role for museum-based research. With the start of this new era of anthropological research, what some scholars would later call the "museum period" of anthropology had come to an end.

The So-Called Museum Period in Anthropology

Toward the end of the nineteenth century a curious thing happened. Around the world there arose a great demand for the curios, artifacts, and handicrafts of "not-yet-civilized" peoples in colonial territories. Sailors had been bringing native curios from the Pacific back to Europe in substantial numbers since Cook's voyages of discovery and even before (see, e.g., Kaeppler 1978), but the demand for curios from exotic places increased rapidly during the industrial revolution, a fact that has variously been attributed to the rapid accumulation of disposable wealth among industrialists, to the loss (because of the availability of factory-made goods) of "traditional" European handicrafts (which loss made the arts and material culture of simpler societies seem more like a reflection of our own primitive past), and to the growth of science, which made such objects important as markers or survivals of the earlier culture histories of the world's diverse peoples.[6]

While there was a demand for curios in museums back home, individual collectors—many of whom, like Lewis, had been sent by museums—flocked to the region. Museums around the world were engaged in an intense competition with one another to get specimens, even threatening lawsuits over particular collections. As new parts of Melanesia were opened up to traders, planters, collectors, and the occasional ethnologist, older pieces were quickly bought up, and villagers started making new objects to replace them. As Lewis observed, these were sometimes made specifically to sell to foreign collectors. Virtually every collector in Melanesia thought that the villages he visited had been picked clean by previous collectors, though few actually left these villages empty-handed. When it became more difficult to find the curios they came for, professional anthropologists and ethnologists did not stop arriving, but they changed the nature of what they collected to adjust to new conditions in the villages as well as a changing demand at home. And after the war anthropologists began collecting other kinds of data rather than museum specimens. What has sometimes been called the "museum period" of anthropology came to an end, setting the stage for more intensive ethnographic studies.

Much has been written over the past quarter-century about the so-called museum period in anthropology. Sturtevant (1969, 622) coined the term to refer to the period from 1840 to 1890, when, he argued, anthropology was centered in the museum rather than in the university. More recently, Lurie (1981, 184) wrote of the museum as anthropology's "institutional homeland," noting that since the Second World War, museums have become almost irrelevant to the discipline of anthropology. As museum anthropologists, both Sturtevant and Lurie were concerned with redefining the museum's role in the discipline today, calling up images of a golden age when anthropology departments in museums played a prominent role in shaping the discipline.

With good reason, Stocking (1985a, 6ff.) took issue with both Sturtevant and Lurie. He pointed out that although ethnological collections may have been held by museums in 1840, the ethnological society was more central to the discipline in the United States until well after the founding of the Peabody Museum in 1866 (see also Hinsley 1985). Stocking (1985a, 6) also suggested that anthropology's presence in the museum "was, even in the so-called 'Museum Period,' always somewhat problematic." By this, Stocking suggests (among other points) that nineteenth-century anthropology developed along a number of diverse institutional and intellectual paths.

One institutional path was certainly the natural history museum in the United States, which played the same role as the ethnology museum in Europe. But in America the great heyday for the museum within the discipline only began in the late nineteenth century, at precisely the moment when university departments were expanding and beginning to train professional anthropologists. As Stocking notes,

> From the point of view of both the employment of anthropological personnel and the support of field research, the great period of museum anthropology only really began in the 1890s. By that time the university was already emerging as a complementary, but in the longer run alternative (and dominating) institutional setting. [Stocking 1985a, 8]

Anthropology did not begin in the museum and move to the university, nor did the discipline move from the ethnological society to the museum and then to the university. All three institutional settings existed simultaneously in the late nineteenth and early twentieth centuries, each playing somewhat different roles in the *practice* of anthropology.

In retrospect, it may seem obvious to us that the university and the museum provided complementary institutional settings for the practice of anthropology. But it seems unlikely that anthropologists were aware of this growing institutional differentiation until about 1920. Before the Great War, most anthropologists were involved with both institutions, and nearly all anthropologists saw their role as educational, irrespective of where they worked.

Lewis and most of his colleagues at Field Museum had done graduate work at one university or another: George A. Dorsey at Harvard (1894); Berthold Laufer at Leipzig (1897); and William Jones (1904), A. B. Lewis (1906), and Fay-Cooper Cole at Columbia (1914). Many curators held joint or dual appointments at a university. Boas, for example, had appointments at both Columbia and the American Museum of Natural History. Dorsey simultaneously held appointments as curator at Field Museum (1894–1915), as professor of comparative anatomy at Northwestern University Dental School (1898–1913), and as assistant (later associate) professor of anthropology at the University of Chicago (1905–1915). Even when curators did not teach, most museum staff saw themselves as educators, giving public lectures, writing books and pamphlets for popular audiences, and installing educational exhibits for the public.[7] Only in the 1920s did Field Museum administrators begin to view university teaching as a conflict of interest with a curator's responsibilities to the museum.[8]

The Changing Practice of Anthropology

In the decade or two before the Great War, the practice of anthropology was in a state of flux, both at museums and in universities. Such changes were partly the consequence of a growing professionalism among the ranks of those who called themselves anthropologists, ethnologists, and archaeologists. To a large extent the discipline was changing because of the kinds of fieldwork anthropologists were conducting (see, e.g., Stocking 1983). Fieldwork changed a great deal during this period, particularly after the Jesup North Pacific Expedition and the Cambridge Torres Straits Expedition. As Herskovits (1953, 19) noted, these two expeditions "dramatized for anthropologists the need to investigate at first hand the cultures of peoples to be studied and confirmed the desirability of field investigation as against the 'arm-chair' research of the older comparative school." Together the Jesup and Cambridge expeditions became a model for fieldwork, the expedition. And each subsequent researcher seems to have tried to improve and innovate on the specific field methods used in those expeditions.

In evaluating ethnological research before the Great War, we should emphasize that there was no single fieldwork standard as there generally is today. Anthropologists were free to do what they pleased in the field, collecting whatever kinds of data, measurements, and specimens they wished. It was all anthropology. Virtually any kind of ethnographic or ethnological observation was viewed as adding to the growing (and much needed) corpus of ethnological data.[9] Most professionally trained anthropologists collected anthropometric data and word lists as well as ethnological specimens for a museum in the field.

Lewis' research in Melanesia epitomized this (apparently) eclectic style of fieldwork practice. As we have seen, his research was primarily ethnological, and he was keenly interested in the variation and distribution of material culture. Although not especially interested in what we now refer to as physical or biological anthropology, he collected more than three hundred human crania[10] because, having trained under Franz Boas, he saw anthropology as a unified discipline. While recovering from blackwater fever in Merauke he even made a series of anthropometric measurements, which he recorded at the back of his diary notebook. Lewis brought back word lists of varying lengths from more than a dozen communities, and he collected local names for objects and raw materials in well over half the communities he visited. He did no excavating, but he collected more than two hundred prehistoric potsherds from several sites (principally in New Guinea) and commented in his diary on other prehistoric materials that he saw (but did not collect); these included the then newly discovered (but now famous) Lapita pottery from Watom Island in east New Britain. Where possible, Lewis took ethnographic notes on dances, village organization, social structure, and the like, in addition to his notes on material culture and technology.

A. B. Lewis was not the only anthropologist or ethnologist with such a broad pattern of data collection, nor was he the only anthropologist to collect for a museum. Anthropologists did many things in the field, and nearly every one of them collected ethnological specimens during fieldwork.

The heyday of museum anthropology arose in the late nineteenth century in large part because of the growing number of professional anthropologists, ethnologists, and archaeologists who collected material for museums in the field. Museums, for their part, wanted exotic, showy material for their exhibits, objects that would have some interest for the museum-going public, particularly objects that could be put to educational ends (Boas 1907; Dorsey 1907). It is important to remember that there was no television or video, either for education or for entertainment, no Public Broadcasting System or National Geographic specials to bring the lives of exotic peoples directly to the American public. In fact, aside from a visit to a natural history museum, the photographs in the *National Geographic Magazine* were as close as most Americans could get to seeing something of native life in remote, primitive places; 16mm documentary films in the 1950s and 1960s and television specials and videos since the 1970s are simply extensions of the concept behind *National Geographic Magazine*. Before the First World War, museums, not television, brought bits of native life directly to the American public, and it was principally the demand for "museum quality" specimens for such exhibition purposes that drove the entire curio market. Because museums, as large institutions, could afford to make major purchases, the prices of curios remained high.

Museums, as institutions, were also able to attract the attention of wealthy donors. These donors funded a growing number of researchers in the field. In most cases, support for the fieldwork was acknowledged by naming the field expedition after the wealthy benefactor. The specimens researchers collected were later prominently exhibited in grand museum buildings, nearly always acknowledging the benefactors by name.

The Joseph N. Field South Pacific Expedition was but one of dozens of "name expeditions" that Field Museum sent off to all parts of the globe. As a natural history museum, Field Museum sent out paleontology expeditions to dig up dinosaur bones, botanists to find specimens for the museum's growing herbarium, and zoologists of every sort to bring back examples of thousands of different species. Lewis, too, collected some botanical specimens that became part of the museum's economic botany collection. He also brought back a dugong and a crocodile skull, some bird of paradise pelts, a cassowary egg, and more than a thousand shells representing fifty-three species of mollusks. Similarly, the museum's biologists often brought some ethnological specimens back from their expeditions, and these specimens were given to the Department of Anthropology to be accessioned with its collections.

It has now been many decades since anthropologists typically went off to the field on such name expeditions, but early in the century nearly all anthropological research was funded in this way. As Stocking (1985b) has shown, this pattern changed midcentury, when scientific foundations became the major source of funding within the discipline. Before the Great War, however, the name expedition was the primary source of funding for all field research in anthropology and related disciplines.

The period from about 1890 until the war was, in many respects, the culmination of museum anthropology. But the character of ethnological research during this period probably owes very little to the fact that museums sent scientists to the field or to the fact that such

564

researchers collected material for museums. This period's essential feature was that fieldwork was organized around expeditions, often by only one or two scientists operating more or less on their own.

In short, the so-called museum period in anthropology is perhaps better understood as the "expedition period" of ethnological or anthropological research.

The "Expedition Period" of Ethnological Research

A. B. Lewis' research was clearly and explicitly oriented toward making collections in the field, but the character of his collection derives from the peripatetic nature of his expedition. As a museum collection, his work in Melanesia is unparalleled; as an expedition, his research was similarly extraordinary. He intended to cover much ground, to visit many communities, and to conduct the sort of ethnological survey he did across as wide a field as possible. In these terms, his work was simply more extensive than that of his contemporaries, and he assembled more collections than most of them. But he was by no means alone; Melanesia was filled with researchers who were similarly conducting extensive research on their own expeditions, nearly always funded by wealthy donors or institutions who wanted credit for their financial support. The Joseph N. Field South Pacific Expedition was thus not a unique event, only the best and most extensive expedition of its kind in Melanesia.

Expeditions were commonplace in various parts of the world by the 1870s; but with the possible exception of Otto Finsch's voyages in 1879–1882 and 1884–1885 and a few coastal surveys, scientific expeditions in Melanesia began in earnest in 1898 with the Cambridge Torres Straits Expedition, under the leadership of A. C. Haddon (1901–1935). After working with Haddon in the Torres Straits, C. G. Seligman (1910) returned to Papua in 1904 on the Cook Daniels Expedition. W. H. R. Rivers, who had also been with Haddon on the Cambridge expedition, returned to Melanesia in 1907 on the Percy Sladen Trust Expedition, accompanied by two young protégés, G. C. Wheeler and A. M. Hocart. A. F. R. Wollaston went to Dutch New Guinea on the British Ornithological Union Expedition in 1909. All of these British scholars made collections of material culture during their expeditions.

Among the Germans, the list of expeditions is even longer. In the fall of 1909 alone, Lewis met Georg Friederici, Richard Neuhauss, Otto Schlaginhaufen, Rudolph Schlechter, and Regierungsrat Wiedenfeld in and around Eitape. Lewis arrived in German New Guinea after the Hamburg *(Peiho)* Expedition had left the Old Protectorate and just missed Thurnwald on his various expeditions to the colony. It is worth noting in particular that each of the German expeditions had quite different goals from the others. Friederici was collecting linguistic data; Neuhauss was primarily seeking anthropometric data; and Schlaginhaufen wanted ethnographic data. Yet each of these scholars collected ethnological specimens from the communities they visited, and the largest part of each of these collections found its way into museum collections.

During his travels Lewis also met Felix Speiser in the New Hebrides and just missed Fritz Sarasin in New Caledonia. In Papua he met Prof. William Patten of Dartmouth College. In Dutch New Guinea he met Wollaston and Kloss on the Second British Expedition to Dutch New Guinea and, later, Captain ten Klooster and Lieutenant Ilgen of the Dutch Military Expedition.[11] Every one of these expeditions collected ethnological specimens, but assembling a museum collection was not a primary objective of any of them except possibly the Speiser and the Sarasin expeditions.

As Lewis' diaries show, Melanesia was alive with scientific researchers before the war, at times resembling Brighton Beach on a warm summer day. The region was criss-crossed by expeditions of all kinds. Melanesia was far from the isolated and rarely visited region our late-twentieth-century biases may suppose it to have been. As each expedition moved from place to place, nearly everyone collected curios and ethnological specimens along the way. But by 1914 the winds of change were already beginning to blow.

The Rise of Intensive Ethnographic Fieldwork

Before the war, the Finnish anthropologist Gunnar Landtman was probably the only anthropologist in all of New Guinea who had conducted intensive ethnographic research in a single location.[12] As a student of Haddon's, Landtman had arranged to live for two years (April 1910 to April 1912) among the Kiwai people at the mouth of the Fly River in western Papua (Landtman 1917, 1927, 1933). His research is probably the first example of intensive ethnographic fieldwork by a trained anthropologist in Melanesia, preceding Malinowski's research in Mailu by four years and in the Trobriands by five years (Sarho 1991; Stocking 1983, 84–85). As Stocking (1983, 83–84) suggests, Landtman's research methods were almost the same as Malinowski's, but Malinowski was better at self-promotion. Malinowski was a prolific writer, had more students than Landtman had, and was fortunate enough to find a prestigious academic appointment in England.

About the same time, A. M. Hocart had more or less settled down in Fiji for some fairly intensive research as well, and G. C. Wheeler spent ten months with the Mono-Alu in the Solomon Islands. In 1914, a graduate student named John W. Layard accompanied Rivers to the New Hebrides. Layard settled in for a year of fieldwork on Atchin, one of the small islands off the northeastern coast of Malekula, while Rivers moved around conducting an ethnological survey, much as he had done on his previous expedition (Slobodin 1978, 52–53).[13]

All of these fieldworkers—together with Bronislaw Malinowski—were responsible for establishing intensive field research as a standard field strategy. All were students of men who were on the Cambridge Torres Straits Expedition. Landtman was a student of Haddon's; Hocart, Layard, and Wheeler were students of Rivers; and Malinowski was a student of Seligman's. Intensive fieldwork—and ultimately the ethnographic method—was the logical elaboration of the innovative field researches begun in the Torres Strait by the Cambridge group.

In July 1914 the British Association for the Advancement of Science held its annual meeting in Melbourne, Australia. This scientific gathering was attended by some 350 scientists, mostly from Great Britain. The group included most of the prominent British anthropologists of the day, among them Seligman, Marret, Rivers, Haddon, and some of the up-and-coming younger anthropologists, including John Layard and a thirty-year-old Pole named Bronislaw Malinowski, both of whom were about to set off on expeditions to Melanesia. Few of the papers given at this gathering of the association are remembered, but this meeting had a tremendous effect on British social anthropology by bringing the young Malinowski to Australasia, where he would conduct the most famous and influential set of expeditions in anthropology's history.

When war broke out in Europe in August 1914, Malinowski found himself officially classed as an enemy alien. Because of his education and scholarly connections, Australian authorities chose not to detain him but allowed him to proceed with his proposed field research in Papua. During the war Malinowski conducted three expeditions to Papua, first to Mailu (1914–1915) and later to the Trobriands (1915–1916 and 1917–1918); the Australian government even subsidized some of this research.[14]

Over the years, considerable attention has been given to Malinowski's founding of the so-called ethnographic method when he pitched his tent in the village next to the huts of the natives (e.g., Kuper 1973; Laracy 1976; Stocking 1983; Young 1988, 1991). But despite the mythologizing about Malinowski, it has become increasingly clear over the years that Malinowski did not immediately invent the ethnographic method on his arrival in Papua.

Like most other anthropologists of his era, Malinowski traveled around a fair bit on his first expedition to Papua. He spent four months in the Mailu district, a month around Port Moresby and Gabagaba, a week on Woodlark, and another month on the coast between Mailu and Samarai (Laracy 1976, 265). He worked in English and Police Motu rather than in the vernacular. His field methods during this first expedition were essentially the same as those of his mentor, C. G. Seligman (see Stocking 1983, 93–97). Malinowski's research on Mailu was detailed and focused on a single community, but he stayed with one of the missionaries and had little opportunity for what we now refer to as participant observation.

When Malinowski returned to Papua on his second expedition, he had still not "invented" the ethnographic method. Following Seligman's advice, during this expedition he planned both to visit Rossel Island and to conduct some research on the Papuan mainland around the Mambare River. Stopping at the Trobriands before going on either to Rossel or to the Papuan mainland, however, Malinowski became fascinated with certain Trobriand rituals and ceremonies and decided to stay a few months. One interesting topic after another presented itself, and he stayed on in the Trobriands to investigate them. He never went on to the other field sites as he had initially planned. When he returned to Australia a year later in 1916 he had considerable grasp of the Kiriwina language; the "ethnographic method" had been born, if not yet accepted by the discipline as a fieldwork standard.

When Malinowski returned to Papua the following year, Lieutenant-Governor Hubert Murray restricted his activities to the Trobriands, forbidding him to visit other islands. This action meant that Malinowski could not easily have begun a survey of several islands or a comparative project had he wanted to (Laracy 1976), so he returned once more to the Trobriands to complete the research that would eventually fill six books and numerous shorter works. All of these publications would help establish functionalism as anthropology's dominant social theory for at least four decades.

Malinowski was a brilliant writer, and his impact on the discipline of anthropology was immense. His influence came in three areas: (1) he trained a large number of the anthropologists in Britain all of whom came of age in the 1920s and 1930s; (2) he established his own style of fieldwork, which he personally christened the "ethnographic method," as the standard against which all research should be measured; and (3) together with Radcliffe-Brown, he established a new research agenda for the discipline by framing all ethnographic problems in terms of his own theoretical orientation (functionalism).

Malinowski's Impact on the Discipline

It is hard to overstate Malinowski's influence on the discipline. At first, of course, his influence was felt almost exclusively in Great Britain and the Commonwealth. But by the late 1940s his field methods and theoretical framework were becoming accepted in the United States.

The effect of these changes in the discipline did not begin until 1922, when Malinowski published *Argonauts of the Western Pacific,* his first full-length publication about Trobriand Islanders. Ironically, while this book is often seen as a primer on the ethnographic method, it is profoundly concerned with regional—rather than local, ethnographic—problems: the circulation of valuables in the *kula* ring. His later books on sexuality, primitive psychology, magic, and religion were inwardly focused on the social life of Trobriand Islanders and suggest a shift from regional, interethnic problems to increasingly local, ethnographic ones.

In later years Malinowski may have presented his research almost as if he had planned from the beginning to revolutionize the entire discipline with his new field methods and theoretical focus, but the evidence suggests that he initially viewed his research as an expedition much like that of every other anthropologist in Melanesia. Thus, in *Argonauts* he wrote of his three "expeditions" to Papua and seems to have seen his researches in Mailu, Gabagaba, Woodlark, the Trobriands, the Amphletts, and Dobu as parts of a single fieldwork experience (1922, xix, 16).

Malinowski also acknowledged his debt to Robert Mond, who provided a large part of the financial backing for these expeditions, and noted that he was "also able to collect a fair amount of ethnographic specimens, of which part has been presented to the Melbourne Museum as the Robert Mond Collection" (1922, xix). Although Malinowski never analyzed these ethnographic specimens and rarely mentioned them in his major publications, he did collect museum specimens, just like virtually every other field researcher before the war.[15]

Despite the resemblance between his initial research and that of nearly every other anthropologist before the war, Malinowski transformed the discipline by establishing both a new research agenda and a new fieldwork strategy. After the publication of *Argonauts* and once he had a secure position at the London School of Economics, he launched (together with Radcliffe-Brown) an attack on speculative historical, diffusionist, and evolutionist studies. He successfully encouraged his students to conduct synchronic studies of social institutions within bounded, functioning societies. These studies largely discounted and dismissed the effects of social change and contact with other functioning societies, including dominant colonial societies.

Most anthropologists now recognize many of the limitations of the functionalist agenda and acknowledge that ethnographies written in the ahistorical "ethnographic present" often misrepresent the effects of contact between different societies. But between the wars, as functionalism and local village-based research gained prominence, earlier kinds of research that focused on regional distributions, culture contact, historical change, in situ development, and social evolution were increasingly dismissed as old-fashioned, superficial, and speculative.

Changes within the Discipline: The Impact on A. B. Lewis

For researchers like Lewis, who had conducted extensive rather than intensive research, such developments in the discipline were problematic. No matter how good prewar research might have been, the regional orientation that had been encouraged during the "expedition period" increasingly came under criticism from younger scholars who now conducted ethnographic, village-based studies. In Britain, local ethnographic research became the standard for nearly all fieldwork after 1930. Americans, who were somewhat slower to adopt functionalism as a theoretical orientation, also increasingly accepted ethnographic village studies as standard in the 1930s. By the Second World War, regional surveys were generally viewed with disdain in the United States as old-fashioned and of marginal significance.

Lewis began writing up his research in 1922 with a series of short popular pieces on masks, sago, and tobacco in New Guinea (Lewis 1922, 1923, 1924a). Next, he prepared three numbers in the museum's new Anthropology Design Series, including one on incised designs in New Guinea (Lewis 1924b, 1924c, 1925). He then began work on a fourth number in the design series (on carved and painted designs) and a more serious analysis of Melanesian shell money for the museum's *Fieldiana (Anthropological) Series*.

About this time Lewis also started planning a monograph about Melanesia for a new series of books intended to explain the new exhibits to the public. Berthold Laufer had inaugurated this series after the new building opened. Although the books in this series were ostensibly written as guides to the museum's exhibits and were thus intended for a general audience, Laufer also wanted the series to provide a major anthropological statement about each of the several regions that were well-represented in the museum's collections.[16]

But in 1926 illness forced Lewis to take a leave of absence from the museum for more than two years. During this time he was unable to complete any of the writing projects he had begun. When he returned to his duties at the museum in the summer of 1928, he applied himself to his writing with renewed enthusiasm and diligence. He completed his paper on shell money in 1929, finished a fourth number in the design series on carved and painted designs in 1931, and finally completed his monograph, *Ethnology of Melanesia,* the following year. (This volume became the fifth volume in the Department of Anthropology's Guide series.)

His book was the first full-length anthropological monograph in English that dealt with Melanesia as a single region, a region filled with diverse peoples who shared certain common cultural features. A small but growing number of books had been published about certain parts of Melanesia, and others described expeditions or dealt with particular topics; but as yet there had been no attempt to describe the range of variation found in Melanesia as a whole, systematically discussing houses, subsistence, clothing, weapons, tools, local products, transportation, music, religion, ceremonies, and other topics.[17]

The book's nonacademic style was popular among the general public, but in the long run this popularity worked against Lewis within the discipline. *Ethnology of Melanesia* was well received by certain anthropologists, and its style well regarded. In a review in the *American Anthropologist,* Robert Lowie (1933) wrote that it was "one of the best museum guide-books it has ever been my good fortune to read," adding that "a special piquancy pervades the little volume from the many notes of personal observations with which the topical discussion is sprinkled." The Australian Ian Hogbin (1932) noted in *Oceania* that "the style in which the book is written is bright and easy to follow" and that "this Guide contains some really excellent descriptions of various material objects made in the Melanesian area, together with some account of their manufacture."

But these reviewers were not uniform in their appreciation of the volume. Although Lowie (1933) praised the book, noting that "Dr. Lewis's treatment is especially noteworthy for its attention to those matters of daily routine which so many pretentious writers treat with lofty disdain," Hogbin (1932) criticized Lewis on what at first glance appears to be essentially the same point, arguing that Lewis had "largely neglected the actual life of the people of Melanesia. He has, in fact, been too interested in objects to bother much about institutions and customs." Hogbin, of course, here means social life, such as the intricacies of marriage arrangements and other "social institutions," rather than Lowie's "daily routine."

By 1932 British functionalism, with its emphasis on institutions, was already becoming established in Australia. Lewis' limited discussion of those institutions that the British school considered important was certain to attract the ire of someone so easily provoked as Ian Hogbin. Hogbin was particularly critical of Lewis for having ignored social functions and was almost indignant that he gave short shrift to Malinowski's discussion of the *kula:*

> In the chapter headed Warfare a good account is given of weapons, but one misses any approach to an analysis of warfare similar to that made by Miss C. H. Wedgwood in the first volume of *Oceania,* and no mention is made of the social function of head hunting. Perhaps the most striking example of the

author's failure to appreciate problems of sociology is to be found in the section
entitled Transportation and Trade. Here the various types of canoe are carefully
described, but the *kula* is dismissed in four lines! It is to be regretted that all
too many guides published by museums suffer from this type of omission.
[Hogbin 1932, 115]

The chapter heading Hogbin refers to here was actually "Weapons and Warfare." His real
criticism was that Lewis had not conducted a village study and was not a British functionalist.

Lowie, also, noted that Lewis paid too little attention to social organization. In fact, Lewis
seems to have understood rather little about Melanesian social organization, in either the British
or the American sense. But while Hogbin and Lowie were accurate in noting that Lewis had little
feel for such social processes *within* villages, Lewis seems to have had a much deeper feel for the
fact that villages (and ethnic groups) were linked to one another, even if he did not always fully
understand how these social and economic linkages operated. He did not reify the village or
ethnic group as an isolated social entity in the ways that ethnographers working in a single
community have tended to do. Such differences in focus between Lewis, on the one hand, and
both Hogbin and Lowie, on the other, suggest a change in the discipline's theoretical paradigm.
Perhaps more noticeably, these differences suggest a dramatic shift from a regional unit of
analysis, with constituent villages and communities, to the society as the unit of analysis with
its constituent social institutions.

Many disciplinary changes were already happening within anthropology in the United
States when Lewis published his monograph in 1932, though at the time it would have been
difficult for anyone to see where anthropology would end up after the dust settled. Only one
other American anthropologist had conducted research in Melanesia since Lewis returned from
the field in 1913. This was Margaret Mead, another (but much younger) student of Franz Boas.
In 1928–1929 Mead conducted a village-based study at Peri village in the Admiralty Islands,
where she stayed for six months with her anthropologist husband, Reo Fortune. Mead's (1930)
study fits the broad framework of Malinowski's ethnographic method, but its theoretical orientation, like virtually everything else Mead wrote (e.g., 1928, 1934, 1935, 1938–1949), was far
from functionalist in character.

American anthropologists did not start arriving in Melanesia in significant numbers until
the 1930s, and even then the flow was still only a trickle. Of the work produced by these
researchers, only Stephen Reed's (1939, 1943) historical study documenting the development of
colonial society in the Mandated Territory is not a local, ethnographic study. Powdermaker's
(1933) study, *Life in Lesu,* was the only intentionally functionalist ethnography, which is not
surprising since Powdermarker studied in London under Malinowski. The publications of the
other Americans working in the region—DuBois (1944), Mead (1935, 1938–1949), Spencer
(1941), and Whiting (1941)—while focusing on a particular society, were not so functionalist
in tone.

Lewis did not live to read most of these monographs; he died following an accident in his
home at the age of seventy-three in October 1940.

Posthumous Reaction to Lewis' Work

Lewis' book became popular during the intensive fighting in Melanesia during the Second
World War. Few Americans had any idea about the exotic island world where their sons and
brothers had been sent, and the *Ethnology of Melanesia* offered practically the only survey of this

little-known area. When the first edition sold out, Field Museum reissued the volume in 1945 as *The Melanesians: People of the South Pacific.* The illustrations, which had originally been at the back of the volume, were interspersed within the text. Lewis' friend and colleague, Wilfrid Hambly, added a brief appendix about physical anthropology and another entitled "Recent Methods of Research." Hambly also attempted to update the original bibliography of recommended readings; Chief Curator Paul Martin added a brief foreword; and subheadings were added throughout the text as an aid to the reader. Hambly also seems to have made a few (mostly minor) changes in Lewis' original text.

This little book was popular enough not only to justify a second printing in 1945 but also to allow a third printing in 1951. The third printing appears to have been made from the plates used in the 1945 edition, though some changes were made. Martin revised and expanded his foreword, and Alexander Spoehr,[18] who had recently been appointed curator of Oceanic ethnology, made many important revisions in the bibliography, successfully updating the original list of suggested reading. Hambly also revised his 1945 appendix on physical anthropology and (probably at Spoehr's urging) eliminated the appendix on research methods.

These two posthumous printings contained only modest changes from Lewis' original 1932 edition. But subtle as these changes are, they tell us a great deal about how Lewis was viewed by Field Museum anthropologists both during and after the Second World War.

When the wartime edition was released in 1945, it had been thirteen years since the first edition and thirty-two years since Lewis' return from the field. At the time, the book was seen as dated and increasingly old-fashioned. Martin (1945), for example, noted in his foreword that with the passage of time "some of the statistical data are now incorrect," and Hambly opened his appendix on "Recent Methods of Research" apologetically, implying that he expected the volume might be criticized as old-fashioned: "Every reader who studies and criticizes a book must ask himself the fundamental questions: For what purpose was this book written? At what period?" (Hambly 1945, 230). He noted that Lewis had written the book to be both entertaining and informative as a handbook for the museum visitor. But Hambly also added that since Lewis' research in 1909–1913 there had been cultural changes in Melanesia as well as "advances in methods of research."

These advances included new techniques in anthropometry and also "in psychology and the social sciences." Although Hambly wanted to protect his late friend and colleague from criticism that his book was just an "old-fashioned monograph," it was hard for him to find anything positive to say about Lewis' findings and conclusions. In the end Hambly could only suggest that Lewis and his contemporaries had laid the foundation upon which the discipline could advance:

> Anthropological science is yet young, and in [the] early days of research investigators often observed and recorded many curious and interesting facts without sufficient analysis of the historical, sociological, and psychological causes that have operated to produce and maintain those phenomena. . . .
>
> These expansions in anthropological method do not represent something entirely new, and a modern writer who speaks disparagingly of the "old-fashioned monograph" does an injustice to much factual material which was laboriously gathered in days when a scientific expedition was more difficult and dangerous than it is today. We must keep an open mind, always ready to welcome and assimilate new techniques, but, while doing so, let us bear in mind that the field work of the period of Lewis, thirty years ago, laid the foundation of anthropological research. With less technicality and verbosity, the older anthropologists assembled—often under most trying physical condi-

tions—the data which today are receiving a fuller and more intelligible explanation. [Hambly 1945, 232, 234]

Despite these ostensibly supportive words, Hambly seems to have viewed Lewis' work as imprecise and hopelessly old-fashioned. These views are most obvious in Hambly's comments on anthropometry. Hambly (1945, 231) noted that his own anthropometric analyses of Melanesian skulls (which Lewis had collected) suggested that the people of Melanesia were more closely related to Australian Aborigines than Lewis had supposed, a finding that clearly differed from Lewis' original comments. Lewis had written that Melanesians had a complex history of migrations and mixing of diverse peoples, but he added that their features resembled those of Africans to whom they were probably related through "intermediate groups in the East Indies and southern Asia" (Lewis 1932a, 8).

In the only significant revision of Lewis' original text, Hambly tried to correct what he felt was an obvious error. Hambly deleted a page of the original text that discussed the so-called pygmy question.[19] In this passage Lewis had made one of the most important arguments contained in his book, suggesting that the short-statured people of Melanesia may have become dwarfed in situ as a result of local environmental forces such as diet. To Hambly's horror, Lewis had suggested that "the dwarfing was relatively recent" (1932a, 11) rather than being a very ancient physical trait or survival that could be detected through anthropometric measurements of modern skeletal material. Nearly half a century later we can see that Lewis' argument was essentially correct; the available evidence suggests that short stature among the so-called pygmies in New Guinea is largely related to environment, especially diet (see Howells 1973, 171–177; Terrell 1986, 66–67; and even Bellwood 1979, 26–27).

Lewis suggested that the issue was a question of process, not of essential types: "The pygmies must have originated some time, and it does not solve the problem to shove it back a few ages," because known prehistoric peoples were not pygmies (Lewis 1932a, 11). The interesting question for him was not whether pygmies migrated to New Guinea from Africa or Southeast Asia, but how short stature developed as a trait. He argued that "pygmy peoples everywhere more nearly resemble their normal neighbors than they do the pygmies of distant regions." To A. B. Lewis this finding suggested local interactive and environmental processes rather than simply the migration of different peoples into Melanesia. Hambly, however, had a much more static, essentialist view and chose to delete the entire argument, substituting a few innocuous lines to the effect that the pygmy question was still unresolved (Lewis 1945, 19; 1951, 19).

Throughout his life Lewis appears to have remained convinced that biological, cultural, and linguistic diversity in Melanesia had a complex history. He acknowledged that there must have been migrations of peoples into the region, and there were also intermarriage, cultural mixing, and even linguistic change among the peoples within Melanesia. Lewis did not presume that the processes of cultural, linguistic, and biological development had happened only outside Melanesia. He assumed that these processes must have continued within the region since human beings first arrived there. Most of all, he argued that Melanesians were not static but had been continuously undergoing change (in language, culture, and biology) from the beginning. On these points, he differed radically from the new generation of ethnographers who focused their attention on local communities and synchronic problems.

Unfortunately, by the time of the Second World War, the broad questions of social, cultural, linguistic, and biological process that interested Lewis and most of his contemporaries had been all but drowned out by the discipline's growing enthusiasm for collecting ever more detailed data about particular communities.

When his book was reprinted once more in 1951, Field Museum no longer viewed Lewis' work as embarrassingly old-fashioned: it had now become historical. Paul Martin could now write in his newly revised foreword to the third printing that "through the years his book, originally written as an aid to understanding the Museum collections, has acquired a value of its own as a historical document on Melanesia." Martin went on to add that it "provides a picture of native Melanesian life, written by a trained observer equipped with the *anthropological techniques and interests of his period,* who had an intimate personal acquaintance with the area and people he describes" (Martin 1951; emphasis added). Spoehr could add at least sixteen publications by American anthropologists to the several new sources Hambly had already included. These younger scholars, all historical figures today, had published a series of (now) classic monographs, the most important being Coulter (1942), Gitlow (1947), Howells (1943), Keesing (1941), Linton and Wingert (1946), Mead (1938–1949), Oliver (1949, 1951), Quain (1948), Reichard (1933), Thompson (1940a, 1940b), and Wingert (1946). From these, it is clear that the kind of expedition Lewis had led to the South Pacific was a thing of the past.

In 1951 Lewis had been gone for barely a decade, and his book had been published only eight years before his death. But his observations in Melanesia had begun forty two years earlier, and his work was now seen as having historical value rather than as being of anthropological interest. Times had changed, and so had the discipline of anthropology.

The Legacy of Albert B. Lewis (1867–1940)

A. B. Lewis' most tangible legacy to the anthropology of Melanesia is his collection of 14,385 objects and his 1,561 surviving photographs from the field.[20] Together with his diaries, field notes, and other documentation, these objects and images provide the only comprehensive museum collection from Melanesia in the United States and one of the most systematic collections from the region made before the Great War. No other scholar has ever assembled such an extensive collection from Melanesia in the field. As a whole, the Lewis Collection is clearly much greater than the sum of its individual parts, whether its constituent parts are seen as objects, photos, and diaries or as the many different parts of Melanesia represented in the collection.

At first glance, we might assume that A. B. Lewis' most important legacy to the discipline is his collection, including his documentation and photos. But the character of the collection suggests a much more important, if less tangible, legacy: a set of research problems that even eighty years later has yet to be solved. As we have seen, Lewis collected showy material that he knew would be put on exhibit at Field Museum. But his correspondence makes it clear that simultaneously he was assembling a research collection that would document cultural variation along the New Guinea coast and among the Melanesian islands. He wanted a collection that provided "a connected view of the coast": not just objects from different places along the coast, but a collection that might demonstrate how these places were and had been connected.

While the number of objects in the Lewis Collection is truly astounding and the pieces themselves remarkable in their breadth, diversity, and beauty as examples of Melanesian art, one must ask why such a large collection is important to a discipline that has largely ignored museum collections for five decades. The number of specimens is incredible, but if such collections offer no special way of better understanding Melanesians, their culture, or their historic (and prehistoric) development, then neither the Lewis Collection nor any other museum collection from the region offers much more than a (large but) quaint set of art objects.

In monetary terms as "curios" on the so-called primitive art market, the Lewis Collection is far more valuable today than it was when Lewis returned from Melanesia some eighty years ago. But today the collection also has even more value to the discipline as a three-dimensional, historical archive documenting what Melanesia was like before the Great War. It is easy for most anthropologists to appreciate the value of Lewis' field notes and photos, even if they are ethnological and comparative rather than ethnographic and local. But the objects in the collection, like his photographs, offer tangible evidence of historic conditions in various parts of Melanesia. From Lewis' work in the field we have a vast reference collection representing all major parts of Melanesia as they were immediately before the Great War.

The aspect of the Lewis Collection that gives it such value as a reference collection is not the number of specimens or their quality. Rather, it is that he collected these pieces planning to use them to analyze Melanesia's remarkable diversity. That Lewis was not successful in *explaining* this cultural, linguistic, and biological diversity in Melanesia goes without saying. In the end the task proved to be too complex for him and for every other prewar scholar. One suspects that the empirical facts of Melanesian diversity were far more complicated than Lewis had initially assumed when in 1909 and 1910 he sat at the harbors now called Aitape or Madang. But, of course, no one else has adequately explained how so many peoples can maintain such (clearly related but) obviously distinct cultural and linguistic patterns when these distinct communities were so actively engaged in trade, exchange, and other kinds of social, political, and economic interaction.

Lewis was clearly not the only early anthropologist to appreciate this conundrum; Malinowski's first book on the Trobriand Islanders, *Argonauts of the Western Pacific* (1922), focused on closely related issues involving the *kula* ring. Before the war many other scholars were interested in distributions, but many of these scholars were all too ready to construct elaborate, hypothetical, or speculative histories to explain the observed diversity. Lewis never constructed a simplistic model of cultural diversity, and his work therefore never achieved the notoriety of Rivers (1914) or even the notice that less prominent figures such as Friederici (1912, 1913), Neuhauss (1911a), Sarasin (1916–1922, 1917; Sarasin and Roux 1929), or Speiser (1923, 1991) had received.

Most of these early scholars failed to explain the distributions of cultural traits they had observed because their empirical data were too limited; more important, their theoretical models of cultural evolution, cultural development, and culture change were also inadequate. Malinowski (together with Radcliffe-Brown) was able to turn the discipline away from these kinds of (admittedly inadequate) theoretical models, but he did so by shifting the intellectual problem away from questions of change to questions of how societies maintain stability and attempt to re-create themselves from generation to generation.

Without denigrating the intellectual problem of how communities transmit their culture and language to their children or how social institutions tend to reproduce similar structural social relations in each generation, most anthropologists now recognize that such cultural transmission and cultural reproduction do not occur in isolation from other communities. Nor do they occur in a historical vacuum (see, e.g., Biersack 1991; Gewertz 1983; Strathern 1988, Terrell 1993). Every community changes within the context of its own social, economic, political, and natural environment. These contexts inevitably involve neighbors with whom members of the community interact and have interacted in previous decades.

The A. B. Lewis Collection provides data about a specific cultural domain, namely material culture. But as I have shown here, the collection offers historically and regionally contextualized data that virtually no other museum collection possesses. By today's standards, the Lewis Collection may seem to have quite limited documentation. In some cases, Lewis was able only to name the village where he obtained an item. But compared to the standards of the time, Lewis brought back rich documentation, often collecting information about where the object was made, what its name was in the local language, what materials were used, and occasionally details about how an item was used or made.

Such documentation is far more detailed than the information most collectors of the time obtained. Even knowledgeable collectors such as Richard Parkinson provided minimal documentation for the collections they sent to museums around the world, regularly omitting even the name of the village where each piece was obtained. Overall, Lewis' documentation is far better than that of nearly every other early collector in Melanesia. For certain kinds of data, such as details about the movement of goods between villages through trade, his collection is in several cases the richest early source of field data (Welsch 1989a, 1989b).

As we have seen, the Lewis Collection is a primary historical document about what kinds of material culture were in use in Melanesian communities immediately before the Great War. It is precisely the kind of collection that offers scholars and field researchers an opportunity to glimpse the rich historical and regional contexts that are increasingly accepted as important in understanding Melanesia and Oceania generally (see, e.g., Biersack 1991; Howe 1988; Terrell 1993).

By all of this I do not mean to suggest that the Lewis Collection is complete or that it is without limitations as a research collection. Every museum collection, like every set of field notes, contains its own set of biases and its own limitations. For some distributional and historical problems, the collection clearly has too many lacunae to be useful by itself. For example, some villages are poorly represented, though neighboring communities are well sampled (such gaps, however, can often be filled in, at least partly, with other early collections; see, e.g., Welsch, Terrell, and Nadolski 1992). In addition, as Lewis tells us in his diaries and letters, he avoided collecting objects that he thought were beyond the scope of his research; in his effort to sample the "ethnographic past" he was particularly reluctant to collect material that made use of European raw materials or that incorporated designs derived from European sources. The Lewis Collection, of course, contains minimal data about social and political relations, domains that rarely leave their mark on objects in direct and obvious ways.

Yet despite these limitations, the collection is a vast (and largely untapped) storehouse of information about Melanesia in the early colonial period. As Corbin (1984, 1989), Barlow and Lipset (1989), Terrell and Welsch (1990a), Torrence (1989, 1993, 1994), and Welsch and Terrell (1991) have shown, the collection can add to our understanding of particular artistic and productive traditions. Much as Lewis had supposed, distributional studies of the collection can address questions about the relative importance of economic relations and cultural traditions in shaping the form of particular kinds of objects and the content of ordinary tool kits in particular places (see, e.g., Newton 1961, 1989; Terrell and Welsch 1989a, 1990b; Welsch and Terrell 1991, 1996).

What is perhaps most startling is that the Lewis Collection contains so much information about economic patterns, suggesting in some areas that many important economic transactions involving relatively small objects such as string bags and wooden bowls have been almost totally overlooked by several generations of scholars (Welsch 1989b). Similarly, by analyzing the collection as assemblages of goods found in particular places, we have been able to address, more or less directly, questions about cultural and linguistic diversity (Welsch, Terrell, and Nadolski 1992).

This collection is—comparatively speaking—so rich in data about historical distributions of particular kinds and styles of objects, and so useful as a historical baseline about the transactions that Lewis glossed as "trade," that it has motivated two new expeditions to Papua New Guinea in 1990 and 1993–1994. Sponsored by Field Museum, these two expeditions have attempted to collect new data about the questions of cultural diversity that had originally interested Lewis. Specifically, we have attempted to understand the mechanisms by which peoples speaking more than two dozen different languages interacted and exchanged objects

Fig. 9.1. Man from Munai village, Ulau district (on the mainland east of Aitape), carrying six earthenware pots up from the beach where he had received them from his hereditary friends from Ali Island, 1993. The Ali Islanders were given these pots by friends on Tumleo, who had made them and to whom the Ali people had given bundles of tobacco, which they in turn had received from other friends on Tarawai Island.

that, as the Lewis Collection documents empirically, moved as much as two or three hundred kilometers along the coast.

This movement of goods suggested to us that the Aitape region, extending to the east and west of Lewis' Berlinhafen, could not be characterized as one of small, hostile, local groups at enmity with one another. Indeed, our research is showing that communities speaking a variety of different languages in this part of Melanesia were organized around a shared concept that we have glossed as "hereditary friendship." What's more, despite more than eighty years, two world wars, missionization, and several waves of economic, social, and political development, these friendship networks are still active and important in people's lives. Friendship networks around Aitape have changed since Lewis observed them, but they have proven to be remarkably (and unexpectedly) resilient (see Welsch 1996; Terrell and Welsch 1991). Moreover, archaeological evidence we collected in 1993 and subsequently in 1996 suggests that these intergroup networks have considerable antiquity in this region, suggesting even greater resilience in the prehistoric past. As our research around Aitape shows, the Lewis Collection has considerable potential for motivating new anthropological research, both in the museum and in the field.[21]

The conclusions from all of these studies—which represent only the first steps toward a proper analysis of this collection—are probably less surprising than the fact that the collection can be analyzed in so many varied ways to address regional and historical questions about diversity.

In retrospect, we should have anticipated that such a range of analyses was possible. A. B. Lewis assembled this collection with questions about diversity in mind, and he built this

576

Fig. 9.2. Munai people helping load up the editor's dinghy with gifts for their hereditary friends from Ali Island: sago, bananas, betel nuts, and other garden products, 1993. Formerly, Ali Islanders would have come to Munai by outrigger sailing canoes, but nowadays people mostly use vessels with outboard motors or boats with diesel engines. Here they took advantage of the resident anthropologist's trip to Munai to visit their friends living down the coast, taking them Tumleo pots and bringing back sago and other foodstuffs.

collection as a "systematic" regional collection, one that would allow both commonalities and differences to be identified. Lewis was not alone in collecting such data to analyze cultural diversity, but he was clearly one of the most systematic among his contemporaries before the Great War.

After the war, of course, when anthropologists in Melanesia turned to more local problems, they largely ceased collecting data and museum specimens that could be used to analyze diversity and cultural change. And because ethnographers were preoccupied with local questions, when they did make museum collections, their collections differed significantly from Lewis'. Modern collections are generally informed by quite different theoretical concerns and assumptions from those that informed Lewis' collecting in the field. Lewis was systematically trying to obtain "a connected view of the coast," which consisted of communities that spoke many different languages but that nevertheless shared many cultural features. Most recent ethnographic collections are intended to illustrate or document the material culture of a single ethnolinguistic group, culture, or society, often materially reifying their social units. As such, these recent collections have their own bias, often being overly rich in items that mark the local distinctiveness and uniqueness of the study community and frequently ignoring commonplace items typical of a larger region.[22]

For the most part Lewis did not directly focus on issues involving recent change during the colonial period. As we have seen, in his field diaries Lewis shows little direct interest in these short-term changes, even though he was well aware of the many forces that were influencing village life. Like every other observer, he made inadvertent observations about the effects of these new ways on the old. But when writing his monograph, Lewis felt it necessary to outline the

577

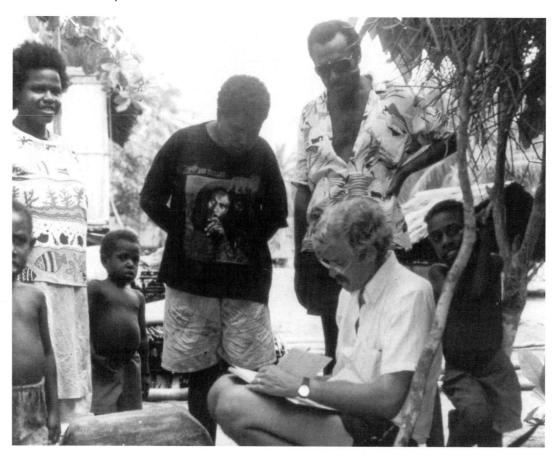

Fig. 9.3. The editor interviewing a family at one of the Yakamul hamlets on the coast east of Aitape, 1993.

history of Melanesia and describe some of the changes colonialism was bringing to these communities.

Most of Lewis' interest in change, however, concerned more gradual processes that we might now describe as cultural development or cultural evolution. His analysis of the so-called pygmy question in his 1932 monograph (discussed above) illustrates his belief that longer-term processual or developmental questions are important in understanding the nature of the Melanesian world he experienced firsthand. Lewis expected environmental factors—by which we should include economic, social, and political relations with neighboring communities—to yield useful clues for understanding contemporary patterns. At times in his diaries, one even senses that these factors, which many of his contemporaries might have glossed (somewhat incorrectly) under the rubric "diffusionism," were more critical in shaping the present than cultural traditions were in preserving older patterns. Unlike so many of his contemporaries, Lewis clearly saw Melanesians as constantly changing and developing. In this sense, his approach now seems an extremely modern one.

In the end, A. B. Lewis was not able to assess systematically the cultural diversity he observed so vividly in the field. But throughout his four long years of fieldwork in Melanesia, he assembled an extraordinary collection, one that he expected would be useful in such an enterprise. He built the largest collection of its kind from this part of the Pacific, overcoming countless obstacles to do so. The Joseph N. Field South Pacific Expedition was an expensive operation, costing the equivalent of something between three-quarters and one million of today's dollars. Throughout the expedition Lewis knew he would have to justify his field expenditures

Fig. 9.4. Archaeologist John Terrell with men from Serra examining a rock shelter in old Sarai village in search of potsherds during a survey of archaeological sites, 1993.

and demonstrate that his collection was worth its cost. As he visited one Melanesian village after another, he knew Director Skiff would scrutinize his collection and the public would later evaluate the exhibit cases he was already planning. But as early as 1910 Lewis knew his extensive collection would find approval from both Skiff and the public, once the full range of his work was seen. Of more consequence for Lewis was his firm belief in the long-term importance his collection would have as a systematic research collection. This feature of the collection—not the large showy specimens or the innovative exhibit cases—was what justified its cost.

Eighty years later we are only beginning to recognize that early museum collections can be used to address many of the same questions that interested A. B. Lewis. He had no way of knowing at the time that his collection and his work in the field would be ignored for so long. But he always believed that his collection would have great significance in the long run. In this respect, his words to Field Museum director Skiff in December 1910 have a prophetic ring to them as we continue to mine his research to try to answer our own questions today: "Of course, sufficient results must be shown to justify cost, but what constitutes results? Some very valuable results may only *materialize* later, even to the advantage of the Museum, which suggestions I very respectfully submit to your consideration" (ABL to Director, 5 December 1910; emphasis in the original).

579

Notes

|||||||||||||||||||||||||||||||||||||||||||||||||||||||||||||||||||||||||||||||||||||||||||||||||||||

INTRODUCTION

The Joseph N. Field South Pacific Expedition of 1909–1913

1. See, e.g., Kuklick (1984), Kuper (1988), Stocking (1984).

2. In the 1890s ethnological field expeditions were understood as an innovative new research strategy in contrast to the armchair anthropology of Tylor and Frazer (see, e.g., Herskovits 1953, 19; Singer 1985; Stocking 1984). It is important to note that until the Second World War virtually all anthropologists in Britain and America saw themselves as conducting expeditions, even though between the wars few moved around much in the field. Today, the notion of an expedition conjures up a sense of peripatetic movement, whereas in the first half of this century it implied simply going and observing exotic communities firsthand.

3. Throughout, I follow A. C. Haddon's use of Torres Straits and Torres Straits Islands instead of the more conventional usage, viz. Strait and Torres Strait Islands. Haddon's usage captures the essentially maritime character of this island region, especially the fact that there are numerous straits and passages among the many scattered islands that lie between Cape York and New Guinea. As will become clear throughout, A. B. Lewis was similarly aware of the maritime character of most accessible parts of Melanesia.

4. Even a loyal protégé like A. M. Hocart (1915) would dismiss Rivers' (1914, vol. 2) naive theorizing as speculative and unsubstantiated, while praising Rivers' deep understanding of individual communities. See Schneider (1968), who makes a similar argument about Rivers' superior understanding of how kinship terminologies worked.

5. Unlike the conceptual reconstructions of society and social institutions presented in studies written in the "ethnographic present," Lewis' collection consists of genuine objects, items that had been used and were still in the villages he visited. He was aware that such items as stone tools were no longer used, a point he expresses frequently in his diaries. Thus, unlike the ethnographic present, this ethnographic past was not a hypothetical reconstruction but a collection of objects that were tangible survivals from a time before European contact.

6. The character of postwar museum collections is different from these early systematic collections insofar as later collections from Melanesia tend to illustrate local uniqueness rather than both similarities and differences as in the Lewis Collection.

7. In a few cases his informants posed with items in his collection to demonstrate how an object was used. Occasionally one of Lewis' tags is even visible in the image (e.g., Lewis 1988, 19), almost certainly because—as often happens even today with museum collections in the villages—an informant wanted to show how a spear, shield, or other object was held. Since fewer than 2 percent of Lewis' photos were of this sort, it is clear he wanted photos of village life as he saw it rather than as a reconstruction of some hypothetical past.

8. The German anthropologist Richard Neuhauss, whom Lewis met several times in German New Guinea, also brought a camera with him and took more than a thousand photos, but a majority of these were physical anthropology front and profile shots (see Neuhauss 1911a, esp. vol. 2). In 1906 the photographer John W. Beattie of Hobart, Tasmania, also made a photo tour of the Melanesian islands, especially the Solomons and Fiji, during which he took a substantial number of pictures; these too are thought to be somewhat fewer than the A. B. Lewis expedition photos, and like Hurley's photos nearly two decades later, many were posed rather than images of ordinary village life.

9. Biographical data about ABL's family, early life, and career up to the time of his departure for Melanesia are drawn from many sources. ABL's cousins, Dorothy Lowrie of Lake Geneva, Wisconsin; Dr. James Anderson of Monroe, Ohio; Martha Benham of Clifton, Ohio; and Margie Mesloh of Tulsa, Oklahoma, offered many details of the family's oral traditions as well as a tour of Clifton's historical sites. They also gave me access to a rich correspondence with ABL's late cousin Merle Rife, whose recollections and interest in family history filled in several key gaps. The most important published sources include *American Men of Science* (3d ed., 1921, 409; 6th ed., 1938, 848); *Book of Chicagoans* (1917, 413); Brien (n.d., 36); Broadstone (1918, 306–308, 715–717); Chapman Bros. (1890, 498–502); *Chicago Daily News* (8 May 1909); *Chicago Daily Tribune* (8 May 1909);

Current Biography (1940; 1:498); Dills (1881; 697–699); *Directory of Protestant Missionaries in China, Japan, and Corea* (1906, 6, 70); Everets (1874, 18); Hambly (1940b, 1941); Robinson (1902, 336); *Who's Who in America* (1914–1915, 8:1407; 1916–1917, 9:1472; 1918–1919, 10:1638; 1934–1935, 18:1449); *Who's Who in Chicago* (1931). Obituary notices appeared in the following newspapers: *Chicago Daily News* (10 Oct. 1940), *Chicago Heights Star* (11 Oct. 1940), *Chicago Tribune* (11 Oct. 1940), *New York Times* (11 Oct. 1940). The following archival sources were consulted: Field Museum of Natural History, archives; Field Museum of Natural History, Department of Anthropology archives; Field Museum of Natural History, minute books; Franz Boas (1858–1942) professional papers (FBPP); microfilm edition of papers in possession of the American Philosophical Society, Philadelphia; National Archives (U.S. Census of Green County, Ohio, for 1850, 1860, 1870, 1880; Census of Lincoln, Nebraska, for 1900; Census of Orange County, California, for 1900, 1910; Census of Chicago, Illinois, for 1920). Information about ABL's education was received from the registrar, College of Wooster, and the registrar, University of Chicago.

10. Just south of town Charles built a spacious, two-story farmhouse for his family; his younger brother Storrs Lewis (ABL's uncle) later built a similar house on the farm next door on land given him by their father.

11. ABL's mother's family, the McKeehans, came from Maryland as farmers in the late 1840s. They had a farm and a large brick farmhouse—where ABL's mother grew up and which is still occupied by younger members of the family—north of town.

12. Bennett Lewis was a prominent and wealthy businessman, merchant, and landowner who had come to Clifton from Connecticut via New York state in 1828. In 1833 he situated the village along the Little Miami River at a site with enough water power for several mills. The village grew and prospered for some years, but its fortunes changed abruptly when the railroad—following intensive lobbying from other villages—chose a route through Yellow Springs rather than Clifton for the Springfield to Xenia line. This decision halted the town's growth and probably limited the elder Lewis' wealth and upward mobility. Nevertheless, Bennett Lewis remained one of Clifton's wealthiest citizens and most prosperous merchants with a series of stores, mills, and even a cotton and woolen factory. Until his death in 1876, he seems to have been the village's largest landowner.

13. Charles moved back to town to his father Bennett's house, where for three or four years young Albert was looked after by his grandmother Eliza and his maiden aunt Harriet.

14. This was a modern brick building that had only recently been completed in 1873 on land donated by his grandfather, Bennett Lewis. It now houses a small municipal museum.

15. For a time he entered the real estate business, but later returned to farming, primarily growing oranges. The move to California was prompted by his elder brother's successes in the northern part of the state.

16. The smaller size of Wooster and similar schools would have seemed more natural than one of the larger eastern universities because he had attended such a small high school. Uncle Storrs had also attended and graduated from a similar college, Miami University of Ohio, before studying engineering at Lafayette College in Pennsylvania.

17. He and a classmate, who was an assistant in chemistry, were listed among the list of faculty and officers in the Collegiate Department in 1893.

18. The most important extant source for this dispute between Boas and Skiff appears in a series of letters or memos in February and March 1894 at the American Philosophical Society, Philadelphia. These are available on microfilm in FBPP. See also Herskovits (1953; 16).

19. Adolph Bandelier (1840–1914) conducted field research in the American Southwest between 1880 and 1892, then lived in Peru and Bolivia from 1892 until 1903, when he joined the staff of the American Museum (see Hyslop 1991). Livingston Farrand (1867–1939) had joined Boas on the Jesup North Pacific Expedition in 1897. The archaeologist Marshall H. Saville (1867–1935) excavated sites in southern Ohio under the direction of Professor Putnam and later conducted extensive field surveys in Yucatan (1890) and Honduras (1891–1892) and expeditions to the ruins at Mitla and Oaxaca, Mexico (1899, 1902, and 1904). In later years he made numerous other expeditions to Peru, Ecuador, Columbia, Honduras, and Guatamala. Throughout his career Clark Wissler (1870–1947) conducted extensive field research among the Plains Indians, especially the Blackfeet (see Freed and Freed 1991). Berthold Laufer (1874–1934) conducted fieldwork in Siberia as a member of the Jesup North Pacific Expedition (1898–1899) and later led the Jacob H. Schiff Expedition to China (1901–1904). While a curator at Field Museum (from 1908), he led the Blackstone Expedition to Tibet and China (1908–1910) and the Marshall Field Expedition to China (1923); see Kendall (1991).

20. These students completed studies as follows: Jones (Ph.D. awarded 1904), Lewis (Ph.D. 1906), Speck (A.B. 1904, A.M. 1905), Lowie (Ph.D. 1908), Goldenweiser (A.B. 1902, A.M. 1904, Ph.D. 1910), Sapir (A.B. 1904, A.M. 1905, Ph.D. 1909), and Cole (Ph.D. 1914, but he had previously studied at Columbia under Boas, 1904–1906).

21. Kroeber was for many years director of the University Museum at the University of California, Berkeley. Jones had gone to Field Museum from Columbia and was killed in the Philippines in 1909 during a museum expedition. Speck was associated with the University Museum at the University of Pennsylvania for much of his career. Lowie played a key role in the development of the University Museum, later renamed in his honor as the Lowie Museum (now the Phoebe A. Hearst Museum) at the University of California, Berkeley. Sapir was at the National Museum of Canada from 1910 to 1925. Cole went to Field Museum in 1904 and maintained ties until 1923, when he left the museum, eventually establishing the anthropology department at the University of Chicago.

22. During his first year at Field Museum, ABL had

been somewhat disenchanted with the position in which he found himself. Dorsey had replaced his preparator with ABL in the capacity of "assistant." Dorsey refused to consider appointing ABL as a "preparator" because he knew that the museum administration would make it difficult to upgrade the position (or ABL in the position) to the assistant curator level. This seems to be the basis on which Dorsey had refused to discuss the matter of ABL's replacing the aging preparator, Wake Stanifield. Dorsey had, in fact, cleverly manipulated the situation by hiring ABL to fill one of the department's preparator's positions under the job title "assistant." This maneuver kept ABL available for an assistant curatorship when Dorsey was able to find some funds in 1908.

23. They had one son, Edgar Bennett Lewis, born in Chicago about 1918.

24. Although there is certainly some hyperbole in this claim, it must be remembered that the published literature about Melanesia was tiny at this time. Only Parkinson (1907) of the classic Melanesian monographs from this century had been published.

THE FIELD DIARIES OF A. B. LEWIS

Book 1: Fiji

1. European flags were raised somewhat earlier in other parts of Melanesia, but claiming sovereignty has little to do with encouraging development. To protect their spice monopoly in the Moluccas, the Dutch in 1828 claimed the western half of New Guinea from 141° east longitude, but more than a century passed before they began to develop the area. The French flag was raised in New Caledonia in 1853. Of all the Melanesian colonies, only New Caledonia was colonized by Europeans at as early a period as Fiji; but its character and history were quite different from the others' because New Caledonia was set up as a penal colony; some twenty thousand convicts were sent to New Caledonia during the penitentiary regime's thirty-year history (from 1864).

2. See, for example, Young (1984). For a summary of the events leading up to the Deed of Cession see also Howe (1988) and Derrick (1950).

3. Derrick (1950), Howe (1988), and Young (1984) provide useful summaries of this eventful period in Fijian history, from which this brief sketch is largely drawn.

4. Of the old settlers ABL met in Fiji, only Wilkinson—who had been secretary to the chief of Bua on Vanua Levu—seems to have had significant ties outside Viti Levu.

5. This includes language. Most of the so-called Polynesian outliers are identified as Polynesian languages though they are spoken by inhabitants of islands in the geographic region universally accepted as Melanesia.

6. When cultural classifications are aimed at groupings larger than a single society or ethnic group, any number of traits may be invoked, typically on an ad hoc basis (see, e.g., Welsch 1987, Welsch, Terrell, and Nadolski 1992; Hays 1993).

Book 2: Humboldt Bay and German New Guinea

1. Roughly four-fifths (549) of the European population were German nationals; the rest were primarily British subjects (including Australians), with a scattering of Dutch, Austrians, Scandinavians, et cetera. Of the total white population, 505 (75 percent) were men and only 71 (11 percent) were children under fifteen. The white population overwhelmingly consisted of single men, as in 1909 only 74 men were married, though quite a number seem to have had relationships with native women. Only 197 Europeans (29 percent) resided in Kaiser Wilhelmsland, the vast majority of the population living on the Gazelle Peninsula.

2. Most residents of Friedrich Wilhelmshafen were associated with the New Guinea Compagnie or the government. Of the 197 Europeans living in Kaiser Wilhelmsland, the majority (at least 129) were either Lutheran or Catholic missionaries, nearly all stationed in at least 28 scattered stations.

3. According to Freytag (1912, 107) thirteen stations had been opened by the end of 1909: Tumleo (1896), Walman (1897), Monumbo (1899), Bogia (1901), Ali (1901), Eitape (St. Anna) (1903), St. Michael (Alexishafen) (1905), Juo (1908), Beukin (1908), Matukar (1908), Mugil (Elisabeth) (1909), Megiar (1909), and Malol (1909). SVD missionaries at these stations numbered 21 priests, 17 brothers, and 29 sisters in 1909 (Sack and Clark 1979, 299). By 1912 their number had grown to 30 priests, 25 brothers, and 40 sisters. Four other SVD stations were opened around Eitape in the intervening years: Jakamul (1910), Ulaū (1910), Eisano (Sissano) (1911), and Arop (1911).

4. In 1908 the entire Eitape district (from Cape Croisilles to the Dutch border) had only 26 European residents: 4 government officers (all at Eitape), 11 male and 8 female missionaries (all SVD), and 3 planters and traders. These numbers had probably risen slightly by the time ABL arrived in Eitape, but these figures illustrate the general pattern up to the First World War.

5. The official German-Dutch boundary commission began its work in March 1910 under the leadership of Leonard Schultze for the Germans and Capt. F. J. P. Sachse and Lt. A. F. H. Dalhuisen for the Dutch. This visit by Hahl and Windhouwer to Humboldt Bay and the Sextroh or Tami River had no official standing as part of the German-Dutch boundary commission. Hahl saw it as an opportunity to build good relations with his Dutch counterpart as well as with villagers in the border area. He also may have wanted to know the lay of the land before any decision about boundaries was made. The official commission party led by Leonard Schultze opened up vast areas of the middle and upper Sepik River to scientific study as well as to labor recruiters. For a discussion of the background to the joint commission see van der Veur (1966, 74–79); for accounts of the various expeditions see Schultze (1910–1911, 1914).

6. Erdweg's essay on Tumleo (1902) remains the most comprehensive ethnography of any community along this coast. Aside from ABL's notes, it offers more detail about trade than any other early source.

7. While ABL collected locality information about

hundreds of objects in and around Eitape, Tiesler's survey listed only twenty-seven specimens with such information that Schlaginhaufen collected. It is possible that Schlaginhaufen got the idea for this field method from ABL. Interestingly, Tiesler (1969–1970) completely ignored ABL's work on the north coast, even though some important and relevant material would have been readily available (e.g., Lewis 1932a).

8. Data for the Eitape coast were presented in Welsch (1989a). For the entire north coast of New Guinea from Humboldt Bay to Cape Croisilles, ABL provides data for nearly as many linkages as all of the more than two hundred published sources summarized by Tiesler (1969–1970); see Welsch (1989b). This volume of data collection by a single field researcher is extraordinary even today.

9. John Terrell (personal communication, 1993) suggests that prehistorically Tumleo and the other Berlinhafen Islands were not the only islands off the north coast of New Guinea but simply the islands farthest from the mainland shore. The hills at Kiap Point, Sumalo Hill, behind Aitape town, and behind Malol, et cetera would once have formed a large offshore archipelago, the waters of which have now been filled in with sand and sediment from the Torricelli Mountains. According to this interpretation, Aitape would once have resembled the islands around Wewak, instead of the long, straight coastline we know today.

10. Ali Islanders claimed in 1993 that only villagers from Malung, the southernmost village on Ali, had led the attack on the Germans. They also suggested that only the southern villages were burned by the German punitive expedition.

Book 3: West New Britain and the Huon Gulf

1. This first set of negatives was given museum negative numbers that sequentially follow ABL's field numbers. Unfortunately, whoever numbered subsequent batches (probably early in 1913 before ABL returned) seems to have assigned museum negative numbers to his plates randomly. This must have caused him considerable consternation and difficulty later.

2. Based in the Bavarian village of Neuendettelsau, the Neuendettelsau Mission Society was established in the 1840s by Pastor W. Löhe. The society sent missionaries to North America and Australia as well as to German New Guinea.

3. In 1884–1885 Dallmann had captained the *Samoa* on Otto Finsch's famous voyage to New Guinea (Finsch 1888a). The settlement at Finschhafen was named in honor of this explorer for the New Guinea Compagnie, not by him. For a general history of the early administration of Kaiser Wilhelmsland see especially Firth (1982) and Hempenstall (1978).

4. From a colonizer's perspective the Dutch East Indies had prospered during the nineteenth century following the imposition of the *cultuurstelsel,* the so-called culture system, better translated as the "cultivation system." This repressive command economy allowed colonial administrators to determine which cash crops were to be grown in particu-

lar districts and to set prices paid to producers at such low levels that they were certain to be profitable exports. On Java and some of the other islands, the native population was relatively large and provided an abundance of labor, nearly everywhere administered through a complex system of indirect rule by sultans, princes, and other indigenous nobles. The combination of monopolies, indirect rule, forced production, and a ready workforce made the Dutch on Java wealthy. Despite the importation of a few dozen Javanese laborers, these conditions were not likely to prevail in Kaiser Wilhelmsland.

5. The first was Friedrich Wilhelmshafen, established by the company in 1892; after 1899 the colonial administration for Kaiser Wilhelmsland was headquartered there. The second was Eitape, which the government opened in 1906.

6. For a summary of the history of the Neuendettelsau Mission see Firth (1982, 145–149), Flierl (1927), Frerichs (1957), Neuhauss (1911b), Paul (1909), and Schmutterer (1954). Pilhofer's (1961–1963) three-volume history of the mission remains the most comprehensive account. For an anthropological view of the mission's effect on the villages, see Hogbin (1951).

7. Radford's (1987) history of Kainantu in the Eastern Highlands gives a feel for what these native teachers experienced in newly contacted areas, particularly up the Markham River and into the central highlands. Conditions in coastal villages along the gulf were probably somewhat easier because virtually all of these communities had preexisting trade relations.

8. For a discussion of the so-called Keysser method, in principle and in action, see Ahrens (1988), Fugmann (1985), Fugmann and Wagner (1978), Keysser (1924, 1980), Koehne (1983), and Pilhofer (1961–1963).

9. Friedrich Müller (1872) had proposed a distinction between Melanesian and Papuan languages (and races). Despite a somewhat different view by Codrington (1885), who saw the Melanesian languages as so diverse that they should not be classed as Malayo-Polynesian, later scholars renewed the Papuan-Melanesian distinction as a linguistic and biological difference. Sidney Ray (1895, 1907) was among the most influential in promoting this dichotomy. The assumption that the distinction between Papuan and Melanesian languages mirrors differences in origin has persisted ever since (see, e.g., Wurm 1967, 1982; but cf. Terrell 1981, 1986, 42ff.). More recent studies using the museum collections suggest that the Papuan-Melanesian distinction is not significantly associated with cultural differences (Welsch, Terrell, and Nadolski 1992; Welsch 1995, 1996).

10. For a comprehensive list of publications by Neuendettelsau missionaries up to the War see Sack's (1980) bibliography.

11. Bamler sold ABL some specimens as well as some photos. He also provided a detailed holographic manuscript about the *balum* cult. This manuscript is preserved in the Department of Anthropology archives at Field Museum.

12. Both Lowie (1933) and Hogbin (1932) criticized ABL's *Ethnology of Melanesia* for ignoring social organiza-

tion. This diary suggests that ABL understood more about this topic than either Lowie or Hogbin had assumed. As a British social anthropologist after Malinowski, Hogbin, of course, would have accepted a study of kinship as the only proper analysis of social organization. Here, ABL makes it clear that unilineal groups were not the only form of social organization found in New Guinea.

Book 4: Friedrich Wilhelmshafen and the North Coast

1. George Dorsey may have recognized bits of this diversity in 1908, but his experiences were so superficial that they could have provided little context for observing, much less appreciating, New Guinea's cultural variations. Margaret Mead (1930), who in 1928, was the next anthropologist to visit the former German New Guinea, did not consider Melanesia's cultural diversity directly until her return to New Guinea in 1931, when she worked among the Arapesh, where she emphasized this theme (1935, 1938–1949).

Diversity has by now become such a basic "fact" of Melanesian ethnology that most anthropologists and art historians merely accept this pattern of cultural, linguistic, and biological variation as a given. For the most part, however, only prehistorians and biological anthropologists have attempted to account for human diversity in Melanesia, largely using quite narrow models in which isolation by geography is the most important cause of differentiation. For a summary of these approaches see Terrell (1981, 1986). ABL was aware of the trade and other kinds of interaction that linked different communities in New Guinea and thus understood that isolation alone could not explain New Guinea's diversity.

2. Conditions may have been somewhat different for a number of German expeditions in the colony, nearly all of which, because of their semiofficial status, had police escorts and long carrier lines. Together these factors were often coercive and either directly or more often indirectly had the effect of forcing villagers to sell objects they may not have wanted to sell (F. Tiesler, personal communication, 1993).

3. O'Hanlon (1993, 12–13, 55ff.) offers one of the most important recent discussions of the practice of museum collecting. He disagrees with claims by postmodern critics like Clifford (1985, 244) that such objects have "been torn from their social contexts of production and reception, given value in systems of meaning whose primary function is to confirm the knowledge and taste of a possessive Western subjectivity." Collecting nearly always involved important decisions by village producers or sellers; it is thus naive to view ethnographic museum collections as simply "cultural hostages." At the time such objects were collected, villagers rarely saw these transactions in such terms.

4. Assembling a systematic collection of similar objects from a series of communities is an extremely challenging task, as I learned firsthand during the A. B. Lewis Project Expedition 1993–1994. In making a collection of some two thousand items from the north coast around Ai-

tape, with the help of Wilfred Oltomo and John Terrell, I systematically tried to collect examples of very commonplace items like limbum buckets, dippers, and nets. It is surprising how easily one can lose track of such mundane items in the excitement of buying many other kinds of things.

5. Field Museum recorder D. C. Davies was later director of the museum from 1921 to 1928.

6. A trip along the Rai coast is never specifically discussed in any surviving documents. It is, however, hinted at in the letter to Dorsey reproduced below.

7. Edward Everett Ayer (1841–1927) had been one of the original founders (with Marshall Field) of Field Museum and served as the museum's first president.

8. In one of his last letters to Dorsey, Voogdt wrote in English rather than his usual German: "I am very sorry to tell you that Mr. Heine is much alarmed about what you wrote in one of the Chicago leading papers. He has returned the little souvenir you so kindly sent him—and your man Mr. Lewis had a good deal of trouble about it. Why did you do that?" (Voogdt 1910). At the time Voogdt wrote this, in fact, ABL had been little bothered by the affair; but Voogdt, who had been in Friedrich Wilhelmshafen working with Heine, knew what steps Heine had already initiated to prevent ABL from obtaining any specimens for Field Museum.

9. It is possible that ABL heard something about the Dorsey articles and the anger they had provoked while he was in Finschhafen, but it is unlikely that the Lutherans in the Huon Gulf would have taken them personally; they too objected to the coarse style of men working in the private sector. ABL may even have known about the affair in west New Britain, though Cape Merkus was isolated from the intense gossip of the capital. In any event ABL did not feel Heine's reaction directly until he arrived in Friedrich Wilhelmshafen in April 1910.

10. The first (reproduced below) was to Dorsey and details the situation as of 1 May 1910, some three weeks after his arrival in Friedrich Wilhelmshafen. The second was written to Field Museum director Skiff two months later. The third, to his colleague and friend Assistant Curator S. C. Simms, was written in September during a short trip to Rabaul to buy lumber for crates for his specimens in Friedrich Wilhelmshafen.

11. One suspects that ABL was especially demoralized because he knew that the columns and the sensationalism they contained served no scholarly purpose but were simply self-serving for Dorsey and publicity for the museum. One of Dorsey's primary motives may have been financial.

12. The Rhenisch Mission Society of Barmen, Germany, was the least successful mission in German New Guinea. This Lutheran society had sent more than fifty ordained and lay missionaries (including women) to Kaiser Wilhelmsland from 1887 to 1914 but had made virtually no converts during that time. Ten men and seven wives were stationed at five stations in 1910. Two of the longest serving of these missionaries were Blum and Helmich (stationed at Siar and Ragetta, respectively), who assisted ABL. In addition Helmich sold ABL five large carved ancestral

figures from Karkar and Rich Islands. For a history of the Rhenisch mission see Bade (1977), Firth (1982, 150–152), Frerichs (1957), and Hempenstall (1975, 1978). The Rhenisch mission later merged with the Neuendettelsau mission.

13. ABL had also met Gramms' partner, Hermann Bröker, the labor recruiter and would-be prospector, in Finschhafen just days before Bröker and his associate, Rudolf Oldörp, were killed during a gale in the Huon Gulf. Gramms managed the plantation and Bröker provided the laborers to work it.

14. This remark is strikingly reminiscent of conditions on the Gazelle Peninsula about this time; Biskup (1969) suggests that lawsuits for slander were so common as to be almost a form of entertainment or a parlor game.

15. The new *kiap* was probably Berghausen, who replaced Dr. Scholz in 1910.

16. There was no standardized orthography for Pidgin in 1910. Throughout his diaries and even after his return to Chicago, ABL generally spelled this term *tamburan*. The modern spelling is *tambaran*.

17. Even Wu (1982), who studied the Chinese in Papua New Guinea, concentrated primarily on the Chinese in East New Britain, largely ignoring similar communities along the Madang and East Sepik coast.

18. A translation of this notice published in the *Deutsche Kolonialzeitung* was reproduced above in the Friedrich Wilhelmshafen part of book 4.

19. This steamer was probably associated with the Dutch-German boundary commission (see Schultze 1910–1911, 1914).

20. There were in fact two other short excursions upriver during this interval. In March 1890 H. C. Bluntschli, the head of a tobacco plantation at Deli, Sumatra, and Capt. H. Sechstroh ascended a few miles in the *Ottilie* during a two-day cruise on the river (Wichmann 1912, 454, 512). Similarly, on 29 August 1906, E. Krauss took the *Seestern* some six miles upstream (see *DKB* 1907; Wichmann 1912, 454).

21. William Jones, Franz Boas' second Ph.D. student at Columbia, was also an assistant curator at Field Museum. In 1908 he went off to Luzon on an expedition for the museum; he was killed by the Ilongot in 1909. Ironically, his untimely death was reported in the *Chicago Tribune* on the same day and in the same front-page story that announced ABL's expedition to the South Pacific. The museum sent another of its assistant curators, S. C. Simms, to the Philippines to make arrangements for Jones' body and to retrieve his personal effects, field notes, and collections. Jones was himself part Native American and before his trip to the Philippines had been working on a manuscript about the Fox Indians, which Boas wanted to publish. Boas had asked Simms to help him find the manuscript, and Simms had inquired of all of Field Museum's curators about the whereabouts of the missing manuscript. Simms recovered the manuscript in the Philippines.

Book 5: The Gazelle Peninsula and Solomon Islands

1. On changing the official name to Rabaul and moving the administrative seat see *Amtsblatt* (1909, 54–55);

Sack and Clark (1979, 304). Regarding the purchase of E. E. Forsayth & Co., see Sack and Clark (1979, 320). On the Bismarck Memorial see *Amtsblatt* (1909, 126–127) and Sack and Clark (1979, 304).

2. The census of 1909 gave the white population of Herbertshöhe district (including Japanese) as 371, of which 73 were non-German. These aliens included nationals from Australia (26), the Netherlands (14), Great Britain (7), Austria (6), Sweden (5), France (4), Greece (3), and Denmark (2), with one resident each from Belgium, Luxembourg, Portugal, Switzerland, the United States, and Japan. These figures are somewhat misleading, as Mrs. Parkinson was counted as German because her husband was a German national; more than one-fourth of the white population living in and around the Gazelle Peninsula were non-Germans. There were 73 missionaries, 56 of whom were German.

3. Ironically, although Mead wrote a sensitive sketch of Phebe Parkinson that acknowledged her role in the history of the colony, Mead's original interest in Mrs. P. was as a Samoan living away from home, not as the New Britain pioneer that she was. Even the title of Mead's essay, "Weaver of the Boarder," suggests that Mead did not see Mrs. P. as fully a part of the expatriate community on Blanche Bay, but as a part-Samoan, part-American living in a sometime German, sometime Australian colony in Melanesia.

4. At the beginning of 1909 there were 24 expatriates in the Kieta district, which included Buka. By 1 January 1911, the white population had grown by more than 60 percent, to 41. This total included 18 Marist missionaries, whom ABL seems not to have met, as well as 3 government officers (with two wives) and 14 planters and traders.

5. From 1877 to 1893, British subjects in the Solomons were under the jurisdiction of the British high commissioner for the Western Pacific, another hat traditionally worn by the governor of Fiji. The commissioner's jurisdiction did not extend to other European nationals and, in any event, his authority was almost negligible, as he had no officers residing in the Solomons and therefore could not effectively police labor recruiting and sales of guns in the group. For a political history of the Solomons and the role of the High Commission, see Scarr (1967). The best general history is that by Bennett (1987).

6. Resident Commissioner Woodford and his deputy, F. J. Barnett, were stationed at Tulagi. The administration also included three district magistrates: T. W. Edge-Partington, N. S. Heffernan in the Shortlands, and R. B. Hill at Gizo. (It is not clear whether ABL met either Heffernan or Hill, though he visited both the Shortlands and Gizo.) For a history of magistrate postings, see Bennett (1987, 397–404).

7. Lever Pacific Plantations, a subsidiary of Lever Brothers, began acquiring land for plantations in the Solomons in 1905. By 1907 LPP held about three hundred thousand acres scattered in the central and western islands of the archipelago. Gavutu was LPP's headquarters. For a history of Lever's operations in the protectorate see Fieldhouse (1978), Pakenham (1985, 134, 242), Scarr (1967, 266–270), and Wilson (1954); Bennett (1987) provides de-

tails about Lever's role in the economic history of the Solomons.

Burns Philp & Co. was established in 1883. The company had a lucrative shipping line to British New Guinea (later Papua) from 1886. From 1898 BP had a shipping service to German New Guinea until Nord-Deutscher Lloyd successfully lobbied the German government to obtain a monopoly in the colony. About 1896 Burns Philp established a regular shipping service to the Solomons. Makambo became BP's major depot in the archipelago. By 1910 BP had also established a number of plantations scattered on various islands in the Solomons. For a history of Burns Philp's economic activities in the Solomons see Bennett (1987); for a photo of Makambo about 1910 see Bennett (1987, 206).

Book 6: To New Zealand, the New Hebrides, and New Caledonia, with a Return to German New Guinea

1. Dorsey was frequently on leave from Field Museum during these years and traveled a great deal. After resigning his curatorship and leaving the museum in 1915, he established a film company in Chicago, and later became a journalist and popular science writer. According to oral tradition around the museum, Dorsey was fired because it was learned that a woman (not his wife) accompanied him on one of his trips abroad. While this story is unsubstantiated, it illustrates Dorsey's bad reputation at the museum, despite the important role he played in building up the department's ethnology collections.

2. General and political histories of the New Hebrides can be found in Howe (1988) and Scarr (1967).

3. Of the original 221 nitrate negatives ABL took during his expedition, 180 survive. These have varying amounts of deterioration. Since 1989 all have been copied onto other media as part of a major Field Museum grant from the National Endowment for the Humanities, for which Nina Cummings was project director.

4. This was Capt. M. Huggett.

5. This was the Anglican missionary Rev. J. W. Blencowe, who was based in the Santa Cruz Islands. On his arrival in the Santa Cruz group, however, the villagers became hostile, and Blencowe was confined to his house for some months. Eventually, Blencowe returned to England, unable to obtain any specimens for ABL.

6. This was N. Hagen, of Noumea, who later sent a collection to Field Museum, but ABL felt he was charging too much for it, and the shipment was returned.

7. In 1911 there were about 19,000 Europeans, mostly French, living on Main Island of New Caledonia (Sarasin 1917, 4). The indigenous population of the entire colony of New Caledonia and the Loyalty Islands had declined from nearly 42,000 in 1887 to fewer than 29,000 in 1911 (Robson 1942, 370). On the main island the indigenous population had fallen to fewer than 17,000 people and represented less than half the population (Sarasin 1917, 5). About 7,000 (roughly a third) of the white population lived in and around Noumea in 1911 (Sarasin 1917, 4).

8. For a general historical survey of the early years of European contact in New Caledonia, see Howe (1988) and Priday (1944). Thompson and Adloff (1971) offer a historical survey that concentrates on the twentieth century. O'Reilly's *Calédoniens* (1980) remains the most important volume containing biographical information on many New Caledonians, both black and white. Sarasin's ethnological work (see especially Sarasin and Roux 1929) supplements Pere Lambert's (1900) early anthropological work; both deal in considerable detail with traditional material culture. The best-known anthropologist who has dealt with New Caledonia within functionalist and ethnographic frameworks is the missionary-anthropologist Maurice Leenhardt (e.g., 1930, 1979), whose writings appeared somewhat later.

9. Sarasin (1917, 73) estimated the entire Pamboa tribe at 350.

10. The total number of specimens is inflated because it includes a large number of sling stones. ABL cataloged the New Caledonia collection with fewer than 130 catalog numbers.

11. This was the planter J. B. Octave Mouton, who was one of the first settlers in the Bismarck Archipelago. He came with the French colonists to Port-Breton on New Ireland and later established himself at Kinigunan on the Gazelle Peninsula. His memoirs were edited by Biskup (1974).

12. See, e.g., Kaeppler (1978).

13. Each of the Komine daggers has a small hole near the end of the handle, and most have a small loop of fiber or string attached. These loops were probably used for hanging the daggers on hooks or nails in the wall and may have been added by Komine's men or by the villagers at Komine's request. The form of these daggers may even have been developed as a new artifact type for selling to foreigners; it is not clear whether such daggers were used in traditional exchanges as the long, fragile, obsidian-bladed spears had been. The overseas curio trade appears to have influenced styles and production among Admiralty spears. Traders may have preferred to buy daggers, which are more easily transported than the awkward spears. See, e.g., Torrence (1989, 1993, 1994).

14. ABL appears to have acquired several expensive items from Tost and Rohu, a major Sydney curio dealer. Among others, these included two full suits of woven armor from Kingsmill Islands, also known as the Gilbert Islands, now Kiribati. Before the Great War, Tost and Rohu also sold Melanesian material to the Australian Museum in Sydney.

15. The MacGregor Collection from Papua, numbering some six thousand items, has been returned to Papua and is now in the collection of the Papua New Guinea National Museum and Art Gallery.

16. Nearly all of these pieces were originally from the Komine collection. While cataloging and packing the Komine collection, ABL seems to have set aside some specimens specifically for the Australian Museum, without even listing them in his list for Field Museum. This collection was sent directly to Sydney, while the others were sent on to Chicago. ABL's visit seems to have prompted Hedley to pay a visit to Field Museum at the end of 1911 or early in

1912, for which ABL hastily drafted a letter of introduction for Hedley to his Field Museum colleague, Assistant Curator S. C. Simms. As Hedley was away, Director Robert Etheridge, Jr., handled the exchange, which was sent to Chicago in mid-January.

Book 7: Papua and Dutch New Guinea

1. The tone of Hall's account seems fully compatible with what we know of ABL's scholarly orientation and his eagerness to learn as much as he could about the villages he visited.

2. See Joyce, Healy, and Legge (1972) and especially van der Veur (1966) regarding the annexation of British New Guinea. For a succinct summary of the history of British New Guinea and Papua see Griffin, Nelson, and Firth (1979). Nelson (1976) is still the best survey of mining in Papua. Souter (1963) offers a good survey of European exploration of Papua but exaggerates the "unknownness" of and lack of commercial development in the colony.

3. The Dutch reasserted these claims and clarified the official boundaries of Dutch New Guinea in 1848 (van der Veur 1966, 9ff.: Souter 1963, 22).

4. R.M.s and A.R.M.s at this time were essentially the same as district officers and assistant district officers of the post–Second World War administration. The Papuan civil service was much more active in opening up the country than their German counterparts had been. Murray has often been criticized for doing little to develop Papua. While it is true that he did little to encourage native-owned businesses and plantations, he worked hard to explore the country, pacify newly contacted populations, and open up the colony to Australian enterprise. He was also eager to identify and exploit mineral deposits. ABL's diaries, like Murray's memoirs (1912b, 1925), contradict the prevailing view.

5. ABL mentions four R.M.s, two A.R.M.s, and nine other officers by name or position. He must have met two or three times as many others as he mentions.

6. Although it is not clear from the diary, Murray (1912a) is explicit that he went along on this trip to the east.

7. ABL systematically uses Baker. Contemporaneous published references identify him as Baker, Massey Baker, and Massey-Baker. In later years he seems to have preferred the last of these.

8. This Port Moresby landmark burned down in 1993.

9. Patten donated 58 specimens (including 27 arrows) to the Dartmouth College Museum in 1914 (accession 14-13). On his death in 1934, his son Dr. Bradley Patten arranged for another 44 specimens (21 arrows) to be accessioned (accession 34-36). In 1953 Mrs. Lincoln Washburn gave Dartmouth College Museum 12 pieces (5 arrows) that had been presented to the Washburn family by Professor Patten some years earlier (accession 53-57). And after Bradley Patten's death in 1971 another 76 pieces (64 arrows and spears) joined the Dartmouth collection (accession 171-29). Like ABL, Patten also took photographs at Goaribari.

About a dozen of these images have survived as lantern slides at the Hood Museum, some with images almost identical to ABL's photos. In a few instances the two photographers may even have lined up their cameras and tripods for essentially the same shot. Patten's original field diary is now lost, but some notes amounting to an expedition log and summary were made from the original by A. F. Whiting in 1960. These notes, which closely correspond with ABL's diary, are currently in the accessions files at the Hood Museum. Patten also donated a few Goaribari arrows to the Peabody Museum in Salem, Massachusetts.

10. In ABL's account, the Papuan Gulf was a busy place indeed. Unlike Eitape in 1909, where most of the activity was scientific, here the activity was aimed at prospecting and other commercial ventures.

11. The standard ethnographic studies of the region are by Beaver (1920), Holmes (1924), Landtman (1927), Riley (1925), and Williams (1924, 1940), of whom only Landtman and Williams were trained anthropologists. All of these monographs are based on observations from about the same period described here by ABL. Here ABL's concern with the "ethnographic past" serves as a useful antidote to presumptions that these monographs were describing a pristine world far removed from Europeans.

12. The best history of the Anglican mission in Papua is by Wetherell (1977). Four missions were established in Papua before the First World War, each with its own sphere of influence. The London Missionary Society was the oldest and had stations from Samarai to Daru, with its headquarters in Port Moresby. The Anglicans were centered at Samarai with stations largely along the northeast coast from Samarai to the German border. The Methodists were situated in the Massim, while the French Catholic mission had stations at Yule Island and on the adjacent mainland. For a survey of the lives and experiences of missionaries in Papua during this period, see Langmore (1989).

13. The Sacred Heart came to the Kei Islands about 1902 and to Merauke in 1905. A station on the Tenimber Islands was opened in 1910. Many of the priests and brothers had previously served the same mission in New Britain. See *Encyc. Ned-Indië* (5:412–413); Vertenten (1935).

14. For a good, succinct history of the Moluccas see Hanna (1978). Legge (1964) and Vlekke (1943) offer good, general overviews of Indonesia's history. For a view that emphasizes the role of Indonesians rather than Europeans see volumes 3 and 4 of the *Sejarah Nasional Indonesia* (Kartodirdjo, Poesponegoro, and Notosusanto 1975). For a summary of sources about the Central Moluccas see Polman (1983); concerning Dutch New Guinea see Galis (1962) and Baal, Galis, and Koentjaraningrat (1984).

15. The UZV had stations on Buru, Halmahera, and Ceram as well as along the north coast of New Guinea. See *Encyc. Ned-Indië* (4:847–849); Klein (1935–1938, 1:319); Polman (1983).

16. Pamela Swaddling (personal communication, 1993) reports considerable time depth to these relations, which she has examined in order to understand the global history of the bird of paradise trade. This important study

(currently in preparation) shows that New Guineans have long been tied into the global economy.

17. British authorities in Papua had complained to the Dutch about Tugeri headhunting since MacGregor's time; see, e.g., Haddon (1891), *Indische Gids* (1892, 1893); Wirz (1933). ABL obtained a set of trophy skulls from the Dutch controleur in Merauke, who had confiscated them from around Okaba a short time earlier in an effort to suppress headhunting.

Return from the Field

1. Marshall Field's will required that a site be selected within six years of his death (*FMNH Annual Report* 1911, 4:105). The structure on the original site was subsequently rebuilt and now houses the Museum of Science and Industry.

2. ABL's notes are unclear about which (if any) specimens were obtained from H. L. C. Johnston of Yule Island. In all likelihood this collection largely consisted of stone clubs from various parts of Papua (field numbers 9324–9369).

3. In some cases, bundles of arrows or other groups of associated objects were cataloged with a single catalog number. When cataloging was complete these specimens produced more than twenty thousand catalog cards.

4. Although ABL had instructed Carpenter to assign museum negative numbers to his negatives following the sequence of field numbers he had already assigned them, more than half of these negatives were inadvertently assigned numbers randomly, probably by one of Carpenter's assistants. A total of 430 different images from ABL expedition photographs—some in multiple copies—have survived as lantern slides in the Department of Anthropology. The large number of these images, many of which were hand tinted by Chicago artists, suggests that over the years ABL was active in presenting public lectures.

CONCLUSION

A.B. Lewis and the Discipline of Anthropology before the Great War

1. Some time after the Second World War, the Department of Anthropology modernized ABL's exhibit by installing lights in the original cases. Some specimens in each case were removed to make room for the electrical lighting. Despite these changes, the original labels written by ABL were retained until 1986, when the entire exhibit was deinstalled. The museum's new Pacific halls, "Traveling the Pacific" and "Pacific Spirits," were opened in 1989 and 1990 and exhibit several hundred pieces that ABL had exhibited, but with a different thematic organization. Most of the Lewis Collection is in storage as a research collection, as it has always been.

2. In biographical entries such as *Who's Who* or for alumni organizations, ABL always emphasized his expedition and the places he visited, rarely mentioning his collection.

3. The only later expedition in German New Guinea was the Kaiserin Augusta River Expedition of 1912–1914, led by Walter Behrmann (1922) and Richard Thurnwald (1916, 1917, 1918). But even during this expedition, which was interrupted by the outbreak of war, Thurnwald worked in a much more restricted region than ABL had and much more intensively (e.g., 1916). In 1914 Rivers also returned to the New Hebrides with his protégé, John W. Layard. While Layard concentrated his researches on Atchin, Rivers moved around the islands in the northern New Hebrides, largely aboard the *Southern Cross,* but "his Melanesian itinerary was much more limited than in 1908" (Slobodin 1978, 52–53).

4. The substance of Freeman's (1983) attack on Mead's Samoan research (1928) is that Boas' research agenda, the attack on eugenics, informed too much of Mead's analysis and data collection. There can be no question that Mead was influenced by Boas and his second research program. It is much less clear that Mead intentionally falsified her data to support Boas' agenda.

5. Thurnwald was on the upper Sepik when the Great War broke out in August 1914. When he returned to Marienburg on the lower Sepik, Australian forces arrested him and took him to Madang for questioning before allowing him to return to the river and continue his research.

6. See, e.g., the papers edited by Stocking (1985) and Cole's (1985) discussions of how and why Northwest Coast collections were assembled.

7. Other career tracks gave curators educational roles as well. When S. C. Simms, for example, left the Department of Anthropology at Field Museum, he was promoted to curator of the Harris Public School Extension Center, which functioned as another department in the museum.

8. While still assistant curator at Field Museum, Fay-Cooper Cole arranged to teach anthropology courses at Northwestern University in the early 1920s. Cole wanted to be appointed professor in a proposed department of anthropology, which was under consideration at the university. Museum director D. C. Davies and anthropology curator Laufer were unhappy with this arrangement because teaching kept Cole away from the museum during ordinary business hours. Although this incident undoubtedly coincides with other tensions between Laufer and Cole, it led to Cole's dismissal from the museum, his subsequent appointment for a time at Northwestern, and his eventual appointment at the University of Chicago. The museum administration's narrow vision in issues of this sort ultimately hastened the demise of museum anthropology in the 1930s by driving away some of its most dynamic staff to nearby universities.

9. This fact alone would seem to explain the eclectic mélange of articles published in Britain's leading anthropological journals, *Man* and *Journal of the Royal Anthropological Institute,* or in the United States in the new series of the *American Anthropologist.* Unlike today, the ethnographic or anthropological map of the world still contained vast blank spaces.

10. Many of these skulls were measured and studied by ABL's colleague and friend, Curator Wilfrid Hambly (1940a, 1946).

11. These expeditions in the north built on the New

Guinea Expedition of 1903 under the direction of Prof. Dr. C. E. A. Wichmann; see Lorentz (1905), van der Sande (1907), Wichmann (1917). Findings from a similar set of expeditions undertaken in the southern part of Dutch New Guinea were also published in formal reports; see, e.g., *De Zuidwest Nieuw-Guinea-Expedition* (1908) and *Verslag van de Militaire Exploratie van Nederlandsch-Nieuw-Guinee* (1920).

12. In 1871–1872, 1876–1877, and 1883, the Russian naturalist N. N. Miklukho-Maklai had lived for a total of almost three years on the Rai coast, east of the modern town of Madang (Sentinella 1975). He was not an anthropologist, but his fieldwork in many ways resembles ethnographic fieldwork today. He collected considerable ethnographic data and made collections of material culture from villages on the Rai coast as well as other parts of Melanesia. Most of these collections are now in the Museum of Anthropology and Ethnography of the Russian Academy of Sciences in St. Petersburg, Russia (Elena S. Soboleva, personal communication, Jan. 1993).

13. The best summary of British social anthropology's increasingly intensive efforts in fieldwork is by Stocking (1983).

14. Oral tradition within the discipline sometimes suggests that Malinowski's movements were restricted by the war and that this restriction produced the ethnographic method; the facts suggest otherwise. For most of the war Malinowski's activities were completely unrestricted by Australian authorities. It was only during Malinowski's third expedition that Lieutenant-Governor Sir Hubert Murray—who had a strong dislike of Malinowski—restricted the Polish ethnographer to the Trobriand Islands (see Young 1988).

15. Malinowski (1934) did write one article about Massim stone axes for the Seligman memorial volume, but the axes in the photographs were from the Seligman collection rather than those Malinowski had himself collected.

16. Laufer, who was himself a prolific writer (see Kendall 1991), seems to have initiated the museum's *Popular Series* of leaflets, the *Design Series*, and this series of *Department of Anthropology Guides*. Ralph Linton, who was assistant curator of Oceanic and Malayan ethnology at Field Museum from 1922 to 1928, wrote the guide for Polynesia and Micronesia (Linton 1926).

17. The Anglican priest R. H. Codrington (1891) had, of course, dealt with many of these and other topics. Although one of the earliest treatments of such anthropological topics in Melanesia, his book deals almost exclusively with the peoples of the Solomon Islands and the New Hebrides. Codrington did not discuss New Guinea, the Bismarck Archipelago, New Caledonia, or Fiji, all of which ABL treats equally as parts of Melanesia.

18. Spoehr, who was born about two months after ABL returned from the field, joined the museum's staff as assistant curator of American ethnology and archaeology in 1940. In 1947 the museum sent him on an expedition to the Marshall Islands, after which he was appointed curator of Oceanic ethnology. His additions and deletions to the bibliography were carefully executed and well chosen.

19. It had long been assumed that wave after wave of migrant groups, each usually assumed to be of different races, had gone to Melanesia. The traditional, now outdated, view was that a dwarf or pygmy group, often called negritos, had been the first to reach New Guinea. See Oliver (1951, 17ff.) for a summary of this now largely abandoned view. This early pygmy or negrito migration theory seemed to draw support from the presence of peoples of short stature in the mountainous interior of New Guinea (e.g., Behrmann 1935; Kirschbaum 1936, 1937; Neuhauss 1911c; Wollaston 1912 Haddon 1912; Festschrift Paul Schebesta 1963: Part I).

20. Nearly all of ABL's specimens are still held by the Department of Anthropology of Field Museum as part of its research and exhibition collections. In addition to the 402 items that ABL exchanged with the Australian Museum, Field Museum is known to have exchanged about 330 pieces (largely from the Komine collection). These were mostly parts of exchanges with major museums, the most important being with the Bishop Museum (in 1925), Buffalo Museum of Science (1925 and 1939), Peabody Museum, Harvard (1918), National Museum of Mexico (1953), and National Museum of Guatemala (1923). Several larger items, particularly canoes, were also sent to the Museum of Science and Industry in Chicago some years ago, as space was at a premium in Field Museum's present building in Grant Park.

During cataloging, ABL seems not to have accessioned about three hundred pieces; about a third of these were probably part of the Australian Museum exchange. Most of the rest were severely damaged, rotten, or badly broken, and ABL seems to have discarded them himself. (Although ABL's specimen lists contain useful information about many of these items, they have been excluded in the appendix and in all tabulations given in the text of this volume.) A handful of pieces is known to have been discarded or "consigned to waste" in the 1920s and 1930s; this group of objects mostly consisted of fragile bands, gourds, pots, and arrows that had suffered severe damage. Inevitably, over the years some pieces have lost their tags or numbers or have been incorrectly numbered and can no longer be associated with ABL's cataloging notes. But for such a large collection this group of problem pieces is surprisingly small. Well over 95 percent of the Lewis Collection is still intact.

21. As Field Museum's own research program, the A. B. Lewis Project, shows, early museum collections can motivate a variety of new field research. The A. B. Lewis Project Expedition 1993–1994 was a collaborative research effort to study regional diversity on the north coast of New Guinea. It involved a research team consisting of Robert L. Welsch and John Terrell from Field Museum, Wilfred P. Oltomo from the Papua New Guinea National Museum and Art Gallery, and Michael Reupana and Alois Kuaso of the University of Papua New Guinea. The project was funded by the National Science Foundation and the National Endowment for the Humanities.

22. Anthropologists have never completely stopped collecting examples of material culture in the villages in which they worked. But trained anthropologists collected far fewer specimens after 1930 than previously. The charac-

ter of the collections brought back by those anthropologists who did make collections changed dramatically as well. Modern collections typically have much better documentation, but they contain fewer specimens and rarely contain material from many ethnolinguistic groups. Most important here is that the narrow ethnographic bias to distinguish one's study community as unique has an impact on the content of these modern collections. These biases are not wrong per se, but they are quite different biases from those informing collections made before 1920.

Bibliography

||||||||||||||||||||||||||||||||||||||||||||||||||||||||||||||||||||||||||||||||||||||||||||||||||||||||||||||||||||

AHRENS, THEODORE

1988   Die aktualität Christian Keyssers: Eine fallstudie protestantischer mission. *Zeitschrift für Mission* 14:94–110.

AKIN, DAVID

1993   Negotiating culture in east Kwaio, Solomon Islands. Ph.D. diss. University of Hawai'i.

ALATAS, SYED HUSSEIN

1977   *The myth of the lazy native: A study of the image of the Malays, Filipinos, and Javanese from the 16th to the 20th century and its function in the ideology of colonial capitalism.* London: Frank Cass.

BAAL, J. VAN; K. W. GALIS; and R. M. KOENTJARANINGRAT

1984   *West Irian: A bibliography.* Koninklijk Instituut voor Taal-, Land- en Volkenkunde, Bibliographical Series, 15. Dordrecht: Foris Publications.

BADE, KLAUS-J.

1977   Colonial missions and imperialism: The background to the fiasco of the Rhenish Mission in New Guinea. In *Germany in the Pacific and Far East, 1870–1914,* ed. J. A. Moses and P. M. Kennedy, 313–346. St. Lucia: University of Queensland Press.

BAMLER, GEORG

1900   Bemerkungen zur Grammatik der Tamisprache (und Vokabular). *Zeitschrift für afrikanische und oceanische Sprachen* 5:198–253.

1911   Tami. In *Deutsch-Neu-Guinea,* R. Neuhauss, 3:489–566. Berlin: Dietrich Reimer.

BARBOUR, THOMAS

1908   Further notes on Dutch New Guinea. *National Geographic Magazine* 19:527–45.

BARLOW, KATHLEEN

1985   The role of women in intertribal trade among the Murik of Papua New Guinea. *Research in Economic Anthropology* 7:95–122.

BARLOW, KATHLEEN AND DAVID LIPSET

1989   The construction of meaning in ethnography and culture: The fabrication of canoes in the Murik Lakes. Paper presented at conference "Object informs, objects in form: The ethnography of Oceanic art." Baltimore Museum of Art. April.

BEAVER, WILFRED N.

1920   *Unexplored New Guinea: A record of the travels, adventures, and experiences of a resident magistrate amongst the head-hunting savages and cannibals of the unexplored interior of New Guinea.* London: Seeley, Service.

BEHRMANN, WALTER

1922   *Im Stromgebiet des Sepik: Eine deutsche Forschungsreise in Neuguinea.* Berlin: A. Scherl.

1935   Pygmäen im Sepikgebiet, Neuguinea. *Tijdschrift van het Nederlandsch Aardrijkskundig Genootschap* 52:407–414.

BELLWOOD, PETER

1979   *Man's conquest of the Pacific: The prehistory of Southeast Asia and Oceania.* New York: Oxford University Press.

BENNETT, JUDITH A.

1987   *Wealth of the Solomons: A history of a Pacific archipelago, 1800–1978.* Pacific Islands Monograph Series, no. 3. Honolulu: University of Hawai'i Press.

BERGHAUSEN, G.

1910   Bericht über eine Expedition nach den Manus-Hermit-Inseln. *Amtsblatt* 2:19–20, 26–28, 34–36, 42–44, 49–50.

BIERSACK, ALETTA, ED.

1991   *Clio in Oceania: Towards a historical anthropology.* Washington, D.C.: Smithsonian Institution Press.

BISKUP, PETER

1969   Hahl at Herbertshoehe, 1896–1898: The genesis of German native administration in New Guinea. In *The history of Melanesia: Second Waigani Seminar,* 77–100. Canberra: University of Papua New Guinea and Research School of Pacific Studies, Australian National University.

————, ED.

1974   *The New Guinea memoirs of Jean Baptiste Octave Mouton.* Pacific History Series, no. 7. Honolulu: University Press of Hawai'i.

BOAS, FRANZ

1907   Some principles of museum administration. *Science* 25:921–933.

1940   *Race, language, and culture.* New York: Macmillan.

BONAPARTE, PRINCE ROLAND

1887   *La Nouvelle-Guinée: IIIe Notice Le Fleuve Augusta.* Paris: Imprimé pour L'auteur.

BONE, ROBERT C., JR.

1958   *The dynamics of the western New Guinea (Irian Barat) problem.* Interim Reports Series, Modern Indonesia Project. Ithaca, N.Y.: Southeast Asia Program, Cornell University.

BRIEN, LINDSAY M.

n.d.   Cemetery records, Green Co., Ohio (incomplete). Typescript, available at the Newberry Library, Chicago.

BROADSTONE, M. A., ED.

1918   *History of Green County Ohio: Its people, industries, and institutions.* Indianapolis: B. F. Bowen.

CHAPMAN BROS.

1890   *Portrait and biographical album of Green and Clark counties, Ohio.* Chicago: Chapman Bros.

CHINNERY, E. W. PEARSON

1927   The blow-gun in New Britain. *Man* 27:208.

CHURCHILL, WILLIAM

1916   *Sissano: Movements of migration within and through Melanesia.* Carnegie Institution of Washington, publication no. 244. Washington, D.C.: Carnegie Institution of Washington.

CLIFFORD, JAMES

1985   Objects and selves—An afterword. In *Objects and others: Essays on museums and material culture,* ed. G. W. Stocking, Jr., 236–246. History of Anthropology, vol. 3. Madison: University of Wisconsin Press.

CLUNE, FRANK

1942a   *Last of the Australian explorers: The story of Donald Mackay.* Sydney: Angus and Robertson.

CODRINGTON, R. H.

1885   *The Melanesian languages.* Oxford: Clarendon Press.

1891   *Melanesians: Studies in their anthropology and folklore.* Oxford: Clarendon Press.

COLE, DOUGLAS

1985   *Captured heritage: The scramble for northwest coast artifacts.* Seattle: University of Washington Press.

CORBIN, GEORGE A.

1984   The central Baining revisited: "Salvage" art history among the Kairak and Uramot Baining of east New Britain, Papua New Guinea. *Res* 7–8:44–69.

1989   Continuity and change in the art of the Sulka of Wide Bay, east New Britain, Papua New Guinea. Paper presented at conference "Object informs, objects in form: The ethnography of Oceanic art." Baltimore Museum of Art, April.

COULTER, JOHN WESLEY

1942   *Fiji: Little India of the Pacific.* Chicago: University of Chicago Press.

1967   *The drama of Fiji: A contemporary history.* Rutland, Vt.: Charles E. Tuttle.

DERRICK, R. A.

1950   *A history of Fiji.* Vol. 1. Suva: Government Press.

DILLS, R. S.

1881   *History of Greene County, together with notes on the northwest and the state of Ohio.* Dayton: Odell and Mayer.

DIXON, ROLAND BURRAGE

1916   *Oceanic mythology.* The Mythology of all Races, vol. 9. Boston: Marshall Jones.

1923   *The racial history of man.* New York: Charles Scribner's Sons.

1928   *The building of cultures.* New York: Charles Scribner's Sons.

DKB

1907   Eine Reise nach Kaiser-Wilhelmsland. *DKB* 18:200–205.

DORSEY, GEORGE A.

1907   The anthropological exhibits of the American Museum of Natural History. *Science* 25:584–589.

1909a   One hundred installments of a diary of a 47,000-mile journey. *Chicago Daily Tribune,* 16 Aug. 1909 to 23 Nov. 1909. (Columns concerning German New Guinea ran 18 Sep. 1909 through 6 Oct. 1909.)

1909b   A visit to the German Solomon Islands. In *Putnam anniversary volume: Anthropological essays presented to Frederic Ward Putnam in honor of his seventieth birthday, April 16, 1909,* 521–544. New York: G. E. Stechert.

DuBois, Cora

1944   *The people of Alor.* Minneapolis: University of Minnesota Press.

Durkheim, Emile

1912   *Les formes élémentaire de la vie religieuse: Le système totémique en Australia.* Original French ed. Paris: F. Alcan.

1915   *The elementary forms of the religious life: A study in religious sociology.* 1st English ed. London: Allen and Unwin.

Ellis, William

1859   *Polynesian researches, during a residence of nearly eight years in the Society and Sandwich islands.* 2d ed., enlarged and improved. London: H. G. Bohn.

Erdweg, Mathias Josef

1901a   Ein Besuch bei den Varópu, Deutsch Neu-Guinea. *Globus* 79:101–105.

1902   Die Bewohner der Insel Tumleo, Berlin-hafen, Deutsch-Neuguinea. *Anthropologische Gesellschaft in Wien, Mitteilungen* 32(3 Folge 2 Band):274–310, 317–399.

Erskine, Captain

1853   *Journal of a cruise among the islands of the western Pacific.* London: John Murray.

Evans-Pritchard, E. E.

1940   *The Nuer: A description of the modes of livelihood and political institutions of a Nilotic people.* Oxford: Oxford University Press.

Everets, L. H.

1874   *Combination atlas map of Green Co., Ohio.* Chicago: L. H. Everets.

Ewers, W. H., and W. T. Jeffrey

1971   *Parasites of man in Niugini.* Milton, Queensland: Jacaranda.

Festschrift, Paul Schebesta

1963   Festschrift Paul Schebesta zum 75. Geburtstag. Studia Instituti Anthropos 18.

Fieldhouse, David K.

1978   *Unilever overseas: The anatomy of a multinational, 1895–1965.* London: Croom Helm; Stanford: Hoover Institution Press.

Finsch, Otto

1888a   *Samoafahrten: Reise in Kaiser Wilhelmsland und Englisch Neu-Guinea in de Jahren 1884 und 1885 an Bord des deutschen Dampfers "Samoa."* Leipzig: Hirt & Sohn.

Firth, Raymond

1936   *We the Tikopia: A sociological study of kinship in primitive Polynesia.* London: George Allen and Unwin.

Firth, Stewart

1982   *New Guinea under the Germans.* Melbourne: Melbourne University Press.

Flierl, Johannes

1927   *Forty years in New Guinea: Memoirs of the senior missionary John Flierl.* Trans. Prof. M. Wiederaenders. Chicago: Board of Foreign Missions of the Synod of Iowa and Other States.

Freed, Stanley A., and Ruth S. Freed

1991   Clark Wissler. In *International dictionary of anthropologists,* comp. Library-Anthropology Resource Group (LARG), Christopher Winters, gen. ed., 763–764. New York: Garland.

Freeman, Derek

1983   *Margaret Mead and Samoa: The making and unmaking of an anthropological myth.* Cambridge: Harvard University Press.

Frerichs, A. C.

1957   *Anutu conquers in New Guinea: A story of seventy years of mission work in New Guinea.* Columbus, Ohio: Wartburg Press.

Freud, Sigmund

1913   *Totem und Tabu.* Leipzig: H. Heller.

Freytag, Anton

1912   *Die Missionen der Geselschaft des Göttlichen Wortes: Handbüchlein zur Geographie, Geschichte und Missionskunde jener Gebiete, in denen die Steyler Missionare gegenwärtig tätig sind.* Steyl: Verlag der Missionsdruckerei.

Friederici, Georg

1909   Die Expedition Sapper-Friederici. *DKB* 20:124–126, 331–336.

1910a   In das Hinterland der Nordküste des Kaiser Wilhelmslandes (Neuguinea). *Petermanns Geographische Mitteilungen* 56(pt. 2):182–185.

1912   *Wissenschaftliche Ergebnisse einer amtlichen Forschungs-reis nach dem Bismarck-Archipel im Jahre 1908.* Band 2: *Beiträge zur Völker- und Sprachenkunde von Deutsch-Neuguinea.* Mitteilungen aus den Deutschen Schutzgebieten, Ergänzungsheft no. 5.

1913   *Wissenschaftliche Ergebnisse einer amtlichen Forschungs-reis nach dem Bismarck-Archipel im Jahre 1908.* Band 3: *Untersuchungen über eine melanesische Wanderstrasse.* Mitteilungen aus den Deutschen Schutzgebieten, Ergäanzungsheft no. 7.

Fugmann, Wilhelm, ed.

1985   *Christian Keysser: Bürger zweier Welten.* Neuhausen-Stuttgart: Hänssler Verlag.

Fugmann, Wilhelm, and Herwig Wagner

1978   *Von Gott erzählen: Das Leben Christian Keyssers 1877–1961.* Neuendettelsau: Friemund Verlag.

FULL, (BEZIRKSASSESSOR)

1909a   Eine Fahrt auf dem Kaiserin Augustafluss. *DKB* 20:739–741, 744–745.

FURNIVALL, J. S.

1944   *Netherlands India: A study of plural economy.* New York: Macmillan.

GALIS, K. W., COMP.

1962   *Bibliographie van Nederlands-Nieuw-Guinea.* Rev. 3d ed. The Hague: Ministrie van Binnenlandse Zaken.

GEWERTZ, DEBORAH B.

1983   *Sepik River societies: A historical ethnography of the Chambri and their neighbors.* New Haven, Conn.: Yale University Press.

GITLOW, ABRAHAM L.

1947   *Economics of the Mount Hagen tribes, New Guinea.* Monographs of the American Ethnological Society, no. 12. Seattle: University of Washington Press.

GOES, H. D. A. VAN DER

1862   Nieuw Guinea, ethnographisch en natuurkundig onderzocht en beschreven in 1858 door een Nederlandsch Indische commissie. *Bijdragen tot de Taal-, Land- en Volkenkunde* 5:1–233.

GOETHEM, EDWARD VAN

1912   String-bags of Mekeo Papua. *Anthropos* 7:792–795.

GOODALE, JANE C.

1966   Blowgun hunters of the South Pacific. With photographs by Ann Chowning. *National Geographic* 129(6):793–817.

GRAEBNER, F.

1909   Die melanesische Bogenkultur und ihre Verwandten. *Anthropos* 4:726–780, 998–1032.

GREUB, SUZANNE, ED.

1992   *Art of northwest New Guinea: From Geelvink Bay, Humboldt Bay, and Lake Sentani.* New York: Rizzoli.

GRIFFIN, JAMES; HANK NELSON; AND STEWART FIRTH

1979   *Papua New Guinea: A political history.* Richmond, Vic.: Heinemann Educational Australia.

HADDON, ALFRED CORT

1891   The Tugeri-headhunters of New Guinea. *Internationales Archiv für Ethnographie* 4:177–181.

1894   *The decorative art of British New Guinea: A study in Papuan ethnography.* Cunningham Memoirs, no. 10. Dublin: Royal Irish Academy.

1900a   A classification of the stone clubs of British New Guinea. *Journal of the Anthropological Institute of Great Britain and Ireland* 30:221–250.

1900b   Studies in the anthropogeography of British New Guinea. *Geographical Journal* 16:265–291, 414–441.

1906   A plea for the investigation of biological and anthropological distributions in Melanesia. *Geographical Journal* 28:155–163.

1912   The Pygmy Question. In *Pygmies and Papuans,* ed. A. F. R. Wollaston, 303–346.

1920   Migrations of cultures in British New Guinea: The Huxley Memorial Lecture for 1920. *Journal of the Royal Anthropological Institute of Great Britain and Ireland* 50:237–280.

1923a   Migrations of peoples in the south-west Pacific. *Proceedings of the Second Pan-Pacific Science Congress, 1923.* 1:220–224.

————, ED.

1901–1935   *Reports of the Cambridge Anthropological Expedition to Torres Straits.* 6 vols. Cambridge: Cambridge University Press.

HALL, MARY

1914   *A woman in the antipodes and in the Far East.* London: Methuen.

HAMBLY, WILFRID D.

1940a   Craniometry of New Guinea. *Fieldiana: Anthropological Series* 25(3):81–290.

1940b   In memoriam Albert Buell Lewis, June 21, 1867–October 10, 1940. *Field Museum News* 11(11):6.

1941   Albert Buell Lewis. *American Anthropologist* 43:256–257.

1945   Recent methods of research. In *The Melanesians: People of the South Pacific,* A. B. Lewis, 230–235. 2d printing (with additions and corrections). Chicago: Chicago Natural History Museum.

1946   Craniometry of Ambrym Island. *Fieldiana: Anthropological Series* 37(1):1–150.

HANNA, WILLARD A.

1978   *Indonesian Banda: Colonialism and its aftermath in the Nutmeg Islands.* Philadelphia: Institute for the Study of Human Issues.

HARDING, THOMAS G.

1967   *Voyagers of the Vitiaz Strait: A study of a New Guinea trade system.* American Ethnological Society, monograph 44. Seattle: University of Washington Press.

HAYS, TERENCE

1993   "The New Guinea highlands": Region, culture area, or fuzzy set? *Current Anthropology* 34(2):141–164.

HAZLEWOOD, DAVID

1872   *Fijian and English and English and Fijian Dictionary.* London: Sampson Low, Marston.

HELD, G. J.

1957   *The Papuas of Waropen.* Koninklijk Instituut

voor Taal-, Land- en Volkenkunde, Translation Series, 2. The Hague: Martinus Nijhoff.

HELLWIG, F. C.

1911　Die Erforschung des Kaiserin-Augusta-Flusses in Deutsch-Neuguinea. *Deutsche Kolonialzeitung* 28:424–425.

1927　Tagebuch der expedition. In *Ergebnisse der Südsee-Expedition, 1908–1910,* ed. G. Thilenius, Vol. 1: *Allgemeines,* 41–359. Hamburgische Wissenschaftliche Stiftung. Hamburg: L. Friederichsen.

HEMPENSTALL, PETER J.

1975　The reception of European missions in the German Pacific empire: The New Guinea experience. *Journal of Pacific History* 10:46–64.

1978　*Pacific islanders under German rule.* Canberra: Australian National University Press.

HERSKOVITS, MELVILLE J.

1953　*Franz Boas: The science of man in the making.* Twentieth Century Library. New York: Charles Scribner's Sons.

HINSLEY, CURTIS M.

1985　From shell-heaps to stelae: Early anthropology at the Peabody museums. In *Objects and others: Essays on museums and material culture,* ed. G. W. Stocking, Jr. 49–74. History of Anthropology, vol. 3, Madison: University of Wisconsin Press.

HOCART, A. M.

1915　[Review of] The history of Melanesian society, by W. H. R. Rivers. *Man* 15:89–93.

HOGBIN, IAN

1932　[Review of] Ethnology of Melanesia, by Albert B. Lewis. *Oceania* 3:114–115.

1951　*Transformation scene: The changing culture of a New Guinea village.* London: Routledge and Kegan Paul.

1963　*Kinship and marriage in a New Guinea village.* London School of Economics, Monographs on Social Anthropology No. 26. London: Athlone Press.

HOLMES, J. H.

1924　*In primitive New Guinea: An account of a quarter of a century spent amongst the primitive Ipi and Namau groups of Tribes of the Gulf of Papua.* New York: G. P. Putnam's Sons.

HOWE, K. R.

1988　*Where the waves fall: A new South Sea islands history from first settlement to colonial rule.* Pacific Islands Monograph Series, no. 2. Honolulu: University of Hawai'i Press.

HOWELLS, WILLIAM W.

1943　The racial elements of Melanesia. In *Studies in the anthropology of Oceania and Asia,* ed. C. S. Coon and J. M. Andrews, *Papers of the Peabody Museum of American Archaeology and Ethnology* 20:38–49.

1973　*The Pacific Islanders.* New York: Charles Scribner's Sons.

HUBER, MARY TAYLOR

1988　*The Bishops' progress: A historical ethnography of Catholic missionary experience on the Sepik frontier.* Washington, D.C.: Smithsonian Institution Press.

HYSLOP, JOHN

1991　Adolph Bandelier. In *International dictionary of anthropologists,* comp. Library-Anthropology Resource Group (LARG), Christopher Winters, gen. ed., 22–23. New York: Garland.

DE INDISCHE GIDS

1892　De Tugeri's. (Het Handelsblad over de venschelijkheid om alsnog een post op de begrooting te brengen voor een posthouder bij de Mariannestraat van Nieuw Guinea.) *De Indische Gids* 14(2):2373–2374.

1893　Een Overleg Tusschen Nederlandsche Autoriteiten en den Administrateur van Britisch Nieuw-Guinea. *De Indische Gids* 15(2):1953–1955.

JOYCE, R. B.

1971　*Sir William MacGregor.* Melbourne: Oxford University Press.

JOYCE, R. B.; A. M. HEALY; AND J. D. LEGGE

1972　British New Guinea. In *Encyclopedia of Papua New Guinea,* ed. P. Ryan, 115–121. Melbourne: Melbourne University Press in association with the University of Papua New Guinea.

KAEPPLER, ADRIENNE L.

1978　*"Artificial curiosities," being an exposition of native manufactures collected on the three Pacific voyages of Captain James Cook, R. N. at the Bernice Pauahi Bishop Museum, January 18, 1978–August 31, 1978, on the occasion of the bicentennial of the European discovery of the Hawaiian Islands by Captain Cook—January 18, 1778.* Bernice P. Bishop Museum, special publication, 65. Honolulu: Bishop Museum Press.

KARTODIRDJO, SARTONO; MARWATI DJOENED POESPONEGORO; AND NUGROHO NOTOSUSANTO

1975　*Sejarah Nasional Indonesia.* 6 vols. Jakarta: Departemen Pendidikan dan Kebudayaan.

KEESING, FELIX M.

1941　*The South Seas in the modern world.* Institute of Pacific Relations, International Research Series. New York: John Day.

KENDALL, LAUREL

1991　Berthold Laufer. In *International dictionary of anthropologists,* comp. Library-Anthropology Resource Group (LARG), Christopher Winters, gen. ed., pp. 383–384. New York: Garland.

KEYSSER, CHRISTIAN

1911   Aus dem Leben der Kaileute. In *Deutsch-Neu-Guinea*, R. Neuhauss, 3:3–242. Berlin: Dietrich Reimer.

1924   Mission work among primitive peoples in New Guinea. *International Review of Missions* 13:426–435.

1925   *Wörterbuch der Kâte-Sprache, gesprochen in Neuguinea*. Zeitschrift für Eingborenen-Sprachen, no. 7. Berlin: Dietrich Reimer (Ernst Vohsen).

1980   *A people reborn*. Trans. Alfred Allin and John Kuder. Pasadena, Calif.: William Carey Library.

KIRCH, PATRICK V., AND ROGER C. GREEN

1987   History, phylogeny, and evolution in Polynesia. *Current Anthropology* 28:431–456.

KIRCH, P. V., AND T. L. HUNT, EDS.

1988   *Archaeology of the Lapita cultural complex: A critical review*. Research Report, no. 5. Seattle: Thomas Burke Memorial Washington State Museum.

KIRSCHBAUM, FRANZ

1936   Pygmies of Ramu-river, N.G. *Pacific Islands Monthly* 7(4):31.

1937   Zur Erforschung der Ramu-Pygmäen (Neuguinea). *Anthropos* 32:661–662.

KLAFFL, JOHN, AND FRIEDRICH VORMANN

1905   Die Sprachen des Berlinhafen-Bezirks in Deutsch-Neuguinea. *Seminar für orientalische Sprachen zu Berlin, Mitteilungen* 8:1–138.

KLEIN, W. C., ED.

1935–1938   *Nieuw Guinee*. 3 vols. Amsterdam: J. H. de Bussy for Molukken-Instituut.

KNAUFT, BRUCE M.

1993   *South coast New Guinea cultures: History, comparison, dialectic*. Cambridge Studies in Social and Cultural Anthropology, 89. Cambridge: Cambridge University Press.

KOEHNE, PETER D.

1983   Justification, the ministry, and the Keysser method. *Lutheran Theological Journal* 17:103–114.

KONING, D. A. P.

1903   Eenige gegevens omtrent land en volk der noordoostkust van Ned. Nieuw-Guinea, genaamd Papoea Telandjang. *Bijdragen tot de Taal-, Land- en Volkenkunde* 55:250–80 (also *Tijdschrift van het Koninklijk Nederlandsch Aardrijkskundig Genootschap* 30:426–428).

KUKLICK, HENRIKA

1984   Tribal exemplars: Images of political authority in British anthropology, 1885–1945. In *Functionalism historicized: Essays on British social anthropology* ed. G. W. Stocking, Jr., 59–82. History of Anthropology, vol. 2. Madison: University of Wisconsin Press.

1991   *The savage within: The social history of British anthropology, 1885–1945*. Cambridge: Cambridge University Press.

KUPER, ADAM

1973   *Anthropology and anthropologists: The British school, 1922–1972*. London: Allan Lane.

1988   *The invention of primitive society: Transformations of an illusion*. London: Routledge.

LAMBERT, PERE

1900   *Moeurs et superstitions des Néo-Calédoniens*. Noumea: Nouvelle imprimerie Nouméenne.

LANDTMAN, GUNNAR

1917   *The folk-tales of the Kiwai Papuans*. Helsingfors: Finnish Society of Literature.

1927   *The Kiwai Papuans of British New Guinea*. London: Macmillan.

1933   *Ethnographical collection from the Kiwai district of British New Guinea, in the National Museum of Finland, Helsingfors (Helsinki): A descriptive survey of the material culture of the Kiwai people*. Helsingfors: Commission of the Antell Collection.

LANGMORE, DIANE

1989   *Missionary lives: Papua, 1874–1914*. Pacific Islands Monograph Series, no. 6. Honolulu: University of Hawai'i Press.

LARACY, HUGH

1976   Malinowski at war, 1914–1918. *Mankind* 10(4):264–268.

LAUFER, BERTHOLD

1914   Letter. Laufer to Skiff, 25 Sept. 1914. Field Museum, Department of Anthropology, director's files.

LEENHARDT, MAURICE

1930   *Notes d'ethnologie néo-Calédonien*. Paris: Institut d'Ethnologie.

1979   *Do Kamo: Person and myth in the Melanesian world*. Chicago: University of Chicago Press.

LEGGE, G. D.

1964   *Indonesia*. Englewood Cliffs, N.J.: Prentice Hall.

LEHNER, STEFAN

1911   Bukaua. In *Deutsch-Neu-Guinea*, R. Neuhauss, 3:397–485. Berlin: Dietrich Reimer.

LEONARD, ANNE, AND JOHN TERRELL

1980   *Patterns of paradise: The styles and significance of bark cloth around the world*. Chicago: Field Museum of Natural History.

LEWIS, ALBERT BUELL

1906b   Tribes of the Columbia Valley and the coast of Washington and Oregon. *Memoirs of the American Anthropological Association* 1(2):147–209.

1916 [Review of] Ein Beitrag zur Ethnologie von Bougainville und Buka mit spezieller Berucksichtigung der Nasioi, by Ernst Frizzi. *American Anthropologist* 18:289–290.

1919 [Review of] Contributions to the ethnography of Micronesia, by Akira Matsumura. *American Anthropologist* 21:315–316.

1922 New Guinea masks. *Department of Anthropology Leaflet,* no. 4. Chicago: Field Museum of Natural History.

1923 The use of sago in New Guinea. *Department of Anthropology Leaflet,* no. 10. Chicago: Field Museum of Natural History.

1924a Use of tobacco in New Guinea and neighboring regions. *Department of Anthropology Leaflet,* no. 17. Chicago: Field Museum of Natural History.

1924b *Block prints from India for textiles.* Anthropology Design Series, no. 1. Chicago: Field Museum of Natural History.

1924c *Javanese batik designs from metal stamps.* Anthropology Design Series, no. 2. Chicago: Field Museum of Natural History.

1925 *Decorative art of New Guinea: Incised designs.* Anthropology Design Series, no. 4. Chicago: Field Museum of Natural History.

1931a *Carved and painted designs from New Guinea.* Anthropology Design Series, no. 5. Chicago: Field Museum of Natural History.

1932a *Ethnology of Melanesia.* Department of Anthropology Guide, part 5, Joseph N. Field Hall (Hall A. Ground floor). Chicago: Field Museum of Natural History.

1945 *The Melanesians: People of the South Pacific.* 2d printing (with additions and corrections). Ed. W. D. Hambly. Chicago: Chicago Natural History Museum.

1951 *The Melanesians: People of the South Pacific.* 3d printing (with additions and corrections). Ed. W. D. Hambly. Chicago: Chicago Natural History Museum.

1988 New Britain notebook. Ed. R. L. Welsch. *Field Museum of Natural History Bulletin* 59(8):1–15.

LIJPHART, A.
1966 *The trauma of decolonization.* New Haven, Conn.: Yale University Press.

LINTON, RALPH
1926 *Ethnology of Polynesia and Micronesia.* Department of Anthropology Guide, part 6. Chicago: Field Museum of Natural History.

LINTON, RALPH, AND PAUL S. WINGERT
1946 *Arts of the South Seas.* New York: Museum of Modern Art.

LITTLE, WILLIAM J.
1911 Expedition by the Honorable W. J. Little, from the Kikori River to the Purari. *PAR,* 1910–1911, 202–203.

LORENTZ, H. A.
1905 *Eenige maanden onder de Papoea's.* Leiden: E. J. Brill.

LOWIE, ROBERT H.
1933 [Review of] Ethnology of Melanesia, by Albert B. Lewis. *American Anthropologist* 35:527.

1937 *The history of ethnological theory.* New York: Holt, Rinehart and Winston.

LURIE, NANCY
1981 Museumland revisited. *Human Organization* 40:180–187.

MALINOWSKI, BRONISLAW
1913 *The family among the Australian Aborigines: A sociological study.* University of London, Monographs on Sociology, vol. 2. London: University of London Press.

1922 *Argonauts of the western Pacific: An account of native enterprise and adventure in the archipelago of Melanesian New Guinea.* London: George Routledge and Kegan Paul.

1932 Introduction. In *Sorcerers of Dobu: The social anthropology of the Dobu Islanders of the western Pacific,* R. F. Fortune, xv–xxviii. New York: E. P. Dutton.

1934 Stone implements in eastern New Guinea. In *Essays presented to C. G. Seligman,* ed. E. E. Evans-Pritchard et al., 189–196. London: Kegan Paul, Trench, Trubner.

1967 *A diary in the strict sense of the term,* ed. R. Firth. London: Routledge and Kegan Paul.

MARTIN, PAUL
1945 Foreword. In *The Melanesians: People of the South Pacific,* Albert B. Lewis, 5. 2d printing (with additions and corrections). Chicago: Chicago Natural History Museum.

1951 Foreword. In *The Melanesians: People of the South Pacific,* Albert B. Lewis, 5. 3d Printing (with additions and corrections). Chicago: Chicago Natural History Museum.

MEAD, MARGARET
1928 *Coming of age in Samoa: A psychological study of primitive youth for Western civilization.* New York: W. Morrow.

1930 *Growing up in New Guinea: A comparative study of primitive education.* New York: W. Morrow.

1934 Kinship in the Admiralty Islands. *Anthropological Papers of the American Museum of Natural History* 34(pt. 2):181–358.

1935 *Sex and temperament in three primitive societies.* New York: William Morrow.

1938–1949 The Mountain Arapesh: (1) An importing culture. (2) Supernaturalism. (3) Socio-economic life. (4) Diary of events in Alitoa. (5) The record of Unabelin with Rorschach analyses. *American Museum of Natural History, Anthropological Papers* 36(3):139–349;

37(3):319–451; 40(3):163–232; 40(4):233–419; 41(3):289–390.

1964   Weaver of the border. In *In the company of man: Twenty portraits of anthropological informants,* ed. J. B. Casagrande, 175–210. Harper Torchbook. New York: Harper and Row.

MEIER, JOSEF

1904   Ein Maskentanz bei den Bainingern von Wuna-Galip. *DKB* 15:367–368.

1907   Primitiv Völker und "Paradies"-Zustand. Mit besonderer Berücksichtigung der früheren Verhältnisse beim Ost-stamm der Gazellehalbinsel im Bismarck-Archipel (Neu-Pommern). *Anthropos* 2:374–386.

1909   *Mythen und Erzählungen der Küstenbewohner der Gazelle-Halbinsel (Neu-Pommern).* Anthropos-Bibliothek, vol. 1(1). Münster: Aschendorff'sche Buchhandlund.

1911   Steinbilder des Iniet-Geheimbundes bei den Eingebornen des nordöstlichen Teiles der Gazelle-Halbinsel, Neupommern (Südsee). *Anthropos* 6:837–867.

1913   Die Zauberei bei den Küstenbewohnern der Gazelle-Halbinsel, Neupommern, Südsee. *Anthropos* 8:1–11, 285–305, 688–713.

1929   Adoption among the Gunantuna. *Publications of the Catholic Anthropological Conference* 1(1):1–98.

MEYER, OTTO

1909   Funde prähistorischer Töpferei und Steinmesser auf Vuatom, Bismarck-Archipel. *Anthropos* 4:251–252, 1093–1095.

1910   Funde von Menschen- und Tierknochen, von prähistorischer Töpferei und Steinwerkzeugen auf Vatom. *Anthropos* 5:1160–1161.

MOORE, CARMELLA C., AND A. KIMBALL ROMNEY

1994   Material culture, geographic propinquity, and linguistic affiliation on the north coast of New Guinea: A reanalysis of Welsch, Terrell, and Nadolski (1992). *American Anthropologist* 96(2):370–392.

MÜLLER, FRIEDRICH

1872   Ueber die Melanesier und die Papua-Rasse. *Anthropologische Gesellschaft in Wien, Mitteilungen* 2:45–49.

MULTATULI (EDOUARD DOUWES DEKKER)

1982   *Max Havelaar or the coffee auctions of the Dutch Trading Company.* Amherst: University of Massachusetts Press.

MURRAY, J. H. P.

1912a   Lieutenant governor's visits of inspection. *PAR,* 1911–1912, 16–22.

1912b   *Papua or British New Guinea.* London: T. Fisher Unwin.

1925   *Papua of today.* London: P. S. King and Son.

MURRAY, STEPHEN O.

1991   Roland B. Dixon. In *International dictionary of anthropologists,* comp. Library-Anthropology Resource Group (LARG), Christopher Winters, gen. ed., 149–150. New York: Garland.

NELSON, HANK

1976   *Black, white, and gold: Goldmining in Papua New Guinea, 1878–1930.* Canberra: Australian National University Press.

NEUHAUSS, RICHARD

1909   Brief des Herrn R. Neuhauss aus Neu-Guinea. *Zeitschrift für Ethnologie* 41:751–753, 962–963.

1911a   *Deutsch-Neu-Guinea.* 3 vols. Berlin: Dietrich Reimer.

1911b   Die 25jährige Tätigkeit der Neuendettelsauer Mission in Deutsch-Neu-Guinea. *Koloniale Rundschau* 6:223–230.

1911c   Über die Pygmän in Deutsch-Neuguinea und über das Haar der Papua. *Zeitschrift für Ethnologie* 43:280–287.

NEWTON, DOUGLAS

1961   *Art styles of the Papuan Gulf.* New York: Museum for Primitive Art.

1989   Mother Cassowary's bones: Daggers of the East Sepik Province, Papua New Guinea. *Metropolitan Museum Journal* 24:305–325.

NOLLEN, H.

1909   Les différentes Classes d'Age dans la Société kaia-kaia, Merauke, Nouvelle Guinée Néerlandaise. *Anthropos* 4:553–573.

O'BRIEN, FREDERICK

1919   *White shadows in the South Seas.* New York: Century.

1921   *Mystic isles of the South Seas.* Garden City, N.Y.: Garden City Publishing Company.

OFFICIAL TOURIST BUREAU, WELTVREDEN

1922   *Come to Java, 1922–1923.* Batavia: G. Kolff.

O'HANLON, MICHAEL

1993   *Paradise: Portraying the New Guinea highlands.* London: British Museum Press.

OLIVER, DOUGLAS L.

1949   Studies in the anthropology of Bougainville, Solomon Islands. *Papers of the Peabody Museum of American Archaeology and Ethnology* 29(1–4):1–194.

1951   *The Pacific Islands.* Cambridge: Harvard University Press.

O'REILLY, PATRICK

1980   *Calédoniens: Répertoire bio-bibliographique de la Nouvelle-Calédonie.* 2d ed. Paris: Société des Océanistes.

PAKENHAM, VALERIE
  1985   *Out in the noonday sun: Edwardians in the tropics.* New York: Random House.

PARKINSON, RICHARD
  1900   Die Berlinhafen-Section: Ein Beiträg zur
Ethnographie der Neu-Guinea-Küste. *Internationales Archiv
für Ethnographie* 13:18–54.
  1907   *Dreissig Jahre in der Südsee: Land und Leute,
Sitten und Gebräuche im Bismarck-Archipel und auf den deutschen Salomo-Inseln.* Stuttgart: Strecker & Schröder.

PAUL, D.
  1909   Die Neuendettelsauer Mission in Kaiser-Wilhelmsland. *Allgemeine Missions-Zeitschrift* 36:411–429,
472–473.

PENCK, ALBRECHT
  1911   Die Erforschung des Kaiserin Augusta-
Flusses durch Leonard Schultze. *Gesellschaft für Erdkunde zu
Berlin, Zeitschrift* 1911:361–365.

PERRY, W. J.
  1923   *The children of the sun.* London: Methuen.

PFARRIUS
  1909   S.M.S. *Cormoran* im Kaiserin Augusta-Fluss.
DKB 20:236–238.

PILHOFER, D. G.
  1961–1963   *Die Geschichte der Neuendettelsauer Mission in Neuguinea.* 3 vols. Neuendettelsau: Friemund Verlag.

POLMAN, KATRIEN
  1983   *The central Moluccas: An annotated bibliography.* Koninklijk Instituut voor Taal-, Land- en
Volkenkunde, Biographical Series, 12. Dordrecht: Foris.

POWDERMAKER, HORTENSE
  1933   *Life in Lesu: The study of a Melanesian society
in New Ireland.* New York: W. W. Norton.

PRIDAY, H. E. L.
  1944   *Cannibal island: The turbulent story of New
Caledonia's cannibal coasts.* Wellington: A. H. and A. W.
Reed.

QUAIN, BUELL
  1948   *Fijian village.* Chicago: University of Chicago Press.

RADCLIFFE-BROWN, A. R.
  1913   Three tribes of western Australia. *Journal of
the Royal Anthropological Institute* 43:143–194.
  1922   *Andaman Islanders: A study in social anthropology.* Cambridge: Cambridge University Press.
  1952   *Structure and function in primitive society: Essays and addresses.* Glencoe, Ill.: Free Press.
  1957   *A natural science of society.* Glencoe, Ill.: Free
Press.

  1958   *Method in social anthropology: Selected essays,*
ed. M. N. Srinivas. Chicago: University of Chicago Press.

RADFORD, ROBIN
  1987   *Highlanders and foreigners in the upper Ramu:
The Kainantu area, 1919–1942.* Melbourne: Melbourne University Press.

RAY, SIDNEY
  1892   On the importance and nature of the
Oceanic languages. *Journal and Proceedings of the Royal Society
of New South Wales* 26:51–59.
  1893   The languages of British New Guinea. *Transactions of the Ninth International Congress of Orientalists*
2:754–770.
  1895   The languages of British New Guinea. *Journal of the Anthropological Institute* 24:15–39.
  1896   The common origin of the Oceanic languages. *Journal of the Polynesian Society* 5:58–68.
  1907   *Linguistics.* Vol. 3 of *Reports of the Cambridge
Anthropological Expedition to Torres Straits,* ed. Alfred Cort
Haddon. Cambridge: Cambridge University Press.

RECHE, OTTO
  1910   Eine Bereisung des Kaiserin-Augusta-
Flusses (Neuguinea). *Globus* 97:285–286.
  1954   *Nova Britannia: Entdeckungsgeschichte—Die
Reise der "Peiho" nach Nova Britania. . . . Ergebnisse der Südsee-
Expedition 1908–1910.* II. Ethnographie: A. Melanesien,
Band 4. Hamburg: Ludwig Appel.

REED, STEPHEN WINSOR
  1939   Acculturation in New Guinea. Ph.D. diss.
Yale University, Department of Anthropology.
  1943   *The making of modern New Guinea, with special
reference to culture contact in the Mandated Territory.* Memoirs of
the American Philosophical Society, vol. 18. Philadelphia:
American Philosophical Society.

REICHARD, GLADYS A.
  1933   *Melanesian design: A study of style in wood and
tortoiseshell carving.* New York: Columbia University Press.

RILEY, E. BAXTER
  1925   *Among Papuan headhunters: An account of the
manners and customs of the old Fly River headhunters, with a description of the secrets of the initiation ceremonies divulged by those
who have passed through all the different orders of the craft.* London: Seeley, Service.

RIVERS, W. H. R.
  1910   The genealogical method of anthropological
inquiry. *Sociological Review* 3:1–12.
  1914   *The history of Melanesian society: Percy Sladen
Trust Expedition to Melanesia.* 2 vols. Cambridge: Cambridge
University Press.

ROBERTSON, HUGH A.

1902   *Erromanga: The martyr isle.* London: Hodder and Stoughton.

ROBIDE VAN DER AA, P. J. B. C.

1879   *Reizen naar Nederlandsch Nieuw Guinea, ondernomen op last der regeering van Nederlandsch-Indie, in de jaren 1871, 1875–1876, door de heeren P. van der Crab en J. E. Teysmann, J. G. Coorengel en A. J. Langeveldt van Hemert en P. Swaan, met geschied- en aardrijkskundige toelichtingen.* The Hague: Martinus Nijhoff.

ROBINSON, GEORGE F.

1902   *History of Greene Co., Ohio.* Chicago: S. J. Clarke.

ROBSON, R. W., ED.

1942   *The Pacific Islands year book 1942.* 4th (wartime) ed. Sydney: Pacific Publications.

RODATZ, HANS

1908   Aus dem neuen Bezirk Eitapé. *DKB* 19:15–20.

1909a   Bericht über eine Expedition Sissano-Leitere-Warapu-Arup-Malol. *Amtsblatt für das Schutzgebiet Deutsch-Neuguinea* 1:124–126.

1909b   Eine Expedition im Norden von Kaiser-Wilhelmsland. *DKB* 20:174–76.

SACK, PETER G.

1976   *The bloodthirsty Laewomba? Myth and history in Papua New Guinea.* Canberra: Department of Law, Research School of Social Sciences, Australian University, and Morobe District Historical Society.

———, ED.

1980   *German New Guinea: A bibliography.* Canberra: Department of Law Research, Australian National University.

SACK, PETER, AND DYMPHNA CLARK, EDS.

1979   *German New Guinea: The annual reports.* Canberra: Australian National University Press.

SAHLINS, MARSHALL D.

1963   Poor man, rich man, big man, chief: Political types in Melanesia and Polynesia. *Comparative Studies in Society and History* 5(3):285–303.

SANDE, G. A. J. VAN DER

1907   Ethnography and anthropology of New Guinea. *Nova Guinea* 3:1–390.

SARASIN, FRITZ

1916–1922   *Anthropologie der Neu-Caledonier und Loyalty-Insulaner.* 2 vols. Berlin: C. W. Kreidel's Verlag.

1917   *Neu-Caledonien und die Loyalty-Inseln: Reise-Erinnerungen eines Naturforschers.* Basel: Verlag von George.

SARASIN, FRITZ, AND JEAN ROUX

1929   *Nova Caledonia: Forschungen in Neu-Caledonien und auf den Loyalty-Inseln. D. Ethnologie.* Vol. 2 contains *Atlas zur Ethnologie der Neu-Caledonier und Loyalty-Insulaner.* Munich: C. W. Kreidel's Verlag.

SARHO, RISTO

1991   Gunnar Landtman. In *International dictionary of anthropologists,* comp. Library-Anthropology Resource Group (LARG), Christopher Winters, gen. ed. 378–379. New York: Garland.

SCARR, DERYCK

1967   *Fragments of empire: A history of the western Pacific high commission, 1877–1914.* Canberra: Australian National University Press.

SCHLAGINHAUFEN, OTTO

1909   Unpublished field diaries. Archives of the Staatlisches Museums für Völkerkunde Dresden.

1910a   Reisen in Kaiser-Wilhelmsland (Neuguinea). *Abhandlungen und Berichte des Königlichen Zoologischen und Anthropologisch-Ethnographisches Museums zu Dresden* 13(1):1–19.

SCHMIDT, W.

1899   Ethnographisches von Berlinhafen, Deutsch-Neu-Guinea. *Anthropologische Gesellschaft in Wien, Mitteilungen* 29 (19 neue Folge):13–29, Sitzungsberichte: [60–70].

SCHMUTTERER, GOTTFRIED

1954   *Dreissig Geschichten aus Neuendettelsauer Mission zum Verlesen.* Neuendettelsau: Friemund Verlag.

SCHNEIDER, DAVID M.

1968   Rivers and Kroeber in the study of kinship. In *Kinship and Social Organization, by W. H. R. Rivers, together with "The Genealogical Method of Anthropological Enquiry" with commentaries by Raymond Firth and David M. Schneider,* 7–16. London School of Economics, Monographs on Social Anthropology, no. 34. London: Athlone Press.

SCHULTZE, L.

1910–1911   Von der Deutsch-holländischen Grenzexpedition in Neuguinea. *DKB* 21:770, 836, 992–993; 22:124–127.

1914   Forschungen im Innern der Insel Neuguinea: Bericht des Fuhrers über die wissenschaftlichen Ergebnisse der deutschen Grenzexpedition in das westliche Kaiser-Wilhelmsland, 1910. *Mitteilungen aus den Deutschen Schutzgebieten, Ergänzungsheft* no. 11.

SCHÜTZ, ALBERT J., ED.

1977   *The diaries and correspondence of David Cargill, 1832–1843.* Canberra: Australian National University Press.

SEEMANN, BERTHOLD

1862   *Viti: An account of a government mission to the Vitian or Fijian islands in the years 1860–1861.* Cambridge: Macmillan.

SELIGMAN, C. G.
1910   *The Melanesians of British New Guinea.* Cambridge: Cambridge University.

SELIGMAN, C. G., AND W. M. STRONG
1906   Anthropogeographical investigation in British New Guinea. *Geographical Journal* 27:225–242, 347–369.

SENTINELLA, C. L., TRANS.
1975   *Mikloucho-Maclay: New Guinea diaries, 1871–1883.* Madang: Kristen Pres.

SIMMS, S. C.
1912   Simms to ABL, 5 Mar. 1912. J. N. Field Expedition correspondence file. Department of Anthropology, Field Museum of Natural History.

SINGER, ANDRE, PRODUCER
1985   *Sir Walter Baldwin Spencer: Fieldwork.* A film in the Strangers Abroad series. Available from Films for the Humanities and Sciences, Princeton, N.J. (800-257-5126).

SLOBODIN, RICHARD
1978   *W. H. R. Rivers.* New York: Columbia University Press.

SMITH, G. ELLIOT
1928   *In the beginning: The origin of civilization.* London: G. Howe.

SOUTER, GAVIN
1963   *New Guinea: The last unknown.* New York: Taplinger.

SPECHT, JIM, AND JOHN FIELDS
1984   *Frank Hurley in Papua: Photographs of the 1919–1923 expeditions.* Bathurst, NSW: Robert Brown.

SPEISER, FELIX
1923   *Ethnographische Materialien aus den Neuen Hebriden und den Banks-Inseln.* Berlin: C. W. Kreidel's Verlag.
1991   *Ethnology of Vanuatu: An early twentieth century study.* Trans. D. Q. Stephenson. Bathurst, NSW: Crawford House.

SPENCER, DOROTHY M.
1941   *Disease, religion, and society in the Fiji Islands.* Monographs of the American Ethnological Society, 2. Seattle: University of Washington Press.

SPRIGADE, PAUL, AND MAX MOISEL, COMPS.
1903–1912   *Grosser deutscher Kolonialatlas.* Berlin: Reimer (for Kolonial-Abteilung des Auswartigen Amts.)

STEEL, ROBERT
1880   *The New Hebrides and Christian missions.* London: J. Nisbet.

STEENIS-KRUSEMAN, M. J. VAN
1950   Cyclopaedia of collectors. *Flora Malesiana,* ser. 1, vol. 1.

STOCKING, GEORGE W., JR.
1983   The ethnographer's magic: Fieldwork in British anthropology from Tylor to Malinowski. In *Observers observed: Essays on ethnographic fieldwork,* ed. G. W. Stocking, Jr., 70–120. History of Anthropology, vol. 1. Madison: University of Wisconsin Press.
1984   Radcliffe-Brown and British social anthropology. In *Functionalism historicized: Essays on British social anthropology,* ed. G. W. Stocking, Jr., 131–191. History of Anthropology, vol. 2. Madison: University of Wisconsin Press.
1985a   Essays on museums and material culture. In *Objects and others: Essays on museums and material culture,* ed. G. W. Stocking, Jr., 3–14. History of Anthropology, vol. 3. Madison: University of Wisconsin Press.
1985b   Philanthropoids and vanishing cultures: Rockefeller funding and the end of the museum era in Anglo-American anthropology. In *Objects and others: Essays on museums and material culture,* ed. G. W. Stocking, Jr., 112–145. History of Anthropology, vol. 3. Madison: University of Wisconsin Press.

———, ED.
1985   *Objects and others: Essays on museums and material culture.* History of Anthropology, vol. 3. Madison: University of Wisconsin Press.

STOLZ, HERR
1911   Die Umgebung von Kap König Wilhelm. In *Deutsch-Neu-Guinea,* R. Neuhauss, 3:245–286. Berlin: Dietrich Reimer.

STRATHERN, MARILYN
1988   *The gender of the gift: Problems with women and problems with society in Melanesia.* Berkeley: University of California Press.

STURTEVANT, W. C.
1969   Does anthropology need museums? *Proceedings of the Biology Society of Washington* 82:619–650.

TERRELL, JOHN
1981   Linguistics and the peopling of the Pacific Islands. *Journal of the Polynesian Society* 90:225–258.
1986   *Prehistory in the Pacific Islands: A study of variation in language, customs, and human biology.* Cambridge: Cambridge University Press.
1989   What Lapita is and isn't. *Antiquity* 63:623–626.
1993   Regional studies in anthropology: A Melanesian prospectus. *Current Anthropology* 34:177–179.

TERRELL, JOHN, AND ROBERT L. WELSCH
1990a   Trade networks, areal integration, and di-

versity along the north coast of New Guinea. *Asian Perspectives* 29:156–165.

1990b   Return to New Guinea. *In the Field: The Bulletin of the Field Museum of Natural History* 61(5):1, 10–11.

THOMAS, K. H.

1941–1942   Notes on the natives of the Vanimo coast, New Guinea. *Oceania* 12(2):163–186.

THOMPSON, LAURA

1940a   *Fijian frontier.* San Francisco: American Council, Institute of Pacific Relations.

1940b   *Southern Lau, Fiji.* Bernice P. Bishop Museum Bulletin, 185. Honolulu: Bernice P. Bishop Museum.

THOMPSON, VIRGINIA, AND RICHARD ADLOFF

1971   *The French Pacific islands: French Polynesia and New Caledonia.* Berkeley: University of California Press.

THOMSON, BASIL HOME

1908   *The Fijians: A study of the decay of custom.* London: William Heinemann.

THURNWALD, RICHARD C.

1916   Banaro society: Social organization and kinship system of a tribe in the interior of New Guinea. *Memoirs of the American Anthropological Association* 3:253–391.

1917   Vorläufiger Bericht über Forschungen im Innern von Deutsch-Neu-Guinea in den Jahren 1913–1915. *Zeitschrift für Ethnologie* 49:147–179.

1918   Drei Jahre im Innern von Neuguinea 1913–1915. *Jahrbuch des Städtischen Museums für Völkerkunde zu Leipzig, 1915–17,* 7:73–76.

TIESLER, FRANK

1969–1970   Die intertribalen Beziehungen an der Nordkuste Neuguineas im Gebiet der Kleinen Schouten-Inseln. *Abhandlungen und Berichte des Staatlichen Museums für Völkerkunde Dresden* 30:1–122; 31:111–195; and plates C1–C14.

1970   Tragbandschilde aus dem Hatzfeldhafen-Gebiet, dem Hinterland der Berlinhafen-Küste und dem Lumi-Gebiet, Nord-Neuguinea. *Jahrbuch des Museums für Völkerkunde zu Leipzig* 27:185–217 and plates.

TORRENCE, ROBIN

1989   Obsidian-tipped spears and daggers from the Admiralty Islands. Research report, Australian Museum, Sydney.

1993   Ethnoarchaeology, museum collection, and prehistoric exchange: Obsidian-tipped artifacts from the Admiralty Islands. *World Archaeology* 24:468–481.

1994   Just another trader? An archaeological perspective on European 'contact' with Admiralty Islanders, Papua New Guinea. Paper presented to the World Archaeological Congress, New Delhi, in the session "Trade, contact, and culture change in Oceania."

VAHSEL, RICHARD

1909   Bericht über einen Zusammenstoss mit Eingeborenen einiger Dörfer am Kaiserin Augustafluss. *Amtsblatt* 1:123–124.

VERSLAG VAN DE MILITAIRE EXPLORATIE VAN NEDERLANDSCH-NIEUW-GUINEE

1920   *Verslag van de Militaire Exploratie van Nederlandsch-Nieuw-Guinee, 1907–1915.* Weltevreden: Landsdrukkerij.

VERTENTEN, P.

1935   *Vijftien Jaar bijde Koppensnellers van Nederlandsch Zuid-Nieuw-Guinea.* The Netherlands: Davidsfonds.

VETTER, KONRAD

1896b   Einige Erzählungen der Eingeborenen von Deutsch Neu-Guinea. *Zeitschrift für afrikanische und oceanische Sprachen* 2:220–240.

VEUR, PAUL W. VAN DER

1966   *Search for New Guinea's boundaries: From Torres Strait to the Pacific.* Canberra: Australian National University.

VLEKKE, BERNARD H. M.

1943   *Nusantara: A history of the east Indian archipelago.* Cambridge: Harvard University Press.

VOOGDT, CAPT. H.

1910   Voogdt to George A. Dorsey, 26 March 1910. Accession file 1088, Field Museum of Natural History archives.

WATSON, JAMES B.

1967   Local variation and its assessment in New Guinea. In *Behavioral science research in New Guinea: A report of a conference, Honolulu, Hawaii, August 18–25, 1965,* 53–71. National Research Council (U.S.) Publication, 1493. Washington, D.C.: National Research Council.

WELSCH, ROBERT L.

1987   C. A. comment on P. Kirsch and R. Green. *Current Anthropology* 28:448–449.

1988   The A. B. Lewis collection from Melanesia—75 years later. *Field Museum of Natural History Bulletin* 59(8):10–15.

1989a   Context and meaning of the A. B. Lewis collection: An example from the north coast of New Guinea. Paper presented at conference "Object informs, objects in form: The ethnography of Oceanic art." Baltimore Museum of Art. April.

1989b   A. B. Lewis's contribution to understanding trade networks along the north coast of New Guinea. Paper presented to the American Anthropological Association, Washington, D.C.

1992   [Review of] Children of Afek: Tradition and change among the Mountain-Ok of central New Guinea. B.

604

Craig and D. Hyndman, eds. *American Anthropologist* 94:494–495.

    1995   CA comment on Roberts, Moore, and Romney. *Current Anthropology* 36:780–782.

    1996a   Collaborative regional anthropology in New Guinea: From the New Guinea Micro-Evolution Project to the A. B. Lewis Project and beyond. *Pacific Studies* 19(3):143–186.

    1996b   Language, culture, and data on the north coast of New Guinea. *Journal of Quantitative Anthropology* 6(4):209–234.

WELSCH, ROBERT L., AND JOHN TERRELL

    1991   Continuity and change in economic relations along the Aitape coast of Papua New Guinea. *Pacific Studies* 14(4):113–128.

    1994   Reply to Moore and Romney. *American Anthropologist* 96:392–396.

    1996   Material culture, social fields, and social boundaries on the Sepik coast of New Guinea. Submitted as part of a collection edited by Miriam Stark to the Smithsonian Institution Press.

WELSCH, ROBERT L.; JOHN TERRELL; AND JOHN A. NADOLSKI

    1992   Language and culture on the north coast of New Guinea. *American Anthropologist* 94(3):568–600.

WETHERELL, DAVID

    1977   *Reluctant mission: The Anglican Church in Papua New Guinea.* St. Lucia: University of Queensland Press.

WHITING, JOHN W. M.

    1941   *Becoming a Kwoma: Teaching and learning in a New Guinea tribe.* New Haven, Conn.: Yale University Press.

WICHMANN, ARTHUR

    1912   Entdeckungsgeschichte von Neu-Guinea (1885 bis 1902). *Nova Guinea* 2(pt. 2):371–1026.

    1917   Bericht über eine im Jahr 1903 ausgefuhrte Reise nach Neu Guinea. *Nova Guinea* 4:1–493.

WILLIAMS, F. E.

    1923   *The Vailala madness and the destruction of native ceremonies in the Gulf Division.* Territory of Papua, Anthropology Report, no. 4. Port Moresby: Government Printer.

    1924   *The natives of the Purari delta.* Territory of Papua, Anthropology Report, no. 5. Port Moresby: Government Printer.

    1940   *Drama of Orokolo.* Oxford: Clarendon.

WILLIAMS, FRANCIS EDGAR

    1977   *"The Vailala Madness" and other essays.* (Ed. by Erik Schwimmer.) Honolulu: University Press of Hawai'i.

WILLIAMS, THOMAS, AND JAMES CALVERT

    1858   *Fiji and the Fijians.* (Ed. G. S. Rowe.) 2 vols. in one. London: Alexander Heylin.

WILSON, CHARLES

    1954   *The history of Unilever: A study in economic growth and social change.* Vol. 1. London: Cassell.

WINGERT, PAUL S.

    1946   *Outline guide to the art of the South Pacific.* New York: Columbia University Press.

WIRZ, PAUL

    1933   Head-hunting expeditions of the Tugeri into the Western Division of British New Guinea. *Tijdschrift voor Indische Taal-, Land- en Volkenkunde* 73:105–122.

WOLLASTON, A. F. R.

    1912   *Pygmies and Papuans: The stone age to-day in Dutch New Guinea.* New York: Sturgis and Walton.

WU, DAVID Y. H.

    1982   *The Chinese in Papua New Guinea, 1880–1980.* Hong Kong: Chinese University Press.

WURM, STEFAN A.

    1967   Linguistics and the prehistory of the southwestern Pacific. *Journal of Pacific History* 2:25–38.

    1982   Papuan languages. In *Melanesia: Beyond diversity,* ed. R. J. May and H. Nelson, 3–10. The Hague: Mouton.

WURM, S. A., AND S. HATTORI

    1981   *Language atlas, Pacific area.* Canberra: Australian National University.

YOUNG, JOHN MICHAEL RENDER

    1984   *Adventurous spirits. Australian migrant society in pre-cession Fiji.* St. Lucia: University of Queensland Press.

YOUNG, MICHAEL W.

    1988   Malinowski among the magi: Editor's introduction. In *Malinowski among the magi: "The Natives of Mailu,"* Bronislaw Malinowski, ed. M. W. Young, 1–76. London: Routledge.

    1991   Bronislaw Malinowski. In *International dictionary of anthropologists,* comp. Library-Anthropology Resource Group (LARG), Christopher Winters, gen. ed., 444–446. New York: Garland.

ZAHN, HEINRICH

    1911   Die Jabim. In *Deutsch-Neu-Guinea,* R. Neuhauss, 3:289–394. Berlin: Dietrich Reimer.

DE ZUIDWEST NIEUW-GUINEA-EXPEDITION

    1908   *De Zuidwest Nieuw-Guinea-Expedition, 1904/5.* Leiden: E. J. Brill.

Index

||||||||||||||||||||||||||||||||||||||||||||||||||||||||||||||||||||||||||||||||||||||||||||

Page numbers in **Bold type** refer to maps.

Abbreviations used in Index:

(Adm.)	Admiralty Islands
(DNG)	Dutch New Guinea
(Fiji)	Fiji
(Gaz.)	Eastern New Britain, especially the Gazelle Peninsula
(Huon)	Kaiser Wilhelmsland, east of Friedrich Wilhelmshafen, especially Huon Peninsula and Gulf
(KWL)	Kaiser Wilhelmsland, west from Friedrich Wilhelmshafen
(Massim)	Islands in Massim district, Papua
(Mol.)	Moluccas in Dutch East Indies
(NB)	New Britain, excluding the Gazelle Peninsula
(N.Cal.)	New Caledonia
(N.Heb.)	New Hebrides
(N.Ire.)	New Ireland and offshore islands (includes New Hanover and St. Matthias)
(Papua)	Papua, from Port Moresby to the west
(SE Papua)	Papuan mainland, east of Port Moresby (excludes the Massim district)
(Sol.)	Solomon Islands (includes Buka, Bougainville, and British Solomon Islands)

629

U

V

About the Editor

||||||||||||||||||||||||||||||||||||||||||||||||||||||||||||||||||||||||||||||||||||||||||||||||||||||||

ROBERT L. WELSCH received his Ph.D. in anthropology from the University of Washington. He is currently adjunct curator of anthropology at Field Museum in Chicago and visiting professor in the Department of Anthropology at Dartmouth College. Among his publications is "Language and Culture on the North Coast of New Guinea" (with J. Terrell and J. A. Nadolski), published in *American Anthropologist* and winner of the American Anthropological Association's Morton H. Fried Prize for best article in 1992.